Dear Readers,

Have you ever wondered why India is often seen as one of the world's top destinations for tourists? Is it the sheer variety – ranging from sandy beaches to majestic mountains, from verdant landscapes to arid deserts? Or is it the food – after all, Hyderabad and Lucknow are both part of UNESCO's Cities of Gastronomy list. Adding to this culinary pride is a fascinating series of food-related records, the latest being set by Bird Airport Hotel Pvt. Ltd, Roseate House, New Delhi, for making the largest *peda*, measuring 3 ft x 3 ft.

No doubt it is also the warmth, empathy, and fellow feeling that define Indians – as we see in the many records on awareness drives. Or perhaps it's all of these and more – strength and stamina (*see the adventure and sports records*), knowledge, acuity, and intelligence (*see education, science and technology, and business records*), creativity (*see the arts and literature records*), and resilience and patience (*see the collection records*).

Speaking of patience, who can forget Santosh Kumar from Thiruvananthapuram, Kerala, who has crafted the smallest devil's knot measuring 8 mm x 2 mm x 2 mm, using his wood sculpting skills? And for courage and stamina, here's a jaw-dropping record from our 2026 edition's record pool: Dr Yagnesh Gohil, Dr Sanjay Karangiya, and Dr Mayur Diwani from Gujarat set a record for the fastest Trans-Himalayan expedition, covering 5,464 km in just 21 hours and 46 minutes. The thrilling journey started in Leh, Ladakh, and ended in Tezu, Arunachal Pradesh, across some of the roughest terrains of the country.

On 22 May 2025, Prime Minister Narendra Modi inaugurated 103 redeveloped railway stations across 18 states and Union territories through video conference, under the Amrit Bharat Station Scheme. Each station now features improved toilet access, new seating arrangements, clear signage, upgraded booking offices, and better lighting. With the world's growing interest in India – as reflected in its thriving tourism sector – such infrastructural development is a must.

And that's not all. On 30 May 2025, the first batch of 17 women (among 336 cadets) graduated from the National Defence Academy – a milestone in an institution that was traditionally all-male. This marks a new era of inclusivity and progressive change.

Every day, India is transforming – and the *Limca Book of Records* continues to be a time-honoured documentation of that journey.

Marketing Team
Coca-Cola India

HACHETTE INDIA LBR TEAM

Consulting Editor: Vatsala Kaul Banerjee

Managing Editor: Anirban Sarkar

Research and Editorial Team:
Shubhali Chopra, Arunima Dharanipragada, Yukta Vats

Administrative Executive: Susheel Kapoor

CONSULTANTS

ADVENTURE
Ajeet Bajaj

CINEMA
Diptakirti Chaudhuri

EDUCATION
Dr Alpana Neogy

MEMORY
Squadron Leader Jayasimha Ravirala

BUSINESS AND ECONOMY
Suparna Pathak

SPORTS

Kamesh Srinivasan: Shooting

K. Arumugam: Hockey

Rakesh Rao: Chess, Golf, and Table Tennis

Aditya K. Halder: Archery, Athletics, Badminton, Basketball, Boxing, Cricket, Cue Sports, Football, Gymnastics, Kabaddi, Powerlifting, Squash, Swimming and Water Sports, Tennis, Weighlifting, Wrestling, General Sports, and Sports Statistics

LAST DATE FOR NEW ENTRIES (COMPLETE WITH DOCUMENTATION) FOR THE *LIMCA BOOK OF RECORDS* 2027 EDITION:

31 MAY 2026

Please see the revised and updated 'Rules and Guidelines' section for details.

Limca Book of Records does not have any branch offices or representatives.

General and Sales enquiries: **sales@hachetteindia.com**

Record applications/queries: **lbr.entries@hachetteindia.com**

Please note that the new number to contact Limca Book of Records is 7292027373. Our team will be available from Monday to Saturday between 10 a.m. and 7 p.m. on this number. Please note that we are not available on WhatsApp.

Dear Readers,

This year has been a remarkable celebration of talent, grit, and achievements for India. The one big landmark that was a proud moment for every Indian was the first ever victory in the ICC Women's World Cup. On 2 November 2025, at the DY Patil Stadium in Navi Mumbai, the Indian women's team defeated South Africa by 52 runs and lifted the coveted trophy for the first time.

The year 2025 has also been a turbulent one – for India, as for the rest of the world. From Operation Sindoor to the Air India crash in Ahmedabad, American tariff tensions to natural calamities – the nation has weathered many challenges. Yet, amid these upheavals came moments that lifted our hearts – forming part of a relentless journey marked by sheer brilliance, diligence, and resilience.

This edition of India's oldest record book celebrates that same indomitable spirit. Within its pages, you will find a rich and diverse chronicle of epoch-making inventions and discoveries, engineering, architectural and creative wonders, medical achievements, and creative pursuits that continue to inspire the country.

In September 2025, the Defence Research and Development Organisation, in collaboration with the Strategic Forces Command, successfully launched an Intermediate Range Agni-Prime Missile from a rail-based mobile launcher system. This specially designed launcher can move freely on the rail network, operate under reduced visibility and provide rapid cross-country deployment.

Infrastructure remains a top priority. The Chenab Bridge, the highest railway bridge in the world, inaugurated in June 2025, stands as a symbol of engineering excellence and human endeavour. Meanwhile, the Chittaranjan Locomotive Works in Paschim Bardhaman District, West Bengal, set a world record by producing 700 locomotives in the financial year 2024–25.

In the field of medicine, Indian doctors achieved extraordinary feats – from removing the largest nasal polyp to excising the largest skull bone tumour. It's no surprise that India ranks among the world's top destinations for medical tourism, placed 10th in the Medical Tourism Index (MTI).

India has also reached new heights in space technology, launching its heaviest communication satellite – weighing 4,400 kg – on 2 November 2025.

And in art and culture, records took on a lyrical note when Ramnath Choudhary of Jaipur, Rajasthan, played an *algoja* (a double flute) through his nose for 20 mins and 35 secs on 18 March 2025 at Bada Padampura, Jaipur.

Through every test – terror threats, tariff wars, or natural crises – the *Limca Book of Records* 2026 is a proof in print of an unwavering spirit, proof that the heart of a champion beats in every Indian. From natural and human-made landmarks to fascinating flora and fauna, from a surge in science and technology to a thriving tourism and start-up ecosystem, from a spirited media and entertainment industry to a formidable defence capability – every facet of India's progress finds a place here.

Yes, India is on the move!

Anirban Sarkar
Managing Editor, *Limca Book of Records*
(Reference Division, Hachette India)

CONTENTS

44

THE HUMAN STORY

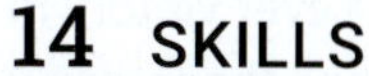

31

34

93

84

AGRICULTURE

STRUCTURES

73

56

EDUCATION

PERFORMING ARTS

VISUAL ARTS

LITERATURE

MEDIA AND COMMUNICATIONS

CONTENTS

GOVERNMENT

221

226

DEFENCE AND MILITARY AFFAIRS

237

250

SCIENCE AND TECHNOLOGY

MEDICAL SCIENCES

280

283

297

THE NATURAL WORLD

307

314

311

CONTENTS

334

357

362

362

380

389

404

387

SPORTS

410

411

415

423

419

447

461

THE HUMAN STORY
KENYA
CENTS
ประเทศไทย
๑๐ บาท
10
HONG KONG
INDIA

I USE ONLY SWEDISH MATCHES
SOLSTICKAN
VULCANS SALONGS TÄNDSTICKOR
TIDAHOLM, SVERIGE
PAMPA
SAFETY MATCH
MANUFACTURED IN SWEDEN
THE TROTTING
SAFETY MATCHES
MADE IN SWEDEN
VULCANS
SALONGS
TIDAHOLM
CANADIAN PACIFIC
S GREATEST TRAVEL SYSTEM
IMPREGNATED SAFETY MATCH
QUALITY GUARANTEED
MADE IN RUSSIA
SÄKERHETS TÄNDSTICKOR
IMPREGNERADE
IMPORT
SARA
Hotel Standard
NORRKÖPING • SWEDEN

SKILLS

Most juggling patterns on a balance board

Jaykishan Vimalbhai Hingu from Jetpur, Gujarat, performed 28 juggling patterns using 3 balls while balancing on a balance board on 5 May 2021 at Radha Park, Jetpur. The patterns were cascade, columns, fake columns, the machine, crossed columns, one going over the top, half shower, false shower, behind the back, box, clawed catches, Mangham's mangle, 'M', infinity, reverse infinity, Georgian shuffle, real tennis, tennis, yo-yo, oy-oy, outside throws, Statue of Liberty, shower, Ripley's rainbow, wiper, 'W', the weave, and Mill's mess.

WR Most tie knots tied – 1 min

Dr Deepak M. Sharma from Ahmedabad, Gujarat, knotted a tie around the neck seven times in 1 min. on 12 February 2020 at a stage performance in Surat.

Most football rolls from eye to eye

Satish Kasi from Bengaluru, Karnataka, performed 164 football rolls from eye to eye in 1 min. from 9:36 a.m. to 9:37 a.m. on 16 May 2019 at Sree Kanteerava Stadium, Bengaluru. He shifts the football from eye to eye while balancing the ball on the forehead.

Satish Kasi

Longest duration of non-stop hitting of a dangling cricket ball

Dr Arjun Anand Shirsath from Ahmednagar, Maharashtra, knocked a dangling cricket ball with a 1.83 m (6 ft) cord length non-stop 10,332 times with a bat for 4 hrs 34 mins 35 secs on 24 April 2020.

Longest basketball shot

Manisha Satyajit Dange from Thane made a 21.4 m long basketball shot in 2 secs 72 millisecs at 10:03 a.m. on 22 May 2021 at the Central Railway Sport Complex, Parel, Mumbai.

Mahir Kumar

Longest time balancing a hockey stick on the middle finger

Arun Kumar Kannan Murthy from Kanchipuram, Tamil Nadu, balanced an on-field hockey stick on his middle finger for 3 hrs 11 mins 50 secs on 18 August 2019 at Neat Trust, Vellore.

Longest duration of non-stop hitting a table tennis ball on a table tennis racket

Mahir Kumar from Gurugram, Haryana, set the record for the longest duration of non-stop hitting a table tennis ball on a table tennis racket by performing it for 3 hours 44 mins from 2:18 p.m. to 6:02 p.m. on 9 December 2022 at the Chenab Boys Hostel, IIT Ropar main campus, Punjab.

Longest time balancing a hockey stick on the little finger

Gagandeep Singh from Fatehgarh Sahib, Punjab, balanced a hockey stick weighing 660 g on his little finger for 1 hr from 4:00 p.m. to 5:00 p.m. on 10 May 2019 in Sirhind, Fatehgarh.

Gagandeep Singh

Manisha Satyajit Dange

Longest duration to play flute by nose

Ramnath Choudhary of Jaipur, Rajasthan, the *algoja* (a double-flute) through his nose for 20 mins and 35 secs on 18 March 2025 at Bada Padampura village.

ENDEAVOUR

Marathon Knitting – solo

Sazida Khan from New Delhi knitted woollen caps for a duration of 27 hrs 28 mins. She started knitting with a number 4 needle at 7:00 a.m. on 26 September 2023 and finished at 10:28 a.m. on 27 September 2023 at Tejas Camp Race Course, New Delhi. She knitted 16 woollen caps as part of the event.

Sazida Khan

YOGA

Longest *ashtavakrasana*

Adesh Motiramji Karnase from Gurugram, Haryana, performed ashtavakrasana (eight-angle pose) for 1 min. 4 secs on 10 June 2020 in Morshi, Maharashtra.

WR Longest *setubandhasana*

Prof. Dr S. Ramesh Babu from Bengaluru, Karnataka, performed setubandhasana (bridge pose) for 24 mins from 8:00 a.m. to 8:24 a.m. on 9 July 2019 at Vidyanjali Academy for Learning, Bengaluru.

Longest *vishvamitrasana*

Nitin Mohanrao Prajapat from Gurugram, performed vishvamitrasana for 1 min. 13 secs on 10 June 2020 in Morshi, Maharashtra.

Longest *parshva poorna dhanurasana*

Amrutha Anand from Chidambaram, Tamil Nadu, performed parshva poorna dhanurasana (full side bow pose) for 15 mins 10 secs, starting at 2:00 p.m., on 2 March 2019 at the Great Wall of China, Beijing.

Amrutha Anand

Longest *padma mayurasana*

Mangal Raj from Sitamarhi, Bihar, performed padma mayurasana (lotus in peacock pose) for 4 mins 14 secs starting at 5:49 p.m. to 5:54 p.m. on 19 November 2021 at Raj Classic Park, Versova, Mumbai.

Longest *purvattanasana*

Sandeep Krishna Murthy Karupakala and Aruna K.S. from Chintamani, Karnataka, held purvattanasana (upward plank pose) for 2 mins 10 secs on 10 April 2021 at Lalitha Nivas, Chintamani.

Longest *mandukasana*

Swapan Kumar Sur from Faridabad, Haryana, performed mandukasana (frog pose) for 47 mins 11 secs starting at 8:33 p.m. to 9:21 p.m. on 14 April 2021 in Chhinamore, Hooghly, West Bengal.

Arooj. K

Longest *padahastasana*

Arooj. K from Thiruvananthapuram, Kerala, performed the padahastasana (forward bending pose) for 3 min 24 sec from 8:26 a.m. to 8:29 a.m. on 24 April 2024 at his home.

Longest *Hanumanasana*

Dr Narendra Kumar Sharma from Jaipur, Rajasthan, performed Hanumanasana (monkey pose) for 23 mins 36 secs on 22 June 2020 in Malviya Nagar, Jaipur.

Longest *ekapada shirshasana*

Virendra Vikram Singh (b. 2 December 1954) from Balrampur, Uttar Pradesh, performed ekapada shirshasana (foot behind the head pose) for 10 mins from 10:00 a.m. to 10:10 a.m. on 20 February 2019 at M.L.K. PG College, Balrampur.

Longest *supta pandangushthasana*

Virendera Vikram Singh from Balrampur, performed the supta pandangushthasana (reclining hand to big toe pose) for 20 mins from 9:50 a.m. to 10:10 a.m. on 19 May 2020 at Late Maharaj Dharmendra Prasad Singh Memorial, Balrampur.

Mangal Raj

Longest *mayurasana* – with one hand
Mangal Raj from Sitamarhi, Bihar, performed mayurasana (peacock pose) with one hand for 56 secs on 4 February 2022 at Raj Classic Park, Versova, Mumbai.

Longest *bakasana*
Virendera Vikram Singh from Balrampur, Uttar Pradesh, performed the Bakasana (crane pose) for 5 mins from 6:10 p.m. to 6:15 p.m. on 16 May 2022 at M.P.P. Inter College, Balrampur.

Longest *janu shirshasana*
Virendera Vikram Singh from Balrampur, performed the janu shirshasana (head to knee pose) for 1 hour from 9:00 a.m. to 10:00 a.m. on 24 February 2021 at Late Ravindra Singh Memorial, Balrampur.

Longest *niralamba ushtrasana*
Dr Narendra Kumar Sharma from Jaipur, Rajasthan, performed niralamba ushtrasana (unsupported camel pose) for 10 mins 38 secs on 30 May 2021 in Bharatpur, Rajasthan.

Dr Narendra Kumar Sharma

Longest *paschima namaskarasana*
Dinesh Kumar Agarwal of Mumbai, Maharashtra, performed the Paschima Namaskarasana (Reverse Namaskar) for 1 hour 21 mins and 20 secs on 26 December 2024 at his residence.

PHYSICAL FEATS

Most sit-ups – 1 min.
Sandeep Arya of Kolkata, attempted 67 sit-ups in 1 min. at Tivoli Court, Kolkata, at 9.30 a.m. on 28 April 2018.

Most abdominal sit-ups – 1 min.– women
Shreya Bhardwaj performed 85 abdominal sit ups in 1 min. from 12:05 p.m. to 12:06 p.m. on 23 May 2019 at H2O Fitness Gym, Gurugram.

Most jumping jacks – 1 min.– women
Richa Maheshwari from New Delhi performed 115 jumping jacks in 1 min. from 12:07 p.m. to 12:08 p.m. on 25 May 2019 at H2O Fitness Gym, Gurugram.

Most jumping jacks – 1 min.
Venkata Sairam Reddy Pulusu from Hyderabad, Telangana, performed 127 jumping jacks in 1 min. from 12:05 p.m. to 12:06 p.m. on 23 May 2019 at H2O Fitness Gym, Gurugram.

Most lunges – 1 hr
Kapil Arora from Mumbai, Maharashtra, performed 948 lunges in 1 hr between 8:16 a.m. and 9:16 a.m. on 28 June 2020 at his residence.

Most abdominal crunches – 1 min.
Mohit Bhardwaj from Gurugram, Haryana, performed 108 abdominal crunches in 1 min. from 12:06 p.m. to 12:07 p.m. on 23 May 2019 at H2O Fitness Gym, Gurugram.

Most superman push-ups – 1 min.
Kuwar Amritbir Singh from Gurdaspur, Punjab, performed 52 superman pushups in 1 min. from 12:05 p.m. to 12:06 p.m. on 5 May 2021 in Umarwala, Punjab.

Most two-finger push-ups – both arms – 1 min.
Arya Rishabh Rameshchandra from Ahmedabad, Gujarat, performed 65 two-finger push-ups (index and middle finger) in 1 min. on 19 May 2019 at I-Can Gym, Ahmedabad.

Arya Rishabh Rameshchandra: most two-finger push-ups in 1 min.

Yoga at the highest altitude

Kavita Singh from New Delhi has performed yogasanas at Umling La Ladakh on 20 April 2024 at an altitude of 19,024 ft for 1 hour 9 mins 34 secs. She performed these asanas along with Surya namaskar at an extremely cold temperature at –17 degree Celsius with 40 per cent less oxygen than average.

Longest *Paschimottanasana*
Virendera Vikram Singh from Balrampur, performed the paschimottanasana (seated forward bend pose) for 40 mins from 9:00 a.m. to 9:40 a.m. on 19 May 2020 at Bagh Palace, Balrampur.

Longest *padma vrischikasana*
Shyam Shamraoji Gawande from Wardha, Maharashtra performed the padma vrischikasana (scorpion in lotus pose) for 2 mins and 8 sec on 18 February 2024 at his home in Wardha.

Longest *sirsasana*
Puran Singh from Mathura, performed the sirsasana (headstand) for 4 hours from 6:15 a.m. to 10:15 a.m. on 29 October 2023 at the Chandralekha Stadium.

Longest *karnapidasana*
Adarsh Pandey from Rewa, Madhya Pradesh, performed the karnapidasana (lifting legs over head and bending knees towards ears) for 30 mins on 14 May 2024 at Dekhaha, Rewa, Madhya Pradesh.

Most burpees – 1 min. – women
Ankita Nagpal from Gurugram, Haryana, performed 48 burpees in 1 min. from 12:05 p.m. to 12:06 p.m. on 23 May 2019 at H2O Fitness Gym, Gurugram.

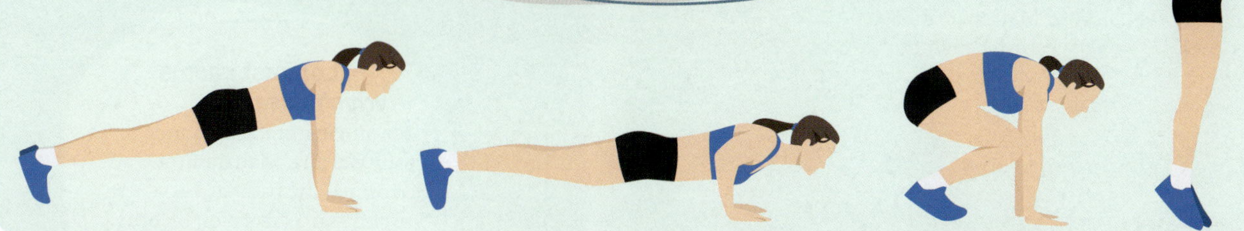

Most jumping jacks – 1 hr
Jasjeet Singh from New Delhi performed 4,479 jumping jacks in 1 hr from 9:12 a.m. to 10:12 a.m. on 17 February 2021 at his residence in Vikaspuri, Delhi.

Most side-jump push-ups – 1 min.
Anand S. from Chennai, Tamil Nadu, performed 42 side-jump push-ups in 1 min. from 1:00 p.m. to 1:01 p.m. on 20 October 2021 in Potheri, Chennai.

Most abdominal push-ups – 1 hr
Prof. Dr S. Ramesh Babu of Bengaluru, Karnataka, did 1,700 non-stop abdominal push-ups in 1 hr, at Prof. Satish Dhawan Park, from 9:00 a.m. on 14 April 2018.

Most clap push-ups – 1 min.
Jatin Goel from Gurugram, Haryana, performed 85 clap push-ups in 1 min from 12:05 p.m. to 12:06 p.m. on 10 May 2019 at H2O Fitness Gym, Gurugram.

Most diamond push-ups – 1 min.
V. Kaliraj from Virudhunagar, Tamil Nadu, did 112 diamond push-ups in 1 min. on 26 May 2019 at D'Pearl Sport Academy, Ramapuran, Chennai.

V. Kaliraj

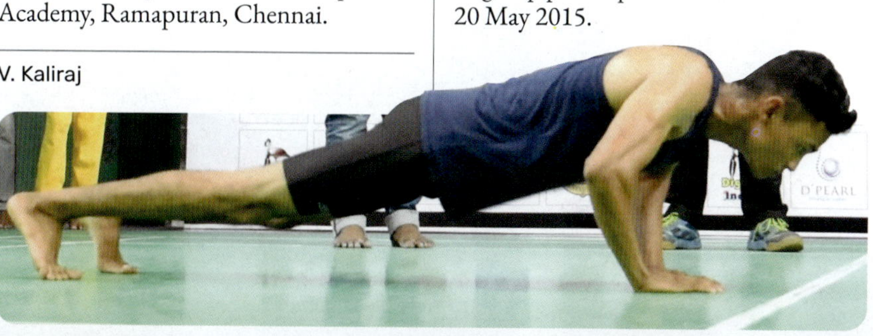

Mandeep Singh Karir and Baldeep Singh

Most tandem push-ups – 1 min.
Mandeep Singh Karir and Baldeep Singh of Singhbhum, Jharkhand, performed 28 tandem push-ups in 1 min. at Paul Fitness and Yoga Hub on 6 July 2022.

Most fingertip push-ups – one arm – 1 min.
Shaikh Rejaul Haque of Ulhasnagar, Maharashtra, performed 45 one-arm fingertip push-ups in 1 min. on 20 May 2015.

Most half-knuckle push-ups – 1 min.
Ashif Khan from Gurugram, Haryana, did 145 half-knuckle push-ups in 1 min. from 12:05 p.m. to 12:06 p.m. on 23 May 2019 at H2O Fitness gym, Gurugram.

Most half push-ups – 1 hr
Umesh Sopan Vyavahare of Adhegaon, Tal Madha, Solapur District, Maharashtra, performed 2,993 half pushups in 1 hr from 5:30 to 6:30 p.m. on 13 July 2017.

Most two-thumb push-ups – 1 min.
Harpreet Singh of Sultanpuri Lodhi, Kapurthala District, Punjab, performed 69 two-thumb push-ups in 1 min. at Lyallpur Khalsa College for Women on 17 April 2017.

Most decline push-ups – 1 min. – women
Shaleni Banthia from New Delhi performed 55 decline push-ups in 1 min. on 24 May 2023 from 5:00 p.m. to 5:01 p.m. at Feet Fit Gym, New Delhi.

Most incline push-ups – 1 min.
Jasjeet Singh from New Delhi performed 90 incline push-ups in 1 min. on 25 August 2023 from 7:39 a.m. to 7:40 a.m. at MMA Warriors Fight Club and Fitness Hub, Delhi.

Most push-ups – 1 min. – women
Sunita Chhabra of Jaipur, Rajasthan, performed 34 full push-ups at Manav Seva Trust's head office in 1 min. on 25 March 2018.

Most contortion push-ups – 1 min.
Rajendra Bishnoi from Bikaner, Rajasthan, performed 132 unique contortion push-ups in 1 min. on 17 March 2019 at Swargiya Shri Balasaheb Thackeray Maidan, Mumbai.

Longest plank
Abhishek Sihag from Sikar, Rajasthan, performed the longest plank for 8 hrs 5 mins from 6:51 a.m. to 2:56 p.m. at the Railway Community Centre, Sikar, on 1 January 2019.

Most parallel dips – 1 min.
Ashish Lohia from Gurugram, Haryana, performed 75 parallel dips in 1 min. from 12:05 p.m. to 12:06 p.m. on 28 May 2019 at H2O Fitness Gym in Gurugram.

Highest unassisted martial arts kick
Chinmay Sharma, from New Delhi, has performed the highest unassisted martial arts 360 degree kick on 4 August 2024. The kick reached a height of 6 ft 9 inches setting a new benchmark.

Most bicycle crunches – 1 min. (woman)
Sunita Chhabra from Jaipur, Rajasthan, performed 88 bicycle crunches in 1 min. from 7:32 p.m. to 7:33 p.m. on 18 February 2020 at the office of JVP Media Group, Jaipur.

Most reverse dips – 1 min.
Ankush Gurjar from Gurugram, Haryana, performed 137 reverse dips in 1 min. from 12:06 p.m. to 12:07 p.m. on 4 May 2019 at H2O Fitness Gym, Gurugram.

Most leg raises – 1 min. – women
Ruhi Chakarvarti of Gurgaon, Haryana, performed 87 leg raises in 1 minute at H2O Fitness, Gurgaon on 14 May 2025.

Most crunches
Nitin Arora of Ghaziabad, Uttar Pradesh, performed 1,000 abdomen crunches in 8 mins from 8:45 a.m. to 8:53 a.m. on 6 May 2018.

Most full-contact kicks on a kickpad – alternate legs – 1 hr
Naman Bhardwaj from Ghaziabad, Uttar Pradesh, performed 6,170 full-contact kicks in 1 hr from 10:20 a.m. to 11:20 a.m. on 26 May 2021 at Vasundhara Taekwondo Academy, Ghaziabad, Uttar Pradesh.

Most full-extension punches – 1 min. – women
Uma Pawan Kedia of Surat, Gujarat, performed 288 full-extension punches in 1 minute at the Premier Warrior Hub in Surat on 15 June 2025.

Most sit-ups – 1 min. – women
Rohini Gera of Gurgaon, Haryana, performed 65 sit-ups in 1 minute at AU Sports Academy Ground, Gurgaon on 17 May 2025.

Effortless Squats

Most pistol squats – alternating legs – 1 min.
Shivam from Lucknow, Uttar Pradesh, performed 45 pistol squats in 1 min. using legs alternately on 4 September 2019 at his residence.

Most alternative squats – 1 min
Gaurav Singh Bhatti of Mandi Dabwali, Haryana, attempted 122 alternative squats in 1 min. at Big Gym on 7 July 2018.

Most squats – 1 min.– women
Priyanka Prasher from Gurugram, Haryana, performed 97 squats in 1 min. from 12:09 p.m. to 12:10 p.m. on 10 May 2019 at H2O Fitness Gym, Gurugram.

Most squats – 1 min.
Apoorv Ashok Mathur performed 96 squats in 1 min. at H2O Fitness Gym, Gurugram, Haryana, on 28 April 2018.

Most jump squats – 1 min.
Himanshu Jadon from Gurugram, Haryana, performed 82 jump squats in 1 min. from 12:05 p.m. to 12:06 p.m. on 28 May 2019 at H2O Fitness Gym, Gurugram.

MEMORY

Fastest to identify all the bones in the human body
Kudrat Kukreja from Shimla, Himachal Pradesh, set a new record by identifying all the bones in the human body in 1 min. 53 secs on 21 August 2020 at Hotel Siddharth, Ram Bazar, Shimla.

Fastest to recall 2,500 digits of π
Vimosh Venugopal from Thrissur, Kerala, recalled 2,500 digits of the value of π correctly in 12 mins 18 secs 90 microseconds on 27 October 2019 at Hotel Joys Palace, Thrissur.

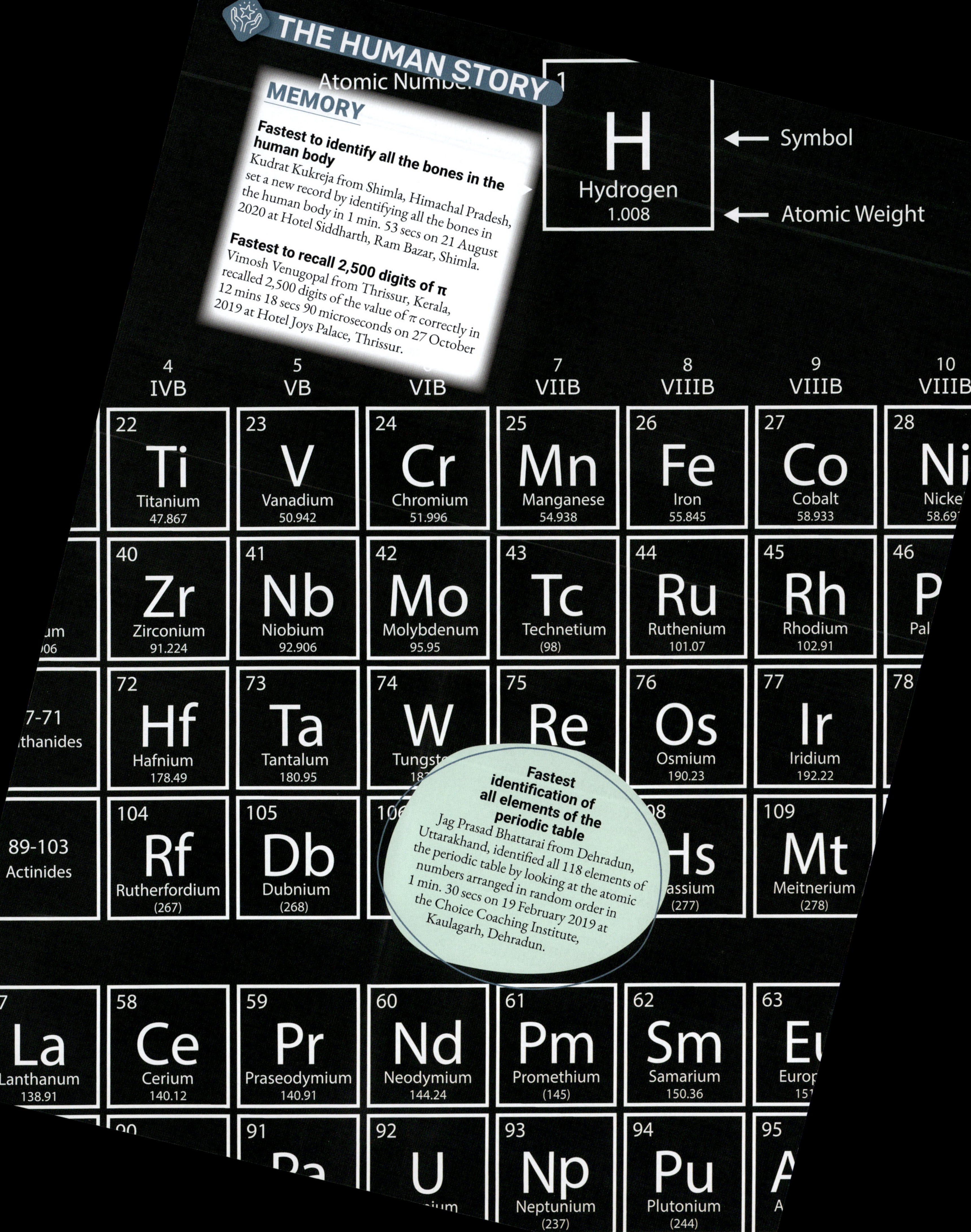

Fastest identification of all elements of the periodic table
Jag Prasad Bhattarai from Dehradun, Uttarakhand, identified all 118 elements of the periodic table by looking at the atomic numbers arranged in random order in 1 min. 30 secs on 19 February 2019 at the Choice Coaching Institute, Kaulagarh, Dehradun.

TALLEST

Tallest Man

Dharmendra Pratap Singh from Meerut, Uttar Pradesh, is the tallest man in India. Standing 8 ft 1 in. tall, he is a feet taller than the Great Khali.

Tallest Mannequin

Shoppers Stop Ltd (SSL) made the tallest mannequin, 35 ft tall with 74 rft (running feet) circumference out of metal and finished in paper and installed it on 10 July 2015 at the SSL Store in GIP Mall, Noida, UP.

Tallest Ravana effigy

Rana Tejinder Singh Chauhan is the founder of Shri Ram Leela Club, Barara, Ambala, Haryana. For Dussehra 2014 the Club made a 64 m (210 ft) tall Ravana effigy and burnt it with firecrackers on 3 October that year. The structure weighed 5 tonnes and used hardware like iron pipes, rods, and angles accounting for 3.5 tonnes while the bamboo, cloth, rope, and paper constituted the remaining 1.5 tonnes. The effigy was burnt as a symbolic representation of the destruction of social vices such as terrorism, communalism, casteism, corruption, foeticide, and adulteration.

Tallest Santa Claus

Shoppers Stop Ltd made the tallest Santa Claus, 75.4 ft, at Inorbit Mall in Malad, Mumbai, for Christmas. Work on the Santa started on 10 December 2015 and was completed on 4 January 2016. Over 30 people worked round the clock to construct it.

Tallest Snowman

Shoppers Stop Ltd made the tallest snowman, 28 ft tall and weighing 200 kg. It was displayed in three metros – Inorbit Mall, Malad, Mumbai; Rajouri Garden, Delhi; and Banerghatta, Bengaluru – from 12 December 2014 to 2 January 2015. Twenty people were involved in its making, and it took 15 days to complete.

Tallest stacked coin tower

Gandhi Institute of Engineering & Technology (GIET), Gunupur, Rayagada, Odisha, organised a Science and Tech Expo from 21 to 23 February 2014 wherein around 350 social and technical models were demonstrated by the students. Sanjeev Kumar Pal, a fourth-semester student of BTech, and his friends used 47,000 ₹1 coins to make a 3.66 m (12 ft) high, 2.74 m (9 ft) long and 1.83m (6 ft) wide replica of India Gate, which was displayed at the expo.

Tallest man-made Christmas tree

Delhi International Airport Ltd, New Delhi, commissioned India's tallest manmade Christmas tree, 30.7 m (101 ft) tall (including the 2.4 m [8 ft] star on top). It had over 16,000 Christmas ornaments and 60,000 pine twigs as decoration. The 12-tonne installation was made in 23 days by a team of 80 members from Karmic Events India. It was inaugurated on 23 December 2019.

MOST

Time for most countries shown on a single analogue clock simultaneously

Surinder Kumar from Ambala, Haryana, designed an analogue clock that showed the time of 29 countries on a single dial simultaneously, in 2024. The list includes countries such as India, China, Japan, US, Russia, Thailand, Viet Nam, Indonesia, Malaysia, Spain, Germany, Italy, Oman, Canada, Australia, Cambodia, New Zealand, Nigeria, and Singapore among others.

WR Most eggs held in one hand – palm down

Lakshmi Manohar Reddy Mavuru from Vijayawada, Andhra Pradesh, equalled the record of holding the most eggs in one hand with the palm facing downwards on 16 April 2024 by holding 13 eggs.

Most eggs held in one hand – palm up

Rajender Singh Mathru of Tilak Nagar, Delhi, held 32 eggs in his right hand for 3 mins 50 secs on 23 September 2017. The eggs were of average size with 59 mm length and 42 mm diameter.

Most diyas lit – multiple venues – group – single day

The Department of Tourism, Government of Uttar Pradesh, in collaboration with District Administration, Ayodhya along with Rammanohar Lohia Avadh University displayed 2,617,215 oil lamps on the banks of the Saryu river on 19 October 2025.

Most mannequins displayed – single day – single venue

Max Fashion, Lifestyle International displayed 100 full body mannequins on 30 September 2023 from 11:00 a.m. to 7:00 p.m. at the Nexus Forum Mall, Hyderabad.

Most kites on a single line

Dharampal Satyapal Foods Limited in association with MOMS Outdoor Media Solutions flew a train of 1,150 kites on a single line between 1:00 p.m. and 2:16 p.m. on 25 February 2023 at the Rann of Kachchh, Gujarat. The thread measured 1,155 m, and around 10 people participated in the event.

WR Most people brushing their teeth simultaneously – multiple venues

Colgate–Palmolive (India) Ltd in association with Indian Dental Association organized most people brushing their teeth simultaneously – a total of 1,77,003 participants in 380 locations – on 9 October 2007.

WR Most people sweeping the floor simultaneously – multiple venues

Prayagraj Mela Authority, Government of India, organized the most people sweeping the floor across multiple venues in locations across Prayagraj, Uttar Pradesh, on 2 March 2019. As many as 10,180 people participated in the event.

Most saree styles draped

Kalpana Bhagwandas Shah from Mumbai, draped a total of 226 unduplicated saree styles in 24 hrs on 9 April 2022. The sarees used varied from chiffon to georgette and crepe to Benarasi silk. A total of 3,914 ft of saree material was draped. The fastest saree drape was done within 1 min.

FASTEST

Fastest assembling of cycles

Hindustan Petroleum Corporation Ltd organized the 'Velocipede Challenge', where 313 participants simultaneously assembled 60 bicycles from different segregated components in 45 mins at the Yuvantage 3.0 Grand Finale on 7 January 2019 at Ramoji Film City, Hyderabad.

WR Fastest time to travel to all seven continents

Dr Ali Irani and Sujoy Kumar Mitra hold the record for fastest time to travel to all seven continents for 3 days 1 hour 5 mins and 4 secs. in Melbourne, Australia on 7 December 2022.

LONGEST

Longest sandwich

The St. Soldier Institute of Hotel Management and Catering Technology, Jalandhar, Punjab, made the longest sandwich on 22 December 2021. Led by Sandeep Lohani, the principal, 5 faculty chefs and 15 students prepared a sandwich, measuring 223 ft 2.4 in. in length and 8 in. in width, in 35 mins from 11:13 a.m. to 11:48 a.m. They

Spectra: longest charcuterie platter

Akanksha Yadav: longest hair

used 123 slices of loaf spread with a combination of vegetables, noodles, cheese, pasta, and dressings for it.

Longest charcuterie platter
Spectra, a restaurant at the Leela Ambience Gurugram Hotel and Residences, Gurugram, Haryana, displayed a 9.448 m (31 ft) long and 30 cm (11.8 in.) wide Christmas charcuterie platter on 24 December 2018. It had a variety of cheeses, meats, compotes, crudités, sandwiches, canapés, truffles, and chocolates, among other dishes.

WR **Longest paper chain**
Vimin M. Vincent from Thiruvananthapuram, Kerala, made the longest paper chain measuring 956.20 m (3,137 ft 1.6 in.) in 24 hours on 11 February 2022.

Longest kebab
NIMS University-Jaipur in Jaipur, Rajasthan, made a kebab measuring 49 ft 8.4 in. in length with a team of 45 participants under the supervision of Prof. Manoj Srivastava in 9 hrs 53 mins on 6 April 2022. The vegetarian tawa kebab was made on a customized tawa, 50 ft long and 2.5 ft wide, using seven industrial gas cylinders with 4 mm hot plate tawa with rail burners underneath. It was displayed at the Sundervan Garden of NIMS University. The kebab was made with 16 kg potatoes, 5 kg chickpea flour, 2 kg green peas, 2 kg ghee, 1 kg mint leaves, 5 kg onion garlic paste, 2 kg capsicum, 1 kg green chillies, 5 kg soya nuggets, 7 kg spinach, and 900 gm ground garam masala.

WR **Longest and largest human chain**
The Government of Bihar, as part of its 'Jan Jeevan Hariyali' campaign, organized an 18,034 km long human chain with 5.16 crore (51.6 million) people on 19 January 2020. It took 7 helicopters and over 100 drones to take aerial images of the human chain. The event championed the cause of conservation of environment along with other social causes.

Longest hair
Akanksha Yadav from Thane, Maharashtra, has the longest hair, which is 3.01 m (9 ft 10.5 in.) long.

Longest bill
Sanjay Dodrajka from New Delhi ordered 420 burgers from the Burger King outlet in Dhaula Kuan for children of MCD School, Nangal Punya, New Delhi, on 7 December 2019. As a result, Sanjay got a 12 ft (144 in.) long bill.

COLLECTIONS

Amitabh Bachchan memorabilia
Mohan Rajgopal Iyer from Nagpur, Maharashtra, an ardent admirer of superstar Amitabh Bachchan, has a collection of his photographs, articles, press clippings, filmography, and

correspondences and articles from the internet. The total number of items were 8,650 up to 31 May 2019.

WR Credit cards

Manish Kumar Dhameja from Lucknow, Uttar Pradesh, has a collection of 1,638 valid credit cards from 25 banks. His first credit card was issued by the State Bank of India in 2014. The collection includes prepaid cards and add-on supplementary cards. His collection was exhibited from 10:00 a.m. to 11:00 a.m. on 30 August 2022 at the Telecommunications Consultants India Limited (TCIL) Southern Regional Office, Hyderabad.

Manish Kumar Dhameja

Airmail envelopes

Jinesh Joseph from Bengaluru, has a collection of 1,858 airmail envelopes from 338 regions including recognized countries, disputed territories, and autonomous republics.

Models of owls

Ramesh Kumar Bhatia from Mumbai, Maharashtra, has a collection of 351 owl models (up to 31 May 2020) since 2013. The models of owls are from different countries including India, Bhutan, China, New Zealand, Australia, Iceland, Uzbekistan, and Morocco, among others.

Ties

Dr Deepak M. Sharma from Ahmedabad, Gujarat, has a collection of 4,589 ties including 2,611 theme-based ones.

Maps

Ravindranath Vishnu Newadkar from Thane, Maharashtra, has a collection of 365 maps up to 31 May 2022. These include 100 maps of various countries and 265 maps of different cities.

Maps

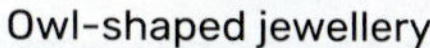

Owl-shaped jewellery

Owl-shaped jewellery

Dr Prashant Laxman Wagh from Nashik, Maharashtra, has a collection of owlshaped jewellery, which he started in 2016. He has 717 items in his collection – 478 pendants, 129 brooches, 62 earrings, and 48 rings. The jewellery is made of materials like zinc alloy, stainless steel, rhinestone, synthetic turquoise stone, and semi-precious metals, among others.

Stickers

Nidhi Bansal from Fatehgarh Sahib, Punjab, had collected 1,03,800 stickers, a hobby since 2007. She had categorized her collection into subjects like smiley faces, flowers, footballs, birds, trains, and cartoons, among others.

Napkins

Parveen Gupta, his wife Anuradha Gupta, and daughter Dr Kanika Gupta from New Delhi have collected 12,246 commercial and 9,325 noncommercial paper napkins from countries like Romania, Egypt, Slovakia, the UK, the US, the UAE, Germany, Australia, Switzerland, and India. They started their collection in 2014.

Napkins

Autographs – national awardees

Praful Thakkar has more than 4,300 autographs of Indian and world celebrities, collected in more than 40 years and arranged thematically into 50 categories. The collection includes autographs of 519 Padma Shri awardees and 101 Nobel laureates.

Chitra Kathayen comics

Ninad Jadhav from Barkuhi, Chhindwara District, Madhya Pradesh, has the largest collection of Hindi-film *Chitra Kathayen*, numbering 123, a collection since 1997. Most of the comics feature Mithun Chakraborty, Dimple Kapadia, Madhuri Dixit, Vinod Khanna, Rajesh Khanna, Shah Rukh Khan, and Navin Nischol. All *Chitra Kathayen* are from Diamond Comics. Amit Jain from Berasia, Bhopal, an ardent fan of Amitabh Bachchan, helped Ninad build this collection.

Autographs of Ajit Laxman Wadekar

Satish Laxman Chaphekar from Dombivli, Maharashtra, has 39 autographs of the late cricketer Ajit Laxman Wadekar, who played 39 international matches during his

Matchboxes featuring horses

career including 37 Tests and 2 ODIs. Satish collected Wadekar's bats, balls, and gloves, among other things.

Matchboxes featuring horses

Sudhir Jain from Satna, Madhya Pradesh, has a collection of 235 matchboxes featuring a horse in the design. None of the matchboxes in the collection is duplicated.

Cinema press booklets – on a single personality

Ninad Jadhav from Chhindwara, Madhya Pradesh, has a collection of 105 cinema press booklets on actor Mithun Chakraborty. The oldest booklet is of the film Mera Rakshak, which was released in 1978.

Obituaries – from a single family

Ninad Jadhav from Chhindwara, Madhya Pradesh, has the most obituary news clippings of the Kapoor family (of Hindi cinema) from 272 multi-language newspapers. The obituaries are of Shammi Kapoor (111), Shashi Kapoor (68), Rishi Kapoor (19), and Rajiv Kapoor (74).

Cinema press booklets on a single personality

Seer (Indian weights)

Ranjeet Kumar Jha from Bhopal, Madhya Pradesh, has a collection of 250 'seer' or 'ser', old Indian weights in various shapes from different Indian princely states like Bhopal, Gwalior, Mewar, Agra, Rajkot, and Indore. In total there are 25 kinds of seer. The scales carry different state seals with different values in different languages.

Hair clips

Hair clips
Sana Fathima from Pudukkottai, Tamil Nadu, has 1,200 hair clips, a collection started on 24 October 2017 and completed on 24 March 2018.

WR Aircraft models
Vikram Rajkumar Tirkannad from Chennai, Tamil Nadu, has collected 719 models of aircraft over the last 38 years. The first model in his collection was an Air India Boeing 747. The largest are the Airways Concorde and a Jet Airways Boeing 737-800 Winglet, both measuring 0.6 m (2 ft). The smallest is the Air India ATR 42-320 measuring only 6 cm (2.36 in.).

Aircraft models

Nokia handsets
Jayesh Umesh Kale from Thane, Maharashtra, has a collection of 1,600 Nokia handsets, a hobby he started in 2013. All the mobile handsets are in working condition.

Soap covers (alphabetical)
Jayadevan Rajagopala from Thrissur, Kerala, has 1,840 unique bath-soap wrappers, a collection spanning more than 30 years. No two covers are the same in his collection, although the same brand might have more than one cover.

Pradhan Mantri Yojana matchboxes
Alok Mehrotra from Kanpur, Uttar Pradesh, has a collection of 1,550 matchboxes of 21 Pradhan Mantri Yojanas including the Awas Yojana, the Amrit Kosh Yojana, the Garib Kalyan Yojana, the Sukanya Samriddhi Yojana, the Namami Gange programme, the Swachh Bharat Mission, the Pradhan Mantri Jan Aarogya Yojna, the National Sports Talent Yojana, the UMANG Yojana, the Jal Shakti Yojana, and the Sovereign Gold Bond Yojana, among others. He started his collection in 2019.

Toothpaste wrappers
Mankeerat Kaur from Gurugram, Haryana, has toothpaste wrappers from different countries, a collection started in April 2020. She has 178 unduplicated toothpaste wrappers from India, the United Arab Emirates (UAE), and the United States of America (US). Her complete collection comprises 204 wrappers.

Lapel pins
Arvind Sinha from Mumbai, Maharashtra, has been collecting lapel pins since 1998 and had 53,228 lapel pins as on 31 March 2015. He exhibits his collection to create awareness on history through lapel pins. The world wars, development of guns, aviation history, space programmes – all these are depicted through his lapel pins.

Lighters
Hamed Husein Patel from Mumbai, Maharashtra, has a collection of 1,042 gas and petrol lighters (till 30 June 2018). The most expensive lighter is the 2008 limited edition St Dupont priced at ₹2,00,000. He also possesses a Dunhill lighter which was once owned by Elvis Presley.

Scales
Ameya Gupta of Delhi has a collection of 2,072 scales (including 1,890 duplicates) from countries like India, UAE, Japan, China, South Korea, Taiwan, Germany, Malaysia, and Egypt as on 30 June 2015. They are made of different materials

like aluminium, steel, wood, paper and plastic. The tallest scale is 6 ft (1.83 m) in length and the smallest is just 3 inches (7.62 cm).

Magazines – Hindi
Dr Jawahar Karnavat from Bhopal, Madhya Pradesh, has 93 Hindi magazines, a collection that started in 2002. The oldest magazine in his collection is the India Opinion published in 1903 in South Africa in Gujarati, Tamil, English, and Hindi. In all, there are 25 weekly, 3 fortnightly, 40 monthly, 18 quarterly, and 7 half-yearly magazines. The Deepawali special issue of Shanti Doot published from Fiji contains as many as 120 pages.

Magazines
Daria Singh Yadav from Haryana has a collection of over 3,000 different magazines and periodicals. The magazines, which are not necessarily first issues, are in 17 languages covering 6 continents.

Magazines – regional languages
A. Ramanan from Vellore, Tamil Nadu, has collected over 1,706 Tamil magazines, some of which have now stopped publication. The oldest Varthaga Mitran is dated 1917, and the second oldest is Ramanujan dated 1919.

Magazines – first issues
Mudappalam M. Sukumar from Mumbai, has been collecting first issues of magazines since May 1979. He has a total of 662 issues of weekly, fortnightly, monthly, and bimonthly magazines in English, Tamil, and Hindi. There are 488 Tamil, 30 Hindi, 112 English, and 32 in other languages. His collection started with the very first issue of the Tamil magazine Chaavi.

Railway platform tickets

Railway platform tickets
Naveen Kumar from New Delhi has a collection of 100 unduplicated railway platform tickets. These tickets have been collected from Uttar Pradesh, Uttarakhand, Delhi, Haryana, Maharashtra, and Rajasthan between 30 April 2023 and 10 June 2023.

Airline magazines
Mallikarjun M. Umadi from Nashik, Maharashtra, has been collecting magazines printed by various airlines since 2006; and as of 30 June 2016, he had 175 different magazines of 33 different airlines, both national and international.

Pencils
Tushar Lakhanpal from New Delhi has the largest unduplicated pencil collection that started in 2001. The collection from 62 countries has over 50 scented pencils in various fragrances, pencils that show temperature variations, pencils depicting the crowns of various Austrian and English kingdoms, and a spoon-like pencil, among others. His collection grew to 16,795 as on 30 June 2017.

Antique matchbox labels – uncut sheets
Samirkumar Hasmukhbhai Arya from Valsad, Gujarat, has a collection of 225 uncut antique matchbox labels.

Magazines – personality covers – featuring a single personality
Anuradha Gupta from New Delhi has collected 317 different magazines in various languages with Prime Minister Narendra Modi on the cover. The collection began in 2017.

WR Bindi
A. Kalaivani has the largest bindi collection with 3,000 unique bindis as verified on 1 February 2016.

WR Airline boarding passes
K. Ullas Kamath has a collection of 3,030 airline boarding passes as verified on 15 August 2014.

Badges – political theme
Ranjeet Kumar Jha from Bhopal, Madhya Pradesh, has 250 badges from different years and of different shapes, sizes, material, and logos of political parties, such as the Congress, BJP, and BSP, in his collection. He started the collection on 9 April 2003 and completed it on 9 April 2021.

Badges – political theme

Playing cards – matchbox theme

Samirkumar Hasmukhbhai Arya from Valsad, Gujarat, has a collection of 242 matchbox themed playing cards. The collection showcases unique cards inspired by Indian and International Matchbox art.

VICTORY HORSE
THE MATCH CORPORATION OF MADRAS SIVAKASI.
SAFETY MATCHES
SANTANU AND GANGA
SAFETY MATCH.
MADE IN SWEDEN.
CHEETA FIGHT
SAFETY MATCHES
MADE IN INDIA
FRANCE
TAMCO
SAFETY MATCHES
SAFETY MATCHES
THE FIGHT
SAFETY MATCHES
MADE IN SWEDEN
TARZAN FIGHT
RETAIL PRICE Rs. 0-0-9
VLINDER
LUCIFERS
NEDERL FABRIKAAT
NATIONALE LUCIFERSFABRIEK
WEERT
THE WHALE
DON'T PANIC
SAFETY MATCHES
KESSEL RUN
WILD CARD
THREE TORCHES
INDEPENDENCE SAFETY MATCH
WINNERS
BRADBURY
ANARCHY BRAND
LION & MOUSE
GOLDING BRAND
FIRESTARTER
EVIL
ANIMAL FARM
TWO FLOWER
VISA
PEACOCK
TAMCO

Toothbrushes

WR

Dr Yogesh Chandrana from Vadodra, Gujarat, has a collection of toothbrushes numbering a total of 2,371 items as on 21 January 2024. The collection has rare pieces from the nineteenth century as well.

Spoons

Shubhangi Apte of Raipur, Chhattisgarh, has 1,852 small and big spoons, a collection started in April 1995. The collection has silver, gold, ceramic, steel, copper, and wooden spoons in a variety of sizes, shapes, and colours. The biggest spoon was 18 inch and smallest measured 1 inch.

Antique clocks

S. Robert Kennedy of Chennai, Tamil Nadu, has been collecting antique clocks (2,200 by March 2018) since 1983. The oldest clock in his collection is 285 years old from the UK. His collection has mechanical and wind-up clocks, pendulum wall clocks, ship clocks, carriage clocks, skeleton clocks, alarm clocks, table clocks, pocket watches, and wristwatches.

Dice

Ankit Shah of Mumbai has the largest collection of dice numbering to 3,131 items. His collection has dice in all shapes and sizes.

Pens

V.T. Jolly of Kochi, Kerala, has 13,000 used pens, both ball-point and fountain, in his possession. Among the many novel pens in his collection, there is a unique golden crown pen, a perfume spraying pen, pens with cigarette lighter, double-sized pen, and more. He has pens from 16 countries.

Candles

Johnson Nayankara of Irinjalakuda, Kerala, has the largest collection of candles. By 30 June 2011, his collection grew to 3,309 candles of different sizes and shapes, and even fragrant ones. He collected them from different parts of the world.

Playing cards

Aditi Shailesh Agarwal from Ahmedabad, Gujarat, has 6,000 sets of Indian and foreign playing cards, the largest such collection, which she started when she was 15 years old. The collection varies in theme, form, size, shape, and material. Aditi has a card deck that was used for a code during the First World War and a celebrity collection on Lady Diana, George Bush, Nelson Mandela, and Bollywood stars Amitabh Bachchan, Madhuri Dixit, Shah Rukh Khan, and others.

Same-day newspapers

Shiju Thomas from Bengaluru, Karnataka, has the largest collection of Mahatma Gandhi's 150th birth anniversary newspapers, dated 2 October 2019. His collection comprises 603 newspapers, which includes 301 newspapers with different titles and 302 newspapers with different place editions in 17 Indian languages. The collection includes weekly, fortnightly, and monthly publications.

Foreign newspapers

Manu Parkash Jindal of Jalandhar has a collection of 3,216 newspapers from 76 countries in 54 languages (including 29 foreign languages). The entire collection is indexed giving detailed explanations on the papers.

Sequential same-day newspaper

Akanksha Jain from Vadodara, Gujarat, has the longest unbroken sequential collection of the same-day newspaper, The Times of India, dated 20 July for 16 years, right from 1994 to 2009.

Newspaper clippings featuring deities

Rekha Gore of Raipur, Chhattisgarh, has been collecting pictures or likenesses of Ganesha since 1950. She has 31,517 such items including 18,309 wedding cards, 9,430 newspaper cuttings, 78 magazine cuttings, 219 books, 102 photographs (foreign), and 3,379 of these from her relatives. She has held an exhibition of these at Raipur on 19 April 2009.

Newspapers

Dayanand N. Manchanda of Lajpat Nagar, Delhi, collected about 1,20,000 newspapers in English and Hindi over the last 15 years. He has been collecting at least 22 papers every day since 1996. He collected them originally as reference material for his research on numerology. He also has a collection of 2,500 magazines on astrology over the last 15 years.

Hindi-language newspapers

Dr Ashok Pandey 'Gulshan' from Bahraich, Uttar Pradesh, has a collection of 12,634 different Hindi newspapers under 655 titles from Indian states, Nepal, China, and Thailand, all received by India Post in Uttar Pradesh since 1990. He has bound volumes alphabetically as daily, tri-weekly, biweekly, weekly, fortnightly, monthly, bimonthly, trimonthly, and annual special issues.

Mugs

Bhupali Nainesh Shah from Mumbai, Maharashtra has a collection of 419 mugs, the largest such collection, as verified in 2025. The collection includes mugs on different themes such as, fruits, animals, cities and celebrities. She started this collection in 2007.

Newspaper clippings featuring Lata Mangeshkar – group

Gaurav Sharma and Manju Lata Sharma have collected 11,505 news clippings on the late singer Lata Mangeshkar. The oldest press clipping dates back to 1955. There are various original press articles on her from 1959 onwards in various languages – Hindi, Marathi, Odia, Bangla, Gujarati, Konkani, Tamil, Telugu, Assamese, Malayalam, Punjabi, Urdu, and English. There are also original newspaper articles on her from Finland, the UK, and Bangladesh.

Newspaper clippings featuring Lata Mangeshkar – solo

Dr Anil Patiram Meshram from Nagpur, Maharashtra, has the largest collection of information and items related to Bharat Ratna Lata Mangeshkar. He has 2,200 newspaper photos, 318 photo clippings with information, and 144 news information pieces without a photo.

Newspapers in most languages
Shashanka Sekhar Dash popularly known as 'Paperboy Shashank' of Jajpur, Odisha, has the largest collection of newspapers totalling 5,000 since 2001. His collection has 3,584 different newspapers from 76 countries in 66 languages.

Newspapers from most countries
Shashanka Sekhar Dash from Jajpur, Odisha, has a collection of 981 newspapers in 63 languages from 102 countries. Started in 2005, his collection has newspapers from countries including Lesotho, Seychelles, Peru, Palestine, East Timor, and Papua New Guinea, and in languages including Estonian, Yakut, Tok Pisin, Tetum, Hebrew, Dari, and Pashto.

Regional-language newspapers
A.S. Muhammed from Kottayam District, Kerala, has been collecting old Malayalam publications like newspapers and magazines, including the 1890 first edition of Malayalam Manorama, and the new edition of Suprabhaatham published in 2014. His archival collection includes 150 newspapers and over 2,000 journals.

Newspaper clippings featuring Mahatma Gandhi – solo
Shiju Thomas from Bengaluru, Karnataka, has a collection of 860 news clippings on Mahatma Gandhi in various Indian languages.

Newspaper clippings featuring Sridevi – solo
Anuradha Gupta from New Delhi has a collection of 1,270 press clippings about late actor Sridevi from newspapers and magazines in many languages starting from 24 February 2018.

Newspaper clippings featuring Atal Bihari Vajpayee – solo
Anuradha Gupta from New Delhi has collected 612 newspaper clippings of former prime minister Atal Bihari Vajpayee. The clippings are in many languages including Hindi, English, Marathi, Gujarati, Tamil, and Telugu.

Newspaper clippings on cinema
Swarnlata Vishwafool from Katihar, Bihar, has collected 100,147 clippings related to Hindi cinema from various Hindi newspapers from 1998 to 2019.

LARGEST

Largest *peda* – group
A team of six chefs, Vaibhav Nehra, Rudra P. Singh, Sandeep S. Mahar, Kuyate M. Rajendra, Sahil Singh, and Rahul, from Bird Airport Hotel Pvt. Ltd, Roseate House, Hospitality District, Aerocity, New Delhi, made the largest *peda* (an Indian sweet dish), measuring 3 ft x 3 ft, in three hours on 27 May 2025 at Roseate House, Aerocity, New Delhi.

Largest decorative display using currency

WR Largest decorative display using currency*
Sri Sathya Ganapathi Shirdi Sai Trust (R) created the largest decorative display, covering an area of 13,000 sq. ft using Indian currency on 18 September 2024 for Ganesh Chaturthi. The impressive display was created over a period of 18 days by 150 artisans under CCTV surveillance. The value of coins and notes used for making the display was ₹7,00,000, and included ₹1, ₹10, and ₹20 coins, and ₹20, ₹50, ₹100, ₹200, and ₹500 notes.

Largest *peda*

*This is a one-time category. Further and future applications for this record will not be accepted.

A delectable Awadhi meal

India's UNESCO 'City of Gastronomy' Designations

Hyderabad was designated India's first **UNESCO Creative City of Gastronomy** in 2019, followed by Lucknow in 2025. The recognition, part of UNESCO's Creative Cities Network, celebrates the rich culinary heritage of these cities – Hyderabad for its iconic biryani and diverse Deccani cuisine, and Lucknow for its famed Awadhi traditions and royal culinary legacy.

A scrumptious Hyderabadi biryani meal

Above: Largest raj kachori; *Below*: Largest flag made from recycled material

Largest human formation – outline

Largest raj kachori
A team of five chefs, Vaibhav Nehra, Rudra Pratap Singh, Gireesh Kumar, Bipin Rawat, and Rahul, from Bird Airport Hotel Pvt. Ltd, Roseate House, Hospitality District, Aerocity, New Delhi made the largest raj kachori (an Indian chaat dish), measuring 76.2 cm (2.5 ft) in diameter. The raj kachori was appropriately filled with stuffing, curd and chutneys, and was made in 40 minutes on 22 May 2024 at Roseate House, Aerocity, New Delhi.

Largest flag – recycled material
Coca-Cola India created the largest flag from recycled material, which was displayed during the ICC Men's Cricket World Cup 2023. They created the Indian national flag from approximately 11,000 PET bottles. It measured 35 meters (114.83 ft) in length and 20 meters (65.62 ft) in width, and weighed 115.55 kgs.

Largest human formation – outline
Chandigarh Group of Colleges, Jhanjeri, Sahibzada Ajit Singh Nagar, Punjab, made the largest human formation – outline with 6,965 participants making an outline of the incubator logo on 3 March 2025 for a duration of five minutes.

SMALLEST

Smallest devil's knot
Santhosh Kumar from Thiruvananthapuram, Kerala, has made the smallest devil's knot measuring 8 mm x 2 mm x 2mm using his wood sculpting skills.

Smallest devil's knot

WR Smallest rugby stadium model

Shaminder Singh from Coventry, UK, constructed a model of the Ricoh Arena rugby stadium, 122 cm (48 in.) long, 76 cm (29.9 in.) wide, and 41 cm (16.1 in.) high, with 45,000 toothpicks. He worked on the model for a total of 900 hours over six months between 1 September 2017 and 2 March 2018.

Smallest rugby stadium model

Smallest scissors

Mattewada Ajay Kumar of Warangal, Telangana, created a miniature working pair of gold scissors in 3 hrs in 2015. It is 11 mm (0.43 in.) long and weighs 0.18 mg.

Smallest microwave oven

Salvendar Ghansheed Baba from Vijayawada, Andhra Pradesh, made the smallest microwave oven, 80 mm (3.15 in.) long, 35 mm (1.38 in.) wide, and 40 mm (1.57 in.) high in 15 days, from 11 to 25 December 2018. He used plywood cardboard, green and orange LED lights of 3 volts, 1,000-ohm resistor, small wires, Nichrome wire, aluminium foil, Fevicol glue, a small switch, a design sticker, a 3.7-volt phone battery and a connecting pin to make the oven.

Above: Smallest scissors; *Below*: Smallest microwave oven

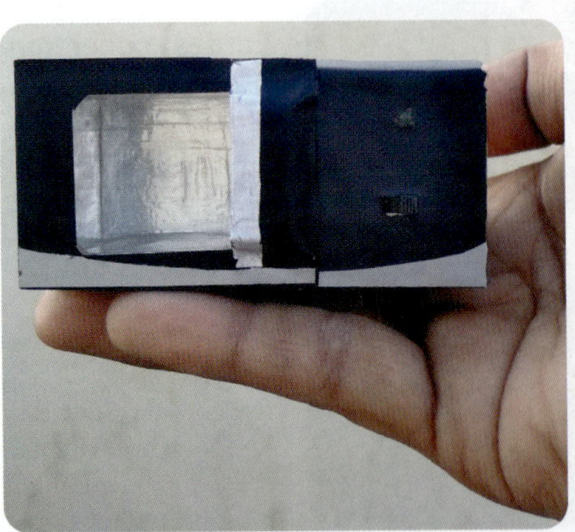

Smallest gold violin

Mattewada Ajay Kumar of Warangal, Telangana, created a 20 mm (0.78 in) long miniature gold violin, weighing 0.74 mg, in 12 hrs in 2009.

Smallest gold violin

Smallest spinning wheel

Jayant Natthuji Tandulkar from Nagpur, Maharashtra, designed the smallest spinning wheel (charkha) to spin yarn from cotton measuring 2.94 mm (0.12 in.) in length, 2.40 mm (0.09 in.) in width, 2.74 mm (0.11 in.) in height, and weighing 0.03 g on 22 April 2023. It took him 8 hrs to make it. He used materials such as steel wire, wooden sticks, and cotton thread to make it. The charkha was measured using a vernier caliper and a digital scale.

Smallest spinning wheel

Smallest iron

Pawan Sharma of Surat, Gujarat, made the smallest electric iron of 17 mm (0.66 in.) height, 9 mm (0.35 in.) width, and 2.5 mm (0.09 in.) thickness, which he completed in seven days spending 1 hr every day until 17 October 2012. The iron is made using aluminium, a plastic handle, asbestos, tungsten wire, a steel stand, and a mobile charger with a 12V DC connection.

Smallest iron

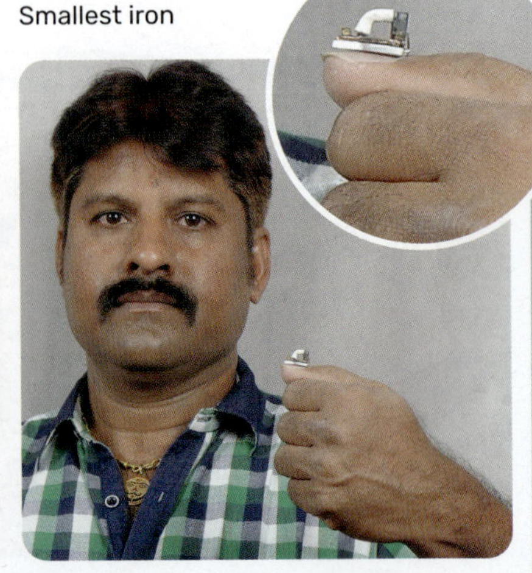

Smallest model of Belur Math

Smallest Wimbledon Centre Court model
Shaminder Singh of Coventry, UK, made a replica of the Wimbledon Centre Court using 12,000 toothpicks over 40 hours each week in 10 months from 2 July to 25 September 2017. The structure is 36 in (91.44 cm) long, 28 in (71.12 cm) wide, and 12 in (30.48 cm) in height.

Smallest Wimbledon Centre Court model

Smallest model of Belur Math
Sudhakar Raghunath Shinde from Pune, Maharashtra, carved the smallest model of the Belur Math out of wood measuring 218.5 cm (86 in.) in length, 102 cm (40 in.) in width, and 98 cm (38.6 in.) in height. The design included details such as carving of elephants, balconies, blooming lotuses, domes, pillars, Lord Ganesha, and Lord Hanuman. He has never visited the Belur Math and made this model using images downloaded from the Internet.

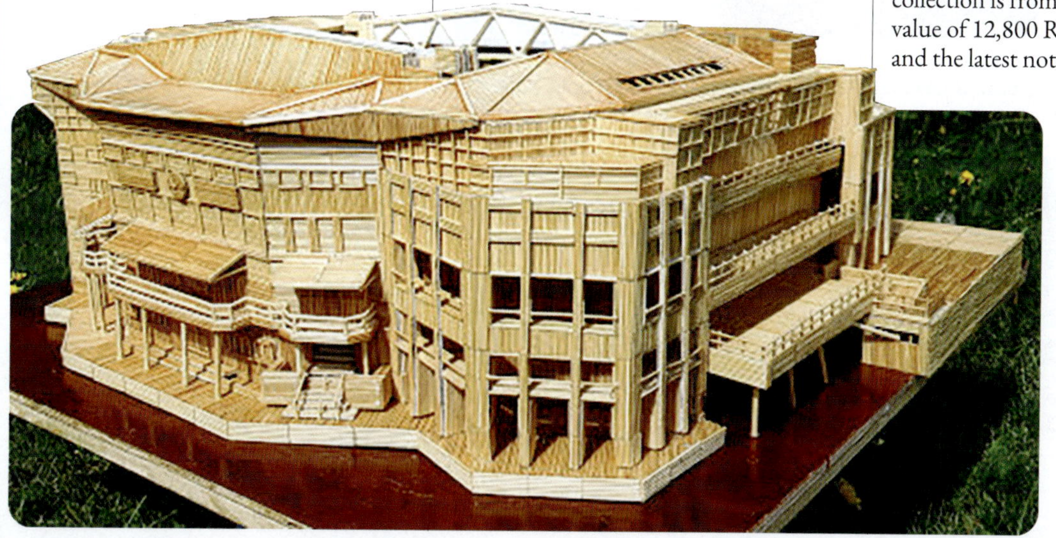

CURRENCY, COINS, AND STAMPS

Largest collection of high denomination currency notes
Putsa Krishna Kameshwar from Amalapuram, Andhra Pradesh, has the largest collection of high denomination currency notes with 306 unduplicated high denomination currency notes of 49 different denominations from 100 to 100 quadrillion from 91 countries. He has been collecting these since 20007. The oldest note in his collection is from Portugal with a face value of 12,800 Ries, printed in 1799, and the latest note is from Iran, 10,000 Rials, released in 2022.

Largest collection of specimen currency notes
Ajay Singh Rawat from Dehradun, Uttarakhand, has 165 unduplicated specimen currency notes from 165 internationally recognized countries. The total notes in his collection, including multiple notes from

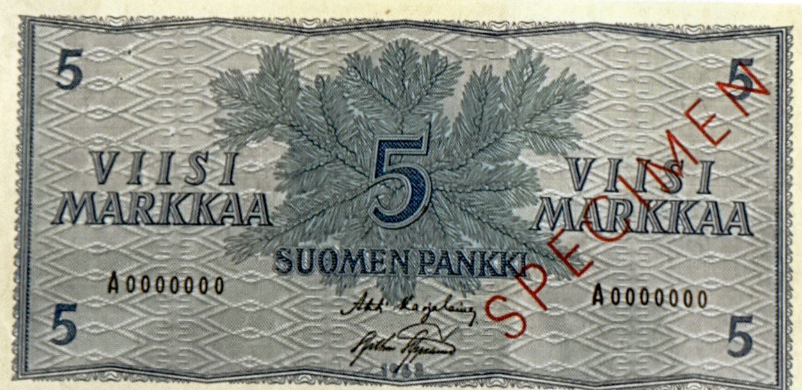

Specimen currency notes

a single country are 313. Some of them are also from unrecognized countries including Bermuda, Cayman Islands, and Transnistria.

Largest collection of COVID-19 themed coins

Paravathina Venkata Narayana from Yedidha, Andhra Pradesh, has the largest collection of unduplicated COVID-19 themed international currency coins which consists of 40 coins from 23 countries and 2 British Overseas Territories. These coins were released between 2020–2023.

Largest collection of ₹75 commemorative coins

Putsa Krishna Kameshwar from Amalapuram, Andhra Pradesh, has the largest collection of

Largest collection of ₹75 commemorative coins

₹75 commemorative coins that he has been collecting since 2010. His collection comprises of 14 coins commemorating events like platinum jubilee of RBI, 75 years of the tricolour, 75th Republic Day celebrations, among others.

Largest collection of COVID-19 themed coins

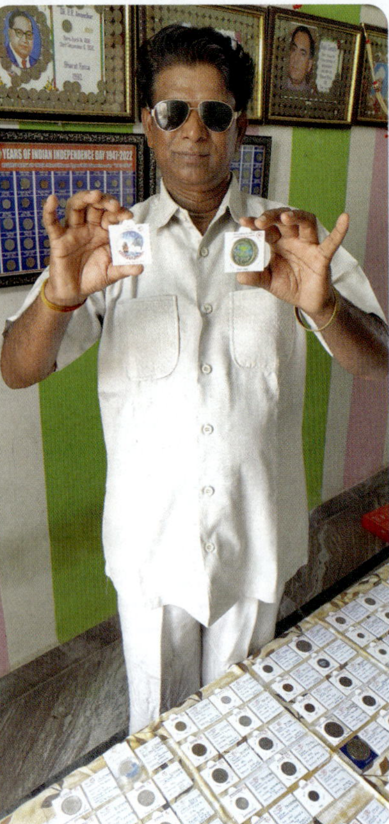

Largest collection of fish-themed coins

Largest collection of fish-themed coins from most countries of the world

Srinivasa Rao Konathala from Visakhapatnam, Andhra Pradesh, has the largest collection of fish-themed coins from most countries, with 230 coins from 90 countries.

Largest collection of 7-digit currency notes

Sagi Satya Narayana Raju from Vishakhapatnam, Andhra Pradesh, has the largest collection of unduplicated 7-digit Indian currency bank notes. There are 116 notes in total in his collection.

Largest collection of solid number currency notes

Sagi Satya Narayana Raju from Vishakhapatnam, Andhra Pradesh, has the largest collection of unduplicated solid number Indian currency bank notes. There are 1,116 notes in total in his collection.

Largest collection of star series currency notes

Sagi Satya Narayana Raju from Vishakhapatnam, Andhra Pradesh, has

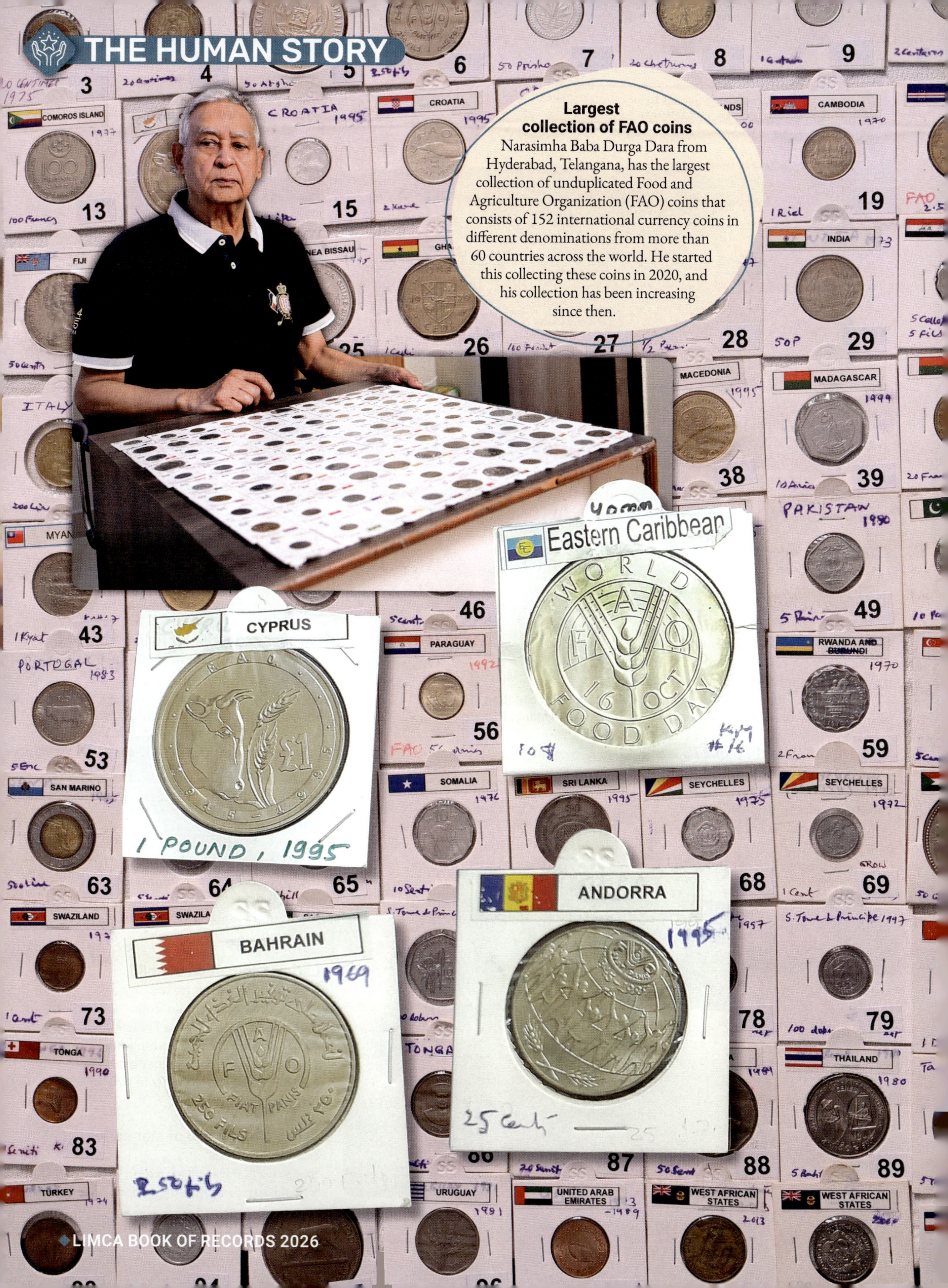

Largest collection of FAO coins

Narasimha Baba Durga Dara from Hyderabad, Telangana, has the largest collection of unduplicated Food and Agriculture Organization (FAO) coins that consists of 152 international currency coins in different denominations from more than 60 countries across the world. He started this collecting these coins in 2020, and his collection has been increasing since then.

the largest collection of unduplicated star series Indian currency bank notes. There are 5,100 notes in total in his collection.

Largest collection of ₹5 notes with the same serial number

Raj Kishore Mahanta from Keonjhar, Odisha, has the largest collection of 5-rupee currency notes with the same serial number. He has 108 notes in his collection with the serial number 999990. All notes have the signature of the former RBI governor D. Subbarao.

₹5 notes with the same serial number

Largest collection of one-quarter British anna coins

Rajendra Agrawal 'Shashi' from Satna, Madhya Pradesh, has collected 10 varieties of one-quarter British anna coins issued between 1835 and 1942. His collection has 90 coins and includes the East India Company, Queen Victoria, King Edward II, King George V, and King George VI.

Largest collection of one-quarter British anna coins

Largest collection of ₹5 stamps

Largest collection of ₹5 stamps

Peddireddi Srinivas from East Godavari district, Andhra Pradesh, has the largest collection of ₹5 Indian postal stamps. He has 603 unduplicated postal stamps in his collection released between 2009 and 2024.

Largest collection of postcards – matchbox theme

Samirkumar Hasmukhbhai Arya from Valsad, Gujarat, has the largest collection of unduplicated matchbox-themed postcards with 170 unused postcards featuring matchbox label art. He believes that his collection showcases art, history, and diversity, and this collection is his way of preserving heritage.

Matchbox-themed postacrds

Largest collection of sports-themed coins from most countries of the world
S.V.V.R. Prasad from Visakhapatnam, Andhra Pradesh, has the largest collection of sports-themed coins from most countries of the world with 400 coins from 81 countries. Out of these, 228 are Olympic coins.

Most craft pieces made out of waste

COMMUNITY DEVELOPMENT

Largest shoe donation
INC.5 Shoes Pvt. Ltd in Mumbai, Maharashtra, distributed 5,000 pairs of shoes to women, girls and the underprivileged in Mumbai and Navi Mumbai between 10:00 a.m. and 5:00 p.m. on 15 March 2019.

Most food donated in a single day – multiple venues
The ISKCON Temple in Dwarka, Delhi, under the chairmanship of Pradyumna Priya Das, in coordination with the district magistrate of southwest Delhi, Rahul Singh, cooked and distributed food to migrant labourers and other needy persons during the lockdown. Beginning in the third week of March 2020 with 5,000 meals a day, they increased the meals to 10,000, and subsequently 1,00,000 a day.

Most craft pieces made out of waste – solo – single day
Ratnamala Rao from Jabalpur, Madhya Pradesh, made the most number of

Most woollen caps donated

handmade craft pieces from waste in a day. She made 53 craft pieces in total and her craftworks included a variety of items, like table, chair, handbag, lamp, bracelet, necklace, cake, and samosa.

Most food packets distributed among the poor
Swami Sunil Das Prabhakaran, chairman of the Muthalamada Charitable Trust in Palakkad, Kerala, has been distributing 1,000 food packets every day to the poor since 1992. He distributed 9 million food packets and 70 million litres of drinking water to the poor up to September 2018.

Most benches donated – 1 year
The Ghanshyamdas Saraf Trust, a charitable trust in Mumbai, Maharashtra, donated 127 three-seater RCC pink benches to temples and police stations in and around Mumbai, between July 2021 and July 2022. A team of eight people were employed in making the benches and it took a week to make 20 benches.

Most woollen caps donated – group – single day – single venue
The Air Force Wives Welfare Association (AFWWA) from New Delhi donated 9,071 woollen caps to Safe Approach, a shelter home in Delhi on 28 October 2022 between 9:55 a.m. and 12:51 p.m. There were 19 people involved in the donation. Each cap measured 22.86–26.67 cm (9–10.5 in.) in length and 43.18–50.8 cm (17–20 in.) in circumference

Most woollen caps donated – group – single day – multiple venues
The Air Force Wives Welfare Association (AFWWA) from New Delhi donated 17,071 woollen caps to three welfare organizations in Delhi on 28 October 2022 between 9:31 a.m. and 12:51 p.m. There were 58 people involved in the donation. Each cap measured 22.86–26.67 cm (9–10.5 in.) in length and 43.18–50.8 cm (17–20 in.) in circumference.

Most ramps constructed – single day
J.K. Cement Ltd, Uttar Pradesh, set a record by constructing 249 cemented ramps for the specially-abled on 5 August 2021 at different government schools around Jaipur, Rajasthan. The ramps were constructed for government schools of Jotwara City and Rural and Sanganer City and Rural.

Most toys donated – single day
Children's University, Gandhinagar, Gujarat, has donated 5,100 toys on a single day, 12 May 2022, on its campus between 9:00 a.m. and 11:00 a.m. The toys were distributed to eight organizations and schools, as well as NGOs working with children. The donation drive was organized by the University's Departments of Toy Innovations and Social Work, and around 30 people participated in the drive.

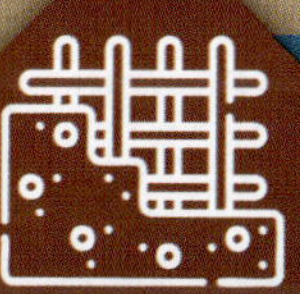

STRUCTURES

EARLIEST STRUCTURES

Earliest extant book on architecture

Several references are found in different literatures including the Rigveda, epics, Puranas and the *Arthasastra*. However, the earliest separate treatise on architecture that is still available is *Manasara*. It is the culmination of all architectural traditions and treatises that were available before. It is believed to have been composed by a person known as Shilpin, a practising architect in roughly 500 – 700 CE. The exact authorship and date are unknown. Another treatise on housing architecture from the same period is the *Mayamata*.

Earliest village settlement

A 4,000-year-old village settlement of the Chalcolithic period (Copper Age), along with remnants of subsequent Iron Age occupation, was unearthed at Balathal near Udaipur, Rajasthan. It included a massive mud rampart. It is the oldest village settlement in India outside of Harappan sites.

First architect on record

Maha Govinda is considered the first architect on record. He designed many north Indian cities in the fifth century BCE. He has been mentioned in the Buddhist work *Dhammapada*.

Earliest extensive drainage system

The Harappan towns of Lothal in Gujarat and Mohenjo-daro (now in Pakistan); with rectangular houses, chessboard streets, brick-lined bathrooms, drainage pipes, and cesspits; were unique in the ancient world. The toilets were equipped with water chutes, which carried dirty water away to covered street drains. The main sewer, about 1.5 m (4 ft 11 in.) deep and 91 cm (2 ft 11 .8 in.) across, is connected to north–south and east–west sewers.

First architect to win the Pritzker Prize

Dr Balkrishna Vithaldas Doshi (b. 26 August 1927) won the famed Pritzker Architecture Prize on 12 March 2018, the first Indian to do so in the award's 40-year history. The Pritzker Prize is referred to as the Nobel Prize in architecture.

Oldest rust-free iron pillar

The iron pillar in the Qutb (Minar) complex in Mehrauli, Delhi, has stood strong since the fifth century CE – during the Gupta period. Udayagiri, in what is now Madhya Pradesh, is most likely where it was built (some also believe Mathura, Uttar Pradesh, was the place where it was made), before it was moved to Delhi. A solid iron shaft, 7.2 m (23.5 ft) high, it has many inscriptions in Sanskrit, among which the oldest, a six-line inscription, states that the pillar was built for a Vishnu temple and at the order of a king called Chandra (often believed to be Chandragupta II).

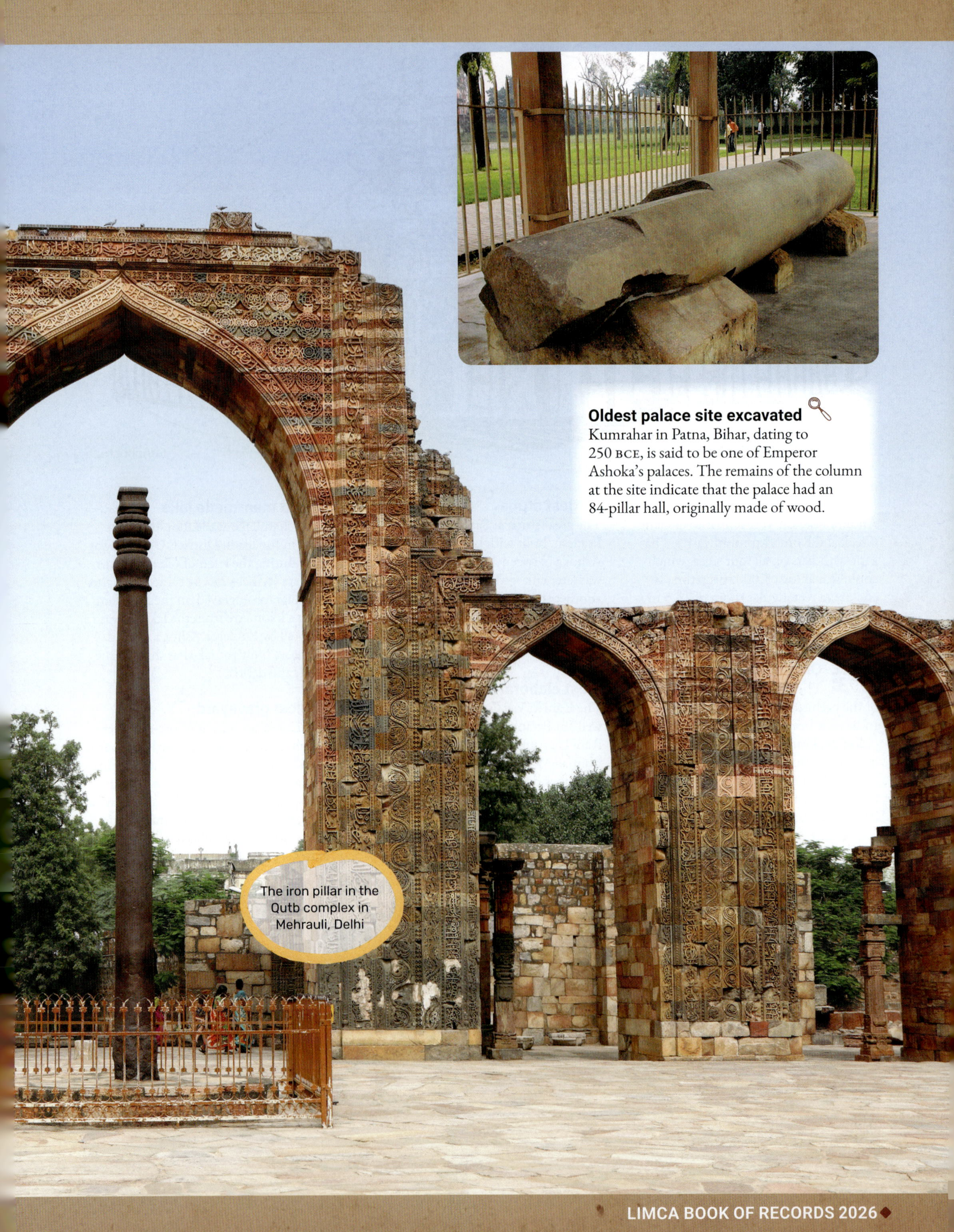

Oldest palace site excavated
Kumrahar in Patna, Bihar, dating to 250 BCE, is said to be one of Emperor Ashoka's palaces. The remains of the column at the site indicate that the palace had an 84-pillar hall, originally made of wood.

Sanchi stupa

Earliest open-air theatre

The earliest open-air theatre was made in the third century BCE at Nagarjunakonda in Guntur District, Andhra Pradesh. It is similar to ancient Greek and Roman amphitheatres – has a pit with tiers on all four sides, which could seat at least 1,000 spectators. It encloses a rectangular room of 16.5 m x 13.7 m (54 ft 1.5 in. x 44 ft 11.4 in.). The structure has good acoustic properties.

WR Oldest dockyard

The most substantial remains of the prehistoric Harappan culture in India have been discovered at Lothal, the oldest dockyard near the Gulf of Cambay in Gujarat. Built in 2300 BCE, the dock is a long, rectangular tank of 218 m x 37 m (715 ft x 121 ft) and about 16 km from its nearest seaport.

Largest stupa

The great stupa at Sanchi in Madhya Pradesh, built with bricks by Emperor Ashoka between 273 and 232 BCE, was later enlarged and enclosed within another stone stupa. In its present form, the stupa now has a diameter of 37 m (121 ft 5 in.) and a height of 16 m (52 ft 6 in.).

Most elaborate stepwell

The Rani ki Vav ('queen's step well') at Patan, Gujarat, was built by Rani Udayamati, the queen of King Bhimadeva I (r. 1022–64 CE) of the Chalukya dynasty, in memory of her husband. It measures 65 m x 20 m (213 ft 3 in. x 65 ft 7 in.) and is over 28 m (91 ft 10 in.) deep. Originally, over 800 sculptures decorated it.

Oldest man-made lake

Sudarshan Lake at the foot of Girnar Hills in Junagadh District, Gujarat, was built during the reign of Chandragupta Maurya (c. 321–297 BCE), according to the epigraph engraved on the Ashokan pillar a kilometre from the lake. It was restored by Emperor Ashoka around 273 BCE. Now the lake has shrunk due to silt and debris.

Earliest graveyard

The largest necropolis of pre-urban era, which is the earliest graveyard discovered in India to date, is located in a Harappan site near Kutch, Gujarat. This 40-acre Harappan burial site predates Dholavira. The graveyard exhibits the transition from earth-mound burials to stone graves – being functional for about

Lothal dockyard

Deepest stepwell

Chand Baori, located at Abhaneri in Dausa District, Rajasthan, is the deepest stepwell in India, extending to 30 m (98 ft 5 in.) down from the ground. It is also considered to be the largest ancient stepwell in the country and among the oldest wells in the world. Its oldest parts were constructed in the 8th century by King Chand and the upper storeys were built during the reign of the Mughals in the 18th century. The stepwell has 13 levels and 3,500 narrow steps. The temperature at the bottom of the well remains 6°C lower than the temperature at its surface.

500 years (between 3,200 BCE and 2,600 BCE). The oldest grave here is 5,200 years old. The excavation began in 2019 and involved more than 150 national and international scientists.

Oldest slide 

The rock-cut slide at Mamallapuram in Chengalpattu District, Tamil Nadu, is said to be the world's oldest children's slide.

Earliest open-air theatre 

The earliest open-air theatre in India could seat 1,000 spectators, if not more! It was built in the third century BCE at Nagarjunakonda in Guntur District, Andhra Pradesh.

First architects to win JK Architecture of the Year Awards (AYA)

The first architects to win the JK Architecture of the Year Awards (AYA), when it was started in 1990, were
a) Laurie Baker (2 March 1917–1 April 2007), a British-born Indian architect from Thiruvananthapuram was the first to win the Great Master's Award. He is often considered a pioneer of sustainable architecture.
b) Anant D. Raje (17 September 1929–27 June 2009) from Ahmedabad was the first to win the Architect of the Year Award. He taught architecture at various universities across the world, including CEPT University, Ahmedabad and University of New Mexico, US.

First Indian winner of the Aga Khan Award for architecture

The first Indian winner of the award was the Mughal Sheraton Hotel, Agra in 1980. Presented in three-year cycles, beginning in 1978, with a prize money of 1 million USD (approx. ₹8.25 crore), the prize recognizes projects, stakeholders, buildings, and teams that translate aspirations of the Muslim society through design and architecture.

MEDIEVAL AND MODERN ERAS

WR Largest corbelled cornice dome

The Gol Gumbaz, built in 1659 in the tomb complex of the Adil Shahi sultans at Bijapur in Karnataka, features a dome that measures 42 m (137 ft 9.5 in.) in diameter. Its corbelled cornice (the ornamental projection that crowns a building) projects more than 3 m (9 ft 10 in.). The dome is the largest of its kind in the world.

Largest silver article 

A 1.8 m (5 ft 11 in.) tall silver jug at the City Palace in Jaipur, Rajasthan, was made for the maharaja of Jaipur to store drinking water during his visit to England in 1901 for the coronation of King Edward VII.

Largest vaulted hall 

The Bara Imambara in Lucknow, Uttar Pradesh, is not only India's but also Asia's largest hall without any external support of wood, iron, or stone beams. The hall measures 49.4 m x 16.2 m (162 ft x 53 ft 2 in.). The ceiling is more than 15 m (49 ft 2.5 in.) high.

Longest corridor 

The longest corridor in India, that of the Ramanathaswamy Temple in Ramaswaram, Tamil Nadu, is 1,220 m (4,002 ft) long. It has 1,212 sculpted and painted pillars. It was built in the 17th century.

Magnificent corridor at the Ramanathaswamy Temple

Earliest known monumental tomb

The Sultan Garhi tomb in Delhi was built over a garhi (cave) in 1231 for Prince Nasiruddin Mahmud by his father Iltutmish, the third sultan of the Slave dynasty, who ruled in Delhi from 1212 to 1236. The octagonal tomb is like a fortress with a courtyard-like layout, uncommon for a tomb.

Largest maze

The Bhul-Bhulaiya, which is a set of passages on the top terrace of the Bara Imambara building in Lucknow, Uttar Pradesh, is a labyrinth of over 1,000 interconnected passages that can be approached through a narrow flight of steps but seem to lead nowhere. These passages reduced the load on the walls, which support the massive 4.88 m (16 ft) thick roof with an estimated weight of about 20,000 tonnes.

Largest brick minaret

The Qutb Minar in Delhi, made in fluted sandstone carved with verses from the Quran, is 72 m (236 ft) high with 379 steps inside leading to the top. It is a tapering tower of five storeys, with a base diameter of 14.3 m (47 ft), which reduces to 2.74 m (9 ft) at the top. Its construction began under Qutbuddin Aibak in 1193 CE, and his successor Iltutmish added 3 storeys. Firuz Shah Tughlaq completed the last storey in 1383 CE. It was built by Asaf-ud-Daula, Nawab of Awadh, in 1784.

First garden tomb

The tomb of Sikandar Lodi (r. 1489–1517) of the Lodi dynasty is located in Lodi Garden near Lodi Road in New Delhi and was built during 1517–18 by his son Ibrahim Lodi.

FORTS AND PALACES

Oldest forts

Though it is difficult to say which is the oldest fort in India, forts found at Harappan sites are surely the earliest. Several parts of a Harappan fort, including its gateways, still exist at Dholavira. Parts of earlier forts that pre-date the Harappan civilization are also found at Dholavira and Kalibangan, which are datable to the last part of the fourth millennium BCE.

Only palace with just a facade wall

Hawa Mahal ('the palace of winds') in Jaipur, Rajasthan, has a facade built on to a wall of the main palace compound. Royal ladies seated in its 953 niches and windows could look down at the street below.

Largest fort in India

The Mehrangarh Fort, sprawling over and area of 1200 acres and perched on sandstone hills about 400 ft (122 m) above the Thar Desert, was built in the fifteenth century by Rao Jodha, the 15th Rathore ruler of Marwar. The fort has 7 gates, and the maximum height of the walls is 120 ft (36 m). The walls are about 65 ft (20m) wide at places.

Oldest surviving fort

Quila Mubarak in Bhatinda is the oldest surviving fort of India. The fort consists of bricks that date back to the era of the Kushan rulers (believed to be built between 90 CE and 110 CE). The original fort was a mud structure built by Raja Dhab. Razia Sultan was imprisoned here, and Guru Govind Singh visited this fort in 1705 CE.

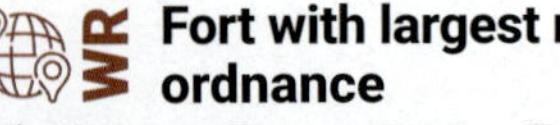

WR Fort with largest metal ordnance

The Bijapur Fort in Bijapur District, Karnataka, houses the famous bellmetal cannon Malik-e-Maidan ('lord of the battlefield'), the largest piece of medieval bell-metal ordnance, which is 4.45 m (14 ft 7 in.) long, with a diameter of 1.5 m (4 ft 11 in.). It weighs 55 tonnes and has a bore of 0.71 m (2 ft 4 in.) from which an iron ball of over a tonne could be fired.

Oldest extant marble structure

The white marble structure over Hoshang Shah Ghori's tomb, built by his son c.1440, at Mandu, Dhar District, Madhya Pradesh, is the oldest extant marble structure known.

Longest fortification wall

A 36 km (22.37 miles) long fortification wall was built by Rana Kumbha (r. 1433–68) along the Aravallis in Rajasthan to protect his kingdom of Mewar. It enclosed 34 fortresses. At its widest sections, the wall is 15 m (49 ft) thick and has stone-brick masonry and decorative flourishes along the top.

Highest gateway

Buland Darwaza, the highest gateway in India, is 53.5 m (175 ft 6 in.) high. It was built by Mughal emperor Akbar (r. 1550–1605) at Fatehpur Sikri, about 40 km from Agra in Uttar Pradesh, and commemorated his conquest of Ranthambore Fort and Khandesh.

Palace with the largest chandelier

The durbar hall of Jai Vilas Mahal of Gwalior, Madhya Pradesh, has two chandeliers, each 12.5 m (41 ft) high and weighing 3.5 tonnes. It is said that three (or eight!) elephants were hoisted to the roof (or suspended from it!) to make sure it would withstand the weight of the chandeliers.

The famous chandeliers of the Durbar Hall of Jai Vilas Mahal

RELIGIOUS STRUCTURES

Earliest mosque

The Cheraman Jama Masjid in Kodungallur, Thrissur District, Kerala, is said to have been built in 629 CE. It is considered the first mosque in India and the second in the world where Juma prayers were started. Malik Ibn Dinar, who made this mosque under instructions from Maharaja Chereman Perumal, used Kerala style of architecture to build this mosque. He also became its first *ghazi*. The mosque is still in use. In the 1970s, it was reconstructed in a way that changed its look completely. In 2021, further renovation took place which brought back the original look.

First revolving minaret

The minaret of the 55-year-old Masjid-e-Chini ki Burj, also known as Chhoti Masjid in Jaipur, Rajasthan, was the first revolving minaret in India. The 10-tonne dome of the 30.5 m (100 ft) high minaret, with a 3 m (9 ft 10 in.) diameter, completed one round in a minute, running on a 1.5 HP motor.

Biggest temple lamp

A lamp with 1,000 wicks at the Chettikulangara Devi Temple in Alappuzha District, Kerala, is made of 1,500 kg of gunmetal. It is 3.3 m (10 ft 10 in.) high with 13 tiers like banyan branches. The lowest rung is 2.1 m (6 ft 10.7 in.) in circumference and holds 101 wicks. The topmost is over 1 m wide with 53 wicks.

Biggest bathing tank

The Brahma Sarovar at Thanesar in Kurukshetra District, Haryana, is 1,370 m x 762 m (4,495 ft x 2,500 ft) and attracts thousands of pilgrims during solar eclipses. Its ancient water reservoir finds mention in the Mahabharata.

Oldest active synagogue

The Paradesi Synagogue in Mattancherry in Kochi, Kerala, was built by the descendants of the European Jews in 1568 CE. The synagogue is also the first one known to be built in a Commonwealth country.

Biggest queue complex

The Vaikuntam queue complex at the Venkateswara Temple complex, Tirumala, Tirupati, Andhra Pradesh,

permits the free flow of around 35,000 pilgrims daily. It has a two-tier seating gallery, two corridors, and a floor at the ground level with amenities within a semicircular length of 238 m (781 ft). A new complex was added later for *sarvadarshan*, or free entry of devotees.

WR Oldest functional Hindu temple

The Mundeshwari Devi temple, in Kaimur District of Bihar, is believed to the oldest functional Hindu temple in the world. Per the Archaeological Survey of India (ASI), this temple was built in 108 CE. The temple is dedicated to Shiva and Shakti and also has other deities like Ganesha, Surya, and Vishnu in it.

The Mundeshwari Devi temple is believed to be part of a religious as well as an educational centre.

Earliest extant structural temple

A third century BCE circular brick-and-timber shrine excavated at Bairat (now Viratnagar) in Jaipur District, Rajasthan, is considered to be the earliest surviving structural temple. The shrine, with a diameter of 8.23 m (27 ft), was built with lime-plastered panels of brickwork alternating with 26 octagonal wooden pillars. The shrine, portico, and a 2 m (6 ft 6.7 in.) wide ambulatory were enclosed in a rectangular compound that measures 305 m x 21 m (1,000 ft 7.8 in. x 68 ft 10.7 in.).

Most sculptures in a temple

The Meenakshi Sundareswar Temple in Madurai, Tamil Nadu, has more than 30 million sculptures in its shrines, halls, and colonnades. It covers an area of 243 m x 228 m (797 ft x 748 ft).

Remains of the temple at Bairat

First Baha'i house of worship 

The Baha'i house of worship, or 'Lotus Temple', in Kalkaji, New Delhi, the first such structure in Asia, is built on 26 acres (10.52 hectares) of land. Built between 1980 and 1986, it is designed as a blossoming lotus. The main structure has three folds of nine concrete petals, each covered with Grecian marble. The temple rises to 35 m (114 ft 10 in.) and is surrounded by pools of water.

Only rat temple 

The 575-year-old temple of Karni Devi (one of the nine incarnations of Goddess Durga) has a large number of rats called *kaba,* believed to be the offspring of the presiding deity. Located at Deshnok, 35 km from Bikaner, Rajasthan, this temple is devoted exclusively to the 'holy' rats, which have the run of the place.

Largest monastery 

The largest Buddhist monastery in the country, and a functioning one, is located in Tawang District, Arunachal Pradesh. The three-storey structure spread over 140 sq. m (1,507 sq. ft) has 65 residential buildings that can house up to 450 lamas. This monastery's Tibetan name – Galden Namgey Lhatse – translates as 'celestial paradise on a clear night'.

Largest cave temple complex 

The cave temples in Ellora in Aurangabad District, Maharashtra, were bu ilt between the fifth and tenth centuries CE. There are 12 Buddhist, 17 Hindu, and 5 Jain cave temples and monasteries. The Kailasa or Kailasanatha Temple in cave 16 is the largest single monolithic rock excavation in the world.

Oldest Buddhist monument

A stupa, which was estimated to be 2,500 years old, was excavated in 1898 in Piprahwa in Siddharthnagar District, Uttar Pradesh, by British colonial engineer and landowner W.C. Peppe. The solid brickwork stupa was 7 m (23 ft) high and its cupola measured 35 m (114 ft 10 in.) in diameter. Most of the other surviving stupas are from the reign of Emperor Ashoka (c. 273–232 BCE).

Largest mosque

The Taj-ul-Masjid, or Taj-ul-Masajid, in Bhopal, Madhya Pradesh, was built by Sultan Shah Jehan Begum between 1868 and 1901. Constructed over decades, the mosque was completed in 1985 by Maulana Sayed Hashmat Ali Sahab and Allama Mohammad Imran Khan Nadwi Azhari. Its name means 'the crown of mosques' and it has an interior area of 23,000 sq. m (247,570 sq. ft). The mosque is made of red stone and can accommodate 175,000 worshippers.

Only shaking minarets

At the Sidi Bashir Mosque in Ahmedabad, Gujarat, the minarets, which are three storeys high and have carved balconies, are known as the *jhulta*, or shaking, minarets. Dated to 1452 CE, the mosque was built either by Sidi Bashir, a slave of Sultan Ahmed Shah, or by Malik Sarang, a noble in the court of Sultan Mahmud Begada. The shaking of either minaret results in the other minaret vibrating after a few seconds, a fact that was first observed in the 19th century by an Englishman and Sanskrit scholar, Monier M. Williams. One minaret has been partly taken down to prevent it from falling over.

Largest Imambara

The Nizamat Imambara located in the Nizamat Kila in Murshidabad, West Bengal, was first built by Nawab Siraj ud-Daulah in 1740. But it was completely destroyed by fire in 1846. Nawab Nazim Mansur Ali Khan built a new structure in 1847. This new Nizamat Imambara, India's largest, is 680 ft long and has varying width at different places. Bara Imambara in Lucknow is the second largest of the country.

Only mosque entirely of marble

Moti Masjid (the Pearl Mosque), built by Mughal emperor Shah Jahan in the 17th century CE within the Agra Fort, is made entirely of marble.

Tallest hollow stone structure

The Global Vipassana Pagoda at Gorai in Mumbai, Maharashtra, is one of the world's largest structures enshrining the relics of the Buddha. It was donated by the Sri Lankan government and the Mahabodhi Society, Bodh Gaya, Bihar. Inaugurated on 8 February 2009, it contains the largest and tallest pillar-less hollow stone pagoda in the world. The height of the dome is 29 m (95 ft 1.7 in.), and the height of the building is 96.12 m (315 ft 4.2 in.). It took around 11 years and 2.5 million tonnes of stone to complete it.

Biggest temple bell

The 110-year-old bronze bell at Tirumala Devaswom, Kochi, Kerala, is more than 1.8 m (5 ft 11 in.) high and weighs over 3 tonnes. The bell is suspended from a huge wooden frame that rests over four massive granite pillars.

WR Tallest temple tower

The 13-storey Sri Ranganathaswamy Temple, built between 1982 and 1987 at Srirangam in Tiruchirappalli District, Tamil Nadu, has a 72 m (236 ft) high *rajagopuram* (main gateway).

Global Vipassana Pagoda

Oldest church

St Thomas Syro-Malabar Church, located in Palayoor in Thrissur District, Kerala, is believed to be built by St Thomas, one of the 12 apostles of Jesus Christ, in 52 CE. It was rebuilt in the 17th century by the Reverend Fenichi. The original altar survives. It is also known as the Malankara Mar Thoma Syrian Church, or the Mar Thoma Church.

Tallest church

The Gothic-style Basilica of Our Lady of Dolours, known locally as Puthanpally, is a minor basilica of the Syro-Malabar Catholic Church in Thrissur, Kerala. Its construction started in 1929. Its two front towers are 45 m (147 ft 8 in.) tall, and the central tower is 79 m (259 ft 2 in.) tall.

Largest church

The 76.2 m x 55 m (250 ft x 180 ft 5 in.) Se Cathedral at Old Goa, around 10 km from Panaji, is the largest in India. It was constructed between 1562 and 1619. It was consecrated in 1640. It had two towers, but one collapsed in 1776 and was not rebuilt.

Se Cathedral at Old Goa

WR Tallest single-stone shikhara

The 80-tonne single-piece granite shikhara atop the Brihadeeswarar Temple at Thanjavur, Tamil Nadu, is the heaviest single-stone object on top of any temple in the world. This marvel of engineering was constructed from 1004 CE, during the reign of Rajaraja Chola, to 1009 CE. It is the world's first temple built with granite. Its *vimana* (a pyramidal tower built over the central shrine of a temple) is also the highest, at 66 m (216 ft 6 in.).

Largest collection of temples

There are as many as 1,000 Jain temples and 12,000 idols in the Shatrunjai Hills of Palitana in Bhavnagar District of Gujarat.

Largest synagogue

Located on Moledina Street in Pune, Maharashtra, the Ohel David Synagogue is a 30 m (98 ft 5 in.) high tower, built in the Gothic style with a spire and four giant clocks.

Largest sun temple

Built by Narasimha Deva I in 1200 CE, the Sun Temple in the historic town of Konark, Odisha, represents a huge chariot with 12 pairs of ornamental wheels, drawn by seven horses rearing up to the east. The original temple consisted of a sanctum sanctorum with a lofty curvilinear shikhara, a 34.14 m (112 ft) long and 38.4 m (126 ft) high jagmohana (assembly hall), and a dance hall. Along with many subsidiary structures, the Sun Temple, which is now the largest extant sun temple, was enclosed within a compound wall 264 m (866 ft) long and 165 m (541 ft) wide, with three gates.

Largest chaitya hall

The Karla Caves near Lonavala, Maharashtra, house the largest known chaitya (Buddhist prayer hall) cave. Its dimensions are 37 m x 14 m x 14 m (121 ft 5 in. x 46 ft x 46 ft).

Highest gurdwara

The gurdwara at Hemkund–Lokpal in Chamoli District, Uttarakhand, stands at a height of 4,328.16 m (14,200 ft) above mean sea level. The place Hemkund finds mention in the Guru Granth Sahib and in Guru Gobind Singh's memoir, *Bachittar* (or *Bichittar*) *Natak*.

Highest monastery

The Tangyud Monastery at Komic Village near Hikkim in Spiti Valley, Himachal Pradesh, is India's highest monastery, at an altitude of around 4,572 m (15,000 ft). Built like a fortified castle, it lies on the edge of the Kibber Wildlife Sanctuary. Tangyud village lies at the foot of the monastery.

STATUES AND IDOLS

WR Tallest statue

A 182 m (597 ft) 'Statue of Unity' of Sardar Vallabhbhai Patel, inaugurated on 31 October 2018, stands on Sadhu Bet River island in the river Narmada near Rajpipla, Gujarat. Designed by sculptor Ram V. Sutar, it took nearly four years to build and cost an estimated ₹29.89 billion (2,989 crore).

WR Tallest monolithic statue

The Gommateshwara statue at Shravanabelagola, Karnataka, is the world's tallest monolithic statue. Dedicated to Bahubali and venerated by the Jains, it is 17.37 m (57 ft) high. It was carved from a single block of granite and weighs 80 tonnes. It was built between 978 and 993 CE by Chavundaraya, a minister of the Western Ganga dynasty.

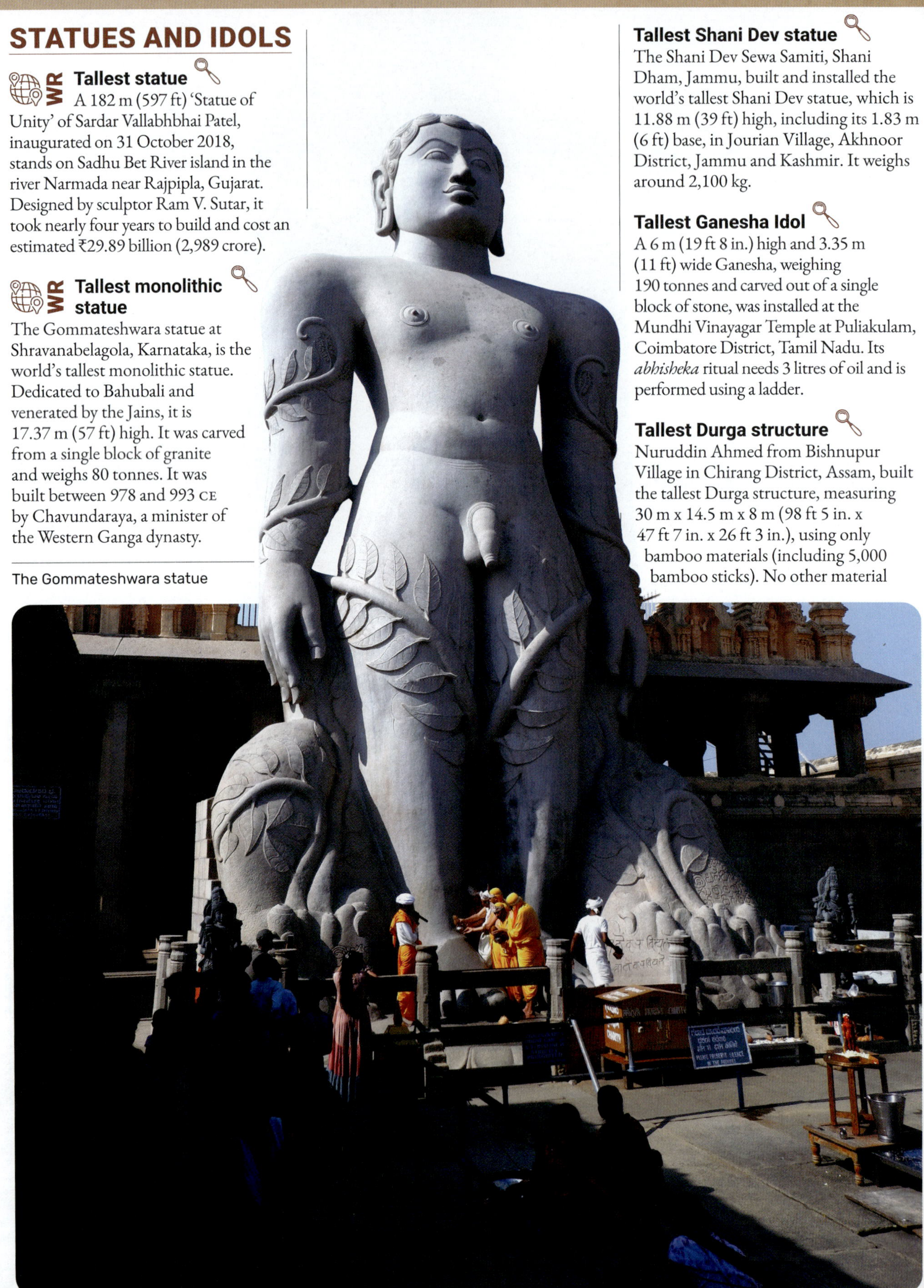

The Gommateshwara statue

Tallest Shani Dev statue

The Shani Dev Sewa Samiti, Shani Dham, Jammu, built and installed the world's tallest Shani Dev statue, which is 11.88 m (39 ft) high, including its 1.83 m (6 ft) base, in Jourian Village, Akhnoor District, Jammu and Kashmir. It weighs around 2,100 kg.

Tallest Ganesha Idol

A 6 m (19 ft 8 in.) high and 3.35 m (11 ft) wide Ganesha, weighing 190 tonnes and carved out of a single block of stone, was installed at the Mundhi Vinayagar Temple at Puliakulam, Coimbatore District, Tamil Nadu. Its *abhisheka* ritual needs 3 litres of oil and is performed using a ladder.

Tallest Durga structure

Nuruddin Ahmed from Bishnupur Village in Chirang District, Assam, built the tallest Durga structure, measuring 30 m x 14.5 m x 8 m (98 ft 5 in. x 47 ft 7 in. x 26 ft 3 in.), using only bamboo materials (including 5,000 bamboo sticks). No other material

WR Tallest shivalinga

The tallest shivalinga in the world was created by Maheswaram Sri Sivaparvathi Temple Trust, Thiruvananthapuram, Kerala. It measures 33.85 m (111 ft) and was constructed in six years and one day between 31 December 2012 and 31 December 2018.

Largest bust

Inaugurated on 24 February 2017, the 34.1 m (112 ft) tall 'Adiyogi' Lord Shiva statue made of steel and located in Coimbatore, Tamil Nadu, at the Isha Yoga Centre, has been funded by the Isha Foundation, and set up by Sadhguru Jaggi Vasudev. Built over 8 months, the structure reportedly weighs 500 tonnes. Its height signifies the 112 chakras in the human system to explore the 112 dimensions of life.

was used except cotton cloth as rope. It was made to promote the bamboo sector in Assam.

Largest sculpture of a mythical creature

Jatayu, the largest sculpture of a mythical creature in India, is located at the Jatayu Earth's Centre (also known as Jatayu Rock or Jatayu Nature Park) in Chadayamangalam, Kollam District, Kerala. The sculpture, conceptualized and built by sculptor and film-maker Rajiv Anchal, is 60.96 m (200 ft) long, 45.72 m (150 ft) wide, and 21.33 m (70 ft) high. It houses a digital museum and a multidimensional theatre, making it a 'functional' sculpture.

Largest Nandi statue

Nandi is the sacred bull and Lord Shiva's vehicle in Hindu mythology. The Nandi statue, about 200 m (656 ft) from the Veerabhadra Temple at Lepakshi Village in Anantapur District, Andhra Pradesh, is 4.57 m (15 ft) tall and 8.23 m (27 ft) long. It is carved from a single piece of granite.

Largest shivalinga

Located in Bhojpur, on the outskirts of the city of Bhopal in Madhya Pradesh, the Bhojeshwar Temple, built by Raja Bhoj (r. 1010–53 CE), houses the largest shivalinga, 5.5 m (18 ft) high and 2.5 m (8 ft 2 in.) in circumference.

Bhojeshwar Temple

BRIDGES

First iron bridge

The first iron bridge was built by Jessop and Company Limited in 1815 over the Gomti River in Lucknow in Uttar Pradesh. Designed by the Scottish engineer John Rennie the Elder, it was made at Butterfly Iron Works, England, for the nawab of Awadh.

Longest balanced cantilever bridge

The 3,015 m (9,892 ft) road bridge across the river Brahmaputra at Tezpur, Assam, called Kolia Bhomora Setu, is the longest bridge that has been provided with a central suspended span of 15 m (49 ft 2.5 in.) length because of its geographical location in a seismic zone. The bridge consists of 24 spans of 120 m (393 ft 8 in.) each and two shore spans of 67.5 m (221 ft 5 in.) each. With a carriageway of 7.5 m (24 ft 7 in.) width, it was constructed between October 1981 and April 1987.

Longest Bailey bridge

The 182.8 m (600 ft) long suspension bridge over the river Chubi in Wokha, Nagaland, connects the Mokokchung District and the Dimapur District of Nagaland.

First cable-stayed rail bridge

India's first cable-stayed rail bridge, Anji Khad Bridge, is in Jammu and Kashmir. It spans across the Chenab River. The total length of cable strand used to build this bridge is 653 km.

Largest cantilever bridge

The Howrah Bridge (officially named Rabindra Setu in 1965) is India's biggest cantilever bridge. It spans the Hooghly River in Kolkata, West Bengal. It was completed in 1943, in the middle of World War II. This technical marvel built without a single nut and bolt took seven years to complete and is the seventh longest cantilever bridge in the world. It is 705 m (2,313 ft) long and 21.6 m (71 ft) wide, with two footpaths of 4.6 m (15 ft) on either side. The 82 m (269 ft) tall bridge is a major tourist attraction in West Bengal. Today this iconic landmark of Kolkata is not only serving millions of people but also has emerged as a famous sightseeing spot.

Busiest bridge

With over 1,00,000 vehicles and over 1,50,000 pedestrians using this bridge a day, Rabindra Setu is also India's busiest bridge.

WR Highest railway bridge

The Chenab Bridge, the highest bridge in India, is also the highest railway bridge in the world.

Only bascule bridge

The only bascule bridge in the country is constructed on Tolly's Nullah

Top: Akkar Bridge in Jorethang
Left: Col Chewang Rinchen Setu, a bridge built by Border Roads Organisation in Eastern Ladakh

First cable-stayed road bridge

The Akkar Bridge in Jorethang, over the Rangit River in Sikkim, is an all-concrete, cable-stayed road bridge built in 1988. It spans a 1.5 km (4,921 ft) wide and nearly 20 m (65 ft 7 in.) deep valley. The bridge consists of two 77 m (252 ft 7 in.) symmetrical spans supported from a single central pylon. With 17 pairs of cable stays, the 55 m (180 ft) high pylon supports the decking 21 m (69 ft) above the riverbed.

WR Bridge at the highest location

Col Chewang Rinchen Setu, a bridge built by Border Roads Organisation (BRO) over River Shyok, connecting Durbuk and Daulat Beg Oldie in Eastern Ladakh, is India's all-weather permanent bridge situated in the highest altitude. It was inaugurated in 2019.

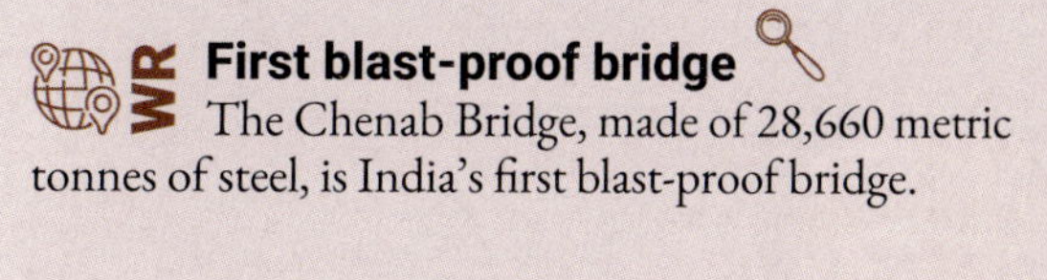

WR First blast-proof bridge

The Chenab Bridge, made of 28,660 metric tonnes of steel, is India's first blast-proof bridge.

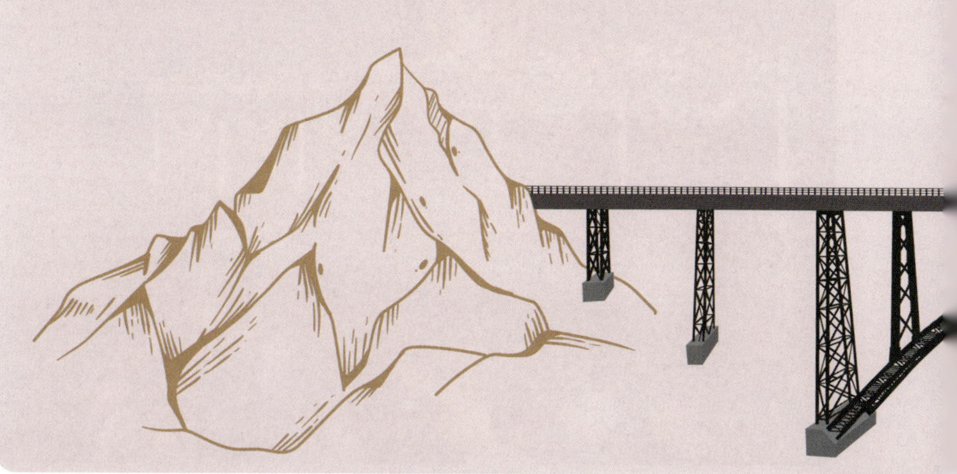

Atal Setu in Mumbai, Maharashtra

(or Adiganga) at Khidirpur in Kolkata, West Bengal. Operated by the Kolkata Port Trust, it is built in two halves, each of which goes up to allow ships to pass through. The bridge has a span of about 35 m (114 ft 10 in.) and was built by Wagner Biro AG, Austria. It was commissioned on 5 November 1966 and replaced a swing bridge built in 1892.

Longest river bridge

The Bhupen Hazarika Setu, also referred to as the Dhola–Sadiya Bridge, connecting Dhola in Dibrugarh District and Sadiya in Lakhimpur District, Assam, is the longest river bridge. The 9.15 km (5.7 miles) long bridge on the Brahmaputra River was inaugurated on 26 May 2017 by Prime Minister Narendra Modi. It is named after Bhupen Hazarika, a well-known Assamese musician and film-maker, who died in 2011.

Longest bridge of India

The Mumbai Trans Harbour Link (MTHL) (later named Atal Bihari Vajpayee Sewri–Nhava Sheva Atal Setu) in Mumbai, Maharashtra, the longest bridge in India, is 21.8 km (71,522.31 ft) long. This six-lane bridge has about 16.5 km length over the sea, making it the longest sea bridge of India as well. About 5.5 km of the bridge lies on land. It connects Mumbai International Airport and Navi Mumbai International Airport. Travelling to Pune, Goa, and south India will now be faster too. across Mahim Bay. This cable-stayed bridge, which carries 8 lanes of traffic, was inaugurated on 30 June 2009.

Tallest bridge

The Chenab Bridge, placed 359 m (1,177 ft 10 in.) above the level of the riverbed – which makes it the tallest bridge – is some 35 m (115 ft) taller than the Eiffel Tower in Paris, France. The rail bridge is part of the Udhampur–Srinagar–Baramulla rail link project (USBRL). Located in the Reasi District of Jammu and Kashmir, the bridge is 1,315 m (4,314 ft 3.6 in.) long and is aimed at boosting connectivity to the Kashmir Valley. The height of its cable crane's pylon at the Srinagar end is 127 m, which is much taller than the Qutb Minar, which is 72 m (236 ft) high. Connecting Bakkal (Katra) and Kauri (Srinagar), the bridge was constructed by the Indian Railways in collaboration with the Defence Research and Development Organization (DRDO). It completed its first successful trial run on 20 June 2024 and finally inaugurated on 6 June 2025.

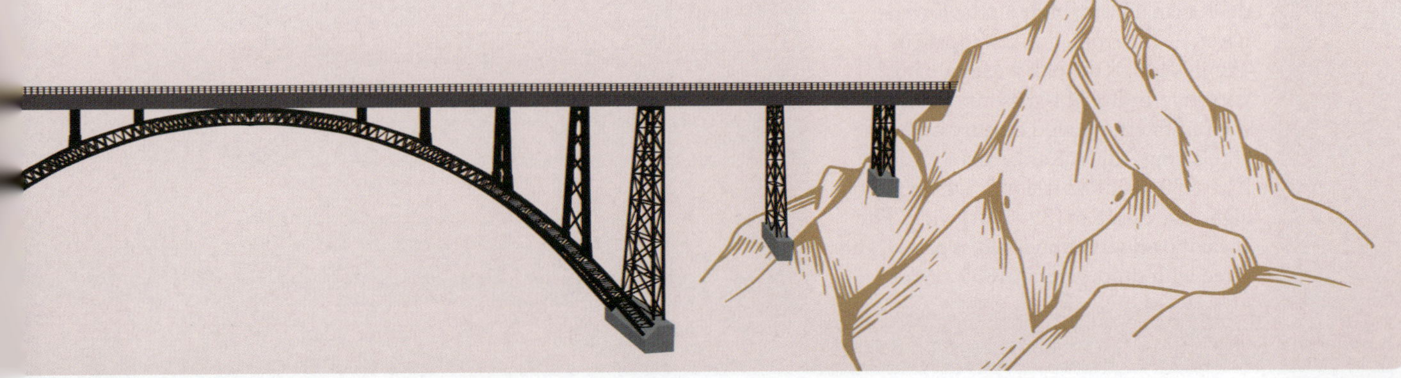

Widest and longest double-decker steel bridge

The North-South corridor of Nagpur Metro Rail Project comprises an 18.9 m (62 ft) wide double-decker viaduct: the lower level has a highway flyover and the upper level has a double-line metro rail. It is a two-level bridge over existing railway lines, crossing the Indian Railways tracks at Gaddigodam at a skew angle of 19 degrees. The span is straight with an effective dimension of 80 m (262 ft) centre to centre of pier. The project's commercial operations began on 11 December 2022.

Longest road-and-rail bridge

Bogibeel Bridge on the Brahmaputra River, between Dhemaji and Dibrugarh Districts, Assam, is the longest road-and-rail bridge, with a length of 4.94 km. Its construction was started in April 2002 and it was completed in December 2018. The bridge has a double-line 1.676 m (5 ft 6 in.) broad-gauge railway on the lower deck and a three-lane road on the upper one. It is India's first bridge with fully welded steel-concrete support beams to withstand earthquakes of magnitudes up to 7 on the Richter scale.

DAMS

Earliest canal system

Canal systems have existed since the pre-Harappan era (around 2500 BCE). Excavations at Dholavira in Gujarat have revealed ingenious systems for diverting water from seasonal nullahs.

Highest dam

The Tehri Dam, near Pratapnagar in Tehri Garhwal District in Uttarakhand, is situated on the Bhagirathi River with a maximum height above foundation of 260.5 m (854.66 ft). It's a rock-

Oldest extant dam

The Grand Anicut Dam, also known as the Kallanai Dam, built on the Kaveri River, 24 km from Tiruchirappalli in Tamil Nadu, is the oldest extant dam known in India. This masonry dam, which was built in the second century CE by the Chola king Aditha Karikalan (or Aditya II), is 330 m (1,083 ft) long, 5.49 m (18 ft) high, and 12–18 m (39–59 ft) wide. The ancient dam was remodelled, repaired, and fitted with sluice gates in 1899–1902.

fill structure and its reservoir holds 21,00,000 acre-feet of water. It also ranks among the world's top ten dams.

Earliest dam 

The earliest dam discovered was built on Sudarshan Lake in Junagadh (then Girinagar) in Gujarat. It dates to 326 BCE.

Longest canal 

The Indira Gandhi Canal, or Rajasthan Canal, which starts in Punjab and ends in Rajasthan, is 649 km long, and is the world's second longest canal. Its schemes include 6,308 km of distributary canals.

Indira Gandhi Canal

The Grand Anicut Dam has irrigated more than a million acres (0.4 million hectares) of land for centuries.

Shivanasamudra Falls

Longest breakwater

The V.O. Chidambaranar Port (earlier Tuticorin Port) North Breakwater in Tamil Nadu is the longest at 4.14 km.

First hydroelectric project

Shivanasamudra Falls hydro-electric project in Chamarajanagar District, Karnataka, opened in 1902 and involved the harnessing of the Kavery River to supply electrical energy to run the machinery at the Kolar goldfields. The power station is still a functioning one.

Largest river dam

The Sardar Sarovar Dam is a gravity dam on the Narmada River near Navagam in Surat District, Gujarat. One of the 30 dams planned on the Narmada River, it is the largest such structure to be built and among the largest dams in the world. Four Indian states – Gujarat, Madhya Pradesh, Maharashtra, and Rajasthan – receive water and electricity supplied from the dam.

Largest barrage

The Farakka Barrage on the Ganga River was opened in 1972 to help maintain navigable depths in Shyama Prasad Mookerjee Port (earlier Kolkata Port). Its length of 2,245 m (7,365 ft 6 in.) contains 108 gated bays of 18 m (59 ft) each and two 8 m (26 ft) fish locks.

Largest water reservoir

Indira Sagar Dam is a multipurpose project on the Narmada River in East Nimar District of Madhya Pradesh. The reservoir has a capacity of 12.2 billion cubic metre (9,890,701 acre feet) and, in terms of water storage, stands as the largest reservoir in India.

LIGHTHOUSES

Oldest lighthouses

In 1766, two signal houses were built, one on Old Woman's Island (now part of Colaba) and the other at Malabar Point, in Bombay, (now Mumbai) Maharashtra. The former was replaced by the first proper lighthouse built in 1768–71.

Highest lighthouse

The highest lighthouse from mean sea level is at Dolphin's Nose at Visakhapatnam, Andhra Pradesh. Its masonry tower rises 19 m (62 ft 4 in.) up from the ground level, and it has an elevation of 173 m (567 ft 7 in.) from mean sea level – which makes it the highest in India.

Visakhapatnam sea port as it looks from the lighthouse

This threw a beam seven leagues seaward in clear weather at 45.72 m (150 ft). It was repaired in 1828 and 1853 but stopped operating when the Prongs Lighthouse was installed in 1874. Prongs Lighthouse is situated in a military area, so it has restricted access.

Oldest functional lighthouses

The lighthouse built in 1821 on Sagar Island, at the mouth of the river Hooghly in West Bengal, was renovated in 1911. Its elevation from mean sea level is 26 m (85 ft 4 in.) and the tower is 25 m (82 ft) high. Its flashing light has a range of 31 km in clear weather. The second oldest was built more than 50 years later. The Prongs Lighthouse in the Colaba area in Bombay, Maharashtra, is recorded to have been constructed in 1874 by Thomas Ormiston. The beam of the lighthouse can be seen at 30 km and it is still operational. Its height is 41 m (135 ft) and range is 43 km.

Tallest lighthouse

The Jakhau Lighthouse in Gujarat is the tallest at 45 m (147.63 ft); from mean sea level it is 46 m (151 ft) high. It was established in 1957 and the present tower was built in 1965. Located on the main quay of Jakhau, a fishing port in western Kachchh, the lighthouse has a range of 33 km.

First unmanned lighthouse

Near Thalassery (earlier Tellicherry) in Kannur District, Kerala, stands the first unmanned lighthouse. It was built in 1835 and renovated in 1924. It is at an altitude of 27 m (89 ft) from mean sea level, and its range is 8 km.

AMUSEMENT ZONES

First indoor amusement play station

Funky Orbit at Ansal Plaza Mall on Khel Gaon Marg in New Delhi was launched on 15 June 2000 by Panoramic Entertainment Pvt. Ltd. The multi-tiered play station had an 8.53 m (28 ft) long curly slide and a ball pool. It closed down in 2011.

First amusement park

Appu Ghar at Pragati Maidan, New Delhi, the first family entertainment centre in India, opened during the 1982 Asian Games in Delhi. It was named after the Games' mascot – Appu the elephant. Shutting down in 2008, it reopened in Gurugram, Haryana.

MECHANICAL AND GENERAL STRUCTURES

First elevator

The first elevator was installed at Raj Bhavan, in Calcutta (now Kolkata), West Bengal in 1892. It used Otis's first design of an electric lift.

First hand-operated crane

The first hand-operated crane was built by Jessop & Company in 1850. The 5-tonne crane was installed at the then Calcutta Port (now Shyama Prasad Mookerjee Port) Customs.

First marine amusement park

In 1998, Dolphin City was set up by Amusements and Picnic Resorts Pvt. Ltd in Chennai, Tamil Nadu, with three performing dolphins and a performing sea lion show. Following the death of the performing dolphins, the marine amusement park featured sea lion performances, underwater viewing, and leisure boating. First live entertainment, theatre, and leisure destination Kingdom of Dreams in Gurugram, Haryana, is India's first live entertainment, theatre, and leisure destination. Spread over 6 acres (2.4 hectares), it is run by the Great Indian Nautanki Company (GINC), a joint venture of Apra Group and Wizcraft. It consists of two theatres, Nautanki Mahal and the Showshaa Theatre as well as a cultural and cuisine area known as Culture Gully. Most names engraved on a monument India Gate in Delhi carries the names of 13,516 British and Indian soldiers of the British Indian Army, who died during 1914–21 at various fronts of the First World War and the Third Anglo-Afghan War. This constitutes the largest number of names inscribed on a monument. Designed by architect Edwin Lutyens, the arch was completed in 1921. It is 42.3 m (139 ft) high and 9.1 m (30 ft) wide.

First floating restaurant

The first floating restaurant was built at Sirhind, Punjab, on the Bhakra Canal in 1979. The eight-room air-conditioned restaurant was part of a tourist complex.

First houseboat

The first houseboat, named *Victory*, was built in 1888 and stationed at the Dal Lake in Srinagar, Jammu and Kashmir.

First revolving restaurant

Neelkanth Patang at Ahmedabad, Gujarat, was the first revolving restaurant at 67.4 m (221 ft) above ground level. Opened in 1984, it has a 90-minute rotation, which unfolds a view of the old and new city of Ahmedabad.

First space-frame concrete structure

The first space-frame structure in reinforced concrete was the Hall of Nations at the Trade Fair Authority of India exhibition grounds in Pragati Maidan, New Delhi. Built during 1971–72, the hall offered an uninterrupted exhibition area of 6,700 sq. m (72,120 sq. ft) in a 82 m x 82 m x 27 m (269 ft x 269 ft x 88 ft 7 in.) pyramid supported at eight points.

Largest auditorium

The Sri Shanmukhananda Hall, inaugurated on 22 August 1963 in Bombay has a total capacity of 3,012 seats. The ground floor seats 1,552, the first balcony 896 and the second balcony 564 people. The stage has a depth and width of 16 m (52 ft) and a height of 6.4 m (21 ft).

Largest glasshouse

A glass-covered hall in Davanagere, Karnataka, completed in 2018, covers 7,334 sq. m (78,942.5 sq. ft). It houses a horticultural information centre and a botanical garden.

First water park

Shanku's Water Park on the Ahmedabad–Mahesana Highway in Gujarat was launched by Shankarbhai Chaudhary in 1993, on a 75-acre (30.35 hectares) campus. It introduced a giant 15.24 m (50 ft) speed slide that ended in a shallow water pool, a spiral ride, a wave pool that simulated sea waves, and a kids' corner.

Largest table

The teakwood table in the Banquet Hall at the Rashtrapati Bhavan in Delhi can seat 104 people at a time.

Largest cooking vessel

The original badi deg (big vessel),

christened Deg-i-Chittor-Kusba, or the 'Chittor-conquering vessel', said to be presented by the Mughal emperor Akbar to the dargah of Khwaja Moinuddin Chishti in Ajmer, Rajasthan, could hold 4,000 kg of food at a time that was enough for 12,000 people.

Largest official residence

The Rashtrapati Bhavan in New Delhi, the official residence of the president of India, has 340 rooms, 18 staircases, 74 lobbies, 37 salons, 1 km of corridors, 37 fountains, and 190 acres (76.9 hectares) of gardens. The residence covers 50 acres (20.2 hectares) of a 330-acre (133.5 hectare) estate.

Largest retractable roof

Kunta International Ltd, Noida, Uttar Pradesh, designed, built, installed, and commissioned an electrically driven retractable roof on a reusable structure on the presidential dais on Rajpath (now Kartavya Path), New Delhi, for Republic Day 2018. Made of steel and polycarbonate sheets with inbuilt sensors, it was 30.5 m (100 ft) wide and 6.4 m (21 ft) deep.

Longest conveyor

The longest single-belt international conveyor stretches from Nongtrai Village near Shella, East Khasi Hills District, Meghalaya, in India, to a cement factory at Chhatak in Sunamganj District, Bangladesh. It is about 17 km long (7 km in India and 10 km in Bangladesh) and conveys limestone and shale at 960 tonnes/hr. The conveyor was engineered by AUMUND France and Larsen & Toubro and installed by Beltpro. Its rollers are unusually designed to deal with both horizontal and vertical terrain curves.

Tallest chimney

The 275.2 m (903 ft) tall chimney of the Reliance Dahanu Thermal Power Station, Dahanu, in Palghar District, Maharashtra, is India's tallest RCC chimney. The base diameter of the chimney is 7 m (23 ft).

Largest multiplex

Mayajaal in Kanathur in Chennai, Tamil Nadu, has the largest movie multiplex with 16 screens and a seating capacity of 2,600. It is part of an entertainment centre that houses a shopping mall, a sports complex, and a resort.

Longest underground pipeline

The Hazira–Bijapur–Jagdishpur (HBJ) gas pipeline is India's first cross–country gas pipeline. This project by GAIL (India) Ltd began in 1986 to supply gas to fertilizer plants in Uttar Pradesh. The first phase, consisting of a non-branched 1,750 km grid, was later expanded to supply gas for industrial and domestic use in Rajasthan, Haryana, and the National Capital Territory (NCT). This extended the grid length to 3,474 km.

Oldest ice-skating rink

The ice-skating rink near Lakkar Bazaar in Simla (now Shimla), Himachal Pradesh, was founded in 1920 by one Mr Blessington. Initially out of bounds for Indians during British rule, it is now managed by the Shimla Ice-skating Club and is open for skating between the winter months of December and February.

MODERN STRUCTURES

First skyscraper

The first skyscraper Usha Kiran, an apartment building of 26 storeys in Bombay was the first of high-rise buildings. It was built between 1964 and 1967.

Tallest building

Lokhandwala Minerva, a 300.6 m (986 ft), 78-floor (above ground, below ground 2) skyscraper in Mumbai, Maharashtra, is the tallest completed building in India. Developed by Lokhandwala Kataria Construction Pvt. Ltd, the building was completed in 2023.

First reinforced-concrete structure

The Golconde dormitory at Sri Aurobindo Ashram in Pondicherry (now Puducherry) was designed by Czech-American architect Antonin Raymond (1888–1976) and completed in 1948. It is the first reinforced-concrete structure in India. All its features evolved from a study of the local climatic conditions and the occupants' needs.

WR Largest office building

Surat Diamond Bourse (SDB), Surat, Gujarat, covers a built-up area of 6,22,450 sq m (67,00,000 sq ft) and can accommodate over 4,500 offices and 67,000 professionals. This 15-storey interconnected building has 131 lifts to connect different floors and has surpassed the Pentagon, US, by almost 55,000 sq ft to become the world's largest office building. SDG was inaugurated by Prime Minister Narendra Modi on 17 December 2023.

First underground market

First underground market Palika Bazaar, the air-conditioned underground market at Connaught Place (now Rajiv Chowk) in New Delhi, was set up in 1978.

First permanent crafts market

First permanent crafts market Dilli Haat in Delhi opened in 1994, with 62 stalls selling handicrafts from all over the country and 25 food stalls.

First all-steel building

The ICICI headquarters in Mumbai, Maharashtra, designed by Raja Aederi and built in 1995, have a superstructure area of 39,948 sq. m (430,000 sq. ft), two-level basements with a total area of 21,368 sq. m (230,000 sq. ft), and a structural area of 14,000 sq. m (150,700 sq. ft).

Tallest escalator

The Janakpuri West metro station on the Magenta Line of the Delhi Metro features India's tallest escalator. The escalator is 15.6 m (51 ft 2 in.) high.

SPECIALIZED STRUCTURES

India's Biggest Demolition

Two illegally constructed towers at the Supertech Emerald Court Housing Society in Sector 93A, Noida, Uttar Pradesh, made headlines on 28 August 2022. The 103 m (338 ft) high towers were demolished by the 'waterfall implosion' technique in a mere 12 seconds! The demolition of these twin residential towers was ordered by the Supreme Court and carried out by a Mumbai-based company, Edifice Engineering, along with the South African firm Jet Demolitions as their expert partner. With the grounding of Apex (32 storeys) and Ceyane (29 storeys) towers, India joined the club of countries that have razed buildings taller than 100 m (328 ft).

First ropeway in Rajgir, Bihar

First ropeway

India opened its first ropeway service in Rajgir, Bihar. It was inaugurated on 25 October 1969 by the then president V. V. Giri.

It is in the ropeway in Rajgir, Bihar, that the famous song 'O Mere Raja' was picturized on Dev Anand and Hema Malini in the film *Johny Mera Naam* (1970)! It has been reported that Hema Malini was stuck on the ropeway with Dev Anand because of a power cut when they were shooting for the song.

First igloo stay

Keylinga's Manali Igloo Stay, near Sethan Village, about 16 km from Manali in Himachal Pradesh, was opened in 2017 by Vikas Kumar and Tashi Dorje of Keylinga Himalayan Adventures. Starting with two fully functional igloos, the duo provide guests sleeping bags with extra fleece, and hot-water bottles.

First igloo cafe

India's first cafe in the shape of an igloo opened in Gulmarg, Jammu and Kashmir, on 24 January 2021, at an altitude of 2,650 m (8,694 ft) in the Pir Panjal Range of the Himalayas. A part of the Kolahoi Green Group of Hotels and Resorts, the cafe is a 4.5 m (14 ft 9.17 in.) high structure completed by a team of 20 members in 15 days, and has a diameter of 7.3 m (23 ft 11.4 in.). The igloo cafe accommodates four tables that can seat around 16 people at a time and is currently the biggest igloo cafe in Asia.

Largest gazebo

Nirmala Nilayam Retirement Community at Theetipalayam near Siruvani in Coimbatore District, Tamil Nadu, completed the largest gazebo on 20 March 2021. It measures 242.25 sq. m (2,607.59 sq. ft). The gazebo serves as a yoga hall, a seminar hall, a space for art and music sessions, and a meditation space.

First eco-hotel

Asia's first certified eco-hotel, the Orchid, opened in Mumbai, Maharashtra, in 1997.

Largest tent structure

The largest permanent tent structure stood at the Osho International Commune in Pune, Maharashtra. Oval in shape – with a 62.75 m (205 ft 10 in.) major axis and a 32.8 m (107 ft 7 in.) minor axis – it had a floor area of 1,582 sq. m (17,029 sq. ft). The roof, which was 3.9 m (12 ft 9.5 in.) high, was a free-spanning, tensile structure on a three-hinged steel arch covering 45.5 m (149 ft 3 in.). It used nylon reinforced PVC material, weighing 1,990 kg.

WR Largest pillar-less dome

The World Peace Monument is located at the Maharashtra Institute of Technology's World Peace University (MIT-WPU) campus at Loni Kalbhor near Pune, Maharashtra. At a height of

STRUCTURES
TERRE ARMEE

29 m (95 ft), the world's biggest pillarless dome is built on top of the World Peace Prayer Hall and Library and has a diameter of 48.7 m (160 ft), larger than the dome of the Vatican 42.5 m (139 ft 5 in.). Completed in 2018, the dome has a bell hanging from the centre.

Largest underground aquarium

The Bagh-e-Bahu Aquarium at the Bagh-e-Bahu Garden that surrounds Bahu Fort in Jammu in Jammu and Kashmir is the largest underground aquarium in India. At more than 220 m (721 ft 9 in.) in length, this fish-shaped aquarium has freshwater and saltwater fish species in 24 caves with 13 smaller caves.

A yellow parrot fish at the Bagh-e-Bahu Aquarium

Highest ropeway

The Gulmarg Gondola, a gondola lift that covers 2,540 m (8,333 ft), is a joint venture of the Jammu and Kashmir government and the French firm Pomagalski SA. Its first stage transfers people from Gulmarg at 2,600 m (8,530 ft) to Kongdori Station in Kongdori Valley. The second stage goes to 3,747 m (12,293 ft) on Kongdori Mountain, with the highest point at 4,200 m (13,780 ft).

Longest river ropeway

A 1.8 km (5,906 ft) long ropeway was opened in August 2020 across the Brahmaputra River in Guwahati, Assam. It connects the southern and northern parts of the city, cutting down travel time from an hour to eight minutes.

Longest transportation railway tunnel

The 11.21 km long Pir Panjal or Banihal RailwayTunnel is the longest transportation tunnel in India. It connects Bichleri Valley, Banihal, to Qazigund in the Kashmir Valley. The first train here was flagged off on 26 June 2013.

WR Tallest reinforced earth structure

World's tallest reinforced earth structure came up in Tindharia town in Darjeeling District, West Bengal, in 2022. This was created by Terre Armée and was part of a landslide restoration process (under National Highway Circle No. III for Rehabilitation of Landslide Location with Slope Protection and Drainage Improvement at Tindharia on NH-55 at locations from 50.155–50.182 km, 52.650–52.929 km, and 53.452–53.475 km – covering a total length of 329 m in Darjeeling, West Bengal. The maximum height of the structure is 102.8 m in location 2 of the three locations where this earth structure was built. The project started in 2017 and took four years to complete.

AGRICULTURE

GENERAL

First nationwide farm loan waiver

The first nationwide farm loan waiver in independent India was the Agricultural and Rural Debt Relief Scheme (ARDRS), announced by the then Finance Minister Madhu Dandavate, under the V.P. Singh government and implemented in 1990–91. It cost the exchequer ₹10,000 crore (100 billion).

Madhu Dandavate

Biggest farm loan waiver

The Agricultural Debt Waiver and Debt Relief Scheme of 2008 under the UPA government was the biggest farm loan waiver in India by value. It cost the exchequer ₹60,000 crore (600 billion) and benefitted over 3 crore small and marginal farmers.

First agricultural theme park

N.K. Kurian, a civil engineer, is the person behind Mango Meadows. It is the world's first man-made agricultural theme park spread on 12 hectares (29.65 acres) of land, in Kottayam, Kerala. Work on the park began in 2004 and it was opened to the public in December 2016. With saplings and seeds collected from 15 countries, currently the park has 4,500 species of plants, including 1,900 medicinal plants, 700 trees, and 900 flowering plants.

First fully organic state

Sikkim was officially declared India's first fully organic state on 18 January 2016. It has succeeded in converting around 75,000 hectares (185,329 acres) of its agricultural land to certified organic land by implementing organic practices as per the guidelines of the National Programme for Organic Production.

Tea garden labourers at the organic tea garden of Temi Tea Estate in Sikkim

First fruit train

A train exclusively carrying fruit – 890 metric tonnes of locally grown bananas – was flagged off from Tadipatri railway station in Anantapur District, Andhra Pradesh. It reached the Jawaharlal Nehru Port in Mumbai, Maharashtra, on 31 January 2020. The train was laden with 43 refrigerator containers of bananas that had been despatched for export to international markets.

First state/UT to regulate crops

Telangana became the first state in the country to stipulate when and how much of which crops to grow for its farmers. From the beginning of the kharif season in 2020, the state decided to regulate the cropping pattern with the help of a detailed cropping map and a seed regulation authority. The emphasis has been to drive supply according to the market demand.

Mango Meadows, Kottayam, Kerala; (*inset*) N.K. Kurian

Earliest ploughed field

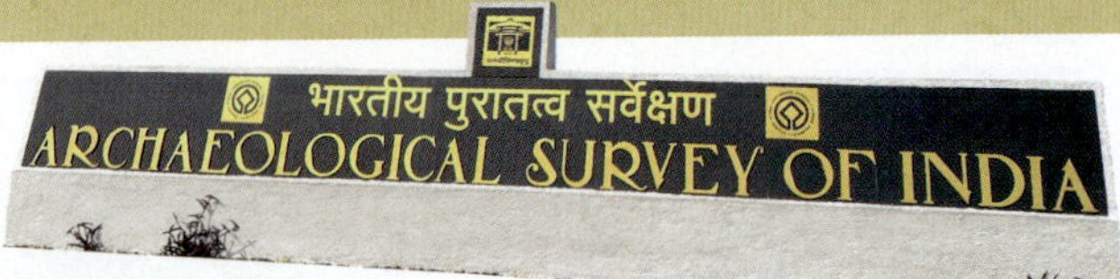

Archaeological Survey of India (ASI)

Archaeologists B.B. Lal and B.K. Thapar of the Archaeological Survey of India (ASI) found a ploughed field dated to c. 2450–2300 BCE during excavations at Kalibangan in Pilibangan Tehsil in Hanumangarh District, Rajasthan.

First state/UT to enact a law on contract farming

Tamil Nadu became the first state in the country to pass a law on contract farming called the Agricultural Produce and Livestock Contract Farming and Services (Promotion and Facilitation) Act in February 2019. Contract farming enables more transparency, and legally safeguards the interests of farmers, producer companies, and purchasers. The Act covers the produce of agriculture, sericulture, horticulture, apiculture, animal husbandry, and forest activities.

HISTORY

Earliest cotton cultivation

The earliest evidence for cotton production comes from the Harappan civilization (2500–1700 BCE). The earliest sample of cotton material was discovered by archaeologist Daya Ram Sahni during 1921–22 in Mohenjo-daro (now in Pakistan). It was a small fragment of cotton clinging to the side of a vase and dyed red with madder pigment (*Rubia tinctorum*).

Earliest irrigation

Evidence of irrigation on agricultural land in the Indian subcontinent dates to the Chalcolithic period (3000–1000 BCE). The Inamgaon area of Maharashtra has a prehistoric mud embankment structure with a stone foundation. This was connected to the Ghod River by a number of channels. Floodwater was used effectively to irrigate the surrounding regions during the dry months by storing it and then distributing it.

Earliest cotton committee

Government of India appointed Indian Cotton Committee (ICC) in 1919. One of the significant recommendations of the committee was to establish an Indian Central Cotton Committee (ICCC), which led to the formation of the same in March 1921. Dr A.J. Turner took charge as its first director in January 1924.

Sir George Campbell

First famine commission

The Campbell Commission set up in 1866 after the famine in 1865–66 (also known as the Odisha famine since it was most severe there), was the first famine commission in the country. Under the chairmanship of Sir George Campbell, it was followed by the appointment of a committee. It blamed the government machinery for the famine and its tragic effects.

Oldest locust control programme

The Locust Warning Organization (LWO), set up in 1939 in Karachi (now in Pakistan) by the British, is the oldest locust control programme in the world. In 1946, the LWO moved to Delhi under the Directorate of Plant Protection, Quarantine and Storage (PPQS), Ministry of Agriculture and Farmers' Welfare, Government of India. It surveys locust populations and issues bulletins.

Aerial view of the ruins of Mohenjo-daro; (*inset*) Daya Ram Sahni

First agricultural society

William Carey

William Carey, a British Christian missionary, social reformer, translator, and anthropologist, founded the Agri-Horticultural Society of India in September 1820 in Calcutta (now Kolkata), West Bengal. It was set up to help disseminate scientific information among the people.

First society of soil sciences

Sir Bryce C. Burt

The Indian Society of Soil Sciences was formed on 22 December 1934 in Calcutta with 28 members. It was formally inaugurated on 3 January 1935 at the Presidency College (now Presidency University). Sir Bryce C. Burt, the then agricultural commissioner in the Imperial (now Indian) Council of Agricultural Research (ICAR), was its first president and Prof. J.N. Mukherjee, its first secretary.

WR First agricultural research institute

The Imperial Agricultural Research Institute, established in 1905 at Pusa, Samastipur District, Bihar, was India's first agricultural research institute. After the building was damaged in an earthquake in 1934, the institute was moved to New Delhi in 1936. It is now known as the Indian Agricultural Research Institute (IARI) and is the oldest agricultural institute in India.

Central Tuber Crops Research Institute, Sreekariyam, Thiruvananthapuram, Kerala

First agricultural university

The G.B. (Govind Ballabh) Pant University of Agriculture and Technology (GBPUA&T), also known as Pantnagar University, was the first agricultural university in India. It was inaugurated on 17 November 1960 as the Uttar Pradesh Agricultural University (UPAU). Later, in 1972, its name was changed to Govind Ballabh Pant University of Agriculture and Technology after the first chief minister of Uttar Pradesh and Bharat Ratna recipient Pandit Govind Ballabh Pant.

WR Only research centre for tropical tuber crops

The Central Tuber Crops Research Institute at Sreekariyam in Thiruvananthapuram District, Kerala, is the only institute in the world dedicated to research on tropical tuber crops. It was established in 1963.

Research institute located at the highest altitude

The Defence Institute of High Altitude Research (DIHAR), situated at 3,505 m (11,499 ft) in Leh, Ladakh, is a laboratory of the Defence Research Development Organization (DRDO). It was established in 1962 to help Indian defence troops as well as farmers of the

College of Agriculture, G.B. Pant University of Agriculture and Technology, Pantnagar

Largest groundwater irrigation system

India has the largest groundwater irrigation system in the world with 39 million hectares (96.4 million acres) of land under this kind of irrigation. Besides groundwater, India's irrigation depends on canals from rivers, well-based systems, tanks, and other rainwater harvesting systems. About two-thirds of farmlands in the country still depend on the monsoon.

Source of Crop Irrigation	Percentage
Canals	22.85%
Tanks	2.82%
Tubewells	49.34%
Other wells	13.46%
Other sources	11.53%

*Source: Annual Report 2024–25, Department of Agriculture and Farmers Welfare, Ministry of Agriculture and Farmers Welfare, Government of India

region with appropriate agro-animal technologies.

First pollen cryobank

The first pollen cryobank (frost bank) was established in 1983 at the Indian Institute of Horticultural Research, Bengaluru, Karnataka, to conserve genetic biodiversity among plants and support the work of crop breeders.

First spices research institute

The regional station for spice research, set up at Kozhikode, Kerala, in 1975 is the apex research organization for spices in the country. It later evolved into the Indian Institute of Spices Research in 1986.

Only weed research centre

The Directorate of Weed Science Research (DWSR), Jabalpur, Madhya Pradesh, set up the National Research Centre for Weed Science on 22 April 1989 – the only one in the world for weed management research.

AWARDS AND HONOURS

First Indian fellow of the Royal Society

Dr Benjamin Peary Pal, the first director of the Indian Council of Agricultural Research, was also the first Indian agricultural scientist to become a Fellow of the Royal Society of London, UK, while in office, in 1972. He was also awarded the top national civilian awards: the Padma Shri (1959), the Padma Bhushan (1968) and the Padma Vibhushan (1987).

A 2008 postal stamp on Dr B.P. Pal

First Indian scientist to receive the Ramon Magsaysay Award

Geneticist Dr M.S. Swaminathan received the Ramon Magsaysay award in 1971 for community leadership and became the first Indian scientist to do so. Known as the 'Father of the Green Revolution' for his leading role in food self-sufficiency in India, he was the director of the Indian Agricultural Research Institute in Delhi at the time. Dr Swaminathan advocated environmentally sustainable agriculture as well as preservation of biodiversity, culminating in what he termed an 'evergreen' revolution.

Dr M.S. Swaminathan

First Indian president of the International Society of Soil Sciences

Dr J.S. Kanwar was elected president of the International Society of Soil Sciences for the period 1978–82. The Society was

WHAT'S THE TEA?

Highest tea garden

The Korakundah Tea Estate of the United Nilgiri Tea Estates Co. Ltd, near Coonoor in the Nilgiris in Tamil Nadu, has its highest tea garden at an altitude of 2,471 m (8,107 ft).

Korakundah Tea Estate, Nilgiris, Tamil Nadu

WR Oldest tea research station

Set up in 1911, the Tocklai Experimental Station in Jorhat, Assam, is the world's oldest and largest tea research station. Its many contributions include the invention of tea machinery and the development of 30 vegetative clones. The transfer of innovative technology to its member estates is carried out through its advisory network. This network covers 1,076 tea estates occupying 341,049 hectares (842,750.4 acres) of land spread over the Brahmaputra Valley, the Barak Valley, Tripura, the Dooars, Darjeeling, and the Terai areas. Tocklai has its regional R&D centre at Nagrakata in Jalpaiguri District, West Bengal.

Tocklai Experimental Station, Jorhat, Assam

Lord William Bentinck

First tea estate

In 1837, the British East India Company set up the first tea estate at Chabua in Dibrugarh District, Assam. Now the estate is owned by Amalgamated Plantations Private Ltd. The first Tea Committee in India was set up in 1834 by the then Governor General of India, Lord William Bentinck.

founded in 1924, mainly by European agro-pedologists interested in establishing standardized methods of soil analysis.

First winner of the World Food Prize

In 1987, Dr M.S. Swaminathan became the first Indian to win the World Food Prize. He was an agronomist, agricultural scientist, and plant geneticist. This global award is given to outstanding individuals who have advanced human development by improving the quality, quantity, or availability of food in the world. So far, eight Indians have won the World Food Prize and the most recent was Dr Rattan Lal, an India-born British scientist from the USA, in 2020.

Dr Rattan Lal

FARMLANDS AND PRINCIPAL CROPS

Largest single farm

The Central State Farm at Suratgarh in Rajasthan, with an area of 6,296 hectares (15,557.8 acres), is said to be the largest farm in Asia.

Largest average farm holdings in a state/UT

As per the 2015–16 Agricultural Census, Nagaland has the largest farm holdings, with 4.87 hectares (12.03 acres) as the average size of an operational unit.

WR First onion hybrid

The world's first onion hybrid was developed at the Indian Agricultural Research Institute, New Delhi, in March 2002 with a potential of increasing yield by 20 per cent.

First genetically modified cash crop approved for commercial cultivation

Bt (*Bacillus thuringiensis*) cotton was the first genetically modified (GM) crop approved for commercial cultivation in 2002 by the Government of India. The Genetic Engineering Appraisal Committee (GEAC) has also approved confined field trials of 20 GM crops for the generation of bio-safety data from both private and public sector

Bt cotton crop

institutions. The crops are cotton, mustard, brinjal, okra, sorghum, groundnut, maize, potato, tomato, chickpea, pigeon pea, banana, castor, papaya, watermelon, sugar cane, wheat, rice, rubber tree, and Indian wormwood.

WR First pigeon pea hybrid (arhar)

The International Crops Research Institute for Semi-Arid Tropics (ICRISAT) released the world's first hybrid pigeon pea, ICPH-8, in 1991. This variety recorded a yield potential of 2,057 kg/hectare.

First cotton hybrid

The first commercial cotton hybrid in the country, named H-4 or Sankar-4, was developed at the Gujarat Agricultural University in 1970 by agricultural scientist Dr Chandrakant T. Patel.

Tallest sugar cane

Vedant Rajendra Yadav from Fursungi Village in Pune District, Maharashtra, grew a sugar cane plant that was 13.1 m (43 ft) tall in January 2021.

WR First hybrid Basmati rice

The IARI, New Delhi, developed and released RH-10 in 2001, the first hybrid superfine-grained, aromatic rice in the world. The optimum yield of this variety of rice, with typical Basmati traits, is 7 tonnes/hectare.

Tallest paddy plant

Tanaji Nikam, a farmer in Vannur Village in Kolhapur, Maharashtra, grew a paddy plant 2.8 m (9 ft 2 in.) tall in 2005 using organic manure.

Tallest jowar

Dodda Ramachandra Reddy from Peddapalli, Karimnagar District, Telangana, grew a jowar plant that was 5.3 m (17 ft 4 in.) tall as on 27 October 2018. It took 161 days to grow to this height.

Tallest papaya plant

Jhantu Paul from Kolkata, West Bengal, owns the tallest papaya tree (*Carica papaya*) measuring 14.07 m (46 ft 2 in.) as verified on 22 January 2017.

Heaviest jackfruit

Kaithakkoli Kurichiya's family found a jackfruit weighing 57.9 kg on their compound in Thallappuzha, Wayanad District, Kerala, in May 2020. The jackfruit was 67 cm (26 in.) long, with a circumference of 1.35 m (4 ft 5 in.).

State/UT with maximum cold storage capacity

Uttar Pradesh has 14,834,695 tonnes of cold storage capacity as on 31 January 2022.

Smallest average farm holdings in a state/UT

The average size of an operational farm in Kerala is 0.18 hectares (0.44 acres) as per the 2015–16 Agricultural Census.

Longest ash gourd

Dr Johnson Nayankara from Mapranam in Thrissur District, Kerala, has grown

Basmati rice

Longest ash gourd

the longest ash gourd as verified on 11 November 2020. It was 47.3 cm (18.62 in.) long, with a 6.2 cm (2.4 in.) stalk.

Longest and biggest coconut

Dr Dilip Kumar Vitthaldas Patil, a scientist at the Central Institute for Cotton Research, Nagpur, Maharashtra, preserved for 12 years, the largest and biggest coconut (and the longest preserved) seen in India. Dr Patil found this giant coconut in a farm in Pilicode Village, Kasaragod District, Kerala. Even in the dried state, it was 27 cm (10.63 in.) from stalk to tip and its equitorial length was 67.5 cm (26.57 in.) as against normal green coconuts, which are 14 to 20 cm (5.51 to 7.87 in.) horizontally and 25 to 45 cm (9.84 to 17.72 in.) long. In its dried state the coconut weighed 1,450 g against an average of 300–500 g.

Highest vineyard

At 1,585 m (5,200 ft) above mean sea level, Kookkal Vineyards (Domaine Kookkal) at Kookkal Village, near Udhagamandalam, Tamil Nadu, are the highest commercial-scale vineyards in the country.

WR Only producer of five commercial silk varieties

India is the only producer of all five commercial varieties of silk, viz. mulberry, oak tussore, tropical tussore, eri and muga. Golden muga is produced only in India. During 2018–19, India produced 31,906 tonnes of raw silk.

Golden muga silk

Mulberry silk

Oak tussore silk

Tropical silk

Eri silk

HORTICULTURE

First seed company

The National Seeds Corporation, set up in 1963 by the Government of India, undertakes the production of certified seeds of nearly 600 varieties of 60 crops through its 8,000 registered seed growers.

First vanilla cultivation

The first cultivation centres of vanilla were set up more than a century ago at the Kallar Fruit Research Station, Thiruvananthapuram District, and the Ambalavayal Horticultural Research Station, Wayanad District, Kerala.

First non-narcotic poppy

Sujata, a poppy variety developed in 1998 at the Central Institute of Medicinal and Aromatic Plants, Lucknow, Uttar Pradesh, was the first poppy variety free of opium and opium alkaloids.

First mustard hybrid

In 2008, NRC Sankar Sarson (NRCHB 506), an Indian hybrid of mustard, was developed by a team of scientists led by Dr K.H. Singh at the National Research Centre on Rapeseed-Mustard (NRCRM; now called the Directorate of Rapeseed Mustard Research) in Bharatpur, Rajasthan.

First castor hybrid

The Castor and Mustard Research Station in Sardarkrushinagar in Banaskantha District, Gujarat, developed the first castor hybrid named GCH 3 and released it in 1968–69 on a commercial scale. GCH 7, released in 2006, has the highest potential productivity (3,000 kg/hectare) in India.

Hottest chilli

The *bhut jolokia*, or 'ghost chilli', is the hottest chilli in India. Rated at 1,041,427 Scoville heat units (SHUs), this variety is cultivated in the north-eastern states of Arunachal Pradesh, Assam, Nagaland, and Manipur.

Bhut jolokia

PERCENTAGE OF FARMERS ISSUED SOIL HEALTH CARD

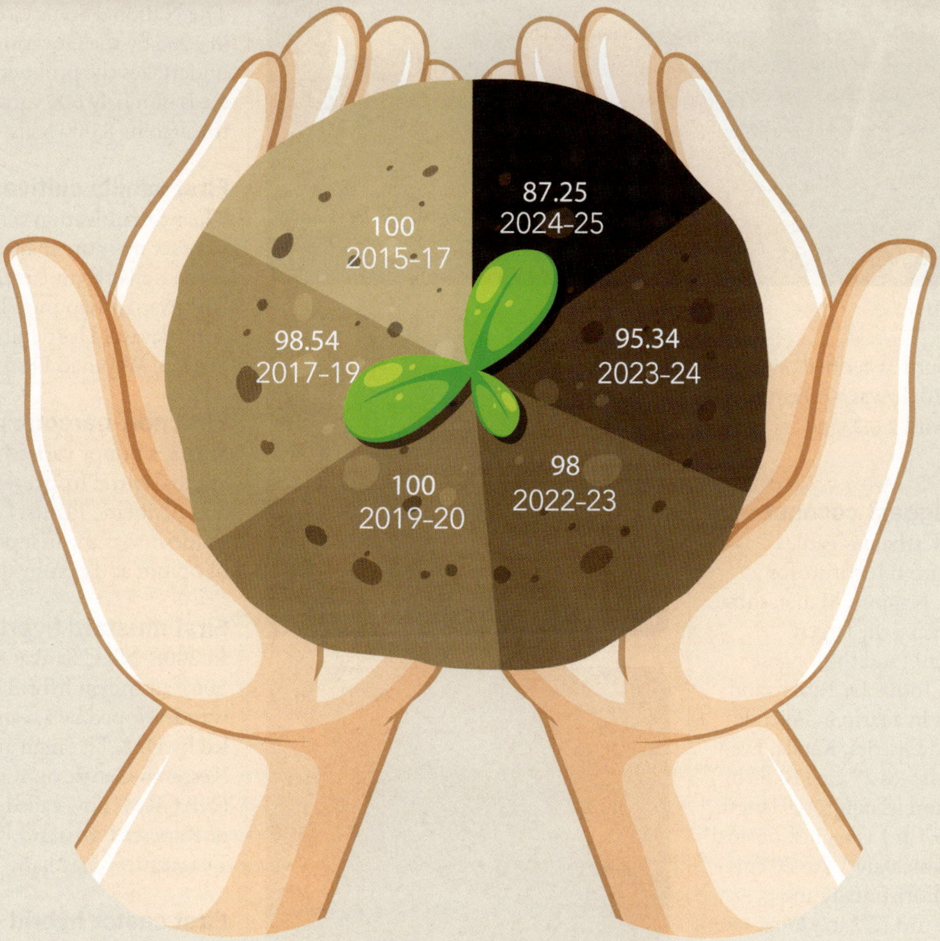

87.25
2024-25

100
2015-17

98.54
2017-19

95.34
2023-24

98
2022-23

100
2019-20

Source: Sustainable Development Goals National Indicator Framework Progress Report 2025, Ministry of Statistics and Programme Implementation, Government of India

ANNUAL GROWTH IN AGRICULTURE SECTOR

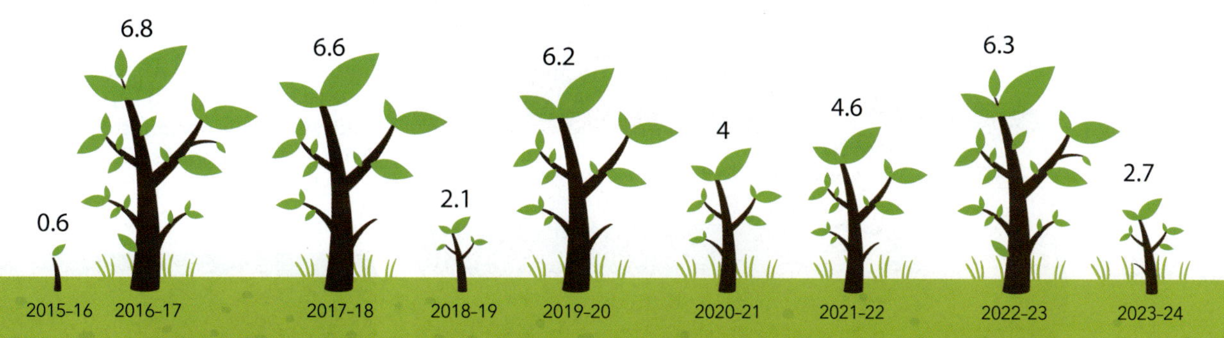

Source: Sustainable Development Goals National Indicator Framework Progress Report 2025, Ministry of Statistics and Programme Implementation, Government of India

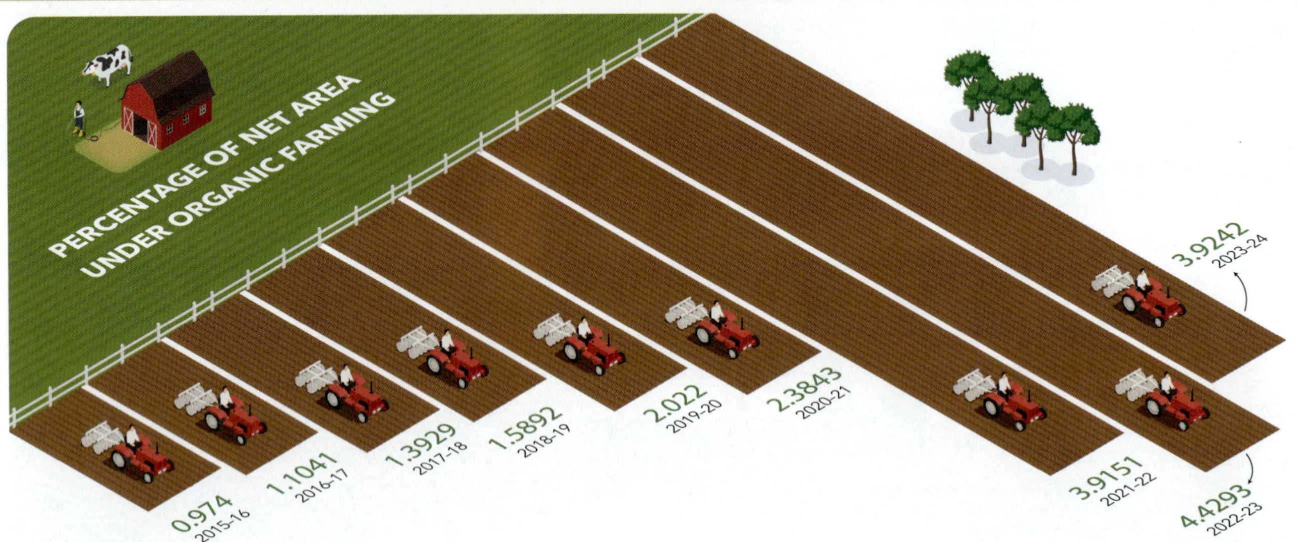

Source: Sustainable Development Goals National Indicator Framework Progress Report 2025, Ministry of Statistics and Programme Implementation, Government of India

PERCENTAGE OF AGRICULTURAL MANDIS ENROLLED IN E-MARKET

Year	Percentage
2016-17	6.49
2017-18	3.1
2018-19	8.41
2019-20	8.55
2020-21	15.1
2021-22	14.4
2022-23	19.21
2023-24	19.56

Source: Sustainable Development Goals National Indicator Framework Progress Report 2025, Ministry of Statistics and Programme Implementation, Government of India

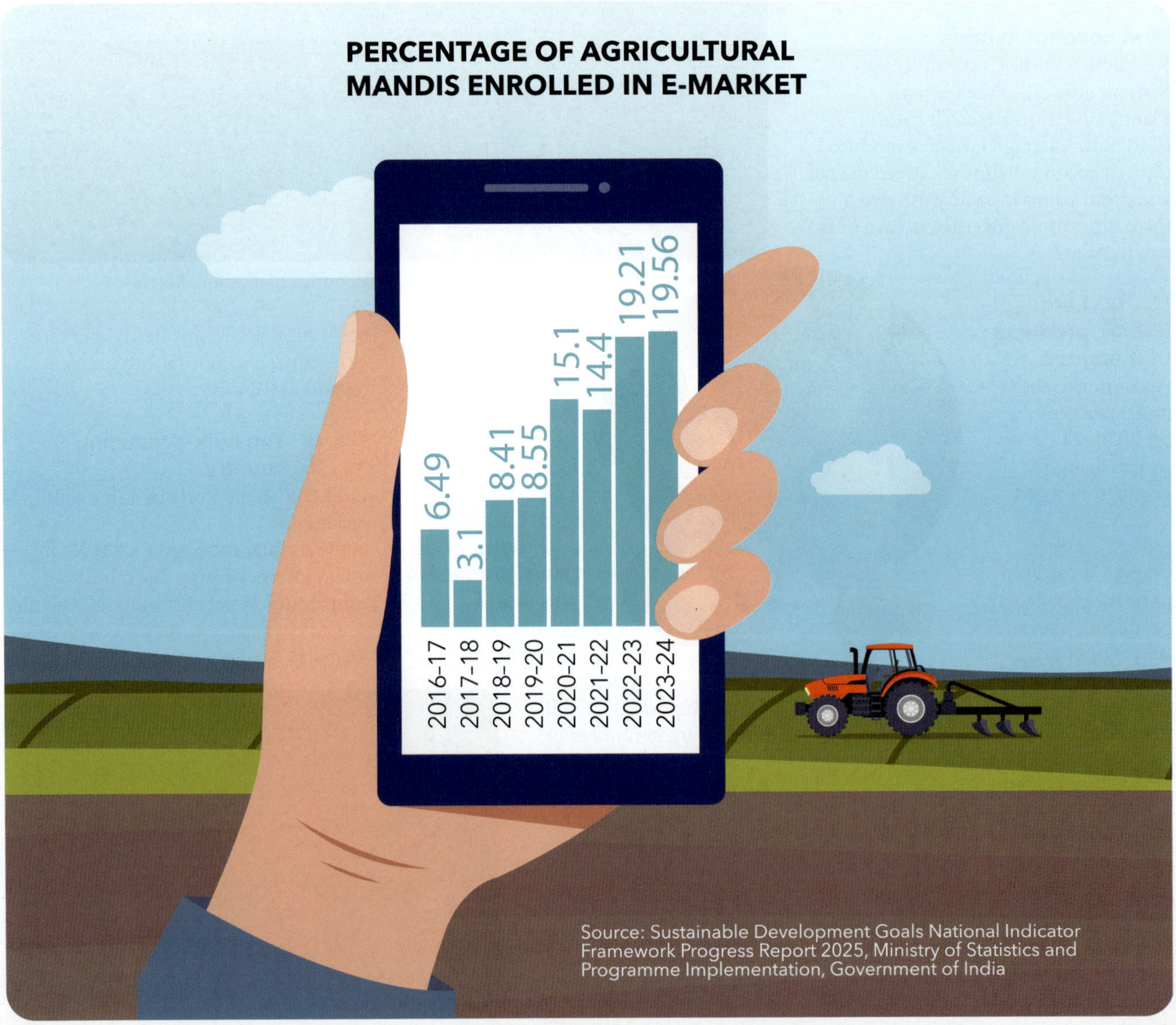

Central Plantation Crops Research Institute (CPCRI), Kasaragod, Kerala

First coconut hybrids

Researchers at the Coconut Research Station, now called the Central Plantation Crops Research Institute (CPCRI), Kasaragod, Kerala, produced the first coconut hybrids between the tall and dwarf palms in 1932, with two to three times more nuts than in each of the parent palms.

Coconut plantation, Kerala

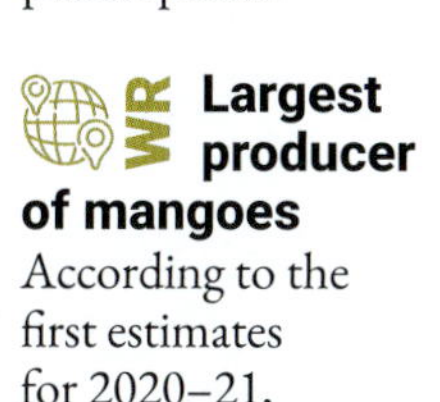

WR Largest producer of mangoes

According to the first estimates for 2020–21, India's mango production stood at 20.82 million tonnes. Andhra Pradesh turned out to be the top mango producing state with the production of 5,001,740 tonnes of mangoes.

Indian mangoes

WR Largest producer of coconuts

India produces 34.73 per cent of the global production of coconuts. As per 2020–21 reports, the area and production of coconuts in the country is 2.18 million hectares (5.8 million acres) and 14.57 million tonnes, respectively. The four southern states of Kerala, Tamil Nadu, Karnataka and Andhra Pradesh account for 88.97 per cent of the area under coconut cultivation and 89.67 per cent of the coconut production in the country.

WR Largest number of organic producers in the world

According to the World of Organic Agriculture Report 2022, India has the largest number of organic producers in the world. With 1,599,010 certified organic producers, the country is home to more than 47.02 per cent of the total number of organic producers (3.4 million) worldwide. However, when it comes to the total area under certified organic cultivation, India only has 1.5 per cent of its entire agricultural area under organic cultivation.

WR Top milk-producing country

India has led the world in milk production since 1997. Milk production in the country increased to 209.96 million tonnes during 2021. India contributes 21 per cent of the global milk

Animal Husbandry in India

Indian spices

production. The top milk-producing states are Uttar Pradesh, Rajasthan, and Madhya Pradesh.

WR Largest producer of spices

India is the largest producer of spices and spice products. In 2020-21, India produced 16.6 million tonnes of spices.

ANIMAL HUSBANDRY

Early vet research

Research on animal healthcare began with the setting up of the Imperial Bacteriological Laboratory at Poona (now Pune), Maharashtra, on 9 December 1889, with Dr Alfred Lingard as the first bacteriologist in 1890. It was moved to Mukteshwar, Uttarakhand, in 1895. The Indian Veterinary Research Institute (IVRI) later began in 1913 at Izatnagar, Bareilly District, Uttar Pradesh.

Dr Alfred Lingard

First veterinary surgeon

William Moorcroft (1767–1825), a Britisher who was appointed veterinary surgeon in 1808 at the Pusa Stud Farm, Bihar, is the first one on record in India.

First frozen semen bank for bulls

The first frozen semen bank for bulls was established in 1963 in Mattupatti, Kerala, with Indo-Swiss collaboration. The objective was to evolve a new breed of cattle adapted to the local environment. The bank dealt with the collection, processing, storage, and transportation of the semen of bull breeds.

First artificial insemination in bulls

Artificial insemination was successfully attempted for the first time in 1939 by Sampath Kumaran, who crossed the Indian Hallikar breed with Holstein Friesian bulls.

First dairy research institute

Established in 1923 as the Imperial Dairy Institute of Animal Husbandry and Dairying in Bangalore (now Bengaluru), Karnataka, it was renamed National Dairy Research Institute (NDRI) after Independence. In 1955, its headquarters was shifted to Karnal, Haryana. It undertakes research, teaching and extension activities in dairy development.

Only camel farm

The National Research Centre on Camel (NRCC), also a camel-breeding farm, was set up in Bikaner, Rajasthan, in 1957 for conducting scientific research on camels. The centre aims to study ways of optimizing the working capacity of camels. It is the only camel farm in the country.

First lamb from frozen embryo

Scientists at the Central Sheep and Wool Research Institute in Avikanagar in Tonk District, Rajasthan, implanted a cryo-preserved Bharat Merino embryo into a Kheri surrogate ewe, which birthed a lamb on 20 January 1999.

Highest stud farm

The Zanskar Pony Breeding and Training Centre at Partapur in Nubra Block, Ladakh, is located at 3,146 m (10,321 ft) above mean sea level.

Most piglets in a single litter

An artificial insemination field project by scientists at the National Research Centre on Pig in Guwahati, Assam, achieved the largest litter size of 19 piglets in a single delivery in 2012.

First cross-bred cow

The first cross-bred cow breed in India, called Taylor, was named after an Englishman, William Taylor, who was the one to initiate cattle cross-breeding in Patna, Bihar, in the mid-19th century.

WR First test-tube yak calf

The first test-tube yak calf in the world, a male weighing 19 kg, was born at the Nyukmadung farm of the National Research Centre on Yak (NRCY), Dirang Dzong, West Kameng District, Arunachal Pradesh, on 15 July 2013. The yak calf was named Norgayal.

WR First buffalo-milk powder

The Kaira District Cooperative

Amul

Milk Producers Union (Amul Dairy), Anand, Gujarat, produced whole and skimmed milk powder from buffalo milk in 1955. They were also the first in the world to commercially produce cheese and baby food from buffalo milk in 1960.

WR Largest population of livestock

India had the largest population of livestock, with an estimated 536.76 million heads of cattle by 2019, making up as much as 31 per cent of the world's livestock population.

Heaviest goat

Asif Ali from Bhopal, Madhya Pradesh, reared the heaviest goat named King on his R.K. Goat Farm. King weighed 171 kg on 25 July 2019.

Heaviest and highest-priced bull

In March 2018, Haryana's first Murrah Ratan Award was won by a buffalo called Shahenshah, which weighed between 1,100 and 1,200 kg and was owned by Narender Singh from Didwari Village, Panipat, Haryana.

State with the most veterinary institutions

Rajasthan leads Indian states and UTs with 7,897 veterinary institutions (31 March 2018).

Largest cattle farm

Mathigiri Cattle Farm and District Livestock Centre near Hosur in Krishnagiri district, Tamil Nadu, is India's and Asia's largest cattle farm. It is spread over 480 hectares (1,200 acres).

Largest dairy development programme

Project Operation Flood, launched in 1970 by the National Dairy Development Board (NDDB) and led by Dr Verghese Kurien, general manager and later chairman, AMUL, and chairman, NDDB and the Institute of Rural Management Anand (IRMA), Gujarat was the largest dairy development programme in India. It involved forming a National Milk Grid that connected milk producers to consumers in over 700 towns and cities in India.

Dr Verghese Kurien

Oldest cow

Ruby, a cow owned by Dr Dipa Panjuani of Pune, Maharashtra, crossed 35 years in 2017. It was milking till six months before it turned 32 years old.

CLONING RECORDS

WR First cloned pashmina goat

Noori, the first cloned pashmina goat, was born at the Faculty of Veterinary Sciences and Animal Husbandry, Sher-e-Kashmir University of Agricultural Sciences and Technology, Srinagar, Jammu and Kashmir, on 9 March 2012. With a birthweight of 1.3 kg, she was cloned by a team headed by Dr Riaz Ahmad Shah, using somatic cell nuclear transfer technique.

WR First cloned buffalo

On 6 February 2009, a team of six scientists – S.K. Singla, M.S. Chauhan, R.S. Manik, P. Palta, R.A. Shah and A. George – all from the Animal Biotechnology Centre at the National Dairy Research Institute, Karnal, Haryana, cloned the first female water buffalo calf in the world from a year-old buffalo of the Murrah breed. Although the calf died five days later, the team of scientists succeeded in testing the cloning and other technologies that helped them achieve one of their objectives of getting the desired gender of the cloned animal.

Most calves cloned from a single bull

The Central Institute for Research on Buffaloes (CIRB), located in Hisar, Haryana, achieved the cloning of seven calves from a single superior breeding bull, named M-29, between October 2019 and January 2020.

First calf cloned from frozen semen

In July 2014, a male calf named Rajat was

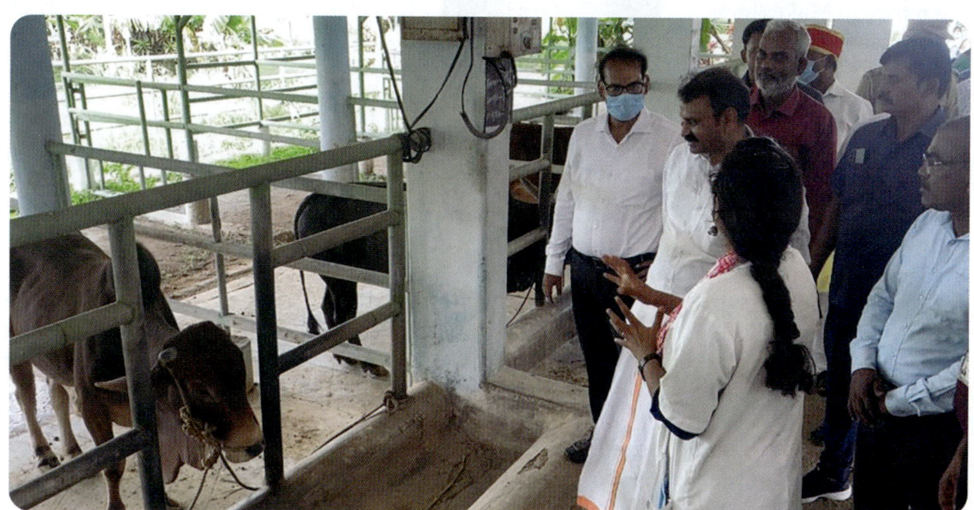

Mathigiri Cattle Farm and District Livestock Centre

cloned by the National Dairy Research Institute (NDRI), Karnal, Haryana, using a donor cell from the frozen semen of a highly ranked Murrah buffalo bull. This was the first time frozen semen was used for cloning a farm animal.

WR First cloned female buffalo by hand-guided technique

In June 2014, scientists of the National Dairy Research Institute, Karnal, Haryana, produced the world's first female cloned buffalo calf through 'hand-guided' cloning, using a donor cell from the ear of a high-yielding Murrah buffalo. The calf was named Lalima.

Ganga – the first cloned cow in India

On 16 March 2023, Ganga, the first cloned cow in India, was born. The scientists at NDRI, Karnal, Haryana, created her. The process of cloning a cow took much longer due to religious sentiments as the technology available back then was invasive. However, in 2018, the scientists got access to a non-invasive technology called ovum pick up that is used to separate oocytes from the cow without harming her. They chose Gir breed as it could withstand harsh weather and produce 2–3 times more milk, i.e., 15 to 20 litres per day.

POULTRY AND FISHERIES

First broiler chicken variety

B-77, the first broiler variety of chicken, was released by the IVRI in Izatnagar in Bareilly District, Uttar Pradesh, in 1977.

Biggest hen egg

A hen at the Dev Research and Breeding Farms of Sukhbir Singh of Ramrai Khera in Jind, Haryana, laid an egg weighing 167 g on 28 September 2014. It was 8.35 cm (3.3 in.) long and 5 cm (2 in.) wide.

Largest poultry company

Suguna Foods Pvt. Ltd, which achieved a sales turnover of over ₹8,700 crore (87 billion) during 2019–20, is the largest broiler chicken company in India. Based in Coimbatore, Tamil Nadu, it ranks among the top 10 poultry enterprises worldwide and operates in 18 states in India, covering over 40,000 farmers in over 15,000 villages. Its products and services include hatcheries, feed mills, processing plants, value-added eggs, and broiler and frozen chicken.

Suguna Foods Pvt Ltd

First and only licensed fisherwoman

In 2017, K.C. Rekha from Thrissur, Kerala, became India's only licensed deep-sea fisherwoman. Rekha accompanies her husband Karthikeyan to work every day.

First deep-sea fishing station

The Deep-Sea Fishing Station, Bombay (now Mumbai), Maharashtra, was set up in October 1946. It was renamed the Exploratory Fisheries Project (EFP) in 1974 when it systematically surveyed the coastal and offshore waters up to a depth of 70 m (230 ft). Engaged in oceanic surveys of Exclusive Economic Zones, it was renamed the Fishery Survey of India in 1979.

First pearl culture

The first cultured pearls, using the Akoya pearl oyster, were produced in 1973 at the Tuticorin Research Centre at the Central Marine Fisheries Research

Central Marine Fisheries Research Institute (CMFRI) building

Top shrimp-producing state/UT
Andhra Pradesh led with 634,672 million tonnes, followed by West Bengal with 35,392 million tonnes, in 2020–21.

Institute (CMFRI) in Thoothukudi, Tamil Nadu, in collaboration with the Tamil Nadu State Fisheries Department.

First research institute for freshwater aquaculture

The Central Institute of Freshwater Aquaculture, Bhubaneswar, Odisha, began in the Pond Culture Division of the Central Inland Fisheries Research Institute, at Cuttack, Odisha, in 1949. The division was later upgraded as the Freshwater Aquaculture Research and Training Centre in 1976. It became an independent institute on 1 April 1987.

Oldest fisheries research institutes

The oldest fisheries research institutes are the Central Marine Fisheries Research Institute (CMFRI), established in 1947, and the Central Inland Capture Fisheries Research Institute (CICFRI), also set up in 1947 under the name of Central Inland Fisheries Research Institute (CIFRI) in Calcutta (now Kolkata), West Bengal.

First marine aquarium for ornamental fish

An aquarium for ornamental fish breeding and multiplication was established in 1998 in Vizhinjam near Kovalam in Kerala.

First transgenic rohu fish

During 2004–05, a team of scientists led by Dr T.J. Pandian at the Madurai Kamaraj University, Madurai, Tamil Nadu, developed a genetically modified rohu fish that could grow 6–7 times faster than a normal one.

FERTILIZERS, PESTICIDES, AND MACHINERY

First synthetic pesticide

DDT (Dichlorodiphenyltrichloroethane) was introduced in 1946 for vector control and used in 1948. Its use was banned in May 1989.

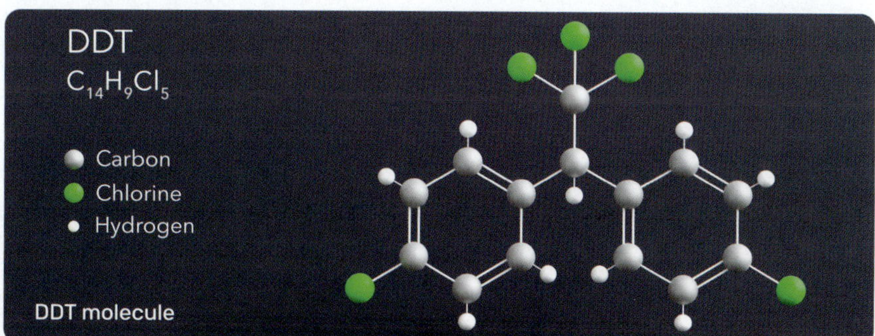

DDT molecule

First neem-based biocide

The first neem-based biocide was tested and commissioned by the National Tree Growers Cooperative Federation during 1997–98.

First use of lift irrigation

In 1926, an experimental lift irrigation system on 1,012 hectares (2,500 acres) of wasteland was started in the Rachna Doab region of Gangapur Village in Punjab (now in Pakistan) by Sir Ganga Ram, a member of the Regional Commission on Agriculture.

Most sold farm equipment with largest market share

Tractors have the biggest share of the farm machinery market in India, at 80 per cent. In 2020–21, overall tractor sales in the country were 842,266 units.

Earliest soil treatment experiments

The earliest methods to find out the effects of inorganic fertilizers on the soil – its physical, chemical, and biological properties vis-à-vis crop yields – were started at the Agricultural College and Research Institute, Coimbatore, Tamil Nadu, in 1909.

First fertilizer factory

The first SSP (single superphosphate) factory that produced fertilizer mixtures, insecticides and fungicides was set up in 1906 in Ranipet District in Tamil Nadu by East India Distilleries Parry Ltd.

First pesticide

Benzene hexachloride (BHC) was first commercialized by the Imperial Chemical Industries Ltd (ICI) in 1952 at Rishra in Hooghly District, West Bengal. A factory was set up in Calcutta (now Kolkata), West Bengal.

State/UT with the highest use of chemical pesticides and biopesticides

Maharashtra was the highest consumer of chemical pesticides (13,175 million tonnes) and biopesticides (934.44 million tonnes) in 2020–21.

First institute for farm machinery training and testing

The Central Farm Machinery Training and Testing Institute (FMTTI), established in 1959 in Budni, Sehore District, Madhya Pradesh, was the first of the four FMTTI centres in India. Since its inception and up to March 2020, the centre has trained a total of 69,056 trainees from across India.

First biocontrol agents

The ladybird beetle of Australia was introduced in 1898 to control mealy bugs on fruit crops.

Ladybird beetle

State/UT with the highest use of fertilizers per hectare

With a total consumption of 312.04 kg/hectare in 2021, Puducherry is the largest consumer of fertilizers (N, P & K).

First agri-plane

Hindustan Aeronautics Ltd's HA-31 Basant monoplane was built in 1972 for agricultural needs. Its use was discontinued in 1980.

Earliest use of tractors

Sardar Sir Jogendra Singh (1877–1946) experimented with steam tractors for wasteland reclamation in 1914 at Aira estate in Lakhimpur, Uttar Pradesh, and at Iqbal Nagar (now in Pakistan) in Punjab.

First semi-autonomous tractor

In April 2018, Mahindra and Mahindra Ltd rolled out a high-tech tractor, the Pack 1. This is an 'intelligent' tractor with a driver-assist system.

Largest seller of tractors

Mahindra and Mahindra Ltd is the largest-selling tractor brand in India, with total sales of 337,052 units in the financial year ended March 2022. It exported 17,646 units in the same period.

State/UT with most tractor exports

Maharashtra with exports worth US $186 million was the state with the most tractor exports in the year 2019–20. According to the Directorate General of Commercial Intelligence and Statistics data, Punjab exported tractors worth US $178 million in 2019–20 while Tamil Nadu exported tractors worth US $156 million.

Mahindra tractor

EDUCATION

73
72

LITERACY

First 100 per cent literate district
In 1990, Ernakulam, Kerala, with a population of 3 million then, became the first completely literate district in the country, with a literacy rate of 98.34 per cent in the age group of 5–60 years.

First national education council
The All India Council for Secondary Education (AICSE) was set up in 1955.

State/UT with the highest literacy rate
Kerala, with 96.2 per cent, has the highest rate of literacy among all states, according to the 75th round of the National Sample Survey (NSS) conducted from July 2017 to June 2018.

State/UT with the lowest literacy rate
Andhra Pradesh, with 66.4 per cent, has the lowest rate of literacy among all states, according to the 75th round of the NSS.

State/UT with highest and lowest female literacy rate
The female literacy rate in Kerala was 95.2 per cent while Rajasthan recorded 57.6 per cent, according to the 75th round of the NSS.

Maulana Abul Kalam Azad

First minister of education
Independent India's first minister of education was Maulana Abul Kalam Azad (1888–1958), during 1947–58. Besides establishing the first Indian Institute of Technology (IIT), the Indian Institute of Science (IISc), the School of Planning and Architecture (SPA), and the University Grants Commission (UGC), he set up key cultural and literary organizations like the Sangeet Natak Akademi, the Lalit Kala Akademi, the Sahitya Akademi, and the Indian Council for Cultural Relations.

State/UT with the highest percentage of graduates
Out of a total of around 68 million graduates in the country, Chandigarh, with 24.65 per cent, has the highest percentage of its population as graduates, according to the Census 2011.

State/UT with the lowest percentage of graduates
Assam has the lowest percentage of graduate population, with only 4.83 per cent as per Census 2011.

SCHOOLS

First school for the hearing-impaired
Established in 1893, the Calcutta Deaf and Dumb School in Calcutta, was the first school for the hearing-impaired.

Earliest schools for girls
St. Thomas School for Girls, which was founded in 1789 for the English-speaking community of Calcutta, Bengal (now Kolkata, West Bengal), was the first girls-only school in India.

Oldest extant school
St. George's Anglo-Indian Higher

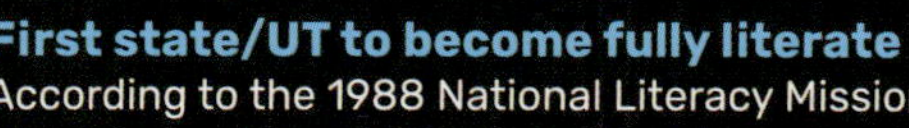

First state/UT to become fully literate
According to the 1988 National Literacy Mission, any state that achieved 90 per cent or above functional literacy was considered fully literate. Kerala was the first to achieve this feat and was declared fully literate. Later, with the introduction of NILP, the threshold of full literacy was increased to 95 per cent. Kerala now fell short of this threshold, and Mizoram emerged as the first fully literate state with 98.2% per cent literacy in 2022/23.

Top: Calcutta Deaf and Dumb School
Bottom: St George's School, Chennai

96

Children from Andh Vidyalaya

Secondary School, founded as the Military Male Orphan Asylum, was established in 1715 in Madras (now Chennai), Tamil Nadu.

Oldest extant institute for the blind

The Institute for the Blind – Andh Vidyalaya – was established in Lahore (now in Pakistan) in 1939 and shifted to Delhi after Independence in 1947.

WR Largest open school

Set up as an autonomous institution under the Ministry of Human Resource Development (MHRD) in 1989, the National Institute of Open Schooling (NIOS) has a cumulative enrolment of 4.13 million students. It works through a network of 23 regional centres, 2 subregional centres, 5 departments, 2 NIOS cells, and over 7,400 study centres (accredited institutions and accredited vocational institutions). These centres are located in various parts of the world, viz., India, Nepal, and the Middle East.

First Indian school abroad

The Indian High School, Dubai, set up in 1957, was the first Indian educational institution situated in a foreign country.

Largest school science fair – single venue – single day

iScience World, a science club formed by science communicators in Prayagraj (formerly Allahabad), Uttar Pradesh, in collaboration with Shri Mahaprabhu Public School, organized a science fair on 14 December 2019 at Delhi Public School, Prayagraj, in which 4,272 students from over 35 schools participated.

Largest chain of government schools

The Kendriya Vidyalaya Sangathan, an autonomous body under the MHRD, Government of India, since 15 December 1963, administers 1,252 schools, including 3 abroad, with 14,28,619 students, as of February 2023.

Largest school science fair – multiple venues – single day

More than 22,500 students from 637 upper primary schools of Bastar District, Chhattisgarh, conducted more than 35,000 scientific experiments at 116 centres on 18 January 2017. The Bastar Vigyan Mela, an annual event, was organized by the Department of Education, Bastar District. The students demonstrated scientific activities and displayed innovative science models.

Oldest co-educational boarding school

Lawrence School Sanawar, near Kasauli in Himachal Pradesh, was established in 1847. It is is the oldest co-educational boarding school in India founded by Sir Henry Lawrence, and was initially intended for the children of British soldiers.

First Sainik school for girls

The Samvid Gurukulam Girls Sainik School was inaugurated in Vrindavan on 1 January 2024. Alongside a CBSE curriculum, military training by ex-servicemen is provided to the students. The Ministry of Defence plans to establish 100 new Sainik schools in partnership with NGOs, private entities, and state government schools.

First solar-powered school

Sri Aurobindo International Centre for Education in White Town, Puducherry, became India's first fully solar-powered educational institute in 2014. It was set up in 1943 by Mirra Alfassa, the spiritual collaborator of Sri Aurobindo.

Sri Aurobindo International Centre

Education Tourism

India has several universities that are not just academic hubs but also architectural, cultural, and historical landmarks. Some universities that can serve as tourist destinations for students interested in educational tourism are:

1. Banaras Hindu University (BHU), Varanasi

Why visit: One of the largest residential universities in Asia, BHU combines sprawling green campuses with historic temples, the Bharat Kala Bhavan museum, and traditional Indian architecture.

Highlights: Vishwanath Temple on campus, Bharat Kala Bhavan museum, beautiful campus gardens.

2. Jawaharlal Nehru University (JNU), New Delhi

Why visit: Known for its vibrant intellectual and cultural atmosphere, JNU hosts seminars, cultural festivals, and open lectures that can enrich student visitors.

Highlights: Campus cultural events, JNU library, murals and sculptures across campus.

3. University of Madras, Chennai

Why visit: Established in 1857, the university has colonial-era buildings and a rich history in research and literature.

Highlights: Marina campus with Gothic architecture, historic libraries, heritage walks.

4. University of Calcutta, Kolkata

Why visit: One of India's oldest universities (est. 1857), featuring colonial architecture, historic lecture halls, and museums.

Highlights: Senate House, Asiatic Society museum, heritage library tours.

5. Osmania University, Hyderabad

Why visit: Known for its Indo-Saracenic style and historic campus, Osmania University is both academically prestigious and visually striking.

Highlights: University Clock Tower, historic libraries, botanical gardens, and heritage buildings.

Old Senate House, University of Madras

Sampurnanand Sanskrit Vishwavidyalaya

Pariksha Pe Charcha

Pariksha Pe Charcha is an annual interactive programme initiated by the prime minister of India, Narendra Modi, where he engages directly with students, teachers, and parents across the country. Launched in 2018, the initiative aims to ease exam-related stress among students by sharing motivational messages, practical tips, and life lessons to build confidence and resilience. Through this unique platform, students get an opportunity to discuss their fears and challenges regarding examinations, while the prime minister offers guidance on managing pressure with a positive mindset. The program has become immensely popular, encouraging a culture of calm and focus during the exam season, and inspiring millions to approach their studies with optimism and balance.

The first Gondi language school

In 2019, the Gond Adivasi community established a primary school in Mohagaon, Gadchiroli, Maharashtra, to teach children in their first language, Gondi.

HIGHER EDUCATION

First steps

The first educational policy in colonial India was articulated in a document called the 'Dispatch of 1854 on "General Education in India"' sent by Sir Charles Wood to the then Governor General Lord Dalhousie. Sir Charles stressed the adoption of vernacular languages in local primary schools, Anglo-vernacular language in high schools and English-medium education in colleges.

First Sanskrit university

The Sampurnanand Sanskrit Vishwavidyalaya in Varanasi, Uttar Pradesh, was the first Sanskrit university in India and is said to have been established in 1791 as a Sanskrit college during the East India Company rule. It has 628 affiliated colleges across India.

First modern university

William Carey, a British Christian missionary, opened the Serampore College, the first missionary college at Serampore, Bengal (now Srirampur, Hooghly District, West Bengal), in 1818. It was granted the status of a university in 1829.

First university act

The Indian Universities Act, 1904, was the first set of educational reforms, which stipulated that universities should offer more teaching and research opportunities and exert more control over affiliated colleges.

Longest functioning ancient university

Nalanda Mahavihara, located about 95 km south-east of present-day Patna in Bihar, functioned uninterrupted as a university from the Buddha's time in the sixth century BCE up to the 13th century CE, when it was destroyed by Muhammad bin Bakhtiyar Khilji. The university's curriculum then included many subjects such as logic, medicine, metaphysics, grammar, and the sciences. In an effort to emulate the ancient centre of learning,

Nalanda University, an exclusively postgraduate and doctoral institution, was started in 2014 in Rajgir, Bihar.

First modern college

The first college to offer modern education in India was the Hindu College of Calcutta, Bengal, established in 1817. Scottish watchmaker and philanthropist David Hare was its first principal. It was renamed Presidency College in 1855. It became Presidency University on 7 July 2010.

Oldest dentist college in south-east Asia

In 1920, the legendary visionary Dr Rafiuddin Ahmed (1890–1965) set up the first Dental College in Calcutta, and since 1949 it is affiliated to Calcutta University, the same year that Dr Ahmed donated his college to the West Bengal government. Dr Ahmed served as principal of the college from 1920 to 1950. He established the Bengal Dental Association, which became the forerunner for the Indian Dental Association. He also started the *Indian Dental Journal* in 1925 and was its editor till 1946. Dr Ahmed helped draft the Bengal Dentists Act in 1939, the first governmental dental regulation in India. It became the model for the Indian Dental Act passed in 1948.

Corridor of Presidency University: First modern college

First medical school

Established on 24 January 1857, the University of Calcutta was the first multidisciplinary and Western-style educational institution in Asia. It was also the first university in Asia to teach European classics, English literature, Indian philosophy, and Occidental and Oriental history. At the time of establishment, it had a catchment area ranging from Lahore to Burma (now Myanmar) and Ceylon (now Sri Lanka). The first medical school, the Calcutta Medical College, was affiliated to the university in 1857. Five Nobel laureates (the highest number in South Asia) are associated with the university. They are Sir Ronald Ross, Rabindranath Tagore, Sir C.V. Raman, Amartya Sen, and Abhijit Vinayak Banerjee.

First institute to teach modern architecture

The first course in architecture can be traced to the founding of a draftsman's class at the Sir J.J. School of Art (established in 1856), Bombay (now Mumbai), Maharashtra, in 1896. In 1913, the course was reorganized, and an independent Department of Architecture was formed.

First intermediate colleges

The University of Punjab (now in Chandigarh) and the University of Allahabad (now in Prayagraj) were the first to establish intermediate colleges in

J.J. School of Art: First institute to teach modern architecture

1917, offering two-year courses between high school and degree college, as proposed by the Sadler Commission.

First five universities

The University of Calcutta, the University of Madras, and the University of Bombay (now renamed as the University of Mumbai), which were modelled on London University, were established in 1857 as non-teaching examining bodies. The University of Punjab in Lahore, Pakistan), was set up in 1881, and the University of Allahabad in 1887.

The oldest centre for Chinese studies

Cheena Bhavana, founded in 1937 at Visva-Bharati University, is the oldest centre for Chinese studies in the subcontinent, offering undergraduate and postgraduate courses in Chinese literature, philosophy, politics, and Buddhist literature.

Oldest centre for German Studies

The University of Mumbai, the oldest centre for German Studies in India, introduced a BA in German in 1913 and an MA in German before 1916. It offers full-time programmes in German Studies (BA, MA, MA (Hons), and PhD) focused on language, literature, culture, translation, and intercultural studies, designed to be research and job-oriented.

Centre of Spanish, Portuguese, Italian and Latin American Studies (CSPILAS)

The Centre of Spanish Studies was originally established in the 1970s. It was later expanded to include Portuguese, Italian, and Latin American Studies and was renamed CSPILAS in 2004. It is part of the School of Language, Literature and Culture Studies at Jawaharlal Nehru University (JNU) in New Delhi. The CSPILAS is one of the leading centres for Spanish and Latin American Studies in south-east Asia and is the first in the country to introduce graduate, master's, and doctoral programmes in Spanish.

The only place to teach ancient Greek

The School of Languages in the Ramakrishna Mission Institute of Culture, Golpark, Kolkata, is the only place in India where ancient Greek is taught. The course is popular among students, teachers, and retired professionals.

First university to introduce Japanese language courses

In 1954, Visva-Bharati University (Shantiniketan) established a Japanese department, making it the first university in India to introduce Japanese language courses.

First rural university

Mahatma Gandhi Chitrakoot Gramoday University, established in 1991 in Chitrakoot, Madhya Pradesh, to promote rural education, was the first rural university in the country.

First pharmacy education course

A chemists and druggists course was initiated in Madras Medical College in 1874. It gained popularity and in 1898, a separate department of chemists and druggists was established at the college. The College of Pharmacy at Madras Medical College is the first institution in India to provide pharmacy education and training by offering a one-year certificate course called the 'Chemist and Druggist Course; training personnel for drug dispensing. However, formal pharmacy education in India was started in 1932 at the Banaras Hindu University (BHU) by Mahadeva Lal Schroff with the support of the vice chancellor of the university, Pandit Madan Mohan Malaviya. Initially, the course was known as B. Pharm (Bachelor of Pharmacy) and in April 1940 the first M. Pharm course was started at BHU.

Clockwise from top left: University of Mumbai; Cheena Bhavana; Jawaharlal Nehru University; Ramakrishna Mission Institute; Visva-Bharati University (Shantiniketan)

First Five Residential Universities

In 1915, the BHU was established as a teaching and residential university, followed by the Universities of Mysore (1916), Patna (1917), Osmania (1918), and the Aligarh Muslim University (1920).

Banaras Hindu University

Patna University

Aligarh Muslim University

Osmania University

Mysore University

First medical school to offer degrees in oncology

The Cancer Institute (WIA–Women's Indian Association), also known as the Adyar Cancer Institute, is a renowned non-profit treatment and research centre located in Chennai, Tamil Nadu. It was established in 1954 under the leadership of Muthulakshmi Reddy, with the motto 'Service to All'. The institute has played a vital role in cancer research and oncology in India. It is the first medical school to offer degrees in various sub-specialities of oncology like radiotherapy, medical oncology, surgical oncology, etc. The Cancer Institute (WIA) is affiliated to both the University of Madras and Anna University, where it offers research programmes leading to M.Phil and PhD degrees in areas of medical physics, psycho-oncology, and molecular oncology. It has also established the first department of nuclear medical oncology in the country and the first ever medical physics department.

Only school of tropical medicine

The School of Tropical Medicine, Kolkata, also known as Calcutta School of Tropical Medicine (CSTM) was established in 1914 by Leonard Rogers. It is the only institution in the country dedicated exclusively in research, post-graduate education, and healthcare for tropical diseases. The institute is presently under the governance of West Bengal University of Health Sciences. The institute focuses on advanced research on HIV/HBV co-infection and Hepatitis B anti-viral therapy.

First virtual medical university

The first virtual medical university, Medvarsity, established in 2000, is an initiative of the Apollo Hospitals Group.

First energy studies university

The University of Petroleum and Energy Studies in Dehradun, Uttarakhand, established in 2003, is India's first university specializing in petroleum, energy, and power.

First college of nursing

The Christian Medical College (CMC) and Hospital, Vellore, is a private educational institute with a network of hospitals in and around Vellore, Tamil Nadu. It was started in 1902 by Dr Ida Scudder, a third-generation American missionary. In 1903, she began training women compounders and started the first school of nursing at CMC in 1909.

First technical university

The Thomason College of Engineering, established in 1847 at Roorkee (now in Uttarakhand), was India's first technical university. Its civil engineering department is the oldest one. It is now IIT, Roorkee.

First science college

The Government Science College, Jabalpur, Madhya Pradesh, was the first Indian science college and was affiliated to the Calcutta University from 1836 to 1890.

First railway university

The National Rail and Transport University was established on 5 September 2018 at the Pratap Vilas Palace in Vadodara, Gujarat. It has now been subsumed by the Gati Shakti Vishwavidyalaya, announced as a central university in July 2022. It provides education and training in the latest technological applications related to the railways, such as radio frequency identification, artificial intelligence, and satellite-based tracking. It offers graduate degrees in subjects such as transportation management, transportation technology, rail infrastructural engineering, and electronics and communication engineering.

First women's university

The Shreemati Nathibai Damodar Thackersey (SNDT) Women's University was established in Pune, Maharashtra, by D.K. Karve (its first principal) on 5 July 1916. Dr R.P. Paranjpye was its first vice chancellor.

First college for women

The Bethune School of Calcutta, Bengal, set up in 1849, was reorganized after it merged with Banga Mahila Vidyalaya. In 1879, Bethune College classes started with one student, Kadambini Bose.

First IIT

The first IIT was established in 1951 at Kharagpur, West Bengal, at the site of the Hijli Detention Camp. There are twenty-three approved IITs in India currently.

First college alumni association

Dr William Miller, principal of Madras Christian College, Madras, Tamil Nadu, formed the first alumni association in 1891.

First technical university for women

The Indira Gandhi Delhi Technical University for Women (IGDTUW), New Delhi, was founded in 1998.

First metro technology institute

The Institute of Metro and Rail Technology (IMRT) opened in October 2013 in Hyderabad, Telangana. It offers short- and long-term courses to design, build, and manage modern rail systems.

First university of fisheries and ocean studies

The College of Fisheries in Panangad, Cochin (now Kochi), Kerala, established in 1979, was a constituent college of the Kerala Agricultural University. The Kerala University of Fisheries and Ocean Studies (KUFOS) was established in 2010 with its headquarters at the College of Fisheries.

Kerala University of Fisheries and Ocean Studies

National Education Policy (NEP) 2020 - at a Glance

- Launch: Announced on 29 July 2020 after extensive consultations with stakeholders.
- Vision: Build an education system rooted in Indian ethos, aiming to make India a global knowledge superpower through equitable, high-quality education for all.
- Access for All: Universal access to schooling from pre-primary to Grade 12, with special focus on early childhood care (ages 3–6).
- New Structure: Shift to the 5+3+3+4 curricular framework, removing rigid separations between arts, sciences, vocational, and academic streams.
- Foundational Skills: National Mission on Foundational Literacy and Numeracy to ensure all children achieve basic reading and maths skills by Grade 3.
- Assessments and Exams: Board exams to be offered twice a year (main + improvement); new National Assessment Centre (PARAKH) for better evaluation standards.
- Higher Education Reforms:
  - Target 50% Gross Enrollment Ratio (GER).
  - Introduce multidisciplinary learning with multiple entry/exit options.
  - Create Higher Education Commission of India (HECI) as an umbrella body with separate verticals for standards, funding, accreditation, and regulation.
- Investment and Collaboration: Increase public spending on education to 6 per cent of GDP; coordinated implementation by centre, states, boards, regulatory bodies, and institutions.

Technology Integration: Establish National Educational Technology Forum (NETF); ensure ICT integration at all levels of learning, assessment, and administration.

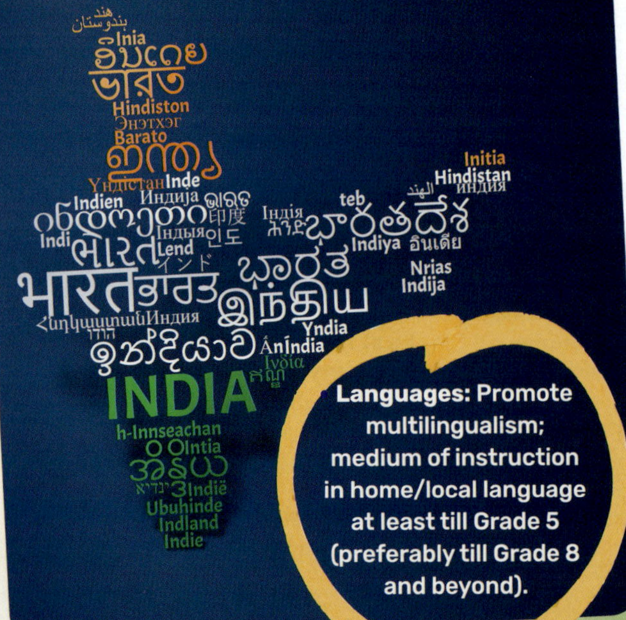

Languages: Promote multilingualism; medium of instruction in home/local language at least till Grade 5 (preferably till Grade 8 and beyond).

Indian Institute of Mass Communication

First institute of mass communication
The first institute to provide a formal education in mass communication was the Indian Institute of Mass Communication (IIMC). Set up by the Government of India in 1965, it is now located on the JNU campus in New Delhi. It is an autonomous institution under the Ministry of Information and Broadcasting, and offers courses related to different media.

First institute for population sciences
The Institute for Population Sciences in Mumbai, Maharashtra, earlier known as the Demographic Training and Research Centre, was established in 1956 to prepare students for administrative, teaching, research, and consultancy careers in population sciences.

First school of mines
The Indian School of Mines – now renamed the Indian Institute of Technology – in Dhanbad, Jharkhand, opened in 1926.

First institute of oceanography
The National Institute of Oceanography, which was founded on 1 January 1966, is an autonomous research organization that undertakes scientific research and studies of special oceanographic features of the northern Indian Ocean. The institute has its main campus in Dona Paula, Goa, and regional centres have been set up in Mumbai, Kochi, and Visakhapatnam.

First university for the study of outer space
The Indian Institute of Space Science and Technology (IIST) in Thiruvananthapuram, Kerala, is the first university in Asia to be solely dedicated to the study and research of outer space. It was set up by the Indian Space Research Organization (ISRO) under the Department of Space, Government of India, in 2007. The institute offers undergraduate, postgraduate, and doctorate programmes with a focus on space science, space technology, geoinformatics, earth system sciences, and their applications.

First gemmological institute
The Gemmological Institute of India (GII), a non-profit public institution founded by the Gem and Jewellery Exporters Association, was established in Bombay in 1971 to promote the scientific knowledge of gemmology.

First statistical institute
The Indian Statistical Institute (ISI) was established in 1931 in Calcutta, Bengal, by scientist and statistician P.C. Mahalanobis.

First institute of fashion technology
The Ministry of Textiles, Government of India, set up the National Institute of Fashion Technology (NIFT) in Delhi on 24 August 1987 to provide professional human resources for the textile industry. There are currently eighteen NIFT campuses in the country.

First home science college
Lady Irwin College, established in 1932 in New Delhi, was the country's first home science college.

First national institute of management
The Indian Institute of Management, Calcutta, was established for the pursuit of postgraduate studies in management on 17 November 1961 by the Government of India, in collaboration with the Sloan School of Management, Massachusetts Institute of Technology (MIT), US, the Government of West Bengal, the Ford Foundation, and several Indian industries.

First radio jockey training academy
The Academy of Broadcasting in Chandigarh, set up in July 2003, was the first academy for training radio jockeys.

First model-training school
Catwalk, set up in Bombay in 1990 by

leading model Lubna Adams, was the first training school in India for fashion models.

First defence academy

The National Defence Academy at Khadakwasla, Maharashtra, was opened on 16 January 1955, to give its students a military orientation to join any of the three services of the Indian armed forces.

First military school

The Prince of Wales Royal Indian Military College in Dehradun, Uttarakhand, now called the Rashtriya Indian Military College (RIMC), was inaugurated on 13 March 1922 by Prince Edward VIII, the Prince of Wales, to provide training to Indian boys to become officers in the armed forces. In a landmark move in 2021, women were allowed admission to the institute.

First college of physical education

The YMCA College of Physical Education in Madras, established in 1920 by Harry Crowe Buck of Pennsylvania, US, was Asia's first college for physical education. It is now affiliated to the Tamil Nadu Physical Education and Sports University, and is considered a pioneer in the promotion of sports for persons with disabilities.

First college for sanitation workers

The Harpic World Toilet College, located in Aurangabad (now Chhatrapati Sambhajinagar), in Maharashtra, was established in August 2018. It is the first of its kind in the country and has trained more than 3,200 sanitation workers. It trains workers in the required skills and also makes them aware of the occupational hazards related to the job. It is run by British consumer goods company Reckitt Benckiser.

First college for the hearing-challenged

The St. Louis Institute for the Deaf and Blind in Madras, Tamil Nadu, which opened on 8 September 1993, was the first college for the hearing-impaired in the country. It is affiliated to the University of Madras and offers graduate degrees.

First law university

The National Law School of India University (NLSIU) in Bangalore was established on 29 August 1987. Currently, there are twenty-three such national law universities in India.

First institute for studying footwear design

The Footwear Design and Development Institute (FDDI), set up in 1986 at Noida, Uttar Pradesh, trains students in footwear technology, computer-aided designing, and pattern making.

First yoga institute

The Bihar School of Yoga, later the Bihar Yoga Bharati in Munger, Bihar, an institute for advanced studies in yoga, set up in 1964, was the first of its kind in Asia.

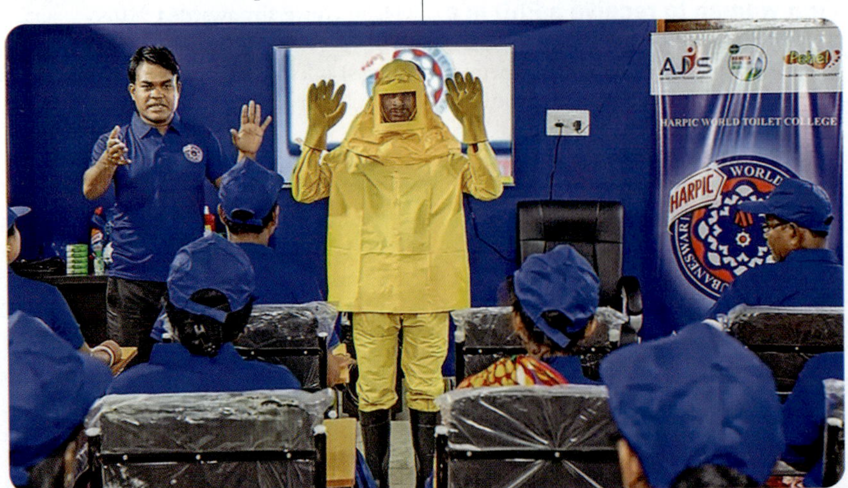

Class in Harpic World Toilet College

First woman doctor

Kadambini Ganguly née Bose obtained a graduate degree from Calcutta Medical College to become the first woman doctor in 1888. She was the first woman to receive the degree from India as well as the first woman to practise medicine in the country.

First university for the disabled

The Jagadguru Rambhadracharya Handicapped University (now renamed as the Jagadguru Rambhadracharya Divyang State University) in Chitrakoot, Uttar Pradesh, was established as a private university on 27 September 2001 to provide higher and professional education only to persons with disabilities in 4 categories – the visually impaired, the hearing-impaired, the mobility-impaired, and the mentally impaired, as defined in the Persons with Disability Act, 1995.

First correspondence courses

The University of Delhi introduced non-formal education in 1962 with its first correspondence course.

First national institute for the visually impaired

The National Institute for the Visually Impaired was established in Dehradun, Uttarakhand, in 1979.

First university only for tribal students

The Kalinga Institute of Social Sciences, founded by Achyuta Samanta in Bhubaneswar, Odisha, became India's first exclusively 'tribal' university when

it was granted university status by the Ministry of Human Resources Development in 2017. It admits students only from indigenous communities and is the only known university in the world to do so.

First National Institute of Watersports (NIWS)

The National Institute of Watersports (NIWS) was established in 1990 at Caranzalem, near Dona Paula Circle, Panaji, Goa, under the Ministry of Tourism. It is the first Institute of its kind in south-east Asia. NIWS serves as a centre for training, education, consultancy, and research for various watersports disciplines, including life-saving, power boat handling, sailing, windsurfing, scuba-diving, river rafting, and kayaking. The institute offers twenty courses designed for watersports professionals and tourists visiting Goa. Certification and licensing from NIWS are mandatory for operators handling different watercraft for tourists, swimming pools, water theme parks, etc.

First master's programme in Hindu studies

Two central universities, BHU and Shri Lal Bahadur Shastri National Sanskrit University, have jointly launched a master's course in Hindu studies in 2022. The curriculum, developed by BHU, aims to provide a comprehensive understanding of the foundational principles underlying Hindu civilization, society, and culture, despite the endless variety. The course is interdisciplinary and covers various subjects, including Hindu philosophy, Mimamsa, the antiquity of Hinduism, and the meaning of the word *Hindu*. The programme is aligned with the recently introduced NEP.

Oldest school of art

Sir J.J. School of Art in Bombay, was founded by Sir Jamsetjee Jeejeebhoy in 1833.

First postgraduate degree

Calcutta University in Kolkata, West Bengal, conferred the first postgraduate degree (MA) in India in 1862.

First woman Bachelor of Medicine

Anandibai Joshi was the first Indian woman to obtain a Bachelor of Medicine degree in 1886 from the University of Philadelphia in the US, but she did not practise medicine.

First Indian to receive a PhD from a foreign university

Agostino Lourenco of Margao, Goa, is considered to have received his PhD in chemistry in Paris, France, in 1860.

First women graduates

Kadambini Ganguly née Bose and Chandramukhi Basu passed the BA examination from Calcutta University in 1883.

First transgender principle

Dr Manabi Bandyopadhyay became the first transgender person to become principal of the Krishnanagar Women's College in Nadia District, West Bengal, on 9 June 2015.

Dr Manabi Bandyopadhyay: First transgender principal

First woman to receive a PhD in a scientific discipline

Kamala Sohonie (1912–98), a biochemist, received her PhD at the Indian Institute of Science (IISc) Bangalore, Karnataka, in 1939, for her work on vitamins and the nutritive values of pulses, paddy, and groups of food items consumed by the poorer sections of society.

First Indian vice chancellor

In 1890, Gurudas Banerjee became the vice chancellor of Calcutta University, Bengal.

First woman vice chancellor

Hansa Jivraj Mehta (1897–1995) made history when she became the first vice chancellor of the Maharaja Sayajirao University of Baroda, Vadodara, Gujarat, in 1949.

First gender-neutral certificate

The National Academy of Legal Studies and Research (NALSAR), Hyderabad, Telangana, issued the first gender-neutral graduation certificate in June 2015.

First woman law graduate

Cornelia Sorabji 1866-1954 graduated in law from the University of Bombay (now University of Mumbai) in 1894.

First to pass the Indian Medical Service examination

Surjo Kumar Chakraborty (1826–74), MRCS (Member of the Royal College of Surgeons), was the first Indian to pass the Indian Medical Service (IMS) examination in 1855. He subsequently became the first Indian professor of Materia Medica at Calcutta Medical College.

First to obtain a doctorate

In 1904, Annoda Prasad Sircar became the first to obtain a doctorate when the University of Allahabad (established in 1887) awarded him a DSc.

First to score 100 per cent in NEET

Kota-based ALLEN Career Institute's student Soyeb Aftab scored 720/720 with all- India rank no.1 at the National Eligibility-cum-Entrance Test (NEET) 2020 (UG).

Most PhDs awarded by a university in a year

Delhi University awarded 910 PhD degrees (512 females and 398 males) at its 99th Convocation on 25 February 2023.

Most master's degrees obtained – woman

Vandana Agrawal (b. 12 November 1954) from Alwar, Rajasthan, has 10 MA degrees, the highest number of postgraduate degrees attained by a woman in India.

WR Postgraduate qualifications from most number of universities

Dr Anil Kumar Yadav (b. 4 June 1968)

from Chandigarh holds fifty postgraduate qualifications (PhD, M.Phil and PG degrees, and diplomas) from twenty-four universities across seventeen states and union territories. His record begins with was in December 2024.

WR First chartered scientist in aviation

Dr Bishnujee Singh (b. 27 October 1972), the chief executive officer of Cayley Aerospace Inc., from Lynnwood, Washington, US, became the world's first chartered scientist in aviation, with the Science Council, UK, in association with the Royal Aeronautical Society, on 26 September 2006.

First woman director of Indian Statistical Institute (ISI)

Dr Sanghamitra Bandyopadhyay, a computer scientist specializing in computational biology, currently serves as director of the Indian Statistical Institute (ISI). She oversees all the five centres of ISI located in Kolkata, Delhi, Bengaluru, Chennai, and Tezpur.

WR Largest open university

The Indira Gandhi National Open University (IGNOU) at Maidan Garhi, New Delhi, has the distinction of being the largest open university in the world, serving more than 3 million enrolled students through its 21 schools of studies, and a network of 67 regional centres, around 2,000 learner support centres, and 25 overseas partner institutions in 15 countries.

First foreign branch campus set up in India

Australia's Deakin University inaugurated a branch campus in GIFT city, Gujarat, on 10 January 2024. This is the first-ever foreign university branch campus in India. Indian students can pursue Master of Business Analytics and Master of Cybersecurity (Professional) from July 2024 without leaving the country.

First university for journalism and mass communication

Makhanlal Chaturvedi National University of Journalism and Communication (MCNUJC) was established in 1992 in Bhopal. It is the country's first university for journalism and mass communication and offers bachelor's, master's, and PhD degrees.

Youngest chancellor

Dileep K. Nair became the youngest chancellor of a university in the country when he took office at the North East Frontier Technical University (NEFTU) in Along (now Aalo), West Siang District, Arunachal Pradesh, in April 2017. He was thirty-eight years old at the time.

ARCHIVES AND LIBRARIES

Biggest public library system

The Delhi Public Library, started as a UNESCO project in 1951 by the Government of India, is the biggest public library system in India and reportedly the busiest set of public libraries in south Asia. The library network consists of a central library, 1 zonal library, 3 branch libraries, 18 sub-branch libraries, 1 community library, 7 resettlement colony libraries, 1 Braille library, 104 mobile library service points, and 30 book-reading centres in the Union Territory of Delhi and the NCR. It has a collection of over 1.8 million books in English and other Indian languages.

Delhi Public Library

Only underground library

In Bhadariya Village in Jaisalmer District, Rajasthan, is an underground library 16 ft (4.88 m) below ground level. Above this library is a temple of Devi Bhadariya Mata. The library can seat 4,000 persons and is maintained by the trustees of the temple. Housing around 9,00,000 books, the library was started by Harbansh Singh Nirmal, an avid reader, popularly known as Bhadariya Maharaj.

Largest university library

The Maulana Azad Library, the central library of Aligarh Muslim University in Aligarh, is the largest university library in Asia. The current 7-floor library houses about 14,00,000 books, periodicals, and pamphlets, 43,000 e-journals and manuscripts, and also paintings and photographs. It was inaugurated by Jawaharlal Nehru, the first prime minister of India, in 1960.

First library

Christian missionaries at Serampore set up their first library (later the William Carey Library) in 1800, which became the hub of their educational activities. The Reverend John Fountain, sent to India in 1796 to assist William Carey, a missionary, was its first librarian.

First operational digital library network

DELNET was the first operational digital library network. It was started as a project of the India International Centre, New Delhi, in 1988 and registered as a society in 1992.

First online Braille library

Launched in 2012 by the National Institute for the Visually Handicapped (NIVH), Dehradun, Uttarakhand, to commemorate the birth anniversary f Louis Braille on 4 January, the online Braille library provides access to 12,000 books in 10 languages in a user-friendly format.

National Digital Library of India

The National Digital Library of India (NDLI) is a comprehensive online repository designed to serve school students, undergraduates, postgraduates, research scholars, and lifelong learners. Offering access to an extensive collection of learning resources in all Indian languages and over 400 foreign languages, the platform hosts diverse content formats including e-books, audiobooks, lecture materials, video lectures, courses, theses, reports, articles, journal papers, question papers, solution banks, datasets, and simulation tools. It covers a wide range of disciplines from science, history, and geography to Humanities, Arts, Engineering, Law, and Medicine. NDLI functions as a one-stop educational hub for learners across age groups and academic levels. Its user interface is available in 11 languages, ensuring accessibility for a broad spectrum of users nationwide.

Under its national licensing agreements, NDLI has integrated vast resources from leading publishers. The World E-book Library contributed over 77 lakh items, and the South Asia Archive added more than 30,000 journals and articles. While the South Asia Archive license is perpetual, allowing continued access to its entire collection, the World E-book Library license was not renewed; however, 6.24 lakh of its e-books remain perpetually available in full text to NDLI users. By bringing together such extensive and multilingual resources on a single digital platform, NDLI plays a crucial role in promoting equitable, open, and lifelong access to knowledge in India.

First university library

The first university library began functioning at the University of Calcutta in 1870.

First mobile library

A bullock cart (in the shape of a small stall), laden with books at Melavasal, a village near Mannargudi in Tamil Nadu, on 21 October 1931, was possibly the first mobile library in the country. The brainchild of Rao Bahadur S.V. Kanagasabai Pillai, a Mannargudi-based engineer, the library was inaugurated by S.R. Ranganathan, called the father of library science in India. The mobile library carried books that dealt with bee-keeping and other cottage industries, aimed at providing vocational training to farmers. The cart would visit neighbouring villages in the months when there was less farming activity. A replica of the cart is now displayed in Tamil University in Thanjavur, Tamil Nadu.

First sports library

The Kanga Library at Wankhede Stadium, Mumbai has a collection of 13,000 books on sports. Around 10,000 of these are on cricket, including the entire collection of *Wisden Cricketers' Almanack* from 1864.

First national medical library

This library was initially conceived as a departmental library with a small collection of books for the use of officers of the erstwhile Directorate General of Indian Medical Services (DGIMS). In 1947, DGIMS was merged with the Office of the Public Health Commission and the Directorate General of Health Services (DGHS), and the library

Left: Anna Centenary Library, Tamil Nadu; *Right*: National Library, Kolkata

became DGHS Library. As the need for a central library grew to support academic, research, and clinical work by medical and health science professionals in the country, the DGHS Library was developed and was renamed Central Medical Library. In 1966, this library, located in New Delhi, was declared as the National Medical Library.

Largest library

- *By built-up area:* The Anna Centenary Library in Chennai, Tamil Nadu, is the largest in terms of constructed area – close to 3,30,000 sq ft (3.07 hectares). It houses around 1 million books.
- *By number of books:* The National Library, Kolkata, with more than 2.6 million books and over 5,00,000 manuscripts, is the largest library by number of books. The campus of the library is spread over 30 acres (12.14 hectares). However, the actual built-up area is around 1.5 lakh sq. ft (1.39 hectares).

Largest film archives

The National Film Archives were set up in 1964 in Poona (now Pune), Maharashtra, as a media unit of the Ministry of Information and Broadcasting, Government of India. Besides over 1,00,000 films, it has 1,57,687 photographs, 23,748 film posters, 14,210 song booklets, over 1,00,000 press clippings, and more.

The National Film Archives

First boat library

The Young Readers' Boat Library was set up on a boat by the West Bengal Transport Corporation in collaboration with a heritage bookshop. It was launched on 26 January 2021, and houses a collection of over 500 titles in English and Bengali. The boat library conducts three-hour ferries on the Hooghly River, starting from Millennium Park to Belur Math Jetty and back. It also offers free Wi-Fi facilities and various readership activities, and conducts 3 trips on all weekdays.

Only bookshop-cum-library on a lake

Gulshan Books, a bookshop-cum-library set up in May 2016, has a reading room, a cafe and over 80,000 books. Located on Nehru Park Island on the Dal Lake in Srinagar, Jammu and Kashmir, it can be reached by a shikara.

Oldest library

The Calcutta Public Library (established in 1836) was merged with the Imperial Library (established in 1891) in 1903. In 1953, it was inaugurated as the National Library with B.S. Kesavan as its first librarian.

The oldest public library

Krishnadas Shama Goa State Central Library in Panaji, inaugurated on 15 September 1832 by the Portuguese viceroy of Goa, is the first public library in India. Initially called the Publica Livaria of the Academia Militar de Goa, it was later renamed Central Library.

MUSEUMS

Largest and oldest museum

The Indian Museum in Kolkata, West Bengal, one of the oldest museums in the world, founded by the Asiatic Society of Bengal in 1814 and has rare collections of antiques, armour and ornaments, fossils, skeletons, mummies, and Mughal paintings.

First public museum in a university

Established in 1937, the Ashutosh Museum of Indian Art, located in the main campus of the University of Calcutta, West Bengal, is the first public museum in any university in India. It is named after Sir Ashutosh Mukherjee, the great educationist, who introduced the study of Indology – including Indian art and archaeology – at the university level and was the vice chancellor of the university from 1906 to 1914 and 1921 to 1923. The museum houses more than 25,000 sculptures, paintings, folk-art objects, textiles, and terracotta items, among other artefacts from various phases of Indian art, with special emphasis on the art of Bengal.

First solar observatory

The Kodaikanal Solar Observatory, operational since 1889, was initially established by the British East India Company in 1792 as the Madras Solar Observatory.

First museum of textiles

The Calico Museum of Textiles in Ahmedabad, Gujarat, was set up by Gautam Sarabhai, chairman of Calico Mills, in 1949, at the suggestion of the pioneering art historian and philosopher Dr Ananda Coomaraswamy. The museum has a comprehensive collection of Indian textiles. The foundation of modern Indian textile studies was laid here and the catalogues of the Calico Museum textile collection are an indispensable reference.

First national museum of Indian cinema

The country's first National Museum of Indian Cinema (NMIC) was inaugurated in Mumbai in January 2019. Conceived in 1997, it has been designed by the National Council of Science Museums and implemented by the Films Division, under the Ministry of Information and Broadcasting, Government of India. It is placed in a period 19th century heritage bungalow called Gulshan Mahal, and extends to another new high-technology 5-floor building with 2 mezzanine floors. On display are projectors, recording equipment, cameras, archival posters of old films, and biographies of actors and other film personalities.

WR First museum of toilets

The Sulabh International Museum of Toilets at Mahavir Enclave in New Delhi, a museum dedicated to toilets, has three hundred objects with a mix of originals, models, and photographs. The museum traces four thousand five hundred years of the history of toilets.

Only kite museum

A museum dedicated to the rarest kites in the world is housed in Ahmedabad, Gujarat, a city popular for its annual International Kite Festival. Established in 1985, the museum was the brainchild of Bhanubhai Shah, who donated his rare collection of over 50 years to the Ahmedabad Municipal Corporation. The only kite museum in the country, it is located in the basement of Sanskar Kendra and boasts of kites of many shapes and sizes, with some that measure up to 6.7 m x 4.88 m (22 ft x 16 ft).

First sports museum – organization

The National Institute of Sports, also known as the Netaji Subhas National Institute of Sports (NSNIS) in Patiala, Punjab, houses within the campus a sports museum. Established in 1972, which showcases a remarkable collection of rare photographs, kits, and medals of renowned Indian sportsmen including the gold medal won by Dhyan Chand at the Amsterdam Olympics in 1928, the Adidas spikes worn by Milkha Singh during the Rome Olympics in 1960, P.T. Usha's shoes, and a doughnut-shaped exercise equipment used by Gama Pehalwan, among others. There is a cricket bat on display signed by the Indian cricket team led by Kapil Dev which won the World Cup in 1983. The museum also houses replicas of different national awards given for sports, like the Arjuna Award and the Dronacharya Award. A part of the museum displays numerous rare photographs and personal items contributed by the royal family of Patiala.

First sports museum – personal collection

Fanattic Sports Museum is located over 6,700 sq ft (622.45 sq. m) at Ecospace in New Town, Rajarhat, around 25 km from central Kolkata. Opened in 2017, this multi-sports museum displays memorabilia from cricket, hockey, football, the Olympics, and Paralympics. It houses memorabilia collected by cricket historian Boria Majumdar for over 25 years. Highlights include Sachin Tendulkar's gloves, Lionel Messi's shoes, Didier Drogba's Chelsea jersey, and many artefacts donated by

National Museum of Indian Cinema

Olympic gold medallist Abhinav Bindra, Paralympics silver medallist Deepa Malik, and bronze medallist Devendra Jhajaria, among others.

First wax museum
Madame Tussauds Delhi, located in the vintage Regal Theatre in Rajiv Chowk, New Delhi, was part of the famed international chain of wax museums, the first of which opened in London in 1835. Set up in December 2017, the Delhi wax museum had on display over 40 life-size wax sculptures of political leaders and celebrities from sports, music, Bollywood, and Hollywood. The 23rd location for Tussauds museums, it was moved to DLF Mall of India, Noida, Uttar Pradesh, in 2022.

First underground museum
India's first underground museum opened in the Rashtrapati Bhavan on 2 October 2016. The museum showcases a collection of artefacts associated with each of the past presidents of India, including their personal belongings and vehicles, with a range of materials highlighting the history of India's freedom struggle. The museum displays more than 2,000 artefacts in a sprawling 12,077.39 sq m (1,30,000 sq ft) space.

Only election museum
Inaugurated in 2016, the Election Museum, located in the office premises of the chief electoral officer at Kashmiri Gate, Delhi, depicts the election journey of the largest democracy in the world. The four sections – library, audio-visual, photo gallery, and electoral management – display more than two hundred archived photographs, maps, artefacts, and references. Possibly the largest of its kind in the world, the museum showcases the electoral journey of India since the first general election in 1952.

First insect museum
An insect museum was unveiled by Tamil Nadu chief minister Edappadi K. Palaniswami, at the Tamil Nadu Agricultural University in Coimbatore, Tamil Nadu, in March 2018. Covering 621.61 sq. m (6,691 sq. ft), this museum displays insect specimens starting from the early 20th century. It has live butterflies in a natural setting, termite mounds, bee species, and insect-eating plants, along with images, video, and models of their behaviour and habitats.

First interactive museum of music
The Indian Music Experience (IME), established in 2018 in Bengaluru, Karnataka, is a rare museum that offers an interactive musical journey during which the visitor is encouraged to touch and feel the instruments on display to create one's own music. IME features a sound garden with 10 playable musical sculptures. It also has touchscreens, musical instruments, small theatres, and audio-video kiosks as well as a learning centre that offers music classes and workshops on a regular basis.

First science museum
The first science museum was set up by the industrialist Ghanshyam Das Birla at Birla Institute of Technology and Science (BITS), Pilani, Jhunjhunu District, Rajasthan, in 1954. Located in a hall 185 sq. m (1,991 sq. ft) of the Tower Building, it depicts the industries and business enterprises of the Birla family along with curricular scientific concepts and shows on current trends in science and technology. It is the only museum of industry and technology located inside a university campus.

First archaeological site museum
The first archaeological site museum was established adjacent to the excavated site of Sarnath, near Varanasi, in Uttar Pradesh. The Archaeological Museum Sarnath is the oldest site museum of the Archeological Survey of India and houses the findings and excavations from the Sarnath archaeological site. The idea of archaeological site museums was first proposed by Sir John Marshal, the then director general of archaeology in India, in 1905. Today there are forty-six archaeological site museums spread over the length and breadth of the country displaying excavated antiquities in close proximity to their original site.

Largest terracotta museum – by collection
The Allahabad Museum was established in 1931 by the Allahabad Municipal Board. The museum has the largest collection of terracotta artefacts in the country. Additionally, its rock art gallery showcases the largest collection of prehistoric paintings dating to 2000 BCE. The museum has achieved self-reliance in power generation by utilizing a solar power system, making it the first museum in the country to do so.

Largest terracotta museum, Allahabad

First transport museum

Opened on 7 December 2013, the Heritage Transport Museum at Tauru, Nuh District, Haryana, has a rich collection of twenty-five hundred objects, including howdahs, bullock carts, palanquins, a 1924 Ford, vintage scooters, a 1946 Piper aircraft, transport toys from the 1920s to now, and other related artefacts.

First railway museum

Inaugurated by Kamalapati Tripathi, the then minister of railways, on 1 February 1977, the Rail Transport Museum at Chanakyapuri, New Delhi, was the first rail museum in India. It was renamed the National Rail Museum in 1995 and features historical exhibits and artefacts related to the history of rail transport in India.

First dinosaur museum

The Dinosaur Museum at the Balasinor Dinosaur Park in Raiyoli Village in Balanisor Taluka in Gujarat's Mahisagar District was inaugurated in June 2019. With an enhanced version of the Dinosaur Museum already existing there, the facility is equipped with modern technology like 3D projection, virtual-reality presentations, interactive kiosks, and life-size dinosaur replicas. Its 10 galleries exhibit dinosaur remains and fossil records from the area as well as other regions of Gujarat and some other states of India, and show the history of these dinosaurs (such as the *Rajasaurus narmadensis*) from their origin to extinction.

Rail Transport Museum

Dinosaur Fossil, Balasinor

Museum on the Partition of India

First Partition museum

The Arts and Cultural Heritage Trust, set up on 24 October 2016 in Amritsar, Punjab, is the world's first museum on partition of India. Housed in a restored portion of the Town Hall, it is dedicated to partition of the subcontinent in 1947. The museum commemorates Partition's victims, its survivors, and its legacy. On display are photographs, clothes, utensils, and other memorabilia of the time.

Largest chain of science museums
The National Council of Science Museums (NCSM), under the Ministry of Culture, Government of India, is the largest chain of science centres/museums under a single administrative umbrella in the world. There are twenty-four science centres or museums and an R&D laboratory and training centre of NCSM, located in different states in India.

First culinary arts museum
Michelin-starred Indian chef Vikas Khanna opened India's first living culinary museum, the Museum of Culinary Arts, at his alma mater, the Welcomgroup Graduate School of Hotel Administration in Manipal, Karnataka, in April 2018. Over 2,000 utensils and artefacts from all over India and dating back centuries are housed in the museum, which is in the shape of a giant pot (similar to Harappan ones). It is spread over 2,322 sq m (25,000 sq. ft), as a part of the Department of Culinary Arts.

First museum of utensils
Vechaar (Vishalla Environmental Centre for Heritage of Art, Architecture and Research), a museum that archives heritage utensils, including more than 5,400 pots, pans, serving vessels, nutcrackers, and other kitchen equipment, is housed in a village-like complex called Vishalla in Ahmedabad, Gujarat. The museum was set up in April 1981 by its collector and owner, Surendra C. Patel, and anthropologist Jyotindra Jain.

Conflictorium
The Conflictorium, a museum in Ahmedabad, Gujarat, was inaugurated on 14 April 2013. It is housed in the Gool Lodge, a two-storey building, located between the Progressive West and the Historical East of the Sabarmati River. The museum was designed by Avni Sethi in collaboration with Janvikas, Centre for Social Justice, and Navsarjan, aiming to document the violent and oppressive history of the state of Gujarat since its establishment in 1960. Originally owned by a Parsi lady, Bachuben Nagarwala, who was the first trained beautician and hairstylist of Ahmedabad, the building is now divided into several galleries each expressing people's voices and thoughts. The purpose of the museum is to enable people to engage in various topics of conflict through artistic and creative ways in various forms of art and culture. It serves as a space for dialogue, reflection, and exploration of conflicts in society. Avni Sethi was declared the recipient of the Jane Lombard Prize for Art and Social Justice for 2020–22 by the Vera List Center for Arts and Politics.

The prime ministers' museum
The Pradhanmantri Sangrahalaya, located on the Teen Murti Estate in New Delhi, is a museum dedicated to celebrating all former prime ministers of India. It was inaugurated on 14 April 2022 by Prime Minister Narendra Modi, marking seventy-five years of Independence. This museum consists of forty-three galleries showcasing the lives and tenures of former prime ministers. It offers various interactive experiences like holograms, virtual reality, augmented reality, and more. The exhibits include personal items, gifts and memorabilia, and medals and commemorative stamps, provided by families of former prime ministers.

Only leprosy museum
The Acworth Leprosy Museum is located at Wadala Acworth Municipal General Hospital in Mumbai. The museum, inaugurated in 2003, showcases the early history of leprosy and honours the contributions by Mahatma Gandhi, Vinobha Bhave, and Ramachandra Vitthal Lad (also called Bhau Daji Lad) towards eradicating the disease and fighting against the discriminations and prejudices associated with leprosy. It is the only leprosy museum in the country and houses panels documenting the history of leprosy, therauptic experiments conducted by Mumbai doctors, social and legal histories related to leprosy, and the efforts of notable figures in the fight against leprosy.

QUIZZES

First live quiz on TV
Neil O'Brien, called the 'father of quizzing', brought the concept of quizzes to India in 1967, after watching them on TV in the UK in the 1960s. He moderated the *Eddie Hyde Memorial Quiz Contest* 1967 in the parish hall

The Conflictorium, Ahmedabad

students from over 200 schools participated.

Most participants in an online quiz – single day

An e-quiz based on the theme 'AatmaNirbhar Bharat: Strengthen the Future', organized by the School of Entrepreneurship Skills, Bharatiya Skill Development University, Jaipur, Rajasthan, and conducted in association with The Employers Association of Rajasthan and the Global Foundation for Skill Development and Entrepreneurship, had 5,058 participants on 1 June 2020. The purpose of this quiz was to disseminate knowledge about the AatmaNirbhar Bharat Abhiyan or self-reliance movement.

of the Church of Christ the King in Calcutta before a forty-strong audience. The open live quiz had four teams with members from all walks of life.

First quiz show on radio

On 12 April 1972, the *Cadbury Bournvita Quiz Contest* for high-school students became the first English quiz show to be broadcast on radio (Vividh Bharati) in India. It became one of India's most famous quiz contests. It ran for over a decade and was later revived as a television quiz in June 1992. The original quizmaster on the radio show was Hamid Sayani, a prominent broadcast personality.

Longest-running open quiz

Instituted in 1992 in Chennai, Tamil Nadu, by the Landmark Bookstores, the annual *Landmark Quiz* is the longest-running open quiz in the country. A preliminary round of about forty questions that come up on a screen is held due to the huge turnout. The quiz is hosted by Dr Navin Jayakumar and his team (which included his mother) since its inception, with the exception of 2006 when Derek O'Brien was the quizmaster.

WR Longest-running school quiz

The *Cadbury Bournvita Quiz Contest* was a weekly televised show that started in 1992 as the first televised school quiz in India. Anchored by reputed quizmaster Derek O'Brien, it ran continuously on Zee TV till 2001, after which it moved to the TV channel Sony, followed by Colors. Now it is conducted in a mobile application format.

First national TV quizmaster

Raman Kumar was the first quizmaster on national television. He hosted *Mashoor Mahal* during 1985–86 in the quiz genre, featuring famous personalities.

Longest-running televised quiz

Prashnottari, a twice-a-week (previously fortnightly) quiz, with participants from schools, colleges, and a general live TV audience, was first telecast on Prasar Bharati's Jaipur Doordarshan Kendra on 23 July 1993. Hosted by former IAS officer Dr Mahendra Surana since it began, it continued without break on the same channel, completing nine hundred episodes on 15 March 2020.

Longest-running state-level quiz

Initiated in 1986 by Vijaya Bank, Karnataka's oldest quiz competition, titled *VGenUth Quiz Contest* (now called the *Baroda Champ Annual Quiz Contest)*, is open to all high-school students across Karnataka. Its 34th edition was held on 2 February 2020 in Bengaluru, in which more than 400

Most participants in an offline quiz – single venue – single day

Under the aegis of Deendayal Vichar Manch, Bhartiya Janata Yuva Morcha conducted 'Jaane Humara Madhya Pradesh', the largest one-day general knowledge quiz with 15,000 participants from all walks of life at Nanakheda Stadium, Ujjain, Madhya Pradesh, on 11 February 2013. Conducted between 9:30 a.m. to 11:00 a.m., there were 80 objective questions with over 900 invigilators present.

Most participants in an offline quiz – multiple venues – single day

The Haryana Police organized an hour-long state-level quiz competition on 8 November 2016 on the theme of road safety. As many as 24,47,744 students participated in it.

ONLINE

Longest lesson – online

Priyanka Sankurushetti (8 January 1995) from Suryapet, Telangana, delivered a marathon lecture on Clinical Research and Clinical Data Management for 24 hours. She began at 9:30 a.m. on 11 December 2022 and ended on 9:30 a.m. on 12 December 2022, on Zoom from Vaagdevi College of Pharmacy, Hanamkonda, Telangana.

PERFORMING ARTS

DANCE

Earliest scriptural mention of dancers

The first known textual mention of dancers can be traced back to the Rig Veda (composed between c. 1500 and 1200 BCE), which has references to mythical *apsaras* (divine dancers) in the story of the celestial dancer Urvashi and the mortal king Pururava.

Earliest known treatise on the performing arts

The *Natyashastra*, said to be the work of Bharata Muni, is dated variously between the second and third centuries BCE and the fourth and fifth centuries CE. It is the earliest known treatise on the performing arts. The *Natyashastra* has 37 chapters with 5,569 slokas. It is the basis of classical Indian dance, music, and drama, and is often referred to as the fifth Veda.

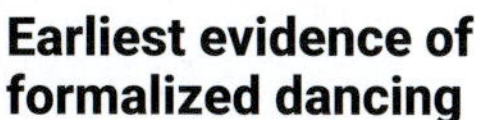

Earliest evidence of formalized dancing

The statuette of a dancing girl from Mohenjo-Daro in the Indus Valley that dates to 2500 BCE is the earliest evidence of formal dance.

Earliest sculptures of Odissi

Sculptures depicting dancers in the Jain cave temples of Khandagiri and Udayagiri, such as the Machapuri and Hathigumpha caves (second century BCE) in present-day Odisha (formerly Orissa), show the existence of a dance form in the region in which the dance of the female temple dancers called *maharis* (devadasis) formed a ritual during worship. Hundreds of figures depicting dance movements are carved on the walls of the Parashurameshwara, Kapileshwara, Brahmeshwara, Mukteshwara, Rajarani, and Lingaraj temples in Bhubaneswar, Puri, and Konark in Odisha, displaying the complex vocabulary of Odissi.

Sandstone statue of Apsara

Krishnanattam Mudra

Sculptures of Odissi in the Parashurameshwara Temple

First known dance drama form

In the early 17th century, Manaveda Raja, Zamorin of Calicut (now Kozhikode), Kerala, was inspired by Jayadeva's *Gita Govinda* to compose the *Krishna Geeti* in Sanskrit. He set it to a new dance drama form known as Krishnanattam – 'the dance of Krishna'. It combined ancient theatre traditions such as Kutiyattam, ritual performances like Theyyam, and folk dances like Kaikottikali.

Oldest surviving dance drama form

Mudiyettu from Kerala, now incorporated in Kathakali, is the oldest extant dance drama form. It is traced back to the ninth century CE.

Earliest text to mention Odissi

Odissi has been traced to a dance form that prevailed in present-day Odisha and Bihar. In ancient times it was in a region referred to as Odhra-Magadha and was first mentioned in the *Natyashastra*. The dance was performed by maharis and male temple acolytes called *gotipuas*. It is also later mentioned in Maheswar Mahapatra's *Abhinaya Chandrika* (15th–16th century CE). This dance form, which includes the *tandava* style and the *lasya* style, has its own repertoire, costumes, music, and grammar.

First modern translation of the *Natyashastra*

In 1950, Manmohan Ghosh translated the *Natyashastra* into English for the Asiatic Society. This was the first successful attempt at translating the definitive text on Indian performing arts.

First English periodical on Carnatic music and dance

Sruti, a periodical on music, was first published in October 1983 in Madras (now Chennai), Tamil Nadu, and gained 30,000 readers in its very first year. It was published by P.N. Sundaresan and edited by N. Pattabhiraman. It was the first-known English periodical on Carnatic music and dance.

Earliest reference to musical performances

The grammarian Panini (c. fourth century BCE) in his comments on *nritya* (dancing) mentions composers of sutras on dancing. The *Pali Pitaka* (c. 300 BCE) mentions 2 disciples of Gautama Buddha attending one such recital.

First classical dance to be revived

The British colonial rule saw the decline of various dance forms, and the devadasi culture associated with Odissi was discouraged by the Christian missionaries and British officials. Odissi was rediscovered by dancer Indrani Rehman, who then popularized it abroad in the early 1940s, though it was recognized as a classical dance form only from the 1960s.

Devadasi

First Kuchipudi dance couple to receive the Padma Shri

Raja and Radha Reddy were the first couple to receive the Padma Shri Award for a single cause, individually and together, in 1984. Widely travelled, they popularized the Kuchipudi form of dance in India and abroad. They also won the Padma Bhushan in 2000.

First dance schools

- Santiniketan, which was founded in 1901 in Bolpur, Birbhum District, Bengal (now West Bengal) by Rabindranath Tagore, had a department of dance to which he invited gurus from regions as far-flung as Manipur and Kerala to live on the campus and teach their dance forms to students. Santiniketan, which later evolved into the Visva-Bharati University, now has an institute of dance, drama, and music, called the Sangit Bhavan.
- Kalakshetra, a premier school for classical dance, was established in 1936 at Adyar, Madras, Tamil Nadu, by Indian classical dancer Rukmini Devi Arundale. Initially called the International Academy of Arts, it was renamed Kalakshetra on the suggestion of Sanskrit and Tamil scholar Pandit P.S. Subrahmanya Sastri. Its first dance production was titled *Kutrala Kuravanji*.

First revivalist dance school

The Kerala Kalamandalam in Trichur (now Thrissur), Kerala was founded in 1930 by the poet Vallathol Narayana Menon to re-establish Kathakali as a major regional theatre art and to revive Mohiniattam, a classical dance form from Kerala. These art forms flourished briefly under Maharaja Swathi Thirunal in the 19th century and then languished, until they were revived by Vallathol Narayana Menon.

First Sangeet Natak Akademi award for creative dance

Dance pioneer Uday Shankar was the first to be honoured by the Sangeet Natak Akademi with an award for creative dance in 1960. Two years later, he received the Sangeet Natak Akademi fellowship. In 1971, Uday Shankar became the first modern dancer to receive the Padma Vibhushan.

Uday Shankar

First national dance seminar

The Sangeet Natak Akademi held the first national seminar on dance from 30 March to 7 April 1958. Dr P.V. Rajammar was the Akademi's chairman then. The seminar's inaugural dance was performed by leading Kathak exponent Pandit Shambhu Maharaj.

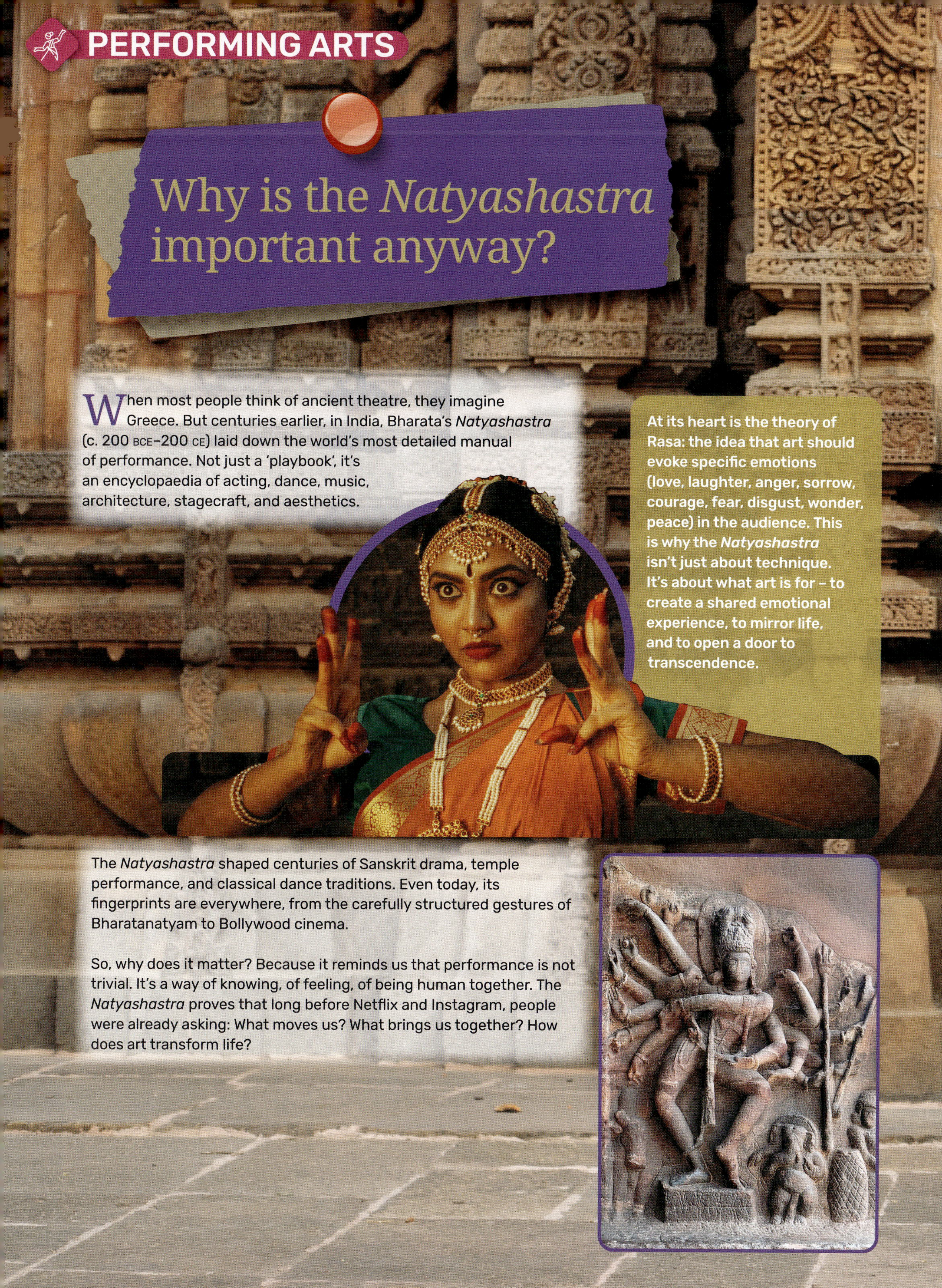

Why is the *Natyashastra* important anyway?

When most people think of ancient theatre, they imagine Greece. But centuries earlier, in India, Bharata's *Natyashastra* (c. 200 BCE–200 CE) laid down the world's most detailed manual of performance. Not just a 'playbook', it's an encyclopaedia of acting, dance, music, architecture, stagecraft, and aesthetics.

At its heart is the theory of Rasa: the idea that art should evoke specific emotions (love, laughter, anger, sorrow, courage, fear, disgust, wonder, peace) in the audience. This is why the *Natyashastra* isn't just about technique. It's about what art is for – to create a shared emotional experience, to mirror life, and to open a door to transcendence.

The *Natyashastra* shaped centuries of Sanskrit drama, temple performance, and classical dance traditions. Even today, its fingerprints are everywhere, from the carefully structured gestures of Bharatanatyam to Bollywood cinema.

So, why does it matter? Because it reminds us that performance is not trivial. It's a way of knowing, of feeling, of being human together. The *Natyashastra* proves that long before Netflix and Instagram, people were already asking: What moves us? What brings us together? How does art transform life?

Let Nāṭya (drama and dance) be the fifth vedic scripture. Combined with an epic story, tending to virtue, wealth, joy and spiritual freedom, it must contain the significance of every scripture, and forward every art.

— Natyashastra 1.14–15

Did you know?

» The *Natyashastra* describes stage lighting using oil lamps 2,000 years before electricity.

» The *Natyashastra* devotes entire chapters to stage construction, right down to acoustics.

First modern work on dance

The book titled *Classical Indian Dance in Literature and the Arts* by scholar Dr Kapila Vatsyayan, published in 1968 by the country's premier institution of dance and music, the Sangeet Natak Akademi, was the first definitive modern work on dance, written in English. Dr Vatsyayan received the Sangeet Natak Akademi fellowship in 1970.

Thickest make-up

The *chutti*, used in Kathakali, is a three- dimensional mask-like attachment made of rice paste and paper, which may extend to 15 cm (6 in.) from the face. It is the thickest make-up used in any dance form in the world.

First woman to perform Chhau

Sonal Mansingh, the well-known exponent of Kuchipudi, was the first woman to learn the Chhau dance form. It is a semi-classical dance with martial and folk origins, and is found in 3 styles drawing their names from the regions where they are traditionally performed – Puralia Chhau (performed in West Bengal), Seraikella Chhau (performed in Jharkhand), and Mayurbhanj Chhau (performed in Odisha).

First campaign for the revival of Bharatanatyam

E. Krishna Iyer, a lawyer based in Madras (present-day Chennai), was the first to fight the anti-nautch campaigns of the 1920s by learning the dance form Bharatanatyam in 1926 from the famous Natesa Iyer from Melattur, Kerala. For 6 years, he lectured and wrote for his cause, and presented devadasis in public performances outside of temples. Finally, it was with T. Balasaraswati's dance performance at the All-India Music Conference in Varanasi, Uttar Pradesh, in 1935, that the dance became accepted as a respectable art form.

First Kuchipudi solo

Vedantam Lakshminarayana Sastri (1886–1956) performed the first solo recital in the traditional dance drama form of Kuchipudi. He learnt the dance form from Sri Vempati Venkatanarayana. He also introduced the popular tarangam into the form, during which the dancers have to balance themselves on the edges of a thali.

First Sangeet Natak Akademi award winners for dance

T. Balasaraswati and Shambhu Maharaj won the first Sangeet Natak Akademi awards for dance in 1955 for their contribution to Bharatanatyam and Kathak, respectively. The awards were instituted in 1952 to honour performing artistes.

First ballet film

Classical–folk fusion guru Uday Shankar's film Kalpana, released in 1948, used the ballet form for a major part of its narration, making it the country's first ballet film.

Sonal Mansingh

First dance theatre form recognized by UNESCO: Kutiyattam

Kutiyattam, a traditional Sanskrit performing art form originating in Kerala, is recognized by UNESCO as a 'Masterpiece of the Oral and Intangible Heritage of Humanity'. It is considered to be at least 2,000 years old and the oldest living theatre tradition globally. UNESCO usually considers only monuments and heritage sites, and this was the first art form recognized for its exceptional value. Mizhavu, a large percussion instrument, is the primary musical instrument that accompanies Kutiyattam. Considered to be sacred, Kutiyattam was traditionally performed only in temple theatres, called *koothambalam*.

T. Balasaraswati

First to win an international dance competition

Madame Menaka (1899–1947), whose real name was Leila Sokhey, was the first Indian to win an international dance competition at the Berlin Dance Olympiad in July 1936. Her troupe, which featured on 2 days, performed Menaka's original ballet, *Deva Vijaya Nritya*, and won the first 3 individual prizes, along with the first prize in the competition.

First celebrity dance competition

Ten famous television couples participated in the first ever celebrity dance competition, *Nach Baliye*, on TV channel Star One. The show premiered on 11 October 2005. The judges were choreographer Saroj Khan, film-maker Farhan Akhtar, and VJ-and-model Malaika Arora Khan. TV stars Sachin and Supriya Pilgaonkar were the first winners of the contest.

First Indian–European fusion

Versatile dancer Uday Shankar (1900–77), who was born in Udaipur, Rajasthan, is known as the father of modern dance in India. He combined European theatrical dance techniques with the classical and folk dance forms of India. Uday Shankar danced with Anna Pavlova, the Russian ballerina, during the 1920s and created *Hindu Wedding* as well as the duet *Radha and Krishna*, which was included in Pavlova's performance *Oriental Impressions*. In 1971, he was awarded the Padma Vibhushan, the second highest civilian award in India.

Only pan-Indian dance text

Jayadeva's Sanskrit book of verse, the *Gita Govinda* (12th century CE), has been choreographed in all major Indian dance styles. It is sung in both Hindustani and Carnatic modes, and has been translated into many European languages.

Oldest recipient of President's Award

Asan Chandu Panikkar (1873–1969), a pioneer of 20th-century Kathakali,

received the President's Award in 1958 at 84 years. He danced at the award ceremony, in front of the then prime minister Jawaharlal Nehru and the then president Dr Rajendra Prasad.

First known Kathak teacher

Pandit Birju Maharaj (1938–2022) is the first known Kathak teacher. Born in Lucknow, Uttar Pradesh, to Shri Achhan Maharaj, a Kathak exponent, he was the popular face of the dance form globally. He was invited to teach Kathak at the age of 13 at Sangeet Bharati, and later at the Bharatiya Kala Kendra, New Delhi. He received the Sangeet Natak Akademi award in 1966 and the Padma Vibhushan in 1986.

Only dance form varied in three states

Chhau, the classical folk dance with martial overtones, has 3 versions based on the regions it is performed in – Seraikela Chhau in Jharkhand (masked), Mayurbhanj Chhau in Odisha, and Purulia Chhau in West Bengal.

Birju Maharaj

Only dance drama performed by women alone

Kuravanji, a form of musical play popular at the beginning of the 18th century, was meant only for devadasis and was performed at the annual festivals of some temples in Tamil Nadu.

Only Persianized classical dance

Kathak is a classical dance form that derives its name from the female professional storytellers or *kathika*s who recited verses from the Ramayana and the Mahabharata, along with explanatory gestures, appropriate choreography, and music, as part of a system of ritualistic worship. This dance form, with its fast and intricate movements, attracted the attention of the Mughal rulers. Over time, the dance form split into 2 main schools: 'Temple Kathak', with its emphasis on *bhava* (or emotion), and a court dance or 'Darbari Kathak', with its focus on rhythmic display.

Only Asthana Nartaki

In 1978, Bharatanatyam exponent Yamini Krishnamurthy was awarded the title of 'Asthana Nartaki', meaning 'resident dancer' of Lord Venkateswara Temple, Tirupati, Andhra Pradesh.

Only classical dancer with an artificial foot

Accomplished Bharatanatyam dancer Sudha Chandran, who lost a leg in a car crash in 1981, resumed her dancing career with a prosthetic Jaipur Foot in 1984. She was rehabilitated by Dr P.K. Sethi of the Sawai Man Singh Hospital in Jaipur, Rajasthan.

Largest arts festival

Soorya Festival, organized annually by the Soorya Stage and Film Society, Thiruvananthapuram, Kerala, is the largest of its kind in India, both in terms

Only extant pre-Vedic dances

Bhutam and Theyyam are ritual dances of Karnataka and Kerala, respectively. The dancers represent local gods and ancestral spirits, based on a pre-Vedic belief system.

Largest Indian Folk Variety Dance – Republic Day 2025

On Republic Day 2025, Kartavya Path turned into a living tapestry of India's cultural diversity when more than 5,000 folk and tribal artists from across the country came together for a single, breathtaking performance titled Jayati Jai Mamah Bharatam. Showcasing over 50 distinct folk dance forms, from Bihu to Ghoomar and from Garba to Wangala, the ensemble celebrated the rhythm and spirit of every region of India. The performance was not only a visual feast of colour, music, and synchronized movement but also a powerful tribute to India's unity in diversity. Its sheer scale and seamless execution earned it a Record for the Largest Indian Folk Variety Dance, making it a historic highlight of the 76th Republic Day celebrations.

of membership and the number of activities. The festival spans 111 days between September and January each year. The 30,000-plus members of Soorya Society, founded in 1978, conduct around 200 programmes annually.

WR Largest Bharatanatyam ensemble

The Department of Tourism, Government of Tamil Nadu, organized the largest Bharatanatyam ensemble with 10,176 dancers on 8 February 2020. The event 'Sathir 10,000', which based the dance on the famous Tamil text *Thirukkural*, was held at S.I.V.E.T College in Chennai.

Largest Kathak ensemble

Keeping the spirit of Indian culture alive, the Nrityachakra team of the Prerana Foundation from Pune, Maharashtra, organized a Kathak event where a total number of 1,188 participants came forward to perform the classical Kathak dance for a duration of 20 minutes. This event was held at Maharashtriya Mandal's Chandrashekhar Agashe College Grounds in Pune on 25 February 2024.

MUSIC

First raga

The first raga is believed to be the Carnatic Mayamalavagowla (equivalent to the Hindustani raga Bhairavi) that Purandara Dasa (c. 1484–1564), the Bhakti poet and musician, also known as Adi Guru, used as the teaching scale. Called Adi Raga, it is said to have emanated from Lord Shiva.

Only multilingual classical songs

Manipravalam *kriti*s are songs in the Carnatic tradition in which two or even three languages are used and the lines are sung alternately in these languages, which include Tamil and Sanskrit.

Earliest form of classical song

The Dhrupad, originally called Dhruvapada, was the prevailing mode of music until medieval times. While this form traces its roots to the *Natyashastra*, it was developed by Swami Haridas and the legendary singer Tansen in the 15th century.

Earliest known royal composer of ragas

Maharaja Swathi Thirunal (r. 1813–46), the ruler of the erstwhile princely state of Travancore (now in Kerala), created more than 400 classical compositions in both the Carnatic and Hindustani modes.

Earliest form of music

The Rig Veda has references to *saman* hymns, the earliest form of music in India. Saman singing is also mentioned in the *Brahmana*s as well as the Upanishads, and features as a part of spiritual observances and exercises.

First medieval treatise on music

The Chalukyan king, Someshvara III, who ruled in the Karnataka region in the 12th century CE, wrote the *Manasollasa*, an encyclopaedic work in Sanskrit on a variety of topics, including music, with 2,500 verses dedicated to the topic. The music section, one of the largest sections in the book, is considered the earliest treatise on music.

Earliest mention of raga

The word *raga* in its modern connotation appears first in the classical Sanskrit text *Brihaddeshi* by Matanga (eighth century CE). It is described as 'a combination of tones which, with beautiful illuminating graces, pleases people'.

Tansen

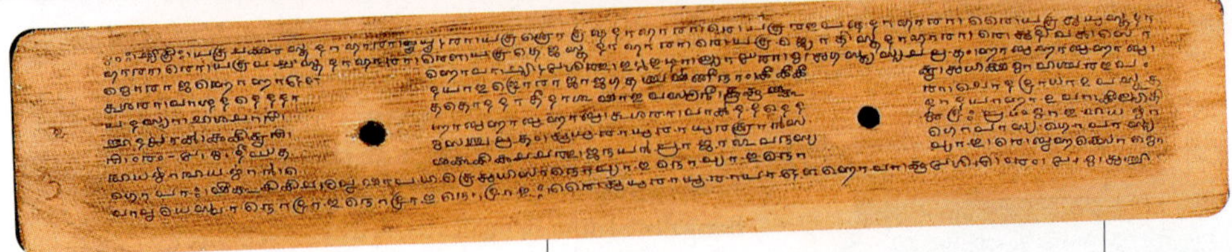

Excerpt from Sama Veda

Earliest musical notes

The Sama Veda, which is believed to date to c. 1200–1000 BCE, mentions seven musical notes in saman singing, viz., Krushta, Prathama, Dvitiya, Tritiya, Chaturtha, Mandra/Panchama, and Antya/Atisvara.

Earliest ballad singing

Both Vedic and epic literature mentions minstrels singing *akhyanas* (texts narrated by professional storytellers), sung to the veena, in the *marga* style of singing. While the Vedas mentions both instrumental music and akhyana recitation in yagnas, the Ramayana also has several references to the singing of ballads.

Earliest Prakrit (popular) songs

The *Natyashastra* mentions *dhruvas*, i.e., songs of 5 different kinds that were an integral part of drama. These songs indicate the context, place, and people in a scene. Dhruvas were originally in Prakrit and were mostly sung by a choir.

First to standardize music

Purandara Dasa (1484–1564) is revered as Sangeet Pitamaha (grandfather of music). He standardized Carnatic music for teaching, besides classifying 35 types of *tala*. He pioneered a musical notation system that is still being used.

Most prolific composer

Purandara Dasa (1484–1564), the philosopher–saint and Bhakti poet, is credited with as many as 4,75,000 compositions.

First codifier of Carnatic concert format

Ariyakudi Ramanuja Iyengar (1890–1967) was the architect of modern Carnatic concert music. He pioneered the transition of the Carnatic concert from temples and courts to modern concert halls, codifying and adapting its format, order, and duration. He introduced the largest number of compositions from the trinity of Thyagaraja, Muthuswamy Dikshitar and Syama Sastri to the concert repertoire, new *pallavis* (opening phrase of a song), the order of *tukkadas* (composition played towards the end of a Carnatic concert,) and *padams* (other songs) that follow the main item of *ragam-thanam-pallavi*.

Purandara Dasa

First fusion melody

The 14th century saw the introduction of Persian models into Indian music. Amir Khusrau (1253–1325), the famous singer at the court of Alauddin Khilji (r. 1296–1316), introduced the qawwali mode of singing, a mixture of Persian and Indian music. He also introduced the sitar, a modification of the veena.

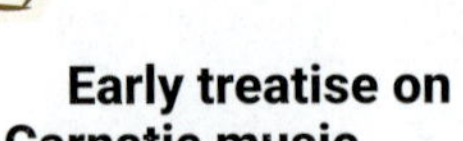

Early treatise on Carnatic music

Rama Amatya, a royal composer at the court of King Ramaraja of Vijayanagar, gave the first detailed exposition of the Carnatic system of music in his text titled *Swaramela Kalanidhi*, around 1550 BCE. He described the first collection of ragas.

Oldest gharana

The Gwalior gharana was founded in the 16th century by Nathan Khan Pir Bakhsh.

Oldest known percussion instrument

The *ghatam* or mud pot, still in vogue in Carnatic concerts, is mentioned in the Ramayana. It was used in folk music for centuries and later elevated to concert status by maestro Palani Krishna Iyer (1876–1908). This tradition continued with maestros, such as Kodandarama Iyer and T.H. 'Vikku' Vinayakram, who popularized it.

An illustrated manuscript of Amir Khusrau's poems

Oldest musical instrument

A lithophone (stone chimes comparable to a xylophone), 3,000–4,000 years old, was identified by German archaeologists in Sankarjang Village in Angul District, Odisha. All the 20 similar-shaped polished basalt stones found possibly formed fragments of a lithophone, with excellent acoustic quality, as the edges were ground thin to achieve a specific pitch.

First mention of the drum

The *Mahajanaka Jataka* (c. second century BCE) mentions the drum, along with horns, gongs, and cymbals.

Bangalore Gayana Sabha

Oldest sabha for dance and music

Sri Parthasarathy Swami Sabha at Triplicane, Madras, was established in 1900. The Bangalore Gayana Sabha, Bangalore (now Bengaluru), Karnataka, set up on 5 August 1905, is the second-oldest private cultural organization with programmes in dance and music.

Oldest south Indian stringed instrument

The *yazh*, a seven-stringed lute is mentioned in Tamil Sangam literature (first to fourth century CE), making it the oldest south Indian stringed instrument known.

First three-in-one classical instrument

The *mridanga veenai*, a stand-up instrument that is framed in wood and played sitting on a chair, was invented by Audanoor P. Haridass, who demonstrated it on 23 September 1984 at the Purasawalkam Arts Academy, Madras. Played with bamboo sticks, it not only reproduces the sounds of percussion and strings, but also simulates the sound of cymbals used in *natuvangam* (rhythmic sound play) and the tinkle of *gajjai* (ankle bells).

Earliest use of the Carnatic veena

Govinda Dikshitar modified the Saraswati veena into the Carnatic veena to enable the playing of all ragas. He was a minister of King Raghunatha Naik of Thanjavur (r. 1614–32 CE), Tamil Nadu.

First female professional saxophone players

Sisters M.S. Lavanya and M.S. Subbulakshmi from Chennai, have given a new dimension to Carnatic music by playing ragas on the saxophone. Daughters of mridangam exponent M.R. Sainath, the duo, called the 'Saxophone Sisters', learnt the instrument from Padma Shri Dr Kadri Gopinath. They performed at venues such as the Soorya Festival in Thiruvananthapuram, Kerala, the Sri Thyagaraja Festival at Thiruvaiyaru, Tamil Nadu, and the Malleswaram Sangeetha Sabha, Bengaluru, Karnataka. They have also performed at the 'One City One World Festival' in Nottingham and the Bath International Music Festival in the UK.

First recorded song

Sashimukhi of Classic Theatre in Calcutta recorded the first song 'Kanha

Earliest extant musical instruments

Drums came into being during the Vedic period. The earliest drums included the *dundubhi* and *adambara*, ordinary drums; *bhumi dundubhi*, an earth drum made by digging a hole in the ground and covering it with hide; and *vanaspati*, a wooden drum. Early stringed instruments included the *skanda veena* and *karkari*, ordinary lutes; *vana*, a lute with a hundred strings; and the veena (similar to the present-day one). Wind instruments included the *tunava*, a wooden flute; the *nadi*, a reed flute; and *bakura*, whose shape is unknown.

From left to right: Anoushka Shankar, Hariprasad Chaurasia, Shreya Ghoshal

Jeevan Dhan' in 1902, from the play *Srikrishna* on a 22.86 cm (9 in.), one-sided disc made by the Gramophone and Typewriter Ltd.

First Indian performer at the Royal Albert Hall

The first Indian singer to perform at the iconic venue, the Royal Albert Hall, in London, UK, was Bollywood playback singer Lata Mangeshkar, who gave a performance at the venue in 1974. Other Indians who have also performed here include sitar players Pandit Ravi Shankar and Anoushka Shankar, flautist Hariprasad Chaurasia, and singer Shreya Ghoshal.

First voices recorded on gramophone

The voices of Dr Harnamdas and Ahmed were recorded by the Gramophone Company in 1899 in London, UK. They sang songs based on the Ramayana and recited the *aayat*s of the Quran for the recordings.

First singer to be recorded on gramophone

Gauhar Jaan (1873–1930) was selected to sing when Fred Ginsberg introduced the gramophone in India with the first disc being cut in Calcutta (now Kolkata), West Bengal, in 1902. She was paid ₹3,000 for the recording session.

Gauhar Jaan

First gramophone company

On 7 July 1901, J. Watson Harrod opened a branch of the Gramophone Company Ltd at Calcutta, which was further developed by T.W. Gainsberg. In 1908, the first factory to process and press records was set up in Beliaghata, Calcutta.

Ustad Ali Akbar Khan

Only gramophone museum

Discs and Machines – Sunny's Gramophone Museum and Records' Archive in Kottayam, Kerala, is a unique repository of around 1,10,000 records and more than 260 gramophones. Owner Sunny Matthew has been collecting them for the last 33 years and opened the museum to public on 25 January 2015. A copy of the first recorded song in India is also on display here. The museum may be visited by appointment.

First gramophone record

Indian music was first produced on a gramophone record in 1898 at the Beliaghata factory of the Gramophone and Typewriter Ltd. In July 1908, the production of disc records was started at the Sealdah factory located on Beliaghata Road, Calcutta. In 1928, the Sealdah factory was closed and building work commenced at the new factory on Jessore Road, Dum Dum, Calcutta.

First electronic instrument

The first electronic tala aid called talometer was invented by M.G. Raj Narayan of Bangalore, in June 1978. It helps musicians to get a precise, unerring, and continuous course of cycles in all the talas.

First duo to introduce jugalbandi

Pandit Ravi Shankar and Ustad Ali Akbar Khan formed the first musical duo to introduce instrumental, duets popularly known as jugalbandi. Shankar and Khan performed the jugalbandi for the first time at the debut performance of the former in 1939, with Shankar playing the sitar and Khan playing the sarod. The duo was also among the first to popularize Indian classical music abroad.

First use of shehnai in Hindustani classical music

The shehnai, like the *sundari* and *surnayi,* was originally a folk instrument that was played on festive occasions. It was Ustad Bismillah Khan (1916–2006) who brought it into the realm of classical music, at par with other classical instruments.

Shehnai in Hindustani Classical Music

First harp player

Meagan Pandian from Mumbai, Maharashtra, is the first harp player from India and the first Indian harpist to participate in A.R. Rahman's concerts. She received the 'Young Musician of the Year' award from the Olga and Jules Craen Foundation in 2014.

First woman instrumentalist

Renowned sarod player Sharan Rani Backliwal (1929–2008) was a leading exponent of Hindustani instrumental music and the first female instrumentalist to give a public recital in the 1930s. She trained under sarod maestros Baba Allauddin Khan and Ustad Ali Akbar Khan. Popularly known as Sarod Rani, she was given the Sahitya Kala Parishad award and the Sangeet Natak Akademi award for classical Hindustani instrumental music in 1974. She received the Padma Shri in 1968.

Sharan Rani Playing at Tehran, Iran

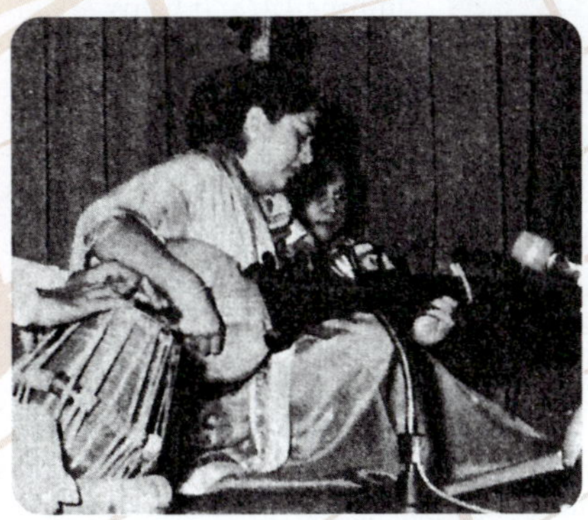

First woman shehnai player

Bageswari Gamar was crowned 'Shehnai Queen' at Chandigarh in 1983, the year she made her debut. A disciple of Ustad Bismillah Khan, she recorded a jugalbandi with the maestro, besides releasing solo cassettes. She represented India at the Bharat Mahotsav in Russia in 1988.

First woman ghatam player

Sukanya Ramgopal (b. 13 June 1957) from Bengaluru, became the first woman to play the ghatam in the Carnatic music tradition. Among many of her innovations are the 'Ghata Tarang', a melody created out of 6 ghatams, and the 'Sthree Taal Tarang', an all-woman percussion ensemble, experiments that have taken her to stages across India and abroad. She received the Sangeet Natak Akademi Award in 2014.

First fusion album

Violinist Yehudi Menuhin and sitar maestro Pandit Ravi Shankar collaborated on a double album called *West Meets East*, which was released in Britain in January 1967, where both played Western and Indian classical pieces alternately.

First to perform at the UN

M.S. Subbulakshmi (1916–2004) was the first Indian to perform at the United Nations (UN) in a concert at the UN General Assembly on UN Day, 23 October 1966. She received the Padma Bhushan in 1954 and the Padma Vibhushan in 1975 and became the first musician to be awarded the Bharat Ratna in 1998. Subbulakshmi was also the first Indian musician to receive the Ramon Magsaysay Award for Public Service in 1974.

First music school

Pandit Vishnu Digambar Paluskar (1872–1931) set up the Gandharva Mahavidyalaya – India's first known music school – in Lahore (now in Pakistan) on 5 May 1901. It was run on public donations and funds raised by his concerts. Another branch was opened by him in Bombay (now Mumbai), Maharashtra in September 1908, and Pandit Vinayakrao Patwardhan started a branch in Poona (now Pune), Maharashtra, on 8 May 1932. Later, the Lahore school was moved to Bombay after Independence in 1947.

First woman nadaswaram player

Madurai M.S. Ponnuthayi from Madurai, Tamil Nadu, was the first professional woman player of the nadaswaram, long considered a male bastion. Born into a family of musicians, she was introduced to the instrument by her father. After receiving training under Natesa Pillai, she gave her first performance at the age of 9 in the 1940s.

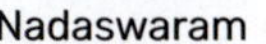

Nadaswaram

WR Most recorded artiste

Asha Bhosle is the most recorded artiste in the history of music. Having begun her career in 1948 with the Hindi film *Chunariya*, she had recorded 11,000 solo, duet, and chorus songs by 2011. In a career spanning more than 6 decades, she has sung in over 20 Indian and foreign languages. She received the Dadasaheb Phalke Award in 2000 and the Padma Vibhushan in 2008. She was also the first Indian singer to be nominated for the Grammy Awards.

First foreign concert tour by a woman instrumentalist

According to a report in *Amrita Bazar Patrika*, dated 11 September 1912, Satyabala Devi, an 18-year-old Bengali girl, had gone to America in the summer of 1911 to play the veena. The article stated that she was the first Indian woman to have gone abroad to perform in an instrumental music concert, and it was declared a great success.

First recorded music

In the 1930s, an organization called Shining Star Society recorded sets of discs with mythological themes. A mix of music and dialogue, the sets ran into several records. A-10 disc *Ramayana* by Saraswati Stores was very popular, followed by other drama sets like *Tukaram* (4 discs), *Purandara Dasa* (5 discs), *Siruthondar* (3 discs), and *Thirugnana Sambandhar* (4 discs). Their recording was supervised by the Katcheri set pioneer, Thuraiyur Rajagopala Sharma.

First compact disc

Pankaj Udhas's album titled *Shagufta* was the first to be formally released in a compact disc (CD) format by Music India in December 1987.

Sandeep Das

Grammy Award for the Best World Music Album

Music composer and tabla player Sandeep Das won a Grammy Award for the Best World Music Album in 2017 for his collaboration with Yo-Yo Ma and the Silk Road Ensemble on the album *Sing Me Home*.

First Indo-jazz (fusion) albums

Indo-jazz came into its own in India in the 1970s with Shakti, a group formed by jazz guitarist John McLaughlin, along with L. Shankar on the electric double violin (which he invented), Zakir Hussain on the tabla and T.H. 'Vikku' Vinayakram on the ghatam.

First set of records

Renowned businessman H. Bose's Talking Machine Hall, a recording shop in Calcutta, released the first set of phonograph records on 19 March 1906. The set featured 8 songs by Rabindranath Tagore and 4 by D.L. Roy.

John McLaughlin

First all-woman Hindustani–Carnatic music band

Tabla soloist Anuradha Pal from Mumbai, founded Stree Shakti, the first all-woman Hindustani–Carnatic music band, in 1996. It performed in India as well as other countries, including in international festivals such as BBC Music Live and Rhythm Sticks.

First whistling LP

An album of Carnatic and Hindustani ragas entirely whistled by Siva Prasad from Hyderabad (now in Telangana) was released on 15 June 1985.

First Indian band on MTV

Rana Banerjee and Sanjoy Sengupta's band, Extinct, was the first Indian group to be featured on MTV Asia, in September 1993.

India's only music director couple

Samir and Mana Raval from Ahmedabad, Gujarat, are India's first and only music director couple, having composed music for more than 100 songs in 35 feature films in Gujarati and Hindi. Having started with music direction for *Teenagers Gang*, a Gujarati film, in 2013, the couple continues to compose music for Hindi and other films, TV serials, and jingles.

First female rapper

Taran Kaur Dhillon (b. 29 July 1979), aka Hard Kaur, was the first female rapper of Indian origin. A British citizen, she topped the UK charts with her song, 'Ek Glassy' in 2007. Her first solo album *Supawoman* released the same year had 11 tracks. She marked her Bollywood debut with the title track (which she co-wrote) of the film *Johnny Gaddaar* (2007).

First Asian to win the Golden Reel Award

Resul Pookutty was the first Asian to win the 63rd American Motion Picture Sound Editor's Golden Reel Award in 2016 for best sound for the documentary *India's Daughter*. A sound designer, editor, and mixer who works in Hollywood and Indian cinema, he also won the Academy Award (Oscar) in 2009 for best sound mixing for the movie *Slumdog Millionaire,* along with Richard Pryke and Ian Tapp. He was awarded the Padma Shri in 2010 and the National Film Award for best audiography in the same year.

From left to right: Ian Tapp, Richard Pryke, Resul Pookutty

WR First portable digital audio player

Carvaan, by Saregama India Ltd, is the world's first portable digital audio player with over 5,000 in - built songs. The songs are categorized based on singers, lyricists, music composers, and moods. Using a jog dial, music stations can be selected, from Kishore Kumar classics and R.D. Burman's hits to timeless love songs and soulful Sufi tracks. Carvaan can function as an FM radio, and also has Bluetooth and USB features.

First disabled DJ

Varun Khullar, aka DJ Aamish, from New Delhi, is the first disabled professional disc jockey (DJ) in India. He began his career in May 2017 and is currently a resident DJ with Kitty Su, New Delhi, a part of the Lalit Group and Hotels. He has performed at festivals like Time Out 72 and Greeshma Utsav.

Only Indian to win both an Oscar and a Grammy Award

Composer and singer A.R. Rahman won two Grammys following his Oscar wins for the soundtrack from Danny Boyle's *Slumdog Millionaire*, becoming the first Indian to win an individual Grammy. He won the first Grammy in the Best Compilation Soundtrack for the Motion Picture category. The second was for the song '*Jai Ho*' in the Best Motion Picture Song category for the same in 2009.

WR Longest innings as a conductor

Western music maestro Zubin Mehta (b. 29 April 1936) from Bombay spent over thirteen years as the music director and principal conductor of the New York

Zubin Mehta conducting an orchestra

Philharmonic Orchestra from 1978 to 1991. Currently, he is the music director of the Israel Philharmonic Orchestra.

First Grammy Award–winning Indian percussionist

T.H. 'Vikku' Vinayakram was the first Indian percussionist to win the Grammy Award in 1991. He won it for his participation in *Planet Drum* by Mickey Hart. Vinayakram, well-known for playing the ghatam and popularizing Carnatic music, was honoured with the Padma Shri in 2002 and the Padma Bhushan in 2014. He also won the Sangeet Natak Akademi fellowship in 2012.

Marathon qawwali performance

Haji Mohammad Idris and Mohammad Ilyas, known as the Qutbi brothers of Dargah Hazrat Qutbuddin, performed Sufi qawwali for 12 hrs. They began at 9:00 p.m. on 12 November 2016 and ended at 9:00 a.m. on 13 November 2016 at the Sangeet Natak Akademi in Delhi. Sixteen singers accompanied them.

Most events in a day

Pernod Ricard India Pvt. Ltd organized 104 musical events on a single day – 29 November 2019. These events were held at different venues across 27 cities in the country, including Delhi, Mumbai, Pune, Chennai, Visakhapatnam, and Chandigarh. Titled 'Play for a Cause', this campaign raised awareness on issues such as pollution, nature, plastic use, and meals for the underprivileged. Bands and artistes including Perfect Strangers (Bengaluru), Parikrama (Gurugram), Ankur Tiwari and the Ghalat Family (Mumbai), Cherry Singh (Chandigarh), and Usha Uthup (Kolkata) performed at these events.

Marathon flute performance

Ananthakrishnan S.R., a flautist from Thiruvananthapuram, Kerala, played the flute for 33 hrs 36 mins, from 6:30 a.m. on 13 July to 6:30 p.m. on 14 July 2017 in Thrissur, Kerala, with a total break time of 2 hrs 24 mins.

Marathon duet singing

Venkatesh and Sangeetha Rajeshkumar from Chennai, sang duets for 28 hours at the Akshaya Mahalakshmi Mahal, Chennai, during 28–29 January 2017. They sang 342 Tamil film songs starting at around 4:00 a.m. on 28 January and ended by 12:30 p.m. the next day. The total break time was 4 hrs 30 mins.

Sunburn Music Festival

First virtual music festival

Sunburn Home Festival, a two-day virtual music festival, was organized from 11 to 12 July 2020. The festival featured a line-up of international stars, such as Bassjackers, Vini Vici, and Ummet Ozcan. The highlight of the event was the application of extended reality (XR) technology offering a mixed reality and holistic environment, also used for the first time.

Marathon Carnatic vocal performance

Sajna Sudheer (b. 1 August 1984) from Thiruvananthapuram, Kerala, performed a marathon Carnatic vocal recital for 37 hrs 50 mins at the Ganesham Natakakalari of Soorya Stage and Film Society. She began her performance at 3:15 a.m. on 21 January 2019 and ended at 9:15 p.m. on 22 January 2019, with a total break time of 4 hrs 10 mins.

Longest ravanhatha

Praveen Singh Rathore along with Shiv Pal Ram, Sugana Ram, and Manwari from Jodhpur, Rajasthan, made the longest ravanhatha, a folk string instrument of Rajasthan. The ravanhatha, measuring 224 cm (7 ft 4.19 in.), was made in 2 weeks at Bhakrasani, Jodhpur, using bamboo, mango wood, goat leather, bull horn, iron, cotton threads, plastic threads, *baval* (babul) wood, *ghungroo* (bells), and fabric.

Most people playing the harmonica together

Hindustan Petroleum Corporation Ltd, as part of its mega festival – Yuvantage BLITZ during 6–7 January 2019 – set a record for most people playing the harmonica simultaneously. The music was played by 457 of the company's employees on their harmonicas for 6 mins 17 secs on 6 January 2019 at Ramoji Film City, Hyderabad, Telangana.

A Man Playing Ravanhatha

Ilaiyaraaja's Symphony Milestone

In a landmark achievement for Indian music, Ilaiyaraaja – fondly known as the 'Maestro' – became the first Indian composer to both compose and perform an original orchestral symphony with the prestigious London Symphony Orchestra. The historic performance, held in 2025, marked the golden jubilee of his musical career, celebrating over fifty years of his pathbreaking contribution to Indian film and classical music. Seamlessly blending Indian ragas with Western symphonic traditions, the composition showcased Ilaiyaraaja's genius for innovation and his ability to transcend genres. The event was hailed as a cultural milestone, placing Indian film music firmly on the global orchestral stage.

THEATRE

First modern Indian plays (translations)

Gerasim Lebedev, a Russian adventurer, founded the first European-style proscenium drama theatre in Calcutta, in 1795. He was helped by the local intellectuals. Along with his Bengali tutor, Goloknath Das, he presented the plays *The Disguise* and *Love Is the Best Doctor* on 7 November 1795. These English comedies, translated into Bengali, were the first urban theatrical performances.

Marathon nukkad natak performance

The Mayaar Group of the Bhopal School of Social Sciences in Bhopal, Madhya Pradesh, organized a street-play marathon to celebrate Mahatma Gandhi's 150th birth anniversary. A record was set with a team of 17 members performing 151 street plays from 5:00 a.m. on 3 March 2019 to 3:56 a.m. on 4 March 2019 at different locations in the city. The performance time added up to 22 hrs 56 mins, with a break time of 2 hrs 26 mins. The plays conveyed the importance of the Swachh Bharat Mission of the Government of India.

First public theatre hall

The Star Theatre in Calcutta, was inaugurated on 21 July 1883 with the play *Daksha Yajna*. Among the first to produce plays here was the acclaimed playwright, novelist, theatre director,

Nukkad Natak Performance

and actor Girish Chandra Ghosh. The theatre moved to its present site on Bidhan Sarani in 1888 and now mainly functions as a cinema hall with plays also being staged.

First full-fledged opera

The Fakir of Benares, an Indo-French opera, was staged at the Siri Fort Auditorium, New Delhi, on 27 February 2002. The opera was directed by Muzaffar Ali while his wife Meera Ali designed the costumes.

First 'protest play'

Nil Darpan, a play in Bengali about the plight, of indigo farmers, was written by Dinabandhu Mitra in 1860. The play was banned by the British authorities.

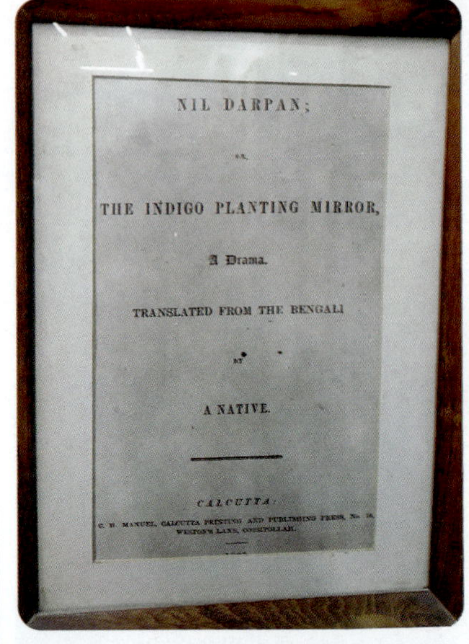

NIL DARPAN;

OR,

THE INDIGO PLANTING MIRROR,

A Drama.

TRANSLATED FROM THE BENGALI

BY

A NATIVE.

CALCUTTA:

C. H. MANUEL, CALCUTTA PRINTING AND PUBLISHING PRESS, No. [illegible]

WESTON'S LANE, COSSITOLLAH.

Title page of Nil Darpan

First dramatic club

The first dramatic club was the Parsi Natak Mandali established in 1853 in Bombay. They performed their first play *Roostum Zabooli and Sohrab* that year, followed by *King Afrasiab and Rustom Pehlvan* and *Padshah Faredun*. Other Parsi theatre clubs were the Elphinstone, established in 1860, and the Victoria, established in 1867. These drama clubs inspired Gujarati theatre.

Play performed in most languages – single day

Yugpurush – Mahatma's Mahatma, a two-hour play based on the relationship between Mahatma Gandhi and his spiritual guide, Shrimad Rajchandra-ji, was performed in five languages, viz., English, Hindi, Bengali, Gujarati, and Tamil, on 11 August 2017. It was organized by the Shrimad Rajchandra Mission in Dharampur, Valsad District, Gujarat, as one of the 808 performances for the 150th birth anniversary celebrations of Shrimad Rajchandra-ji.

First commercial theatre

The first commercial theatre, generally known as the 'Parsi theatre', started by Pestonji Framji in 1870, was aimed at mass entertainment, while dealing with social problems. Though based in Bombay, the theatre company travelled widely all over north India.

WR Most theatrical performances

The Gujarati stage actor Pransukhlal Nayak (1910–89) had 22,455 theatrical performances to his credit by December 1986. He had played 241 roles in stage productions in a career he started at the age of 9.

Most stage plays performed in a day – solo

Akash Bhadsavle (9 February 1996) has performed a total of 12 shows in 3 plays of 45 min each on Sunday, 9 October 2022. The plays were performed in Gadkari Rangayatan, Thane, in 2 sessions from 8:00 a.m. to 11:00 p.m. and 11:00 a.m. to 2:30 p.m.; in Dada Kondake Amphitheatre, Thane, from 4:00 p.m. to 7:30 p.m.; and in Mahakavi Kalidas Natya Mandir Mulund from 8:30 p.m. to 11:45 p.m.

First foreign translation of a Sanskrit play

Poet Kalidasa's *Abhijnana Shakuntalam* was translated into German in 1791 by revolutionary Georg Forster and into English by Anglo-Welsh philologist Sir William Jones in 1795.

Longest-serving director of the NSD

Ebrahim Alkazi (1925–2020) was appointed as the second director of the National School of Drama (NSD) in 1962 and served till 1977.

First recipient of the Kalidas Samman (theatre)

Shambhu Mitra (1915–1997) from Kolkata, was the first recipient of the Kalidas Samman for his contribution to Bengali theatre.

Raja Ravi Verma's Shakuntala

Most performances as a character (mythological) – stage

V.S. Narayanan (b. 20 November 1943) from Mumbai, has been performing the role of Hanuman for the annual Ramnavami festival held by the Mulund Bhajana Samaj, Mumbai, since 1967. He has performed each year for 53 years.

Most performances as a personality – stage and screen

Deepak Madhukant Antani (b. 20 August 1964) from Ahmedabad, Gujarat, is a professional actor who has performed the most times as Mahatma Gandhi on screen and stage. His maiden venture enacting the role of the Mahatma was on 20 June 2000 in *Sardar Patel*, a play written by him for Sardar Vallabhbhai Patel's 125th birth anniversary celebrations. As a Gandhi- lookalike, he has performed in 1 advertisement, 2 feature films, 21 short films, 1 TV serial, 190 stage plays, 3 documentaries, 4 voice-overs, and a 200-km padyatra completed in 9 days.

First and only play on Broadway and West End

The Ramayana by Gopal Sharman, enacted in a one-woman tour de force by Jalabala Vaidya, was played at the Barbizon Plaza Theatre, Manhattan, New York, in February 1975. The play was also performed at other venues, such as the Smithsonian Institution, Washington DC, the United Nations headquarters, New York, USA, and Sedler's Wells Theatre, London, UK.

Jalabala Vaidya

Annasaheb Kirloskar

First Marathi musical

Shakuntala was staged as a Sangeet play on 31 October 1880 by Balwant Pandurang 'Annasaheb' Kirloskar and his Kirloskar Natak Mandali. Written in Marathi, it featured simple songs. This format was followed by Marathi stage in the musical drama genre called Sangeet plays. It attracted giants like Bal Gandharva (Narayanrao Rajahansa) and Keshavrao Bhonsle.

Asia's biggest theatre festival

Bharat Rang Mahotsav, the annual theatre festival of the National School of Drama (NSD), is the biggest theatre festival in Asia. Established in 1999, the Bharat Rang Mahotsav includes theatre groups from around the world. The 23rd edition of the Bharat Rang Mahostav was conducted in February 2024 and featured around 150 performances, and also included workshops, discussions, and master classes.

Early dramatic references

There are references to drama, dancing, music, and acting in the Ramayana, the Mahabharata, and the Puranas. Buddhist and Jain texts mention that monks were forbidden from watching dramatic performances. Panini (c. fourth century BCE) mentions dramatic works in his *Ashtadhyayi*. Patanjali (variously dated from second century BCE to the fourth century CE), describes the conditions of dramatic performers. Kautilya also refers to music, dance, and drama in the *Arthashastra*.

Earliest plays

- Patanjali mentions plays such as *Kamavadha*, *Balibandhan*, and *Sariputra-Prakarana* in his text *Mahabhashya* (c. third century BCE).
- Bharatamuni also mentions plays

such as *Devasura Sangrama*, *Amrita Manthana*, and *Tripuradaha* in his *Natyashastra*.

• *Uparupaka*s (secondary dramas) are found in the Rig Veda in the form of dialogue hymns. The most famous one tells the story of Pururava and Urvashi. Eighteen such uparupakas are mentioned in *Sahitya Darpana*, a book on rhetoric and dramaturgy from the 14th century, authored by Pandit Vishwanath Kaviraj. These plays pre-date even the *Natyashastra*. Uparupakas were probably enacted before the public on royal occasions and temple festivals.

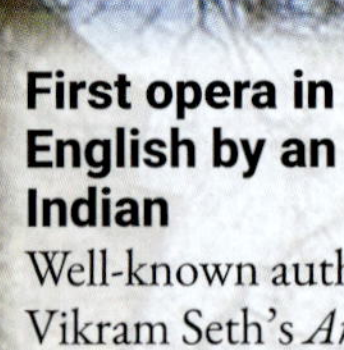

First opera in English by an Indian

Well-known author Vikram Seth's *Arion and the Dolphin*, which premiered in the UK in June 1994, was the first opera written in English by an Indian Commissioned by the English National Opera, it was performed at the 964-seat drill shed of HMS *Drake*, a high-security naval base. The opera was directed by Rebecca Meitlis.

Early political plays

Mrichchhakatika by Shudraka (dated between the third and the fifth century CE) and Vishakhadatta's *Mudrarakshasa* (dated between late fourth and the eighth century CE), both depict clashes between different powers, political intrigue, espionage, and counter-espionage. They are considered to be the first plays with political themes.

Earliest playwright

Bhasa (third to fourth century CE) of the Chola era in south India is believed to be the earliest playwright. Well-known plays by him include *Abhisheka*, *Swapnavasavadattam*, and *Pratimanatakam*.

Oldest extant play

Palm-leaf fragments belonging to the Kushana period (around first century CE) feature a 9- act Buddhist play titled *Sariputra Prakarana*, by Ashvaghosha, the court poet of King Kanishka. It follows all the rules for drama laid down in the *Natyashastra*.

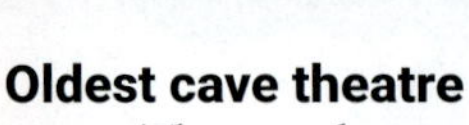

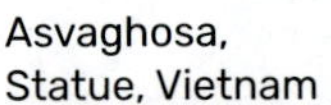

Asvaghosa, Statue, Vietnam

Oldest cave theatre

The cave theatres at Sitabenga and Jogimara in the Surguja District of Chhattisgarh are estimated to be around 3,000 years old. Sita Bengra, which pre-dates the Lomas Rishi caves of the Mauryan period (322–187 BCE), was chiefly used for dance and drama.

Earliest street plays

Therukoothu, a theatre form originating during 200 BCE–200 CE in ancient Tamil Nadu, literally means 'street play'. It was performed on streets on an improvised stage with very few props and hardly any special costumes. Themes were taken from the epics. Therukoothu as well as other forms of street plays like Pallu, Kuravanji, and Nandi Natakam are still performed in south India.

Oldest children's theatre

Children's Little Theatre, the oldest children's theatre in the country, was founded in Calcutta, by Samar Chatterjee (1908–86) in May 1951. It included dance, drama, music, and puppetry.

VISUAL ARTS

CINEMA

FIRSTS

First films exhibited

The first screening of six short films, by France's famed Lumière Brothers, Louis and Auguste, was held on 7 July 1896. They were: *Entry of Cinematographe*, *Arrival of a Train at la Ciotat Station*, *Sea Bath*, *Workers Leaving the Factory*, *A Demolition*, and *Ladies and Soldiers on Wheels*.

Lumière Brothers

First film shot in India

Coconut Fair is said to be the first short film shot in India in 1897, and it was made by an unknown foreign photographer. Shortly after, another 'film' made in India, a short dancing scene from the Bengali opera *The Flower of Persia* was exhibited on 9 February 1898 at the Star Theatre, Calcutta (now Kolkata), West Bengal.

First female actor of the talkies

After silent performances in 36 movies, Zubeida Begum acted in the first Indian talkie *Alam Ara* (1931).

First child artiste

Dadasaheb Phalke's son, Bhalchandra, was the first child actor in Indian cinema. He played the role of the king's son Rohitashva in *Raja Harishchandra*. His daughter Mandakini was the first female child artiste and became popular for her role as Krishna. Her first film was *Krishna Janam* in 1918.

First advertisement for a film

The first advertisement for a film appeared in the *Times of India*, Bombay (now Mumbai), on 7 July 1896. It gave the night's programme for the screening of the six short films by the Lumière Brothers and called the event, 'the marvel of the century' and 'the wonder of the world'.

First indigenous feature film

Dadasaheb Phalke's silent feature film *Raja Harishchandra* was released at the Coronation Theatre in Bombay (now Mumbai), Maharashtra, on 3 May 1913. It was a fully Indian venture and was shown along with four imported short films, together making up a 90-minute show. It ran for 23 days and was screened again later at multiple venues.

First film concern

Royal Bioscope Company was started in 1898 by Hiralal Sen and his brother Motilal. Initially, they bought films that were made in England and showcased them in India.

First talkie

Alam Ara, made in Hindustani language by Ardeshir Irani and released on 14 March 1931 in Bombay, Maharashtra, became India's first talkie feature. The first talkie stars were Master Vithal as hero, Zubeida as heroine, Prithviraj Kapoor in a supporting role and W.M. Khan as a singing fakir. The first music directors were Pirojshah Mistry and B. Irani. It was a costume fantasy with seven songs. The film reel was 3,048 m (10,000 ft) long and it ran for seven weeks.

Alam Ara: First talkie

Dadasaheb Phalke and QR code for *Raja Harishchandra*

First film serial

Ram Vanvas (The Exile of Rama) was made by Patankar Friends and Company and released on 14 September 1918. It was shown in four parts, each running for a period of a few weeks.

First film review

In 1899, the *Times of India* started a film review column.

WR First one-actor, one-set film

Sunil Dutt made *Yaadein* in 1964, the first experiment of its kind in the world with only one actor (himself) emoting on only one set. In 2005, Kannada film *Shanthi* became the second movie with a single actor.

First adult film

Social Evil, a docudrama, was made by the Social Purity League of Bombay, Maharashtra, in 1929 to provide information about sex problems. It was also the first sex educational film. It was shown free of cost and was the first film given the label 'For adults only'.

First cinema hall

Elphinstone Picture Palace was started by J.F. Madan in Calcutta, West Bengal, in 1905. It was first renamed the Minerva Theatre and then Chaplin Cinema. This piece of history was demolished in 2013 by the Kolkata Municipal Corporation (which owned it).

First studio

Khan Bahadur Ardeshir Irani (1886–1969) started his first studio – Star Films – in 1920.

First 'trick' effects

Ankurachi Wadh (1912) by Dadasaheb Phalke showed a bud bursting into a flower with the single-frame exposing technique.

First experiments with colour

The very first colour venture was by Madan Theatres of Calcutta in 1932. Their talkie feature *Bilwamangal* was sent abroad for printing. Prabhat Company under V. Shantaram tried a colour-processed film *Sairandhri* (1935), which was taken to Germany for printing. Ardeshir Irani tried a local process called Cine Colour in his *Kisan Kanya* (1937) and *Mother India* (1938). Bhavnani's *Ajit* (1948) and Mehboob's *Aan* (1952) were shot in 16 mm Kodachrome and processed abroad. *Aan* had the first Technicolour prints. Sohrab Modi's *Jhansi ki Rani* (1953) was the first Technicolour film shot in India by foreign technicians and printed abroad. Ambalal Patel's *Pamposh* (1954) was the first film in Gevacolour to be completely shot and processed in India. The first Technicolour film to be completely shot by an Indian was V. Shantaram's *Jhanak Jhanak Payal Baaje* (1955) with prints made abroad.

THE BENGALEE SATURDAY NOVEMBER 1, 1919

AMUSEMENTS

Cornwallis Theatre.

ELPHINSTONE BIOSCOPE
138, CORNWALLIS ST.

THE GREATEST PLAY INDIA HAS KNOWN

"BILWAMANGAL"
OR
"BHAGAT SOORDAS"

ON THE SCREEN
ON THE SCREEN

ELPHINSTONE BIOSCOPE CO.

MISS GOHUR
MISS GOHUR

Above: A still from *Sairandhri* (1933); *Above left*: *Kisan Kanya* poster; *Above right*: Advertisement for *Bilwamangal*

First box office hit

Dadasaheb Phalke's *Lanka Dahan* (1917), which ran for 23 weeks, was India's first box office hit. It is on record that the money collected at the ticket counters had to be transported in bullock carts protected by armed guards!

QR code for *Lanka Dahan*

First censor boards

• The first film censor boards were set up in Bombay, Calcutta, and Madras (now Chennai) in 1920.

• Film censorship was centralized under a central board, the Central Board of Film Certification (CBFC) in Bombay, Maharashtra, in 1951.

First women on screen

Durgabai Gokhale and her daughter Kamalabai Gokhale were the first women to feature as actors as part of Dadasaheb Phalke's film, *Mohini Bhasmasur* (1913). Prior to this, male actors played female roles as well, such as A. Salunke in *Raja Harishchandra*.

First film in 70 mm

• The first Indian film in 70 mm (using the blowing-up method) was director Pachhi's *Around the World*, starring Raj Kapoor and Rajshree, in 1967. It was in Technicolor and had stereophonic sound.

• G.P. Sippy's multi-starrer blockbuster *Sholay* in 1975 was shot on the 70 mm format in India, along with stereophonic soundtrack, the four channels of which could be connected to amplifiers in cinema theatres. Those not equipped for it were provided flat (35 mm) single-track prints.

• Tarachand Barjatya's *Maine Pyar Kiya* (1989) was made in Cinemascope with a new system of four-track magnetic stereophonic sound. This could be fitted in theatres. Later, mobile equipment was provided for the stereophonic effect in small towns and touring cinemas.

Above: Raj Kapoor; *Below*: A set depicting elements from *Sholay* in Dubai

TRAVELLING TALES

An itinerary of 26 places (real and imaginary) that have been made iconic by films, or made films iconic, made the travel bug bite people. Or put them off travel forever!

1 **New Zealand's Canterbury Plains** (172.1007° E) was the location where a *Kaho Naa... Pyaar Hai* song was shot and could be the easternmost location for a Bollywood film.

2 Indian cinema's first tryst with The Land of the Rising Sun – and its capital **Tokyo** – happened via *Love in Tokyo* (1966), a classic Bollywood romcom that gave the vicarious pleasure of an exotic international location to a largely unexposed Indian audience.

3 The seven North-Eastern states have been under-represented in Indian cinema, with only a few examples of cinema from outside these states being shot here. **Assam**: *Ek Pal* (1986), *Dil Se* (1998). **Meghalaya**: *Rock On 2* (2016), *Anek* (2022). **Nagaland**: *Saaya* (2003), *Neelakasham Pachakadal Chuvanna Bhoomi* (2013), *Paatal Lok Season 2* (2025). **Arunachal Pradesh**: *Koyla* (1997). *Rangoon* (2017), *Bhediya* (2022).

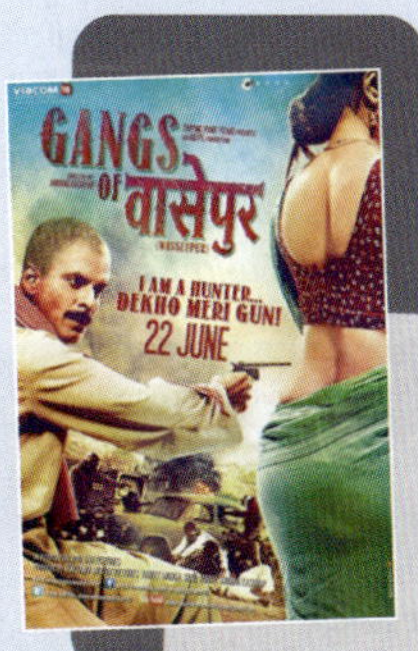

4 **Wasseypur** is a suburb of Jharkhand's Dhanbad but received unprecedented attention – both positive and negative – when Anurag Kashyap's *Gangs of Wasseypur* (2012) exploded as a cult classic and joined neighbourhoods like (*Shootout at*) Lokhandwala and Wadala to have featured in a movie title.

5 **Pollachi taluk** in **Tamil Nadu** is estimated to be the location of some 5,000 Tamil films – including full sequences, songs or parts thereof, and village scenes. Starting with MGR's *Malaikkallan* (1954), it has hosted many classic and even TV serials and advertisements.

6 Ooty in **Tamil Nadu** is yet another super-popular destination for Hindi and Tamil movies that started with *Anbe Vaa* (1966) but really exploded when Bollywood star Mithun Chakraborty shifted here and offered his Hotel Monarch for the crew to stay in and use the surroundings for the films he would star in. It is estimated that a staggering 75 films starring Mithun were shot here.

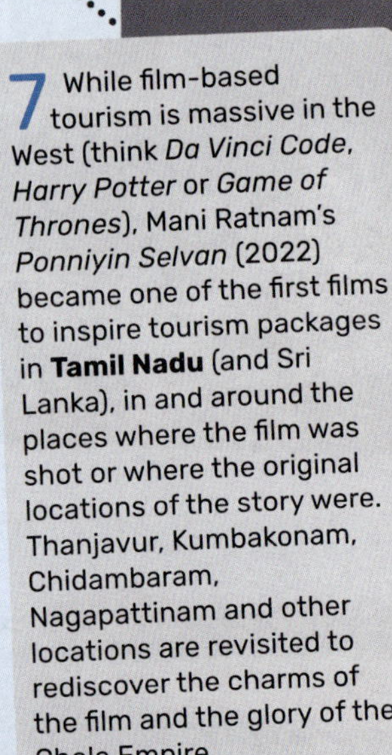

7 While film-based tourism is massive in the West (think *Da Vinci Code*, *Harry Potter* or *Game of Thrones*), Mani Ratnam's *Ponniyin Selvan* (2022) became one of the first films to inspire tourism packages in **Tamil Nadu** (and Sri Lanka), in and around the places where the film was shot or where the original locations of the story were. Thanjavur, Kumbakonam, Chidambaram, Nagapattinam and other locations are revisited to rediscover the charms of the film and the glory of the Chola Empire.

8 Originally called **Devil's Kitchen** near **Kodaikanal**, the caves became known as Guna Caves after Kamal Haasan-starrer *Guna* (1991) was shot here. The caves' deep recesses have led to many visitors going missing and only one person survived. This tale became the central premise of *Manjummel Boys* (2024) – the second highest grossing Malayalam film of all time. Immediately afterwards, tourism shot up and nearly 1 lakh visitors thronged the caves in February 2024, the month of the film's release.

9 It is an interesting coincidence that the fictional village of Ramgarh was located in a real location called **Ramanagaram**, 50 kms from Bangalore, and now considered an iconic place thanks to the monumental success of *Sholay*. Ramesh Sippy placed his dacoit tale far away from the ravines of Chambal, amidst the massive boulder-filled terrain of Karnataka. Writer Javed Akhtar has said Ramgarh is located 'somewhere between Meerut and Mexico' and the imposing landscape of Ramanagaram made us believe that.

10 Mysore has Vrindavan Gardens, a grand location for songs and dances for films in Hindi and most South Indian languages as well. Mysore was also the location for Bharatiraja's *16 Vayathinile* (1977) – a benchmark for realistic depictions of the rural – which is considered as the first Tamil film to be shot mostly outdoors, a major departure because Tamil cinema shot in studios till then.

11 Goa is not new territory for Hindi cinema, with filmmakers hopping on to a *Bombay to Goa* bus or telling the story of the state's Liberation. Farhan Akhtar's *Dil Chahta Hai* made Goa super-cool and aspirational, when he got his three protagonists to spend a few luxurious days on its beaches and shacks. Their banter while lounging on the ramparts of Chapora Fort made the destination super popular as the 'DCH Fort'.

12 Marine Drive. Gateway of India. Jahangir Art Gallery. Churchgate. The local train. Dharavi. Juhu chowpatty. Hiranandani. Arrey Colony. The nerve centre of Bollywood – **Bombay, (now Mumbai)** – is the most frequent location for Hindi cinema. It is the allure of this *mayanagari* that attracts as many jobseekers as it does tourists. People who spend hours in front of a Jalsa or a Mannat, hoping to own the city one day!

13 In Satyajit Ray's *Shonar Kella* (*The Golden Fortress*), a young boy seemed to remember a golden fortress from his previous birth, which led to him, a doctor, two miscreants and a Bengali detective landing up in **Jaisalmer** in **Rajasthan**. Popular sleuth Feluda identified the 'gold' to be the brightly coloured sandstone found in the region and the film triggered off a tourism craze among Bengalis that is continuing unabated.

14 The giant-size Hanuman image overlooking an overhead Metro line is the most famous image of **Delhi** in Indian cinema. Be it Chandni Chowk of *Delhi 6*, or the statuesque Akashvani Bhavan in *Rang De Basanti*, or the verdant Talkatora Gardens in *Chashm E Buddoor*, or Central Delhi in *Dil Se*, or the courts in so many legal thrillers... the national capital is one of the most frequent venues of our films.

16 ...Mani Ratnam's *Roja* – which was shot in **Manali** (among other places). It's ironic that a film that brought Kashmir back into cinema was not shot in the state. **Himachal Pradesh** (especially its capital, Shimla) was the location for *Love in Simla*, *Black*, *Jab We Met*, *Yeh Jawaani Hai Deewani*, *Animal* and many others.

15 The first Indian film to be shot in **Kashmir** was *Junglee* (1961) starring Shammi Kapoor and Saira Banu, which opened the floodgates for commercial filmmakers to make a beeline for the Heaven on Earth. This continued unabated till the 1980s when unrest in Kashmir halted film shooting. After that, films set in Kashmir explored the insurgency and the troubled times of the state including Vidhu Vinod Chopra's *Mission Kashmir* or...

18 The rough and rugged **Afghanistan** first became the location of a Bollywood when Feroze Khan landed there to shoot *Dharmatma* (1975). In the early 1990s, Mukul S. Anand shot *Khuda Gawah* in Afghanistan and then President Najibullah was such a fan of Amitabh Bachchan that he deployed the Afghan Air Force to provide security for the superstar.

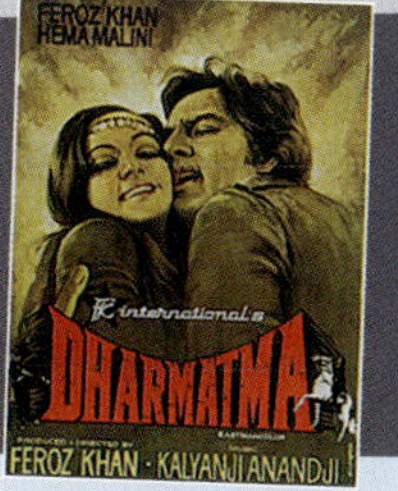

17 Chetan Anand was supposed to direct his home production, *Guide*, when he got to know that he had received permission to shoot in **Ladakh** for his war-drama *Haqeeqat* (1964) that became the first Indian film to shoot there. The icy desert was the location for his grim and gritty film based on the 1962 Sino-Indian war. More than forty years later, Rajkumar Hirani's hero in *3 Idiots* ran a school in Ladakh and reunited with his friends on the banks of Pangong Lake and this time, Ladakh was a bright, optimistic shade of blue.

21 The city of **Rovaniemi** in **Finland** (66.5039° N, 25.7294° E) is on the Arctic Circle and is the northernmost location where an Indian film has been shot. Siddharth Anand's *War* placed a high-voltage car chase in this stunning expanse of white snow. This narrowly beats Iceland's Sólheimasandur (63.4595° N, 19.3646° W) – made famous by the wreckage of a crashed DC3 aircraft – where Shah Rukh Khan and Kajol filmed the song *Gerua* in the film *Dilwale*.

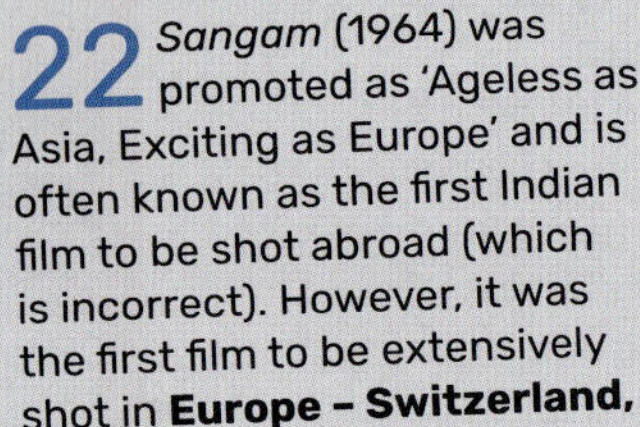

22 *Sangam* (1964) was promoted as 'Ageless as Asia, Exciting as Europe' and is often known as the first Indian film to be shot abroad (which is incorrect). However, it was the first film to be extensively shot in **Europe – Switzerland, France,** and the **UK** – thus kicking off a craze for foreign locales in Bollywood.

23 Ten years before *Sangam*, director Hirendra Kumar Basu took his film *Naaz* (1954) to **Egypt** on an ocean liner. Ashok Kumar and Nalini Jaywant played out a rich-girl-poor-boy romance in the presence of the Sphinx, with Kumar scorching the screen with his bare-chested shenanigans!

20 **Switzerland's Interlaken** has – among other things – a life-sized statue of Yash Chopra, which was installed by the tourism department and is a worthy tribute to the man who singlehandedly kick started the Indian tourism boom to Switzerland. Some of Chopra's 1980s films (*Faasle*, *Chandni* etc.) had key songs or scenes in Switzerland and with *Dilwale Dulhania Le Jayenge*, it became a rage.

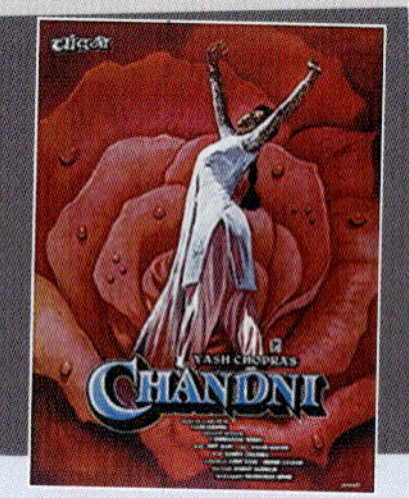

24 Even *Naaz* was not the first Indian film to go abroad. That distinction belongs to director Hirendra Kumar Basu's *Afrika Mein Hind* (1939), who was invited by freedom fighter Seth Govind Das to shoot a film about the early Indian settlers who reached Africa to trade – even before Western people. Shot entirely on location in **Kenya** and **Tanzania**, the crew witnessed several incidents of racism before managing to complete filming and return.

19 When Zoya Akhtar took her three heroes on a road trip around **Spain** in *Zindagi Na Milegi Dobara*, the country's tourism department didn't know what they had bargained for. The trip around Barcelona, Costa Brava, Buñol, Seville, and Pamplona led to a doubling of Indian tourists in the very first year after the film – and a healthy increase every year after that.

25 The fitting way to showcase the most beautiful woman in the world would be to film her around the **Seven Wonders of the World**. Shankar's *Jeans* (1998) did exactly that when they took Aishwarya Rai and Prashanth on a 30-day tour to shoot the song *'Poovukkul'* at the Taj Mahal, the Eiffel Tower, the Colosseum, the Leaning Tower of Pisa, the Empire State Building, the Pyramids, and the Great Wall of China.

26 Raj Kapoor was stranded with just eight dollars during this trip ***Around the World*** (1967) which was all about him (kind of) circumnavigating the Earth for a pittance. He managed to cover Niagara Falls and Disneyland in the USA, while putting Japan, Canada and the Caribbean, Islands (where he met legendary West Indies cricket captain, Frank Worrell).

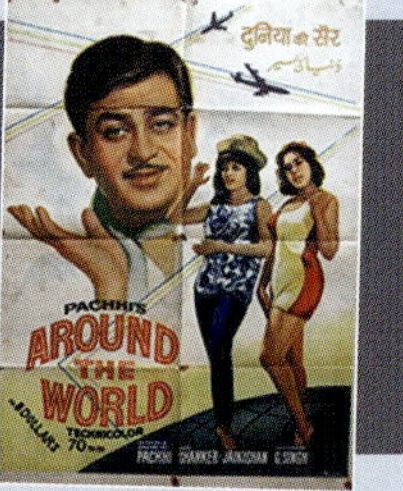

First feature film to be shot on indigenous camera

Baburao Painter (and his brother Anandrao) were inspired by Phalke and they built a camera entirely by themselves and shot *Sairandhri* that was released in 1920 after a lot of hardship. (This film was also the first time a film was censored as the themes were perceived to be anti-British by the censors)

First recorded film song

The song 'De de Khuda ke Naam Pyaare' from *Alam Ara* was the first recorded song and was sung by W.M. Khan.

First animated film

Directed by R.C. Boral, *On a Moonlit Night* (1934) was the first Indian animated film with a soundtrack.

First cinemascope films

- Guru Dutt made *Kaagaz Ke Phool* in 1959 in black-and-white Cinemascope.
- Mahesh Kaul made *Pyar Ki Pyaas* in Cinemascope and colour in 1961.

First film with background music

The film *Chandidas* (Bengali) introduced the concept of background music in 1932.

QR code for *Chandidas*

First 3D film

My Dear Kuttichathan (1984), produced by M.C. Punoos and directed by his son, Jijo, was the first Indian 3D. It was a Malayalam-language film.

First use of surround sound

Khuda Gawah (1992), when screened in big cities, used stereophonic four-track sound with special gadgets fitted into theatre walls and ceilings. This gave the impression of sound surrounding the audience, to give more impact to scenes of fights, horse riding, and the Afghan game of *buzkashi*, among others.

LANGUAGE

First film in multilingual versions

J.B.H. Wadia's *Court Dancer* (*Raj Nartaki*), directed by Madhu Bose and featuring Sadhana Bose and Prithviraj Kapoor, was shot in Hindi, Bengali, and English in 1941.

QR code for *Raj Nartaki*

First Films in Different Languages/Dialects

Language	Dialects	Film Year Of Release
Assamese	*Joymoti*	1935
Bengali	*Dena Paona*	1931
Bruj	*Brij Bhumi*	1982
Garhwali	*Jagwal*	1983
Haryanvi	*Bahurani*	1983
Hindi	*Raja Harishchandra*	1913
Kashmiri	*Naizraat*	1964
Konkani	*Suzanne*	1982
Maithili	*Mamta Gawae Geet*	1982
Odia	*Sita Bibaha*	1934
Rajasthani	*Jeevi Rabaran*	1981

First Indian film in English

Ardeshir Irani's *Noor Jahan*, directed by Ezra Mir in 1931, starring Mazhar Khan, Nayampally, Mubarak, and Vimala, was given an English version a year later for foreign markets.

Films edited in most languages/dialects

A. Sreekar Prasad from Chennai, Tamil Nadu, has edited films in 17 languages/dialects English, Hindi, Tamil, Telugu, Malayalam, Kannada, Odia, Assamese, Bengali, Punjabi, Nepali, Marathi, Sinhalese, Karbi, Mishing, Bodo, and Pangchenpa.

INTERNATIONAL

First Academy Award

Bhanu Athaiya (1929–2020) became the first Indian to win an Academy Award (Oscar) in 1983. She designed the costumes for the acclaimed film *Gandhi* (1982), directed by Sir Richard Attenborough.

First to act in a Hollywood film

The first Indian actor to feature in a role that was credited in a Hollywood movie was Dastagir, who was also known as 'Sabu' in the film world. He hailed from the princely state of Mysore (now Mysuru), Karnataka. He acted in Robert Flaherty's film *Elephant Boy* (1937). His other films included *The Thief of Baghdad* (1940), and *Jungle Book* (1942).

First Indian winner of the Legion d'Honneur

Satyajit Ray is the only Indian film personality to be awarded the Commandeur level of France's highest civilian award, the Legion d'Honneur, on 2 February 1989 – one of only two film-makers in the world to have received it. He is also the only Indian filmmaker to receive the Magsaysay Award.

Satyajit Ray

First South Asian to win the Pardo alla Carriera

Shah Rukh Khan won the coveted Pardo alla Carriera Award, the first South Asian to win it, on 10 August 2024. He received it at the 77th Locarno Film Festival in Switzerland. Also known as the Career Leopard, it is a lifetime achievement award for contributions to cinema and collective imagination.

A still from *Seeta* by East India Films Co.

First foreign film award
The film *Seeta* (1934) by East India Films Co., Calcutta, which was directed by Debaki Bose, was the first film from India to win the gold medal at the Third International Exhibition of Cinematographic Art in Venice, Italy, in 1935.

First Academy Award for Best Documentary (short subject)
The Elephant Whisperers, directed by Kartiki Gonsalves, was awarded the Best Documentary (short subject) award at the 95th Academy Awards held on 13 March 2023 in Los Angeles, US.

PERFORMANCE

First woman stunt actor
Nadia, India's legendary woman stunt actor, has been described as 'Zorro, Tarzan, and John Wayne rolled into one'. Born Mary Evans, she swung from chandeliers, jumped from moving trains, and performed many other incredible stunts that earned her the title of 'Fearless Nadia'. Her best-known film is the 1935 hit, *Hunterwali*.

Oldest debut actor in a film
Ninety-three-year-old Chinnakrishnan Kaliyaperumal from Ariyalur, Tamil Nadu, acted as the lead in the Tamil short (20-minute) film, *93* Not Out* (2016), directed by engineer-turned-film-maker Arudra Saravanakumar. It is the story of an old man who, after a pacemaker implant, has the desire to ride a cycle and to buy a book, and how he finally achieves it at the age of ninety-three. The film has won several awards, for editing, direction and more, besides a jury mention at the Dadasaheb Phalke Film Festival 2017, and has been showcased at national and international film festivals.

First double role
Dadasaheb Phalke's discovery, A. Salunke, is the first artiste to have played both hero and heroine in the same film. He played Rama and Sita in Phalke's *Lanka Dahan* in 1917. In the talkie era, Sahu Modak played the double role of a prince and a pauper in *Awara Shahzada* (Vagabond Prince) directed by Master Vithal in 1933. Neetu Singh, then known as Baby Sonia, is the only child star of India to have played a full-length double role of twin sisters in *Do Kaliyan* made in 1968.

Most roles in a single film
• Harish Raj enacted 16 roles in the Kannada film *Shri Sathyanarayana*, which released on 11 March 2016. He essayed the role of the lead character named Sathyanarayana as well as 15 other cameo roles with screen time ranging from one to five minutes for each.
• Priyanka Chopra played 12 roles (one for each sign of the zodiac) in Ashutosh Gowariker's *What's Your Raashee?* (2009).
• Kamal Haasan played 10 different roles in K.S. Ravikumar's *Dasavathaaram* (2008), including one as former US president George W. Bush.

Most films as a lead
Prem Nazir, born as Abdul Kadar in Chirayinkeezhu, Kerala, played the lead role in as many as 600 films. He starred in Malayalam, Tamil, Kannada, and Telugu films, and co-starred in films with at least 85 female actors.

WR Roles in most films
• *Women*: Manorama, a popular Tamil heroine of the 1950s and '60s, who later became a character actor, acted in over 1,000 films. Her first film was *Malayitta Mangai* (1958). Her real name was Gopishantha. She received the Padma Shri in 2002.
• *Men*: Brahmanandam Kanneganti, a well-known comedian of Telugu cinema, has received credits for acting in 1,178 films. He achieved this feat over an acting career of more than 30 years and he is still going strong. He received the Padma Shri in 2009.

WR Most pairings
Actors Prem Nazir and Sheila paired together in 107 films and hold a world record for the highest number of movies done together. They did 92 films more than the Hollywood husband–wife pair of Charles Bronson and Jill Ireland, who starred together in 15 films.

Most awards won by a film
Kaho Naa... Pyaar Hai, featuring Hrithik Roshan and Amisha Patel in lead roles and a production of Rakesh Roshan's Film Kraft Production (I) Pvt. Ltd, bagged an unprecedented 89 awards between 2000 and 2001 in various categories. The millennium's biggest blockbuster swept awards in both the national and international arena including 9 Filmfare awards, 14 Zee Cine awards, 4 Zee Sangeet awards, 10 Screen awards, 11 Sansui awards, and 9 International Indian Film Academy (IIFA) awards, among others.

Priyanka Chopra

NATIONAL FILM AWARDS - 2025

The 71 National Film Awards – given out on 23 September 2025 – honoured films released in 2023. Here is a selection of some awards.

Dadasaheb Phalke Award – Mohanlal: Affectionately called Lalettan by fans and colleagues, Mohanlal's secondary identity is as a superstar of Malayalam cinema, but that is derived from his almost unbelievably versatile career as an actor par excellence. Winner of four National Awards (including two jury awards) and countless other honours for his acting, Mohanlal's stellar run is still going strong, both on critical and commercial fronts.

Best Film – *12th Fail*: Vidhu Vinod Chopra – known for action, music, and grand spectacles in his films – made this uncharacteristically stark underdog story that was all heart and oh-so-real, tracing the struggles of a UPSC aspirant from a Chambal village to the final step in New Delhi.

Best Direction – Sudipto Sen (*The Kerala Story*): Marred by controversy during the release, run and the award, the film told a fictionalised story of the forced religious conversion of three women from Kerala and their trafficking to ISIS camps.

Best Actor – Shah Rukh Khan (*Jawan*) and Vikrant Massey (*12th Fail*): SRK's popular turn as a vigilante-police officer and Massey's acclaimed role as a real-life UPSC aspirant got them their first awards for films that created waves at the box office and in the review columns.

Best Actress – Rani Mukerji (*Mrs Chatterjee vs Norway*): Another first-time winner, Mukerji played an Indian mother fighting the might of a nation's legal and societal structure to win back custody of her children – again based on a true story.

Best Feature Film Promoting National, Social, and Environmental Values – *Sam Bahadur*: India's most loved soldier came alive in this Meghna Gulzar film where Vicky Kaushal became the character he was playing. The award-winning makeup and costumes, as well as the other elements contributed to the rousing feeling of national pride that the film brought.

Best Popular Film Providing Wholesome Entertainment – *Rocky aur Rani Kii Prem Kahaani*: Karan Johar directed this cross-cultural love story with hilarious dialogues, over-the-top acting, and flamboyant costumes, as it poked fun at patriarchy, misogyny, the 'woke culture', and the circus that is the Indian family.

Best Film in AVGC (Animation, Visual Effects, Gaming, & Comic) – *Hanu-Man*: In this newly created category (in 2022), the winner merged Indian mythology with present-day superhero narratives to create a combination that wowed audiences across languages.

Best Children's Film – *Naal 2*: The second* sequel to win this award, Sudhakar Reddy Yakkanti's film traces the journey of a little boy – with his adoptive parents – getting reunited with his biological parents and exploring the nuances of his extended family.

*The first sequel to win the Best Children's Film award was Satyajit Ray's *Joy Baba Felunath*, starring the popular detective Feluda.

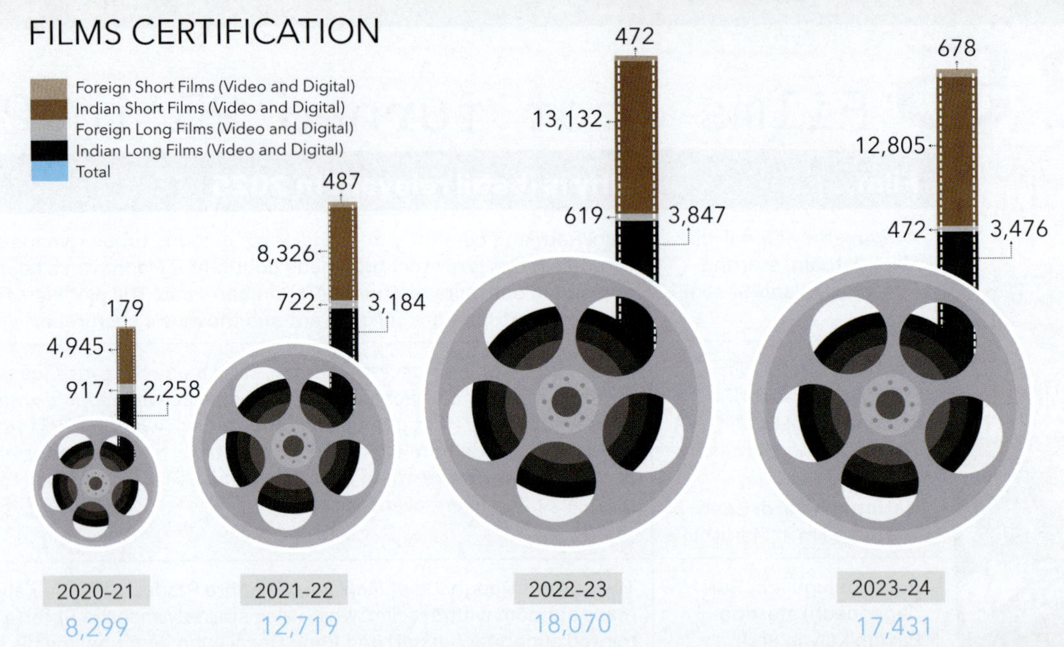

Universes in Indian Films

While sequels have always been around and popular characters became 'franchises', the concept of a Universe is comparatively new to Indian cinema. Unlike the linearity of a sequel, a universe consists of a film (with a main storyline) being overlapped by characters and events from earlier or later films. 2025 saw the release of *Lokah Chapter 1: Chandra* – a hugely successful Malayalam film starring Kalyani Priyadarshan as Chandra and the film ended with the entry of Dulqer Salman (who's also the producer) and Tovino Thomas. A mid-credits scene hinted at Thomas' character becoming the main character of Chapter 2 while Chandra might have a cameo. Here's a look at some popular film universes:

Maddock Horror Comedy Universe

With *Thamma*, the Maddock Horror Comedy Universe got its fifth instalment. The story started with *Stree* (2018) but without any indications of a universe. *Bhediya* (2022) had characters from *Stree* making appearances and the universe started falling in place. With *Munjya* (2024), *Stree 2* (2024) and *Thamma* (2025), we have a full-blown universe that has managed to reprise Indian folktales and fables into modern-day thrillers – with likeable characters and identifiable locales.

Upcoming films: *Shakti Shalini, Bhediya 2, Chamunda, Stree 3, Maha Munjya, Pehla Mahayudh, Doosra Mahayudh, Chhoti Stree.*

YRF Spy Universe

YRF had produced three films – *Ek Tha Tiger, Tiger Zinda Hai,* and *War* – when the production house decided to build a universe out of the spies they had created. Shah Rukh Khan-starrer *Pathaan* (2023) had a cameo by Tiger (Salman Khan) while *Tiger 3* had cameos by SRK and Hrithik Roshan (Kabir of *War*). *War 2* didn't have any appearances, but both the Khans were mentioned and there was a cameo by another star who is likely to be a major character in the next film.

Upcoming films: *Alpha, Pathaan 2, Tiger vs Pathaan.*

Rohit Shetty Cop Universe

Rohit Shetty also started his jeep-spinning, bullet-spewing, jingoism-brewing cop films without any thought of a universe. The first *Singham* (2011) – starring Ajay Devgn – was based on a Tamil superhit and the second film Singham Returne (2014) was a straight sequel. In *Simmba* (2018) starring Ranveer Singh, Bajirao Singham made an appearance while Veer Sooryavanshi (Akshay Kumar) from a forthcoming film was teased. The subsequent films (*Sooryavanshi, Singham Again*) became a revolving door of cameos with two stars popping up in the third's film (along with others, who would – probably – appear in a future instalment).

Srijit Mukherjee Cop Universe

Bengali director Srijit Mukherji's second film, *Baise Srabon* (2011) had a disgraced ex-cop Probir Roy Chowdhury (Prosenjit Chatterjee) investigating serial murders in Kolkata along with Abhijit Pakrashi (Parambrata Chatterjee). *Dwitiyo Purush* (2020) follows Pakrashi solving yet another serial killing case that ends in a twist. In between, *Vinci Da* had Bijoy Poddar as yet another cop. *Dawshom Awbotaar* (2023), where Roy Chowdhury and Poddar tackled yet another murder mystery, was a prequel to all the above films – becoming a sort of origin story.

Upcoming films: At least two more films featuring Roy Chowdhury and Poddar.

Lokesh (Kangaraj) Cinematic Universe

Kaithi (2019) – starring Karthi – was planned loosely to become the part of a universe. *Vikram* (2022) – starring Kamal Haasan – featured the voice of Karthi and a last-scene cameo by Suriya (playing the intriguingly named Rolex). In Vijay-starrer *Leo* (2023), Haasan's voice is heard – all contributing to the anticipation for the forthcoming instalments. Given the pre-thought given to the characters and the timeline, this is likely to be the best planned universe.

Upcoming films: *Benz, Kaithi 2, Vikram Returns*, film featuring on Rolex, two spin-off shows featuring characters from *Kaithi* and *Vikram*.

25 Films that turned 25 in 2025

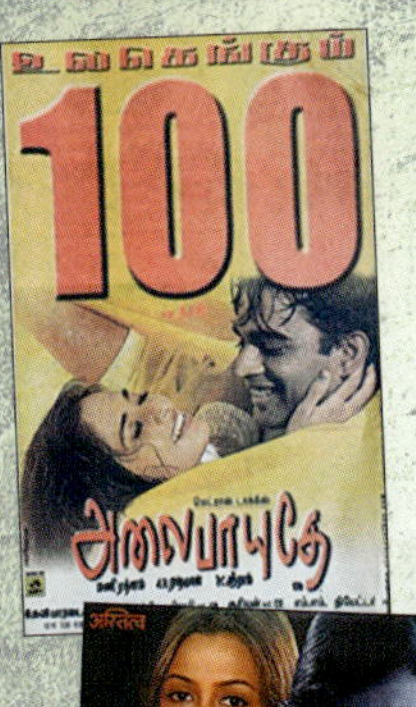

Film	Why is it still relevant in 2025
Alaipayuthey (Tamil, dir: Mani Ratnam) starring R Madhavan and Shalini	Mani Ratnam's comfort with the idiom of modern, urban romance came through in this love story that made debutant R Madhavan a heartthrob and added one more feather to AR Rahman's cap. The plot elements – living in, startups – are still relevant and the music evergreen.
Astitva (Marathi, dir: Mahesh Manjrekar) starring Tabu, Sachin Khedekar and Mohnish Behl **National Award**: Best Feature Film in Marathi	After a string of box-office successes, Tabu made her presence felt with strong performance-backed roles. What started with *Maachis* reached a peak with *Astitva* (that got her the third Critics' Award for Best Actress at Filmfare). Made from a feminist perspective, the film's performances as well as theme have stood the test of time as Tabu continues to be a premier acting talent event today.
Badri (Telugu, dir: Puri Jagannadh) starring Pawan Kalyan and Ameesha Patel	The current Deputy Chief Minister of Andhra Pradesh, Pawan Kalyan, hit mass stardom with this film, which also starred Ameesha Patel (a freshly minted superstar herself) and Renu Desai (who later became his second wife). The debutant director is also going strong – though his recent box-office performances have not been up to the mark.
Bariwali (Bengali, dir: Rituparno Ghosh) starring Kirron Kher, Roopa Ganguly and Chiranjit **National Award**: Best Actress in a Leading Role (Kirron Kher, 1999)	A film crew arrives at a sprawling, crumbling mansion to shoot a film based on Tagore's *Chokher Bali* and the reclusive landlady is suddenly thrust into a limelight. Ghosh's study of loneliness and emotional manipulation had great performances, though Kher's award was marred by the controversy of her voice being dubbed by Bengali actress, Rita Kayral.
Gaja Gamini (Hindi, dir: Maqbool Fida Husain) starring Madhuri Dixit	M.F. Husain's obsession with Madhuri Dixit started with Hum Aapke Hain Koun and culminated in this surreal film that had her travelling through time and inspiring the likes of Kalidasa and Da Vinci. An unabashed ode to the star, the film wasn't as much a story as it was a montage of how women fought oppression down the ages and inspired great art along the way.
Josh (Hindi, dir: Mansoor Khan) starring Shah Rukh Khan, Aishwarya Rai, Chandrachur Singh, Sharad Kapoor	West Side Story came to Goa as the film told the story of the tussles between the residents and the immigrants over land-grabbing. SRK and Aishwarya played twins and had a quirky chemistry, while the music topped charts. The last of Mansoor Khan's four directorial ventures, Josh was commercially successful and reasonably well-reviewed but still didn't meet the high expectations from the director and the stars.
Hera Pheri (Hindi, dir: Priyadarshan) starring Akshay Kumar, Sunil Shetty and Paresh Rawal	Remake of the Malayalam hit *Ramji Rao Speaking*, this Priyadarshan classic kickstarted Akshay Kumar's career in the comedy space and started a franchise (whose third instalment is currently in the works). However, the standout performance was by Paresh Rawal as the hilarious Baburao Ganpatrao Apte, the avaricious landlord – for which he won the Filmfare Award for Best Performance in a Comic Role.
Hey Ram (Tamil/Hindi, dir: Kamal Haasan) starring Kamal Haasan, Rani Mukerji and Shah Rukh Khan	Kamal Haasan's magnum opus travelled from the ruins of Mohen-jo-Daro to Partition-era Calcutta to Thanjavur to New Delhi, with the journey of a regular Indian becoming communalised till he comes face to face with Gandhi. While the film didn't do very well commercially, it was well received by critics and the message of communal harmony has become more relevant with time.

Film	Why is it still relevant in 2025
Kaho Naa... Pyaar Hai (Hindi, dir: Rakesh Roshan) starring Hrithik Roshan and Ameesha Patel	If instant stardom needs a case study, Hrithik Roshan is one – immediately after the release of his home production, *Kaho Naa Pyaar Hai*. Roshan's presence as a dancing-fighting-romancing superstar eclipsed pretty much everything in Hindi cinema and he still retains his starry charisma. The film became – and still holds the record for – the most awarded Indian film including Filmfare Awards for Best Film, Director, Best Actor and Male Debut. And about 80 others.
Kandukondain Kandukondain (Tamil, dir: Rajeev Menon) starring Mammooty, Ajith Kumar, Tabu, Aishwarya Rai and Abbas **National Award**: Best Male Playback Singer (Shankar Mahadevan)	Based on Jane Austen's *Sense and Sensibility*, director Rajiv Menon took a potent mix of acclaimed actors and charismatic young stars to create the intertwined love stories of two sisters. The soundtrack was sold for a then record sum and was awarded, adding to the allure of the story that flowed smoothly despite having many characters and multiple subplots.
Mohabbatein (Hindi, dir: Aditya Chopra) starring Amitabh Bachchan, Shah Rukh Khan and Aishwarya Rai	Aditya Chopra returned to the director's chair (after the record-breaking *DDLJ*) and the expectations were sky-high. His story of teenage romance in the face of parental romance was cliched, but the look was ultra-modern and lavish. The film gave a boost to Amitabh Bachchan's flagging career and launched four debutants on the way to becoming the highest grossing film of the year. It also had the highest number of nominations at the year's Filmfare Awards.
Mission Kashmir (Hindi, dir: Vidhu Vinod Chopra) starring Sanjay Dutt, Hrithik Roshan and Preity Zinta	Vidhu Vinod Chopra had signed Hrithik Roshan before his debut film had released and gave a dream role to the new star. The locales, the music and the action were all grandly mounted, while the story examined the alienation of the Kashmiri youth in the face of foreign propaganda. Chopra and Roshan are still winning awards, 25 years on.
Narasimhan (Malayalam, dir: Shaji Kailas) starring Mohanlal	This film is a (yet another) example of how Mohanlal –Dadasaheb Phalke winner in 2025 – merged acting brilliance with box-office success. *Narasimhan* earned more than 20x its budget and its dialogue ('*Nee po mone, Dinesha*') became a rage. His popularity and stature have only expanded manifold in the last 25 years.
Nuvve Kavali (Telugu, dir: K. Vijaya Bhaskar) starring Tarun, Richa Pallod **National Award**: Best Feature Film in Telugu	A sleeper hit featuring a debutant lead pair, *Nuvve Kavali* was not only the highest grossing Telugu film (at that time) but also won critical acclaim with a National Award. The lead pair – who were child artistes earlier – were charming in front of the camera, the music and dialogues became popular, all of which made a runaway hit.
Paromitar Ekdin (Bengali, dir: Aparna Sen) starring Rituparna Sengupta, Aparna Sen and Soumitra Chatterjee	Aparna Sen's film looked at the unusual relationship between a mother-in-law and daughter-in-law as they navigated familial responsibilities, the weight of patriarchy and the misfortunes of life. Sen herself played the mother-in-law, bringing a sympathetic view to the initially conservative woman – her talents as an actress and director both shining through.
Phir Bhi Dil Hai Hindustani (Hindi, dir: Aziz Mirza) starring Shah Rukh Khan, Juhi Chawla and Paresh Rawal	Shah Rukh's first production venture didn't meet the sky-high commercial expectations from it but was surprisingly prescient about a two unscrupulous news anchors creating fake news and building a grotesque tamasha around an execution (for a fake crime). The story remains relevant, much more than the time when it first came out.
Pukar (Hindi, dir: Rajkumar Santoshi) starring Anil Kapoor, Madhuri Dixit **National Award**: Best Feature Film on National Integration, Best Actor (Anil Kapoor)	A full-on masala film with song, dance, action, love triangle and a treason subplot was a surprise entrant at the National Awards this year, winning one for the leading man. Anil Kapoor and Madhuri Dixit's hit pairing continued its charm, as did Dixit's magnetism as a dancer, this time in the form of a partnership with Prabhu Deva.

Refugee (Hindi, dir: J.P. Dutta) starring Abhishek Bachchan and Kareena **National Award**: Best Music (Anu Malik), Best Lyrics (*Panchhi nadiyaan* – Javed Akhtar)	*Refugee*'s music topped the charts even before the release, but that was not the only reason for the buzz. Two scions of Hindi cinema's first two families – Abhishek Bachchan and Kareena Kapoor – made their debuts in this film, and they are both continuing to wow the audiences.
 *Sasurbari Zindabad* (Bengali, dir: Haranath Chakraborty) starring Prosenjit Chatterjee and Rituparna Sengupta	A remake of the Hindi film, *Jamai Raja* (1990), this commercial blockbuster then became the highest grossing Bengali film of all time, further enhancing the reputation of Chatterjee as the no. 1 crowd-puller in Bengali cinema. Chatterjee starred in one of the highest collection films of 2025 (*Devi Chowdhurani*) as well, while Sengupta produced and starred in the critically acclaimed *Puratawn*.
 *Vaanathaippola* (Tamil, dir: Vikraman) starring Vijayakanth **National Award:** Best Popular Film Providing Wholesome Entertainment	The most successful Tamil film of the year – buoyed by a superhit songs, great comic performances and an evergreen social plot – also received significant critical acclaim and several major awards at both state and national levels. The lead actor, Vijayakanth, known as an action star, got glowing notices for his role.
 *Utsab* (Bengali, dir: Rituparno Ghosh) starring Madhabi Mukherjee, Mamata Shankar, Prosenjit Chatterjee and Rituparna S **National Award**: Best Direction (2000)	Rituparno Ghosh's third film was an uncomfortable study of fraying familial ties as a joint family got together to celebrate Durga Puja in Kolkata. He used reigning superstars – Prosenjit and Rituparna – in difficult roles and coaxed great performances out of them – cementing his reputation as the leading Bengali director after Ray.
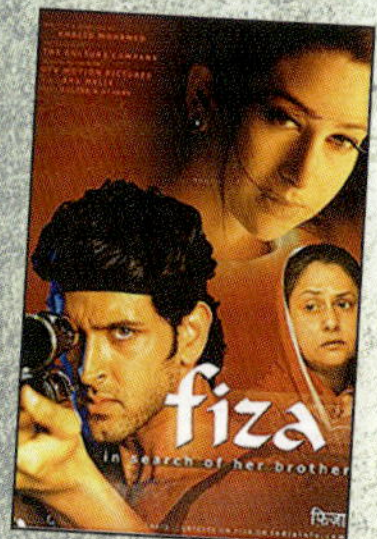 *Uttara* (Bengali, dir: Buddhadev Dasgupta) starring Tapas Paul and Jaya Seal **National Award**: Best Direction (1999)	An allegorical story about two wrestlers and their ongoing sparring as one's wife remain neglected, unfolding in a landscape of increasing communalism and injustice. Buddhadev Dasgupta brought his light lyrical touch to the film that won acclaim at national and international film festivals, the themes of religious fundamentalism and chauvinism still as relevant as ever.
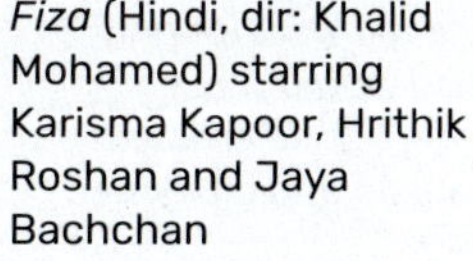 *Fiza* (Hindi, dir: Khalid Mohamed) starring Karisma Kapoor, Hrithik Roshan and Jaya Bachchan	A gut-wrenching tale of a Muslim boy, who joins a terrorist group after being unfairly targeted during the 1993 Mumbai riots, the film was conceived as a small-budget vehicle focused on the boy's sister (Fiza, played by Kapoor). With the stardom of Roshan, his role increased along with commercial elements like songs and action. Both the actresses (Kapoor and Bachchan) won Filmfare awards for their roles.
 *Bharathi* (Tamil, dir: Gnana Rajasekaran) starring Sayaji Shinde, Devayani and Nizhagal Ravi **National Award: Best** Feature Film in Tamil	A biopic of legendary Tamil poet, Subramania Bharti, starred Marathi actor – Sayaji Shinde – who made his Tamil debut a year after his breakout Hindi role (in Shool) and managed to wow critics despite the language barrier. Nearly all the lyrics of the film were taken from Bharti's poems and the poet's journey from penury to an iconic figure of Tamil Nadu is well narrated.
 *Kochu Kochu Santhoshangal* (Malayalam, dir: Sathyan A.) starring Jayaram, Lakshmi Gopalaswamy, Kalidas Jayaram **National Award:** Best Feature Film in Malayalam, Best Choreography (Kala)	The story of a cute little boy caught in the crossfire of his estranged parents, who come from different backgrounds and have different views about the mother's career ambitions. Jayaram and his real-life son, Kalidas, played the father-son duo. Kalidas won praise for this role (which was his debut) and even won a National Award for Best Child Artiste for his second film.

50 Years of NFDC

In a year that saw some of the biggest blockbusters and the most momentous films of Hindi cinema, the Government of India started NFDC (National Film Development Corporation) to foster excellence in cinema and promote the development of the film industry. The body has since then become synonymous with tastefully made and socially significant films – many of which have stood the test of time.

Film financing was not new to India. Film Finance Corporation was founded in 1960 as a state body for funding a new Indian cinema as an alternative to commercial films – giving rise to the term 'parallel cinema'. With the formation of FTII (Film and Television Institute of India) in 1961, a new breed of filmmakers – trained in the craft and aware of the global cinematic trends – started their journeys and took advantage of the state funding to create meaningful cinema. FFC had a stellar lineup of films in its portfolio as it extended production loans to classics like Satyajit Ray's *Charulata*, *Nayak*, *Goopy Gyne Bagha Byne* as well as Mrinal Sen's *Bhuvan Shome* and Mani Kaul's *Uski Roti* – all of them winning international recognition and reasonable commercial success in India. Eventually, FFC was merged into NFDC (in 1980).

NFDC's roster of films includes several National Awards for Best Film (in different languages as well as the overall prize) in almost every year from 1980 till the early 2000s. While this includes a documentary as a record for posterity (Utpalendu Chakraborty's *Music of Satyajit Ray*), a film to boost a classical language (*Adi Shankaracharya* in Sanskrit), a milestone film of a legend (Satyajit Ray's *Agantuk*), it also has a trenchant satire like *Jaane Bhi Do Yaaro* that trains its guns on governmental corruption in all forms. In a way, it is to the credit of NFDC that they produced films of quality, mostly without censorship or governmental pressure. It is also a testament to their process that almost every widely acclaimed filmmaker of India across languages have made films with NFDC.

NFDC's crowning glory came when they co-produced Richard Attenborough's *Gandhi* that swept the Oscars with eight awards. In fact, NFDC put up the first tranche – $10 million – of the budget that allowed the director to secure the balance funding from other producers.

Over the years, NFDC has also become the nodal body for organising festivals, preserving film-related archival material, and promoting India as a filmmaking destination. NFDC has produced over 300 films, though their activity and success rate have both come down a bit in the last two decades – with the advent of savvy private producers who know how to secure funding and how to generate revenue by targeting film festivals, multiplexes, television and (more recently) streaming.

In the five decades of its existence, NFDC is easily the most impactful single 'producer' of Indian cinema – almost like a port of call for established filmmakers as well as new makers starting off on their journey.

LENGTH

Most episodic films in a single feature film

BSB Films, a film-making company from Jaipur, Rajasthan, made a Hindi-language film, titled *Prabhu Mahaveer Ki Divyavani,* under their banner. The film features 23 episodic films as part of it, the highest in a single feature film. The film has a total duration of 157 mins and 27 secs and was released on 30 September 2021.

Longest use of reused archival footage

Camellia Productions Pvt Ltd, a film production company in Kolkata used recycled footage of Uttam Kumar from his previous films for 24 minutes 48 seconds in their film, *Oti Uttam* (2024). It was directed by Srijit Mukherji.

Films with longest footage

• Vithalbhai Jhaveri's documentary on Mahatma Gandhi, *Mahatma: Life of Gandhi, 1869–1948* (1968), was 5 hrs 30 mins long, and was broken up into many segments for general screening.
• R.K. Films' productions *Mera Naam Joker* (1970) that had a runtime of 248 minutes, along with *Sangam* (1964) with a run time of 238 minutes, were the first to be run with two intervals.

MUSIC

Most songs recorded in a day

In 1993, playback singer Kumar Sanu recorded 28 songs in a single day at the Musicians Studio in the Juhu area in Mumbai, Maharashtra. The session was made for Sterling Records and Cassettes and the chief recordist was Vishram More, who was on the machines for 24 hours.

WR Most number of songs in a Hindi film

Indra Sabha, made in 1932, featured 71 songs. Based on an Urdu play and opera written by Agha Hasan Amanat and first staged in 1853, the 211-minute long film was made by Jamshedji Framji Madan's company, Madan Theatre.

WR Most prolific lyricist

Shitala Pande, better known as Sameer 'Anjaan', holds the world record for writing lyrics for the most number of songs. Starting in 1983 with the Hindi film *Bekhabar*, he had written lyrics for 3,524 songs for Hindi and Bhojpuri films by 15 December 2015. He has also written lyrics for music albums. He has done the highest number of films (146) with the music director duo Anand–Milind, writing around 899 songs for them.

MAKERS

First woman film-maker

The first woman to produce, direct, and script a film in the silent era was Fatma Begum. She formed the Fatma Film Corporation and made *Bulbule Paristan* in 1926.

Most film-making aspects handled

Narasimha Raju from Bengaluru, Karnataka, handled 18 segments of film-making for the Kannada film *The Fire* (2017). He was credited for direction, story, screenplay, dialogues, fight, stunt, direction of cinematography, editing, special effects, grading, Digital intermediate (DI), sound, dubbing, voice dubbing, Background music (BGM) placing, re-recording, poster design, and acting in the film. The 113-minute film participated in the 10th Bengaluru International Film Festival in March 2018.

WR Largest film poster

Global United Media Co. Ltd, in collaboration with Impresario Event Management (I) Ltd, unveiled a 75.28 m (247 ft) long and 63.39 m (208 ft) wide poster of *Baahubali,* to mark the launch of the film's Malayalam audio, at the Sacred Heart College football field in Thevara, Kochi, Kerala, on 27 June 2015. The poster, designed by the director of the movie, S.S. Rajamouli, and made by Sign Maker Digital Solution at Vyttila, Kochi, took 30 hrs to print.

WR Tallest film cut-out

The world's tallest cut-out – 65.5 m (215 ft) high – advertised a film in Thiruttani town, Tiruvallur District, Tamil Nadu. It featured actor Suriya (in a folded *veshti*, holding a flaming torch) to promote his film *Nandha Goalan Kumaran (NGK)* in 2019.

WR Largest film city/studio

Ramoji Film City in Hyderabad, Telangana, spread over a little more than 1,666 acres (674 hectares), is the largest film city/studio in the world. It has sound stages and permanent sets ranging from railway stations and temples to gardens and residential streets, among others. It is also a tourist attraction because of its unique cinema-like experience.

Highest number of screens

RRR – a period drama about two legendary revolutionaries and their journeys and directed by S.S. Rajamouli – was released worldwide on over 10,200 screens.

Most tickets booked in advance

BookMyShow, a ticket-booking app, saw a record sale of advance tickets when it sold over a million tickets online in a day. The tickets for Marvel's *Avengers: Endgame* were booked in a manic frenzy as soon as they were available on 22 April 2019. The sale averaged about 18 tickets per second!

Most films produced

Well-known director and producer of Telugu films, Dr D. Ramanaidu holds the record of having produced 110 films (including 11 dubbed films) in six languages over a span of 36 years. He started his career with *Anuragam* in 1963.

Most feature films directed

Dr Dasari Narayana Rao (1947–2017) has directed 148 films. Among women, Vijaya Nirmala has directed 35 films in Telugu and Tamil.

Most horror films produced

The seven Ramsay brothers – Kumar, Keshu, Tulsi, Kiran, Shyam, Gangu, and Arjun – made more than 30 horror films on low budgets, of which the well-known ones are *Purana Mandir* (1984), *Veerana* (1988), and *Purani Haveli* (1989).

WR Longest-running film

Yash Raj Films' *Dilwale Dulhania Le Jayenge* (*DDLJ*) is still running at Mumbai's Maratha Mandir theatre – thirty years after the film premiered there. The single show at 11:30 a.m. is the result of an arrangement between Yash Raj and the theatre, which agreed to run the film there for (what seems like) eternity. But even before the arrangement, *DDLJ* ran to semi-packed houses for over two decades, making it the longest-running film in the world.

PHOTOGRAPHY

First commercial photographer

Lala Deen Dayal of Hyderabad, the 'photographer of kings', is India's best-known photographer from the British times. His career began in the mid-1870s, and he went on to set up studios in three cities in three different states – Indore, Madhya Pradesh; Bombay, Maharashtra; and Hyderabad (now in Telangana). He was appointed the photographer to the viceroy of India in 1885. His lens captured India's rich culture, architecture, and landscapes.

Earliest recorded commercial album

A gilded and bound album of a hundred photographs of Indian buildings, scenery, races, costumes, and bazaar incidents was sold for ₹12 in Bombay in 1884. It used to be a popular souvenir among the British.

Earliest book on photography

Pagoda Hallibee written by R.B. Gakley in 1859 was the first book on photography published in India.

First use of the daguerreotype

Within a year of its first use in England, the daguerreotype (early photography process using an iodine-sensitized silvered plate and mercury vapour) was used in Calcutta, in January 1840. It was brought to document India's architecture and landscape.

Earliest commercial studio

Bourne and Shepherd was well known for its studio portraits of the ruling classes, both Indian and British. Its photographers attended royal events, state visits and the imperial durbars of 1877, 1903, and 1911. After Independence, Bourne and Shepherd was bought over by Indian proprietors, who operated under the same name in Calcutta. The studio was closed down on 20 April 2016 after 176 years of operations.

First woman photojournalist

Homai Vyarawalla (1913–2012), born into a priestly family in Navsari, Gujarat, in December 1913, was the first Indian woman photojournalist to document Indian life. Her very first photographs were published in *Bombay Chronicle* in 1936. She and her husband even covered wartime activities for *The Illustrated Weekly of India* and the *Far Eastern Bureau* of the British Information Service. *Life* and *Time* magazines also featured her photographs of the Indian independence movement.

First photo exhibition

The first All-India Photographic Exhibition Bourne and Shepherd was organized by the Photographic Society of India in Bombay, in 1856. The exhibition was inaugurated by the then governor general of India, Lord Canning.

WR Largest camera museum

The Museo Camera Centre for the Photographic Arts, Gurugram, Haryana, houses more than 2,500 cameras, which is the world's largest collection of vintage and other cameras on display. Inaugurated on 27 September 2019, it is spread over 1,672.2 sq m (18,000 sq ft) of built-up space and can accommodate up to 200 visitors at a time. It is a collaboration between acclaimed photographer Aditya Arya and the Municipal Corporation of Gurugram.

First Kodak Express outlet

Established in 1978, Skylab was the first colour lab in suburban Bombay. Initially the lab catered to advertising agencies, but gradually the focus shifted to providing a photo colour lab and studio for amateurs and ordinary people.

First photo film-manufacturing company

Hindustan Photo Films Manufacturing Co. (HPF), a public sector unit, was set up in 1960 at Ooty (now Udhagamandalam), Tamil Nadu, to make photosensitive materials for the Indian film industry, still photography, and X-ray films for medical and industrial use. It introduced the Indu brand of raw film.

First personal studio

Maharaja Sawai Man Singh of Jaipur, Rajasthan, was a nineteenth-century amateur photographer. Thousands of photographic plates of his work were discovered in the 1980s in the storerooms of the City Palace in Jaipur. He recorded the life of the people in his state.

Oldest extant portrait studio

Sir Victor Sassoon, who was passionate about photography and constructed many public buildings in Bombay, set up Hamilton Studios in the E.D. Sassoon Building, which he owned, in 1928. Photography sessions at these studios were held by appointment, and the rich and famous personalities of Bombay were seen coming for quick and glamorous shoots. Currently, the studios are run by Ajita Madhavji and can be found in Ballard Estate.

First photographic society

The Bombay Photographic Society was founded in October 1854 with British captain Harry J. Barr as its first president. It had more than 200 people as members, many of them Indian. Divisions in Madras and Bengal followed in 1856.

First course in photography

The first photography course began in Elphinstone College, Bombay, in 1855. The J.J. School of Art, Bombay, and the Madras School of Art, Madras, Tamil Nadu, began similar courses around the same time.

Largest unit for photo production/distribution

The Photo Division, Press Information Bureau, under the Ministry of Information and Broadcasting, Government of India, provides photographs to media units, and Central and state government departments. In the year 2023–24, it acquired 6,95,776 digital images in-house and supplied 2,541 digital prints.

WR Largest collection of cameras
Dilish Parekh, a photojournalist from Mumbai, has a collection of 4,425 cameras, some dating back to 1906. It includes brands such as Leica, Nikon, Kodak, Canon, Hasselblad, and Royal Mail Postage, besides types such as watch, binocular, and button cameras. He began the collection in 1977 with 600 cameras given to him by his grandfather.

Marathon photography – city/structures
Hariohm N. Gurjar from Vadodara, Gujarat, set out to document his city's various dimensions at 7:00 a.m. on 14 March 2014. He travelled 95 km in the city, shooting Elphinstone College, Bombay for 13 hrs. He captured 3,555 unduplicated images of people, architecture, markets, monuments, and more.

Marathon photography – models
Photographer Vivek Ashok Somani from Surat, Gujarat, conducted a marathon photo shoot on 12 May 2019. He clicked 11,076 photographs in 15 hrs 55 mins. Using a Nikon D5300 camera, and an 18–55 mm lens, he photographed 70 models at Future Dance Studio, Surat.

Most people in a selfie
On 26 March 2016, during Ragam, the annual cultural festival at the National Institute of Technology Calicut (NITC) in Kozhikode, Kerala, actor Sreenath Bhasi clicked a selfie with a camera mounted on a selfie stick at the open-air theatre on the campus, with 2,151 students.

AWARDS AND HONOURS

First to receive the Hasselblad Award
Dayanita Singh from New Delhi became the first Indian and the first South Asian laureate to receive the Hasselblad Award. She was handed the award on 14 October 2022 in a ceremony held in Gothenburg, Sweden. She won two million Swedish krona, becoming the first to receive the prize since it was upgraded. Awarded annually since 1982, the Hasselblad Award is considered to be one of the most prestigious awards in photography worldwide. Dayanita received commendation for her 'mobile museums' (she uses objects that allow for the artwork to be constantly arranged and rearranged) in the official citation for the award.

First Indian fellow of the British Photographic Society
Sir Prodyot Coomar Tagore, a prominent landowner of the time in Calcutta, was an art collector besides being a keen photographer. He was the first Indian to be elected a Fellow of the British Photographic Society in 1896. He had a studio in his Tagore Castle home and exhibited his works. He was the founder and first president of the Academy of Fine Arts, Calcutta.

First Asian to win the International Photography Awards
Sharad Haksar from Chennai, Tamil Nadu, won one gold, one silver, two bronzes, and 21 nominations in the International Photography Awards 2004. India finished fourth behind the US, the UK, and Canada.

First winner of the Wildlife Photographer of the Year title
The Wildlife Photographer of the Year, organized by the Natural History Museum, London, UK, is one of the most famed contests in the world. Rajesh Bedi became the first Indian to win the grand title in 1986 for his photograph of the Asiatic black bear.

First winners of the Pulitzer Prize for feature photography
- Anushree Fadnavis and Adnan Abidi were part of the Reuters team that won in the 'Breaking News Photography' category of the Pulitzer Prize for photography in 2020, for their work on the Hong Kong protests.
- Dar Yasin, Mukhtar Khan, and Channi Anand from Associated Press won in the 'Feature Photography' category of the Pulitzer Prize for photography in 2020 for their coverage of Jammu and Kashmir.

WR First winner of the Académie des Beaux-Arts Photography Award – William Klein
Raghu Rai won the first-ever Académie des Beaux-Arts Photography Award – William Klein (Fine Arts Academy award for Photography). He was named the laureate and was awarded the prize at the Palais de l'Institut de France on 30 October 2019. The award carries a prize money of € 1,20,000 (approximately ₹10.79 crore). It was instated in honour of William Klein, a celebrated US-born French photographer and film-maker.

WR First permanent photo exhibition in space
Dr Hersh Chadha is the first person to organize a permanent photo exhibition in space on the International Space Station (ISS). Five images of different flowers were sent to the ISS on 16 October 2016 with the ISS 49/50 team. The purpose of this was to help the astronauts staying in space for months to remain connected with nature. On 1 March

Paintings at Ajanta Caves

2017, Dr Chadha was honoured by the Yuri Gagarin Cosmonaut Training Centre, Russia, for this.

PAINTING AND CRAFT

FIRSTS AND EARLIESTS

Earliest use of tempera method

The Ajanta Caves are rock-cut Buddhist cave monuments in Aurangabad, Maharashtra, dating back from the 2nd century BCE to about 650 CE. The paintings in these caves used the tempera method. In this technique the rough mud plaster containing some organic matter like cow dung and animal hair was first pressed on the surface of the rocks and then a coat of fine lime plaster was laid all over it. This layer was allowed to dry thoroughly before applying colour on it. The scenes represented in these caves are mostly from Buddhist texts and events from the Buddha's life.

First auction of contemporary Indian paintings abroad

Sotheby's hosted the first-ever auction of contemporary Indian paintings in New York, US, on 12 June 1995. The 38 artists whose works were displayed included Jogen Chowdhury, M.F. Husain, Arpita Singh, Ganesh Pyne, S.H. Raza, and Jamini Roy.

Earliest rock paintings

The largest and the oldest collection of rock paintings in India is at Bhimbetka, about 46 km from Bhopal, Madhya Pradesh. The paintings, found in more than 700 rock shelters dated to around 30,000 years ago, depict people's everyday lives such as hunting, dancing, and decoration of bodies.

Oldest extant murals

Two 1,000-year-old Chola paintings, which were found at the Brihadeeswarar Temple in Thanjavur, Tamil Nadu, are believed to be the oldest existing mural paintings. They depict two women who are watching a procession from a balcony.

First painting gallery

Maharaja Ram Singh, a nineteenth-century king of Jaipur, built a unique hall in the garden of the Ram Niwas Bagh Palace. It was fully displayed with paintings and called the Ram Vilas. The walls of this hall were covered with imitations of several Greek, Roman, Persian, and Chinese paintings.

First realist painter
Raja Ravi Varma (1848–1906) from the princely state of Travancore (now in Kerala) painted themes mainly from Indian mythology and legends in the realistic style of the West, making him the first realist painter in the country and the pioneer of a new movement in Indian art. In 1904, the then viceroy Lord Curzon bestowed the Kaisari-i-Hind Gold Medal on him.

Raja Ravi Varma

Scenes from the Ramayan

Goddess Lakshmi

Scene from the Mahabharat

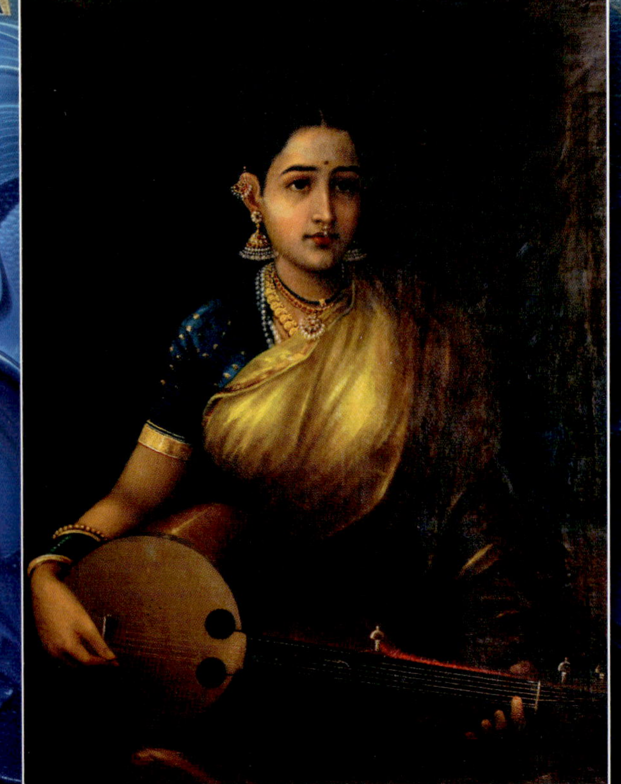

Lady playing the swarbat

The Maharashtrian Lady

Earliest paintings discovered

Painted pottery, mostly in fragments, excavated at Mohenjo-daro, Chanhu-Daro, Harappa, and other places in the Indus Valley, are dated to 3000–2250 BCE.

First fine arts exhibition

The first fine arts exhibition was held in the Public Library, Calcutta, on 1 February 1831, by the Brush Club, with paintings drawn by foreign artists in India.

Lalit Kala Akademi, Delhi

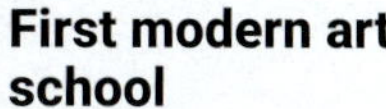

First modern art school

The Mechanical Institute was founded by Frederick Corbyn and Tarapada Chakrabarty in Calcutta, on 2 February 1839. First named Society for the Promotion of Industrial Art, it was finally called the School of Industrial Art on 16 August 1854. It held its first exhibition from 22 January to 3 February 1855.

Frederick Corbyn

First art summit

The first India Art Summit was held at Pragati Maidan, New Delhi, during 22–24 August 2008. The 34 exhibition galleries exhibited over 550 artworks and sold more than half of them. The summit was brought to India by Hanmer MS&L Communications Pvt. Ltd.

First academy for visual arts

The Lalit Kala Akademi, which was established in Delhi in 1954, started its work by organizing national exhibitions of contemporary Indian art. It also gives awards and honours and conducts Triennale-India (a global art show) and a Rashtriya Kala Mela (national art fair), where artists from across the country come together to present their work.

First art bank

The Art Bank, set up in 2007 and started by curator Adishwar Puri, primarily for novice collectors apprehensive of making bad choices, now has corporations, government institutions, banks, and hospitals as clients. The artists who register benefit by receiving 50 per cent of the rental value of the work.

Logo of Indian Institute of Cartoonists

First cartoon gallery

The Indian Institute of Cartoonists opened its 186 sq m (2,000 sq ft) gallery, the Indian Cartoon Gallery, at Midford House, Bangalore (now Bengaluru), Karnataka, on 16 August 2007. It has a seminar hall, a library, and a cartoon bibliography from across the world.

First officially recognized female graffiti artist

Kajal Singh from New Delhi, who goes by the moniker 'Dizy', is the first recognized female graffiti artist from India. Her art form includes the use of bright colours and different font styles that instantly pop out. Besides India, she has left her signature in countries like Germany, China, the United States, Russia, and Indonesia. She was part of the Indo-German Hip-Hop Urban Art Project (2012), Each One Teach One (2013), 25 Years of the Berlin Wall (2014), Hip-Hop Cultural Exchange (2015), and On The Run Exhibition (2016). She was honoured as the 'First Lady' of graffiti in India by the Ministry of Women and Child Development, Government of India on 20 January 2018.

First published in 2025 by Hachette India
(Registered name: Hachette Book Publishing India Pvt. Ltd)
An Hachette UK company
www.hachetteindia.com

1

Information in the book has been updated to 31 August 2025, except in the Science and Technology, Human Story, and Sports chapters, where select information relates to later dates.

All maps in this work are pictorial representations, not to scale, and are not meant to represent exact political boundaries. They are for general illustration only, and are not intended to be used for reference purposes or reproduction elsewhere. It is clarified that the representation of a particular theme, or data set across regions with colour demarcations do not reflect political boundaries. It is also reiterated that such pictorial maps do not either represent or contradict India's national sovereignty, jurisdiction, or the recognition of political regions as mandated by the Surveyor General of India for maps showing political boundaries.

Old place names (such as Madras, Calcutta, and Bombay) may have been used to retain the historicity of the information as well as avoid confusion with earlier presidencies and provinces of the same name.

All QR codes included in the book lead to video links which belong to the respective channels/video platforms that have posted them. Their availability is subject to the period till the respective channels/video platforms continue to feature them.

All efforts have been made to verify the copyright ownership of photographs as well as the correctness of the information included in this edition. Any omissions are unintentional and regretted, and, following written communication, will be rectified in the next edition.

Subsequent edition/reprint specifications may be subject to change, including but not limited to cover or inside finishes, paper, text colour, and/or colour sections.

Hardback edition ISBN 978-93-5731-505-0
Ebook edition ISBN 978-93-5731-733-7

Hachette Book Publishing India Pvt. Ltd
4th & 5th Floors, Corporate Centre
Plot No. 94, Sector 44, Gurugram 122003, India

Designed and typeset
by Syed Salahuddin

Printed and bound in India by
Manipal Technologies Limited

hachette
INDIA

First Mughal illuminated manuscript
Emperor Humayun engaged Mir Sayyid Ali and a group of painters to paint the 'Dastan-i-Amir' (the story of Amir Hamza), which featured as many as 1,375 miniatures painted on cotton cloth in the Persian Safavid style. The work on the manuscript was under way in the 1560s.

GENERAL

Most National Awards won in a family

Nine members of the Jangid family have won the Master Craftsman Award, the national award for artisans and craft people between 1971 and 2017. Mal Chand Jangid, Richotmal Jangid, Vinod Kumar Jangid, Mahesh Chand Jangid, Sitaram Jangid, Kamlesh Jangid, Pawan Kumar Jangid, Navatmal Jangid, and Om Prakash Jangid won these awards.

Highest price at an auction for a work of Indian art

On 19 March 2025, a 1954 untitled painting (Gram Yatra) by M.F. Hussain was auctioned at the Christie Auction in New York for ₹118 crore (US $13.8 million) – a new record for the highest price achieved for a work of Indian art in an auction worldwide.

M.F. Hussain

First public art district

The Lodhi Art District in New Delhi, inaugurated by the Central Public Works Department on 1 March 2019, is the first public art district in the country. Conceptualized and realized by the St+Art India Foundation, a not-for-profit that works on art projects in open spaces, the artistic transformation of the district began in 2015. With the support of the local community and civic and cultural bodies, more than 50 artists of 23 nationalities have reimagined the area's facades by creating murals that bring the viewer into a contemporary urban art museum. A total of 56 walls with an area of approximately 16,310 sq m (1,75,565 sq ft) have been painted by the artists. This was followed by the Mahim (East) art district in Mumbai, Maharashtra; the Maqta art district in Hyderabad, Telangana; and the Panjim (Panaji) art district in Goa.

LARGEST, SMALLEST, AND MARATHON ARTWORK

Largest collage – group

Forty-four students and three teachers from Christ University, Bengaluru, created the largest collage on 2 March 2018. The collage, which measured 85.34 m x 9.14 m (280 ft x 30 ft), was made in 2 hrs 12 mins.

Largest Zentangle Art

Twenty-five students from the National Institute of Fashion Technology – Tiruppur Exporters Association (NIFT-TEA) College of Knitwear Fashion, Tiruppur, Tamil Nadu, created the largest Zentangle artwork measuring 185.8 sq m (2,000 sq. ft), with 'Make in India' as its theme. The students completed the artwork in 34 hrs during 17–18 August 2018.

Largest drawing – pencils – solo

Megha Harsha from Bikaner, Rajasthan, created the largest pencil drawing by an individual. The artwork measured 455.21 sq m (4,900 sq ft) and was completed in 86 hrs over the course of 17 days from 16 October to 1 November 2019 at Bikaner Boys School, Bikaner. The artwork created awareness regarding the United Nations' Sustainable Development Goals (SDGs) related to climate change, safety of women, and pollution, among others.

Largest painting – oil paints – solo

Sandeep Sinha, an artist from Pune, Maharashtra, made an oil-on-canvas painting titled 'HiMakhan'. The artwork measures 48.78 sq m (525.06 sq ft) and is a single-scene painting of the Himalayas. He began in August 2018 and completed the work by October 2018. His painting was exhibited at the Raja Ravi Varma Art Gallery, Pune. Sinha dedicated this work to acid attack survivors.

Largest mandala artwork – group

NIFT-TEA College of Knitwear Fashion in Tiruppur, Tamil Nadu, created a mandala artwork, which was 101.17 sq m (1,089 sq ft) in area, in 25 hrs over two days in the college premises. The participants began the artwork on 27 February 2021 and finished on 28 February 2021.

Largest quilling artwork – solo

Dr Jiji S. Deepak from Thrissur, Kerala, created a 6.71 m x 3.66 m (22 ft x 12 ft) artwork, using the paper-quilling technique. It took her 45 hrs 10 mins over a period of nine days. The artwork is based on the theme 'Mother Earth'.

Largest portrait – pencils – solo

Aman Gulati from Lakhimpur, Uttar Pradesh, created the largest pencil portrait, which measured 410.25 sq m (4,416 sq ft) in area. The portrait of Mahatma Gandhi was completed on 2 October 2019 to mark Gandhiji's 150th birth anniversary.

Largest wall painting – single wall – solo

NIFT-TEA College of Knitwear Fashion,

Sandeep Sinha: artist of the largest oil painting – solo

Tiruppur, Tamil Nadu, created a wall painting measuring 46.82 sq m (504 sq ft) in 250 hrs over 25 days in the college premises. The painting was made by R. Sanjay Kumar for the college. He started his painting on 17 June 2020 and finished on 11 July 2020.

Largest portrait – acrylic paints – solo

Rajeev Ranjan from Purnea, Bihar, who is popularly known as Rajeev Raj, created a painting of former prime minister Atal Bihari Vajpayee with acrylic paints on canvas. He began painting on 3 December 2018 at 4:43 p.m. and completed the artwork at 11:18 p.m. on 4 December 2018 at the Vidya Vihar Residential School. He took 30 hrs 35 mins and used 225 pieces of canvas, each 0.762 m x 0.762 m (2.5 ft x 2.5 ft). The artwork covered a total area of 130.6 sq m (1,406 sq ft).

Marathon sand painting

Neha Umak from Thane, Maharashtra, completed 133 pieces of sand painting artwork in 24 hrs 49 mins 19 secs from 9:16 a.m. on 30 June 2019 to 10:05 a.m. on 1 July 2019 at Kundan Talent Academy, Thane. The total break time was 1 hr 37 mins 40 secs. The artworks were a mix of portraits and sceneries.

Marathon pencil-art session

Dinesh K. Gupta from Mumbai, completed 201 drawings in a marathon pencil-art session, starting at noon on 5 April 2019 and ending at noon on 6 April 2019. Using 6B pencils, he sketched famous people, natural sceneries, religious figures, and still life on A3 sheets. The event took place at Dr Babasaheb Ambedkar Art Gallery, Kalyan. The total break time was 1 hr 50 mins.

Marathon sculpture-making

Ramita Bhaduri from Nazir Bagan, Kolkata, West Bengal, completed a marathon sculpture-making session during 29–30 April 2019, using clay and cement. She logged 15 hrs of sculpting and 3 hrs break time (30 mins after every 3 hrs), making 29 sculptures in all. The average dimensions of the sculptures were 30.48 cm x 30.48 cm x 33.02 cm (12 in. x 12 in. x 13 in.) for standing figures, 25.4 cm x 30.48 cm x 38.1 cm (10 in. x 12 in. x 15 in.) for lying down ones, and 25.4 cm x 25.4 cm x 30.48 cm (10 in. x 10 in. x 12 in.) for sitting figures.

Largest mandala artwork – solo

Radha Shankar Narayanan from Bengaluru, created a 58.06 sq m (625 sq ft) mandala artwork in 89 hrs 20 mins over 14 days at BGS National Public School, Bengaluru. He started his painting on 15 June 2021 and finished on 28 June 2021.

Largest mandala artwork – solo

Largest cross-stitch artwork – solo

Marathon portrait making – marker and ink – solo

Srushti Sandeep Ingale from Kolhapur, Maharashtra, completed 157 portraits in a marathon marker-and-ink session, starting at 7:00 a.m. on 20 November 2021 and ending at 8:00 p.m. on the same day. Using four Montex Mega Tap black ball pens, she sketched portraits of political and sports personalities, among others, on A3 sheets. The event took place at Hotel Pearl, Kolhapur. The total break time was 50 mins.

Most towel origami made – group – 1 hour

CT Institute of Hospitality Management, Punjab, created 150 unduplicated towel origami designs with 76 participants between 11 a.m. and 11:03 a.m. on 18 April 2025 at the university premises.

Largest single-item origami (widest) – solo

Glendale Academy International created the largest single-item origami artwork on 21 February 2019. Radhika Chintalapati, a teacher from the school, created a butterfly with nine folds in 15 mins at Glendale International School, Hyderabad. The width of the butterfly was 2.438 m (8 ft), and the wing-to-wing length was 4.267 m (14 ft).

Smallest pencil-lead carving

- Muna Mahana from Odisha created the smallest pencil-lead carving of 'India Gate' on a graphite pencil lead. The artwork measures 4 mm (0.15 in.) in length and 2 mm (0.07 in.) in width. It was made on 26 April 2025.
- Dr Gattam Venkatesh from Andhra Pradesh created the smallest pencil-lead carving of 'Taj Mahal' on a graphite pencil-lead. The artwork measures 4 mm (0.15 in.) in height. It was made on 27 April 2025.

Largest cross-stitch artwork – solo

Neelam Ashwin Samant from Mumbai, Maharashtra, created the largest cross-stitch artwork measuring 4.83 sq ft over a period of 12 months and 21 days. The artwork is on a 14-count cross-stitch cloth with 252 stitches x 540 stitches and a avergae of 14 stitches per inch of embroidery.

LITERATURE

BOOKS

Oldest living language
Tamil, which belongs to the Dravidian group of languages, is the oldest living language of India. *Tholkappiyam,* the oldest known work in Tamil, is a work on Tamil grammar. Its composition has been variously dated to between the second century BCE and the fifth century CE.

Oldest surviving book
The oldest surviving Indian book is the Tamil work *Christiya Vanakkam,* a revised edition of the *Doctrina Christiana.* It was first published in 1560 in Goa and followed by its Tamil version published in 1564.

Christiya Vanakkam, 1572

DOCTRINA CHRISTAM
en Lingua Malauar Tamul.

Earliest known grammar text
The Sanskrit grammar treatise *Ashtadhyayi,* which was composed around 500 BCE by Panini, a grammarian, is said to be the earliest formalized book on Sanskrit grammar. It contains 4,000 precise rules of grammar in as many *sutras,* expounding an array of topics such as syntax, root derivatives and moods.

First known printed book
The first known printed book in India, titled *Conclusoes e Outras Coisas,* was printed in Portuguese in Goa by Joao de Bustamante, a Christian missionary.

Earliest known anthology
Therigatha, the ninth book of the *Khuddaka Nikaya,* is the earliest known anthology. This Buddhist scripture, written in Pali, consists of short poems that were recited by the early members of the Buddhist sangha. It has 73 poems, which are organized into 16 chapters, and the text comprises 522 stanzas.

First printed book to use Bengali type
A Grammar of the Bengal Language written in 1778 by Nathaniel Brassey Halhed constituted the first grammar book in Bengali. It was printed in Hoogly, Bengal (now West Bengal).

A Grammar of the Bengal Language

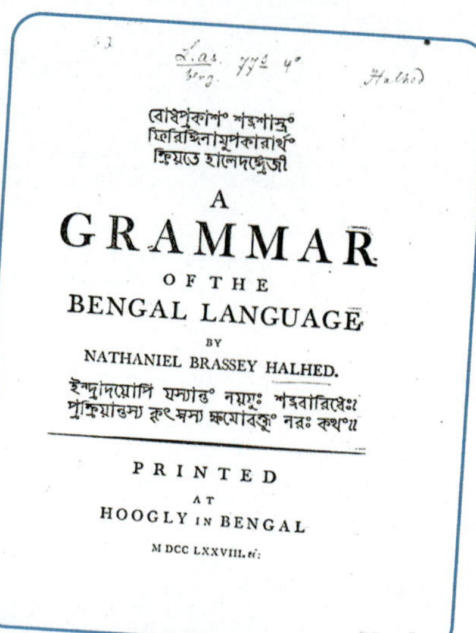
বোধপ্রকাশং শব্দশাস্ত্রং
ফিরিঙ্গিনামুপকারার্থং
ক্রিয়তে হালেদঙ্গ্রেজী

A
GRAMMAR
OF THE
BENGAL LANGUAGE
BY
NATHANIEL BRASSEY HALHED.

ইন্দ্রাদয়োপি যস্যান্তং নযযুঃ শব্দবারিধেঃ
প্রক্রিয়ান্তস্য কৃৎস্নস্য ক্ষমোবক্তুং নরঃ কথং

PRINTED
AT
HOOGLY IN BENGAL
M DCC LXXVIII.

First printed book in Bengali
Krister Mangal Samacar (*The New Testament*) published in 1819, written by William Carey was the first translation of the Bible in Bengali. It was printed by the Serampore Mission Press, Serampore, Bengal (now Srirampur, West Bengal).

First known printed books in local languages
- **Assamese:** An early translation of the New Testament, titled *Dharmapustak,* printed by the Serampore Mission Press, Serampore, Bengal, in 1813. • **Devanagari/Hindi:** *Grammar of Sanskrit and Grammar of the Hindustani Language,* published by the Chronicle Press, Calcutta (now Kolkata), in 1796.
- **Dogri:** *Valmiki Ramayana,* published by Sri Saraswati Press, Jammu, in Jammu and Kashmir, in 1858.
- **Gujarati:** *Dabestan-e-Mazaheb,* the Gujarati translation of a Persian book, published by Fardoonjee Marazban in Bombay (now Mumbai), Maharashtra, in 1815.
- **Kannada:** *A Grammar of the Karnatic Language* by William Meckerell, published by the Serampore Mission Press, Serampore, Bengal, in 1820.
- **Konkani:** *Doutrina Crista,* printed at the Society of Jesus Press, Goa, in 1556.
- **Maithili:** *Krishna Janma,* edited by Grierson, published by Vidyapati Press, Laheriasarai, Bihar, in 1936.
- **Malayalam:** *The Bible,* printed at the Courier Press, Bombay, Maharashtra, in 1811.
- **Odia:** A translation of the New Testament by Pandit Mrityunjaya Vidyalankar, printed at the Serampore Mission Press, Serampore, Bengal, in 1807.
- **Tamil:** *A Book of Prayers,* published by the Society of Jesus Press, Goa, around 1560.
- **Telugu:** *A Grammar of Telugu,* printed at the Serampore Mission Press, Serampore, Bengal, in 1813.
- **Urdu:** Halhed's Urdu translation of Kannada laws, published by Honourable Company Press in Calcutta, in 1792.

First poet in English in India
Henry Louis Vivian Derozio, assistant headmaster of Hindu College, (now Presidency University, Kolkata), West Bengal, is considered to be the first Indian

Fakeer of Jungheera and Other Poems

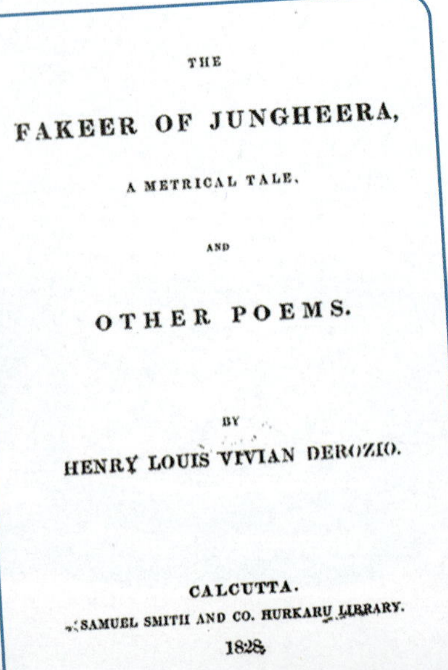
THE
FAKEER OF JUNGHEERA,
A METRICAL TALE.
AND
OTHER POEMS.
BY
HENRY LOUIS VIVIAN DEROZIO.

CALCUTTA.
SAMUEL SMITH AND CO. HURKARU LIBRARY.
1828.

poet who wrote in English. The poems that he submitted to the newspaper *India Gazette* under the pseudonym 'Juvenis' were published as a collection in 1827. The second edition of the collection was released in the following year and included his most famous poem, 'The Fakeer of Jungheera', which featured aspects of life in colonial India.

Most translated Indian work

The most translated Indian work is the Bhagavadgita, which is an integral part of the Mahabharata. The Bhagavadgita was first translated into English in 1785 by British typographer and founder of the Asiatic Society, Charles Wilkins. Since then, it has been translated into as many as 55 languages.

Bhagavadgita (English Translation), 1785

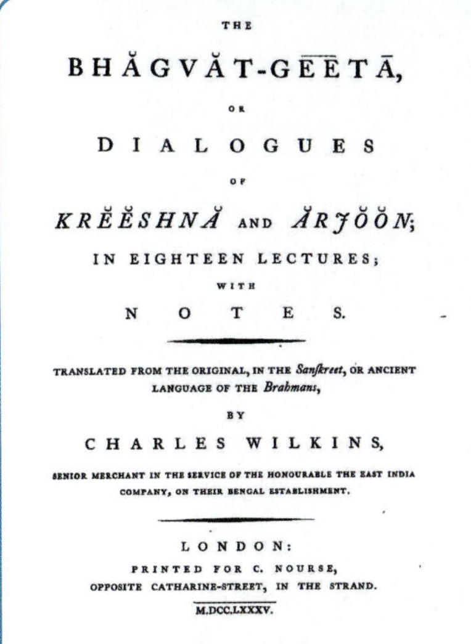

THE

BHĂGVĂT-GĒĒTĀ,

OR

DIALOGUES

OF

KRĒĒSHNĂ AND ĂRJŌŌN;

IN EIGHTEEN LECTURES;

WITH

NOTES.

TRANSLATED FROM THE ORIGINAL, IN THE *Sanskreet*, OR ANCIENT LANGUAGE OF THE *Brahmans*,

BY

CHARLES WILKINS,

SENIOR MERCHANT IN THE SERVICE OF THE HONOURABLE THE EAST INDIA COMPANY, ON THEIR BENGAL ESTABLISHMENT.

LONDON:

PRINTED FOR C. NOURSE,

OPPOSITE CATHARINE-STREET, IN THE STRAND.

M.DCC.LXXXV.

Earliest known works in different languages

Earliest known Malayalam work

Samkshepa Vedartham, a catechism book by the Reverend Clement Pianius, was printed in movable type in Rome in 1772.

Earliest known Gujarati work

The earliest work in Gujarati prose was *Balavabodha,* written by Tarunaprabha and dated to 1355 CE.

Earliest known Tamil work

Tholkappiyam, a treatise on the grammar of the Tamil language, is the earliest known extant work in Tamil. It has been dated to between the second century BCE and the fifth century CE. The authorship is loosely attributed to the sage Tholkappiyar.

Earliest known Kannada works

• The earliest extant work in Kannada, the second oldest living language in India, is the *Kavirajamarga,* which was written (possibly in parts) by a Rashtrakuta king – Nrupatunga Amoghavarsha I (r. 814–78 ce). It is a work on the rhetoric, poetics, and grammar of Kannada.

• The Kannada text in prose, titled *Vaddaradhane* (sixth to ninth century ce), which is believed to have been written by Shivakotiacharya, consists of inspiring stories of 19 great Jain saints.

Earliest known Marathi works

• *Viveka Sindhu* was written by Mukundraj (1128–1200 ce) in Marathi verse, and preached Advaita bhakti. Mukundraj was a follower of Adi Shankaracharya's philosophy of Advaita or 'non-dualism', which inspired him to write this religious composition.

• *Leela Charitra* by Mahim Bhat is a biography of Chakradhara, a thirteenth century saint who founded the Mahanubhava sect and socio-religious movement. The work contains more than a hundred stories on the subject.

Earliest extant English work

Cavelly Venkata Boriah's *Account of the Jains,* published in 1809, is the first extant evidence of Indian writing in English.

Earliest original Odia work

Lavanyavati, the first Odia epic, was an original work featuring the love story of a prince of Karnataka and a princess of Sri Lanka, by Upendra Bhanja (1680–1720), who belonged to a ruling feudatory family in Ghumsar in Bhanjanagar in present-day Odisha. Called *'Kavi Samrat',* he is said to have written many books.

Earliest known Telugu work

The first printed prose work in Telugu, which was a part of the New Testament, was translated by Reverend Benjamin Schultze in the early eighteenth century.

Only Shakespeare folio

A rare copy of Shakespeare's *First Folio* (1623) was found at the Mahatma Gandhi Central Library, University of Roorkee, Uttar Pradesh (now IIT Roorkee, Uttarakhand) as reported in 2019. The 900-page volume titled *Mr William Shakespeare's Comedies, Histories and Tragedies* was found in an old trunk in the librarian's office. It contains 36 of Shakespeare's 37 plays.

1623 Shakespeare Folio Edition p-xvii

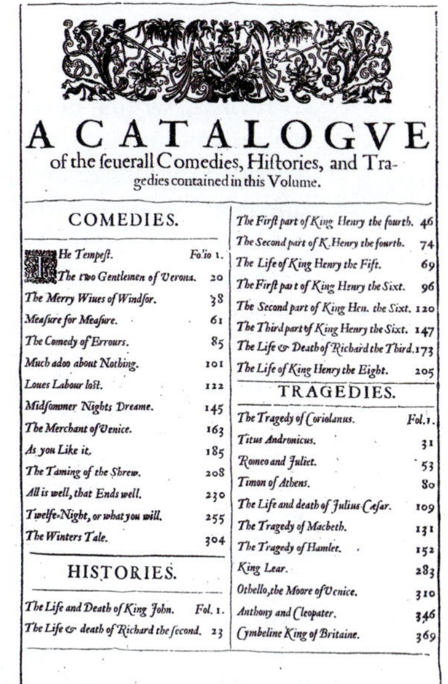

A CATALOGVE

of the feuerall Comedies, Hiſtories, and Tragedies contained in this Volume.

COMEDIES.			
The Tempeſt.	Folio 1.	The First part of King Henry the fourth.	46
The two Gentlemen of Verona.	20	The Second part of K. Henry the fourth.	74
The Merry Wiues of Windſor.	38	The Life of King Henry the Fift.	69
Meaſure for Meaſure.	61	The First part of King Henry the Sixt.	96
The Comedy of Errours.	85	The Second part of King Hen. the Sixt.	120
Much adoo about Nothing.	101	The Third part of King Henry the Sixt.	147
Loues Labour loſt.	122	The Life & Death of Richard the Third.	173
Midſommer Nights Dreame.	145	The Life of King Henry the Eight.	205
The Merchant of Venice.	163	TRAGEDIES.	
As you Like it.	185	The Tragedy of Coriolanus.	Fol. 1.
The Taming of the Shrew.	208	Titus Andronicus.	31
All is well, that Ends well.	230	Romeo and Juliet.	53
Twelfe-Night, or what you will.	255	Timon of Athens.	80
The Winters Tale.	304	The Life and death of Julius Cæſar.	109
HISTORIES.		The Tragedy of Macbeth.	131
		The Tragedy of Hamlet.	152
		King Lear.	283
		Othello, the Moore of Venice.	310
The Life and Death of King John.	Fol. 1.	Anthony and Cleopater.	346
The Life & death of Richard the ſecond.	23	Cymbeline King of Britaine.	369

Below: *Lavanyavati*, the First Odia Epic; *Right*: Benjamin Schultze

THE LONG AND SHORT OF IT!

Longest novel

Avakasikal, written by M.K. Menon in Malayalam, runs into 3,958 pages, in 4 volumes, making it the longest novel in any Indian language. Menon received the Sahitya Akademi Award in 1981 and the Vayalar Award in 1983 for the novel.

Longest audiobook

The longest audiobook, titled *Shree Haricharitramrut Sagar*, was voiced by Gyanjivandasji Swami – 'Kundaldham' and Ishwarcharandasji Swami – 'Kundaldham', and published on 27 October 2017. The audiobook is 1,46,444 mins 52 secs long.

Largest book

A special edition of the Bhagavadgita at the ISKCON temple in New Delhi is the largest-sized book. The book measures 2.8 m x 2 m (9 ft 2.2 in. x 6 ft 6.7 in.) and has 670 pages. Weighing 800 kg, it was printed in Milan, Italy, on YUPO synthetic paper, making it untearable and waterproof. It was unveiled on 26 February 2019.

Thickest book

Povitr Pustokantlem Bhanddar (*Roman Konkani Biblical Concordance*) is the thickest book. It is 149.09 cm (58.7 in.) thick, and measures 30.5 cm (12 in.) in length, and 43.2 cm (17 in.) in width. The book was launched on 28 February 2021 at the Our Lady of Carmel Chapel, Navelim, Goa. The copyright owner of the book is Ives Joaquim Tavares.

Smallest book

B. Jameela from Madras (now Chennai), Tamil Nadu, had a copy of the Quran, which is 27 mm (1.06 in.) long, 19 mm (0.74 in.) wide and 10 mm (0.39 in.) thick, and weighed only 4.4 g.

First pseudonym

'Sujatha' was the pseudonym of the popular Tamil author S. Rangarajan (1935–2008), who wrote more than 100 novels, 250 short stories, 10 books on science, 10 stage plays, and a volume of poems. He was a regular contributor to topical columns in Tamil periodicals such as *Ananda Vikatan, Kumudam,* and *Kalki.* He served for a brief period as the editor of *Kumudam,* and also wrote screenplays and dialogues for Tamil movies.

First official sign language dictionary

Bridging the gap for the deaf and speech-disabled communities, *The Indian Sign Language Dictionary,* a first-of-its-kind book, was launched on 23 March 2018. Developed by the Delhi-based Indian Sign Language Research and Training Centre, it contains 3,000 words in Hindi and English, and their corresponding graphic representations. Available in both print and video formats, it brings uniformity to the various sign languages used. It divides the words into five categories: Everyday, Legal, Academic, Medical, and Technical terms.

PUBLISHING AND BOOK SELLING

Largest trade publishing house

Penguin Random House India is the subcontinent's largest English-language trade publisher. It publishes more than 300 new titles every year and has an active backlist of over 3,000 titles.

Largest literary publisher

DC Books in Kottayam, Kerala, started in 1974 by Dominic Chacko Kizhakemuri, is considered the publishing hub of south India. The translation programme of DC Books is considered to be the largest in India. It publishes around 1,500 books in a year (2024).

Largest book market

College Street in Kolkata, West Bengal, is the venue of the largest book market in the country and possibly the largest used-books market in the world. Known locally as *boi para* (the neighbourhood of books), this 1.5 km long street sees a large number of book lovers and buyers every day.

First literary agency

Neville Tuli of Osian, Rajasthan, set up the first professional agency for authors on 9 April 2007. The first author they signed on was Omair Ahmad on 1 June 2007. The literary agency was a division of Osian's Connoisseurs of Art Pvt. Ltd.

First comic book convention

The Annual Indian Comic Book Convention (Comic Con) was organized for the first time on 19 February 2011 by Twenty Onwards Media at Dilli Haat, New Delhi. Fifty publishers participated in it, bringing together writers, gamers, cosplayers, games, and films.

First book fair

The First International Book Fair opened at New Delhi's Pragati Maidan on 18 March 1972 during the International Book Year. Around a hundred Indian publishers took part, displaying about 10,000 books in English and local Indian languages. Foreign participants included those from the USSR, the USA, France, New Zealand, Turkey, and Sri Lanka.

Display at world Book Fair

First book village

Bilhar, located in Satara District of Maharashtra, was identified as the first book village in India on 4 May 2017. Known as *Pustakanch Gaav*, the village has a genre-specific libraries in 25 locations, housing more than 15,000 books, mostly in Marathi. The village is decorated with murals, paintings, and artworks on the theme of books. The aim of the initiative is to share a passion for books and an appetite for knowledge.

Logo of Pustakanch Gaav

First virtual literary festival

LitFest X, organized between 23 October and 1 November 2015 was the country's first virtual literary festival. The event used multiple platforms like YouTube, Google Hangouts, Facebook, and Twitter to present the interactive sessions to readers including book launches and book readings.

First independent publisher

The first Indian publisher to set up a press was Gangakishor Bhattacharya in 1821 in Calcutta, West Bengal, a former employee of the Serampore Press, Serampore, Bengal. He published eighteenth century ballads in Bengali and adaptations from classics.

Biggest retail bookshop chain – high street

Crossword Bookstores Ltd, a wholly owned subsidiary of Shoppers Stop Ltd, is the largest high-street bookstore chain in India. Established in October 1992, the company had 88 stores, including franchises, across India by August 2023. These stores are across the country in cities such as Mumbai, Bengaluru, Ahmedabad, Gurugram, Delhi, Chennai, and Pune, among others.

Largest-selling bilingual dictionary

The *English–English–Malayalam Dictionary* by T. Ramalingam Pillai was first published in May 1983. Published by DC Books, based in Kottayam, Kerala, it is in its 55th impression now. As on September 2019, around 2.4 million copies had been sold.

BRITANNIA
Zindagi mein Life
Presents
BOOKaROO
India's First Ever Children's Literature Festival
19th – 23rd November 2008

Images from the first Bookaroo

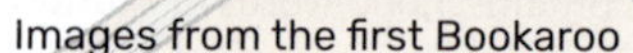

First children's literary festival

Co-founded by Swati Roy, Jo Williams, and Venkatesh M. in 2008, Bookaroo was the first children's literary festival in India, with its first edition held in New Delhi. Since its inception, the festival has travelled to 17 cities (15 cities in India, and one each in Malaysia and Sri Lanka). It has completed 49 editions in 16 years. It is the winner of the Literary Festival Award at the London Book Fair's International Excellence Awards, 2017.

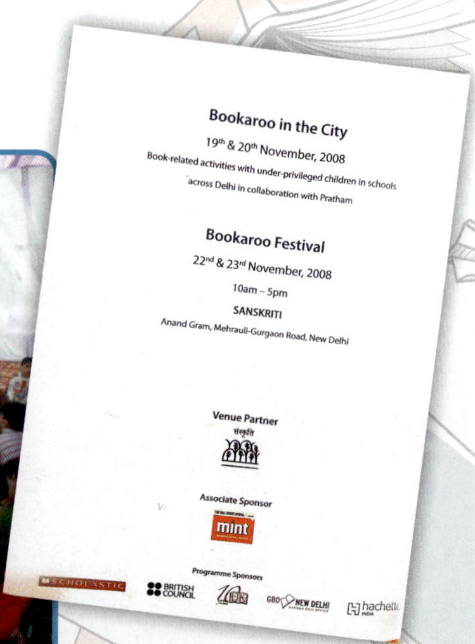

Bookaroo in the City

19th & 20th November, 2008

Book-related activities with under-privileged children in schools across Delhi in collaboration with Pratham

Bookaroo Festival

22nd & 23rd November, 2008

10am – 5pm

SANSKRITI

Anand Gram, Mehrauli-Gurgaon Road, New Delhi

Venue Partner

Associate Sponsor

mint

Programme Sponsors

SCHOLASTIC BRITISH COUNCIL NEW DELHI hachette

Brochure of the first Bookaroo

First feminist publishing house

Kali for Women, a not-for-profit trust, publishing a wide variety of books by women and on women, was started in 1984 by Urvashi Butalia and Ritu Menon in New Delhi.

Largest adult non-fiction seller – hardback

Cricket legend Sachin Tendulkar's autobiography, *Playing It My Way,* coauthored with Boria Majumdar, was published in India by Hachette India, Gurugram, Haryana, and released on 6 November 2014. It broke all previous records in the adult non-fiction (hardback) category with 1,50,289 copies confirmed on order subscriptions.

Oldest bookshop

Higginbothams, the oldest bookshop in the country, was opened in 1844 by Abel Joshua Higginbotham in Madras, Tamil Nadu. It has a subscription division that helps educational institutions, corporate bodies, and professionals to get journals and periodicals from more than 3,000 publishing houses abroad. It currently has 22 branches in India.

Largest sales on release for a fiction title – hardback

Dan Brown is a best-selling American author of thrillers. His book *Origin* was the fifth in his Robert Langdon series, following *Angels & Demons, The Da Vinci Code, The Lost Symbol,* and *Inferno.* It was released in India on 3 October 2017 by Penguin Random House India, with an initial subscription of 1,25,000 copies, breaking all records in the fiction hardback category.

Dan Brown: Best-selling author

Largest literary festival

The Jaipur Literature Festival, founded in 2006, is an annual literary festival in Jaipur, Rajasthan, which brings together some of the most prominent thinkers and writers from across the world every January. The festival directors are authors Namita Gokhale and William Dalrymple, and it has been produced by Sanjoy Roy of Teamwork Arts since 2008. The festival has seen a footfall of 4,31,000 people, conducted 238 sessions in over 46 languages by around 370 speakers in 2023.

Largest sales for a children's book – hardback

Harry Potter and the Cursed Child (Parts One and Two) is the official script book for the play of the same name written by J.K. Rowling, John Tiffany, and Jack Thorne. It is the eighth story in the Harry Potter book series. Released in India by Hachette India, Gurugram, Haryana, in July 2016, it sold 2,59,537 print copies (as of October 2017), making it the largest-selling children's book in India.

Largest bookshop

Sapna Book House in Gandhinagar, Bengaluru, Karnataka, was started in 1967 by Suresh C. Shah. Spread over 3,716 sq m (40,000 sq ft), it has more than 2,20,000 titles covering many genres and topics. Sapna Book House has four more branches in Bengaluru and Mysuru – adding up to retail space of about 9,290.3 sq m (1,00,000 sq ft).

Largest lifetime sales

The Secret by Rhonda Byrne, published by Simon and Schuster, US, in 2006, is a best-selling self-help book, based on the pseudoscientific 'law of attraction', which claims that a person's thoughts can change the world directly. The book has sold over 7,00,000 copies in India and has also been translated into 50 languages.

Rhonda Byrne

TOP 10 FRONT-LIST TITLES * 2024

	Title	Author	Volume
ADULT FICTION	*I Don't Love You Anymore: Moving On and Living Your Best*	Rithvik Singh	39,343
	Lucifer was Innocent: The Red Pill	Tirth Raj Parsana	24,025
	The Naga Warriors: Battle of Gokul	Akshat Gupta	23,062
	Acts of God	Kanan Gill	16,764
	More Days at The Morisaki Bookshop:	Satoshi Yagisawa	16,039
	The Hidden Hindu Trilogy: A Mythological Adventure (Boxset)	Akshat Gupta	15,756
	Never Lie	Freida Mc Fadden	15,679
	Warmth	Rithvik Singh	11,343
	Butter	Asako Yuzuki	9,606
	Blue Sisters	Coco Mellors	8,594
ADULT NON- FICTION	*11 Rules For Life: Secrets to Level Up*	Chetan Bhagat	69,882
	Make Epic Money	Ankur Warikoo	68,524
	Own Your Body: A Doctor's Life-Saving Tips	Dr Shiv K. Sarin	46,142
	The Art of Being Alone: Loneliness Was My Cage, Solitude Is My Home (HB)	Renuka Gavrani	42,803
	The Satvic Revolution: 7 Life-Changing Habits to Discover Peak Health and Joy	Subah Saraf & and Harshvardhan Saraf	32,623
	The Golden Road: How Ancient India Transformed the World	William Dalrymple	31,106
	The Wealth Money Can't Buy: The 8 Hidden Habits to Live Your Richest Life	Robin Sharma	28,859
	The Art of Laziness: Overcome Procrastination & Improve Your Productivity	Library Mindset	28,554
	Spiritual Anatomy: Meditation, Chakras, and the Journey to the Center	Daaji Kamlesh D. Patel	22,999
	Mastering the Data Paradox: Key to Winning in the AI Age	Nitin Seth	20,832
CHILDREN'S FICTION	*Diary of a Wimpy Kid: Hot Mess (Book 19): Diary of a Wimpy Kid*	Jeff Kinney	22,098
	Grandpa's Bag of Stories	Sudha Murty	16,455
	Percy Jackson and the Olympians: Wrath of the Triple Goddess	Rick Riordan	11,755
	Sad-Glad	Sidhartha Mallya	9,895
	Gopi's Day Out!: The Gopi Diaries	Sudha Murty	9,850
	Dog Man: The Scarlet Shedder (Graphic Novel)	Dav Pilkey	9,473
	Reckless	Lauren Roberts	8,189
	Grandma's Bag of Stories (HB)	Sudha Murty	6,223
	The Adventures of Ed-a-Mamma: Ed Finds a Home	Alia Bhatt	5,088
	Diary: of a Wimpy kid: No Brainer	Jeff Kinney	4,088
CHILDREN'S NON- FICTION	*Unstoppable Us: Why the World Isn't Fair* (Volume 2)	Yuval Noah Harari	5,898
	A History of South India For Children	Pradeep Chakravarthy	2,344
	The Padmas: Fifty Stories of Perseverance	Neha J. Hiranandani	2,220
	The Book of Emperors: An Illustrated History of the Mughals	Ashwitha Jayakumar	1,811
	Poor Economics for Kids	Cheyenne Duflo, Esther & Olivier	1,473
	Revolutionaries: Fight For Freedom	Sanjeev Sanyal	1,021
	Virat Kohli	Clive Gifford	843
	The Talking Book: The Wild Journey of Communication-From Caveman to AI	Jane De Suza	690
	The Gutsy Girls Who Led India	Ilina Singh	659
	A Really Short History of Nearly Everything	Bill Bryson	644

**NOTE: Titles published between 1 January and 31 December 2024. Data sourced from Nielsen Bookscan retail panel market and © Nielsen BookData. Volume indicates the number of copies sold. The list includes new re-issues, changes in format or any other change by publishers.* This list contains English-language trade titles.

From top: Akshat Gupta, Daaji Kamlesh D. Patel, Sudha Murty, Pradeep Chakravarthy, cover of *A History of South India for Children*

AWARDS AND HONOURS

First recipients of the Sahitya Akademi Award

• *Man*: Makhanlal Chaturvedi (1889–1968), a poet, was the first person to receive this award for *Him Tarangini* (Hindi) in 1955.

• *Woman*: The Punjabi poet and writer Amrita Pritam (1919–2005) received the award in 1956, the year after its inception, for *Sunehre* (Punjabi), a collection of poems.

Top: Makhanlal Chaturvedi; *Above*: Amrita Pritam

First Sahitya Akademi Bhasha Samman Award

The Bhasha Samman Awards are given annually for contribution towards the development of a language. The first of these awards were given in 1996 to:

• Dharikshan Mishra for Bhojpuri,
• Bansi Ram Sharma and M.R. Thakur for Pahari (Himachal Pradesh),
• K. Jathappa Rai and Mandara Keshava Bhat for Tulu (Karnataka), and
• Chandra Kanta Murasingh for Kokborok (Tripura).

First Sahitya Akademi Fellowship

• *Man:* Former Indian president and eminent scholar Dr S. Radhakrishnan (1888–1975) was the first to receive this honour in 1968 for his contribution to Indian thought and universal humanism.

• *Woman:* The first woman to be elected Fellow of the Akademi was the poet Mahadevi Varma in 1979.

Portrait of Dr Radhakrishnan

First Indian winner of the Neustadt Prize

The Neustadt International Prize (given for an author's body of work) is one of the few international prizes for which poets, novelists, and playwrights are all eligible. Raja Rao was the first Indian to win it in 1988. Indian-Canadian writer Rohinton Mistry won the prize in 2012.

First winner of the Nobel Prize for Literature

Rabindranath Tagore won the Nobel prize for literature in 1913. He is currently the only literature Nobel laureate from India. His prize motivation is cited as, "because of his profoundly sensitive, fresh and beautiful verse, by which, with consummate skill, he has made his poetic thought, expressed in his own English words, a part of the literature of the West".

First Indian winner of the Ondaatje Prize

Sports journalist Rahul Bhattacharya's *The Sly Company of People Who Care* won the Royal Society of Literature Ondaatje Prize in 2012. It also won the Hindu Literary Prize (2011) and was the Kirkus Fiction Book of the Year in the US.

First novel in an Indian language to win the International Booker Prize

Tomb of Sand by Geetanjali Shree became the first Indian-language (Hindi) novel to win the prestigious International Booker Prize in 2022. Translated from *Ret Samadhi* into English by Daisy Rockwell, it is set in north India and follows the story of an 80-year-old woman. *Heart Lamp* by Banu Mushtaq, translated from Kannada by Deepa Bhasthi won the accolade in 2025.

First Indian winner of the Commonwealth Writers' Prize

Author Nayantara Sahgal won the Commonwealth Writers' Prize for Best Book in 1987, for her novel *Plans for Departure*.

First to win the DSC Prize for South Asian Literature

• *Man*: Poet and novelist Jeet Thayil won the DSC Prize for South Asian Literature 2013 for his novel *Narcopolis* (Faber & Faber).

• *Woman*: Jhumpa Lahiri was judged as the winner of the DSC Prize for South Asian Literature 2015 for her book *The Lowland*. The US $50,000 prize and the specially designed trophy was awarded to her on 22 January 2015.

Jhumpa Lahiri

First Indian winner of Newbery Medal

Dhan Gopal Mukerji

Dhan Gopal Mukerji (1890–1936), who was born in a village near Calcutta, West Bengal, and later went to the US, was the first Indian winner of the Newbery Medal for his novel, *Gay-Neck, the Story of a Pigeon,* in 1928.

First winners of the Saraswati Samman

The Saraswati Samman was instituted by the K.K. Birla Foundation in 1991. Award winners receive ₹15 lakh along with a citation and a plaque. The first winners are:

- *Man*: Harivansh Rai Bachchan for Autobiography in four volumes (Hindi) in 1991.
- *Woman*: Balamani Amma for *Nivedyam* (Malayalam) in 1995.

Harivansh Rai Bachchan

First Winners of the Sahitya Akademi Translation Prize

Established in 1989, the award is presented for outstanding translation works in 24 languages. The awardees receive a plaque and a cash prize of ₹50,000. Here is a list of the first winners:

Language	Translator	Translation	Title Year
Assamese	Narendranath Sarma	*Atmajivan Charit*	1990
Bengali	Nilina Abraham	*Patummar Chhagal O Balyaskhi*	1989
Bodo	Pramila Narzary	*Aswini Solo*	2005
Dogri	Ram Nath Shastri	*Mitti Di Gaddi*	1989
English	Bikram K. Das	*Paraja*	1989
Gujarati	Nagindas Parekh	*Na Hanyate*	1989
Hindi	Noor Nabi Abbasi	*Malabar Se Masko Tak*	1989
Kannada	S.V. Parameshwara Bhatta	*Kannada Kalidasa Mahasamputa*	1990
Kashmiri	Syed Rasool Pompur	*Pranwaar*	1991
Konkani	Ravindra Kelekar	*Ani Tankan Manshant Hadle*	1990
Maithili	Upendranath Jha 'Vyas'	*Vipradas*	1990
Malayalam	K. Ravi Verma	*Ganadevata*	1989
Manipuri	T. Thoibi Devi	*Drishtipath*	1989
Marathi	Uma Virupax Kulkarni	*Vamsavriksha*	1989
Nepali	Karna Thami	*Sakanta Ka Kavitaharu*	1994
Odia	Basanta Kumari Devi	*Ganadebata, Parts I and II (Panchagram)*	1989
Punjabi	Rattan Singh Jaggi	*Tulasi Ramayan (Ramcharitmanas)*	1989
Rajasthani	Deo Dutta Nag	*Sapano*	1990
Sanskrit	Ganesha Sharma	*Vijananam Samajasca*	1990
Santhali	Sobha Nath Beshr	*Rahla Raybar*	2010
Sindhi	Jagat Assudomal Advani	*Rolak Ji Atam Kahani*	1989
Tamil	M.G. Jagannatharaja	*Aamukta Malyada*	1990
Telugu	B. Gopala Reddi	*Ravindruni Natikalu*	1989
Urdu	Hameed Almas	*Farmoodat*	1989

First Indian to win the Booker Prize

Arundhati Roy (b. 24 November 1961) won the prestigious Booker Prize in 1997 for her first novel, *The God of Small Things.*

First winners of the Yuva Puruskar Award

The Yuva Puraskar Award is given by the Sahitya Akademi annually to writers below the age of 35 in 24 Indian languages. This award was introduced in 2011 and the Dogri and Sindhi languages were added later, in 2011 and 2015 respectively. The first year had only 22 languages. The first winners are:

Assamese: Arindam Borkataki for *Anusilon.*

Bengali: Binod Ghosal for *Danaowla Manus.*

Bodo: Jaishree Baro for *Jeu Saharani Beduin.*

Dogri: Yash Raina for *Do Kandhe* in 2012.

English: Vikram Sampath for *My Name is Gauhar Jaan! – The Life and Times of a Musician.*

Gujarati: Dhwanil Parekh for *Antim Yuddha.*

Hindi: Uma Shankar Choudhary for *Kahte Hain Tab Shanshaah So Rahe The.*

Kannada: Veeranna Madiwalara for *Nelada Karuneya Dani.*

Kashmiri: Nisar Azam for *Patte Leji Zoon Daras.*

Konkani: Jofa Gonsalves for *Nirnay.*

Maithili: Anand Kumar Jha for *Hathat Parivartan.*

Malayalam: Sushmesh Chandroth for *Marana Vidyalayam.*

Manipuri: Devchand for *Nongthangna Mutkhrabada.*

Marathi: Aishwarya Patekar for *Bhuishastra.*

Nepali: Kamal Regmi for *Srijana Ra Abhista.*

Odia: Gayatribala Panda for *Gaan.*

Punjabi: Paramveer Singh for *Amrit Vela.*

Rajasthani: Dula Ram Saharan for *Peer.*

Sanskrit: Paramanand Jha for *Kavyakaveri.*

Santali: Satilal Murmu for *Jagron.*

Sindhi: Manoj Chawla 'Tanha' for *Pinjraa* in 2015.

Tamil: M. Thavasi for *Sevalkattu.*

Telugu: Vempalli Gangadhar for *Jumma.*

Urdu: Vishal Khullar for *Dhund Mein Amaan.*

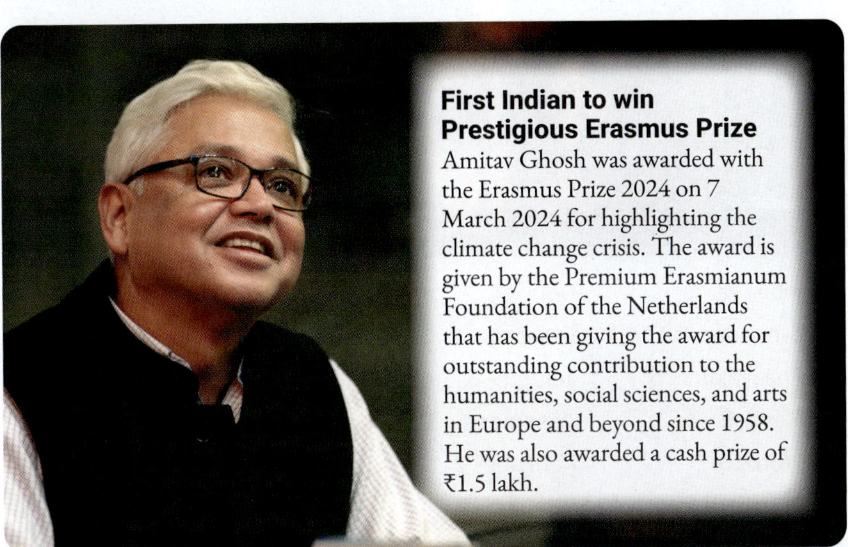

First Indian to win Prestigious Erasmus Prize

Amitav Ghosh was awarded with the Erasmus Prize 2024 on 7 March 2024 for highlighting the climate change crisis. The award is given by the Premium Erasmianum Foundation of the Netherlands that has been giving the award for outstanding contribution to the humanities, social sciences, and arts in Europe and beyond since 1958. He was also awarded a cash prize of ₹1.5 lakh.

First winner of Grinzane Cavour Prize

Anita Desai won the lifetime achievement award of the Grinzane Cavour Prize on 18 July 2005 in Piedmont, Italy.

Highest monetary prize

• *Fiction:* The JCB Prize, established in 2018, is the most valuable prize in Indian literature, amounting to ₹25 lakh (2.5 million). Funded by JCB, a British manufacturing firm, the prize is awarded to the best work of fiction by an Indian citizen in English or translated from another language into English. Each of the five shortlisted books is awarded ₹1 lakh (0.1 million) and a separate prize of ₹5 lakh (0.5 million) is given if the winning entry is a translation. Mita Kapur, founder and CEO of Siyahi, a literary consultancy organization, now serves as its director.

• *Non-Fiction:* The richest prize for non-fiction writing is the New India Foundation Prize, valued at ₹15 lakh (1.5 million).

First Indian-origin winner of the Pulitzer Prize – fiction

Jhumpa Lahiri's *Interpreter of Maladies* (Mariner Books/Houghton Mifflin) won the Pulitzer Prize for Fiction in 2000.

First winner of the Rabindranath Tagore Literary Prize

The Rabindranath Tagore Literary Prize, started in 2018, is awarded annually for valuable contributions to literature and poetry. Kabir (awarded posthumously) was the first awardee for *One Hundred Poems of Kabir* in 2018.

First winners of the JCB prize

The JCB Prize was established in 2018 and is awarded annually. The first winners were:

• *Man*: Benyamin for *Jasmine Days* in 2018.

• *Woman*: Madhuri Vijay for *The Far Field* in 2019.

First winners of the Kamaladevi Chattopadhyay NIF Book Prize

Established in 2018, the Kamaladevi Chattopadhyay NIF Book Prize is an annual award for non-fiction books published in the preceding year. The first winner of the award was Milan Vaishnav in 2018 for *When Crime Pays: Money and Muscle in Indian Politics.*

The Jnanpith Award

The Bharatiya Jnanpith confers the Jnanpith Award annually to the authors with an 'outstanding contribution towards literature'. The highest literary award and also the oldest, the first award was conferred in 1965.

First recipients of the Jnanpith Award

The Jnanpith Award is presented annually by the Bharatiya Jnanpith to an Indian author for their contribution to literature. The first winners were:

- *Man*: Malayalam poet G. Sankara Kurup (1901–78) was the recipient of the first Jnanpith Award in 1965, the year of its inception, for his anthology of poems, *Odakkuzhal*.
- *Woman*: Ashapurna Devi (1909–95), Bengali novelist and poet, was the first woman author to receive the Jnanpith Award in 1976 for her novel *Pratham Pratishruti* (which was published in 1965), the first of a trilogy that included *Subarnalata* and *Bakul Katha*.

Languages with the most Jnanpith Awardees

Hindi:- 12
Kannada:- 8
Malayalam:- 6
Bengali:- 6
Urdu:- 5
Marathi:- 4
Odia:- 4
Gujarati:- 4
Telugu:- 3
Assamese:- 3
Konkani:- 2
Punjabi:- 2
Sanskrit:- 2
Tamil:- 2
English:- 1
Kashmiri:- 1

Jnanpith Awardees

Year	Awardee	Language
1965	G. Sankara Kurup	Malayalam
1966	Tarasankar Bandyopadhyay	Bengali
1967	Umashankar Joshi	Gujarati
	Kuppali Venkatappa Puttappa 'Kuvempu'	Kannada
1968	Sumitranandan Pant	Hindi
1969	Firaq Gorakhpuri	Urdu
1970	Viswanatha Satyanarayana	Telugu
1971	Bishnu Dey	Bengali
1972	Ramdhari Singh 'Dinkar'	Hindi
1973	D.R. Bendre	Kannada
	Gopinath Mohanty	Odia
1974	Vishnu Sakharam Khandekar	Marathi
1975	Akilan	Tamil
1976	Ashapoorna Devi	Bengali
1977	K. Shivaram Karanth	Kannada
1978	Sachchidananda Vatsyayan 'Agyeya'	Hindi
1979	Birendra Kumar Bhattacharya	Assamese
1980	S.K. Pottekkatt	Malayalam
1981	Amrita Pritam	Punjabi
1982	Mahadevi Varma	Hindi
1983	Masti Venkatesha Iyengar	Kannada
1984	Thakazhi Sivasankara Pillai	Malayalam
1985	Pannalal Patel	Gujarati
1986	Sachidananda Routray	Odia
1987	Vishnu Vaman Shirwadkar 'Kusumagraj'	Marathi
1988	C. Narayana Reddy	Telugu
1989	Qurratulain Hyder	Urdu
1990	Vinayaka Krishna Gokak	Kannada
1991	Subhash Mukhopadhyay	Bengali
1992	Naresh Mehta	Hindi
1993	Sitakant Mahapatra	Odia
1994	U.R. Ananthamurthy	Kannada
1995	M.T. Vasudevan Nair	Malayalam

Year	Awardee	Language
1996	Mahasweta Devi	Bengali
1997	Ali Sardar Jafri	Urdu
1998	Girish Karnad	Kannada
1999	Nirmal Verma	Hindi
	Gurdial Singh	Punjabi
2000	Mamoni Raisom Goswami	Assamese
2001	Rajendra Shah	Gujarati
2002	Jayakanthan	Tamil
2003	Vinda Karandikar	Marathi
2004	Rehman Rahi	Kashmiri
2005	Kunwar Narayan	Hindi
2006	Ravindra Kelekar	Konkani
	Satya Vrat Shastri	Sanskrit
2007	O.N.V. Kurup	Malayalam
2008	Akhlaq Mohammed Khan 'Shahryar'	Urdu
2009	Amarkant	Hindi
	Shrilal Shukla	Hindi
2010	Chandrashekhara Kambara	Kannada
2011	Pratibha Ray	Odia
2012	Ravuri Bharadhwaja	Telugu
2013	Kedarnath Singh	Hindi
2014	Bhalchandra Nemade	Marathi
2015	Raghuveer Chaudhari	Gujarati
2016	Shankha Ghosh	Bengali
2017	Krishna Sobti	Hindi
2018	Amitav Ghosh	English
2019	Akkitham Achuthan Namboothiri	Malayalam
2021	Nilamani Phookan	Assamese
2022	Damodar Mauzo	Konkani
2023	Rambhadracharya	Sanskrit
	Gulzar	Urdu
2024	Vinod Kumar Shukla	Hindi

MEDIA AND COMMUNICATIONS

{Sunday}
Hindustan Times
M3M
दैनिक जागरण
policybazaar.com
HAR FAMILY HOGI INSURED
कहीं हॉस्पिटल का
लाखों का बिल
NBT

PRINT

First printing press

The first printing press came to India accidentally, in 1556, when the patriarch designate of Abyssinia (now Ethiopia, Africa) broke his journey at Goa and later died there. The printing press was left behind. The printers were a Spaniard named João de Bustamante and his Indian assistant, whose name is not known.

First paper-making machine

William Carey (1761–1834), a British Christian missionary, translator, social reformer, and cultural anthropologist, who founded Serampore College in Bengal, first set up a paper-making machine in Calcutta (now Kolkata), West Bengal in 1830.

Top: Reference image of a printing press
Below: Serampore College in Bengal

First indigenous typewriters

- Godrej & Boyce Manufacturing Company Ltd manufactured India's first manual typewriter in 1955. It was designed and created entirely by Indian engineers.
- Blackwood India Ltd in Calcutta, established in 1960 and renamed J.K. Business Machines in 1961, were the first makers of portable typewriters in the country.
- The first indigenous electronic typewriters were manufactured by Hindustan Teleprinters Ltd in 1975.

First lithographic printing

Lithographic printing was introduced by the Calcutta Art Studio in 1878 in Calcutta (now Kolkata), West Bengal.

First multilingual press

A multilingual press for all the main local Indian languages was first set up in Serampore, Bengal (Srirampur, West Bengal), in 1800 by Christian missionaries.

Earliest type

The first types in any Indian language were cast in Goa in 1577 by João Gonçalves reportedly assisted by Father Pero Luis, who was a Tamil Jesuit priest.

First typewriters

The first typewriters were imported into India in 1896.

First press regulation

The Censorship of Press Act of 1799 was the first censorship regulation to enforce wartime restrictions on the press. It was enacted by the then Governor General Lord Wellesley, who anticipated a French invasion of India. All news was scrutinized, including 'pre-censorship' before publication, by a special security administration unit with a view to preventing information leaks.

First news agency

The Press Trust of India (PTI), which is a non-profit sharing cooperative of Indian newspapers, was established on 27 August 1947. It took over the Associated Press of India and the Indian operations of Reuters. It provided news, photographs, features, and infographics from February 1949 onwards.

First news agency to supply news in Urdu

On 5 June 1992, the United News of India (UNI) became the first agency in the world to supply Urdu news. It remains the only agency to do so.

The only handwritten newspaper

The Musalman, the oldest Urdu language daily newspaper, published from Chennai, Tamil Nadu, is the only handwritten newspaper in the world. It is a four-page evening paper handwritten by four calligraphers or *katibs*, and printed. Established in 1927 by Syed Azmatulla, it has not missed a single day's publication. The paper has correspondents all over India and sells at 75 paise a copy to around 25,000 subscribers.

First newspaper

Hicky's Bengal Gazette or the *Original Calcutta General Advertiser*, India's and Asia's first newspaper, was launched on 29 June 1780 by James Augustus Hicky, an Irishman.

First newspaper for visually impaired people

Swagat Thorat's *Sparshdnyan*, launched in February 2008, is India's first newspaper for visually challenged people. Its name means 'knowledge by touch', and it is published in Marathi on the 1st and 15th of every month.

First non-English newspaper

In 1794, the Reverend Harutyun Shmavonyan edited and published *Azdarar* in the Armenian script in Madras (now Chennai), Tamil Nadu. This was the first Armenian journal in the world and the first non-English one in India.

HICKY's
BENGAL GAZETTE;
OR THE ORIGINAL
Calcutta General Advertiser.

A Weekly Political and Commercial Paper, Open to all Parties, but influenced by None.

From Saturday March 3d to Saturday March 10th 1781. No. VII

Hicky's Bengal Gazette

First newsprint factory

The first paper mill in India to manufacture newsprint was a factory at Nepanagar, Burhanpur District, Madhya Pradesh, set up in January 1955.

First vernacular paper

Samachar Darpan was published in Bengali from Serampore, Bengal, by William Carey and John Clark Marshman from May 1818 onwards. Marshman was a British journalist, historian, and publisher of the *Friend of India* from which *The Statesman* newspaper descended.

Reverend Harutyun Shmavonyan and the Armenian Newspaper *Azdarar*

First Hindi newspaper

Banaras Akhbar began in 1845, under the editorship of Govind Narayan Thatte, as the first Hindi newspaper.

First financial daily

The Economic Times, India's first financial daily, was launched by the Times of India Group in March 1961. Like the London-based *Financial Times*, it too was printed on salmon-pink paper.

Old Image of the *Times of India* Building

English daily with the largest readership

The Times of India, headquartered in Mumbai, Maharashtra, has a recorded readership of 1,73,44,000 (2019 Q4; Indian Readership Survey [IRS]).

First daily with an international edition

In February 1994, India's global newspaper *The Asian Age* was launched simultaneously from Delhi, Mumbai, and London. It has a Kolkata edition too.

William Carrey

First magazine for visually challenged people

White Print was the first lifestyle magazine in English in India for visually challenged people. It was launched in May 2013 by Upasana Makati, a former communications student from the University of Ottawa, Canada. This sixty-four page monthly, printed at the National Association for the Blind, Mumbai, Maharashtra, and circulated across India, features articles about sports, politics, culture, fashion, and technology, besides short stories and reader contributions. *White Print* has also released Braille-tactile alphabet books in Braille, in both English and Hindi, which are called 'Tactabet'.

First newspaper to be printed in colour

The Hindu, with its headquarters in Madras began as a weekly in 1878 and turned into a daily in 1889. A family-run newspaper, it was the first to be printed in colour in 1940. It was also the first Indian newspaper to own aeroplanes to distribute newspapers (1963), and the first newspaper to digitize and be available online (1995).

First magazine in Hindi

Saraswati, India's first Hindi monthly magazine, was published in January 1900. Its founder was the well-known printer and publisher Chintamani Ghosh and the magazine was published by the Indian Press, which was based in Allahabad (now Prayagraj), Uttar Pradesh.

First women's magazine in English

The Indian Ladies' Magazine was first published in English in 1901 by Kamala Satthianadhan in Madras.

First women's magazine in an Indian language

Masik Patrika in Bengali, published from Calcutta, in 1854, was the first women's magazine in an Indian language.

THE INDIAN LADIES' MAGAZINE

Vol. 1.] AUGUST, 1901. [No. 2.

CONTENTS.

	PAGE
Ourselves	25
Queen Victoria and Queen Alexandra.—(Illustrated)	26
Social Intercourse between European and Indian Ladies	29
Col. Meadows Taylor's "Seeta": A Study	31
The Vedic Wife	34
In the Forest:—A Poem	36
"A Little Child shall lead them":—A Hindu Story	37
Pundita Ramabai and her Work.—(Illustrated)	40
Miss Marie Corelli on "Sovran Woman"	43
Friendly Chats between Ourselves:—The Home	45
Seriousness: A Fancy	46
The Low-Caste Wife: A Sketch from Life	48
An Indian Lady's Appreciation	49
Editorial Notes:—Women's Work in the Handicrafts; Miss Ghosal on the Education of Indian Girls	50
Things Seen:—The Marina	52
Indian Cookery	[illegible]
Correspondence:—Lady Ampthill's Women's Memorial to Queen Victoria; The Maharani's Girls' College, Mysore; A Famous Indian Lady	53
News and Notes	55

Top: Chintamani Ghosh; *Below*: *The Indian Ladies' Magazine*

First vernacular periodical

Digdarshan, a Bengali monthly, first appeared in April 1818.

First letters to the editor column

The letters to the editor column was introduced in the biweekly magazine *Calcutta Journal*, first published in 1878 in Bengal.

Multi-edition daily with the largest readership

Dainik Jagran, which has its headquarters in Kanpur, Uttar Pradesh, leads with 37 editions across 11 states and a readership of 6,86,67,000 (2019 Q4; IRS).

State/UT with the most Indian-language publications

Delhi leads among all states and UTs in the most number of Indian language publications in as many as languages. It is followed by Maharashtra, Uttarakhand, and Tamil Nadu with publications in fourteen languages each. Gujarat comes after that with publications in eleven languages as of 2020–21.

Daily with largest readership – Hindi

Dainik Jagran, which is headquartered in Kanpur, Uttar Pradesh, has a readership of 6,86,67,000 (2019 Q4; IRS).

State/UT with most registered newspapers

Uttar Pradesh, with 21,336 registered publications, is the state with the most registered newspaper publications.

Largest read regional-language daily

Malayala Manorama, with its headquarters in Kottayam, Kerala, has a readership of 1,77,63,000 (2019 Q4; IRS).

100 years of *Malayala Manorama*

First newspaper run entirely by women

Khabar Lahariya is the first newspaper in India that is entirely staffed, edited, and published by women. The 8-page rural weekly newspaper in Hindi is sold in 600 villages. It was launched in 2002 in Chitrakoot District, Uttar Pradesh. In 2009, it was awarded the UNESCO King Sejong Literary Prize for its contribution to literacy. It has become fully digital since 2015, and publishes on its Youtube channel and website.

Representative image of newspapers

State/UT with the most newspaper and periodical publications

Uttar Pradesh, with 21,166 publications, leads with the maximum number of publications in India. It is followed by Maharashtra, with 19,796 publications, and Delhi with 16,351 of them as of 2020–21.

Most read English magazine

India Today, a weekly published from Noida, Uttar Pradesh, by the India Today Group, has a readership of 94,93,000 (2019 Q4; IRS).

Oldest children's magazine

Chandamama, founded by Telugu film-makers B. Nagi Reddy and Aluri Chakrapani was launched in July 1947 in Telugu. It was edited by Kodavatiganti Kutumba Rao. The magazine ceased publication in 1998. In 2007, it was acquired by Geodesic Ltd. Its last edition came out in March 2013 and since then its status is unknown. In its heyday, *Chandamama* was published in 13 languages and had a readership of around 2,00,000 across the country.

Chandamama, Hindi Edition

Most circulated government publication

Employment News, an English weekly published from New Delhi by the Publications Division, Ministry of Information and Broadcasting, Government of India, has the highest circulation of 2,39,498 among government publications (as of 2019).

Most read Hindi magazine

India Today (Hindi), a weekly published from Noida, Uttar Pradesh, by the India Today Group, has a total readership of 66,41,000 (2019 Q4; IRS).

Most read magazine in a regional language

Vanitha, a Malayalam fortnightly magazine, published from Kottayam, Kerala, by the Malayala Manorama Group, has a readership of 58,86,000 (2019 Q4; IRS).

State/UT with most publications in a single language

Uttar Pradesh, with 16,557 publications in Hindi, leads among all states and UTs with the most publications in a single language (Hindi). It is followed by Madhya Pradesh, with 11,973 Hindi-language publications, and Maharashtra, with 9,982 publications in Marathi.

First Indian-origin journalist to win the Pulitzer Prize

Gobind Behari Lal (1889–1982), a science journalist in the USA, won the Pulitzer Prize in 1937.

Longest-running women's magazine

Femina Magazine

Femina, which started in July 1959 with Frene Talyarkhan as its first editor, continues to be published. It is now published by Worldwide Media, which is owned by the Times Group. It was also the first lifestyle magazine of the country in English, and has the highest circulation in its category (1,08,560 in August 2019).

Oldest extant newspaper – English

The Times of India began on 3 November 1838 as a biweekly, initially called *Bombay Times and Journal of Commerce*. It was renamed *The Times of India* in 1850, with J.E. Brennan as its editor.

Longest spell as editor

Tushar Kanti Ghosh

Tushar Kanti Ghosh (1898–1994) was editor of the *Amrita Bazar Patrika*, based in Kolkata for 64 years. He had founded the newspaper in 1928.

Most pages in a newspaper supplement

Kannada daily *Vijayavani*'s Mysuru edition brought out a special issue with 320 pages in 10 volumes on 25 March 2020. This supplement was dedicated to Shri Mayakara Madappa, a social reformer and spiritual leader of the 16th century. The newspaper was sold at a price of ₹4.

OWNERSHIP PATTERN OF REGISTERED PUBLICATIONS

(As on 31.03.2025)

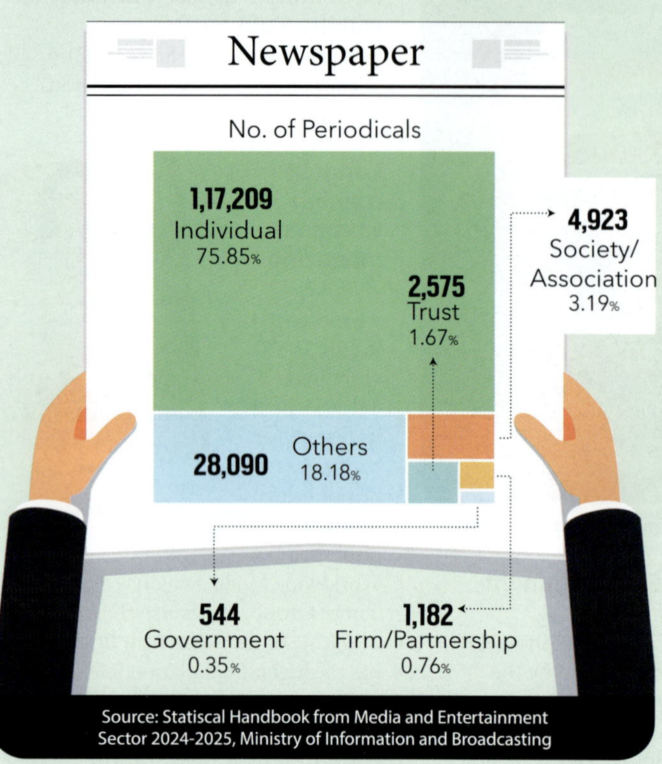

Source: Statiscal Handbook from Media and Entertainment Sector 2024-2025, Ministry of Information and Broadcasting

NUMBER OF REGISTERED PUBLICATIONS AND GROWTH FROM 2019-2025

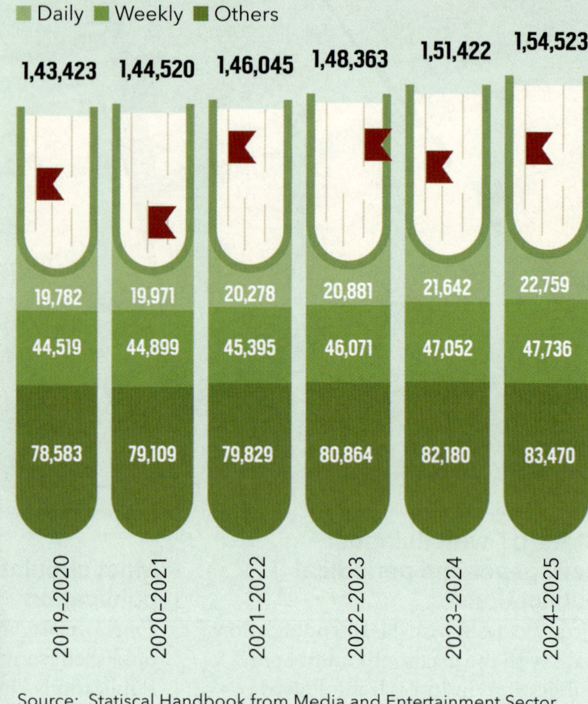

Source: Statiscal Handbook from Media and Entertainment Sector 2024-2025, Ministry of Information and Broadcasting

LANGUAGE WISE REGISTERED PUBLICATIONS (As on 31.03.2025)

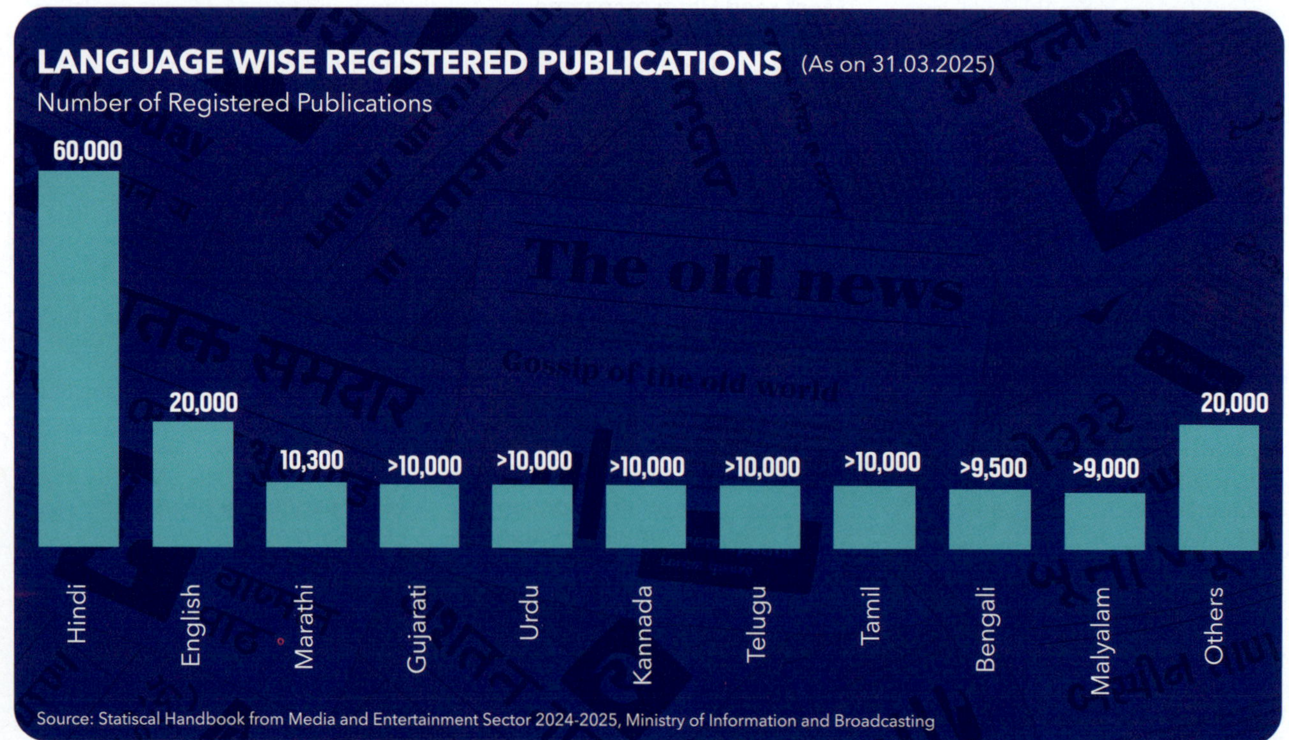

Source: Statiscal Handbook from Media and Entertainment Sector 2024-2025, Ministry of Information and Broadcasting

Building of *Bombay Samachar*

Oldest extant newspaper – regional language

The *Bombay Samachar*, now titled *Mumbai Samachar*, is the oldest continuously published newspaper in any language in India, and continues to be published. Launched on 1 July 1822 by Fardoonjee Marazban (1787–1847), the daily is published in both Gujarati and English. Marazban, who was from Bombay (now Mumbai), Maharashtra, was a printer and a newspaper editor. He established vernacular journalism in India and initiated the production of Gujarati types.

Most pages in a newspaper

Dainik Bhaskar's Indore edition brought out a special issue with 128 pages on 17 September 2020. This issue was on the theme 'Aatma Nirbhar Indore'.

Most articles published in a year – single publication

Vinod Chanrashekhar Dixit has written a total number of 4,505 articles in Free Press Gujarat between the period of 15 June 2024 to 15 May 2025.

Longest career as a journalist

B.P. Sharma, a journalist from Jammu and Kashmir, who died in 2005 at the age of 97, was an active journalist for over 70 years. He established the Jammu station of Radio Kashmir (All India Radio), and was its first director. He also worked with the news agency Reuters, *The Times of India, Hindustan Times* and *The Tribune*. Later, he served as the principal information officer of Jammu and Kashmir.

Longest letter to the editor

Vinod Chandrashekhar Dixit (b. 1 December 1964) from Ahmedabad, Gujarat, wrote the longest letter to the editor, which was published in *Free Press*, Gujarat, on 28 March 2024. He wrote a total of 3,973 words on the topic *'Sant Mavji Maharaj - an incarnation of Lord Krishna'*.

Most columns published in a year – multiple publications

Dr Prem Kumar Sharma (b. 9 November 1958) has the most number of columns published in a year. He has written nearly 1, 275 columns for multiple publications. His columns have been published in *Haribhoomi, Punjab Kesari, Voice Weekly, Hindustan Times* and other dailies.

Most articles published in a year – multiple publications

Vinod Chandrashekhar Dixit (b. 1 December 1964) from Ahmedabad, Gujarat, published the most number of articles in newspapers and magazines in a year. The total number of articles published by him between 1 March 2022 and 28 February 2023 was 1,846.

RADIO

First broadcasting service

The Madras Presidency Radio Club, under the stewardship of C.V. Krishnaswamy Chetty, started a broadcasting service in 1924, using a tiny 40 W transmitter with an effective range of only 8 km.

First controller of broadcasting

Lionel Fielden took over as the first controller of broadcasting for the Indian State Broadcasting Service (ISBS) on 30 August 1935 in British India. A senior BBC producer, he spent 5 years in India, establishing a countrywide radio service. On 8 June 1936, the ISBS was renamed All India Radio.

First direct relay

A historic occasion, the first direct relay coincided with India's 'freedom at midnight' from British colonial rule. The ceremonies for the transfer of power from Britain to an independent India on the night of 14–15 August 1947 at the Central Hall of the Parliament House in Delhi were relayed by All India Radio (AIR).

Emblem of Akashvani Bhavan

First private radio station

On 10 September 1935, Akashvani Mysore, a private radio station, was set up in present-day Karnataka by Dr M.V. Gopalaswamy, professor of psychology and principal of the Maharaja's College, at his residence.

Longest running commentary

Melville de Mellow's running commentary on the last journey of Mahatma Gandhi on 31 January 1948, a day after his assassination, lasted for more than 7 continuous hours.

First national broadcast of music

AIR broadcast its first national music programme on 20 July 1952 with sitar maestro Pandit Ravi Shankar as the music conductor.

First private FM broadcaster
Times FM from the Times Group commenced operations in 1993 from Ahmedabad, Gujarat. It ran till June 1998 and was relaunched as Radio Mirchi in 2000. Over the years, Radio Mirchi has expanded its presence across 63 cities in India and multiple stations in the UAE and the US.

First private FM station
Radio City Bangalore, based in Bengaluru in Karnataka, started on 3 July 2001, becoming the country's first private FM radio station, after the Government of India opened up the FM broadcasting industry to private companies and competition.

First frequency modulation (FM) service
AIR inaugurated the first ever FM service from Madras, on 23 July 1977.

Largest media organization
All India Radio, established in 1936, today reaches almost the entire population across the length and breadth of the country and nearly 92 per cent of the total area, making it the largest media organization by reach. It broadcasts in 23 languages and 179 dialects. Programmes of its External Services Division are broadcast in 11 Indian and 16 foreign languages.

First broadcasting company
The Indian Broadcasting Company (IBC) was set up in Bombay, on 23 July 1927, with a medium-wave transmitter that had a range of 50 km.

First broadcast
In June 1923, the Radio Club of Bombay made the first ever broadcast in the country from Bombay. This was followed by the setting up of the Calcutta Radio Club in West Bengal around 5 months later.

First national broadcast of a play
In July 1956, AIR first aired a play that was broadcast countrywide. The play was *Prafulla* by Girish Chandra Ghosh. It was a Bangla stage play.

First news bulletin
The first news bulletin over radio was aired in English on 23 July 1927 from the Indian Broadcasting Company's station in Mumbai. As the station did not have a news bureau, the bulletin was based on news supplied by Reuters.

First sponsored programme
A musical programme, *Saridon Ke Saathi*, sponsored by Saridon, was aired on 3 May 1970 on the Mumbai–Pune–Nagpur radio network.

First cricket commentary
On 1 January 1936, Bertie Meyer provided commentary for a match between the All-India XI and the Maharaja of Patiala's Australian XI, from the Bombay station of AIR from 12:46 p.m. to 1:00 p.m.

First phone-in programme
Phone-in programmes were introduced on 10 January 1993 at AIR, Delhi.

Highest radio station
The Himbotingla station of AIR in Ladakh, located at an altitude of 4,053.84 m (13,300 ft) above mean sea level, is the highest radio station in the world. The 10 kW, high-power transmitters were inaugurated on 25 September 2021.

First national programme of talks
On 29 July 1953, AIR aired the first national programme of talks in English.

First relay between radio stations
On 18 January 1939, an inter-station relay took place between Delhi and Bombay.

WR Most commercial radio programmes anchored
The legendary radio announcer and programme anchor Ameen Sayani started his broadcasting career in 1951. During his career, he compèred more than 10,000 commercial radio programmes, and voiced 12,000 spots and jingles. He produced more than 38,920 publicity programmes for feature films.

Ameen Sayani

TELEVISION

First national telecast
Doordarshan (DD) started nationwide telecasts on 15 August 1982 from its TV studio in Mandi House, New Delhi.

Longest running non-fiction TV series
Krishi Darshan, a TV programme aimed at disseminating useful information on farming to rural areas and agricultural communities, started on 26 January 1967 on DD National and still continues on the channel as well as on DD Kisan. It is considered to be the longest-running non-fiction TV series.

First simultaneous tele-broadcast
Om Namah Shivay, directed by Dheeraj Kumar, was the first tele-serial to be telecast and broadcast at the same time on television and radio from March 1999.

First central production centre
Set up in 1989 at the Siri Fort Complex, New Delhi, the Central Production Centre began with 2 large studios equipped with modern facilities to produce high-quality, well-researched programmes.

First private producer of national news
In February 1995, New Delhi Television Ltd (NDTV) became the first private producer of national news with the show titled *The News Tonight*, which was hosted by Prannoy Roy at 8:00 p.m. They were the first private broadcasters for news on Doordarshan.

First director general of Doordarshan
P.V. Krishnamoorthy became the first director general of Doordarshan on 1 April 1976, the day Doordarshan and AIR were each given separate status.

Doordarshan Kendra

Tallest TV tower
The tallest TV tower in India is located in Rameswaram, Tamil Nadu. The height of the tower is 323 m (1,060 ft). The tower was built in 1995 and is used by Doordarshan for television broadcasting. It is made of reinforced cement concrete, and the mast is of lattice steel.

First telecast
The first experimental telecast was carried out in Delhi on 15 September 1959 from a makeshift studio with the help of a single transmitter of 500 W which carried signals up to 25 km for an operational time of an hour a day. The studio was relocated to Rajpath for the first live telecast of the Republic Day parade in 1960.

Most watched daily soap
Anupamaa, starring Rupali Ganguly and Sudhanshu Panday, is the most watched daily soap in India between 21 and 27 October, according to the Broadcast Audience Research Council (BARC).

Stamps to mark the 60th Anniversary of Doordarshan

First newsreader
Doordarshan began a five-minute news bulletin in 1965 with Pratima Puri as the first TV newsreader.

First teleshopping programme
Shopping through TV was introduced on 1 January 1995, with an hour-long home-shopping show on Doordarshan's Metro channel in Delhi.

First colour TVs
In 1982, the year India hosted the Asiad (Asian Games), colour TVs were introduced in India.

First satellite linkage
The first satellite linkage experiment was launched on 1 August 1975 in 6 states in the country for a year. Later, satellite channels were available for the first time in 1991 to a select few who had access to the powerful dish antennas in embassies and five-star hotels.

First private channel
Zee TV, the first private television channel in the country, was launched in October 1992 in collaboration with Star TV and Zee Telefilms Ltd.

First business channel
Asia Business News International (ABNI), a 24/7 business channel, was launched on 14 February 1996 by the Hinduja Group in collaboration with Asia Business News (ABN) and TV18.

First Indian animation serial
Featuring Ghayab, the do-gooder ghost, *Ghayab Aya* was the first fully 'made-in-India' serialized animation film telecast on Doordarshan in 1986. The animator director was the well-known painter–illustrator Suddhasattwa Basu.

First colour transmission
An experimental telecast was conducted from the Madras TV station on 18 July 1980 for an hour. It was transmitted to Delhi viewers.

Podhigai Tower – the TV tower of Doordarshan in Chennai

First TV station to get a second channel
Delhi was the first TV station to get a second channel on 17 September 1984.

First 24-hour news channel
Star News, India's first 24-hour news channel, started on 3 February 1998, with news updates every hour from 6:00 a.m.

First private satellite channel
Aaj Tak was the first private satellite channel permitted in 2000.

Aaj Tak: First private satellite channel

First infotainment channel
DD-3, which was Doordarshan's dedicated channel for infotainment, was launched on 14 November 1995.

First video film
Teri Meri Kahani, the first video film, was produced by B.R. Chopra in 1981.

First serial
Teesra Rasta was the first fiction serial telecast from Doordarshan Kendra, New Delhi, starting from 2 May 1962.

First high-definition channel
The first high-definition (HD) channel was introduced in India by Discovery Communications in March 2010.

First sci-fi serial
Space City Sigma, produced by Studio Ifekt, was telecast from 21 May 1989.

First telefilm
Satyajit Ray's *Sadgati* was telecast on the national network on 13 April 1981. This 52 -minute. telefilm was based on Munshi Premchand's short story. Produced by Doordarshan, it starred well-known actors, such as Om Puri and Smita Patil.

Dialogue writer with most credited episodes – TV series – fiction
Munisha Rajpal, from Andheri West, Mumbai has been the dialogue writer for the TV show Yeh Rishta Kya Kehlata Hai for over 10 years, 11 months, and 14 days. She has been credited with 2,863 episodes.

First DTH service
Launched on 2 October 2013, Dish TV was the first Direct-to-Home (DTH) service in India.

A satellite dish on the roof of a house (representative image)

GROWTH OF PRIVATE SATELLITE TV CHANNELS IN INDIA FROM 2019-2025

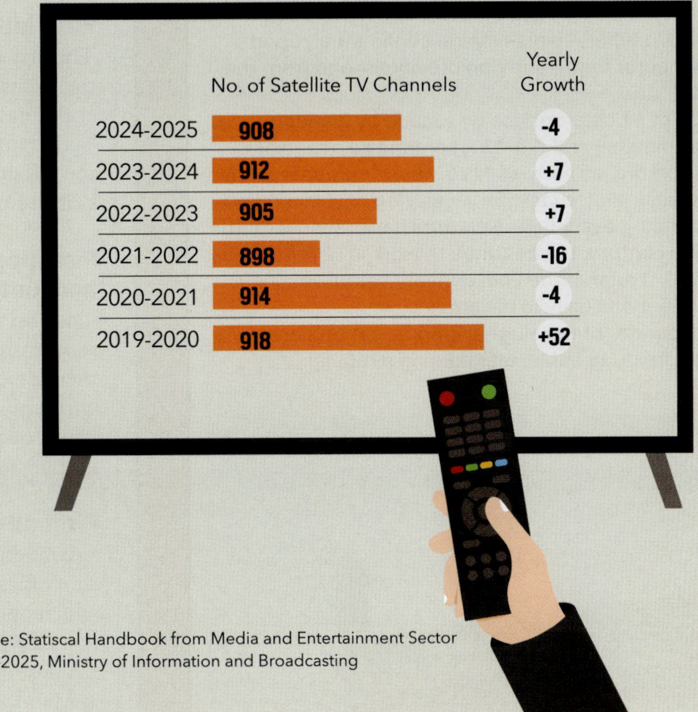

Source: Statiscal Handbook from Media and Entertainment Sector 2024-2025, Ministry of Information and Broadcasting

POST AND PHILATELY

First mail by steamboat

In 1828, mail was sent by a steamboat service between Calcutta (now Kolkata), West Bengal and Allahabad (now Prayagraj), Uttar Pradesh, along 1,266 km of the Ganga River. This is the earliest instance of mail delivery by steamer in Asia.

First window delivery of letters

The Madras General Post Office or GPO (now in Chennai, Tamil Nadu) began the window delivery of letters from 1 June 1786 in the then Fort St George Square.

First postal training centre

Established on 2 April 1951, the postal training centre at Saharanpur, Uttar Pradesh, was the first training centre in Asia, set up exclusively for postal and telegraph personnel.

Madras General Post Office

WR First electronic Indian Postal Order

On 22 March 2013, the first electronic Indian Postal Order (E-IPO) was introduced for Indian nationals living abroad. On 14 February 2014, the service was also extended to all Indian citizens.

WR Largest postal network

With a network of 1,56,434 post offices, the Indian Department of Posts has the world's largest postal network as recorded till 31 March 2021.

First postcard

The Postal and Telecommunications Department issued the first postcard on 1 July 1879.

First dead letter office

A post office for undelivered, unclaimed letters and letters with incomplete addresses was set up during 1834–37 in Benson Town in Bangalore. It was also called a Returned Letter Office.

Earliest postal communication

- In India, the earliest evidence of a systematic mail service is found during the reign of Chandragupta Maurya (r. 321–297 BCE), who ruled from Magadha (now in southern Bihar). In his empire, confidential reports were dispatched from the emperor to the outlying provinces, and from the provinces back to the ruler.
- The first recorded mention of a postal service was made by Ziauddin Barani, who wrote that Alauddin Khilji (r. 1296–1316) organized a regular foot-runner service, called *harkara*, as early as 1296. These *harkaras* carried a baton with bells and ran across allotted territory, carrying mail in a relay system with the runners changing every mile. *Harkaras* have faded with the advent of railways in the 19th century, but continue to work in remote areas.
- Sikandar Lodi (r. 1488–1518), a ruler of the Lodi dynasty set up small posts across his kingdom and sent *firmans* daily to his armies.
- Babur (r. 1483–1530), the founder of the Mughal Empire, set up horse couriers from his capital at Agra up to Kabul, maintaining a regular 'postal' system.

First hot-air balloon carrying mail
A special postal cover was carried in a hot-air balloon carrier of India Post from Sakthi Mills Ground, Pollachi, Coimbatore District, Tamil Nadu, to the postmaster of Kovipalayam, Pollachi, on 3 January 2016.

First delivery peons
• *Men:* Postmen or delivery peons were first engaged on a security bond with a specific responsibility, as part of postal reforms carried out in Bengal in 1840. They were dressed in uniform and wore badges supplied by post offices. They were allowed to earn *baksheesh* of 2 pies (1 pie = 1/192 of a rupee) on each letter delivered, in addition to the collection of postage due to the post office.

• *Women:* K. Padmakshi Amma, who worked in the Thiruvananthapuram postal division in Kerala, joined service on 19 February 1959 as the country's first postwoman.

First Indian postmaster general
• *Man:* Rai Bahadur Saligram became the first Indian postmaster general for the North-Western Provinces in 1881.

• *Woman:* Sushila Chaurasia, who was born in Bijapur, Karnataka, in 1923, was the first woman to become postmaster general in the country. She assumed charge of the Madhya Pradesh circle on 24 May 1979.

First woman postal inspector
R. Santhakumari, who was from the Thiruvananthapuram postal division, Kerala, passed the inspector's examination in 1968 to become the first woman postal inspector.

First letter by airmail
The first airmail letter was introduced in the country in November 1944. Priced at 6 annas, the airmail letter was called an 'aerogramme' and could be sent to the UK and other countries under the British Empire.

First post office savings bank account
The post office savings bank, which started on 1 April 1882, introduced the then revolutionary concept of banking with a post office instead of a bank, which had been the usual method of keeping one's savings.

First all-woman post office
• Avinashilingam Home Science College post office in Coimbatore, Tamil Nadu, which opened in January 1966, was the first all-woman post office in India.

• A post office, which started functioning at Manoramaganj in Indore, Madhya Pradesh, on 31 March 1976, is also fully run by women employees only.

First insured mail service
The system of insurance post for letters and parcels, which was then called the 'insured mail service', was introduced on 1 January 1878.

First computerized registration centre
The first computerized registration centre (CRC) was opened in June 1996 at the Market Road wing of the New Delhi General Post Office (GPO).

First drive-in post office
A drive-in post office was inaugurated on 11 November 1975 in Pune, Maharashtra.

First mobile post office
On 1 November 2011, the Department of Post, Government of India, launched the Post Office on Wheels initiative with its first mobile van running in Pune, Maharashtra. The van worked from 8:00 a.m. to 8:00 p.m. daily covering 30 locations in a week, stopping at each location for 2 hours. The van offered all types of postal services, including e-enabled services, selling postcards,

opening a new savings account, and selling postal life insurance, among others. The services were resumed during the lockdown period in 2020 due to COVID-19, to deliver pensions and provide mobile services in states such as Kerala and Uttar Pradesh.

First parcel service

Originally known as Bhangy post, parcel service was introduced on 2 December 1884. Its name came from the *bhangy* or bamboo stick with parcels on either end that the parcel carriers balanced on their shoulders.

First letter boxes away from post offices

A great reform in the history of Indian post took place in October 1854 with the introduction of letter boxes located away from post offices.

First automatic mail processing centre (AMPC)

The first AMPC was launched at the Mumbai GPO, Maharashtra, on 29 April 1993, and a second one was established at Chennai, Tamil Nadu, in October 1995.

The services were resumed during the lockdown period in 2020 due to COVID-19, to deliver pensions and provide mobile services in states such as Kerala and Uttar Pradesh.

First registered mail service

The first mention of a system of registration being adopted by a post office to secure the safety of coins or documents in transit was found in an advertisement published on 20 February 1795. Actual registered post was introduced in Bombay Presidency on 1 November 1849 with a postal notice on 16 October 1849. In Bengal, it was established at Calcutta GPO on 1 January 1851 and later at Madras GPO. The fee was 8 annas for registering a letter.

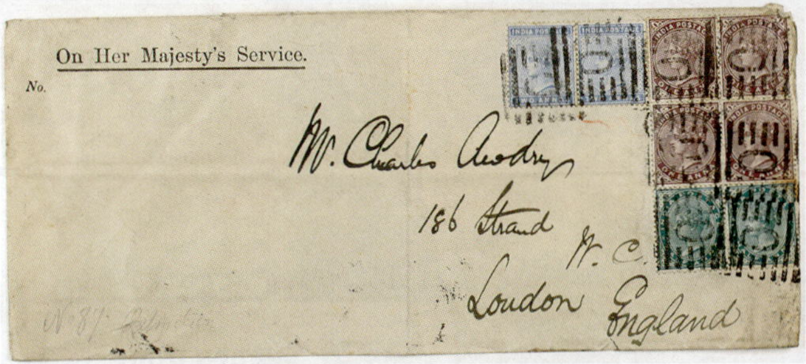

Official letter with half, one and two anna stamps

First fully-computerized post office

The Head Post Office located at Sansad Marg, New Delhi, became fully computerized on 24 June 1998.

WR First stamp

The Scinde Dawk (Provincial), India's first half-anna stamp, was issued with the help of Edward Lees Coffey, the postmaster of Karachi, on 1 July 1852 in Scinde District, Karachi (now in Pakistan). It was embossed on circular red wafers used as seals on letters, with the East India Company emblem and the legend Scinde District Dawk around the circumference. It was Asia's first ever adhesive stamp. It was withdrawn in 1854.

First stamp to be jointly issued with another country

India and the erstwhile USSR issued a set of 2 stamps on the Festival of India in the USSR, which was held in August 1990. Both countries issued the stamp with similar designs.

First express mail service

Speed Post was introduced by the Government of India on 1 August 1986, connecting 7 cities in the country, and 5 other countries to India.

Mumbai GPO

WR Stamps from most countries in honour of a person

Stamps in honour of Mahatma Gandhi have been issued from over 150 countries up to 2019.

1869-1948
МАХАТМ
ГАНД
GRANDS LEADERS MONDIAUX DE LA PAIX
tma Gandhi
SHAMIR
$1.0
CENTENARY OF THE BIRTH OF GANDHI
Re 1
MAURITIUS
MAHATMA GANDHI
2 OCT 1869 30 JAN 1948
INDIA POSTA
COURVOISIER S.A.
HAPPY CHILD-NATION'S PR
INTERNATION
YEAR OF THE CH
Centenary of Gandhi's Visit to
Mauritius 1901-2001
MAURITIUS Rs15
B/ 0.50
NDHI
Nevis
Gandhi, South Africa, 1914
भारत INDIA
O DE
E LA INDIA
SRI LANKA
.75

Longest-serving postmaster

Brother K.V.S.J. Peter, who received a Padma Shri in 1983, was the longest-serving postmaster, for 68 years. He took charge of the Shenbaganur post office in Dindigul District, Tamil Nadu, on 12 September 1913, and was in service till 8 February 1982.

First state to issue a stamp (pre-1947)

Kathiawar state in Saurashtra (later Gujarat) issued a 1-anna stamp in November 1864 with the inscription 'Saurashtra Post 1864–65'.

First customization of stamps

Initially introduced in India during the World Philatelic Exhibition 'INDIPEX-2011', 'My Stamp' is the scheme for personalized sheets of postage stamps of India Post. Such a sheet has a thumbnail image, for example–the customer's photograph, logos of institutions, artwork, famous tourist places, historical cities, heritage buildings, or wildlife, on a selected template sheet featuring postage stamps. The facility is available for both non-corporate and corporate entities.

First differently shaped stamps

• **Polygonal:** The 4- anna indigo-and-red stamp of India, issued on 15 October 1854, was polygonal, with the top and side panels raised from the main frame, which was slightly curved.
• **Circular:** The earliest circular stamp was the Scinde Dawk, though only the first printing was circular in the true sense since the later versions were issued on sheets that were usually cut square. It was the first circular stamp issued not only in India but in all of Asia. Later, the states of Indore (1889) and Jammu and Kashmir (1866–78) issued similar circular stamps.
• **Triangular:** Stamps of this shape were issued on 10 October 1985 by the Border Roads Organization.
• **Oval:** The half-anna red stamp, issued by the Indian state of Bhor (now in Maharashtra) in 1879, was oval in a horizontal format. It was imperforate and had to be cut out.

First Indian stamp featuring a woman

The Indian saints and poets series, issued on 1 October 1952, featured Mirabai, the 16th-century Bhakti poet-saint.

• **Diamond-shaped:** Depicting Raja Ram Mohan Roy, these stamps were issued on 27 September 1964.
• **Trimmed:** These revenue stamps, reissued for postal use in 1866, had their inscriptions cut off at the top and bottom.
• **Octagonal:** A set of 6 octagon-shaped commemorative stamps to mark the 150th birth anniversary of Mahatma Gandhi was released on 2 October 2019 for the first time.

First airmail

India became the first country in the world to send mail by plane when 6,500 letters and postcards were flown from Allahabad to Naini (a distance of only 18 km!) in Uttar Pradesh in a Humber- Sommer biplane by Henri Pequet on 18 February 1911. A pictorial postmark showing the aeroplane was used.

First stamp designer (pre-Independence)

Captain H.E.L. Thuillier, the deputy surveyor general of India, who was then stationed in Calcutta designed the first lithographic stamps, which were issued in 1854 and said to be engraved by an artist called Munirooddin.

Polygonal Stamp, Circular Stamp and Diamond Stamp of Raja Ram Mohan Roy

First one-rupee charity stamp

The first charity stamps were issued on 26 January 1950. Three 'Healthy India' charity stamps were brought out in denominations of 1 anna, 4 annas, and 1 rupee.

First miniature sheet

To commemorate the India International Philatelic Exhibition 1973 in Delhi, a miniature sheet with a face value of ₹4.65 was issued on 14 November 1973.

Miniature Stamp Sheet 1973

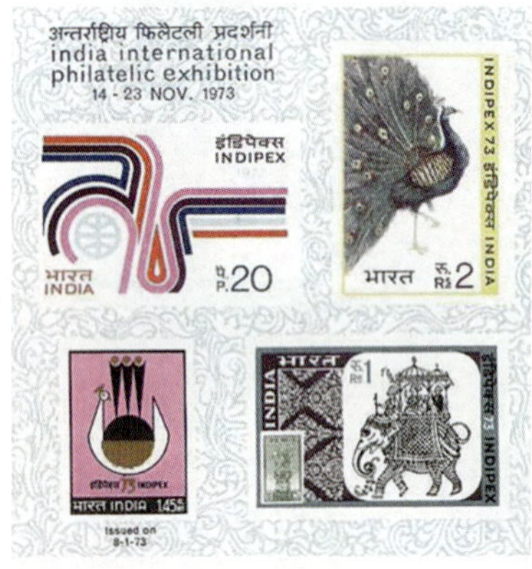

First national philatelic museum

The National Philatelic Museum of India was established in New Delhi on 6 July 1968. It has large collections of postage stamps printed and issued by India and former princely states of India, early essays, proofs, and colour trials, Indian stamps used abroad, early Indian postcards, postal stationery, and other thematic collections. It also has a philatelic bureau and postal objects, such as letter boxes from Victorian times.

First Indian president of Federation Internationale de Philatelie (FIP)

Late D.N. Jatia, a reputed philatelist, was elected president at the 59th Congress of the FIP in London, UK, on 14 May 1990.

Largest philatelic bureau

Mumbai General Post Office Philatelic Bureau also an international philatelic bureau, is the largest in the country.

First philatelic exhibition

The Philatelic Society of Bengal held an exhibition of postage stamps at the art gallery of the Government School of Art (now renamed the Government College of Art and Craft) in Calcutta in December 1894.

First philatelic society

The Philatelic Society of India, the country's first philatelic society, was formed in Mumbai on 6 March 1897.

First stamp of independent India

A 3.5-anna stamp with the inscription 'Jai Hind' was issued on 21 November 1947.

Jai Hind stamp

First autograph-inscribed stamp

A stamp issued on 7 May 1961 to commemorate the birth centenary of Nobel laureate Rabindranath Tagore had his signature inscribed on it.

First Indian to design a stamp for the United Nations

Dipok Dey (b. 1938) from Calcutta was the first Indian to design a stamp for the UN in 1985. The stamp was based on the theme of child survival.

First commemorative stamps

A set of 6 stamps was issued on 9 February 1931 on the laying of the foundation of New Delhi as the new capital of India. These were the first pictorial stamps depicting the important landmarks of the city.

First stamp featuring wildlife

The first Indian stamp depicting an animal was released in 1962, and it was a 15-paisa stamp showing the Indian rhinoceros. Next year, 5 more such stamps came out, featuring the Indian gaur (10 paise), the red panda (15 paise), the Indian elephant (30 paise), the Bengal tiger (50 paise), and the Asiatic lion (1 rupee).

A wildlife stamp

First international stamp exhibition

'India 80' was the first international stamp exhibition held in Asia under the patronage of the Federation Internationale de Philatelie (FIP), held from 25 January 1980 to 3 February 1980.

TELECOM

First Indian radio telegraphy company

The Indian Radio Telegraphy Co. was established in 1923, which ushered in the era of wireless telegraphy.

First Indo-European telegraph line

The first independent double line of telegraph from London, UK, to Karachi via Tehran, and Iran, which was constructed by M/s Siemens and Co., was opened for operations on 31 January 1870.

First fibre-optic link

India's first fibre-optic link was made in 1979 when Hindustan Cables Ltd's office at Shivaji Nagar, Pune, Maharashtra, was linked to the Cotton Telephone Exchange, a distance of 4 km.

First submarine cable link

Madras was linked to Penang, Malaysia, in 1886 with a submarine telegraph cable.

First director general of the telegraph service

Sir William O'Shaughnessy was appointed as chief superintendent of telegraphs in 1857 in colonial India.

First manufacturer of telephones

- A telecommunication maintenance and repair shop was set up at Alipore, Calcutta, in 1860. The manufacture of minor components that were needed for the Baudot Telegraph and Line stores was initiated at the P&T workshop in 1913.
- The Indian Telephone Industries Ltd was established at Doorvaninagar near Bangalore, in July 1948 for manufacturing automatic and carrier equipment. The local assembly of phones from imported parts began in 1948, and the first phone off-the-line was produced on 26 January 1949.
- The first telephone with indigenous components was made in 1951.

First known use of SOS signal

On 1 November 1977, the duty operator in the astral wireless station at Ennore, near Madras, received a weak SOS call from a cargo ship in the Bay of Bengal, stating that its engine room was on fire. The call was acknowledged and rescue ships reached in an hour.

First automatic telephone exchange

The first automatic telephone system in the country was commissioned at Simla (now Shimla), Himachal Pradesh, in 1914. The exchange had 400 working lines and another 300 lines in reserve.

First radio phone link

On 1 May 1933, Sir Samuel Hoare, the then Secretary of State for India under British rule, spoke from London, UK, to Sir Frederick Sykes, governor of Bombay, on radio phone, thus establishing a communication network between Britain and India.

Samuel Hoare

Last telegram

India's 163-year-old telegram service ended at 11:45 p.m. on 14 July 2013. Its last message was booked at the Central Telegraph Office, Janpath, New Delhi, by Ashwani Mishra, who sent telegrams to Congress leader Rahul Gandhi and the DD news director general S.M. Khan.

First SMS provider

Hutchison Max Telecom Ltd. offered a global text messaging service (SMS) in India in 2001.

First STD service

The facility for subscriber trunk dialling (STD) was first started between Lucknow and Kanpur in Uttar Pradesh on 26 November 1960.

First push-button telephone

The first Indian firm to manufacture electronic push-button phone answering machines was Bharti Telecom Ltd. It was also the first Indian company to launch cordless phones that were called 'Beetel'.

First call using a mobile phone

On 31 July 1995, the then Union telecom minister Sukh Ram and the then West Bengal chief minister Jyoti Basu spoke to each other using handheld mobile phones, over Modi Telstra's MobileNet service.

First ISD service

The Arvi earth station for satellite communication, set up in 1971 in Arvi near Poona (now Pune), Maharashtra, marked the introduction of the first operator dialled service to international subscribers. The first intercontinental telephone exchange was commissioned in 1973, and the first international subscriber dialling (ISD) telephone service was introduced between Bombay, and London in 1976.

First carrier to demonstrate 5G service capability

Bharti Airtel became the first carrier to successfully demonstrate live 5G service over a commercial network on 28 January 2021 in Hyderabad, Telangana. The carrier was capable of delivering 10x speed, 10x latency (the time it takes for data to pass from one point on a network to another), and 100x concurrency (the execution of multiple instruction sequences at the same time) in comparison with existing technologies.

Bharti Airtel Store, Udaipur

Stalls to make STD calls

First cellular operators' association

The Cellular Operators Association of India (COAI), Delhi, was set up in 1995.

Stamp depicting Arvi Earth Station

First circle launch

In 1996, Bharti Mobile Ltd, which was a joint venture of Bharti Enterprises with Telia Company of Sweden, launched Airtel, the first to provide services in a circle (outside metros) in Himachal Pradesh.

First national/international roaming service

On 12 September 1997, the Department of Telecommunications (DoT), Ministry of Communications, Government of India, cleared a national automatic roaming facility for cellular operators in Delhi, Mumbai, Calcutta, and Chennai. International roaming facility was approved on 12 January 1998.

Mobile tower at the highest altitude

Installed by BSNL with the help of the Indian Army's Trishul Signallers, the highest mobile tower is located at 4,877 m (16,000 ft) in Chongtash in Ladakh. With this tower, even the remotest regions of Ladakh are connected by a communication link.

Largest wireline service provider

Reliance Jio is the largest wireline service provider in India with a market share of approximately 34.7 per cent as of December 2023. Airtel is the second-largest provider with a market share of 25.24 per cent.

First net fax service

Satyamfax, launched by Satyam Infoway on 25 April 2000 at Chennai, Tamil Nadu, in technical association with Singapore Telecom, was the first to provide fax to fax, web to fax, email to fax, and PC desktop to fax services.

First telephone exchange

In 1881, the Government of India licensed the Oriental Telephone Company to set up telephone exchanges in Calcutta, Bombay, Madras, and Karachi. A 50-line exchange was set up in Calcutta in 1881 as one of the oldest exchanges in the world. It was set up only 5 years after the invention of the telephone.

First internet telephony service

On 25 July 2018, government-owned Bharat Sanchar Nigam Limited launched India's first internet telephony service that allows users to dial any phone number in India through its mobile App.

Service area with largest access subscriber base
Uttar Pradesh (East), with 9.814 crore (98.14 million) wireless and wirelinesubscribers, has the largest subscriber base (September 2020).

Service provider with number of rural subscribers – wireless
Reliance Jio has 17.931 crore (179.31 million) rural subscribers, which amounts to 33.47 per cent of total rural wireless subscribers. It is followed by Bharti Airtel with (168.63 million) rural subscribers, and Vodafone Idea with 149.93 rural subscribers up till March 2021.

First cellular service
Modi Telstra, a joint-venture company of the B.K. Modi Group and the Telstra Corporation of Australia, inaugurated the first commercial cellular service in India on 23 August 1995. The network was constructed by Telecommunication Engineering Centre and the Modi Telstra team.

Largest wireless service provider
Reliance Jio was the leading wireless service provider with 45.981 crore (459.81 million) subscribers, followed by Bharti Airtel with 38.173 crore (381.73 million) subscribers, as of 2024.

Jio Building in Navi Mumbai

State/UT with highest tele-density
Delhi has the highest tele-density (number of fixed landline telephone connections) with over 278 telephones per 100 people as of December 2023.

INTERNET, SOCIAL MEDIA, AND APPS

First private Internet service provider (ISP)
Satyam Infoway (Sify) became the country's first private internet service provider company on 22 November 1998.

First mobile app store
Airtel App Central was the first Indian mobile application store in the country. It was launched by Bharti Airtel Ltd on 9 February 2010.

First 3G operators
• The public sector telecom service provider Mahanagar Telephone Nigam Limited (MTNL) first provided 3G mobile service to parts of Delhi. This service started on 11 December 2008.
• Tata Docomo launched its 3G mobile service in many states – Rajasthan, Uttar Pradesh (West), Gujarat, Maharashtra (except Mumbai), Haryana, Punjab, Kerala, Karnataka, and Madhya Pradesh – on 5 November 2010. It was the first private 3G operator in India.

WR **First free email service**
Conceived by Sabeer Bhatia (and colleague Jack Smith), Hotmail was the first free email service that took the whole world by storm in 1996. Bhatia was a Bengaluru-born Indian-American businessman and led Hotmail as its

president and CEO, until its eventual acquisition by Microsoft in 1998.

Top Internet subscription – service areas – both wired and wireless

The highest-subscription service areas in the country are the states of Uttar Pradesh (East+West) 8.78 crore (87.88 million), Maharashtra 6.14 crore (61.42 million), Andhra Pradesh 5.67 crore (56.73 million), Tamil Nadu5.04 crore (50.42 million), and Madhya Pradesh 4.72 crore (47.23 million)

Largest Facebook user base

With 31 crore (310 million) active users, India emerged as Facebook's largest audience in July 2020.

Largest WhatsApp user base in the world

India remained WhatsApp's biggest market with 40 crore (400 million) monthly active users, who exchange around 6,000 crore (60 billion) messages daily (as of July 2019). The country has been the biggest market for WhatsApp since November 2015.

WR First Aadhaar-based payment app

The Government of India launched Bharat Interface for Money (BHIM) app, an Aadhaar-based mobile app for digital payments, on 30 December 2016.

BHIM App

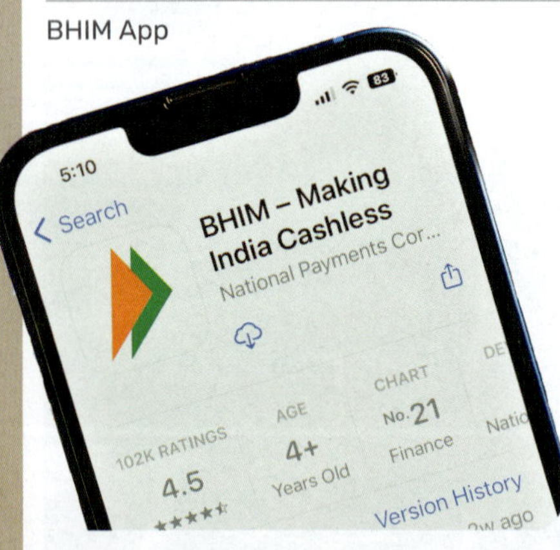

Most number of mobile app downloads

India had the most number of mobile app downloads, 7 billion (700 crore), on the Apple iOS App Store as well as on Google Playstore in the second quarter of 2020. It is followed by the USA with 375 crore (3.75 billion) and Brazil with 300 crore (3 billion).

First provider of Internet services

Videsh Sanchar Nigam Limited (VSNL), under Department of Telecommunications (DoT), Ministry of Telecommunications, Government of India, was the first provider of Internet services in the country. It was launched on 15 August 1995.

VSNL manhole cover in Delhi

Highest data consumption

India has the highest data consumption of 11 gigabyte/month per user on an average.

Most popular search engine

Google, with a user base of 93.4 per cent, is the favourite search engine in India.

Most popular mobile operating system

The favourite mobile operating system in India is Android with 62 per cent usage; next is Windows with 19.4 per cent usage.

WR Most viewed Indian video on YouTube

'Phonics Song with TWO Words', an alphabet learning video by ChuChu TV has garnered 4,348,214,171 views on YouTube as on 14 December 2021. The video was posted on 7 March 2014.

Most popular browser

The most popular browser in India is Google Chrome, with a share of 51.91 per cent among all browsers.

First and only 4G, all-Internet protocol network

Reliance Jio, which revolutionized the mobile Internet market in India when it rolled out 4G services in 2016, is the only network in the world to rely solely on 4G Long-Term Evolution (LTE) network, based on Internet telephony, without the backing of the legacy 3G/2G services.

WR Most subscribed YouTube channel

T-Series (Super Cassettes Industries Pvt. Ltd), a music record label and film production company, became the first YouTube channel in the world to reach 100 million subscribers in May 2019. As of October 2022, it had 22.6 crore (226 million) subscribers.

WR Fastest 4G service provider

Vodafone Idea Ltd is the provider of the fastest 4G network in the country with a download speed of 13.74 megabyte per second Mbps and an upload speed of 6.19 Mbps. It is followed by Bharti Airtel and Reliance Jio.

Highest concurrent video viewership

A new world record of 2.57 crore (25.7 million) concurrent viewers was set by Jio Cinema, the official digital streaming partner of the India Premier League (IPL). The record was set for the IPL 2023 match. Viewers came to watch Chennai Super Kings play with the Royal Challengers Bangalore. The previous record was held by Disney+Hotstar which had a record of 2.53 crore (2.53 million).

Most downloaded mobile application

Aarogya Setu, a COVID-19 contact-tracing app launched by the Government of India became the most downloaded application in India and the seventh most downloaded application in the world. It recorded 127.6 million (12.76 crore) installations up till July 2020.

Largest social network penetration

India is the world's second largest market with 34.997 crore (349.97 million) users in 2020. While there are many apps available to the Indian public, YouTube leads with 82 per cent market penetration. It is closely followed by Facebook (76 per cent), WhatsApp (70 per cent), Instagram (64 per cent), and Facebook Messenger (53 per cent), according to the 2019 Q3 figures.

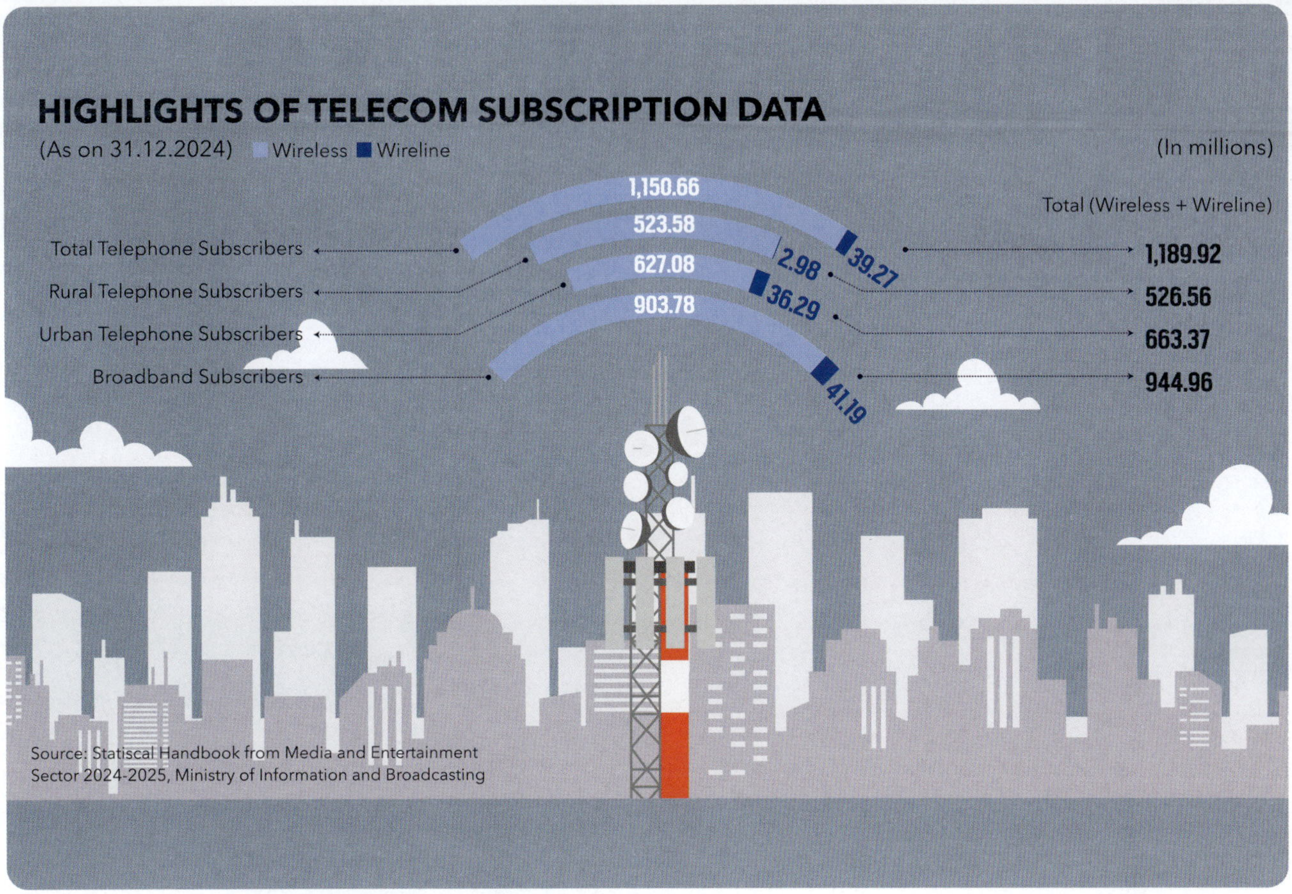

HIGHLIGHTS OF TELECOM SUBSCRIPTION DATA

(As on 31.12.2024) Wireless Wireline (In millions)

	Wireless	Wireline	Total (Wireless + Wireline)
Total Telephone Subscribers	1,150.66	39.27	1,189.92
Rural Telephone Subscribers	523.58	2.98	526.56
Urban Telephone Subscribers	627.08	36.29	663.37
Broadband Subscribers	903.78	41.19	944.96

Source: Statiscal Handbook from Media and Entertainment Sector 2024-2025, Ministry of Information and Broadcasting

World's Most Affordable Data & 5G Rollout

India today combines the world's most affordable data rates with one of the fastest 5G rollouts globally. Backed by government initiatives such as timely spectrum allocation and streamlined infrastructure development, 5G services have expanded at record speed. With hundreds of thousands of base stations already deployed and massive investments flowing into the sector, digital connectivity is reaching wider sections of the population, making access to high-speed internet more equitable than ever before.

Nearly 1 Billion Broadband Connections

By May 2025, India's broadband subscriber base had surged to 97.487 crore (974.87 million) encompassing both mobile and wired internet users. This represents a sharp increase in just a month, up 3.37 per cent from April's figure. Among providers, Reliance Jio led by a wide margin, holding approximately 49.447 crore (494.47 million) broadband users (wired + wireless), giving it just over 50 percent market share. This boom in broadband adoption reflects increased demand for high-speed internet, especially from mobile users and via fixed wireless access (FWA) services. It also signals growing connectivity in rural and semi-urban areas, as more affordable data plans and infrastructure reach beyond metro centers. With wired broadband still making up a smaller part of the total but rising steadily, India's digital landscape continues to broaden in both depth and scale.

GOVERNMENT

THE
CONSTITUTION
OF

HISTORICAL PERSPECTIVE

Earliest republic on the subcontinent

Vrijji, a mahajanapada (republic) of ancient India, dating to the sixth century BCE, is believed to be the earliest republic on the Indian subcontinent. It did not have a monarch, but instead a popular assembly of elders carried on the business of state. Vrijji was formed by the union of several clans, including the Lichchhavis, Jnatrikas, and Videhas. Its capital was at Vaishali, in the present-day region of Mithila, Bihar.

First Indo-European alliance

Chandragupta Maurya met Alexander III of Macedon in 327 BCE – after the battle with Porus (or Puru) and the capture of Punjab – and teamed up with him for the capture of Magadha in what may be termed the first Indo–European treaty.

Chandragupta Maurya seated on the left

Shortest reign — monarchy

Following the death of Alauddin Khilji (Khilji dynasty) in 1316, Malik Kafur captured the throne of Delhi. His reign lasted between 25 and 30 days. He was ousted by Alauddin's son, Shihabuddin Omar.

First woman rulers

Nayanika from the Satavahana dynasty (first century BCE) is considered the first woman ruler of India. She was a queen regent, who was holding the fort for her son, Satakarni II, when he was a child. She was the first woman ruler to have coins struck in her name. She was the wife of King Satakarni I. In 1236 CE, when Razia Sultan of the Mamluk dynasty ascended the Delhi throne, she became the first queen regnant in India. Unlike a queen regent, Razia ruled her territory in her own right. She was also the only woman ruler of the Delhi Sultanate.

First Republic Day parade

India became an independent nation on 15 August 1947 and declared itself a sovereign and democratic republic with the promulgation of the Constitution of India on 26 January 1950. The first Republic Day parade was held in 1950 at Irwin Stadium (now known as Major Dhyan Chand National Stadium) in New Delhi. Five years later in 1955 the R-Day parade found a new and permanent venue at Rajpath (now Kartavya Path), New Delhi.

PARTIES AND ELECTIONS

First political organization

The first recorded political organization in the country was the Zamindari Association of Calcutta (now Kolkata), West Bengal. Formally launched in 1838, it was a body of landlords, which changed its name to Landholders' Association shortly after its inception. Its principal organizers were Radhakanta Deb and Prasanna Kumar Tagore. Set up to defend the landlords against government policies that the Zamindars thought were against their interest, it became defunct in 1851.

First chief election commissioner

Sukumar Sen (1898–1963) was India's first chief election commissioner, in office from 21 March 1950 to 19 December 1958. Under his leadership, the Election Commission of India conducted India's first two general elections, in 1951–52 and 1957. He also administered the first parliamentary elections in Sudan in 1953.

First voter of independent India

Shyam Saran Negi (1 July 1917–5 November 2022), a schoolteacher in Kalpa of Himachal Pradesh, was declared by the Election Commission in 2012 to have been the first to cast his vote in the first general elections of independent India.

Longest tenure as chief election commissioner

K.V.K. Sundaram (1904–92), India's second chief election commissioner, served for 8 years, 9 months, and 11 days, from 20 December 1958 to 30 September 1967.

Shortest tenure as chief election commissioner

V.S. Ramadevi (1934–2013), the first woman chief election commissioner (acting) of the country, held the post of chief election commissioner for only 17 days from 26 November 1990 to 12 December 1990.

First general election

India went to the polls as an independent country for the first time during 1951–52, with 314 constituencies with one seat, 86 constituencies with two seats, and one with three seats. There were also 2 nominated Anglo-Indian members. At the time, the Election Commission of India recognized 14 political parties as multi-state parties and 39 parties as state parties. Voting in the election was based on the 'balloting system', i.e., casting votes in ballot boxes allotted to the respective candidates.

National party with most votes

The Congress (I) secured a record 11,52,21,078 votes (78.5 per cent of the total votes) and won 412 out of the 513 parliamentary seats in the elections held in December 1984. This is the largest victory margin of any political party on record.

First use of single ballot paper and single ballot box

The general election of 1962 introduced the single ballot paper system, in which

WR Largest electorate

The number of eligible voters in the 2024 general election was 96.9 crore (969 million), making India the largest electorate in the world. In other words, more than 10 per cent of the global population were eligible to cast their vote in the largest democratic exercise in history. Chief Election Commissioner Rajiv Kumar explained that India set a world record in the 2024 general election, as 64.2 crore (642 million) voters, including 31.2 crore (312 million) women, participated in the polls. Thus, the total number of voters participating in 2024 parliamentary polls turns out to be 1.5 times of the total number of voters of all G7 countries, which are the United States, United Kingdom, France, Germany, Italy, Japan, and Canada. In terms of the number of women voters who participated, 312 million is also the highest in India as well as the world.

the voter had to mark one choice from the candidates and drop the paper in a ballot box. Earlier, during the 1951–52 and 1957 general elections, there were separate ballot boxes for each candidate with their name and party symbol on them.

Oldest political party

Allan Octavian Hume (1829–1912), a member of the Imperial Civil Service, initiated the events that led to the formation of the first political party in India. Speaking out against British policies in India, in 1883, he exhorted Calcutta University graduates to form their own national political movement. This led to the first session of the Indian National Congress in Bombay (now Mumbai), Maharashtra, in 1885.

First use of indelible ink

It is generally believed that indelible ink was used for the first time in the third Lok Sabha elections in 1962. Mysore Paints and Varnish Ltd, based in Mysore (now Mysuru), Karnataka, was authorized to manufacture the ink. The company continues to supply this ink to this date. However, there are sources that date similar use of indelible ink back to the 1952 general election.

First app launched for voter vigilance

For the first time in elections, an application called 'cVIGIL' was launched for citizens to report any malpractice

Congress headquarters, New Delhi

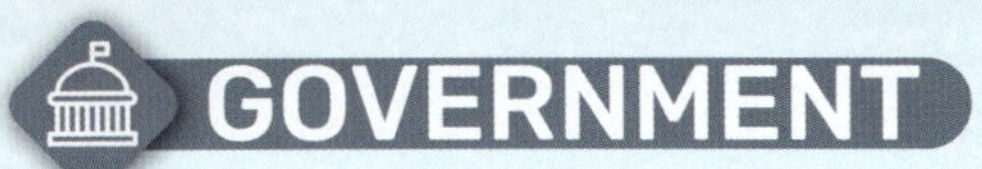

Colonial Rule

First colonial rule

Dom Francisco de Almeida was appointed the first Portuguese viceroy in India by King Manuel I of Portugal in 1505 – marking the first colonial rule in India.

Longest colonial rule

Goa, Daman, and Diu were under colonial rule for the longest period in Indian history – over 450 years. For over a decade after the British had left India, the Portuguese ruled these pockets as 'Estado da India Portuguesa' (the Portuguese State of India). They were liberated by the Indian Army on 19 December 1961.

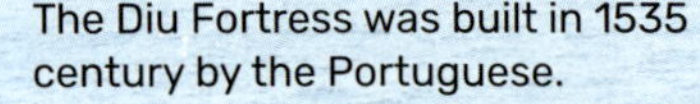

The Diu Fortress was built in 1535 century by the Portuguese.

Old Portuguese gun in Goa.

The Basilica of Bom Jesus is an extraordinary example of Portuguese colonial architecture. This Renaissance Baroque structure was built between 1594 and 1605 in what is now called Old Goa, which was the original capital of the Portuguese colony of Goa in India. The Roman Catholic church was listed as a World Heritage site in 1986.

Remains of Saint Francis Xavier have been preserved here in the Basilica of Bom Jesus.

or violation of the model code of conduct before or during elections. This app includes a combination of live photo/video and time-stamping with auto-location. A government official is bound to respond within 100 minutes. Launched in July 2018, the app was rolled out across India before the 2019 Lok Sabha election.

First electronic voting machines

Electronic voting machines (EVMs) were used for the first time in the assembly by-elections in Kerala in April 1982. The election commission used EVMs on a trial basis at 50 of 84 polling stations in the Paruvar constituency by-election that year. The machines were developed by the Electronics Corporation of India Ltd (ECIL). However, when the Parur (a village in the Paruvar constituency) contest was challenged by the losing side in the courts, the Supreme Court annulled the elections on account of the use of EVMs, saying the Representation of Peoples' Act 1951 clearly laid out that votes were to be cast by ballots, not voting machines.

Persisting with its recommendation for EVMs, the Election Commission of India (ECI) recommended an amendment to the said law, which came through in 1989 – even though a general consensus about their use came about nearly a decade later in 1998. That year a pilot-run was carried out in 25 assembly constituencies in Delhi, Madhya Pradesh, and Rajasthan. The first state assembly elections to have EVMs operationalized in all constituencies were held in 2001 in Kerala, Pondicherry (now Puducherry), Tamil Nadu and West Bengal. The first general elections to see EVMs deployed (more than a million) in all 543 Lok Sabha constituencies was that of 2004.

A replica of the electronic voting machine

First 'Others' category of voters

A third gender category of voters, called 'Others', was introduced in the electoral rolls in 2014. As many as 28,314 voters enrolled in this category in 2014 and 38,970 voters in 2019.

First teenage vote

The 61st amendment of the Constitution of India in 1989 lowered the voting age for election to the Lok Sabha and the state legislatures from 21 years to 18 years. As a result, 35.7 million voters in the age group of 18–21 years voted.

First NOTA option

The 2014 general elections were the first to offer Indian voters the option of choosing 'None of the Above' (NOTA), also known as the 'against all' or a 'scratch' vote internationally. The NOTA option provides a neutral vote to those electors who do not wish to vote for any candidate on the electoral ballot. Around 1.04 per cent of voters polled NOTA in the 2019 elections – NOTA received 65.2 lakh votes. However, the number dipped significantly in 2024 to a meagre 1.48 lakh votes.

Lowest voter turnout in the Lok Sabha general election

In the 1951 – 52 general election, which was the first election to be held in independent India, only 44.87 per cent of the electorate was recorded as having cast their votes.

Highest voter turnout in the Lok Sabha general election

The 2019 general election had the largest voter turnout to date with 61,31,36,854 voters, constituting 67.1 per cent of the total electorate of the country.

Most female candidates in a Lok Sabha general election

The 2024 general election registered a total of 796 female candidates.

Fewest women elected in a general election

Only 19 women were elected in the 1977 general election, which was the fewest ever in the history of general elections.

Most independent candidates elected in a general election

In the history of Indian elections, independent candidates had the most successful run in the 1957 general election, winning 42 seats.

Most independent candidates in a general election

The 1996 general election had a total of 10,636 independent candidates, the highest ever to date.

Fewest independent candidates elected in a general election

Only 3 of the 3,235 independent candidates in the 2014 general election were successful, the lowest win by independents in the history of general elections in India.

Voter-verifiable paper audit trail in all constituencies for the first time

The ECI set up the voter-verifiable paper audit trail or VVPAT system in all constituencies in 2019. The VVPAT prints a slip with the

MP Diya Kumari, who won the 2019 Lok Sabha election from Jaipur, Rajasthan, among the voters.

Most women elected in a Lok Sabha general election

Seventy-eight women were elected in the 2019 Lok Sabha general election, making it the election with the highest number of successful female candidates. The number slipped to 73 in 2024.

MP Mahua Moitra from West Bengal is known for her fiery speeches in the Parliament.

serial number, name, and symbol of the candidate for whom the vote was cast.

State/UT with the largest electorate

Uttar Pradesh had the largest electorate in the 2024 general election, with 1,54,103,670 eligible voters. This is the largest ever in India.

State/UT with most Lok Sabha seats

Uttar Pradesh had 80 Lok Sabha seats up for grabs in the 2024 general election. Whereas, there were 9 states with just 1 seat each.

First election where disabled elderly people could vote from home

In 2024, for the first time, all people above 85 and with 40% benchmarked disability could cast their votes from home through postal ballot. Postal ballots are available only for service voters, special voters, wives of service and special voters, voters in preventive detention, voters on election duty, and notified voters (this category included the disabled elderly people in 2024).

Youngest winning candidate in Lok Sabha

Prakash Chandra (b. 29 September 1959) won the Lok Sabha election from Bihar's Barh constituency in 1984. He was 25 years, 3 months, and 3 days old when the eighth Lok Sabha began its term on 31 December 1984. He was a member of the Indian National Congress. His father Ram Lakhan Singh Yadav was a freedom fighter and also a politician of independent India from Bihar.

Samajwadi Party (SP) member Pushpendra Saroj (b. 1 March 1999) is a close contender for the record and lost it just by a day – he was 25 years 3 months, and 4 days old when the 18th Lok Sabha began its term. He contested and won the Kaushambi Lok Sabha seat in Uttar Pradesh in the 2024 general election.

Smallest Lok Sabha constituency – by number of electors

The New Delhi Lok Sabha constituency in Delhi is currently the smallest constituency in the country with 15,25,071 eligible voters. In 2019, it was Chandni Chowk constituency in Delhi, with 1,561,828 voters. The number of voters in New Delhi came down by 90,923 in 2024 from 1,615,994 in 2019.

Win by highest margin

Shankar Lalwani of the BJP won from Indore parliamentary constituency by 11.72 lakh votes, which is the highest ever victory margin in Indian parliamentary polls.

State/Union Territory (UT) with the smallest electorate

The Union Territory of Lakshadweep had the smallest electorate in the 2024 general election, comprising a total of 57,784 eligible voters. The UT also holds the record for being the constituency with the smallest electorate in the country.

Indian women voting in the 2019 Lok Sabha

Most women candidates in an election

In the 2024 election, 797 women contested (up by 81 candidates from 2019), constituting 9.6 per cent of the total 8,337 candidates. Despite an increase in the number of women candidates, the total number of women elected to the 18th Lok Sabha dipped to 74 from what was 78 in 2019. Thus, the record is retained by the 17th Lok Sabha election, in 2019.

Highest polling station

The polling station at Tashigang in Spiti Valley, Himachal Pradesh, situated at an altitude of 4,650 m (15,256 ft), is the highest polling station in the world.

Most voter IDs distributed – 1 hr

The district administration of Allahabad (now Prayagraj), Uttar Pradesh, led by District Magistrate Sanjay Kumar and Chief Development Officer Andra Vamsi, conducted the largest ever voter ID distribution camp on 16 February 2017, distributing 12,594 voter ID cards in an hour. The distribution event took place from 11:00 a.m. to 12:00 noon at the Parade Ground in the city.

Representative image: Voter ID distribution

Only booth with 100% turnout

A polling booth was set up deep inside the Gir Forest of Gujarat, the last surviving natural habitat of Asiatic lions, to ensure that the solitary voter of the booth could cast his vote without facing any hassle. Though political parties did not carry out campaigns there for the fear of lions and other wild animals, a polling team of 10 people traversed through the forest to set up a booth for the one and only voter – Haridas Udasin. Udasin, a Hindu monk, cast his vote on 7 May 2024. The polling station was set up adjacent to the Hindu temple that Mahant Haridas Udasin is in charge of. Thus Udasin, being the single registered voter, ensured a 100 per cent turnout at the polling booth.

PRESIDENTS AND VICE PRESIDENTS

First presidential election and first president

The first presidential election in the country was held in 1952 when Dr Rajendra Prasad (1884–1963) became the president of India.

First woman president

Pratibha Patil (b. 19 December 1934) became the first woman to be appointed president of India. Earlier, Pratibha Patil had held the office of governor of Rajasthan during 2004–07. She was affiliated with the Indian National Congress. Pratibha Patil started the Shram Sadhana Trust. The trust runs hostels for working women in New Delhi, Mumbai, and Pune.

Pratibha Patil

First vice president

Dr S. Radhakrishnan (1888–1975) was vice president of India during 1952–62. He also had the longest tenure as vice president, that of 10 years, a record he shares with Hamid Ansari, who was in office from 11 August 2007 to 11 August 2017.

of India, was in office from 1966 until 1977. She was re-elected in 1980 and her second tenure lasted four years, until her assassination in 1984.

Most presidents from a state

With 3 presidents to date, Tamil Nadu is the state that has given the country the most number of presidents. They are S. Radhakrishnan, R. Venkataraman, and A.P.J. Abdul Kalam. Dr S. Radhakrishnan, the first vice president and second president of India, held the position of president from 1962 to 1967. R. Venkataraman, the eighth president of India, held office from 1987 to 1992. A.P.J. Abdul Kalam, the 11th president of India, held the presidential office from 2002 to 2007.

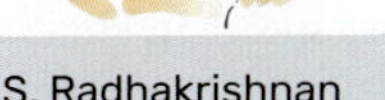

S. Radhakrishnan

R. Venkataraman

A.P.J. Abdul Kalam

Longest tenure as president

Dr Rajendra Prasad (1884–1963), a lawyer and freedom fighter who became the first president of India, remained in office for 12 years, 3 months, and 18 days – from 26 January 1950 to 13 May 1962.

Shortest tenure as president

Dr Zakir Hussain (1897–1969), the third president of India, held the office of president from 13 May 1967 until his death, for a little less than 2 years. He was also the first president to die in harness.

Oldest vice president to assume office

Bhairon Singh Shekhawat (1923–2010) became vice president on 19 August 2002, when he was 79 years of age.

Oldest to become president

K.R. Narayanan (1920-2005) became India's oldest president when he assumed the office on 25th July 1997. He was 76 years and 271 days old.

PRIME MINISTERS

First prime minister

Jawaharlal Nehru (1889–1964) became the first prime minister of India on 15 August 1947. Previously, he headed the interim government as prime minister, starting 2 September 1946. He served as prime minister until he died on 27 May 1964.

First prime ministers to die in harness

Jawaharlal Nehru, the first prime minister of India, passed away on 27 May 1964, after serving the office for 17 years. He was the first prime minister of India to die in harness.

Jawaharlal Nehru's successor, Lal Bahadur Shastri, died at Tashkent, Uzbekistan, on 11 January 1966. He was the first prime minister of India to die in harness abroad.

Only woman prime minister

Indira Gandhi (1917–84), the first and only woman to become prime minister

Right: Indira Gandhi;
Below: Jawaharlal Nehru

Oldest to become prime minister

Morarji Ranchhodji Desai (1896–1995), a freedom fighter during India's struggle for independence, became prime minister at the age of 81 years and 24 days on 24 March 1977. Earlier he had held many offices, such as those of minister of home affairs, deputy prime minister, and finance minister. He was also the chief minister of undivided Bombay state from April 1952 to October 1956.

First prime minister to resign

Morarji Ranchhodji Desai was the first prime minister of India to resign from the office. He assumed office on 24 March 1977 and resigned from his post on 28 July 1979, following a split in the Janata Party, which he was heading at the time.

Longest tenure as prime minister

Jawaharlal Nehru (1889–1964), the first prime minister of India served as prime minister until he died on 27 May 1964. His tenure lasted 16 years and 286 days.

Shortest tenure as prime minister

- Chaudhary Charan Singh (1902–87) was prime minister for 171 days from 28 July 1979 to 14 January 1980, making him the shortest-tenured prime minister on record. He was the only prime minister of India who never faced the Parliament.
- Gulzari Lal Nanda had 2 shorter tenures as acting prime minister, once from 27 May to 9 June 1964, after Jawaharlal Nehru's death, and again from 11 to 24 January 1966, following Lal Bahadur Shastri's demise.

Youngest to become prime minister

Rajiv Gandhi assumed office on 31 October 1984, when he was 40 years and 72 days, following the assassination of his mother, Prime Minister Indira Gandhi.

First prime minister born after Independence

Narendra Modi (b. 17 September 1950) is the first prime minister of India who was born after Independence.

First deputy prime minister

Sardar Vallabhbhai Patel was sworn in as the first deputy prime minister of India on 15 August 1947 in the first cabinet of independent India, which was headed by the then prime minister Jawaharlal Nehru.

Narendra Modi

First woman cabinet minister

Vijaya Lakshmi Pandit (1900–90) was elected to the provincial legislature of the United Provinces as minister for local government and health in 1937, making her the first woman cabinet minister. Later, she was president of the United Nations General Assembly from September 1953 to September 1954.

First woman full-time finance minister

Nirmala Sitharaman (b. 18 August 1959) became the first woman to be a time finance minister of India on 31 May 2019. She is the second woman finance minister after former prime minister Indira Gandhi, who held the finance ministerial office for some time while she was prime minister during 1970–71. Sitharaman was also the first woman minister with defence as her sole portfolio from 2014 to 2019.

UNION GOVERNMENT

First non-Congress government

The Janata Party, led by Jayaprakash Narayan, overthrew the Indira Gandhi government in the 1977 general election to form the first non-Congress government in the history of independent India. Morarji Desai was appointed prime minister of the government formed by the Janata Party.

Jayaprakash Narayan

First electoral win by an Indian political party

In the elections held under the provisions of the Government of India Act, 1935, the Indian National Congress formed governments in 7 states, in addition to a coalition ministry in Assam. They lasted till October–November 1939, after which they unanimously resigned in protest against the inclusion of Indians in the Second World War.

First Union minister to die in harness

Sardar Vallabhbhai Patel (1875–1950), India's first home minister and first deputy prime minister, who died on 15 December 1950, was the first Union minister to die while in office.

First Union minister to resign

Dr Shyama Prasad Mookerjee (1901–53) resigned from the Union cabinet on 19 April 1950. After leaving the Nehru government and the Congress party, he foundedthe Bharatiya Jana Sangh in 1951.

Shortest tenure of a cabinet minister

Justice H.R. Khanna (1912–2008) was in office as the minister for law and justice in the Charan Singh ministry for five days from 30 July to 3 August 1979.

Sardar Vallabhbhai Patel

Longest serving cabinet minister

Babu Jagjivan Ram (1908–86) was a Union minister for over 28 years from 15 August 1947 to 25 July 1979 with a break from 31 August 1963 to 24 January 1966. Some of the portfolios held by him included the Ministry of Labour, the Ministry of Defence, and the Ministry of Transport and Communications.

First use of Hindi at United Nations (UN)

Atal Bihari Vajpayee (1924–2018), former prime minister of India, gave a historic speech in Hindi at the United Nations General Assembly in 1977 as India's minister for external affairs. This was the first time when any Indian leader had given a speech in Hindi at any international platform. It was translated into English by an Indian diplomat. Vajpayee spoke again in Hindi in 1978.

Atal Bihari Vajpayee

THE STATES

First modern Indian states/UTs

The Indian states of Bihar and Orissa (now Odisha) were the first to be formed in British India. The Bihar and Orissa province of Bengal Presidency was carved out as a separate province on 1 April 1912, which included the present-day states of Bihar, Jharkhand, and parts of Odisha. On 1 April 1936, the then Bihar and Orissa province was divided into the separate provinces of Bihar and Orissa.

State sharing borders with most states

Uttar Pradesh shares its borders with

First linguistic state (pre-1947)
The Orissa (now Odisha) province that was formed as a result of the division of the Bihar and Orissa province in 1936, was the first to be formed on a linguistic basis.

nine Indian states – Rajasthan, Haryana, Himachal Pradesh, Delhi, Uttarakhand, Bihar, Madhya Pradesh, Jharkhand, and Chhattisgarh.

State with the largest area
With an area of 3,42,239 sq. km, Rajasthan is the largest state. It covers around 10.4 per cent of India's total area.

State with the smallest area
Goa is India's smallest state with a total area of 3,702 sq. km.

State with the longest international border
West Bengal shares a 2,216.7 km long border with Bangladesh, making it the state with the longest international border.

Youngest state
Telangana was formed on 2 June 2014, after its separation from the state of Andhra Pradesh.

Youngest UTs
After abrogation of Article 370 on 5 August 2019, the former state Jammu and Kashmir was bifurcated into two Union territories: a) Jammu and Kashmir and b) Ladakh.

First state to implement a uniform civil code
Uttarakhand is the first state in India to enact a uniform civil code (UCC). It passed the bill on 7 February 2024, and on 13 March the president of India assented to the same. The UCC aims to create a uniform and equal set of rules on personal matters (marriage, divorce, succession, inheritance, and so on) for all citizens of the state without making any differences in terms of religion. The scheduled tribes of the state, however, have been kept out of the bill's purview.

Lowest suicide rate
According to the Accidental Deaths and Suicides in India 2022 report of the National Crime Records Bureau (NCRB), Bihar has the lowest suicide rate in the country, which is 0.6 per 1,00,000 population.

Highest suicide rate
Sikkim's suicide rate is the highest in the country – 43.1 per 100,00 populaiton.

First woman chief minister
India's first woman chief minister was freedom fighter Sucheta Kripalani (1908–74). She was chief minister of Uttar Pradesh (1963 to 1967).

First state under president's rule
President's rule was imposed on Punjab from 20 July 1951 to 17 July 1952. The proclamation came after the resignation of the Congress ministry headed by Dr Gopichand Bhargava.

First elected communist government
On 5 April 1957, the Communist Party of India in Kerala formed the first communist government in the world to come to power by voting. It was led by E.M.S. Namboodiripad. It was dismissed by the Centre in 1959.

Longest tenure as chief minister
Pawan Kumar Chamling (former chief minister of Sikkim) has been India's

First linguistic state (post-1947)
The Telugu-speaking Andhra state was carved out of Madras (now Chennai) state on 1 October 1953, with its capital at Kurnool. It was later merged with the Telugu-speaking areas of Hyderabad state to form Andhra Pradesh on 1 November 1956.

Devi Lal

Om Prakash Chautala

Banarsi Das Gupta

Hukam Singh

Most chief ministers in a year

Haryana had four chief ministers in nine months from November 1989 to July 1990: Devi Lal (November 1989), Om Prakash Chautala (December 1989), Banarsi Das Gupta (May 1990), and Hukam Singh (July 1990).

longest-serving chief minister, having served in that post for five terms from 12 December 1994 to 26 May 2019 (24 years 165 days). He has surpassed the record of Jyoti Basu, who held the office of chief minister of West Bengal from 1 June 1977 to 6 November 2000 (23 years 137 days).

Shortest tenure as chief minister

Jagdambika Pal was chief minister of Uttar Pradesh for one day – on 21 February 1998. Harish Rawat's second term as chief minister of Uttarakhand also lasted a day – 21 April 2016.

First woman chief minister

India's first woman chief minister was freedom fighter Sucheta Kripalani (1908–74). She was chief minister of Uttar Pradesh (1963 to 1967).

Youngest chief minister

M.O. Hasan Farook Maricar, three-time chief minister of Pondicherry (now Puducherry), was the youngest chief minister when he came to power at 29 years in 1967. He died in office in 2012 as governor of Kerala.

Pema Khandu, elected as chief minister of Arunachal Pradesh in 2016 at the age of 38 years, is the youngest serving chief minister of a state.

First 'film star' chief minister

M.G. Ramachandran (popularly known as 'MGR') was the first film star to become chief minister when he assumed office in Tamil Nadu on 4 July 1977. He was elected chief minister of Tamil Nadu while he was admitted in a New York hospital. His nomination papers for the Andipatti assembly constituency were flown in from the United States and he was elected in absentia. He was sworn in on 10 February 1985, forty-three days after the election. Thus, he was also the first chief minister of India who got elected while staying abroad.

Most Legislative Council elections won

Basavaraj Shivalingappa Horatti (b. 14 April 1946), currently chairman of Karnataka Legislative Council, scripted history in June 2022, when he got re-elected to the Legislative Council from the Karnataka West Teachers' Constituency for a record eighth time. He is the longest-serving member of a legislative council in India, a member since 1980.

GOVERNANCE

First Indian in the Imperial Civil Service

Satyendranath Tagore, elder brother of Rabindranath Tagore, was the first Indian to join the service in 1863. He was recruited into the Covenanted Civil Service (later named the Imperial Civil Service). His first posting was in the Bombay Presidency (which included parts of present-day Maharashtra, Gujarat and Sindh).

First Indians in the Privy Council

In 1907, K.G. Puta and Syed Hussain Bilgrami were admitted to the Privy Council of India, the supreme appellate authority in British India, which advised the British monarchy.

First woman IAS officer

Anna Rajam George (b. 17 July 1927) from Calicut (now Kozhikode), Kerala, was the first woman to qualify for the Indian Administrative Service (IAS), in 1950. She was posted as a subdivisional officer in a small town in Tamil Nadu in 1951.

First woman ambassador

Vijaya Lakshmi Pandit, the sister of India's first prime minister, Jawaharlal Nehru, was India's first woman ambassador, to the erstwhile USSR from 1947 to 1949. She also served as ambassador to the US and Mexico (1949–51) and Ireland (1955–61). She held a post in the cabinet in pre-Independence India, the first Indian woman to do so. Her longest tenure was in London, as high commissioner to the UK, serving from 1954 to 1961. Her last posting as ambassador was in Spain. She served as governor of Maharashtra from 1962 to 1964 and as member of the Lok Sabha from 1964 to 1968.

First woman career diplomat

Chonira Belliappa Muthamma from Coorg (now Kodagu), Karnataka, qualified for the Indian Civil Service and joined the foreign service in 1949. She served in France, the UK, and Burma (now Myanmar), and later as ambassador to Hungary and Ghana.

Youngest governor

Swaraj Kaushal (b. 12 July 1952) was appointed governor of Mizoram in February 1990 when he was 37 years and 7 months old.

Swaraj Kaushal and his wife Sushma Swaraj, former foreign minister

AADHAAR

State/UT with highest Aadhaar coverage
Estimated count of Aadhaar number holders in Uttar Pradesh is 22,44,40,893 as on 31 August 2025. This is the highest in the country. In terms of saturation, Lakshadweep holds the record with 109.28 per cent.

State/UT with least Aadhaar coverage
Interestingly, Lakshadweep also holds the record for the lowest number of Aadhaar number holders – 69,000. Nagaland occupies the lowest spot when it comes to saturation, at just 62.45 per cent.

LAW AND ORDER

First Indian sheriff
Manackjee Rustomjee, a Parsi businessman and judge from Bombay (now Mumbai), Maharashtra, was appointed as the sheriff of Calcutta (now Kolkata, West Bengal) in 1873, the first Indian to be appointed to the position.

First forensic science laboratory
In 1853, the Government Examiners' Laboratory was established in Calcutta followed by labs in Madras, Bombay, Lahore (now in Pakistan), and Agra, Uttar Pradesh. At present, there are seven central forensic science labs in India, viz., Hyderabad, Kolkata, Chandigarh, New Delhi, Guwahati, Bhopal, and Pune.

First Indian director of the Intelligence Bureau
T.G. Sanjeevi Pillai took over as the first Indian director of the Intelligence Bureau, Ministry of Home Affairs, from Sir N.P.A. Smith in April 1947 and held office till July 1950.

Incumbent director of the Intelligence Bureau

First woman IPS officer
Kiran Bedi (b. 9 June 1949) was the first woman to join the Indian Police Service (IPS) on 16 July 1972. She retired in 2007 and was later the lieutenant governor of Puducherry (May 2016–February 2021).

First all-woman police station
The first all-woman police station in the country was started in October 1973 at Calicut (now Kozhikode) in Kerala. Sub-inspector Padmini was in charge of it.

WR First fingerprint bureau
The first fingerprint bureau in the world was set up in Calcutta in June 1897. A murder case in 1898 in Jalpaiguri was the first to be solved on the basis of dactyloscopy, which is the science of fingerprint identification.

First Police Act
The Police Act of 1861 led to the creation of a police service. This Act introduced a uniform system applicable to entire British India.

First police dog squad
The Madras City Police Dog Squad, now called the Chennai City Police Dog Squad, was started in 1952 by a sub-inspector of police, Kanniah Naidu, in Chennai, Tamil Nadu. It was the first police dog squad in India.

First open prison
The first open prison in India, Durgapura Open Camp, was started in Rajasthan in 1956 by the then governor, Dr Sampurnanand, in the Government Agriculture and Research Centre campus at Jaipur. Prisoners who had spent six years behind bars could live with their families and go out in the day to earn.

First transgender sub-inspector
India's first transgender sub-inspector, K. Prithika Yashini, joined the Tamil Nadu police force on 2 April 2017. She was posted to Dharmapuri District in Tamil Nadu after a legal battle with the Madras High Court ruling in her favour.

Kiran Bedi

Largest prison complex
Tihar Prisons, which started with the Central Jail in 1958, now includes nine central jails, apart from a district jail at Rohini, New Delhi, making it the largest prison complex in Asia. Its current capacity is of 5,200 prisoners.

LEGAL MATTERS

First Penal Code
The Indian Penal Code (IPC) and the Criminal Procedure Code (CrPC), which were introduced in Bengal in 1862, were drafted on the recommendations of the first Law Commission of India set up in 1834, chaired by British historian and politician Thomas Babington Macaulay.

First British Indian Code
The East India Company's proposal for separate civil and criminal courts in districts of Calcutta (now Kolkata), West Bengal, on 15 August 1772 was the first British Indian Code.

First chief justice of India
India's first chief justice was Justice Sir Harilal J. Kania (1890–1951), who held the position from 26 January 1950 to 6 November 1951.

First woman judge
Justice Anna Chandy (1905–1996) was the first ever woman judge of India, appointed in 1937. She was also the first female judge in any high court in India (appointed in Kerala High Court in 1959).

First high court judge
Shambhunath Pandit, a Kashmiri domiciled in Calcutta was appointed judge at the Calcutta High Court on 2 February 1863. His tenure ended in 1867.

Oldest civic body
The Greater Chennai Corporation, Tamil Nadu, was inaugurated under a royal charter issued by King James II of England, on 29 September 1688, as the Corporation of Madras. It is the oldest civic body in the country and the second oldest in the world. The first is in London, UK.

First municipalities
Municipal corporations for civic amenities were set up first between 1880 and 1884, when Lord Ripon was the viceroy of India.

First woman mayor
Tara Cherian (1913–2000) was appointed mayor of Madras (now Chennai), Tamil Nadu, in 1957. She received the Padma Bhushan in 1967.

Greater Chennai Corporation at night

Youngest mayor

Arya Rajendran (b. 12 January 1999), the Left Democratic Front (LDF) councillor from the Mudavanmugal ward, became the mayor of Thiruvananthapuram Corporation, Kerala, in December 2020 when she was 21 years old.

First panchayats

Panchayats were first established in villages under the Panchayat Act in 1912, but with little success. It was in 1952 that a new Panchayat Act revived the system.

First woman sarpanch

Chhavi Rajawat, the first woman sarpanch (head of the village panchayat) in India, looks after Soda, a village in Tonk District, Rajasthan. She assumed office in February 2010 at the age of 30 years. She is an alumna of Rishi Valley School, Madanapalle, Andhra Pradesh; Mayo College Girls' School, Ajmer, Rajasthan; and Lady Shri Ram College, New Delhi. She also holds an MBA degree from Balaji Institute of Modern Management, Pune, Maharashtra. She left her corporate job to work in rural India.

Oldest high court

The Calcutta High Court, established on 1 July 1862, under the Indian High Courts Act, 1861, is the oldest high court in India. It has jurisdiction over West Bengal, and the Union Territory of Andaman and Nicobar Islands. Its building was designed by British architect Walter Granville, who based it on the Cloth Hall at Ypres in Belgium. The seat of the high court is Kolkata. It also has a permanent circuit bench in Port Blair, the capital of the Andaman and Nicobar Islands. It has a sanctioned strength of 72 judges. T.S. Sivagnanam (b. 16 September 1963) is its current serving chief justice.

High court with the most judges

Allahabad High Court has the largest sanctioned strength of 160 judges but has never held its full complement. As on 21 March 2023, it had 82 permanent judges and 21 additional judges (total 103).

First woman chief justice

Justice Leila Seth (1930–2017) was appointed the chief justice of Himachal Pradesh on 5 August 1991, becoming India's first woman chief justice of a high court. She was also the first woman to top the Bar exam of England and Wales (in 1958).

First barrister-at-law

Gyanendramohan Tagore (1826–90) passed the barrister-at-law examination from Lincoln's Inn in England on 21 June 1862, becoming the first Indian to do so. In November 1865, he was enrolled into the Calcutta High Court in the then Bengal Presidency (now in Kolkata, West Bengal) as the first Indian barrister.

First public prosecutor

S. Subramania Iyer (1842–1924), jurist and freedom fighter, was appointed public prosecutor in Madras (now Chennai), Tamil Nadu, in 1887.

First woman judicial officer

Anna Chandy (1905–96), a member of the Travancore Legislative Council during 1923–24, graduated in law in 1930 and was appointed munsif by the erstwhile state of Travancore in 1937. She became a district and sessions judge in 1948, and a judge of the Kerala High Court in 1959.

Youngest advocate general

Swaraj Kaushal (b. 12 July 1952) holds the record for the youngest advocate general of any state in India when he became advocate general of Mizoram in 1987.

S. Subramania Iyer

First Indian president of the International Court of Justice

Dr Nagendra Singh (1914–88) was the first Indian president of the International Court of Justice, serving from 1985 to 1988. He was also the first Indian to be a judge of the court. He received the Padma Vibhushan in 1973.

First Indian judge of ITLOS

P. Chandrasekhara Rao (22 April 1936 –11 October 2018) was a judge at the International Tribunal for the Law of the Sea (ITLOS) from 1996 to 2017. He was president of ITLOS from 1999 to 2002.

First transgender judge

Joyita Mondal Mahi, India's first transgender judge, was appointed as a judge in the Lok Adalat in West Bengal in 2017. She was 29 years old at the time.

First Indian woman judge of ITLOS

Neeru Chadha (b. 27 March 1955), an international law expert, became the first Indian woman to be appointed to the International Tribunal for the Law of the

First woman advocate

Cornelia Sorabji (1866–1954) was the first woman to graduate in law, in 1894. However, law being a male bastion then, she was enrolled in the Allahabad High Court Bar only in 1923.

Sea (ITLOS), being elected to the UN body in June 2017. She was elected as a judge and has been its vice president since October 2023.

First citizen to have a 'no caste, no religion' certificate

M.A. Sneha Parthibaraja, a lawyer from Tirupattur, Tamil Nadu, became the first Indian citizen to win the right to not have a caste or religion, on 5 February 2021. She was granted the certificate after a nine-year-long court battle.

First transgender lawyer

Sathyasri Sharmila, a lawyer in the Bar Council of Tamil Nadu and Puducherry, is the first transgender lawyer in India. Although she completed her education in 2007, she enrolled as an advocate after the National Legal services Authority of India (NALSA) judgment of 2014, which recognized the third gender.

First judge to face impeachment proceedings

In 1993, impeachment proceedings were initiated against Justive V. Ramaswami, then a Supreme Court judge. On the day of voting in the Lok Sabha, 196 members supported the motion, but 205 members abstained. Thus, he escaped the impeachment. The charges brought against him was that of financial misconduct.

On 14 March 2015 a fire broke out in a property of Justice Yashwant Verma, then a Delhi High Court judge. This incident led to the discovery of unaccounted cash, which further set a series of judicial, administrative and executive action in motion. If these finally leads to his impeachment, he would be the first judge to have been successfully impeached.

THE CENSUS*

First census

The first all-India census was conducted in 1872 in British India. However, the first regular census in the country was conducted in 1881, and then every 10 years. The last census was conducted in 2011. The census is conducted by the registrar general and census commissioner under the Ministry of Home Affairs, Government of India.

Most populated state

Uttar Pradesh is India's most populated state, with a population of 19,98,12,341.

Most populated UT

Delhi is India's most populated UT with a population of 1,67,87,941.

Least populated UT

Lakshadweep, with a population of 64,473, is the least populated UT.

Most densely populated state

Bihar has a population density of 1,106 persons per sq. km, making it the most densely populated state in India. Most densely populated Union Territory Delhi, with a population density of 11,320 persons per sq. km, is the most densely populated UT.

Gangtok, the capital of Sikkim, is a popular tourist destination.

Least populated state

Sikkim is India's least populated state, with 610,577 people.

*On the basis of the 2011 census of India

Least densely populated UT
Andaman and Nicobar Islands have a population density of 46 persons per sq. km, making it the least densely populated UT.

The Cellular Jail was an infamous colonial prison in the Andaman and Nicobar Islands

State/UT with the highest sex ratio
Ladakh has the highest sex ratio at birth among all states and UTs, with 1,125 females per 1,000 males.

State/UT with the lowest sex ratio
Dadra and Nagar Haveli and Daman and Diu has a sex ratio at birth of 817 females per 1,000 males.

Least densely populated state
Arunachal Pradesh, with a population density of 17 persons per sq. km, is the least densely populated state in India.

STATE LEGISLATURE

First paperless assembly
Himachal Pradesh Legislative Assembly became India's first to use the e-Vidhan system and become completely paperless in 2014. This high-tech assembly was the first to implement the e-Governance solution called e-Vidhan with financial and technical help from the then Department of Electronics and Information Technology (DeitY), Government of India, in 2014.

First state legislative assembly
The maharaja of Travancore, Sree Moolam Thirunal Rama Varma, constituted an eight-member assembly in March 1888. A bicameral system was introduced on 28 October 1932 by King Chithira Thirunal Balarama Varma, who abolished the existing council and set up the Sree Moolam Assembly (Lower House) and the Sree Chitra State Council (Upper House).

Largest legislative building
Vidhan Soudha, Bengaluru, Karnataka, is a rectangular building made with granite measuring 213.36 m (700 ft) north–south and 106.68 m (350 ft) east–west, with 2 inner open quadrangles on either side of the central wing measuring about 70.10 m (230 ft) by 70.10m (230 ft) each.

Largest legislature

Uttar Pradesh Legislative Assembly is the largest state legislative assembly in India with 403 seats. Uttar Pradesh Legislative Council consists of 100 seats, which is also the highest in the country.

Most legislative council elections won

Basavaraj Shivalingappa Horatti (b. 14 April 1946), currently chairman of Karnataka Legislative Council, scripted history in June 2022, | when he got re-elected to the legislative council from the Karnataka West Teachers' Constituency for a record eighth time. He is the longest-serving member of a legislative council in India, a member since 1980.

Shortest session of state legislative assembly

There was a one-minute session of the Rajasthan Legislative Assembly from 11:00 a.m. to 11:01 a.m. on 14 August 1972, the shortest session of a legislative assembly on record.

PARLIAMENT RECORDS

First session of Parliament

The first session of Parliament in free India was held on 13 May 1952 with Jawaharlal Nehru as prime minister and Dr Rajendra Prasad as president.

First Speaker of the Lok Sabha

Freedom fighter 'Dadasaheb' G.V. Mavalankar was the first Speaker of the Lok Sabha, holding the post from 15 May 1952 to 27 February 1956.

First deputy Speaker of the Lok Sabha

On 30 May 1952, Madabhushi Ananthasayanam Ayyangar was elected as deputy Speaker of the Lok Sabha.

First visually impaired member of Parliament

Sadhan Chandra Gupta (1917–2015), an Indian lawyer and politician, became the first visually impaired member of Parliament (MP) in 1953. He later served as the advocate general of West Bengal. Gupta was elected to the Lok Sabha from the Calcutta (now Kolkata), West Bengal, South-east constituency in a 1953 by-election on a Communist Party of India (CPI) ticket.

First Lok Sabha dissolution

The fifth Lok Sabha was dissolved by Indira Gandhi in 1971, for the first time in the history of the Indian Parliament. The second Lok Sabha dissolution came in 1979 under Charan Singh, and the third was the ninth Lok Sabha on 6 March 1991 under Chandra Shekhar.

First representative in the British House of Commons

The 'Grand Old Man of India', Dadabhai Naoroji, was the first Indian-origin and non-white member of the British House of Commons, when he was elected as a Liberal Party member of Parliament in London from Central Finsbury in July 1892, by a bare majority of three votes. He held the position till 1895.

Shortest term as Speaker

Neelam Sanjiva Reddy was Lok Sabha Speaker from 26 March to 13 July 1977, thus serving the shortest term as Speaker. He was the sixth president of India, from 1977 to 1982.

Neelam Sanjiva Reddy

Youngest member of Rajya Sabha

Anubhav Mohanty (b. 24 December 1981), the film star-turned-politician from Odisha, became a member of the Rajya Sabha on 13 June 2014. He was 32 years, 5 months, and 19 days old then. The youngest member's tenure at the upper house of Indian Parliament ended in 2019. Later he was elected to the Lok Sabha (2019–24). He started his political career with the Biju Janata Dal (BJD) and switched to the Bharatiya Janata Party (BJP) in 2024.

First woman secretary general of Rajya Sabha

V.S. Ramadevi was the first woman to be appointed as the Secretary General of the Rajya Sabha on 1 July 1993, for three years. She was also acting chief election commissioner for some time in 1990.

First woman legislator

Dr S. Muthulakshmi Reddy was a social worker, educationist, and physician, with many firsts to her credit. In 1926, she became the first woman legislator (Madras Legislative Council member) and in 1930, by way of the All India Women's Conference, pushed through the Child Marriage Restraint Act. She was also the first woman alderman of the Madras Corporation in 1937.

First hung Parliament

A hung parliament is a situation where no single political party has an absolute majority of seats in the Parliament. For the first time in nine general elections,

India's electorate did not give a decisive verdict in 1989. The Congress (I) was ousted in the north and the ruling regional parties were similarly ousted in the south.

First couple in Parliament

Joachim and Violet Alva from Karnataka were the first couple in Parliament. While Violet was elected to the Rajya Sabha in 1952, Joachim became a Lok Sabha member in the same year.

Longest tenure as Rajya Sabha chairman

Dr S. Radhakrishnan, the second president and first vice president of India, had the longest tenure as chairman of the Rajya Sabha, from 1952 to 1962.

Longest term as Speaker

Balram Jakhar served as Speaker from 1980 to 1989, for eight years and 329 days in two terms, becoming the Speaker with the longest tenure.

Shortest Lok Sabha term

The 12th Lok Sabha lasted from 10 March 1998 to 26 April 1999, a duration of around 13 months, due to the withdrawal of support by the All-India Anna Dravida Munnetra Kazhagam (AIADMK) from the National Democratic Alliance (NDA) government led by Atal Bihari Vajpayee.

Shortest session of state legislative assembly

There was a one-minute session of the Rajasthan Legislative Assembly from 11:00 a.m. to 11:01 a.m. on 14 August 1972, the shortest session of a legislative assembly on record.

Lok Sabha with highest average age

The average age of the elected MPs in the current 17th Lok Sabha is 54 years, making it the Lok Sabha with the highest average age in the history of the Indian Parliament.

Lok Sabha with lowest average age

The first Lok Sabha (1952–57) had the lowest average age of 46.5 years.

Most bills passed in a year

The Parliament passed 118 bills in 1976, which is the highest number of bills ever passed by it in a single year.

DEFENCE AND MILITARY AFFAIRS

भारतीय वायु सेना
INDIAN AIR FORCE
C-17 GLOBEMASTER III

ARMY

PERSONNEL

K.M. Cariappa

Major Somnath Sharma

General Bipin Rawat

First Indian commander-in-chief

General (later field marshal, in 1986) K.M. Cariappa (1899–1993) took over from the British commander-in chief (C-in-C), General Sir Roy Bucher, on 15 January 1949 and held office till 14 January 1953. The only other C-in-C was General M. Rajendra Sinhji Jadeja, who took over as the first chief of army staff (CoAS) in April 1955, after which the post of C-in-C was abolished.

First chief of integrated defence staff

On 1 October 2001, Lieutenant General Pankaj Joshi was appointed the first chief of integrated defence staff (CIDS) in the country, reporting to General Sundararajan Padmanabhan, chairman of the Chief of Staff Committee at the time.

MEDALS AND HONOURS

First Victoria Cross

The first Indian to be awarded the Victoria Cross was Sepoy (later Subedar) Khuda Dad Khan of the 129 Baluchis, on 31 October 1914, for gallantry at Hollebeke, Belgium, in the First World War.

Victoria cross

Youngest to receive the Victoria Cross

At nineteen, Sepoy Kamal Ram of the Royal Indian Army was the youngest Indian to receive the Victoria Cross in 1944. Born in Bholupura Village of Karauli District, Rajasthan, he was with the 3rd Battalion of the 8th Punjab Regiment during the Second World War.

Sepoy Kamal Ram: Youngest to receive the Victoria Cross

First Param Vir Chakra

Major Somnath Sharma, heading a detachment of the Kumaon Regiment at Badgam, Jammu and Kashmir, laid down his life in the effort to save Srinagar city and airport from a Pakistani attack during the Kashmir operations in 1947. He was given the award posthumously in 1950.

First prisoner of war and first Kirti Chakra recipient

Flying Officer Ulrich Anthony D'Cruz, whose aircraft was shot down by ground fire on 1 December 1947 in the 1947–48 Kashmir war, was taken prisoner by Pathan tribesmen and later by the Pakistan Army, and released after a year. He was awarded the Kirti Chakra in 1952 for bravery during captivity.

First chief of defence staff

On 31 December 2019, after demitting office as chief of army staff, General Bipin Rawat (1958–2021) took over as India's first chief of defence staff (CDS), serving as a tri-services chief and principal military adviser to the defence minister on all matters related to the army, navy, and air force. He also headed the Department of Military Affairs created within the Ministry of Defence.

First women in the army

The first batch of 25 women outside the Army Medical Corps (AMC) was commissioned in the Indian Army on 6 March 1993 at the Officers Training Academy in Madras (now Chennai), Tamil Nadu. They were inducted into non-combat departments, such as supply, legal, education, and logistics.

First Ashok Chakra

Naik Nar Bahadur Thapa of 5 Gurkha Rifles was awarded the Ashok Chakra Class I (now known as the Ashok Chakra). On 15 September 1948, during the Hyderabad police action, as the No. 2 Platoon of the A Company came under fire on the banks of the Tungabhadra River, he dashed across the 100-yard open ground and single-handedly silenced the gun crew.

First George Cross

Havildar Nandlal Thapa of the Gurkha Rifles received the George Cross in 1935 for exceptional courage and devotion to duty. He was about 32 years old at the time and was serving in the 2nd Battalion of the 8th Gurkha Rifles.

Nandlal Thapa: First George Cross

First Republic Day commander and first army officer to receive Padma Bhushan

The first Republic Day parade of independent India, which featured interservice contingents from the army, navy, air force, and police forces, was held on 26 January 1950, and was commanded by Brigadier (later Lieutenant General) Joginder Singh Dhillon, a Bengal Sapper. On 24 November 1965, as lieutenant general, he became the first Indian Army officer to receive the Padma Bhushan.

First Indian peacekeeper to win the United Nations Military Gender Advocate Award

Major Suman Gawani, an Indian Army officer, was awarded the UN (United Nations) Military Gender Advocate of the Year award on 29 May 2020 in a virtual ceremony, becoming the first Indian peacekeeper to receive the honour. She served as a peacekeeper in a UN mission in South Sudan (UNMISS) in 2019.

Most decorated regiment

The Sikh Regiment has to its credit the highest number of gallantry awards, viz.; 1,652. These include two Param Vir Chakras, eight Maha Vir Chakras, sixty-four Vir Chakras, and four Ashok Chakras among other decorations.

First field marshal

S.H.F.J. (Sam) Manekshaw, the then general, became field marshal in 1973. He was honoured with the Padma Bhushan in 1968 and the Padma Vibhushan in 1972.

Field marshal Sam Manekshaw

First women in military police

First commissioned officer

Major General K. Bhagwati Singh (ID I-O-No. 1) was the first officer to be commissioned into the Indian Military Academy (IMA). He passed out of the Indian Military Academy in 1934, with his batchmate (and later field marshal) Sam Manekshaw.

First woman Subedar

On 28 January 2024, Havildar Preeti Rajak was promoted to the rank of Subedar, becoming the first woman to be promoted to this rank in the army. She is also a trap shooter and joined the army on 22 December 2022.

First woman lieutenant general

Dr Punita Arora from Saharanpur, Uttar Pradesh, was promoted to the rank of lieutenant general on 1 September 2004. She was the first woman in any of the four services (army, navy, air force, and coast guard) to reach a three-star rank.

First women in military police

On 25 April 2019, the Indian Army issued a formal notification inviting women applicants for the post of soldier – general duty. This was the first time that the army opened its ranks to women for personnel below officer rank (PBOR). The soldiers were to be inducted into the Corps of Military Police (CMP) to investigate offences such as theft, molestation, and rape. Their portfolio also included assisting civil police and the prevention of breach of regulations by army personnel.

Dr Punita Arora

First women cadets to pass out from NDA

On 30 May 2025, the first batch of 17 women (among 336 cadets) passed from the National Defence Academy. Traditionally, an all-male institution, the supreme court directed for doors to be opened for women cadets in 2022.

First Woman DG Medical Services

On 1 August 2024, Lieutenant General Sadhna Saxena Nair assumed the office of Director General Medical Services (Army), becoming the first woman to be appointed to this prestigious position. Prior to this, she was the first woman to hold the post of DG Hospital Services (Armed Forces) on promotion to the rank of Air Marshal.

Lieutenant General Sadhna Saxena

UNITS

First artillery unit

On 15 January 1935, A Field Brigade (now 1 Field Regiment SP), with four batteries of horse-drawn guns, was raised at Bangalore (now Bengaluru), Karnataka. This date was adopted by the Regiment of Artillery as its raising day.

First administrative unit

The Army Service Corps (ASC) was established in 1748 when Stringer Lawrence, commander-in-chief in India, appointed Robert Clive as commissary. It was formally set up in 1760 in the Bengal, Madras, and Bombay Presidencies, and became a formal Supply and Transport Corps in 1901. The ASC was the oldest administrative component of the East India Company and was then known as the Commissariat.

Stringer Lawrence

First artillery company

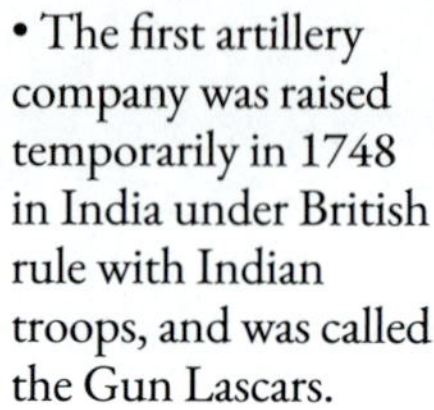

- The first artillery company was raised temporarily in 1748 in India under British rule with Indian troops, and was called the Gun Lascars.
- A company of Bombay Artillery, which still exists as 5 Bombay Mountain Battery, was raised on 28 September 1827, the date being celebrated as Gunners' Day.

First cavalry unit

The first Indian cavalry unit was raised in 1787 as 5 Regiment of Madras Native Cavalry. It became 1 Regiment in 1788 under Major Tonyn. Renamed 26 Light Cavalry in 1903, it was amalgamated with 30 Lancers in 1922 and became the 8th Light Cavalry.

First cavalry regiment

The first cavalry regiment before India's independence, the Scinde Horse, was raised in 1838 as the Scinde Irregular Horse by Captain Ward in Hyderabad (in Sind, now in Pakistan) under the command of Captain John Jacob. It last paraded its horses in April 1938 at Rawalpindi (now in Pakistan).

First Special Operations Division

India's first Special Operations Division was announced on 15 May 2019. At its peak, this tri-services division will have around 3,000 commandos from the Indian Army's special forces, the Indian Air Force's Garud force, and the Indian Navy's marcos commando units. The raising is the first step for counterterrorism operations. Major General A.K. Dhingra, from the 1 Para Special Forces Regiment, was the first chief of the division.

Oldest infantry brigade

In September 1933, 5 Mountain Brigade was raised. Deployed in the Along (now Aalo) sector of Arunachal Pradesh, its area of responsibility comprises a frontage of more than 460 km.

Oldest infantry unit

Raised on 4 August 1768, the 1 Maratha Light Infantry or Jangi Paltan is the only unit that does not hang captured enemy flags upside down in its mess. It is also the only unit that was in constant battle for 20 years after it was raised, and in this duration, it earned 18 battle honours and 5 theatre honours.

An illustration of the Maratha Light Infantry

First rifle regiment

The rifle regiment as a tactical unit was introduced in 1841 and the first such unit was the 4 Bombay Native Infantry, which till 1947 was 1 Battalion Rajputana Rifles, and is now 3 Guard. They were issued Enfield muzzleloaders and 577 bullets.

First and oldest extant armament checker

The Proof and Experimental Establishment in Chandipur in present-day Odisha, called the Proof

Department, was set up on 7 November 1895. It has been associated with major armament developments. Included under the Defence Research and Development Organization (DRDO) in 1958, it had Lieutenant Colonel B.N. Mitra as its first Indian director.

Bengal Sappers

First tri-services affiliation
Bengal Sappers has been affiliated with the Indian Navy and Indian Air Force since 2002. Originally known as the Bengal Sappers and Miners, and headquartered in Roorkee (now in Uttarakhand), it has won 80 battle honours and 11 theatre honours.

EQUIPMENT

First gun foundry
The Board of Ordnance was constituted in April 1775, but it took 27 years to establish a factory at Cossipore in Calcutta (now Kolkata), West Bengal, on 18 March 1802 as the Gun Carriage Agency. In 1830, it was renamed the Gun Foundry and, in 1905, this name was changed to Gun and Shell Factory.

Earliest tanks
The first three tanks of the Indian Army were two varieties of Medium-D tanks brought in 1920 before Indian independence. Fifty Vickers MkII-B light tanks were acquired for use in India in 1933.

First flying spy
Unmanned aerial vehicles (UAVs) were used first in the Kargil conflict in 1999 to detect the movement of enemy troops and locate bunkers. UAVs were brought in to counter Pakistan's Gultari guns and the US-made AN/TPQ-36-37 gunlocating radars.

First rifle factory
A rifle factory, set up at Ichhapore, Bengal (now Ishapore, West Bengal), began production on 20 September 1904. It produced the .303-inch Bolt-action rifles in large quantities for the First and Second World Wars.

First indigenous training simulator
On 20 February 2002, the Simulator Development Division, Secunderabad (now in Telangana), introduced the aiming-training simulator (ATS) for infantry combat vehicles.

First indigenously manufactured bulletproof vests
Shantanu Bhowmik, professor at the Department of Aerospace Engineering at the School of Engineering, Amrita University, Coimbatore, Tamil Nadu, designed the first indigenous bulletproof vest for the armed forces in 2017. The 20-layer vest, made with indigenous-ultra-modern lightweight thermoplastic technology, is being developed in collaboration with DRDO. The vest is effective up to a temperature of 57°C and weighs 1.5 kg while the earlier jacket weighed 15 kg.

First bulletproof helmets
In July 2017, the army obtained bulletproof helmets for the first time. The 1.2–1.4 kg lightweight helmets are being made in Kanpur, Uttar Pradesh, by MKU Systems, which is manufacturing them for the Indian Army for the first time. The company had earlier manufactured such helmets for the UN and the North Atlantic Treaty Organization (NATO) forces.

RFI company logo

First indigenous armoured personnel carrier
In 1987, the first BMP-2 infantry fighting vehicle, Sarath, was assembled at the ordnance factory at Shankarapally, Andhra Pradesh (now in Telangana), from Soviet-supplied components. Sarath was subsequently made indigenously in 1991.

Longest-range nuclear missile

On 26 December 2016, India successfully test-fired Agni-V, a surface-to-surface nuclear-capable missile with the longest range, from Abdul Kalam Island off the Odisha coast. Designed and developed by DRDO, this 17 m (55 ft 9 in.) long missile can carry a nuclear warhead of about 1.5 tonnes reportedly over 5,000–8,000 km. India is the sixth country after France, China, Russia, the US, and the UK to have a missile with a range of over 5,000 km.

Agni-V night trial footage

Agni-V ICBM cutaway diagram

First indigenous tank

The first military tank that was made in India, named Vijayanta, rolled out of the assembly line on 12 December 1965 at the Heavy Vehicles Factory in Avadi in Madras (now Chennai), Tamil Nadu. It entered service on 29 December 1965.

First indigenous revolver

In 2002, the research and development wing of the Ishapore Rifle Factory near in Barrackpore, West Bengal, after around two years of research, developed a lowcost and high-tech revolver, which weighs barely 380 g. The .22-in. automatic revolver has a range of 20 m (65 ft 7 in.).

Lightest towed artillery

On 18 May 2017, the Indian Army received the first batch of two M-777 A-2 ultralight howitzers (ULH) from the USA. These ULHs, with a maximum range of 30 km, manufactured by BAE Systems, were test-fired at Pokhran, Rajasthan. The 155 mm, 39-calibre guns are equipped to fire Indian ammunition.

First robot sentry

In 2017, the Indian Army built Robot Sentry, a mobile robot specifically meant for patrolling and surveillance applications in urban campuses of the army. Another robot, the Snake, has 14 active joints for lateral undulation, sidewinding, and rolling. These help the robot to navigate difficult passages.

First set of next-gen Armoured Engineer Reconnaissance Vehicle

Indian Army chief General Manoj Mukund Naravane flagged off and inducted the first set of indigenously developed next-generation Armoured Engineer Reconnaissance Vehicles (AERVs) at Bombay Engineering Group (BEG) on 21 December 2021. The AERV, which can match the speed of tanks, will upscale the existing engineer reconnaissance capabilities of the Indian Army significantly, keeping in view the possibility of future conflicts.

First indigenous sniper rifles

SSS Defence, based in Bengaluru, has developed the country's first indigenous sniper rifle prototypes with 7.62 mm x 51 mm calibre and .338 Lapua magnum platforms. The barrel length ranges from 20 to 24 in. (50.8 to 60.96 cm) based on use environments and specific missions.

OPERATIONS

First heli-lifted battalion

The First Guards (2 Punjab), raised in 1762 as 10 Battalion of the Coastal Sepoys and redesignated 18 times since, was heli-lifted during the counter-insurgency operations in Nagaland during 1969–70.

First para regiment in action

The 17 Para Field Regiment supported operations at Tangail in Bangladesh in 1971 by sending 49 Para Field Battery, a sub-unit of the regiment along with 2 Para.

First use of air cavalry

In May 2018, during Exercise Vijay Prahar carried out in the Mahajan Firing Range near Suratgarh, Rajasthan, Indian troops worked on the first use of the concept of air cavalry unleashed by the US Army in Vietnam during 1955–73. In these operations, weaponized attack helicopters carried out combined action against the 'enemy' in coordination with tanks and mechanized ground forces, while conventionally helicopters are called in only when ground forces cannot neutralize ground targets. This requires very precise coordination but speeds up the operation.

First heli-borne operations

In 1971, the Indian Army used helicopters to capture the 7,000-strong Sylhet garrison in East Pakistan (now Bangladesh). The 5 Gurkha Rifles (Frontier Force), which was led by Major M.M. Malik, landed with the first sortie of seven helicopters at Mirpara on the banks of the Surma River.

WR Highest tank battle in the world

On 1 November 1948, an Indian brigade group, supported by the 7th Cavalry (using Stuart Tanks), broke through the Himalayan range at Zoji La in Jammu and Kashmir at 3,528 m (11,575 ft) to drive out a group of invaders from Pakistan intermixed with Pakistan-occupied Kashmir (PoK) battalions and tribal groups.

GENERAL

First counter-insurgency school

The Counter-Insurgency and Jungle Warfare School was established at Mynkre, Meghalaya, in 1967. It was relocated to Vairengte in Mizoram on 1 May 1970.

Logo of Counter-Insurgency and Jungle Warfare School

First army veterinary school

A veterinary school was started at Kirkee in Poona (now Pune) District,

Maharashtra, in 1862, for officers and men of artillery, cavalry, and mounted police. Similar schools also came up in Hapur (Uttar Pradesh) in 1877, Lahore (now in Pakistan) in 1882, Ambala (now in Haryana) in 1889, and Simla (now Shimla, in Himachal Pradesh) in 1891.

A board at the Siachen glacier: Highest Battleground

WR Highest Battleground

Siachen is a 76.8 km glacier of ice abutted by knife-edged, fluted, serrated ridge lines, sometimes exceeding 6,400 m (20,997 ft and 4.5 in.), where temperatures dip to as low as –55°C. Army posts at altitudes from 4,572 m to 6,096 m (15,000 ft to 20,000 ft) face bitterly cold 200 km/hr blizzards.

First military dog school

The War Dog Training School was opened in 1959 at the Indian Army Remount and Veterinary Corps Centre and School (now RVC Centre and School) in Meerut, Uttar Pradesh. Training for avalanche rescue operations began here in September 1976.

First military intelligence school

Opened in Karachi (now in Pakistan) on 20 January 1941, the first military intelligence school moved to Mhow (Dr Ambedkar Nagar) in Madhya Pradesh, and was renamed the Intelligence Corps Training School and Depot. It soon moved to its current location in Pune in 1952. On 29 February 1984, its name was changed to Military Intelligence Training School and Depot.

Directorate of Military Intelligence Corps Insignia

An illustration of Fort William, Calcutta

First board of ordnance

The Board of Ordnance was set up in 1775 at Fort William, Calcutta. Currently, the Indian Ordnance Factories Organization – a set of 41 ordnance factories under the aegis of its corporate headquarters, the Ordnance Factory Board (OFB), Kolkata – has more than 200 years of experience in the development and marketing of a range of land, sea, and air defence systems. At present, the OFB has nine training institutes, three regional marketing centres, and four regional controllers of safety under it.

First drone show

For the first time ever a drone show was held during the Republic Day celebrations in the 75th year of Indian independence in 2022. The 10-minute show involved around 1,000 drones and they were conceptualized, designed, produced, and choreographed under the 'Make in India' initiative. It was organized by the start-up 'Botlab Dynamics' and supported by IIT Delhi and Department of Science and Technology, Government of India.

Longest bridge built during war

The Indo-Pakistan war in 1971, termed the Sappers War, saw the construction of a 421.8 m (1,384 ft) composite bridge across the River Madhumati in East Pakistan (now Bangladesh) in a matter of 34 hours. It was the longest 'war' bridge to be constructed by India after the Second World War and the longest operational bridge constructed during a war involving India.

First high altitude warfare school

Instituted as a formation ski school at Gulmarg, Jammu and Kashmir, the High Altitude Warfare School came into being on 8 April 1962. The courses at this institute include those on skiing and mountaineering.

First nuclear shelter

DRDO, the Pune-based research and development laboratory, introduced an integrated battlefield shelter for all three services in 2002 to withstand nuclear or chemical strikes for up to 96 hours. The portable shelter, 28 m (91 ft 10 in.) long and with a diameter of 2.5 m (8 ft 2 in.), has chemical toilets, water tanks, pumps for sewage disposal, and two power generators. It can accommodate 30 people and can be used as a command post, an observation post, and a communication centre.

First win at International Scout Masters Competition

Held in India for the first time, the host Indian Army team, trained by the Southern Command, won the Fifth Army International Scout Masters Competition (ISMC). Part of the International Army Games, it was held at Jaisalmer Military Station, Rajasthan, during 6–14 August 2019 and included five stages of competitions. Participants included teams from the armies of Armenia, Belarus, China, India, Kazakhstan, Russia, Sudan, and Uzbekistan.

National War Memorial

First national war memorial

The armed forces first proposed a National War Memorial way back in 1960. On 25 February 2019, the memorial, designed by the Chennai-based WeBe Design Lab, led by Yogesh Chandrahasan, was inaugurated near India Gate, New Delhi. Covering over 40 acres (16.2 hectares), it has the names of Indian soldiers martyred in 1947–48 (Kashmir), 1961 (Goa), 1962 (China), 1965 and 1971 (Pakistan), 1987 (Siachen), 1987–88 (Sri Lanka), 1999 (Kargil) and other operations. It has concentric circles, with the Amar Chakra (Circle of Immortality) and an Eternal Flame in the centre. Around it are the Veerta Chakra (Circle of Bravery), a gallery depicting iconic battles and the Rakshak Chakra (Circle of Protection). The circles represent the *chakravyuh* or traditional Indian war formation. The Param Yodha Sthal has busts of 21 recipients of the Param Vir Chakra.

First Bactrian camels join the army

Since February 2017, the Bactrian camel was put through the paces at the Defence Institute of High Altitude Research (DIHAR), a DRDO laboratory in Leh, Ladakh. Bactrian camels are used to patrol the Line of Actual Control (LAC) in Ladakh and carry loads for the army.

An illustration of a Bactrian camel

First all-girls Sainik School

On 1 January 2024, the Samvid Gurukulam Girls Sainik School at Vrindavan in Mathura, Uttar Pradesh, was inaugurated with a strength of approximately 870 students by Union minister of defence, Rajnath Singh. Samvid Gurukulam Girls Sainik School, Mathura.

First rail-based mobile missile launcher system

On 24 September 2025, the DRDO, in collaboration with the Strategic Forces Command (SFC), carried out the successful launch of an Intermediate Range Agni-Prime Missile from a rail-based Mobile launcher system. The launcher was specially designed has the capability to move on the rail network without any pre-conditions. It can launch within a short reaction time even with reduced visibility and can provide a cross-country reach.

First Indian dog breed in active duty

The Indian Army began to use dogs for active duty in 1959, the preferred breeds being the Labrador retriever, the Great Swiss Mountain dogs, and the German shepherd. In 2017, the Remount and Veterinary Corps introduced the first Indian breed, the Mudhol hound (or caravan hound), a sight hound used as a hunting hound first in Central Asia and later in the Deccan region, especially Karnataka. It is known for its courage, speed, and loyalty.

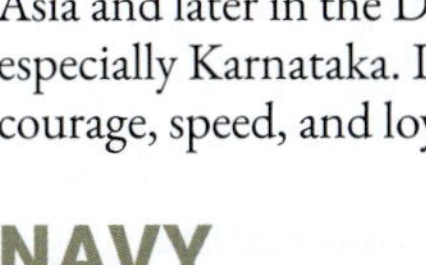

Mudhol hound dog

NAVY

PERSONNEL

Operational activites of the Indian Navy

First four-star admiral

Admiral A.K. Chatterji (1914–2001) became a four-star admiral on 1 March 1968. He joined the Royal Indian Marines as a cadet in 1933 and became chief of naval staff in 1966.

First naval pilot

Lieutenant Y.N. Singh of the Royal Indian Navy was deputed to England in 1941 for basic training and later to Canada where he obtained his wings in 1944 before serving in the escort carriers of the Royal Navy in the Second World War.

First chief of naval staff

• Admiral Sir Mark Pizey was the first chief of naval staff in 1955.
• The first Indian chief of naval staff was Vice Admiral Ram Dass Katari in 1958.

Vice Admiral Ram Dass Katari

First commander-in-chief

• The first commander-in-chief of the Royal Indian Navy was Admiral Sir Edward Parry in August 1948.
• Rear Admiral I.T.S. Hall was the first post- Independence commander-in-chief of the Royal Indian Navy. The word 'Royal' was dropped on 26 January 1950.

First woman maritime reconnaissance pilot

Shubhangi Swaroop became the first woman pilot in the navy who was trained to fly maritime reconnaissance aircraft in 2017. Three other women cadets – Astha Segal, Roopa A., and Sakthi Maya S.– passed out with her in the first batch of women officers from the Indian Naval Academy, Ezhimala, Kerala, on 22 November 2017, and were inducted into the naval armament inspection (NAI) branch. The Indian Navy had inducted its first woman officer in 1991. Its aviation branch had women working as air traffic control officers and as observers in aircraft.

First woman pilot of naval aircraft

On 2 December 2019, 24-year-old sub-lieutenant Shivangi Singh graduated with two other trainee officers from the seventh Dornier Conversion Course (DOCC) at Kochi, Kerala. Originally from Muzaffarpur, Bihar, this Short Service Commission pilot entry scheme officer was commissioned into the Indian Navy in June 2018 and underwent a year of flying training at the Air Force Academy (AFA), Dundigal, Telangana, and Indian Naval Air Squadron (INAS) 550 and INS *Garuda* in Kochi. During training, she flew aircraft such as Pilatus PC 7 Mk II, a basic trainer, at AFA before the Dornier Conversion Course.

First woman officers as 'Observers'

Sub-lieutenant Kumudini Tyagi and Sub-lieutenant Riti Singh graduated as 'Observers' (airborne technicians) in the Indian Navy's stream of helicopters to be deployed on warships for short- or long-term missions. They were awarded their wings in a graduation ceremony held at INS *Garuda* on 21 September 2020.

First nuclear submarine

INS *Chakra*, the navy's first nuclear-powered submarine belonging to the Victor 1 SSN class had a speed of 32 knots and a dive displacement of 5,000 tonnes. It carried 90 sailors. On lease from the USSR, it was commissioned on 3 February 1988 and sent back in 1991.

First woman naval helicopter pilot

At the passing out parade held at naval air station INS *Rajali*, Arakkonam, in Ranipet District, Tamil Nadu, on 7 June 2024, Sub-lieutenant Anamika B. Rajeev graduated as the first woman naval helicopter pilot.

First woman commander of an Indian naval ship

Lieutenant Commander Prerna Deosthalee became the first woman officer to command an Indian naval warship in December 2023. She assumed command of INS *Trinkat*, a fast attack craft based in the western seaboard.

UNITS

First navy air squadron

On 17 June 1959, the Fleet Requirement Unit was commissioned as the Indian Naval Air Squadron 550. INS *Vikrant*, formerly HMS *Hercules*, joined the Indian Navy on 16 February 1961 as the first aircraft carrier and saw action during the Goa liberation struggle in December 1961. It has flown 14 types of aircraft, starting with Sealands to the Dornier maritime reconnaissance aircraft flown currently.

Only training command

The Southern Naval Command is the only training command of the Indian Navy. It was augmented by INS *Magar*, which arrived at Kochi, Kerala, on 10 April 2018 to join the first Training Squadron for sea training of officers.

First exclusive naval base

INS *Kadamba*, inaugurated on 31 May 2005 near Karwar in Karnataka, is India's third operational naval base after Mumbai and Insignia of the Southern Naval Command Visakhapatnam, and the first under the sole control of the navy. Signifying another first, the inauguration speech was read out in Sanskrit. Sanctioned in 1985 as Project Seabird, its foundation stone was laid in 1986.

First unmanned aerial vehicle squadron

The navy's first unmanned aerial vehicle (UAV) squadron, intended to patrol the seas, was commissioned on 6 January 2006, with 12 UAVs from Israel. The Intensive Flying and Training Units were based in Kochi, Kerala.

EQUIPMENT

First submarine depot ship

INS *Amba*, an ex-Soviet Ugra-class ship with a displacement of 6,750 tonnes, is a submarine tender and was commissioned on 28 December 1968. INS *Amba* has two cranes (6 tonnes and 10 tonnes) and it can accommodate 750 personnel.

First missile boat

INS *Vinash*, a Soviet OSA (Russian word meaning 'wasp') 1 commissioned on 21 January 1971, was fitted with four SS-N-2A surface-to-surface missiles and four 30 mm guns. With a complement of 30 crew, it could reach speeds exceeding 35 knots.

First submarine base

On 19 May 1971, INS *Virbahu*, the Indian Navy's first submarine base, was commissioned near Visakhapatnam, Andhra Pradesh.

First cruiser and flagship

HMS *Achilles*, a 7,030-tonne battleship, formerly of the Royal Navy, was commissioned as HMIS *Delhi* on 5 July 1948 in England, and became the first cruiser and flagship of the Indian Navy. It arrived at Bombay, on 15 September 1948. HMIS *Delhi* (renamed INS *Delhi*) was 169.1 m (554 ft 9 in.) long and 16.77 m (55 ft) across its beam, with a speed of 32 knots. Its armaments included six 152 mm guns, eight 102 mm guns, fifteen 40 mm guns, four anti-aircraft three pounders, and eight torpedo tubes.

First submarine rescue ship

INS *Nistar* was converted from a fleet minesweeper to a submarine rescue ship and commissioned on 29 March 1971. An ex-Soviet Valday-class ship, it features a diving bell, a recompression chamber, two rescue chambers, and a lift of 10 tonnes.

First indigenous patrol boat

Godavari-class frigate INS *Ajay*, commissioned on 21 September 1960, is a front-line warship equipped with missiles, guns, and anti-submarine equipment, as well as early warning navigation and electronic warfare systems. Built by Garden Reach Shipbuilders and Engineers (GRSE) Ltd, it could carry two Sea King helicopters.

Longest-serving warship/aircraft carrier

INS *Viraat* – the second Centaur-class aircraft carrier in service – served India for 30 years after 27 years of service in the Royal Navy of the UK as HMS *Hermes*. The UK Royal Navy commissioned it in 1959, and it was later sold to the Indian Navy in 1986. It was decommissioned on 6 March 2017.

First indigenous nuclear-powered ballistic missile submarines

The Arihant-class submarines are India's first indigenously developed nuclear powered ballistic missile submarines. The lead submarine of the class, INS *Arihant*, was commissioned in 2016. These submarines are designed to carry and launch nuclear ballistic missiles. It completed its first deterrence patrol on 5 November 2018.

First indigenous diving support vessel

INS *Nistar*, was commissioned in Vishakhapatnam on 18 July 2025. It is the first of two vessels being built by Hindustan Shipyard Limited, has been designed for complex deep sea saturation diving and rescue missions. With top notch diving equipment such as diving compression chambers, remotely operated vehicles and self-propelled life boats, it can undertake operations upto 300 m depth. The 118 m ship, with a displacement of over 10,000 tons incorporates over 80 per cent indigeneous content.

First missile corvette

INS *Kora*, the first indigenously built missile corvette, was commissioned on 10 August 1998. Capable of operating in nuclear, biological, and chemical confrontation zones, it has a displacement of 1,300 tonnes and an overall length of 91.16 m (299 ft). INS *Kora* has two indigenous, fuel-efficient diesel engines and can touch 26 knots. Along with a helipad for advanced light helicopters and Chetaks, it has a complement of 11 officers and 110 sailors.

First indigenous submarine

INS *Shalki*, the first of SSK Type-1500 submarines, built at Mazagon Dock Ltd, Bombay, was commissioned in February 1992. It has a displacement of 1,450 tonnes and carries 14 AEG SUT torpedoes.

First ocean minesweepers

INS *Pondicherry* and INS *Porbandar*, built at the Isora Yard, Leningrad, USSR (now Russia), were given to the Indian Navy in 1978. These Natya-1-class sweepers have steel hulls with active mine detection sonars.

First dedicated cadet training ship

INS *Tir* (A86), named after HMIS *Tir*, a River-class frigate of the Royal Indian Navy that had served in the Second World War as HMS *Bann* (K256), was the first dedicated cadet-training ship built at Mazagon Dock Ltd. It is

INS *Nistar*

the senior ship of the First Training Squadron under the Southern Naval Command. Commissioned on 21 February 1986, it carries 120 cadets and 20 instructors.

First anti-ship missile

On 2 March 2017, the first anti-ship missile was fired from an indigenously built Kalvari-class submarine, the first in a series of Scorpene-class submarines being built in India. The submarine was stationed in the Arabian Sea and the missile successfully hit a surface target.

First multiwarships

INS *Talwar* was launched in May 2000, INS *Trishul* in November 2000 and INS *Tabar* in May 2001. These Talwar-class guided missile frigates were designed and built by Russia.

First 'green' ship

In February 2017, the survey vessel INS *Sarvekshak*, based at the Southern Naval Command in Kochi, became India's first naval ship to go green by installing a zeromaintenance solar power system that can generate 5.4 kW of electricity. It replaces the ship's emergency diesel alternator. The customized power-generating system has flexible, razor-thin solar panels on the canopy of the retractable helicopter deck, which use no-fume solid electrolyte batteries and are maintenance-free for 24 years. The solarpowergenerating system can be used to run communication equipment and on-board lights, and charge batteries. With an annual carbon emission of 60,225 kg, it will replace about 22,995 litres of diesel.

INS *Sarvekshak's* flexible solar panels in use at sea

First indigenous fleet replenishment tanker

INS *Aditya*, built by GRSE, Calcutta was commissioned at Visakhapatnam, Andhra Pradesh, on 3 April 2000. Manned by 16 officers and 140 sailors, the 172 m (564 ft) long fleet tanker has a deadweight tonnage of 1,700. It can touch a speed of 24 knots with an endurance of 10,000 nautical miles, and load six ships simultaneously on the high seas. It also carries a Sea King helicopter.

INS *Aditya*

Decommissioning of *INFAC T-80*

First fast attacker

INFAC-T-80 (Indian Navy's extra-fast attack craft), commissioned at the Naval Dockyard in Mumbai, on 24 June 1998, was the first fast-attack, high-speed vessel and the first of an Indo-Israeli defence project. This aluminium-hull vessel could sustain 45 knots and it was the smallest ship in the Indian Navy.

First indigenous ammunition

The Indian Navy received its first made-in-India, 30 mm ammunition for AK-630 rotary cannons fitted on warships, as reported on 29 August 2022. The production of AK-630 guns was carried out by M/s Economic Explosives Ltd (EEL), Nagpur, Maharashtra, a subsidiary of Solar Industries India Ltd.

First Integrated Automatic Aviation Meteorological System

On 28 March 2017, the then chief of naval staff, Admiral Sunil Lanba, inaugurated the first Integrated Automatic Aviation Meteorological System (IAAMS) at INS *Rajali* (informally also known as the Arakkonam naval air station) in Tamil Nadu. The IAAMS has been established with the objective of modernizing the meteorological infrastructure and aviation safety of the nine naval air stations of the Indian Navy through automated monitoring of weather.

First indigenously developed naval anti-ship missile

The first indigenously developed naval anti-ship missile for the Indian Navy was test-fired on 18 May 2022. The missile was launched aboard a Sea King 42B Naval Helicopter from the Integrated Test Range (ITR) at Balasore in Odisha.

First pilotless drone

India's first passenger drone *Varuna* will be introduced in the navy. It is a pilotless drone with an ability to carry one person inside. Designed by the start-up Sagar Defence Engineering Company, this drone can cover a distance of 25 kilometres and can carry a payload of 130 kg. Its demonstration was held on 20 July 2022.

First indigenous aircraft carrier

IAC *Vikrant*, commissioned on 2 September 2022, in Kerala was designed by Warship Design Bureau (WDB) and built by Cochin Shipyard Limited. It is the largest ship ever built in the maritime history of India. With the commissioning of IAC Vikrant, India joins US, UK, France, China and Russia as countries with capacity to design and construct an aircraft carrier locally.

Largest aircraft carrier

INS *Viraat*, commissioned on 12 May 1987 at Devonport, UK, is the second and largest aircraft carrier of the Indian Navy. The 28,700 tonne INS *Viraat* (R-22), earlier called HMS *Hermes*, was launched in 1953 as the flagship of the South Atlantic Task Force in the Falklands War in 1982. The Indian Navy is among eight navies in the world to have aircraft carriers.

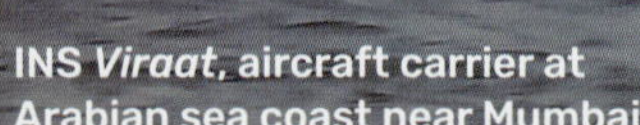

INS *Viraat*, aircraft carrier at Arabian sea coast near Mumbai

- The **first aircraft carrier**, INS *Vikrant* was launched on 22 September 1945 as *Hercules*.
- It was commissioned as Vikrant on 4 March 1961, under the command of Captain Pritam Singh Mahindroo.
- It was the first ever carrier for an Asian country.
- It marked its importance in the Goa Liberation Operation (1961) and the 1971 war.
- In 1984, it emerged as a Vertical/short take off and Land carrier.
- It was decommissioned on 31 January 1997.

- The **second aircraft carrier**, INS *Viraat* was originally commissioned as HMS *Hermes* on 18 November 1959.
- Indian Navy acquired it on 24 April 1986, and it was commissioned on 12 May 1987.
- It played a pivotal part in Operation, Jupiter (1989), Operation Parakram, and Operation Vijay.
- It launched 22,034 hours of flying and spent a total of 2,250 days at sea sailing over 5.8 lakh Nautical Miles. It was decommissioned from service on 6 March 2017.

- INS *Vikramaditya* was commissioned into the Indian Navy at Severodvinsk, Russia on 16 November 2013.
- The ship has the capacity to carry 30 aircraft.
- It has about 1,600 personnel onboard.

IAC *Vikrant*, an Introduction

GENERAL

First modern shipbuilding yard

Garden Reach Shipbuilders and Engineers (GRSE) Ltd, located on the eastern bank of the Hooghly River in present-day Kolkata, dates to 1884. The company's name was changed to Garden Reach Workshop in 1916 and on 1 April 1960, it was taken over by the Government of India. The name was changed back to Garden Reach Shipbuilders and Engineers on 1 January 1977. It builds a range of ships, including warships, sophisticated commercial vessels, harbour craft and fast, powerful patrol vessels for the Indian Navy and the Indian Coast Guard. It built INS *Ajay*, India's first indigenous patrol boat, in 1960.

An illustration of the Bombay Harbour, Bunder Pier

First naval academy

The first naval academy was established in Kochi, in January 1969. The first batch of cadets graduated in December 1970. Commander K. Ramdas was the first officer-in charge. Earlier, cadets used to be trained in England.

Above: Garden Reach Shipbuilders & Engineers Headquarters
Below: The first naval academy, Kochi

First naval dockyard

The Naval Dockyard at Bombay started with the Bunder Pier in 1693. A tiny dry dock was constructed in 1750. The old Bombay Dock and the Duncan Dock were built in 1765 and 1810, respectively. A wet basin was constructed in 1892. The largest naval dockyard today, it is the premier maintenance facility for ships and submarines of the Indian Navy.

First naval school

The Signal School on INS *Venduruthy* was established at Bombay's Carnac Bunder in 1919 in Maharashtra. The next year, it was shifted to the Naval Dockyard, Bombay, and in 1941, to HMIS *Talwar*, also in Bombay. In 1946, it finally moved to Kochi.

A brochure of the Signal School

Wadia shipbuilders

First modern shipbuilder

In 1736, the East India Company invited Lowji Nusserwanji Wadia to build the first shipyard in Bombay (now Mumbai), Maharashtra. Since then, seven generations of the Wadias have built ships, including HMS *Minden* (the first constructed outside of Great Britain), HMS *Trincomalee* and HMS *Cornwallis*.

HMS *Trincomalee*

HMS *Minden*

HMS *Cornwallis*

DEFENCE AND MILITARY AFFAIRS

DEFENCE PRODUCTION

- Defence Public Sector Undertakings
- New Defence Public Sector Undertakings
- Other Defence Public Sector Undertakings/Joint Ventures
- Defence Private Companies

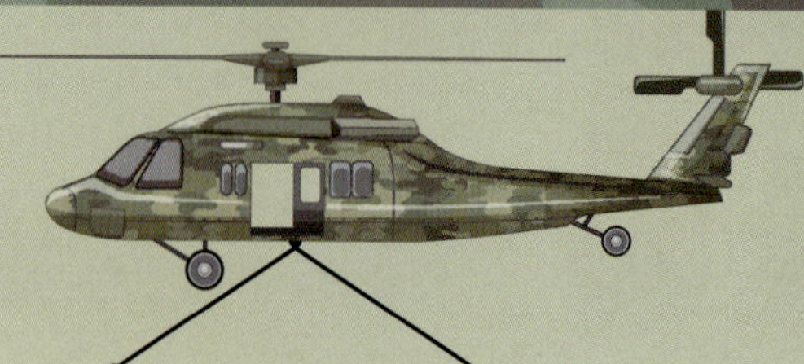

Figures (In ₹ Crore)

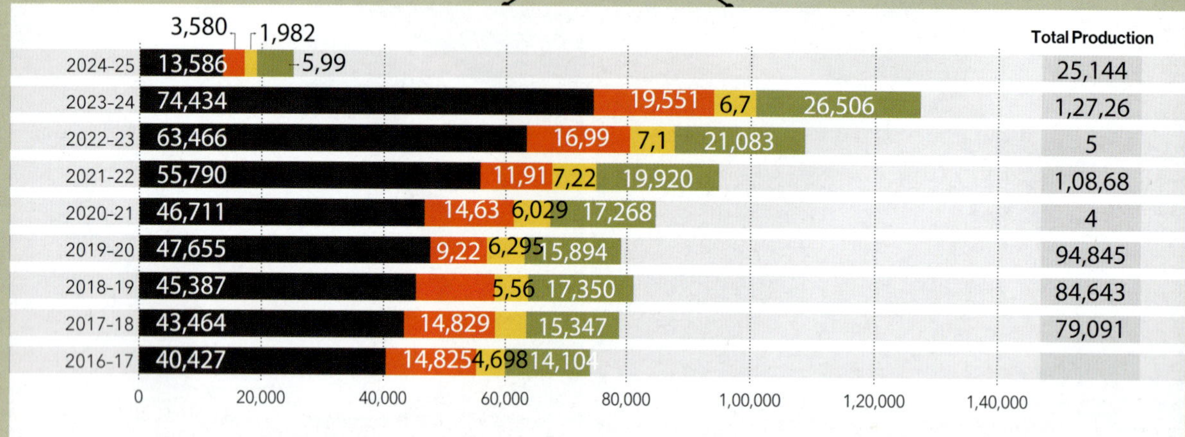

Source: Department of Defence Production, Government Open Data Licence

INDIAN COAST GUARD SEARCH AND RESCUE DATA

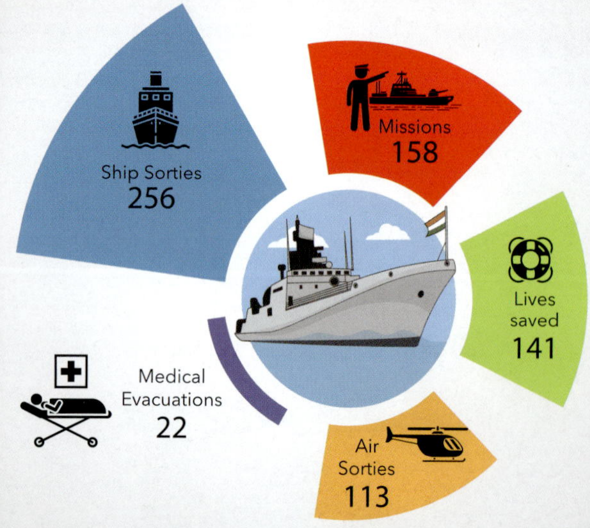

Source: Year-end Review 2024, Press Information Bureau

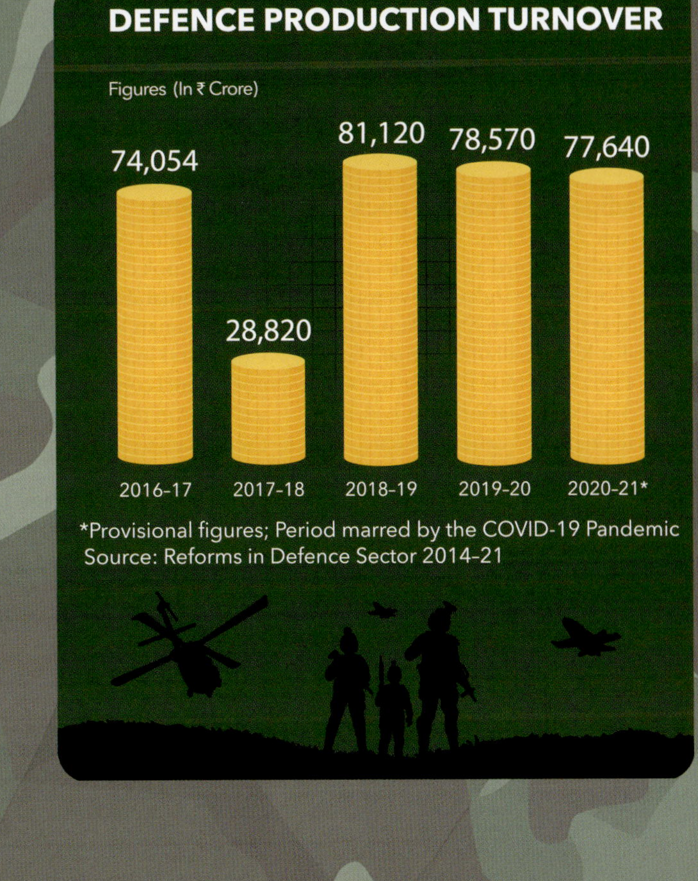

MILITARY EXPENDITURE AS PERCENTAGE OF GDP

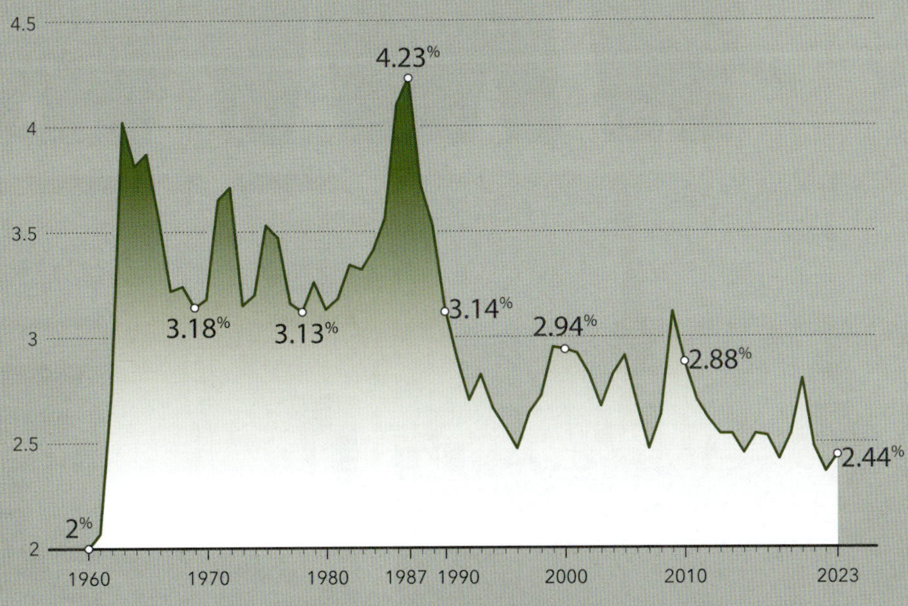

4.5
4
3.5
3
2.5
2

4.23%
3.18%
3.13%
3.14%
2.94%
2.88%
2.44%
2%

1960 1970 1980 1987 1990 2000 2010 2023

Source: Yearbook: Armaments, Disarmament and International Security, Stockholm International Peace Research Institute (SIPRI)/World Bank Data

First floating dry dock

The floating dry dock at Port Blair, Andaman and Nicobar Islands, commissioned in 1987, has a lifting capacity of 11,500 tonnes and can accommodate vessels that have a deadweight of up to 30,000 tonnes.

First indigenous floating dock

On 20 June 2017, FDN-2, the first indigenously designed and constructed floating dock of the Indian Navy was launched at the Larsen & Toubro Ltd shipyard at Kattupalli in Chennai, Tamil Nadu. The 185 m (607 ft) long and 40 m (131 ft 3 in.) wide platform has best-in-class machinery and control systems. It accommodates up to 8,000-tonne ships with draught up to 7 m (23 ft), including submarines.

First helicopter training school

INS *Rajali* at Arakkonam, Tamil Nadu, houses the Indian Naval Air Station (INAS), which is a base for training helicopter pilots.

First aircraft carrier dry dock

On 28 September 2019, the first aircraft carrier dry dock was inaugurated at the Naval Dockyard in Mumbai. The largest dry dock of the Indian Navy, it can accommodate INS *Vikramaditya* (IAC-I), the indigenous aircraft carrier under construction at Cochin Shipyard Ltd, and ships with a tonnage of up to 90,000 tonnes. Started in 2010, the completed dock is 281 m (921 ft 11 in.) long, 45 m (147 ft 8 in.) wide and 17 m (55 ft 9 in.) deep. Unlike most dry docks that are made by excavating land, this one is built into the sea, for which 38 caissons or watertight steel sections drained out seawater before construction could begin.

First unified theatre command

Vice Admiral Arun Prakash took over as the first commander-in-chief of the Andaman and Nicobar Command in 2001, with operational control of all three services and the Indian Coast Guard in the Andaman and Nicobar theatre.

Vice Admiral Arun Prakash

First all-woman crew to circumnavigate the world

On 21 May 2018, a six member all-woman crew completed circumnavigating the globe in 254 days on-board INSV *Tarini*, becoming the first Indian allwoman crew to do so. The journey ended at INS *Mandovi* jetty in Panaji, Goa, from where they had set sail on 10 September 2017. The crew included Lieutenant Commanders Vartika Joshi, Pratibha Jamwal, P. Swathi, and Lieutenants S. Vijaya Devi, B. Aishwarya, and Payal Gupta. The 17 m (56 ft) sailing vessel was captained by Lieutenant Commander Joshi. The crew was mentored by Commander Dilip Donde, who became India's first solo circumnavigator in 2010.

Longest expedition with a mixed crew

INSV *Mhadei* and INSV *Tarini* set sail for the Bay of Bengal Offshore Sailing Expedition on 22 February 2020 from

Below: First all-woman crew to circumnavigate the world; *bottom*: Model of INSV *Tarini*

First aircraft carrier dry dock, Mumbai

the Indian Naval Ocean Sailing Node in Goa. The crew comprised five naval officers, including two women officers in each boat, covering 6,100 nautical miles over 55 days. Captain Vipul Meherishi, the skipper of INSV *Tarini*, led the expedition. Captain Atool Sinha was the skipper of INSV *Mhadei*. The sailing vessels had scheduled halts at Colombo (Sri Lanka), Yangon (Myanmar), Chittagong (Bangladesh) and Phuket (Thailand).

First deep-sea submarine rescue system

On 12 Dec 2018, the Indian Navy's first flyaway deep-sea submarine rescue system was inducted by Admiral Sunil Lanba at the Naval Dockyard, Mumbai. The system has a non-tethered Deep Submergence Rescue Vehicle (DSRV) and associated equipment, which give the navy the capability to search, locate, and rescue crew. The rescue system can be mobilized from the naval base at Mumbai, to the nearest mobilization port by air, land, or sea to expedite rescue. On 5 June 2019, an entirely Indian crew conducted its first full submarine rescue drill on the Kilo-class submarine, INS *Sindhudhvaj*, off the eastern coast of India.

First combat management system

A combat management system (CMS) for indigenous aircraft carriers has been developed by the Indian Navy along with the Tata Power Strategic Engineering Division (TPSED), in collaboration with the Weapon and Electronics System Engineering Establishment and MARS, Russia. On 28 March 2019, it was handed over to the navy. All tests and trials conducted on its hardware and software were successful. This is the first CMS developed by a private company for the Indian Navy.

First virtual reality centre

On 12 April 2019, Admiral Sunil Lanba inaugurated the first virtual reality centre (VRC) at the Directorate of Naval Design (Surface Ship Group). This centre boosts the design of indigenous warships and collaborative design reviews between designers and end-users of warships. It has developed 19 warship designs.

Admiral Sunil Lanba

AIR FORCE

PERSONNEL

IAF showcasing platforms for 89th anniversary celebrations

First air chiefs

Air Marshal Subroto Mukerjee became the first Indian chief of air staff when he succeeded Air Marshal Sir G.E. Gibbs on 1 April 1954. However, the IAF chief's rank was only equivalent to that of a lieutenant general of the Indian Army at the time. The IAF got its first air chief marshal only in 1966 when Air Marshal Arjan Singh was promoted to the post in recognition of the IAF's role in the 1965 war with Pakistan.

First air chiefs

First marshal

On 26 January 2002, former chief of the Indian Air Force, Air Chief Marshal Arjan Singh, was given the rank of marshal, equivalent to a field marshal.

Air Chief Marshal Arjan Singh (Centre)

First Indian station commander

Wing Commander Subroto Mukerjee was given command of the airbase RAF Kohat (now in Pakistan), the first all-Indian station with only Indian Air Force (IAF) squadrons, in 1944.

Longest tenure as air chief

Air Marshal Subroto Mukerjee served the longest tenure as air chief, from 1 April 1954 to 8 November 1960.

First squadron commander

Flight Lieutenant Subroto Mukerjee took over command of 1 Squadron on 3 September 1939 – later becoming the first officer to command a flight, a squadron, a station and finally the IAF.

First woman in the Defence Services Staff Course

Padmavathy Bandopadhyay (later air marshal) joined the Indian Air Force as a medical officer. Bandopadhyay was also the first woman to attend the prestigious Defence Services Staff Course (DSSC) in 1978, the first woman in Asia to specialize in aerospace medicine, and the first Indian woman to visit the North Pole (1989–90).

First women combat pilots

In July 2016, for the first time, women combat pilots were inducted into the Indian Air Force with the then defence minister Manohar Parrikar commissioning Mohana Singh, Avani Chaturvedi, and Bhawana Kanth.

DEFENCE AND MILITARY AFFAIRS

A stamp commemorating Indra Lal Roy

A stamp commemorating Sardar Hardit Singh Malik

A stamp commemorating Lieutenant Errol Sharat Chandra Sen

Jeejeebhoy Piroshaw Bomanjee

First Indian pilots

• Lieutenant Indra Lal Roy from Calcutta, was the first Indian pilot with the Royal Flying Corps and later in the Royal Air Force during the First World War. He claimed 10 victories in air combat, all within two weeks, in July 1918. He was killed in action when only 19 years old and was posthumously awarded the Distinguished Flying Cross.

• The only other Indian pilots known to have flown in the First World War were Sardar Hardit Singh Malik, Lieutenant S.G. Welingkar, Lieutenant Errol Sharat Chandra Sen, and Lieutenant Naoroji.

Lieutenant S.G. Welingkar

An image with Lieutenant Errol Sen (sitting on the floor)

First woman flight commander

Wing Commander Shaliza Dhami was the first woman to become a flight commander in the IAF. She was commissioned to the position on 26 August 2019 and took command of a Chetak Helicopter Unit at Hindon Airbase, Ghaziabad, Uttar Pradesh. She is also the first woman to be granted a permanent commission and the first to be an authorized instructor for IAF helicopters.

First woman air marshal

Air Marshal Padmavathy Bandopadhyay, AVSM, VSM, took over as the director general of medical services (Air) on 1 October 2004. Having joined the IAF in 1968, she was also the first woman to reach the rank of air vice marshal in 2002.

First to command an IAF combat unit

Group Captain Shaliza Dhami took command of a frontline combat unit in the western sector on 27 March 2023, becoming the first woman officer to do so. She has a flying experience of over 2,800 hours with 1,935 hours on the Chetak helicopter.

First helicopter pilot

On 28 March 1954, Flight Lieutenant A. Neil Todd and his co-pilot Squadron Leader S.K. Majumdar flew the then prime minister, Jawaharlal Nehru, from Palam, Delhi, to Tilpat Range in Faridabad, Haryana, and back.

First commissioned woman pilot by order of merit

Squadron Leader Priya Nalgundwar was commissioned in the Indian Air Force in the Flying Branch on 17 December 1994 as part of the first batch of seven women pilots and stood first in the order of merit in her batch.

She received her wings from the then chief of air staff Air Chief Marshal S.K. Kaul.

First woman medical officer

Dr Vijayalakshmi Ramanan (later, wing commander), an army doctor, was inducted into the IAF in 1955.

First chief of foreign air force

Air Commodore K. Jaswant Singh, who was on deputation to Ghana to plan and establish the Ghana Air Force, took charge on 25 March 1959 as its air chief.

Above: Air Marshal Padma Bandopadhyay; below: Group Captain Shaliza Dhami

First technical officer

Harjinder Singh, one of 19 Hawai Sepoys recruited to the IAF in 1931 (who later became air vice marshal), was promoted to the rank of warrant officer in 1941 Medals and Honours and became a flying officer in 1942. He was 41 years old when he learned to fly, earned his wings, and became the air officer commander-in-chief of the then newly formed Maintenance Command in Kanpur, Uttar Pradesh, in 1955.

First couple to be awarded the Vishisht Seva Medals

Flight Lieutenant (Dr) Sati Nath Bandopadhyay and his wife Flight Lieutenant Padmavathy Bandopadhyay were honoured with the Vishisht Seva Medal (VSM) at the same investiture ceremony by Air Chief Marshal O.P. Mehra for their service to the nation in the 1971 Bangladesh operations. They are the only Indian Air Force couple to be awarded such a commendation.

First woman to be awarded the Yudh Seva Medal

Squadron Leader Minty Aggarwal, a woman fighter controller who essayed a stellar role in intercepting retaliatory air attacks by the Pakistan Air Force after the Indian Air Force's Balakot air strikes in February 2019, was awarded the Yudh Seva Medal on 15 August 2019. Aggarwal thereby became the first woman in India's military history to be awarded the medal for distinguished service of a high order during war, conflict, or hostilities. Aggarwal was among seven fighter controllers on duty in an underground bunker at the Ambala airbase. She joined the air force in 2011.

First and only Sarvottam Yudh Seva Medal

On 15 August 1999, Air Marshal Vinod Patney was awarded the Sarvottam Yudh Seva Medal (SYSM) for his exemplary leadership during the Kargil conflict in 1999. The award is the highest wartime distinguished service decoration. The medal has been conferred thrice to date and he is the only IAF officer to receive it.

First woman pilot to lead the Republic Day fly-past

Flight Lieutenant Swati Rathore became the first woman pilot to lead the Republic Day fly-past on 26 January 2021. She flew an Mi-17 V5 with the IAF flag in a formation of four choppers. Flight Lieutenant Bhawana Kanth also participated in the Republic Day fly-past. A total of 38 IAF and four army aircraft were part of the parade.

First Param Vir Chakra

Flying Officer N.J.S. Sekhon of 18 Squadron is the only Indian Air Force officer to have been decorated with the Param Vir Chakra, the highest gallantry award. It was given posthumously after he was killed in an air battle over Srinagar in Jammu and Kashmir on 14 December 1971.

Flying Officer N.J.S. Sekhon

LIST OF GALLANTRY AWARDEES 2025

Sarvottam Yudh Seva Medal

- Air Mshl Narmdeshwar Tiwari, PVSM, AVSM, VM
- Air Mshl Nagesh Kapoor, PVSM, AVSM, VM
- Air Mshl Jeetendra Mishra, AVSM, VSM
- Air Mshl Awadhesh Kumar Bharti, AVSM, VM

Uttam Yudh Seva Medal

- Air Mshl Manish Khanna, AVSM, VM
- Air Mshl Praveen Keshav Vohra, AVSM, VM
- Air Cmde Ajay Kumar Chaudhary, VM
- Air Cmde Prabhat Malik, VM
- Gp Capt Kamran Nazeer

Vir Chakra

- Gp Capt Ranjeet Singh Sidhu
- Gp Capt Manish Arora, SC
- Gp Capt Animesh Patni
- Gp Capt Kunal Kalra
- Wg Cdr Joy Chandra
- Sqn Ldr Sarthak Kumar
- Sqn Ldr Siddhant Singh
- Sqn Ldr Rizwan Malik
- Flt Lt Aarshveer Singh Thakur

Shaurya Chakra

- Wg Cdr Abhimanyu Singh

Yudh Seva Medal

- Avm Joseph Suares, VM
- Avm Prajual Singh, VM
- Air Cmde Shashi Kant
- Air Cmde Sagar Singh Rawat, VM
- Air Cmde Ashok Raj Thakur, VM
- Air Cmde Pradeep Batra
- Air Cmde Kanwal Preet Singh Dham, VM
- Air Cmde Devashish Kukreti, VM
- Air Cmde Rohit Kapil, VM
- Gp Capt Alok Kumar Sharma
- Gp Capt Vikas Verma, VM
- Gp Capt Ankit Mehrotra, VM
- Wg Cdr Gobind Singh

Vayu Sena Medal (For Gallantry)

- Gp Capt Ankur Hakim
- Gp Capt Manav Bhatia
- Gp Capt Yasir Faruqi
- Gp Capt Varun Bhoj
- Gp Capt Anuraj Singh Minhas
- Gp Capt Omar Browne, VM
- Gp Capt Deepak Chauhan
- Gp Capt Kunal Vishwas Shimpi
- Wg Cdr Rupak Roy
- Wg Cdr Devendra Babasaheb Autade
- Wg Cdr Mayank Paliwal
- Wg Cdr Deepak Dogra
- Wg Cdr Ravinder Kumar
- Wg Cdr Adarsh Gupta
- Wg Cdr Abhay Singh Bhadoria
- Wg Cdr Amandeep Singh Dihot
- Sqn Ldr Kaustubh Nalawade
- Sqn Ldr Mihir Vivek Chaudhari
- Sqn Ldr Rakesh Sharma
- Sqn Ldr Malapati Nv Naveen Kumar
- Sqn Ldr Shubham Sharma
- Sqn Ldr Aman Singh
- Sqn Ldr Gaurav Khokher
- Flt Lt A Naveen Chandar
- Sgt Surendra Kumar
- Cpl Varunkumar S

Mention-in-Despatches (For Op Sindoor)

- Gp Capt Sumit Prasad
- Gp Capt Vipin Rehani
- Gp Capt Mohan Namdeo
- Gp Capt Samar Veer Saharan, VSM
- Gp Capt Prashant Arora, VSM
- Gp Capt Sanjeev Rao
- Gp Capt Tara Dutt Karnatak
- Gp Capt Ritam Kumar, VM
- Gp Capt Sunil Kumar Deshwal
- Gp Capt S Parameswaran
- Gp Capt Parijat Saurabh, VM
- Gp Capt Charles Shorabh Simon
- Gp Capt Vishwas Ashok Jamkar
- Gp Capt Laxman Singh Charan
- Gp Capt Jijo Jose Ovelil, VM
- Gp Capt Parijat Jha
- Gp Capt Tanmay Khare
- Gp Capt P Sajini
- Gp Capt Rajesh Agarwal, VM
- Gp Capt Yathartha Johri
- Gp Capt C Clement Chelliah Anantharaj
- Gp Capt Saurabh Karmakar
- Gp Capt Rakesh Kumar Yadav
- Gp Capt Gurinder Singh
- Gp Capt Sameep Nijhawan
- Gp Capt Chikkanayaknahalli Jagadeesh Chethan
- Gp Capt Gaurav Kundalia
- Gp Capt Vipul Kumar
- Gp Capt Danpreet Paul Singh Bali
- Gp Capt Sushil Kumar
- Gp Capt Abhishek Raina
- Gp Capt Sameer Yadav
- Gp Capt Abhishek Tripathi
- Gp Capt Gowdhaman Karthikeyan
- Gp Capt Amol Sudhir Kelkar
- Gp Capt Sachin Kumar
- Gp Capt Gunadnya Ramesh Kharche, Sc
- Gp Capt Bharat Malhotra
- Gp Capt Inderjeet Singh
- Gp Capt Manish Joshi
- Gp Capt Sahil Kapoor
- Wg Cdr Pankaj Pant
- Wg Cdr Somraj Mitra
- Wg Cdr Bhaskar Aaruni
- Wg Cdr Ankur Dagar
- Wg Cdr Neeraj Singh
- Wg Cdr Rajat Devendra Gupta
- Wg Cdr Maria Ismenia Sanchia Pereira
- Wg Cdr Chintamani Telang
- Wg Cdr Milind Londhe
- Wg Cdr Keshav Sharma
- Wg Cdr Ashutosh Bhadola
- Wg Cdr Jugal Kishor Lohani
- Wg Cdr Suvojit Dutta
- Wg Cdr Manish Kumar Singh
- Wg Cdr Shree Krishna
- Wg Cdr Shrey Tomar, Vm
- Wg Cdr Joyanta Mukherjee
- Wg Cdr Sandeep Waila
- Wg Cdr Avdesh Tripathi
- Wg Cdr Prashant Kondal
- Wg Cdr Satender Kumar Barar
- Wg Cdr Saurabh Kumar
- Wg Cdr Md Rakibur Mirza
- Wg Cdr Kaushal Kumar Jha
- Wg Cdr Nitin Sehra
- Wg Cdr Manoj Yadav
- Wg Cdr Yathish N
- Wg Cdr Sourabh Suryakant Ambure
- Wg Cdr Danish Handa
- Wg Cdr Raveesh Vashisht

- Wg Cdr Sunil Kumar
- Wg Cdr Deepak Upadhyay
- Wg Cdr Hareen Mukesh Joshi
- Wg Cdr Priti Yadav
- Wg Cdr Dhann Singh
- Wg Cdr Retaish Wali
- Wg Cdr Poonam Gulia
- Sqn Ldr Dhruv Trehan
- Sqn Ldr Amol Vijay Shitole
- Sqn Ldr Manoj Kumar
- Sqn Ldr K Muthamil Selvan
- Sqn Ldr Sanket Shrikant Pande
- Sqn Ldr Sanjay Kumar Kalkhuriya
- Sqn Ldr Nikhil Sanjay Mahagaonkar
- Sqn Ldr Ranmay Ranjan Ghosh
- Sqn Ldr Ankita Singh
- Sqn Ldr Sumangla Sharma
- Sqn Ldr Kuldeep Singh
- Sqn Ldr Swapnika Saxena
- Sqn Ldr Kirti Pandey
- Sqn Ldr Sehaj Veer Singh Sidhu
- Sqn Ldr Sudhir Kumar
- Sqn Ldr Kunal Verma
- Sqn Ldr Brijraj Singh Rathore
- Sqn Ldr Bendhi Rohan Reddy
- Sqn Ldr Anup Omprakash Singh
- Sqn Ldr Nishant Srivastava
- Sqn Ldr Naman Bhatt
- Sqn Ldr Khsitij Singh Sehlot
- Sqn Ldr Anoop Rawat
- Sqn Ldr Kartik Menon
- Sqn Ldr Amol Garg
- Sqn Ldr Kaustubh Sandip Muley
- Sqn Ldr Dharmadhikari Saurabh Shrirang
- Sqn Ldr Sahil Sahu
- Sqn Ldr Harpreet Singh
- Flt Lt Iqbal Singh Gill
- Flt Lt Samarth Shukla
- Flt Lt Bichkar Shubham Santosh
- Flt Lt Digvijay Charak
- Flt Lt Ankit Sharma
- Flt Lt Akash Makarand Bibikar
- Flt Lt Vikram Jaywant
- Flt Lt Mihir Singh
- Flt Lt Hrithik Gaur
- Flt Lt Saanand Dudpuri
- Flt Lt Shakti Panchal
- Flt Lt Ankit Thapa
- Flt Lt Dhruv Bhardwaj
- Flt Lt Ashish Kumar
- Flt Lt Ravi Kumar
- Flt Lt Ananya Sharma
- Flt Lt Anurag Kushwaha
- Flt Lt Swastika Jamwal
- Flt Lt Anish Singh Sisodiya
- Fg Offr Pranav Bellur
- Fg Offr Abhishek Suryawanshi
- Mwo Girish Kumar Jha
- Mwo Mohan Kishor Thakur
- Wo Suresh Kumar M P
- Wo Rajesh Prasad Gupta
- Wo Krishna Moorthy Poornaiyan
- Jwo Krishna Kumar Yadav
- Jwo Suneesh Ambat
- Naresh Kumar
- Jwo Santosh Kumar
- Jwo Deepak Kumar
- Jwo Rajesh Potta
- Jwo Bharat Singh Bhakuni
- Sgt Nilesh Kumar
- Sgt Zubair Ahmad Khan
- Sgt Bhale Singh (Retd)
- Sgt Ramjeewan Choudhary
- Sgt Prateek Singh
- Sgt Deepak Singh Rawat
- Sgt Deepak Kumar
- Sgt Manoj Kumar Yadav
- Sgt Renju Pr
- Sgt Abhishek Kumar
- Sgt Raghvendra Tiwari
- Sgt Sorabh Yadav
- Sgt Pravesh Yadav
- Sgt Karamavir
- Sgt Rahul Kumar Singh
- Sgt Deepak Sharma
- Sgt Suresh Vishnoi
- Sgt Pawan Kumar Singh
- Cpl Ankit Shukla
- Cpl Jahid Beg
- Cpl Vishal Kumar Pandey
- Sep Mohd Zabair

Mention-In-Despatches (Miscellaneous)

- Gp Capt Sagili Sai Kiran
- Wg Cdr Girish Rajkumar Boldara
- Wg Cdr Mayank Kukreti
- Wg Cdr Deepak Prasad
- Sqn Ldr Shashank

Abbreviations used

- Air Mshl: Air Marshal
- Air Cmde: Air Commodore
- Gp Capt: Group Captain
- Wg Cdr: Wing Commander
- Sqn Ldr: Squadron leader
- Flt Lt: Flight Lieutenant
- Fg Offr: Flying Officer
- Mwo: Master Warrant Officer
- wo: Warrant Officer
- Jwo: Juniour Warrant Officer
- Sgt: Sergeant
- Cpl: Corporal
- Sep: Sepoy

UNITS

First squadron

1 Squadron was formed on 1 April 1933 at Karachi's Drigh Road Airfield with Royal Indian Air Force (RAF) officer Flight Lieutenant C.A. Bouchier as the first commanding officer. The first six Indian officers commissioned into the IAF were: Subroto Mukerjee, H.C. Sirkar, A.B. Awan, Bhupendra Singh, Amarjeet Singh, and J.N. Tandon, along with 19 technicians who formed the complement. The six officers were pilots except Tandon, who was commissioned as first ground duty officer.

Air Commodore Bouchier

First heavy-lift transport squadron

In 1961, 44 Squadron, known as 'Himalayan Geese', was raised and equipped with the An-12 four-engine turboprop transport aircraft. In the 1980s, it was renamed the 'Mighty Jets'.

44 Squadron

First squadron to have a jet bomber

106 SPR Squadron, though technically tasked with photo reconnaissance work, was the first unit to fly the famous English Electric Canberra in April 1957. The first squadron to have a jet bomber role again was No. 5 Squadron that took charge of the bomber variant of the Canberra in September 1957.

The biplane aircraft Westland Wapiti: first aircraft

First transport squadron

The first transport squadron of the RIAF was raised with Spitfire fighter aircraft under the command of Squadron Leader S. Sajad Haider at Kohat (now in Pakistan). It moved to Bhopal, Madhya Pradesh, in 1946 and converted to Dakotas, which it flew till 1954, when it then converted to Packets, a twin-engine cargo aircraft.

First attack helicopter squadron

On 1 November 1983, 125 Helicopter Squadron (also known as Gladiators), a fighter squadron, was formed with the Mil Mi-25 attack gunships. It was re-equipped with Mi-35 helicopters in April 1990. The squadron saw action in Sri Lanka during the operations of the Indian Peacekeeping Force (IPKF) between 1987 and 1990. It is currently based at the Pathankot air force station, Punjab.

First bomber squadron

The No. 5 Squadron (Tuskers) was raised on 2 November 1948 on the Consolidated B-24 Liberator bomber. It is now equipped with Jaguar IS and based in Ambala, Haryana.

5 Squadron

EQUIPMENT

First aircraft

The biplane aircraft Westland Wapiti with a maximum speed of 362 km/hr was inducted into the IAF on 1 April 1933. Fitted with two machine guns, this aircraft could carry a load of 263 kg. Four Wapitis, which are believed to have been procured for 10 pounds sterling each, formed the A Flight of 1 Squadron, commanded by Flight Lieutenant C.A. Bouchier of the Royal Indian Air Force (RIAF).

First indigenous advanced light helicopter

The naval version of the advanced light helicopter (ALH), developed by HAL, took its first flight from INS *Viraat* on 8 March 1998. It had an integrated dynamic system, hinge-less main rotor and composite blades, bearing-less tail rotor, advanced cockpit, and high-power engines with electronic control. It could exceed a speed of 250 km/hr.

Apache Attack Helicopter

First supersonic aircraft

In February 1957, 1 Squadron (The Tigers) was equipped with the Dassault MD-452 Mystere Iva. The Mystere could break the sound barrier in a dive. However, the first squadron to fly a level-flight-capable supersonic aircraft was the 28 Squadron, raised in October 1963 on the MiG-21F. Aptly christened First Supersonics, 28 Squadron also has the honour of being the first squadron to fly a Mach 2-capable fighter.

1 Squadron

First jet bomber

The twin-engine English Electric Canberra, which is a long-range and reconnaissance air craft, was inducted into the Indian Air Force in 1957. Six IAF Canberras of 5 Squadron served with the UN forces on the Congo peacekeeping assignment in October 1961.

First indigenous aircraft (trainer)

The HT-2-piston-engined elementary trainer was designed at HAL. It made its maiden flight on 5 August 1951 and was in operation from 1953 to 1990. It replaced the Tiger Moth and was used to train over 5,000 Indian and foreign pilots.

First indigenous tandem-seat jet trainer

The intermediate jet trainer (IJT) was designed in India, with the fastest design to first-flight time, and flown officially by Squadron Leader Baldev Singh for 20 mins on 21 March 2003. With a 10 m (32 ft 10 in.) wingspan and an overall length of 11 m (36 ft), the 3,500 kg aircraft can touch 750 km/hr. However, the credit of being the first tandem-seat jet trainer used for intermediate flying training in the IAF goes to the Polish PZL TS-11 Iskra.

First Apache helicopters

On 3 September 2019, eight Boeing-made Apache Guardian attack helicopters were inducted into service at the Pathankot air force station. The AH-64E (I) Apache helicopter has been built keeping in mind the high mountainous terrain that the IAF operates in. It can also carry out precision attacks. This helicopter can receive and transmit images from the ground to its weapon systems and likewise transmit images from its weapon systems to the ground. The air crew and ground crew were trained to operate the helicopter at the US Army base, Fort Rucker.

First indigenous AEW&C system class of aircraft

On 14 February 2017, the IAF was given its first indigenous Airborne Early Warning and Control (AEW&C) System class of aircraft in initial operational configuration (IOC) by DRDO, during Aero India 2017, a biennial air show and aviation exhibition, at the Yelahanka airbase in Bengaluru, Karnataka. It is built on an Emb-145 platform, and has an air-to-air refuelling capability to enhance surveillance time.

First jet

The British single-seat Vampire was inducted in 1948, making India the first Asian country with jet fighters. In 1950, India entered into a licence agreement with de Havilland Aircraft Company Ltd, UK, and the first Vampire built by Hindustan Aeronautics Ltd (HAL) flew on 21 February 1952. Vampires were phased out in 1975.

Havilland Vampire

First indigenous light combat aircraft

Tejas is the first advanced fly-by-wire light combat aircraft (LCA) designed, developed, and manufactured indigenously by HAL, DRDO, NAL (National Aerospace Laboratories), and ADA (Aeronautical Development Agency). It is a lightweight single-seat multi-role jet fighter, and pegged as the world's smallest and lightest supersonic fighter. It is equipped with a satellite-aided inertial navigation system, a digital, computer-based attack system, and autopilot mode. Tejas can fire air-to-air missiles, and carry bombs and precision-guided ammunition with a reach of over 400 km. It is mainly for use in close air-to-ground operations.

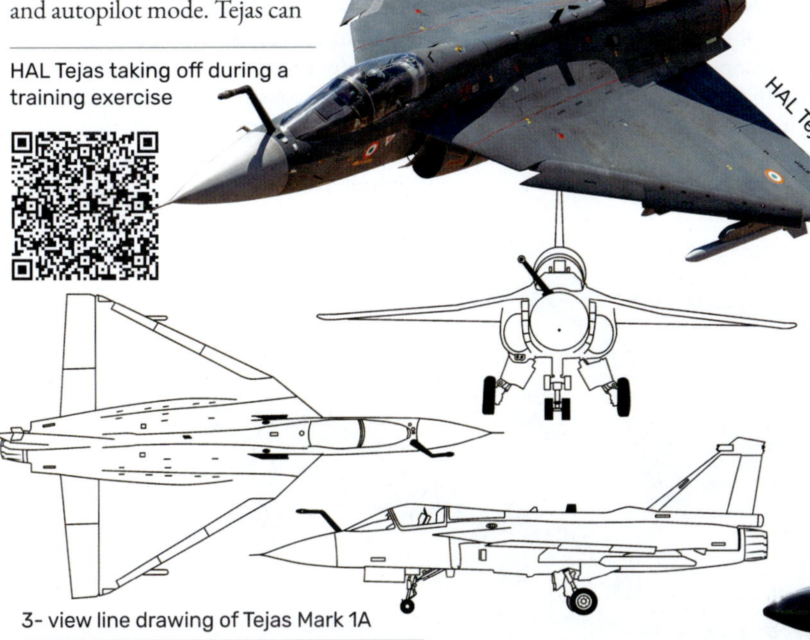

HAL Tejas taking off during a training exercise

HAL Tejas

3- view line drawing of Tejas Mark 1A

First Gnat

The first Gnat or Ajeet, a single-seat, light, fighter bomber, about a third in size and half the weight of a conventional fighter, was inducted into the IAF in 1958. The first Gnat, made by HAL, flew on 18 November 1959. It helped Flying Officer Nirmal Jit Singh Sekhon win the IAF its only Param Vir Chakra, and was in front-line service for more than three decades.

HAL Ajeet

First indigenous fighter aircraft

The single-seat Mach-2 combat jet fighter HF (Hindustan Fighter)-24 Mk I (Marut Ground Attack Fighter), with two single-shaft turbojet engines, was designed at HAL, Bengaluru. It took its maiden flight on 17 June 1961.

First AESA radar for IAF

The IAF gave the nod in July 2017 for the first Active Electronically Scanned Array (AESA) radar to be integrated with its aircraft. The radar is fitted on to the Jaguar fighter aircraft. In conventional radars, the antenna is moved manually to scan enemy targets. The AESA radar moves electronically and rapidly, tracking multiple and long-distance targets, while also jamming enemy communications and radars.

First S-400 air-defence system

The Indian Air Force deployed the first S-400 Triumf air-defence missile system in the Punjab sector near Pakistan border, as reported on 21 December 2021. The deployment was to take care of any aerial threat from either Pakistan or China, using its capability to shoot down enemy fighter aircraft and cruise missiles at a long range (400 km).

First indigenous anti-radiation missile

Rudram-1, a new-generation air-to-surface anti-radiation missile (NGARM), developed by DRDO for the Indian Air Force was test-fired on 9 October 2020 on a radiation target on Wheeler Island off the coast of Odisha. The missile Rudram-1 was fired from a Sukhoi-30 Mk I fighter aircraft, the potential launch source aircraft for the same. With its ability to detect radio sources from 100 km away, the missile can disarm enemy radars and target the range of emitters. Its strike range is between 100 and 250 km.

Rudram-1

OPERATIONS

First flight to the true North Pole

The IL-76 aircraft of the 44 Squadron, representing the IAF, flew over the true North Pole in Exercise Cope Thunder-03 in Alaska, USA, with 14 crew members. The mission was launched on 19 June 2003 at 8:15 p.m. IST from USA's Eielson air force base, south-east of Fairbanks, Alaska, and the crew flew over the true North Pole on 20 June 2003 at 00:16 a.m. IST. The aircraft returned to base on 20 June 2003 at 5:51 a.m. IST after a flight lasting 9 hrs 36 mins.

First airlift of Indian troops

During the Kurdish uprising in April 1923, the Royal Air Force flew 280 Sikh troops from Kingarban to Kirkuk, Iraq. Covering the distance that would normally require a five-day march, the flight covered 120.7 km in 10 hours.

First active operation

In September 1937, 1 Squadron operated from Miranshah in North Waziristan (now in Pakistan) against hostile tribesmen. The IAF men lived inside a fort for safety and had to wheel in their aircraft into the fort every evening. Flying Officer (later Air Marshal) Aspy Merwan Engineer was the first officer to be Mentioned-in-Dispatches for the operations.

Biggest rapid airlift

On 18 December 2018, the Western Air Command of the IAF airlifted a record 463 tonnes from the Chandigarh airbase and dropped the load in Ladakh. The massive airlift was done in a single wave and proved the IAF's rapid airlift capability. The feat was completed by 16 fixed-wing transport aircraft including the C-17 Globemaster, the Ilyushin-76 Gajraj and the medium-lift tactical aircraft, Antonov-32. The airdrop was done in less than six hours.

GENERAL

Only vintage flight

A vintage aircraft flight was raised in Palam, Delhi, in 1988 for heritage aircraft, such as the Howard, Tiger Moth and Dakota planes.

First forward surgical centre

During an IAF military exercise, Gaganshakti-2018, which was conducted from 8 to 22 April 2018, the IAF set up a Forward Surgical Centre (FSC) at Naliya air force station in Gujarat. An FSC can be used for life- and limb-saving surgeries as also to help stabilize a patient.

First private military aircraft plant

In October 2024, Tata Advanced Systems Limited partnered up with Airbus to open a private military aircraft plant in Vadodra, Gujarat. Inaugurated by Prime Minister Narendra Modi and President, Pedro Sánchez Pérez-Castejón of Spain, the facility will manufacture the Airbus C295 aircraft.

COAST GUARD

PERSONNEL

First director general of the Indian Coast Guard

Vice Admiral V.A. Kamath, PVSM, was the first director general of the Indian Coast Guard (ICG) from 19 August 1978 to 31 March 1980.

First and only Integral ICG contingent operating abroad

An ICG Dhruv helicopter – CG 853 – has been operating in Maldives along with an ICG contingent since 2019. Since its induction, the helicopter has aided in 168 medivac (medical evacuation) missions, saving 178 lives.

First woman hovercraft pilot

In 2017, Assistant Commandant Sneha Khatayak became the first woman hovercraft pilot in India.

First woman pilot

Assistant Commandant Monica Seth joined the Indian Coast Guard on 5 June 1998. She flew a total of 1,500 hours during her tenure. She flew on missions during the Kargil conflict in Jammu and Kashmir in 1999 and also for earthquake relief in Gujarat in January 2001.

First women combatants

In 2017, the Indian Coast Guard became the first Indian armed forces service to deploy women in combat roles onboard ships. Assistant Commandants Anuradha Shukla, Sneha Khatayak, Shirin Chandran, and Vasundhara Chouksey were trained at the Indian Coast Guard station at Mandapam, Tamil Nadu.

MEDALS AND HONOURS

First Yudh Seva Medal

Deputy Commandant S.P.S. Basra and Deputy Commandant B.A.S. Bhar were awarded the Yudh Seva Medal (YSM) on 26 January 1989. Commanding the Indian Coast Guard ships ICGS *Ahalya Bai* and ICGS *Tara Bai*, respectively, they prevented the infiltration of the Liberation Tigers of Tamil Eelam (LTTE) in the Palk Bay.

First to receive President's Tatrakshak Medal

Commandant A.K. Dey received the award for his efforts in firefighting during the construction of an Indian Coast Guard ship, and preventing an oil spill off the coast of Goa in June 1994.

Dhruv MK-III

EQUIPMENT

First indigenous offshore patrol vessel

On 21 February 2019, ICGS *Sachet*, the first indigenous offshore patrol vessel (OPV) of the Indian Coast Guard was launched at Goa Shipyard Ltd (GSL). This OPV is part of an indigenous project that was launched on 13 November 2016. Designed in-house, these OPVs will be used for protecting the Exclusive Economic Zone. The vessel weighs 2,400 tonnes and is equipped with features like quick-response boats for rescue and anti-piracy, gunnery simulators, and many more advanced features.

Commissioning of ICGS *Sachet*

Latest training vessel

On 24 October 2018, ICGS *Varuna*, an indigenously designed training vessel built by Reliance Naval and Engineering Ltd (RNAVAL), was launched at the Pipavav Shipyard, Gujarat. ICGS *Varuna* is a 105 m (344 ft 6 in.) long vessel with a crew of 242 officers and sailors. It is powered by twin diesel engines and can reach a speed of 20 knots. It has ultra modern navigation and communication systems. This is the largest ship built yet for the Indian Coast Guard.

OPERATIONS

First and longest deep-sea passage by hovercraft

On 13 January 2015, Indian Coast Guard Air Cushion Vehicle (ACV) H-198 undertook area deployment from New Mangaluru, Karnataka, to Androth Island in Lakshadweep, across the Arabian Sea. The ACV hovercraft, piloted by Commandant Amitabh Banerjee and Deputy Commandant Konark Sharma, covered 142.5 nautical miles (264 km) in five hours. The ACV H-198 is the only hovercraft in India to venture into the lagoon islands of Lakshadweep. The return run of 146 nautical miles (270.39 km) was made on 22 January 2015.

First vessels

ICGS *Kuthar* and ICGS *Kirpan* (formerly of the Indian Navy) were commissioned on 19 August 1978 under Commander N.S. Achreja and Commander V.K. Tuli, respectively.

INS *Kirpan*

First underwater clean-up

On 5 June 2019, celebrated as World Environment Day, the Indian Coast Guard (Eastern Region) conducted an underwater debris clean-up exercise in the Bay of Bengal near the Chennai coast, in association with Dive India. The operation lasted two hours during which nearly 500 kg of trash was collected. This was the first underwater clean-up in India to remove debris, nets, and plastic from the ocean.

GENERAL

An introduction to Indian Coast Guard

Youngest defence service

The Indian Coast Guard or Sea Police was constituted under the Coast Guard Act on 18 August 1978, for the preservation and protection of the 2.01 million sq. km Exclusive Economic Zone. The force is under the direction and control of the director general, Indian Coast Guard.

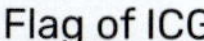

Flag of ICG

First hovercraft berthing platform

In 2001, the first hovercraft berthing platform was built at Haldia, West Bengal, in eight months by the Military Engineering Services.

Largest integrated shipbuilding facility

Reliance Naval and Engineering Ltd (RNAVAL), known earlier as Reliance Defence and Engineering Ltd and Pipavav Shipyard Ltd, headquartered in Mumbai, Maharashtra, is one of the largest shipbuilding yards of its kind in the world. RNAVAL is the first private sector company in India to earn a licence and contract to construct warships. It has India's largest integrated shipbuilding facility with the shipyard located in Pipavav, Gujarat. Its dry dock measures 662 m x 65 m (2,172 ft x 213 ft). It has the only modular shipbuilding facility in India.

SCIENCE AND TECHNOLOGY

FORMAL SCIENCES

MATHEMATICS

WR Earliest mention of mathematical series

Arithmetic and geometric series were mentioned in Vedic literature as early as 2000 BCE in the *Taittiriya Samhita* and in the Panchavimsa Brahmana.

WR Earliest treatise on geometry

The *Shulba Sutras* are the earliest known treatises that are related to geometry. Dating to the Vedic period, these texts are focused on the measurement and the building of altars. Baudhayana, who lived around 800 BCE, wrote the first *Shulba Sutra*.

WR First application of geometry

In the first millennium BCE, Apastamba, the founder of a Vedic school, propounded practical geometry for the construction of sacrificial altars, which describes acute, obtuse, and right angles.

Patna) in Bihar is credited with the invention of algebra. He was also the first to approximate the value of π (pi) to 3.14159..., which is accepted today.

WR Earliest magic squares

The oldest magic square that can be dated in India occurs in polymath Varahamihira's encyclopaedic work the *Brihat-Samhita* (c. 550 CE). Varahamihira used a modified 4 x 4 magic square to indicate combinations and quantities of ingredients for making perfumes.

Earliest use of the decimal system

A Gupta inscription from 448 CE found in Allahabad (now Prayagraj) District, Uttar Pradesh, indicates that the decimal system was known in India at the beginning of the fifth century CE.

WR Use of sines and cosines in place of chords

In a significant contribution to trigonometry, Indian mathematicians

WR Firsts to understand the idea of 'zero'

Brahmagupta (c. 598–668 CE) was the first mathematician to treat zero as a number and present its mathematical operations. Bhaskara I (c. 600–680 CE) was the first mathematician to understand the properties of both zero and infinity and to state that any number divided by zero equals infinity.

First study of infinite series

Founded in the 14th century by Madhava (c. 1340–1425 CE) of Sangamagrama, who is said to have been born in present-day Irinjalakuda in Thrissur District, Kerala; the Kerala school of astronomy and mathematics (or the Kerala school) was responsible for notable contributions to the study of infinite series, trigonometry, geometry, algebra, and calculus. The foundations for calculus laid by Madhava were further developed by his successors at the Kerala school, with many results that would later be repeated in Europe, including the infinite series for circular and trigonometric functions.

First textbook on arithmetic

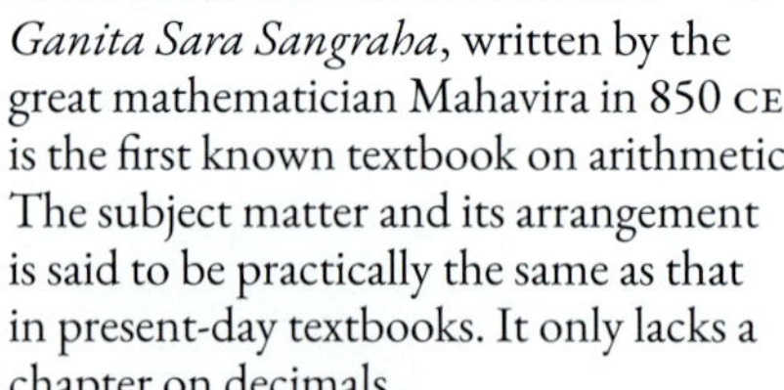

Ganita Sara Sangraha, written by the great mathematician Mahavira in 850 CE, is the first known textbook on arithmetic. The subject matter and its arrangement is said to be practically the same as that in present-day textbooks. It only lacks a chapter on decimals.

Apastamba

WR Earliest use of irrational numbers

The use of irrational numbers dates back to the *Shulba Sutras* (c. first millennium BCE).

WR Invention of algebra

Aryabhata (476–550 CE) from Kusumapura near Pataliputra (today's

changed the use of chords to sines and cosines, making the system much more convenient and the various theorems on triangles much neater. Starting with the *Arya-siddhanta* (c. fifth and sixth centuries CE), Aryabhata used a simple table for sines. Varahamihira gave the first clear statements of sin2A and sin2A + cos2A.

Madhava of Sangamagrama

WR Discovery of differential calculus

Bhaskara II (c. 1114–85 CE), said to have been born in Bijapur (now Vijayapura) in Karnataka, conducted mathematical operations that showed that he had invented calculus long before Isaac Newton and Gottfried Leibniz, who are considered its pioneers. Bhaskara II used calculus to determine the area and volume of a sphere and the daily motion of planets.

First to give the Gregory series

In 1502, Keḷallur Nilakantha Somayaji (1444–1545 CE) from Tirur in present-day Malappuram District, Kerala, devised the *Tantrasangraha* equation, which is employed to give the approximate value of π or pi (3.14159...). This is known today as the 'Gregory series' after it appeared in the works of later mathematicians James Gregory (1638–75) and Gottfried Leibniz (1646–1716).

Discovery of the Kaprekar Constant

D.R. Kaprekar (1905-81) discovered in 1946 what is known as the Kaprekar Constant in mathematics. Explained thus: Take a number, arrange its digits in descending order and in ascending order and calculate the difference. Arrange the digits of the result of the subtraction in the same way and find the difference. Keep repeating the process. For any four-digit number, this leads in a few steps to 6,174 and then it becomes a constant. This does not work for repetitive numbers like 1,111 and 2,222, which lead to a difference of zero in the first step itself. So the numbers should have at least two different digits.

First mathematical society

The Indian Mathematical Society (IMS) was the oldest organization in India devoted to the promotion of the study of and research in mathematics. With its headquarters in Pune, Maharashtra, it was founded by V. Ramaswamy Aiyer in April 1907. The society's first president was Dr B. Hanumantha Rao.

Invention of the Mahalanobis distance

Pioneering statistician P.C. Mahalanobis (1893–1972) invented statistical tools such as the Mahalanobis distance and fractile graphical analysis in 1936. He was the first statistician to be elected a Fellow of the Royal Society, UK, in 1945.

First to propose a theory on infinite dimensional representations

Indian-born American mathematician–physicist Harish Chandra (1923–83) created a theory for infinite dimensional representations in 1947, which was used in quantum mechanics when it was necessary to analyse the effect of symmetries on the motions of particles and waves.

First Indian to win MSO

Twenty-year old Neelakantha Bhanu Prakash (b. 13 October 1999) became the fastest human calculator in the world after winning the gold for India in the Mental Calculation World Championship at Mind Sports Olympiad (MSO) in September 2020.

PHYSICAL SCIENCES

ASTRONOMY

First manual on the astrolabe

The astrolabe is an instrument for measuring the altitude of stars. Mahendra Suri (c. 1340–1400 CE), an astronomer, wrote a manual on the astrolabe in Sanskrit while under the patronage of ruler Firuz Shah Tughlaq of the Tughlaq dynasty.

Two firsts in astronomy

Lagadha, who lived around 900 CE near Srinagar, Jammu and Kashmir, was the first to systematize astronomy, the first to complete a text – Vedanga Jyotisha or *Jyotishavedanga* – on astronomy, and the first to work out simple formulae to derive unknown quantities from known ones. Aryabhata was the first astronomer to deduce that the earth is round and that it rotates on its own axis, causing day and night.

Earliest extant astrolabe

The Yantraraja, which was 276 mm (10.87 in.) in diameter, was designed and built in Ahmedabad, Gujarat, in 1607 for astronomer Damodara during the reign of the Mughal ruler Jahangir.

First modern catalogue of stars

The Madras or Taylor catalogue was made by T.G. Taylor, astronomer to the British East India Company, in 1844. The catalogue contained the positions of 11,015 stars, based on his observations of the night sky in Madras (now Chennai), Tamil Nadu.

Rings of Uranus discovered

Prof. J.C. Bhattacharya and Sri Kuppuswamy from the Indian Institute of Astrophysics, Bangalore (now Bengaluru), Karnataka, discovered the rings of planet Uranus in 1976 at the Vainu Bappu Observatory in Kavalur, Tamil Nadu. Around the same time, US astronomer James Elliot and his team, aboard the airborne Kuiper Observatory, discovered the same rings during an occultation of a star by the planet.

Vainu Bappu Observatory

WR First liquid mirror telescope only for astronomical observations

Aryabhatta Research Institute of Observational Sciences (ARIES), an autonomous institute under the Department of Science and Technology, now has the first liquid mirror telescope that is meant only for astronomical observations. It is called International Liquid Mirror Telescope (ILMT). This is also India's, as well as Asia's, largest. This telescope was inaugurated on 22 March 2023. It was designed and built by Advanced Mechanical and Optical Systems (AMOS) Corporation and the Centre Spatial de Lie'ge in Belgium. The telescope will generate 10–15 gigabytes of data, which in turn will allow application of big data and machine-learning algorithms that will be used for classifying the objects observed through the ILMT.

First facility for ground-based, infrared observations of celestial objects

The Mount Abu Infrared Observatory in Mount Abu, Rajasthan, is the first Indian facility that offers ground-based infrared observations of celestial objects. This facility is operated by the Physical Research Laboratory and began its journey with a 1.2-m telescope. Currently it has five telescopes, a new 2.5-meter primary mirror telescope equipped with the PARAS-2 spectrograph being the most powerful.

Indian Astronomical Observatory, Hanle, Ladakh

Highest astronomical observatory

Established in 2001, the Indian Astronomical Observatory, under the aegis of the Indian Institute of Astrophysics, Bangalore, is located in Hanle (at Digpa-Ratsa Ri, atop Mt Saraswati) in Ladakh. It has the world's second highest optical telescope at 4,500 m (14,764 ft) above mean sea level.

Oldest planetarium

The M.P. Birla Planetarium at Calcutta (now Kolkata), West Bengal, was established on 29 September 1962 by the Birla Education Trust. The planetarium coordinates the various activities of the Amateur Astronomers Association, which include telescope fabrication, astrophotography, and organizing skywatching sessions.

Discovery of the Bappu–Wilson effect

Indian astronomer M.K.V. Bappu (1927–82), in collaboration with Colin C. Wilson at Mount Wilson and Palomar Observatories, USA, discovered a relationship between the luminosity of particular types of stars and their spectral characteristics. Known as the 'Bappu–Wilson effect', this helps determine the luminosity and distance of these types of stars. It was discovered in 1957.

First discovery of an asteroid

R. Rajamohan (b. 1944), associate professor at the Indian Institute of Astrophysics, Bangalore, and his team discovered an asteroid (No. 4130) in 1988, through the optical telescope at Kavalur, Tamil Nadu.

First to observe a nova

Radha Gobinda Chandra (1878–1975) from Jessore (now in Bangladesh) was the first Indian astronomer to observe a nova. A nova is a transient astronomical event that causes the sudden appearance of a bright and seemingly 'new' star that slowly fades over weeks or months. He sighted the nova in the Aquila constellation on 7 June 1918. A pioneer of observational astronomy in Bengal – now split into two parts, Bangladesh (a country) and West Bengal (an Indian state), Chandra was one of the first international members of the American Association of Variable Star Observers.

Radha Gobinda Chandra with his telescopes

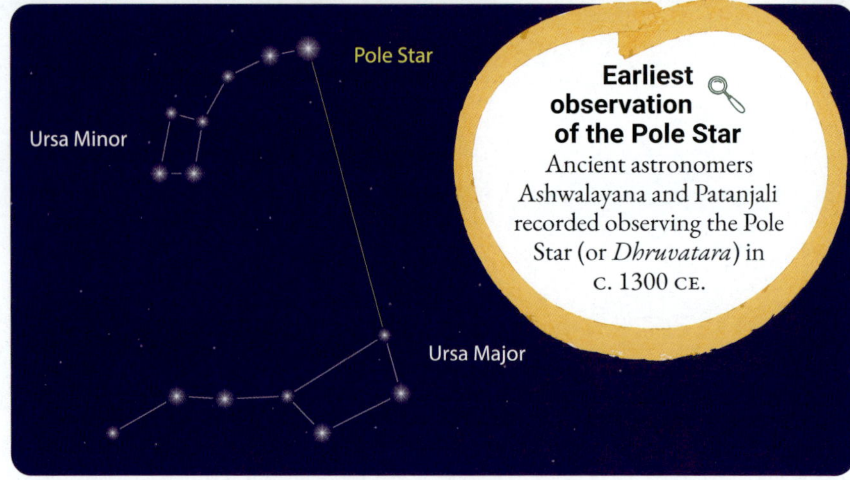

Earliest observation of the Pole Star

Ancient astronomers Ashwalayana and Patanjali recorded observing the Pole Star (or *Dhruvatara*) in c. 1300 CE.

Discovery of the variability of stars

In 1958, astrophysicist K.D. Abhyankar (1928–2007), professor of astronomy at the Osmania University in Hyderabad, discovered the variability of two types of stars, called dwarf cepheid and the short period eclipsing binary.

WR First chain of observatories

Sawai Jai Singh II (1686–1743), the maharaja of the kingdom of Amber in Rajasthan, was the first in the world to build a chain of astronomical observatories, in Mathura, Varanasi, Delhi, and Jaipur; from 1719 to 1737. It was about a century after European astronomers had verified Polish scientist Nicolaus Copernicus's theory that the sun (and not Earth) was at the centre of the universe.

Discovery of solar radio burst

In 1958, Prof. Govind Swarup (b. 1929) and A. Maxwell discovered a burst, called 'type U solar radio burst'. A pioneer of radio astronomy, Swarup was behind the concept, design, and installation of the Ooty Radio Telescope near present-day Udhagamandalam, Tamil Nadu, and the Giant Metrewave Radio Telescope (GMRT) near Poona (now Pune) in Maharashtra.

First modern astronomical observatory

On 5 December 1786, William Petrie, an officer of the East India Company, made the first astronomical observations to calculate the latitude and longitude of the Masulipatnam Fort from his private observatory. This observatory on the terrace of his residence was fitted with an astronomical clock, a transit instrument, and two or three telescopes. The first modern astronomical observatory, the Nizamia Observatory, was set up more than a century later in Hyderabad (now in Telangana) in 1908 by the Nizam's government.

First university to teach astronomy

Osmania University, based in Hyderabad

Radio telescope in Ooty

(now in Telangana), was the first educational institution in the country to start teaching astronomy and astrophysics at postgraduate and research levels in 1959. The Astronomical Society of India was also registered in Hyderabad, in 1972.

First woman president of the Astronomical Society of India

In 2019, the Astronomical Society of India elected its first woman president, Dr G.C. Anupama, a senior professor and dean at the Indian Institute of Astrophysics in Bengaluru. She has projects such as the Himalayan Telescope at the Hanle Observatory in Ladakh to her credit and is a member of an international team setting up a 30 m (98 ft 5 in.) telescope (TMT) in Hawaii, USA.

WR Biggest sundial

The Samrat Yantra built by Sawai Jai Singh II, ruler of the kingdom of Amber in Rajasthan, in 1728 CE at Jaipur, Rajasthan, is the biggest sundial in the world. Its gnomon rises to 22.6 m (74 ft).

First robotic telescope

India's first robotic telescope became functional on the night of 12 June 2018 at Hanle, Ladakh. It is the first one designed to observe dynamic or transient events in the universe. GROWTH-India, the facility at Hanle, is part of a multi-country collaborative initiative, known as the 'Global Relay of Observatories Watching Transients Happen' (GROWTH), to observe transient events in the universe.

PHYSICS

Earliest atomistic theory

Kanada, an ancient Indian natural scientist and philosopher, who lived between the sixth and second centuries BCE, composed the *Vaisheshika Sutra*, a text in which he explored and presented the relationship between cause and effect for the first time in relation to physics and philosophy.

WR First double radio source

Mrinal Kumar Dasgupta from the Institute of Radio Physics and Electronics, Calcutta, West Bengal, discovered the first double radio source Cygnus A in 1953 in collaboration with R.C. Jennison at the Jodrell Bank Experimental Station in Cheshire, UK.

First solar heater

Prof. Shri Krishna Joshi from Almora, who lived in Allahabad (now Prayagraj), Uttar Pradesh, invented an apparatus for utilizing solar heat as a substitute for fire, named 'Bhanu Taap'. Also called the 'heliotherm', it was patented in 1900 and awarded a gold medal at the Industrial Exhibition of Calcutta in 1901.

First optical fibre 

Narinder Kalpany from the Imperial College, University of London, UK, invented optical fibre in 1955. This is a thin and long fibre of glass through which light can travel without hindrance, whether it is bent or not. Optical fibres have a wide variety of applications in a range of fields, including medicine, computers, communications, and the automotive industry.

First semiconductor laser 

The Bhabha Atomic Research Centre, Bombay developed a semiconductor laser in 1965.

First to measure ozone in the atmosphere 

In 1985, M. Vivekananda and R.S. Arora from the Raman Research Institute, Bangalore, first measured the density and height distribution of ozone in the atmosphere over Bangalore by a simple ground-based technique using radio waves.

Top: Digitally altered image of the Bhabha Atomic Centre, Mumbai; *Below*: Raman Research Institute, main building

First nuclear reactor

Apsara was the first Asian research reactor to achieve criticality, when it became operational, at the Bhabha Atomic Research Centre (BARC) in Bombay in 1956. It was shut down in 2010.

Above: Apsara- U reactor complex; *Left*: Apsara-U pool-top view from viewing gallery

Only nuclear safety institute

With the inauguration of the Safety Research Institute at Kalpakkam, Tamil Nadu, on 20 February 1999, India became the second country after France to have such a facility.

Kudankulam Nuclear Power Plant (KKNPP) Units 1 and 2 at Kudankulam in Tirunelveli district of Tamil Nadu, India

First synchrotron radiation facility

The first synchrotron radiation facility in India was INDUS-1, set up in 2002. An advanced, indigenously built nuclear particle accelerator, it is part of the Centre for Advanced Technology at Indore, Madhya Pradesh.

First nuclear implosion

On 18 May 1974, India imploded its first nuclear device at Pokhran in Rajasthan. The test, code-named 'Smiling Buddha', was conducted at a depth of 107 m (351 ft). It yielded energy equivalent to 8–10 kilotonnes of TNT, and produced a 47 m (154 ft) wide and 10 m (33 ft) deep crater.

First multicore fibre

STL Multiverse launched India's first multicore fibre and cable in October 2022. This development allows the fibre to carry multiple beams of light (separated within the body of the optic fibre cable) through it making it more efficient than single-core fibre.

First molecular distillation unit

Major General Sir Singh Sokhey of Haffkine Institute, in Bombay (now Mumbai), Maharashtra, installed the first molecular distillation unit in India to separate vitamin A from shark liver oil in the early 1940s. He was also the first Indian scientist to receive the Lenin Peace Prize in 1947.

First advanced heavy water reactor

In 2016, the Bhabha Atomic Research Centre (BARC) in Mumbai, designed an advanced heavy water reactor, which employed thorium instead of uranium as fuel. It was the centrepiece of India's nuclear power programme.

Discovery of mesons

Indian nuclear physicist Dr Homi Jehangir Bhabha and German physicist Dr Walter Heinrich Heitler presented the 'Cascade Theory of Electron Showers', called the 'Bhabha–Heitler Cascade Theory' in 1937 in Cambridge, UK, which explains the process of electron showers in cosmic rays. Bhabha recognized heavy electron particles in cosmic rays, which he named 'mesons'.

Discovery of the 'Krishnan effect'

In the 1930s, physicist Rappal Sangameswaran Krishnan (1911–99) from the Indian Institute of Science (IISc), Bangalore, discovered the 'Krishnan effect' – a new optical effect in the scattering of light. This led to the discovery of the presence of large clusters of molecules in liquid mixtures, glasses, and colloidal solutions. It also helps in assessing the size of the scattering particles.

First Nobel Prize in physics

Sir Chandrasekhara Venkata Raman (1888–1970) from Tiruchirappalli, Madras Presidency (now Tamil Nadu), won the 1930 Nobel Prize in physics for his groundbreaking work in the field of the scattering of light, or the 'Raman effect'.

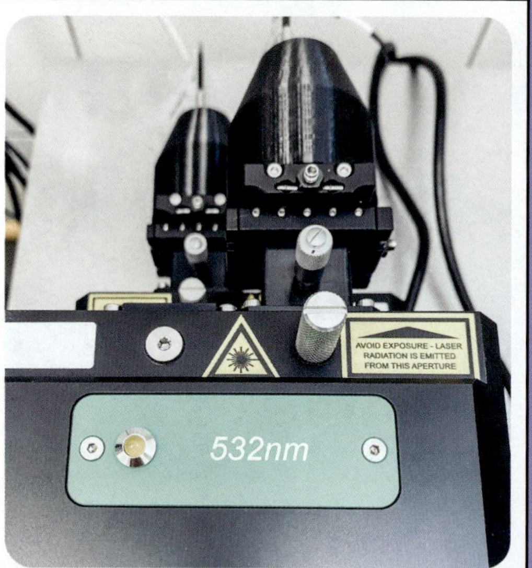

A Raman microscope-spectroscope, which uses the Raman effect to analyse a sample and provide detailed chemical information about it.

First prediction of hot superconductors

S.N. Ekbote and A.V. Narlikar from the National Physical Laboratory (NPL), New Delhi, were the first scientists to predict the presence of 'hot' superconductors based on their new theory of superconductivity formulated in 1981, which challenged the then accepted Nobel Prize–winning theory.

New method for thermal conductivity

Suresh Chand Jain (1926–2009), former director of the Solid State Physics Laboratory and Defence Research and Development Organization (DRDO), and his mentor R.S. Krishnan developed a new method known as the Jain–Krishnan method in 1952, which is now a standard method for measuring the thermal conductivity of solids at high temperatures.

Discovery of helium isotope in cosmic rays

Dr K.M.V. Apparao (b. 1933), a scientist at the Tata Institute of Fundamental Research in Bombay discovered in 1961 an isotope of helium in cosmic rays, the energetic particles that fall down on earth like a continuous rain from outer space, in 1961.

Discovery of bosons

In the late 1920s, famous physicist and German Nobel Prize–winner

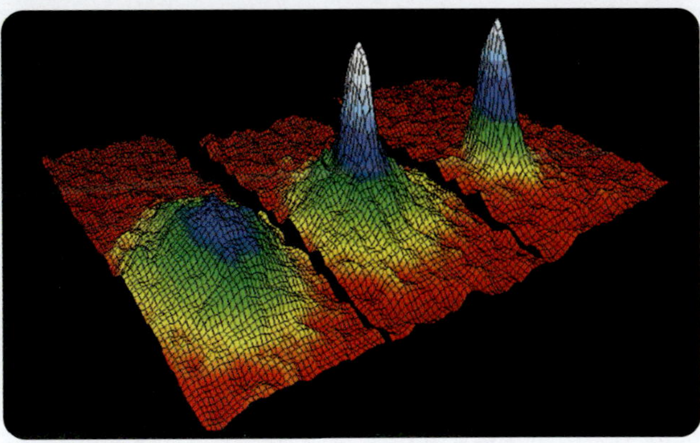

Velocity-distribution data for gas of rubidium atoms. *Left*: just before the appearance of a Bose–Einstein condensate. *Center*: just after the appearance of the condensate. *Right*: after further evaporation, leaving a sample of nearly pure condensate.

Albert Einstein and Indian scientist Satyendra Nath Bose worked together on the Bose–Einstein equations, which pointed to a state of matter comprising particles, now known as 'bosons'. As researchers at the Joint Institute of Laboratory Astrophysics, Colorado, USA, they cooled thousands of atoms of rubidium to create the 'Bose–Einstein condensate'.

Discovery of quantum Zeno paradox

Indian theoretical physicists Baidyanath Misra and E.C.G. Sudarshan, then conducting research at the University of Texas at Austin, US, discovered the quantum Zeno effect (or paradox) in 1977. It is the quantum mechanical analogue of the proverbial adage 'a watched kettle never boils'. In 1989, the paradox was experimentally proven – under continuous measurement, an unstable atomic nucleus that normally decays was found not to decay.

CHEMISTRY

First heavy chemicals company

Behramji Sorabji Lalkaka (1880–1957) started the Pioneer Magnesia Works Ltd in 1915 at Kharagodha in the Little Rann of Kachchh, Gujarat, for the manufacture of magnesium chloride, the import of which was stopped from Germany due to the First World War. Magnesium chloride is used in a variety of ways in the chemical industry.

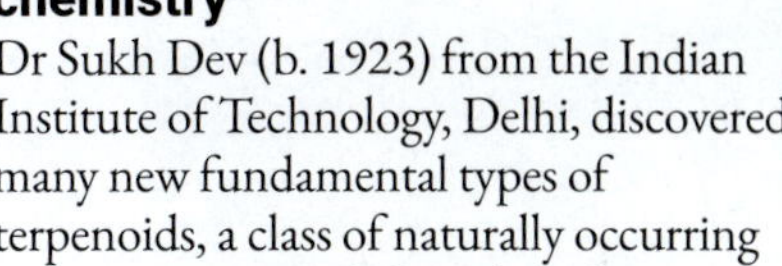

Discoveries in terpene chemistry

Dr Sukh Dev (b. 1923) from the Indian Institute of Technology, Delhi, discovered many new fundamental types of terpenoids, a class of naturally occurring organic compounds found in plants.

Discovery of tetracycline

Tetracycline, a life-saving drug, was discovered as a natural product and developed in 1948 by a research group headed by Dr Yellapragada Subbarow at the Lederle Laboratories in New York, US. An anti-plague drug, it helped save many lives in the 1994 plague epidemic in Surat, Gujarat.

First observation of spontaneous fission

Prof. Shyamadas Chatterjee (1909–95) from the Indian Physical Society in Calcutta, West Bengal, first observed spontaneous fission – the splitting of a heavy nucleus on its own in uranium – in 1940, almost at the same time when scientists in Western countries reported its discovery.

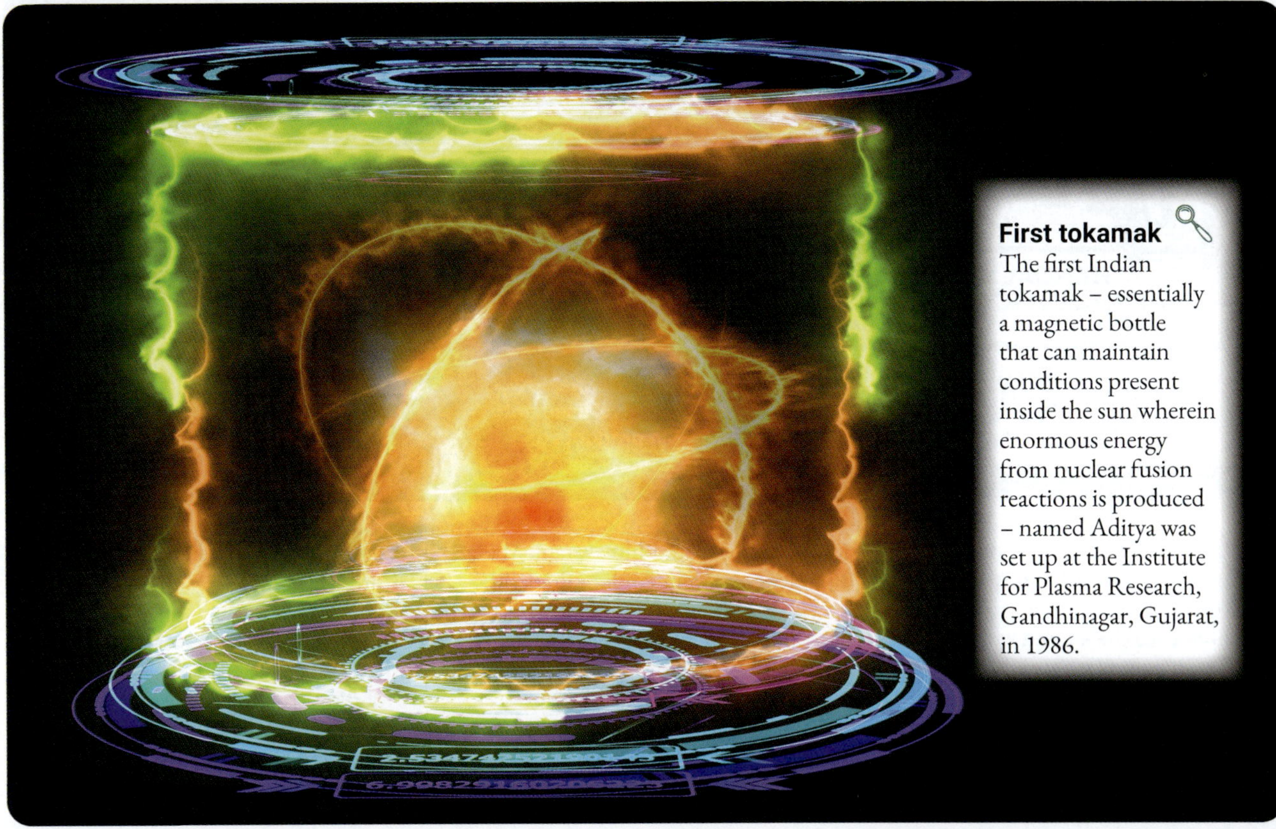

First tokamak

The first Indian tokamak – essentially a magnetic bottle that can maintain conditions present inside the sun wherein enormous energy from nuclear fusion reactions is produced – named Aditya was set up at the Institute for Plasma Research, Gandhinagar, Gujarat, in 1986.

Bengal Chemicals celebrating 150th birth centenary of Acharya Prafulla Chandra Ray in 2010

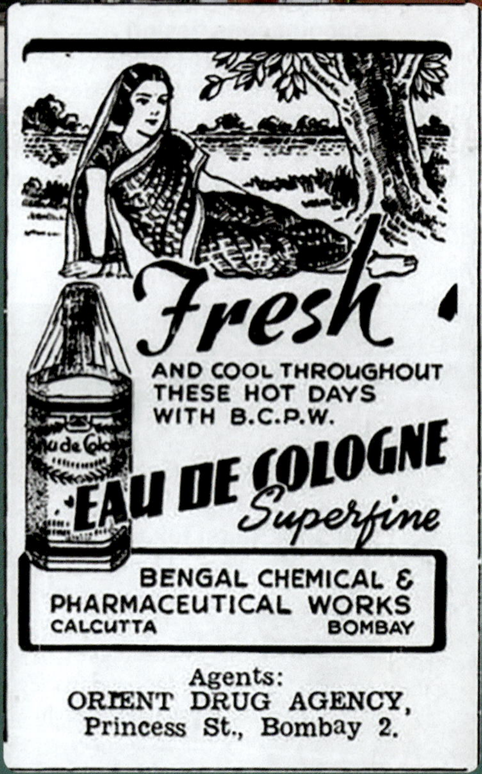

First chemicals company

In 1892, Prafulla Chandra Ray (1861–1944) set up Bengal Chemicals and Pharmaceutical Ltd at Calcutta, West Bengal, using locally available materials, which led to the production of many chemicals and medicines indigenously. He was also the first person to synthesize ammonium nitrite (NH_4NO_2) in its pure form.

Left: A 1943 Bengal Chemical advertisement; *Right*: Old products of Bengal Chemicals

First Indian to receive the Chemical Landmark Plaque award

The Royal Society of Chemistry in 2011 honoured the life and work of Prafulla Chandra Ray with the first ever Chemical Landmark Plaque awarded to anyone from a country outside Europe.

Discovery of phosphocreatine

In 1927, Dr Yellapragada Subbarow (1895–1948) from Bhimavaram, Madras Presidency (now in Andhra Pradesh), and Cyrus H. Fiske discovered the function of adenosine triphosphate, an organic phosphorous compound, as an energy source in the human cell, connected with the chemical mechanism of muscle contraction. He also discovered methotrexate (still used in chemotherapy) and diethylcarbamazine (DEC), which is used for effectively treating filariasis).

Discovery of the isomerism of thiosulphuric acid

Prof. Priyada Ranjan Ray (1888–1982), director, Indian Association for the Cultivation of Science, Calcutta, established for the first time the isomerism (compounds that have the same molecular

A close-up of industrial carbon dioxide laser cutting

formulae but different molecular structures) of thiosulphuric acid.

First wireless demonstration

In 1894, scientist Jagadish Chandra Bose (1858–1937) at Presidency College, Calcutta, Bengal (now Presidency University, demonstrated the transmission of radio waves before Italian inventor Guglielmo Marconi did it in Europe, using very short radio waves or 'microwaves'. Jagadish Chandra Bose also scientifically proved that plants have feelings. He also wrote the first science fiction in Bengali.

First carbon dioxide laser

Chandra Kumar Naranbhai Patel (b. 1938), an Indian-origin scientist in the United States, invented the powerful carbon dioxide laser in 1963, which resulted in making lasers a valuable tool in scientific research.

A carbon dioxide laser

Largest scientific and industrial research organization

The Council of Scientific and Industrial Research (CSIR), which was set up in 1942, is India's largest research and development organization for scientific and industrial research for economic and environmental development.

First chemistry department

Chemistry was first taught as a subject in 1872–73 at Presidency College, (now Presidency University, Kolkata, West Bengal). Postgraduate courses were introduced in 1886. In 1889, chemist Prafulla Chandra Ray set up the first organized laboratory here for research.

First course in geology

Geology as a degree course leading to postgraduation was started at Presidency College, Calcutta, for the first time in the country in 1892.

First woman director general of CSIR

Dr Kalaiselvi N. became India's first

woman director general of the Council of Scientific and Industrial Research (CSIR), India's largest research organization. She primarily works on electrochemical power systems. She was appointed to the post in August 2022.

GEOLOGY

First mention of seismological zones

Varahamihira, the ancient astronomer and scientist, was the first to mention seismological zones and the most earthquake-prone areas in his treatise Brihat- Samhita (c. 550 CE).

First geomagnetic observatory

The Colaba Geomagnetic Observatory in Bombay was the first geomagnetic observatory to be set up in pre-Independence India. It was established in 1846 by the scientists of the East India Company to study the earth's magnetic field by using geomagnetic instruments.

First geologist

Dr Henry Wesley Voysey, a doctor by profession, became the first professional geologist in India under British rule in 1818.

First megafossil from the Himalayas

In 1984, R.N. Lakhanpal, a scientist at the Birbal Sahni Institute of Palaeosciences, Lucknow, Uttar Pradesh, and his team discovered a leaf of the temperate palm *Trachycarpus*, the first definite megafossil record of the Miocene period (23 million to 5.3 million years ago) in Ladakh in the Himalayas.

First dinosaur fossils

The Geological Survey of India (GSI) discovered dinosaur bone fossils from the Lameta formation of the late Cretaceous age (145 to 66 million years ago) at Raiyoli near Balasinor in the Kheda District, Gujarat, in 1981. Dinosaur egg clutches were also found at the site in 1982. Both the eggs and bones are preserved at the Indian Museum in Calcutta (now Kolkata), West Bengal.

First underwater mining system

The National Institute of Ocean Technology, Chennai, Tamil Nadu, in collaboration with the University of Siegen, Germany, devised an underwater mining vehicle called the crawler, which extracts mineral-rich polymetallic nodules from the ocean floor. The mining system consists of a crawler, cutter, and slurry pump. Mounted on board the ship ORV *Sagar Kanya*, its first test was conducted successfully on 14 March 2000 near Tuticorin (now Thoothukudi), Tamil Nadu.

First president of the International Geological Congress

Dr D.N. Wadia (1883–1969), president of the 22nd International Geological Congress, which was held in New Delhi in 1964, was the first and only Indian to become president of the International Geological Congress.

WR Periodicity of geomagnetic reversals

J.G. Negi and R.R. Tewari from the National Geophysical Research Institute, Hyderabad (now in Telangana), put forward, in 1983, the theory that the flipping of the earth's magnetic field, i.e., the North Pole becoming the South Pole and vice versa, is related to variations in the gravitational force of the earth. They found that the frequency with which the earth's magnetic field flips is directly correlated to the periodicity of the orbit of the sun.

First geoscientific data centre

The Geological Survey of India (GSI) set up a geoscientific data centre at Calcutta (now Kolkata) on 3 November 1998. It is the largest repository of knowledge on earth sciences in Asia, Australia, and Africa.

Largest mineral explorer

The Mineral Exploration Corporation Ltd, established in October 1972, is a public sector company under the Ministry of Mines, Government of India with its corporate office at Nagpur, Maharashtra, and regional offices at Kolkata, Hyderabad, Ranchi, Jaipur, and Nagpur. Its functions include mineral targeting, deposit assessment, and mine development.

First official Indian geologist

Pramatha Nath Bose is considered to be the first official Indian geologist. He

GSI members in China in 1870

joined the Geological Survey of India (GSI) as an officer in 1880. He is known to have mapped the Vindhya Range as well as the igneous rocks of Raipur and Balaghat areas of what was then the Central Province.

Discovery of vanadium

Abani Kumar Dey and J.A. Dunn discovered a new vanadium-bearing mineral in the Singhbhum–Mayurbhanj area, which is in present-day Jharkhand and Odisha, in the 1930s and called this mineral coulsonite (composition FeV_2O_4), the main source of vanadium in India. It is of strategic importance for making special steels. Abani Dey was the recipient of the First National Mineral Award in 1968.

Discovery of iron ore deposits

Pramatha Nath Bose discovered the first iron ore deposit in Mayurbhanj region in present-day Odisha, in 1904, paving the way for the modern iron industry.

OCEAN STUDIES

First course in oceanography

The first postgraduate course in oceanography was introduced in 1948 at Andhra University in Visakhapatnam in Andhra Pradesh.

First marine research institute

On 3 February 1947 the Central Marine Fisheries Research Institute was established in Chennai. Since 1971, it is headquartered in Kochi, Kerala.

First oceanographic research vessel

RV *Gaveshani*, commissioned on 1 December 1975, was the first oceanographic research vessel. It carried teams of scientific personnel on various marine expeditions that could last from a few days to months.

First Antarctic expedition

Dr S.Z. Qasim, director, National Institute of Oceanography, Goa, reached Antarctica on 9 January 1982. The 21-member team left Mormugao Harbour, Goa, on 6 December 1981 on a Norwegian ship, MV *Polar Circle*, and returned on 21 February 1982. During the expedition, the team built Dakshin Gangotri, the first Indian scientific research base station in the Queen Maud Land area in Antarctica.

First women on Antarctica

Structural geologist Sudipta Sengupta and marine biologist and oceanographer Aditi Pant were the first Indian women to visit Antarctica, during the third Indian expedition to Antarctica from 3 December 1983 to 25 March 1984. The expeditions aimed to study atmospheric, biological, earth, chemical, and medical sciences in the region.

Highest wave

Scientists on board the ship RV *Gaveshani* of the National Institute of Oceanography recorded a wave 13 m (42 ft 7.8 in.) high in the Arabian Sea off the coast of Goa in June 1979.

Rama Brahma Sanyal

LIFE SCIENCES

BIOLOGY

Discovery of earliest multicellular organisms

In October 1998, Pradip K. Bose, a professor at Jadavpur University, Calcutta, found a site close to Churhat town in Sidhi District, Madhya Pradesh, where multicellular organisms with body fluid existed around 1.1 billion years ago. He discovered tracks on sandstone rock left by wormlike creatures about half a centimetre thick, while burrowing through the sea floor ages ago. This was the first evidence of macroscopic animals in India.

Oldest biological fossils

Fossils of 3-billion-year-old photosynthetic blue-green algae of the Archaean era (4 billion to 2.5 billion years ago) were discovered at Kashia in Orissa (now Odisha) in 1998 by scientists of the Birbal Sahni Institute of Palaeosciences in Lucknow, Uttar Pradesh. The latest find includes 1.6-billion-year-old red algae fossils in the Chitrakoot region of central India.

First zoologist

Rama Brahma Sanyal (1850–1908) joined the Calcutta Zoological Gardens in Calcutta in 1876. He wrote scientific papers on birds and sea snakes and books on zoology.

First methane plant

Biomethane was first put to use in India in 1857, when a methane plant was installed in a colony near Bombay.

First national gene bank

R.S. Paroda, director general of the Indian Council of Agricultural Research, Delhi, established the first National Gene Bank in Delhi in 1985.

First clone of hepatitis E virus

Dr S.K. Panda, professor of pathology, and his support team of scientists at the All India Institute of Medical Sciences (AIIMS), New Delhi, genetically engineered a clone of the hepatitis E virus in 1996.

Hepatitis E virus

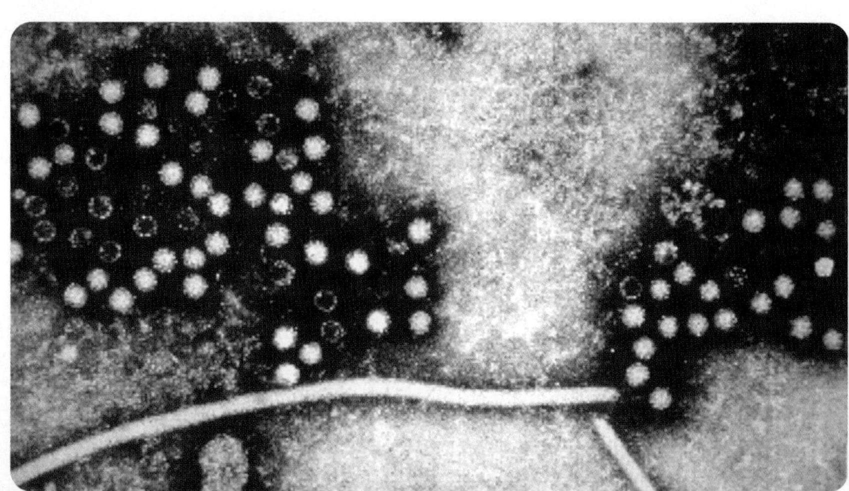

First anther culture

S.C. Maheswari and Sipra Mukherjee from Delhi discovered the anther culture technique in 1967, in which anthers (part of a stamen that contains pollen, in a plant) were placed on a synthetic culture medium.

First to extract insulin from a plant

In the early 1980s, Pushpa Khanna, professor at the University of Rajasthan, Jaipur, was the first to extract an insulin-like substance from bitter gourd. That substance is an active ingredient called polypeptide-P, which lowers blood sugar in the body. Insulin is currently extracted from animal pancreas for the treatment of diabetes.

Detailed macro photograph focusing on the stamen of a flower

First biocentre

The M.S. Swaminathan Foundation, Chennai, Tamil Nadu, opened a biocentre in Pillayarkuppam Village in Pondicherry (now Puducherry) on 10 April 1999. This centre functions as a demonstration, training, information dissemination, and service unit for sustainable food security.

First biologist to win the Linnean Medal

In 2018, Dr Kamaljit Bawa, president of the Ashoka Trust for Research in Ecology and the Environment (ATREE) and distinguished professor of biology at the University of Massachusetts, Boston, US, was awarded the Linnean Medal for his pioneering research in the field of conservation biology. He researched biodiversity, the evolution of tropical plants, deforestation, and non-timber forest products in Central America, the Western Ghats, and the Himalayas.

First synthesis of a workable gene
Indian-born US resident Dr Har Gobind Khorana (1922–2011), using off-the-shelf chemicals, synthesized a total gene of the simple microbe *Escherichia coli* (which lives in the intestines of humans and animals) in 1976. He was awarded the Nobel Prize for physiology or medicine in 1968 for discovering the genetic code, which opened up the possibility of producing DNA in a laboratory. He shared the prize with US scientists Robert W. Holley and Marshall W. Nirenberg.

First to isolate insulin-blocking enzyme
In 2013, Indian-born Kanwal Gambhir from Harvard University, US, and his co-workers isolated an insulin-blocking enzyme. As insulin controls sugar levels in blood, this discovery had far-reaching implications in the control of diabetes, cardiovascular diseases, and cancer.

Discovery of seminal plasmin
Pushpa M. Bhargava and E.S.R. Reddy from the Regional Research Laboratory, Hyderabad (now in Telangana), discovered the protein seminal plasmin in the seminal fluid of a bull in 1979. This is a potent antimicrobial agent active on a wide range of micro-organisms, such as yeast.

Discovery of the cholera exotoxin
S.C. Seal from the All India Institute of Hygiene and Public Health, Calcutta, discovered cholera exotoxin in the early 1940s. The vaccine based on this helped in the eradication of cholera epidemics in India.

Discovery of gymnosperms
In 1948, Birbal Sahni (1891–1949), a pioneering palaeontologist, discovered Pentoxyleae (gymnosperms), a plant group belonging to the Jurassic period (208 to 145 million years ago).

First human organ regeneration
In 2001, Dr Balakrishna Ganpatrao Matapurkar from Maulana Azad Medical College, New Delhi, was granted US Patent No. 6227202 (from 1995) for enabling regeneration of mammalian organs in the body at the site of old and diseased organs. He used unique stem cells in the body to regenerate organs like the uterus, urethra, and ureters in animals and large tendons in the human abdomen.

First bamboo tissue culture
A.F. Mascarenhas, R.S. Nadgauda, and V.A. Parasharami from the National Chemical Laboratory in Pune, Maharashtra, worked to produce a tissue culture of bamboo in 1990.

INTER-DISCIPLINARY AND APPLIED SCIENCES

COMPUTERS

First indigenous chip
The Graphics and Intelligence-based Script Technology (GIST), developed by the Centre for Development of Advanced Computing (C-DAC), hit the market in the 1990s. While it was designed especially for land records departments based in different climatic zones, where protection from dust and other vagaries is not always available, it was also used by industries and public information systems.

First analogue computer
The first electrical analogue computing machine was developed by the Indian Statistical Institude (ISI) in 1953-54 by a team led by Samarendra Kumar Mitra (14 March 1916–26 September 1998). This invention eventually led to the building of an Electronic Computer Division at the ISI.

First digital computer
The British-built HEC-2M was installed at the Indian Statistical Institute in Calcutta in 1955. In 1964, the first indigenous computer, ISIJU-1, was developed by the Jadavpur University and the Indian Statistical Institute.

Fastest supercomputer
AIRAWAT–PSAI is currently India's fastest supercomputer, with a peak power of 13,170 teraflops (13.17 petaflops). The system is installed under National Programme on AI by Government of India. It was manufactured by Natweb Technologies and is currently installed in C-DAC, Pune, Maharashtra. It is currently ranked 75th among the top 500

First human brain–like computing developed

A team of scientists led by Dheemahi Rao from the Jawaharlal Nehru Centre for Advanced Scientific Research (JNCASR), Bengaluru, have developed brain-like computing using industry-compatible nitride semi-conductors on 25 January 2023. For this, the scientists have used scandium nitrite, a semiconductor with great stability. The human brain is an extra-ordinary biological computer that is smaller than a traditional man-made computer and is more efficient because of a synapse (the connection between two neurons) that plays the role of both the processor and the memory storage units. Traditional computers take enormous energy and time to transfer data between these units because they are physically partitioned. The invention of brain-like computation will take artificial intelligence to new heights.

Buckyball at Pauling Building in JNCASR, Jakkur, Bangalore. This was designed by famous Indian architect Charles Correa.

supercomputers in the world (details on page 199). Earlier, in January 2018, India unveiled Pratyush and Mihir, an array of computers that are able to output a peak power of 6.8 petaflops. This was followed by PARAM Siddhi–AI, which was conceived by C–DAC, Pune, Maharashtra. Able to output a peak power of 6.5 petaflops, the supercomputer is used for research efforts in a wide range of areas, such as healthcare, agriculture, cybersecurity, and robotics. It was ranked 63rd among the top 500 most powerful supercomputers in the world in November 2020 (its current ranking is 131st).

First indigenous palmtop computer

In 1995, a team of engineers working for Signals and Systems India Private Ltd, headquartered in Gurugram, Haryana, built the country's first indigenous palmtop computer suitable for a variety of industrial and field applications.

Dr Raj Reddy is one of the pioneers of artificial intelligence

First powerful commercial computer

In 2001, Tata Consultancy Services (TCS) commissioned the 64-bit z-Series e-Server from IBM to become the first organization in South Asia to adopt the then latest technology being used in mainframe computing.

First powerful indigenous supercomputer

PARAM 10000, also developed by C-DAC under Dr Vijay P. Bhatkar's directorship, in 1998, was the first powerful indigenous supercomputer, capable of 100 billion calculations per second. It is housed at the National PARAM Supercomputing Facility (NPSF) at C-DAC, Pune.

First indigenous microprocessor for space applications

Vikram Sarabhai Space Centre of Indian Space Research Organisation (ISRO) released VIKRAM3201 & KALPANA3201, microprocessors meant for space applications, on 5 March 2025. The processor was fabricated at the 180 nm CMOS semiconductor fab of the Semiconductor Laboratory (SCL), Chandigarh. This 32-bit microprocessor is the first fully indigenous microprocessor that can be used in launch vehicles for space exploration.

Indian microprocessor

First Indian to obtain a PhD in computer science

Dr Raj Reddy (b. 13 June 1937), the dean of the School of Computer Science, Carnegie Mellon University, Pittsburgh, US, was the first Indian with a PhD in computer science, which he obtained in 1966 from Stanford University, US. He was also the first person of Asian origin to receive the Association for Computing Machinery (ACM) Turing Award, in 1994, then the highest award in computer science, for his work in the field of artificial intelligence.

First indigenous supercomputer

Developed by C-DAC in Pune, in 1991, PARAM 8000 was capable of one billion calculations per second. The then director of C-DAC, Dr Vijay P. Bhatkar, under whom this project was conducted, is considered to be the architect of India's national initiative in supercomputing.

First supercomputer

On 25 March 1989, the Supercomputer Cray XMP-14 was installed as a key facility at the National Centre for Medium Range Weather Forecasting, New Delhi, to facilitate medium-range weather forecasting and agrometeorology programmes.

First to invent a new and speedy algorithm

In 1984, Indian-born mathematician Dr Narendra Karmarkar from Bell Laboratories in New Jersey, USA, introduced a new algorithm, called 'Karmarkar's algorithm', which solved linear programming efficiently, and helped computers find solutions to simultaneous inequalities very quickly. It solved problems 50 to 100 times faster than the methods known at the time.

First smallest multimedia notebook

In 1997, Bangalore–Ncore Technology's multimedia sub-notebook computer called the Yantra, which weighed just 2.1 kg, was the lightest laptop in the world. The Yantra occupied less than half of a briefcase, had a CD-ROM, a built-in sound blaster, two PCMCIA (Personal Computer Memory Card International Association) card slots, and a small yet powerful battery built to last for more than three years.

First Super Fab Lab

The first super fab lab (fabrication laboratory) of the country was inaugurated via remote control from the Government Polytechnic College, Palakkad, Kerala, on 25 January 2020. Located at the Integrated Startup Complex of the Kerala Start-up Mission (KSUM), Kalamassery, Kochi, the lab offers digital fabrication and computation and was launched in collaboration with MIT (Massachusetts Institute of Technology, US). The brainchild of Dr Neil Gershenfeld, director of the MIT Centre for Bits and Atoms, it aims to enable researchers, innovators, and developers to do things beyond the purview of the existing fab labs of the country.

METALLURGY

Earliest zinc use

An artefact (No. 4189) containing 6.04 per cent zinc was found at the Harappan site of Lothal (dated to 2200–1500 BCE in Gujarat. It indicated that the Harappan people could generate temperatures of above 1,000°C required for zinc metallurgy.

Earliest copper kiln

A copper smelting kiln, 35 cm (13.8 in.) high with an 18 cm (7 in.) rim diameter and 10 cm (3.9 in.) base diameter, was discovered at the Harappan site of Lothal (2200–1500 BCE) in Gujarat. Lothal copper was found to be very pure.

Earliest use of iron

Around 1000 BCE, iron was used in eastern Punjab, western Uttar Pradesh, and Rajasthan. Excavations show that iron weapons such as arrowheads and spearheads were commonly used in western Uttar Pradesh from about 800 BCE. Iron is called *shyama* or *krishna ayas* (black/dark metal) in later Vedic texts.

Earliest iron furnace

An iron furnace was found at Pandu Rajar Dhibi in Burdwan (now Bardhaman District), West Bengal, and was dated to 1100–800 BCE.

First metallurgist to work with plutonium

Dr P.R. Roy, a scientist and director at the Bhabha Atomic Research Centre (BARC), Bombay, was the first Indian metallurgist to handle plutonium. He played a crucial role in India's first nuclear implosion at Pokhran, Rajasthan, in 1974.

First manufacture of steel

Indian smiths manufactured crucible steel, known as *wootz*, which was exported to many countries in medieval times. Indian craftsmen were known around the world at the time for their steel swords. After the British banned the production of weapons following the Indian Rebellion of 1857 wootz technology was lost.

New class of quasicrystals

In 1985, P. Ramachandra Rao and G.V.S. Sastry from the National Metallurgical Laboratory, Jamshedpur, now in Jharkhand, discovered a new class of quasicrystals composed of aluminium, manganese, and zinc metals.

SPACE

First space venture

Launched from the base in Thumba near Trivandrum (now Thiruvananthapuram), Kerala, on 21 November 1963, a Nike-Apache rocket supplied by NASA kick-started the Indian space programme. Parts of this first sounding rocket launched by India were transported to the Thumba base on the carrier of a bicycle! St Mary Magdalene Church in Thumba is a preferred site for rocket launches because of its proximity to the magnetic equator. Quite fittingly, the church houses the Vikram Sarabhai Space Centre (VSSC) space museum.

First satellite centre

ISRO's Satellite Centre (ISAC), established in 1972, conducts research in satellite technology. Aryabhata, the first Indian satellite, Bhaskara I and II, and Rohini and APPLE satellites were all designed and built at ISAC. The spacecraft of the Indian Remote Sensing satellite series and the Stretched Rohini satellite series were also designed at ISAC.

First Indian space organization

Indian National Committee for Space Research (INCOSPAR) was India's first space research organization. It was formed in 1962 and helmed by Dr Vikram Sarabhai. When Indian Space Research Organization was formed in 1969, it superseded INCOSPAR.

First weather-cum-communications satellite

Indian National Satellite INSAT-1A, launched on 10 April 1982 on an American Delta-3920 launch vehicle, was India's first satellite employed for meteorological observations over India and the Indian Ocean, as well as for domestic telecommunications, including nationwide direct TV broadcasting, TV programme distribution, and meteorological data distribution.

First remote-sensing mission

IRS-1A, the first of a series of indigenous state-of-the-art remote-sensing satellites, was launched into a polar sun-synchronous orbit on 17 March 1988 from the then Soviet Cosmodrome at Baikonur. It carried two cameras, LISS-I and LISS-II, with a swathe width of 140 km during each pass over India.

First indigenous satellite series

Designed and built by ISRO, INSAT-2A was launched by the Ariane launch vehicle from Kourou, French Guiana, on 10 July 1992. INSAT-2B was also launched by Ariane on 23 July 1993. INSAT-2C, the third in this series of satellites, was launched on 7 December 1995 and put into operation in February 1996.

ISRO headquarters, Bengaluru

Highest-resolution imaging satellite

CARTOSAT-3, considered to be India's highest-resolution civilian satellite to date, was successfully launched into space along with 13 US nanosatellites by ISRO on 27 November 2019. Weighing 1,625 kg, the observation satellite lifted off from the Satish Dhawan Space Centre, Sriharikota High Altitude Range (SHAR), Sriharikota, Andhra Pradesh. It is an advanced imaging and mapping satellite with a mission life of five years and a panchromatic resolution of 0.25 m (9.8 in.).

First oceanographic satellite

IRS-P4 (OceanSat), the first satellite built for ocean applications, was launched into a polar sun-synchronous orbit, 720 km high, by the PSLV from SHAR, Sriharikota, Andhra Pradesh, on 26 May 1999. A 1,050 kg satellite measuring 2.8 m x 1.98 m x 2.57 m (9 ft 2 in. x 6 ft 6 in. x 8 ft 5 in.), the IRS-P4 orbited Earth in 99.31 mins. It completed its mission on 8 August 2010. former Indian president A.P.J. Abdul Kalam as its first chancellor. The university offers undergraduate, postgraduate, and doctorate programmes in engineering, focusing on space science, technology, and their applications.

First man in space

Squadron Leader Rakesh Sharma (b. 13 January 1949), then an Indian Air Force pilot, flew aboard spacecraft Soyuz T-11, launched on 2 April 1984, as part of the Intercosmos programme and spent over seven days orbiting Earth. He was the first Indian person to travel to space.

First privately developed launch vehicle

Skyroot Aerospace is credited with India's first privately developed rocket, Vikram-S, was launched into space on 18 November 2022.

First interplanetary mission

On 5 November 2013, PSLV-C25, the 25th flight of PSLV launched Mangalyaan, the Mars Orbiter Mission (MOM) spacecraft, from SHAR, Sriharikota, Andhra Pradesh. Under the aegis of ISRO, the mission was conducted to observe the physical features of Mars and the Martian atmosphere. With this mission, ISRO became the fourth space agency in the world to reach Mars. India is the first Asian nation to reach the Mars orbit and the first nation in the world to do so in its first attempt.

Statue of Rakesh Sharma in Bengaluru

India's first private rocket builder

Skyroot Aerospace, India's first private rocket builder, started operations in 2018. It is founded by a group of people that includes former ISRO scientists.

First dedicated commercial satellite mission

India's Polar Satellite Launch Vehicle PSLV-C51 successfully launched the satellite Amazonia-1, developed by Brazil, along with 18 co-passenger private satellites, from SHAR, Sriharikota, Andhra Pradesh, on 28 February 2021. The first dedicated commercial mission of NewSpace India Ltd (NSIL), under the Department of Space, Government of India, it was part of space reforms aimed at increasing the participation of private companies in the space sector. The co-passenger satellites included four from Indian National Space Promotion and Authorization Centre (IN-SPACe) and 14 from NSIL.

First ESCES

India's first Experimental Satellite Communication Earth Station (ESCES) was operationalized in 1967 in Ahmedabad. This also worked as a training centre for the Indian and international scientists and engineers.

First woman in space

Dr Kalpana Chawla (1962–2003), an American cosmonaut who was born in Karnal, Haryana, was the first woman of Indian origin in space. She zoomed into orbit aboard space shuttle Columbia on 19 November 1997 on a 16-day scientific mission, along with five fellow astronauts, and returned to Cape Canaveral on 5 December 1997. In 2003, Chawla was one of the seven crew members who died in the space shuttle Columbia disaster when it disintegrated during its re-entry into Earth's atmosphere.

First private satellite launched

Exseed SAT-1, built by Exseed Space Innovations Private Ltd, founded by scientists Kris Nair and Asshar Farhan, became the first private Indian satellite to be launched in space. The amateur (ham) radio satellite hitched a ride on the Elon Musk–led company SpaceX's Falcon 9 rocket on 4 December 2018.

WR Smallest spacecraft launched

On 23 June 2017, the world's smallest spacecraft, Sprites, was launched by ISRO's PSLV rocket and placed in the low earth orbit. The 3.5 cm x 3.5 cm (1.38 in. x 1.38 in.) space probe weighs just 4 g and runs on sunlight.

WR Lightest satellite in orbit

Kalamsat-V2 was launched by ISRO on 24 January 2019 from the Satish Dhawan Space Centre, SHAR, Sriharikota. Weighing only 1.26 kg, it is said to be the world's lightest satellite to be put into orbit. It was made by students belonging to Space Kidz India, a Chennai-based aerospace start-up pioneering in design, fabrication, and launch of small satellites, spacecraft, and ground systems. The satellite will also serve as a communications device for ham radio transmission, which is a form of wireless communication used by amateurs for non-commercial activities. It took six days to make and cost around ₹12 lakh (1.2 million).

India's first solar mission

ADITYA-L1 is India's first satellite dedicated to studying the outer atmosphere of the sun. It has been indigenously developed by ISRO and launched on 2 September 2023.

Heaviest satellite launched

GSAT-11, weighing 5,854 kg and laying claim to being the heaviest Indian satellite ever launched, was sent into space by ISRO on 5 December 2018 from the Ariane Launch Complex at Kourou in French Guiana. The satellite is expected to help boost communication services across India.

First lunar probe

India's first lunar probe, Chandrayaan-1was launched by ISRO, using a PSLV-XL rocket, on 22 October 2008 from Satish Dhawan Space Centre (SDSC), SHAR, Sriharikota, Andhra Pradesh. It operated until August 2009.

XPoSat being tested on Earth

First polarimetry mission

XPoSat, X-ray Polarimeter Satellite, is the first dedicated scientific satellite launched by ISRO with the purpose of research in space-based polarisation measurements of X-ray emission from celestial sources. It was launched on 1 January 2024.

First space technology gallery

India's first space technology gallery came up in 28 November 2017 at the Visvesvaraya Industrial and Technological Museum, Bengaluru. It has been set up in an area of 7534.74 sq ft (700 sq m) on the second floor of the museum.

Heaviest communication satellite

ISRO launched the heaviest communication satellite of India, CMS-03 (also known as GSAT-7R), on 2 November 2025 from the Satish Dhawan Space Centre in Sriharikota, Andhra Pradesh. This is indigenously developed and weighs 4,400 kg. ISRO's most powerful launch vehicle, LVM3, was used to achieve this feat. This satellite would help Indian Navy secure communication links between ships, aircraft, and submarines.

LVM3 M5 during the launch of CMS-03/GSAT-7R Mission for Indian Navy

MEDICAL SCIENCES

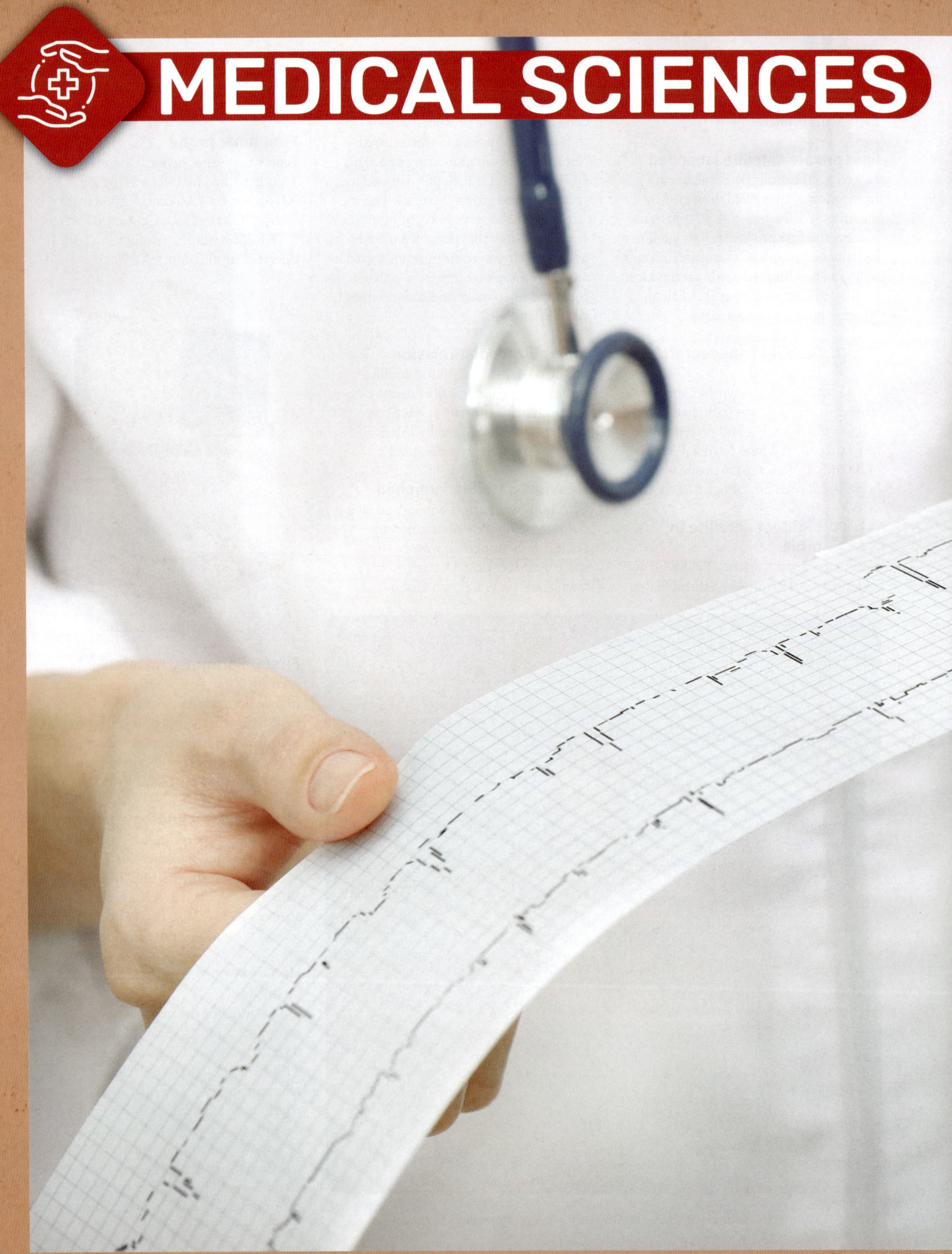

GENERAL

Earliest treatise on medicine

The Atharva Veda (1500–1200 BCE) is the earliest known treatise on human diseases and medicine.

First text on Unani medicine

Persian translation of *Kitab-ul Saidana* (Materia Medica and Pharmacology) of Al-Beruni is the first traceable medical book on Unani medicine written in India. It was translated by Abu Bakrbin Alibin Uthman, who lived at the court of Iltutmish.

A 1973 Soviet stamp featuring Al-Beruni

WR Largest healthcare scheme

Ayushman Bharat Yojana, announced as a universal healthcare plan by the Government of India in February 2018, is the largest healthcare scheme in the world. Aimed at providing free healthcare access to around 50 crore (0.5 billion) people in the country, the Ayushman Bharat Pradhan Mantri Jan Arogya Yojana (AB-PMJAY) was launched in September 2018. A paperless and cashless scheme, it involves e-cards being issued to beneficiaries and health insurance coverage of up to ₹5,00,000 per family per year.

Pradhan Mantri Jan Arogya Yojana

Largest survey sample

India's Annual Health Survey (AHS) is the first nationwide survey initiative to provide district-level fertility and mortality statistics. Begun with a baseline study in 2010–11 and a sample of 18.2 million people (3.6 million households), it is conducted in all 284 districts in eight Empowered Action Group (EAG) states, viz., Madhya Pradesh, Jharkhand, Bihar, Uttar Pradesh, Chhattisgarh, Uttarakhand, Odisha, and Rajasthan. It reports vital indicators such as crude birth and death rates, sex ratios (at birth, 0–4 years, and all ages) and mortality rates (maternal, infant, neonatal, and under-5), separated by urban/rural and male/female data.

Only state to legislate right to health

Rajasthan is the only state where all residents have the right to health. Everybody in the state can have free-of-cost emergency treatment at both government and private hospitals. The bill was passed in March 2023.

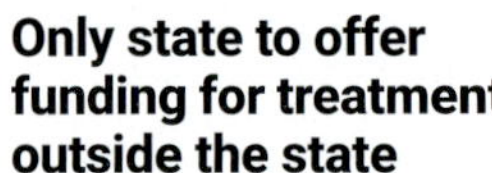

Only state to offer funding for treatment outside the state

Sikkim is the only Indian state where residents get government aid in getting treatment outside the state under the Chief Minister's Medical Assistance Scheme Rules, 2022.

WR First and only global outpost for traditional medicine

In 2022, WHO along with the support of the Indian government established the Global Centre for Traditional Medicine (GCTM) in Gandhinagar, Gujarat, which is the first and the only global outpost for traditional medicine in the world. It is a collaborative project involving the Ministry of Ayush and WHO. It was established to provide leadership on matters related to traditional medicine as well as support to member countries in shaping various policies pertaining to public health and traditional medical research and practices. It had its first summit in August 2023.

FERTILITY, CHILDBIRTH, AND BABIES

WR Oldest IVF mother

On 12 October 2019, 75-year-old Prabha Devi became the oldest woman to give birth, after conceiving through IVF. She delivered a baby girl, weighing 680 g, prematurely by Caesarean section performed at Kinker Hospital, Kota, Rajasthan.

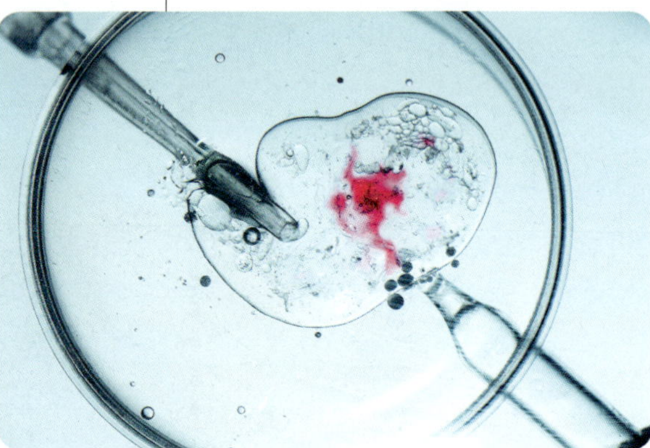

Microscopic view of IVF procedure

First IVF baby

Baby Harsha was born to Mani and Shyami Chawda on 6 August 1986 by the in vitro fertilization and embryo transfer (IVF-ET) method. This technique was used after three years of research by Dr Indira Hinduja of King Edward Memorial Hospital and Seth Gordhandas Sunderdas Medical College, Bombay, Maharashtra.

First woman to give birth after a uterine transplant

Meenakshi Valand from Bharuch District, Gujarat, became the first Indian woman to deliver a baby after undergoing a uterine transplant on 19 October 2018 at Galaxy Care Hospital, Pune, Maharashtra.

First GIFT twins

The first twins, both male, were born through the gamete intra-fallopian transfer (GIFT) technology to Renuka and Vijay Thakkar on 5 September 1990 in Bombay (now Mumbai), Maharashtra.

Heaviest baby at birth

On 26 May 2016, Nandini, a 20-year-old mother, gave birth to a baby girl by Caesarean section at a hospital in Hassan, Karnataka. The baby, whose birthweight was 6.8 kg, was reported to have been the heaviest one ever born in the country. The heaviest baby boy till then, who weighed 6.7 kg at birth, was recorded to have been born in November 2015.

Lightest baby

A premature baby girl, weighing 400 g and measuring 8.6 in. in length, was born by Caesarean section on 15 June 2017 at Jivanta Children's Hospital in Udaipur, Rajasthan. She was kept in the neonatal intensive care unit (NICU) at the hospital for 210 days under the care of Dr Sunil Janged, Dr Nikhilesh Nain, and trained nursing staff, and was discharged when she weighed close to 2.4 kg.

MEDICAL INSTITUTIONS AND LABORATORIES

Oldest eye hospital

The Madras Eye Infirmary (MEI) in Madras was set up in 1819. It is said to be the oldest eye hospital in India and Asia, and second oldest in the world. It was renamed the Government Ophthalmic Hospital in 1886 and is now officially called the Regional Institute of Ophthalmology and Government Ophthalmic Hospital (Egmore Eye Hospital, Egmore, Chennai, Tamil Nadu).

WR First governmental family planning programme

India was the first country in the world to have government-sponsored family planning programmes in 1952. The first private family planning clinic was opened even earlier in Mysore (now Mysuru), Karnataka, in 1930.

First hospital

The first modern hospital was established at Fort St George, Madras (now Chennai), Tamil Nadu, in 1664. Today, it exists as Rajiv Gandhi Government General Hospital.

First medical school to offer oncology degrees

The Adyar Cancer Institute in Chennai, Tamil Nadu, is a non-profit cancer treatment and research centre set up in 1954 under the leadership of Dr Muthulakshmi Reddy. It was the first medical school in India to offer degrees in various sub-specialities of oncology, recognized by the Medical Council of India.

First homoeopathic college

Dr L. Salzar from Austria began homoeopathic education in India in 1867. He influenced Dr P.C. Majumdar and Dr B.L. Bhaduri in Bengal, and in 1878, Dr Majumdar along with Dr D.N. Roy, Dr B.N. Banerjee, and Dr Younan set up the Calcutta Homoeopathic Medical College, Calcutta (now Kolkata), West Bengal, which was India's first homoeopathic college.

First homoeopathic company

M. Bhattacharya and Company Pvt. Ltd in Calcutta was established in 1889 by Mahesh Chandra Bhattacharya from Comilla (now in Bangladesh), for making homoeopathic medicines.

Dr Muthulakshmi Reddy

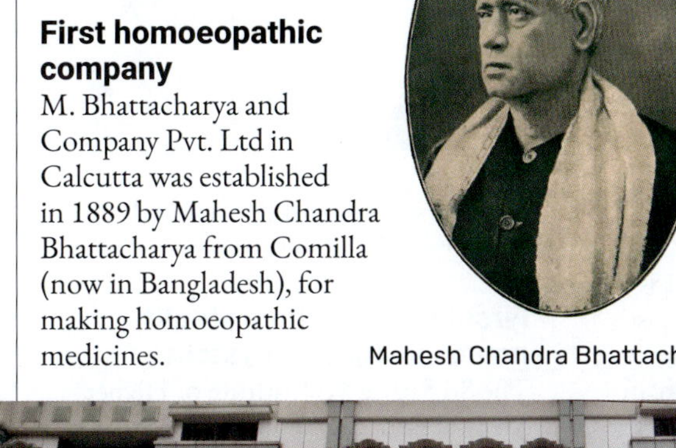
Mahesh Chandra Bhattacharya

First college of nursing

Christian Medical College and Hospital (CMCH), Vellore, Tamil Nadu, set up the first college of nursing in India in 1946.

First organized medical service

The Indian Medical Service was the formal collective name for the top echelon of the East India Company's and British Indian Army's medical service from the early 19th century up to 1896. Its three divisions – Bengal Medical Service, Madras Medical Service, and Bombay Medical Service – were combined into a single service under government control in January 1897.

First biotechnology department

Dr Indira Nath set up the first department of medical biotechnology at the All India Institute of Medical Sciences (AIIMS), New Delhi, for teaching and research in 1986.

First medical laser facility

India's first medical laser to destroy tumours with minimal blood loss was set up at the K.B. Bhabha Hospital in Bombay in October 1993.

Rajiv Gandhi Government General Hospital

First dental college

Dr Rafiuddin Ahmed, the 'father of modern dentistry' in India, founded the Calcutta Dental College in Calcutta, in 1920. By 1928, it was a well-known institution for scientific dental education in India.

Left: Dr Rafiuddin Ahmed; *right*: Dr Mukesh Batra

First medical college

Calcutta Medical College (now renamed Medical College and Hospital, Kolkata) set up on 28 January 1835 in Calcutta, was the first medical college to be established in India and Asia.

Calcutta Medical College

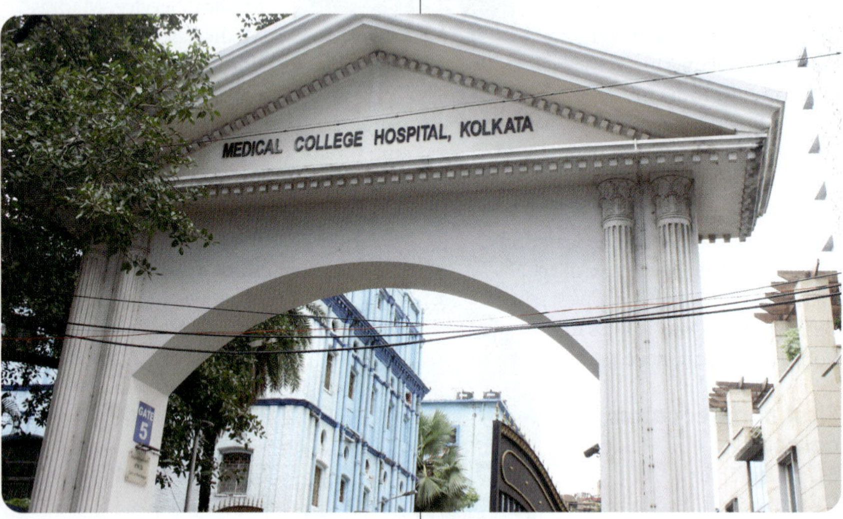

First online clinic

Homoeopath Dr Mukesh Batra set up Dr Batra's Positive Health Clinic in Bombay in 1982, which now has 230 clinics across 122 cities in India, Bangladesh, Dubai, and the UK. He went online in 1997, which made him the first online medical consultant in the country.

First hospital with a stealth neuro-navigation system

The Sri Sathya Sai Institute of Higher Medical Sciences, Whitefield, Bangalore (now Bengaluru), Karnataka, set up in 2001, is the first in India and second in the world to acquire a stealth neuro-navigation system (for image-guided surgeries). It is one of the cutting-edge technologies in precision neurosurgery.

First low-vision rehabilitation centre

L.V. Prasad Eye Institute, Hyderabad (now in Telangana), opened the Meera and L.B. Deshpande Centre for Sight Enhancement on 18 February 1997, to provide complete low-vision rehabilitation for patients by restoring optimal physical, psychological, and social functioning.

First hormone replacement therapy clinic

A hormone replacement therapy (HRT) clinic was started by Urvashi P. Jha in March 1993 at the P.D. Hinduja National Hospital in Mumbai, Maharashtra, to deal with aspects of menopause.

P.D. Hinduja National Hospital, Mumbai

First centre for cancer rehabilitation

Dr Darab Jehangir Jussawala (1915–99) was a medical and surgical oncologist, medical writer, and director of the Lady Ratan Tata Memorial Centre in Bombay (now Mumbai), Maharashtra. Dr Jussawala was the co-founder of the Indian Cancer Society with Naval Tata in 1951 and established the Indian Cancer Rehabilitation Centre in Parel, Bombay, Maharashtra, in 1956, which was the first such centre in India. He received the Padma Bhushan in 1975 from the Government of India.

भारत INDIA
200
टाटा स्मारक केन्द्र TATA MEMORIAL CENTRE
1991

Postal stamp on Tata Memorial Centre

First institute of advanced virology

The first Institute of Advanced Virology was inaugurated in February 2019 at Thiruvananthapuram, Kerala. It is affiliated to the Global Virus Network, which has 45 centres of excellence in more than 29 countries.

First corporate hospital

Apollo Hospitals, founded by Dr Prathap C. Reddy in Madras, Tamil Nadu, in 1983, was the first corporate hospital in the country.

Vaccine manufacturing facility, Serum Institute of India, Pune, Maharashtra; (*inset*) Serum Institute of India logo

WR Largest vaccine company

The Serum Institute of India in Pune, Maharashtra, founded by Cyrus Poonawalla in 1966, is the world's largest vaccine-making company by the number of doses produced and sold globally, with 1.2 billion vaccine doses supplied yearly to 147 countries.

First indigenously developed vaccine

Rotavac, a rotavirus vaccine, was India's first indigenously developed vaccine, launched in 2015. It was developed by Bharat Biotech India Limited and the Gates Foundation, and supported by the Government of India and National Institute of Health of the US Government. Rotavirus is the most common cause of serious (often fatal) diarrhoea in children.

Rotavac

First liver clinic

The first liver clinic was opened at Sir Ganga Ram Hospital, New Delhi, in 2002 for treating patients with liver diseases.

Indian postal stamp commemorating Sir Ganga Ram and Ganga Ram Hospital

First department of minimal access surgery

Dr Pradeep Kumar Chowbey from Sir Ganga Ram Hospital, New Delhi, set up the first dedicated department of minimal access surgery (MAS) in Asia in 1995 and has trained nearly 1,000 doctors in laparoscopy in India and abroad.

First rural medical college

Kasturba Health Society's Mahatma Gandhi Institute of Medical Sciences (MGIMS) in Sevagram, Wardha district, Maharashtra, was the country's first rural medical college. It was founded by Dr Sushila Nayar, a physician and politician, in 1969, and was affiliated to the Maharashtra University of Health Sciences.

First endoscopy lab

The first fully equipped endoscopy centre was established at the Bhatia General Hospital in Mumbai, in October 1994. An endoscopy is performed to examine the interior of a hollow organ.

AIIMS: A hub of medical firsts

The All India Institute of Medical Sciences (AIIMS) is a public hospital and medical Endoscopy equipment research university based in New Delhi. Established in 1956, it operates autonomously under the Ministry of Health and Family Welfare. It was:

- The first to start a medical toxicology lab in a medical college in 1986,
- The first to develop a DNA profiling lab in a medical college in 1990,
- The first Indian centre to perform a successful cardiac transplant in 1994,
- India's first minimally invasive surgery training centre,
- The first in the public sector to have an in vitro fertilization (IVF) facility, in February 2008.

First hospital with a rooftop helipad

The eleven-storey Lakeshore Hospital and Research Centre, Kochi, Kerala, is the first super-speciality hospital in the country to have air, water, and road ambulance services at its doorstep. Inaugurated in January 2003, this hospital with its state-of-the-art medical services, has a helipad on its roof to facilitate heli-lifting of critically ill patients from airports in Kerala.

Top left: All India Institute of Medical Sciences (AIIMS), New Delhi; *left*: Lakeshore Hospital and Research Centre, Kochi, Kerala

Banking on Life: Medical Banks

First stem cell bank
Reliance Life Sciences, through its Relicord service, established South Asia's first cord blood repository, which began stem cell banking in 2002. This facility is located at the Dhirubhai Ambani Life Sciences Centre in Navi Mumbai.

First blood bank
Upendranath Brahmachari (1873–1946) set up a blood bank in Calcutta, (now Kolkata), West Bengal, in September 1939.

First sperm bank
Dr Aniruddha Malpani and Dr Anjali Malpani from Bombay (now Mumbai), Maharashtra, opened a sperm bank in 1990 to help infertile patients. It also had facilities for storing sperm of people who may be critically ill, for implantation at a later date.

First breast milk bank

Dr Armida Fernandez pioneered the establishment of Asia's first human milk bank at the Lokmanya Tilak Municipal General Hospital in Bombay, in November 1989.

First eye bank

Dr R.E.S. Muthayya established the first eye bank in 1945 in the Regional Institute of Ophthalmology and Government Ophthalmic Hospital in Chennai. He also performed the first corneal transplant in India in 1948.

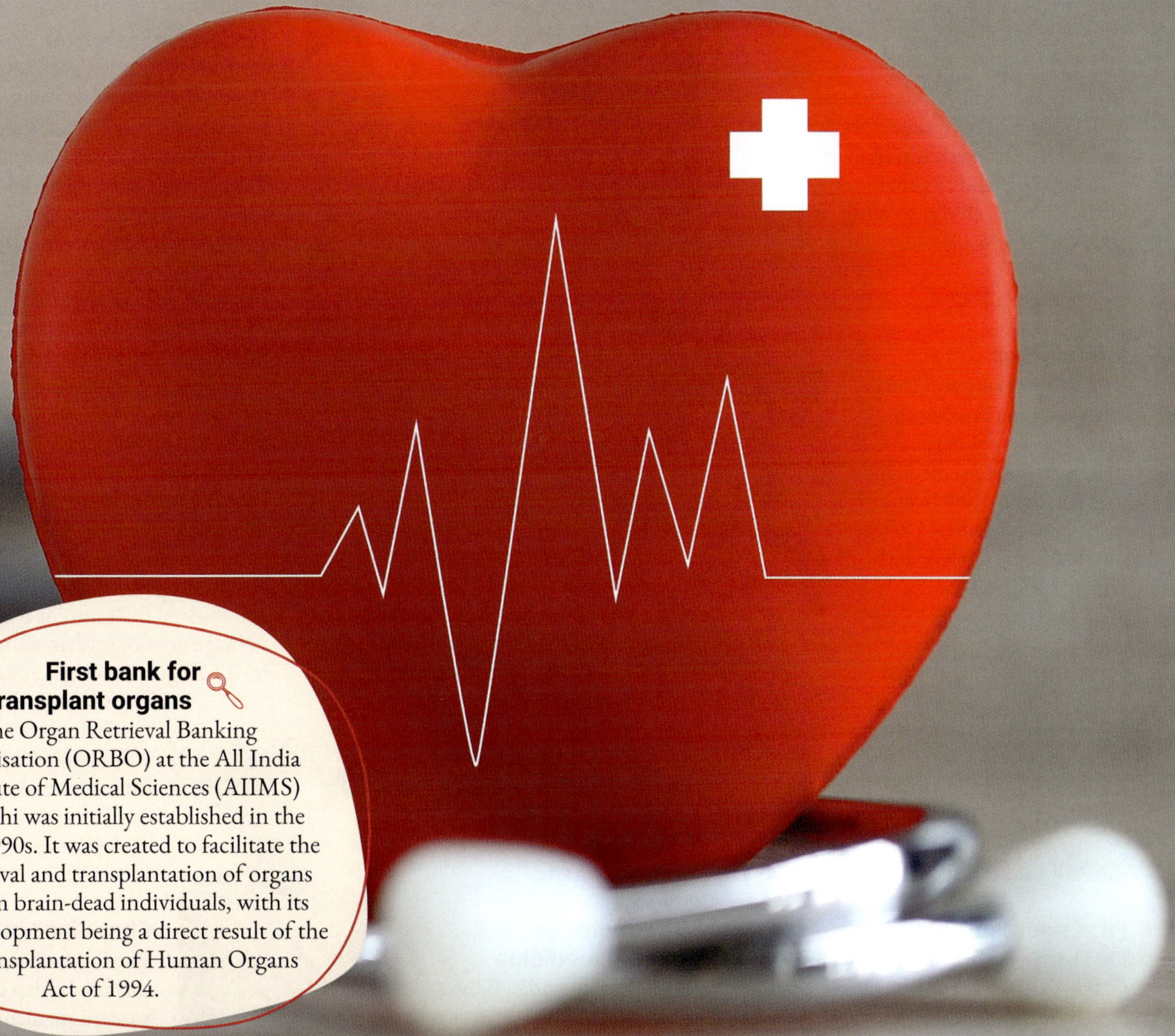

First bank for transplant organs

The Organ Retrieval Banking Organisation (ORBO) at the All India Institute of Medical Sciences (AIIMS) in Delhi was initially established in the mid-1990s. It was created to facilitate the retrieval and transplantation of organs from brain-dead individuals, with its development being a direct result of the Transplantation of Human Organs Act of 1994.

PUBLICATIONS AND INNOVATION

First to win a Pulitzer Prize for a health/medicine-related publication

Indian-origin American oncologist Siddhartha Mukherjee won the Pulitzer for General Non-Fiction in 2011 for *The Emperor of All Maladies: A Biography of Cancer*, published in 2010 by Scribner, New York, US. The book was acclaimed as one of the 100 most influential books of the last 100 years by *Time* magazine and one of the 100 best works of non-fiction by the *New York Times Magazine*.

Smallest medical robot

The smallest medical robot measuring 120 nm (one nanometre is one-billionth of a metre) was created by Soutik Betal, a doctoral research student from India, at the University of Texas, San Antonio, Texas, US, on 10 November 2016. Capable of being remotely controlled electromagnetically and of interacting with biological cells, these robots may be used to advance research in cell-based therapy and to provide direct medication to cells for treating cancers and Alzheimer's disease.

DOCTORS

First doctor

Kadambini Ganguly (1861–1923) was the first South Asian female physician trained in Western medicine to graduate in 1888 from the Calcutta Medical College (now Medical College and Hospital, Kolkata, West Bengal).

Kadambini Ganguly

First surgeon general

Mary Poonen Lukose (1886–1976) from Kerala graduated from the University of Madras (now in Chennai), Tamil Nadu, in 1909, and studied medicine in the UK. She became the first woman surgeon general of India in 1938 and was awarded the Padma Shri in 1975.

First neurosurgeon

Dr Thanjavur Santhanakrishna Kanaka (1932–2018) was the first female neurosurgeon in Asia. She was also the first neurosurgeon in India to perform chronic electrode implants in the brain, having performed deep-brain stimulation as early as 1975.

First anaesthetist

Dr Rupa Bai Furdoonji was one of five female students to join the Hyderabad Medical School in 1885. She received her diploma in 1891. As a medical student, she achieved great proficiency in delivering chloroform anaesthesia. She went to Edinburgh in 1909 to gain greater knowledge in the field of anaesthesia. She is probably the first lady anaesthetist in the world who took on anaesthesiology as a full-time career.

Dr Rupa Bai Furdoonji with surgeon Major Edward Lawrie (*sitting on her right*) and Sir Thomas Lauder Brunton, F.R.S. (*sitting on her left*)

First aerospace doctor

Dr Parvathi Gopal from Bengaluru, Karnataka, joined the Institute of Aerospace Medicine in the Department of High Altitude Physiology in 1992. Her field of work included research and treatment to determine whether a fighter pilot is medically and mentally fit to fly.

First doctor of western medicine

Pandit Madhusudan Gupta was the first Indian doctor to study western medicine in India. Initially an Ayurvedic practitioner based in Calcutta in the nineteenth century, he was trained in western medicine in 1835–36.

Pandit Madhusudan Gupta

First nurse 

Bai Kashibai Ganpat of Thane, Maharashtra, was the first Indian woman to undertake training to become a nurse at a hospital of Jamsetjee Jeejeebhoy Group in Bombay (now Mumbai), Maharashtra, in 1891.

Most innovations by a medical professional

Dr Pankaj Garg (b. 27 December 1972), a colorectal surgeon from Panchkula, Haryana, has 16 innovations in the medical field to his name. Consisting of seven surgery procedures and nine treatment concepts, these have been published in national and international surgical journals from April 2015 to May 2019.

First neurosurgeon

Dr Jacob Chandy (1910–2007) started the department of neurology and neurosurgery in 1949 at Christian Medical College and Hospital, Vellore, Tamil Nadu. He initiated the first training programmes in neurosurgery in 1958 and in neurology in 1962.

First psychosurgeon

M.S. Govindaswamy (1904–62) was the first psychiatrist to start psychosurgery in India. He combined psychological, medical, psychiatric and nursing aspects for holistic treatment.

First doctor-to-doctor online session

A doctor-centric portal with the URL www.ranbaxyfordoctors.com hosted a discussion on 'Current trends in the management of cardiac arrhythmia' on 28 August 2000, where 69 doctors chatted online. It was moderated by Prof. (Dr) K.K. Sethi, director, interventional cardiology and cardiac arrhythmia services, Sir Ganga Ram Hospital in New Delhi.

First dissection 

Pandit Madhusudan Gupta, the first Indian doctor of western medicine, was also the first to perform human dissection in Asia in 1836.

Postgraduate Institute of Medical Education and Research (PGIMER), Chandigarh

First government-run department for disorders of sex development

The Postgraduate Institute of Medical Education and Research (PGIMER), Chandigarh, in July 2019, established the country's first government-run facility for children with disorders of sex development (DSD). The facility provides diagnosis of genetic and hormonal issues, surgical correction and psychological support for such children. Around 200 children per year can be treated here.

First cardiologist

Dr S. Srinivas from Bihar was the first cardiologist of India, who started his medical practice in 1950. He was trained by Dr Paul Dudley White and was also the first to bring ECG machine in India.

Discovery of a 'feeding' centre in the hypothalamus

Prof. Bal Krishan Anand (1917–2007) was a famous physiologist and pharmacologist, born in Lahore (now in Pakistan). He was credited with the discovery of the 'feeding' centre in the hypothalamus in 1951 and regarded as the founder of modern neurophysiology in India.

MEDICINE AND SURGERY

Christian Medical College and Hospital's many firsts

Christian Medical College and Hospital (CMCH), Vellore, Tamil Nadu, is a private educational and research institute, which includes a network of primary, secondary, and tertiary care hospitals. Founded in 1900 by an American missionary, Dr Ida S. Scudder, CMCH has many firsts to its credit:

- First reconstructive surgery for leprosy in the world (1948),
- First department of neurological sciences (1948),
- First successful open-heart surgery in India (1961),
- First kidney transplant in India (1971),
- First virology department (1978),
- First bone marrow transplant (1986),
- First successful ABO incompatible (organ donated by a donor of a different blood type) kidney transplant (2009).

Father of plastic surgery

Sushruta is considered the 'father of plastic surgery'. He is believed to have lived around the sixth century BCE and pioneered the advancement of medicine in ancient India. His teachings of anatomy, pathophysiology, and therapeutic strategies, featured in his *Sushruta Samhita*, were far ahead of his time.

First medical symposium

The Vedic sage Bharadwaja, who is believed to have founded the Indian Ayurvedic system of medicine, presided over the first-ever symposium on medicinal plants in the seventh century BCE, possibly in the Himalayan region.

First international homoeopathic congress

The first International Homoeopathic Congress in India was held in 1967. It was organized and presided over by the renowned homoeopathic doctor Diwan Harish Chand. All the earlier ones, commencing from 1876, had been held in Europe and North America.

First separation of conjoined twins

Dr J. Dalal, paediatrics and neonatology specialist, surgically separated a set of conjoined twins (also known as Siamese twins) born to one Mrs Kambli on 11 August 1962 at Bhatia Hospital, Bombay (now Mumbai), Maharashtra.

First open-heart surgery

Dr Reeve H. Betts, an American missionary, founded the first department of thoracic and cardiovascular surgery in 1948 at the Christian Medical College and Hospital, Vellore, Tamil Nadu, with cardiac surgical work beginning in 1950. Along with Dr N. Gopinath, he performed the first successful open-heart surgery here on a 12-year-old patient, Beulah, in 1961.

Christian Medical College and Hospital (CMCH), Vellore, Tamil Nadu

PHARMACEUTICALS
The Backbone of Medical Science

First pharmaceutical degree course

The first pharmacy degree course started in 1937 at Banaras Hindu University (BHU) as a 3-year course in Bachelor of Pharmacy (B. Pharm). It was initiated by Prof. Mahadeva Lal Schroff, and this was the beginning of formal pharmacy education in India.

First pharmaceutical company

Bengal Chemicals & Pharmaceutical Works Ltd. (BCPW), the forerunner of today's Bengal Chemicals & Pharmaceuticals Ltd. (BCPL), was founded in 1901 by the eminent scientist Acharya Prafulla Chandra Ray. It was the first Indian enterprise to manufacture quality drugs, pharmaceuticals, chemicals, and home products using indigenous technology.

First indigenous antibiotic

Nafithromycin, the medicine developed with the support of the Biotechnology Industry Research Assistance Council (BIRAC), Department of Biotechnology, and marketed as 'Miqnaf' by the pharmaceutical company Wockhardt, is India's first indigenous antibiotic targeting Antimicrobial Resistance (AMR). It was launched in the market in 2024 and is intended for the treatment of Community-Acquired Bacterial Pneumonia (CABP), a serious infection caused by drug-resistant bacteria that poses a higher risk to children, the elderly, and immunocompromised patients.

WR Largest producer and exporter of generic drugs

India is the world's largest producer and supplier of generic medicines, accounting for about 20% of the global export volume of generic drugs. Its pharmaceutical exports were valued at approximately US$27.9 billion in FY 2023–24.

First pharmacopoeia

The first official Indian Pharmacopoeia (IP) was published in 1955, following the establishment of the Indian Pharmacopoeia Committee in 1948. It was a landmark publication providing authoritative standards for drugs manufactured and sold in India, covering both Western and traditional Indian systems of medicine. Prior to this, the country relied on the British Pharmacopoeia and its colonial addenda for drug standards. A crucial step toward a national pharmacopoeia came in 1946, when the Government of India issued The Indian Pharmacopoeial List, which compiled monographs of both British and indigenous drugs and laid the foundation for the IP.

Father of Pharmaceuticals in India

Professor Mahadeva Lal Schroff (1902–1971), hailed as the Father of Indian Pharmacy Education, introduced India's first pharmacy course at BHU in 1932 and went on to establish the country's first full B. Pharm (1937) and M. Pharm (1940) programmes. He was the founding President of the Indian Pharmaceutical Association (1939), the Indian Pharmaceutical Congress (1948), and the Association of Pharmaceutical Teachers of India (1966), and also led the Pharmacy Council of India. He launched the Indian Journal of Pharmacy in 1939 and played a pivotal role in shaping drug standards and legislation. His legacy is honoured annually on National Pharmacy Education Day on 6 March.

Earliest cataract surgery

Ancient Indian physician Sushruta (c. sixth century BCE) had diagnosed that cataract was a disease of the eye lens, characterized by its opacity resulting in impaired vision, and had prescribed surgery as the only remedy. It was performed with a curved needle used to loosen the lens and push the cataract out of the field of vision. The eye would later be soaked with warm butter and then bandaged.

Statue of Sushruta

First bloodless breast surgery

A team of doctors at the Dr B.R. Ambedkar Institute Rotary Cancer Hospital, AIIMS, New Delhi, carried out a major bloodless breast cancer surgery in September 1998, using ultrasonic waves.

First laser surgery on trachea

Dr Deepak Talwar, a leading pulmonologist, and his team at the Metro Hospital and Heart Institute, Noida, Uttar Pradesh, successfully opened up the lower part of a patient's windpipe, which had narrowed to 0.5 cm (0.2 in.) from the usual circumference of 2 cm (0.79 in.), in 1998. This was the first such surgery performed using laser technology.

First conference

The first medical conference, inaugurated by the then viceroy of colonial India, Lord Elgin, was held in Calcutta, Bengal (now Kolkata, West Bengal), between 24 and 29 December 1894.

First craniopagus surgery

A team of 125 doctors and paramedical staff, led by Dr Deepak Kumar Gupta and Dr Ashok Kumar Mahapatra from the Department of Neurosurgery at the All India Institute of Medical Sciences (AIIMS), New Delhi, successfully separated 28-month-old twins Jagga and Kalia, who were joined at the cranium. The twins belong to Milipada Village of Kandhamal district in Odisha. The complex surgery was conducted in two stages, on 28 August 2017 (25 hrs long) and 25 October 2017 (20 hrs long).

First video-assisted heart surgery

Video-assisted thoracic surgery (VATS) was used for the first time in heart surgery at the B.M. Birla Heart Research Centre, Calcutta (now Kolkata), on several children suffering from a congenital heart disease called patent ductus arteriosus (PDA), in August 1994.

Camera

Diagram depicting Video-Assisted Thoracic Surgery (VATS)

First Maze III (atrial fibrillation) surgery

A heart surgery to cure atrial fibrillation (fast and irregular heartbeat) was performed for the first time in India by Dr Amit Banerjee, cardiothoracic surgeon, on 25-year-old Kiran Bir at the Govind Ballabh Pant Hospital, New Delhi, on 25 August 1994.

First global telecast of surgery

On 11 June 1998, a team of doctors, led by leading cardiovascular and cardiothoracic surgeon Dr Naresh Trehan, operated upon six patients with heart ailments at the Escorts Heart Institute and Research Centre, New Delhi. The procedure was beamed live to 200 cardiac specialists and 1,000 delegates in San Francisco, US. The back-end support was provided by the Medical Products Group at Hewlett-Packard.

First heart-shrink surgery

Dr Naresh Trehan (b. 12 August 1946), a cardiovascular and cardiothoracic surgeon, performed the first successful heart-shrink surgery in India, which was also the first in Asia, with his team of cardiac surgeons, on a 50-year-old patient, Mani Ram Gurera, at the Escorts Heart Institute and Research Centre, New Delhi, on 21 May 1996.

Dr Naresh Trehan

Pioneering cataract removal

Cataract surgery was normally done through a 10–12 mm incision until 15 August 1998, when Dr Amar Agarwal pioneered the technique called Phakonit, in which a cataract was removed through a 0.9 mm incision at Dr Agarwal's Eye Hospital, Chennai, Tamil Nadu. This technique has now been adopted all over the world.

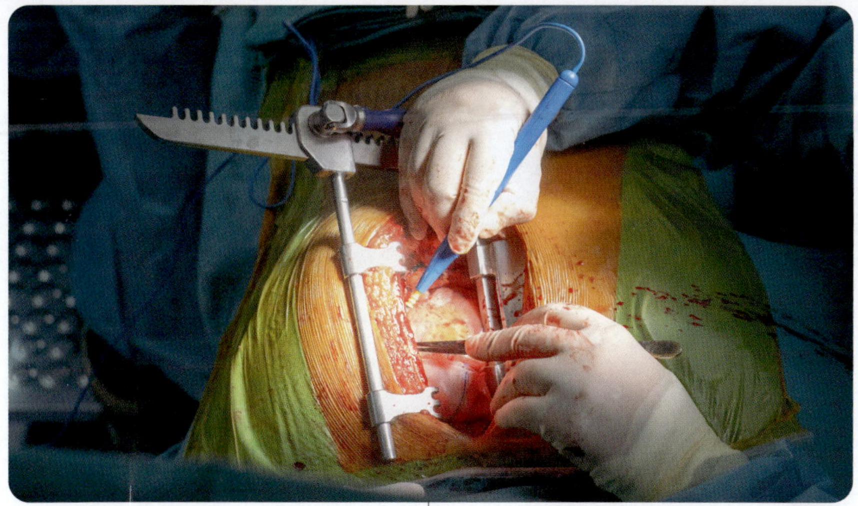

Coronary artery bypass surgery

First coronary artery bypass surgery

Dr K.M. Cherian performed India's first successful coronary artery bypass surgery in 1975. He has pioneered several transplants at the Madras Medical Mission and Institute of Cardiovascular Diseases in Chennai, Tamil Nadu.

First bi-ventricular pacemaker

Prof. Kewal Kishan Talwar, cardiologist and former chairman of the Medical Council of India, New Delhi, and Dr T.S. Kler of Escorts Heart Institute and Research Centre, New Delhi, implanted biventricular pacemakers (also known as cardiac resynchronization therapy {CRT}) on end-stage heart-disease patients on 8 May 2000 in two separate surgeries. This pacemaker ensures that all chambers of the heart contract and expand simultaneously.

First cochlear implant

Dr Sandra Desa Souza was the first surgeon to perform a cochlear implant surgery in the human ear to treat complete deafness. The surgery was performed at Jaslok Hospital, Bombay, Maharashtra, in November 1987.

Cochlear implant

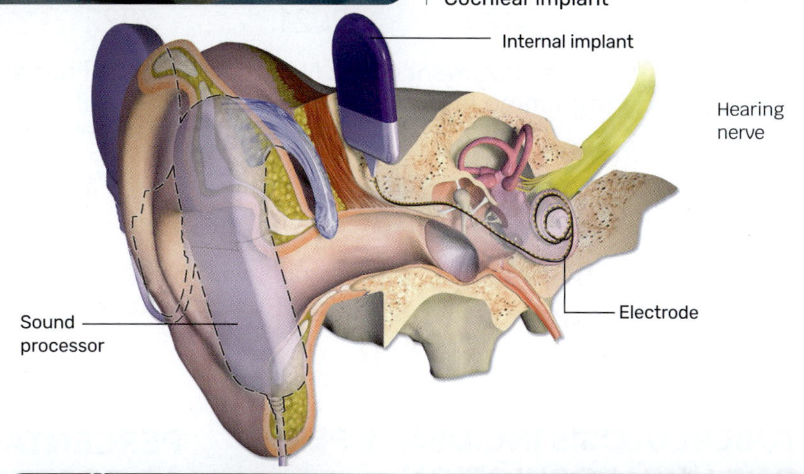

Left: Biventricular pacemaker (CRT-P device) and an implantable cardioverter-defibrillator (ICD) device; *right*: Implantation of the same

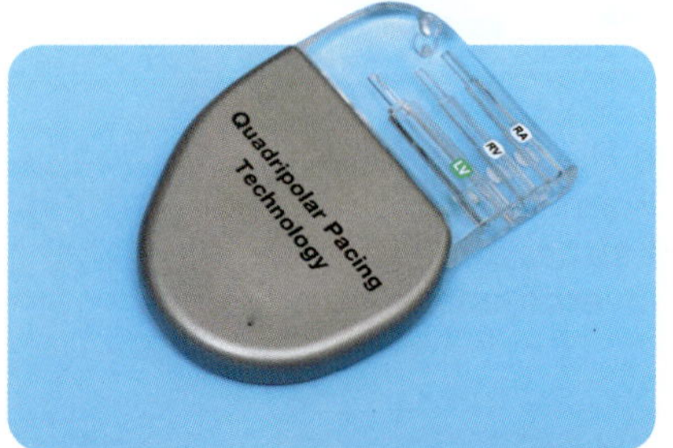

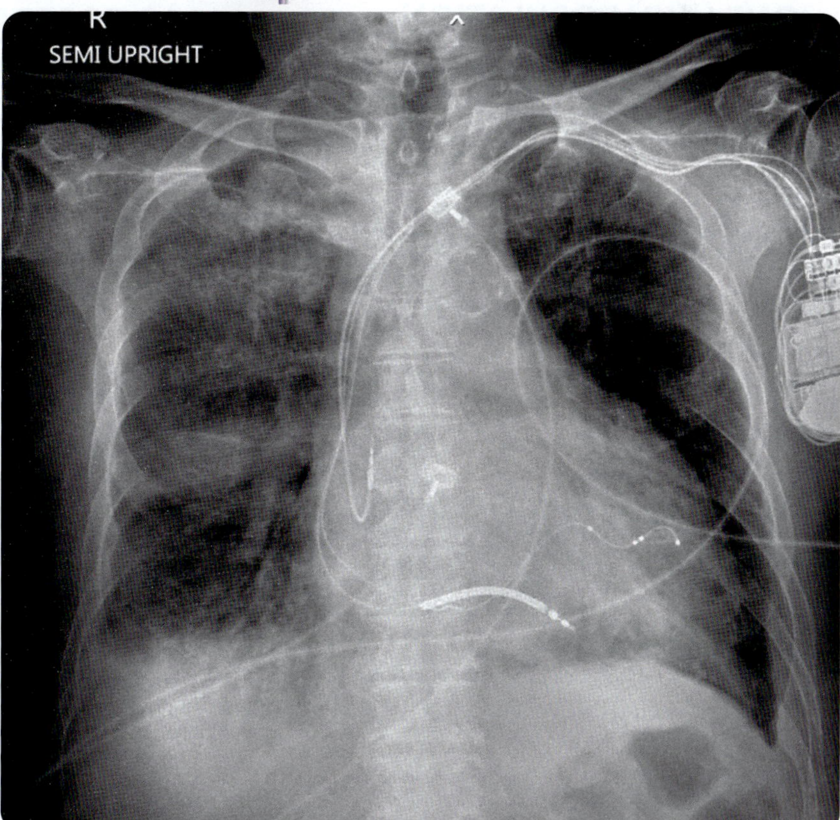

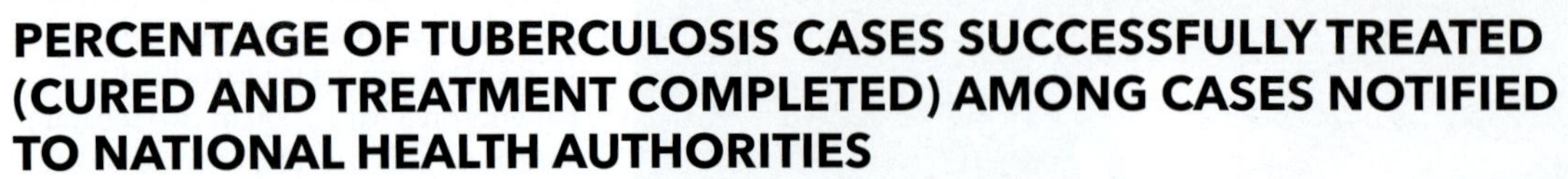

PERCENTAGE OF TUBERCULOSIS CASES SUCCESSFULLY TREATED (CURED AND TREATMENT COMPLETED) AMONG CASES NOTIFIED TO NATIONAL HEALTH AUTHORITIES

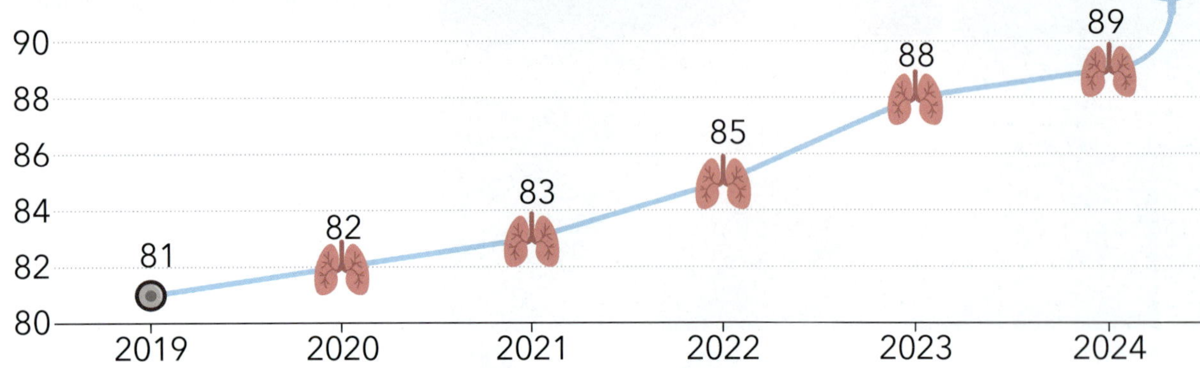

Source: Sustainable Development Goals National Indicator Framework Progress Report 2025, Ministry of Statistics and Programme Implementation, Government of India

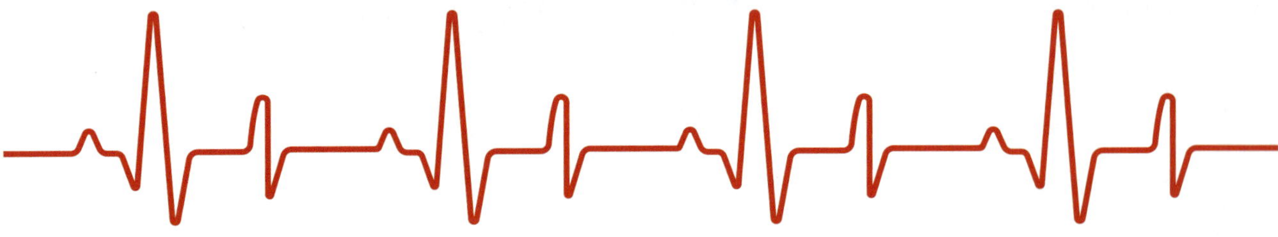

TUBERCULOSIS INCIDENCE PER ONE LAKH POPULATION

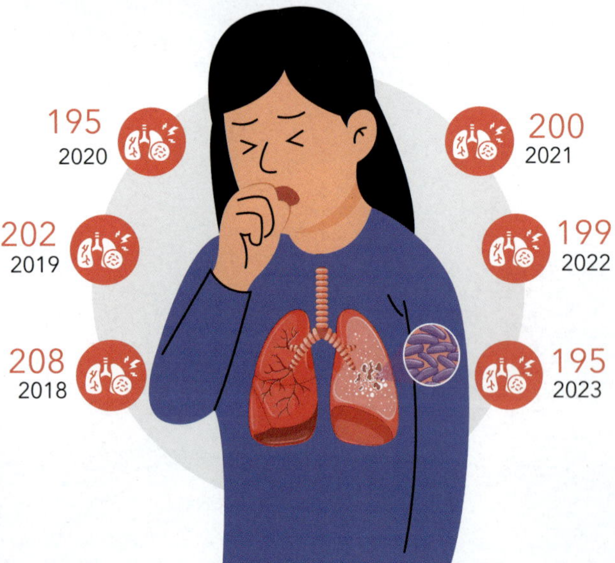

Source: National TB Elimination Programme, India Tuberculosis Report 2024, Central TB Division, Ministry of Health and Family Welfare, Government of India

PERCENTAGE OF CHILDREN AGED 12-23 MONTHS FULLY VACCINATED WITH BCG, MEASLES AND THREE DOSES OF POLIO AND DPT/PENTA VACCINE

(Excluding polio vaccine given at birth)

Source: Sustainable Development Goals National Indicator Framework Progress Report 2025, Ministry of Statistics and Programme Implementation, Government of India

BUDGETARY ALLOCATION FOR DEPARTMENT OF HEALTH RESEARCH

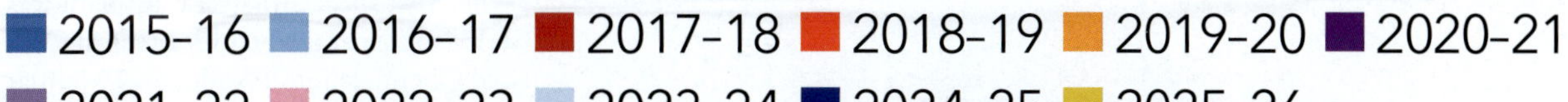

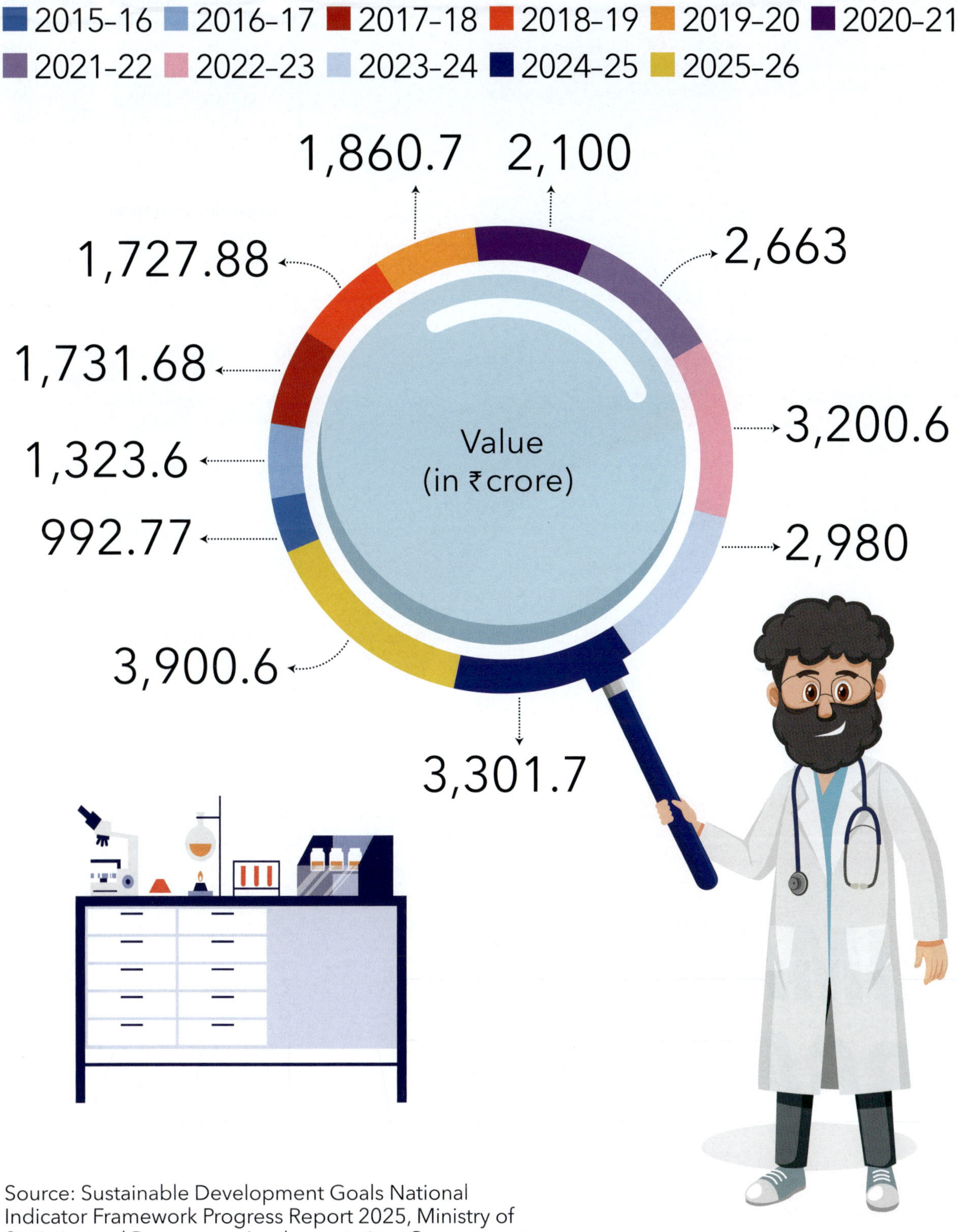

2015-16
2016-17
2017-18
2018-19
2019-20
2020-21
2021-22
2022-23
2023-24
2024-25
2025-26
1,860.7
2,100
1,727.88
2,663
1,731.68
3,200.6
1,323.6
Value
(in ₹ crore)
992.77
2,980
3,900.6
3,301.7

Source: Sustainable Development Goals National Indicator Framework Progress Report 2025, Ministry of Statistics and Programme Implementation, Government of India

TRANSPLANTS

First successful liver transplant

The first successful liver transplant was performed at the Stanley Medical College in Chennai, Tamil Nadu, on 19 January 1996. It was the third transplant, the first two having been performed at Apollo Hospital, Chennai, and AIIMS, New Delhi, respectively. In both cases, the patients died within a few days.

First womb transplant

Doctors at Galaxy Care Hospital, Pune, Maharashtra, successfully conducted India's first womb transplant on 18 May 2017 by transferring a woman's uterus to her 21-year-old daughter, who was unable to conceive. The procedure, which took 9 hrs using the laparoscopic technique, was performed by a team of 12 doctors.

First successful heart transplant

A team of doctors led by Dr P. Venugopal at the All India Institute of Medical Sciences (AIIMS), New Delhi, performed a successful heart transplant surgery in 5 hrs on 3 August 1994.

First paediatric heart transplant

On 14 June 1997, an 11-year-old boy underwent a successful heart transplant at the Institute of Cardiovascular Diseases, Madras Medical Mission, Chennai, Tamil Nadu. The surgery took three-and-a-half hours.

First successful thumb transplant

Dr Tapeshwar Anand and Dr Mohan Das were part of a team of specialists who performed a 12-hour limb-transplant surgery on a seven-hour-old baby Amy, at St Bart's Hospital, London, UK, on 24 March 2001. Her twin sister's thumb was transplanted on her hand (born thumbless) after her sister died at birth.

First double (liver and kidney) transplant

Ganesh Nehru became the first recipient of a liver from his maternal uncle Mohan Ram and a kidney from his mother Hemlata simultaneously. The double transplant lasted 18 hrs on 17 April 2007 and involved 50 doctors and paramedics, besides intricate coordination between three operating theatres at Sir Ganga Ram Hospital, New Delhi. Dr A.S. Soin was the transplant surgeon in charge of the case.

MEDICAL MARVELS

First scalp replantation

A completely avulsed scalp was replanted microsurgically on Gurkripal Singh by Dr Abraham Thomas and Dr Jaychandran of Christian Medical College and Hospital, Ludhiana, Punjab, in March 1985.

Oldest to undergo hip surgery

• A team of doctors at the Postgraduate Institute of Medical Education and Research (PGIMER), Chandigarh, performed a hip replacement surgery on a 110-year-old woman (age based on her Aadhaar card), Manjauki, on 8 January 2020. The team comprised Prof. Vijay G. Goni, Dr Tanvir Samra, Dr Deepak, Dr Karan, Dr Pradeep and Dr Sumeet.
• Ram Lal, a 105-year-old patient, was the oldest to undergo a bipolar replacement of the right hip when he sustained a fracture around the hip joint. The surgery was carried out under Dr Sujoy Kumar Bhattacharjee, director, joint replacement surgery, at Metro Heart Institute with Multispeciality Hospital in Faridabad, Haryana, on 23 March 2018. The operation lasted 2 hrs 52 mins.

Oldest woman to deliver twins

Seventy-four-year-old Mangayamma Yaramati gave birth to a pair of twin girls on 5 September 2019 at the Ahalya Hospital, Guntur, Andhra Pradesh. Dr Sankayalla Uma Shankar delivered the babies by Caesarean section. Conceived through IVF, the babies were the first children of the couple.

WR Heaviest ovarian tumour removed

• The world's heaviest ovarian tumour, weighing 50 kg, was removed on 18 August 2020 at the Indraprastha Apollo Hospital, New Delhi, from a 52-year-old patient, by a team of surgeons led by Dr Arun Prasad. The surgery lasted for three-and-a half hours.
• *Malignant*: Kavita Khoiwal, assistant professor, Department of Obstetrics and Gynaecology, AIIMS, Rishikesh, Uttarakhand, along with her team of doctors, operated on a 24-year-old female patient on 21 August 2020 and removed the heaviest abdominopelvic mass. The weight of the cancerous ovarian mass was 41.1 kg, from which 36 litres of mucinous fluid was removed prior to removal and the remaining mass of 5.1 kg was removed subsequently. The size of the mass was 60 cm x 50 cm x 40 cm (23.62 in. x 19.68 in. x 15.75 in.) approximately.

Longest object removed from the brain

Dr Rahul Prakash Modgi, neurosurgeon, and Dr Rajendra Gawatre, anaesthesiologist, operated on Pallavi Vijay Shelke, 17, at Shri Saibaba Hospital, Shirdi, Maharashtra, on 29 December 2012. They removed a 12 cm (4.72 in.) long iron rod, weighing 47 g, from her right frontotemporo-parietal region.

Heaiest kidney removed

Dr Puvvada Sandeep and three other doctors from his team at Ramaiah Medical College, Bengaluru, Karnataka, removed a kidney weighing 7.72 kg on 21 November 2019. Containing 3.12 litres of fluid, the kidney was removed from a 53-year-old patient suffering from bilateral adult polycystic kidney disease (APKD) and chronic kidney disease.

Longest foreign body removed

Dr Sanjay Kolte, urologist and kidney transplant surgeon at Sparsh Urology and Kidney Hospital, Dhantoli, Maharashtra, removed a 154 cm (5 ft 0.6 in.) long soft electric wire from the urinary bladder of a patient by percutaneous cystoscopy extraction of foreign body surgery on 28 August 2012.

Largest cystic tumour of the liver removed

Dr N. Bheerappa from the department of surgical gastroenterology at the Nizam's Institute of Medical Sciences, Hyderabad, Telangana, successfully removed the largest known cystic liver tumour (mucinous cystic neoplasm) in 2017. The 24-year-old female patient was operated on for a tumour measuring 40 cm x 28 cm x 15 cm (15.74 in. x 11.02 in. x 5.91 in.).

Largest oral (head and neck) tumour removed – in one piece

Dr Saurabh Gupta, assistant professor and consultant, Surgical Oncology, Max Superspeciality Hospital, Shalimar Bagh, New Delhi, as operating surgeon, removed a head-and-neck tumour from a 38-year-old male patient in a left commando surgery. This, along with free alt flap reconstruction, took 11 hrs from 9:00 a.m. to 8:00 p.m. on 30 April 2020. The size of the tumour in this case of oral cancer was 18 cm x 12 cm x 8 cm (7.09 in. x 4.72 in. x 3.15 in.).

Largest kidney stone removed

Dr Hemendra Shah at R.G. Stone Urological Research Institute, Mumbai, Maharashtra, removed a 13 cm (5.12 in.) wide kidney stone from a patient on 18 February 2004.

Largest urethral calculus removed

Dr Neeraj Kumar Agrawal removed a 5.6 cm (2.2 in.) long stone from a patient at Neeraj Lifecare and Stone Centre, Bareilly, Uttar Pradesh, on 21 August 2019.

Largest thoracic tumour removed

On 13 September 2021, the largest thoracic tumour was successfully removed by Dr Anshuman Darbari of the cardiothoracic department, AIIMS, Rishikesh, Uttarakhand. The tumour was removed from a 51-year-old female patient. The tumour measured 26 cm x 24 cm x 12 cm (10.23 in. x 9.44 in. x 4.72 in.).

Largest urinary bladder stone removed

Dr D.C. Patel operated on Maheshbhai Patel, a 49-year-old suffering from blocked urine, at Shree Sainath Surgical and Maternity Hospital, Dharampur, Gujarat, on 6 April 2017. Dr Patel removed a bladder stone measuring 15 cm x 12 cm x 10 cm (5.90 in. x 4.72 in. x 3.94 in.) and weighing 1.365 kg. He was assisted by Dr Hemant Patel and Dr Nital Patel.

Largest breast tumour removed

The largest breast tumour recorded, which measured 41 cm x 39 cm x 37 cm (16.14 in. x 15.35 in. x 14.57 in.), was removed from a patient by Dr Vikas Jain at the B.J. Hospital, Gondia, Maharashtra. The surgery was conducted on 25 July 2019 from 3:30 p.m. to 6:00 p.m. The tumour weighed 5.6 kg after it was removed.

Longest fistula removed

A 110 cm (43.30 in.) long fistula was removed from a patient by Dr Ashwin

Porwal at Healing Hands Clinic, Pune, Maharashtra, on 10 May 2019. The surgery was conducted from 3:00 p.m. to 7:00 p.m. using the distal laser proximal ligation (DLPL) technique.

Largest small-intestinal tumour removed

A tumour measuring 21 cm x 19 cm x 13 cm (8.26 in. x 7.48 in. x 5.12 in.) was removed from the small intestine of a patient by Dr Karthik Babu Perumalla at Ramesh Sanghamitra Hospital, Ongole, Andhra Pradesh. The surgery was conducted on 1 March 2019 from 11:00 a.m. to 4:00 p.m.

Longest foreign body removed from the windpipe

Dr Himanshu Jagdishchandra Thakkar surgically removed the longest foreign body – a sapodilla seed – measuring 02 cm in length and approximately 01 cm in breadth from the left main bronchus (windpipe) of the respiratory system of a 50-year-old female patient on 07 February 2017 between 9:30 and 9:45 am at Dr Thakkar's ENT and Dental Hospital, Rajkot, Gujarat.

Most loose bodies removed from a joint

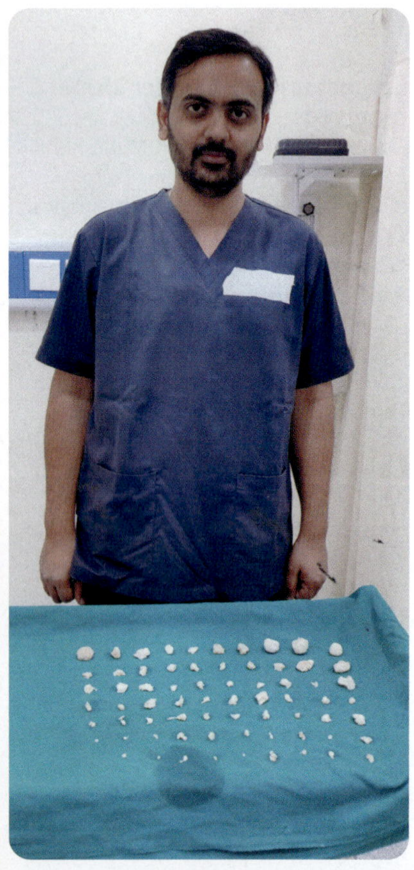

Longest foreign body removed from the windpipe

Largest nasal polyp removed

Dr Himanshu Jagdishchandra Thakkar surgically removed the largest nasal polyp of size 10 cm x 3.5 cm x 01 cm from the nose of a 47-year-old male patient on 20 May 2025 between 11:15 and 11:45 am at Dr Thakkar's ENT and Dental Hospital, Rajkot, Gujarat.

Most loose bodies removed from a joint

Dr Ajinkya Bhaskarrao Desale surgically removed 69 loose bodies (joint stones) from the left knee joint of a 54-year-old female patient on 20 July 2023 at Apex Wellness Hospital, Nashik, Maharashtra. Usually, 2–3 such loose bodies are encountered but 69 of such in a single knee joint was a unique occurrence.

Longest blood clot removed

On 24 September 2022, Dr Anne Sai Pavan, a cardiothoracic surgeon at Aayush Hospital, Vijayawada, performed a femoral artery embolectomy from 9 p.m. to 11 p.m. and removed the longest clot measuring 20 cm (7.87 in.).

Largest bone tumour removed

On 9 June 2021, a team of doctors from the orthopaedics department of ACPM Medical Hospital, Dhule, Maharashtra, removed the largest tumour from the left femur of a 28-year-old patient. The team comprised Dr Yashwant Mahale, Dr James Kuris, Dr Ameya Thaware and Dr Akash Metkar. The tumour measured 43.18 cm (17 in.) in length, 30.48 cm (12 in.) in breadth and 25.4 cm (10 in.) in width. It had a circumference of 102 cm (40.16 in.). The surgery took a total of 3.5 hours.

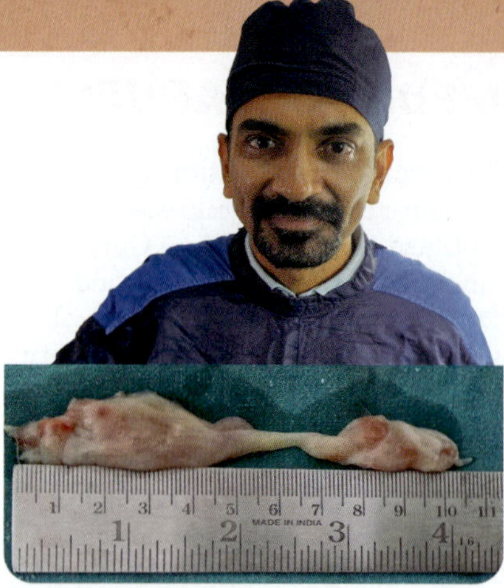

Largest nasal polyp removed

Largest adrenal cyst removed

On 24 January 2023, a team of urologists from ACE Hospital and Research Centre, Pune, Maharashtra, removed the largest adrenal cyst measuring 23 cm laparoscopically. The cyst was removed from a 58-year-old female patient. The team included Dr Suresh B. Patankar, Dr Gururaj R. Padasalagi, Dr Mayur M. Narkhede and Dr Kashinath V. Thakare.

Longest foreign body removed from the spine

Dr Saraj Kumar Singh, Chief Surgeon, and Dr Kranti Bhavana, Assistant Surgeon, along with their assisting team, removed a fish bone measuring 35 mm x 02 mm from the cervical

Longest foreign body removed from the spine

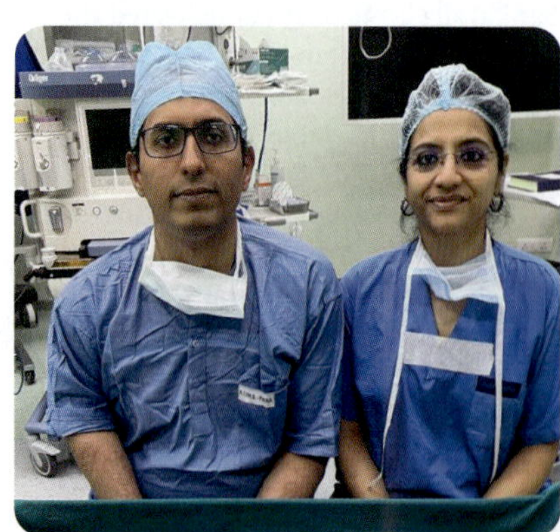

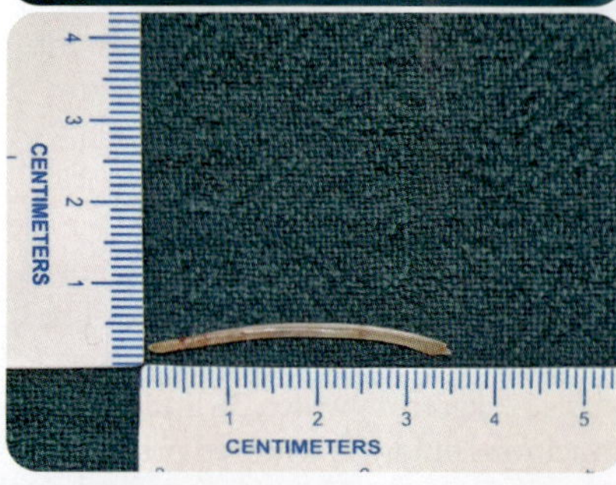

spine of a 42-year-old male patient on 09 March 2025 at the neurosurgical operation theatre, AIIMS, Patna, Bihar. The surgery took place between 9:00 am to 1:05 pm, lasting four hours and five minutes.

Largest skull bone tumour removed

Dr Saraj Kumar Singh, Associate Professor, Neurosurgery, AIIMS, Patna, along with his team, removed a skull bone tumour measuring 22 cm x 16 cm x 07 cm and weighing 830 gms from a 29-year-old male patient via craniotomy and tumour resection on 21 February 2024 at the hospital. The surgery started at 9:00 am and ended at 4:45 pm, lasting 7 hours and 45 minutes.

Largest skull bone tumour removed

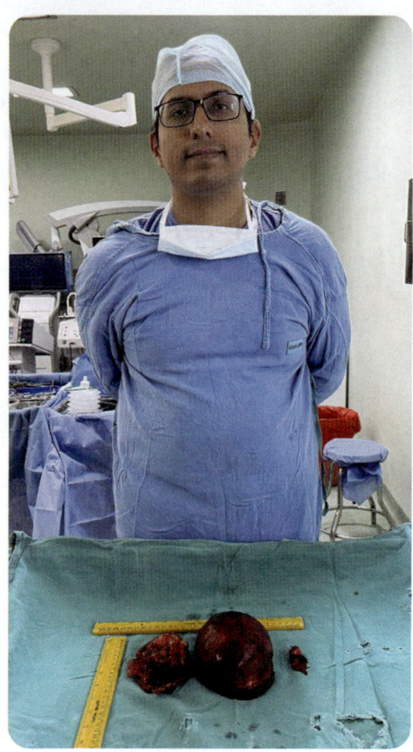

Most uterine fibroids removed

Dr Ravindra Keshavrao Shelmohkar removed 63 uterine fibroids from a 34-year-old female patient in an open abdominal myomectomy conducted on 14 April 2021 from 9:45 a.m. to 10:45 a.m. at Pune District Education Association's Ayurved Rugnalaya and Sterling Multispeciality Hospital in Nugdi, Pune, Maharashtra.

Surgery on the heaviest woman

Forty-two-year-old Amita Rajani, weighing 300 kg, underwent bariatric surgery performed by Dr Shashank Shah at his hospital in Pune, Maharashtra, in 2015. She was bedridden for eight years before the surgery and had multiple risk factors. She lost 214 kg as a result of the surgery.

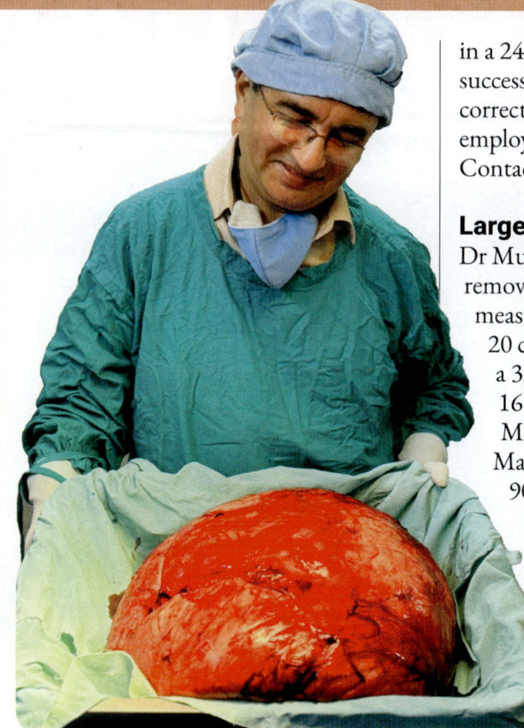

Largest uterine fibroid removed

WR Surgery on the world's heaviest teenager

Mihir Jain, then 14 years old, became the world's heaviest teenager to undergo bariatric surgery. He weighed 237 kg at the time, with a BMI of 92 kg/sq. m. The surgery was performed by Dr Pradeep Kumar Chowbey at Max Hospital, Saket, New Delhi, and a team of six doctors in 2 hrs 20 mins in July 2018.

Largest spinal disc removed

Dr Saraj Kumar Singh surgically removed the largest spinal disc of size 08 cm x 03 cm x 01 cm from a 55-year-old male patient on 25 September 2023 at AIIMS, Patna. The method employed for the surgery was endoscopic discectomy.

Highest spectacle power corrected surgically

The highest spectacle power of – 32.5 D was corrected surgically by Dr Rahil Chaudhary on 22 March 2021 at Eye7 Eye Hospital, Lajpat Nagar, New Delhi. Myopia of right eye –25.00 diopter and –32.50 diopter of left eye in a 24-year-old female patient was successfully corrected using a vision correction refractive eye surgery that employed Customized Implantable Contact Lens (ICL).

Largest uterine fibroid removed

Dr Mukesh Ramesh Rathi surgically removed a single largest uterine fibroid measuring 34.8 cm x 29.5 cm x 20 cm and weighing 16.75 kgs from a 32-year-old female patient on 16 March 2025 at Laxminarayan Memorial Hospital, Akola, Maharashtra. The surgery lasted 90 minutes, and the uterus of the patient was preserved for future pregnancy.

WR Heaviest brain tumour removed

Dr Saraj Kumar Singh, assistant professor, AIIMS, Patna, Bihar, and his assisting team removed a brain tumour weighing 2.280 kg (2,280 g) from a 50-year-old male patient on 22 November 2021 at the hospital. The surgery to excise the tumour began at 12:26 p.m. and ended at 3:42 p.m., lasting 3 hrs 16 mins. The tumour measured 24 cm x 24 cm x 14 cm (9.44 in. x 9.44 in. x 5.51 in.).

Largest tumour removed

Dr Saraj Kumar Singh surgically removed the largest eye tumour of size 12 cm x 10 cm x 04 cm and weighing 180 gms from the left eye of a 14-year-old male patient on 28 August 2023 at AIIMS, Patna.

Largest ear tumour removed

Dr Saraj Kumar Singh surgically removed the largest ear tumour of size 10 cm x 10 cm x 04 cm and weighing 110 gms from the left ear of a 35-year-old male patient on 11 September 2023 at AIIMS, Patna.

First home-grown anti-cancer CAR-T cell therapy

In April 2024, the President launched India's first home-grown anti-cancer CAR-T cell therapy in Mumbai for cancer treatment, developed by IIT Bombay, Tata Memorial Centre and ImmunoACT. It is not only a first for India, but also deemed as the most affordable CAR-T therapy.

THE NATURAL WORLD

PHYSICAL FEATURES

Longest land mountain range

The Himalayan range is the loftiest and most rugged mountain barrier in Asia. Out of the 7,300 mountain peaks in the world, 96 are in the Himalaya–Karakoram range. The range stretches over 2,500 km and varies in width from around 500 km in Jammu and Kashmir to around 200 km in Arunachal Pradesh. Some of the higher ranges are composed of 600-million-year-old Precambrian rocks.

Largest glacier

Siachen Glacier, Ladakh, near the India–Pakistan border, is India's largest glacier. It is 75.6 km long and 2–8 km wide. It is also the second longest glacier outside the polar regions of the Earth.

Largest river system

Of the total river discharge in India, 65 per cent is from the Himalayan group of rivers. The Ganga, Indus, and Brahmaputra Rivers are part of this river system.

Longest river

The 2,525 km long Ganga River is the longest river in the country. Its source is in the western Himalayas in Uttarakhand, from where the river flows south and east through the Gangetic Plain and Bangladesh, finally merging into the Bay of Bengal.

WR Largest delta

The triangular landmass formed by the Hooghly River, the Ganga, Padma, and Meghna Rivers combined, and the Bay of Bengal is called the Ganga-Brahmaputra Delta or the Sundarbans Delta or the Bengal Delta. It is the largest delta in the world with an approximate subaerial surface area of 1,10,000 sq. km. Around 60 per cent of this delta is in Bangladesh, and the rest lies in West Bengal, India.

Largest brackish water lagoon

Chilika Lake in Odisha is the largest brackish-water lagoon and has an area of around 1,100 sq. km.

Largest catchment area

The Ganga–Brahmaputra–Meghna system is the biggest river system in the country, with a catchment area of 272

Panoramic view of the Himalayas from Kullu Valley

Aerial view of the Ganga in Rishikesh, Uttarakhand

Aerial view of Chilika Lake, Odisha

Largest mangrove forest

Sundarbans is the largest contiguous mangrove forest in the world with an approximate area of 10,000 sq. km. It is part of the largest delta of the world, the Ganga-Brahmaputra delta. It is also a UNESCO World Heritage Site since 1987.

Aerial view of the Sundarbans

Wular lake, Kashmir

Largest freshwater lake

Wular Lake, in Bandipora, Jammu and Kashmir, is India's largest freshwater lake, and Asia's second-largest freshwater lake with an area of 260 sq. km. The main source of water for the lake is River Jhelum.

million acres (110 million hectares), which is more than 43 per cent of the catchment area of all the major rivers of the Indian subcontinent..

Amarnath cave

Largest cave

The Amarnath Cave, about 44 km from Pahalgam in Jammu and Kashmir, is the largest cave and a popular pilgrimage. It is a natural cave located at an altitude of 3,800 m (12,467 ft). The cave is 50 m (164 ft) wide and 25 m (82 ft) high. The Shivalinga worshipped in the cave is a remarkable example of a stalagmite.

Lonar crater, Maharashtra

Largest crater

The Lonar meteorite crater in the Buldhana District of Maharashtra is India's largest meteorite crater. It measures 1,800 m (5,906 ft) across and is 170 m (558 ft) deep. It is estimated that it was formed 50,000 years ago by a meteorite that was around100 m (328 ft) in diameter, weighed a million tonnes and was travelling at a speed of around 90,000 km per hour.

Only cold desert

Ladakh, at an average altitude of 4,878 m (16,004 ft), is the only cold desert in India.

Highest peak

Kanchenjunga, with its base partly in India and partly in Nepal, is 8,586 m

Largest desert

The Thar Desert is the largest desert in India that stretches over an area of about 200,000 sq. km and spreads over four states: Punjab, Haryana, Gujarat, and Rajasthan. It is interspersed with hillocks, gravel plains, salt marshes, and lakes. Aeolian dunes are a prominent feature of the landscape.

Dunes of Thar Desert

Mt Kanchenjunga

(28,169 ft) high. Yalung Kang (also on the India–Nepal border) is the second highest at 8,505 m (27,903 ft) and Nanda Devi comes in third at 7,817 m (25,646 ft).

Maximum average annual rainfall

Mawsynram, a village in the East Khasi Hills District, Meghalaya, about 65 km from Shillong, gets a mean annual rainfall of 11,873 mm (467 in.) in about 147 days and is considered the wettest place in India. Earlier the record for the highest average annual rainfall was held by Cherrapunji (now Sohra) in the same district. The latter continues to hold the record for highest annual rainfall received with 26,470 mm.

Minimum average rainfall area

Jaisalmer in Rajasthan receives an average rainfall of only about 200 mm (around 7.87 in.) in a year and is considered the driest place in India.

Largest meteorite shower

On 14 July 1860, a heavy meteorite shower fell at Dharamshala (32°14′N, 76°28′E) in Kangra District, Himachal Pradesh. It consisted of many stones, the largest of which weighed 150 kg.

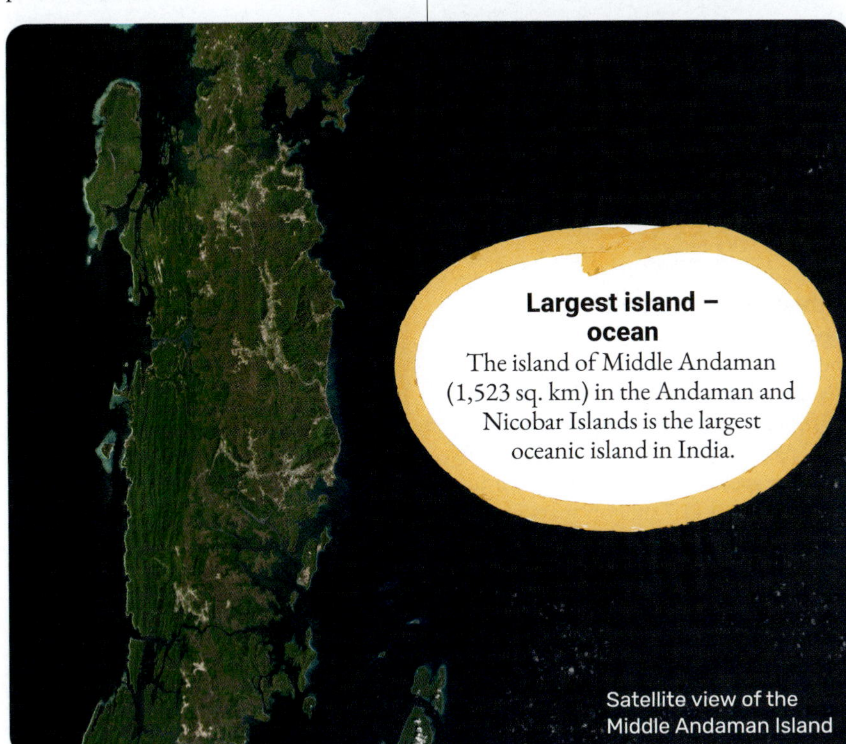

Largest island – ocean

The island of Middle Andaman (1,523 sq. km) in the Andaman and Nicobar Islands is the largest oceanic island in India.

Satellite view of the Middle Andaman Island

Largest island – freshwater

The island of Majuli, with an area of 352 sq. km in the Brahmaputra River in Assam, is the largest freshwater island in the world.

Highest waterfall

Kunchikal Falls in Nidagodu Village near Masthikatte in Shivamogga District, Karnataka, falls down a total height of 455 m (1,493 ft), making it the highest waterfall in India.

Highest surface salinity

The surface salinity in the Gulf of Kachchh, off the coast of Gujarat, varies from a maximum of 45.5 psu (practical salinity units) near the head of the gulf to 36.6 psu at the mouth. A practical salinity unit is equivalent to parts per thousand.

Lowest surface salinity

Salinity near the surface in the northern Bay of Bengal can be as low as 31 psu because the bay receives fresh water as rain as well as run-off from the Ganga, Brahmaputra, Irrawaddy, and other rivers.

Longest natural sandstone cave

Krem Puri, found in East Khasi Hills District, Meghalaya, is the world's longest sandstone cave with a length of about 24.58 km. It is also known for its dinosaur fossils from 66–76 million years ago. It is 6 km longer than the previous record holder – the 18.2 km long Cueva Del Saman sandstone cave in Edo Zulia, Venezuela.

Only active volcano

Barren Island, which lies 110 km north-east of Port Blair in the Andaman and Nicobar Islands, is India's only active volcano. On 10 April 1991, it blew up nearly two centuries after it erupted in 1803. It last erupted in 1995.

Highest temperature

On 19 May 2016, India recorded its highest-ever temperature, 51°C, in Phalodi, a town in Jodhpur District, Rajasthan.

Lowest temperature
The lowest temperature recorded in Dras, Ladakh, was –60°C on 9 January 1995, making it the coldest inhabited place in India.

FOSSILS

Oldest dinosaur fossil discovery

The first dinosaur fossils in India were discovered by a British palaeontologist named William Henry Sleeman in 1828 in Jabalpur, Madhya Pradesh. The specimens were lost in 1877 and found in 2013 in the office of the Geological Survey of India, Kolkata, West Bengal.

W.H. Sleeman

MAMMALS

Oldest living mammal

One of the oldest living mammals is the Indian one-horned rhinoceros (*Rhinoceros unicornis*). The Indian and Javan rhinoceroses first appeared in the fossil record of Asia 1.6–3.3 million years ago. The species may have diverged much earlier, around 11.7 million years ago.

Smallest mammal

• ***Land:*** The white-toothed pygmy shrew or the Etruscan shrew (*Suncus etruscus*), which has a head and-body length of 3–5.5 cm (1.18–2.17 in.) and a tail length of 2.5–3.2 cm (0.98–1.26 in.), is the smallest Indian land

Above: Indian one-horned rhinoceros in Kaziranga; *below*: Etruscan shrew

mammal by weight. It weighs around 1.8 g. This shrew can be found across the Indian subcontinent, except in Jammu and Kashmir and arid areas of Gujarat and Rajasthan.

• ***Water:*** The smallest water mammal in the country by weight is the Indo-Pacific finless porpoise (*Neophocaena phocaenoides*), with an average adult being 1.5–1.8 m (5–6 ft) long and 30–45 kg by weight. It is found in the waters of peninsular India.

Indo-Pacific finless porpoise

100 days. Females have an average count of 11.32 pregnancies a year with a total break of 32.3 days in between. The female may produce as many as 70 young ones a year.

Slowest breeders

The elephant's main breeding season is the summer and the beginning of monsoon. Only one calf is born at a time and at intervals of three years.

Largest litter

The Indian mole rat (*Bandicota bengalensis*), found in most plains and forests, is known to have litters of over 12 young ones at a time.

Asian elephant

Largest land mammal

The adult Asian elephant found in India (*Elephas maximus indicus*) belongs to the species of the largest land mammal *Elephas maximus.* An adult bull elephant averages 2.74 m (9 ft) in height at the shoulder and weighs around 4.5 tonnes. The female elephant or cow measures 2.35 m (7 ft 8.5 in.) at the shoulder and weighs around 3 tonnes. Elephants are found in four clusters in the plains of north, south, east and central India and the north-east.

Fastest breeders

The Indian mole rat (*Bandicota bengalensis*) is the fastest-breeding mammal. The males mature in 58 days after birth and the females in 90–

Longest-living

• Humans are the longest-living mammals.

• The average lifespan of a blue whale (*Balaenoptera musculus*) is 80–90 years.

• The Indian elephant follows with an average lifespan of around 60 years, but they can live up to 80–90 years.

Primate with the longest tail

The tail of the common langur (*Semnopithecus entellus*) measures around 1 m (3 ft 3.4 in.) on average.

Fastest mammal – Land

The blackbuck (*Antilope cervicapra*), which is native to India, can run at a speed of up to 80 km per hour. It is found in regions ranging from Rajasthan to Punjab in the north, up to Odisha in the east and Tamil Nadu in the south. The cheetah (*Acinonyx jubatus*), recently introduced in India, in Madhya Pradesh, can sprint at speeds of up to 120 km per hour.

Slowest mammal – Land

The Bengal slow loris (*Nycticebus bengalensis*), which measures 30–40 cm (11.8–15.7 in.), is the slowest land mammal in the country. It is found in Assam.

Fastest mammal – Water

The 2–2.5 m (6 ft 6 in.–8 ft 2 in.) long-beaked common dolphin (*Delphinus capensis*), found off the coast of peninsular India, swims at 30 knots or 55.5 km per hour, and is the fastest mammal in water.

Slowest mammal – Water

The slowest mammal in water is the 3.2 m (10 ft 6 in.) long dugong or sea cow (*Dugong dugon*), found in the Gulf of Kachchh, off the Malabar Coast, and in the Andaman Islands.

Longest gestation

The elephant has a gestation period of about 20 months.

Shortest gestation

Rodents have a gestation period averaging a month.

Only herbivorous marine mammals

Dugongs and manatees (*Trichechus manatus latirostris*/*Trichechus manatus manatus*) form the only group of herbivorous marine mammals.

They are found in the Gulf of Mannar and Palk Bay, where seagrass meadows provide them with food. Highly

Common langur

endangered, dugongs are also found in the Gulf of Kachchh and near the Andaman Islands. They are 1 m to 3 m (3 ft 3 in. to 9 ft 10 in.) long and weigh around 400 kg.

The only apes

The western hoolock gibbon (*Hoolock hoolock*) and the eastern hoolock gibbon (*Hoolock leuconedys*) are the only ape species found in India. They are the tallest gibbons, and the only ape species too. Their average height, standing on hind legs, is about 0.9 m (3 ft).

Smallest feline

The world's smallest cat, about half to three fourths the size of a domestic cat, is the rusty-spotted cat *(Prionailurus rubiginosus)* found in southern and central India. The male has a head-and body length of 35–48 cm (14–19 in.) and the tail measures 15–30 cm (5.9–11.8 in.). Males weigh around 1.5–1.6 kg, while females weigh about 1.1–1.5 kg.

Above: Western hoolock gibbon; *left*: Rusty-spotted cat

Feline found at the highest altitude

The snow leopard (*Panthera uncia*) is found at around 3,650–3,960 m (12,000–13,000 ft) in the Himalayan mountains.

Himalayan Snow Leopard

Largest/heaviest feline

Male tigers have a head-and body length of 3.55–4.20 m (11 ft 7 in.–13 ft 9 in.). Females have a head-and-body length of 2.40–2.65 m (7 ft 10 in. – 8 ft 8 in.). The height at shoulder is around 90–110 cm (35–43 in.). The average weight of males is 175–260 kg and that of females is 100–160 kg.

WR The only camels that swim

The Kharai camels (*Camelus dromedarius*) from the Kachchh region in Gujarat are the only ones of their kind in the world that can swim. They live with nomadic camel herders, who are indigenous to the region. The camels have padded hooves that help them navigate wet and salty coastal land and they can swim up to 3 km.

Smallest bat

The Indian pygmy bat (*Pipistrellus tenuis*) has a head-and-body length of 3.3–4.5 cm (1.3–.8 in.). Its tail is 3.5 cm (1.38 in.) and its forearm is 2.5–3 cm (1.0–1.2 in.) long.

Largest bat

The large flying fox (*Pteropus vampyrus*) is the largest bat at 19.8–30 cm (7.8–11.8 in.) in the country and is found in the Himalayas and peninsular India.

BIRDS

Largest round nests

The largest nests are made by the megapodes (*Megapodius nicobariensis*). They reach a height of 1.5 m (4 ft 11 in.) and have a circumference of 10 m (32 ft 10 in.).

Smallest wingspan

The Nilgiri flowerpecker (*Dicaeum concolor*) male has a wingspan of 43–48 mm (1.69–1.89 in.). The female has an even smaller wingspan of 42 –45 mm (1.65–1.77 in.).

Smallest and lightest

The Nilgiri flowerpecker (*Dicaeum concolor*) is only 7 cm (2.7 in.) long and weighs around 4.5 g.

Largest wingspan

The bearded vulture (*Gypaetus barbatus*) or the lammergeier, found along the lower Himalayas in Jammu and Kashmir, Himachal Pradesh, Uttarakhand, Sikkim, Assam, and Arunachal Pradesh, has a wingspan of 2.31–2.83 m (7 ft 7 in.– 9 ft 3 in.).

Bearded vulture

Nilgiri flowerpecker

Largest egg

Longest claws

The hind claw of the bronze winged jacana (*Metopidius indicus*) measures around 6.5–7 cm (2.5–2.7 in.) in length. Its leg (tarsus) is 6.5–6.8 cm (2.5–2.6 in.) long.

Smallest egg

The average size of the egg of the scarlet backed flowerpecker (*Dicaeum cruentatum*) is 14 mm x 10.3 mm (0.55 in. x 0.4 in.).

Largest egg

The average size of the sarus crane's (*Grus antigone*) egg is 10.4 cm x 6.4 cm (4 in. x 2.5 in.).

Rosy pelican; Dalmatian pelican

Longest beak

The beaks of the rosy pelican (*Pelecanus onocrotalus*) and the Dalmatian pelican (*Pelecanus crispus*) are 43–45 cm (1 ft 4.9 in.–1 ft 5.7 in.) long.

Slowest bird

The Eurasian woodcock (*Scolopax rusticola*) flies at a speed of around 8 km per hour.

Shortest legs

The crested tree swift (*Hemiprocne coronata*) has around 7–9 mm (0.27 – 0.35 in.) long legs.

Longest legs

The legs (tarsus) of the sarus crane (*Grus antigone*) measure 31–35 cm (12–13 in.), making them the longest among birds.

Swiftest/fastest dive

The peregrine falcon (*Falco peregrinus*) reaches speeds of over 320 km per hour. It can dive at a speed of up to 360 km per hour – faster than a moving racing car.

Only breeding ground for flamingos

The only known breeding ground in India for the lesser and greater flamingos is the Rann of Kachchh in Gujarat. Thousands of flamingos nest every year in the seasonal marshes of both the Great Rann and the Little Rann of Kachchh.

First bird hospital

The Charity Birds' Hospital in Chandni Chowk, Delhi, caters to about 20,000 birds a year and is the only exclusive hospital for birds in the country.

WR **Tallest flying bird**

The sarus crane (*Grus antigone*) is the world's tallest bird, standing 1.52 m (5 ft) tall. This greyish crane with a red head is common around the *jheel*s of northern and central India. Of the 14–15 species of cranes in the world, six are found in India.

Most intricate nest

The weaver bird species, like the baya (*Ploceus philippinus*), makes the most intricate nests. Shaped like the pipe of a snake charmer, the nests have many chambers.

Baya bird's nest

AMPHIBIANS

Smallest frog

In February 2017, Indian scientists found seven new endemic species of *Nyctibatrachus*, or night frogs, which make insect-like calls. Four species of these nocturnal amphibians, including Vijayan's night frog *(Nyctibatrachus pulivijayani)*, were found in the Agasthyamala Biosphere Reserve (spread across several districts in Tamil Nadu and Kerala). They all measure around 12.2–15.4 mm (0.5–0.6 in.).

Largest frog

The Indian bullfrog (*Hoplobatrachus tigerinus*), found all over the country, can grow up to 15 cm (5.9 in.). Some weigh as much as 1 kg.

Flying frog

The Malabar gliding frog *(Rhacophorus malabaricus),* found in Karnataka and the Wayanad District of Kerala, glides from the top of a tree to the base of another using its concave body and webbed feet as a parachute.

Malabar gliding frog

Rarest frog

The black, narrow-mouthed Galaxy frog or Malabar frog or Kerala Hills frog (*Melanobatrachus indicus*), found in the Anaimalai Hills of the Western Ghats, inhabits moist evergreen forests at 1,220 m (4,000 ft) and is considered one of the rarest frogs in the country.

Galaxy frog

REPTILES

LIZARDS

Only flying lizards

Norvill's flying lizard (*Draco norvillii*), found in north-east India, and the Indian flying lizard (*Draco dussumieri*) in the Western Ghats and south India are endemic to India. Their average length is 23 cm (9 in.) and they can glide through the air for around 17 m (55 ft 9 in.).

Indian flying lizard in camouflage

BUTTERFLIES

Largest moth
The Indian atlas moth (*Attacus atlas*) is the largest moth in India and possibly in the world too. The average length of males is 16.7–27.1 cm (6.57 –10.67 in.) and females is 14.2–26.2 cm (5.59–10.31 in.).

Smallest butterfly
The grass jewel butterfly (*Freyeria trochylus*) has a wingspan of only 1.5 cm (0.6 in.).

Butterfly at the highest altitude

The blue Apollo (*Parnassius hardwickii*) is found at altitudes of 4,267–4,876 m (14,000–16,000 ft) in the Green Lake area at the base of Mt Kanchenjunga. This bluish white butterfly, with orange spots, has a wingspan of 4.5 cm (1.8 in.).

Biggest butterfly

The female golden birdwing (*Troides aeacus*) has a wingspan of 19.4 cm (7.6 in.) and was seen in Didihat, Uttarakhand. The male is much smaller with a wingspan of 10.6 cm (4.2 in.).

Water monitor lizard

Norvill's flying lizard

Largest lizard

The water monitor lizard (*Varanus salvator*) reaches a length of 2.5 m (8 ft 2 in.) and can weigh up to 14 kg. It is a carnivorous lizard of the Sundarbans, Odisha and the Andaman Islands. Land monitor lizards (*Varanus bengalensis*) also grow up to 61–175 cm (24–69 in.) from snout to tail end.

Longest tongue

The chameleon's (family Chamaeleonidae) tongue is three-fourths the length of its body (30 cm/11.8 in.) and has a viscid club-shaped tip. It can flick out its tongue and catch prey in 1/25th of a second.

Chameleon catching prey with its tongue

Longest tail in relation to body

The long-tailed grass lacertid (*Takydromus sexlineatus khasiensis*) measures only 5 cm (2 in.), but its tail is 35 cm (13.7 in.) long – a ratio of 1:7. It is found in the Khasi Hills of Meghalaya.

Only legless lizard

The Asian glass lizard or Burmese glass lizard (*Ophisaurus gracilis*) is found at altitudes of 820–1,500 m (2,690–4,920 ft) in Darjeeling, West Bengal, and the Khasi Hills, Meghalaya. It crawls and uses its tongue in a snake-like fashion.

GECKOS

Smallest gecko

A 4 cm (1.6 in.) Persian sand dwarf gecko (*Tropiocolotes persicus*), or the dwarf or pygmy gecko, was recorded in Rajasthan in 2011.

Largest gecko

The *Hemidactylus frenatus* or the common house gecko, found in Bihar, Bengal and north-east India, grows to around 34 cm (13.4 in.) in length. It feeds on insects, rats, birds and small snakes.

'Flying' gecko

The gliding gecko (*Ptychozoon kuhli*), found in the Nicobar Islands and north-east India, can glide over 13 m (43 ft). It has skin flaps on the side of its head, body and tail, which help it glide when the animal launches into the air.

Rarest gecko

The golden hill gecko (*Calodactylodes avreus*), found in the Tirumala Hills of Andhra Pradesh, is a very rare species. Its body is golden yellow with brown spots.

CROCODILES

Heaviest crocodile

The estuarine or saltwater crocodile (*Crocodylus porosus*) is the heaviest reptile in the country. The adult male crocodile may weigh around 1,000–1,300 kg while the adult female weighs around 76–100 kg.

Longest crocodile

The estuarine or saltwater crocodile grows to a recorded length of 7 m (23 ft). It is found in tidal estuaries, marine swamps and coastal waters in and around the Sundarbans, Odisha and the Andaman and Nicobar Islands.

First known white crocodile

Gori, an albino white crocodile, was artificially hatched at the Bhitarkanika Dangamal Crocodile Research Centre in Odisha on 26 June 1975.

Shortest crocodile

The mugger crocodile (*Crocodylus palustris*), found in streams, is only 3 m

(9 ft 10 in.) long. It is found almost all over India except at higher altitudes such as in the Himalayan mountains.

Rarest crocodile

The rarest of the three crocodile species found in India, the gharial (*Gavialus gangeticus*) grows to 6.25 m (20 ft 6 in.) and is the only living member of the family Gavialidae in India. The surviving population is found in the tributaries of the Ganga River like the Girwa (Uttar Pradesh), Son (Madhya Pradesh), Ramganga (Uttarakhand), Gandak (Bihar), Chambal (Uttar Pradesh, Madhya Pradesh, and Rajasthan) and the Mahanadi River (Odisha). It is classified as critically endangered by the International Union for the Conservation of Nature (IUCN).

First and largest crocodile bank

The Madras Crocodile Bank Trust and Centre for Herpetology, 40 km from Madras (now Chennai), Tamil Nadu was founded in 1976 by the naturalist Romulus Whitaker and had over 8,000 crocodiles of 10 different species.

Right: Romulus Whitaker; *below*: Madras Crocodile Bank Trust and Centre for Herpetology

Above: Mugger crocodile; *below*: Reticulated python

SNAKES

WR Longest snake

The reticulated python (*Python reticulatus*) is the longest snake in the world. It is found in the Nicobar Islands. The average length is between 3 and 6 m (10 and 20 ft). While the reticulated python prefers small mammals, it can take larger animals up to the size of a full-grown wild boar.

Longest sea snake

The yellow sea snake (*Hydrophis spiralis*) grows 1.8 m (6 ft) long. Specimens up to 3 m (10 ft) long are not uncommon. It is found both in the Bay of Bengal and the Arabian Sea.

Fastest snake

Rat snakes and bronze-back tree snakes can reach a speed of 10 km per hour.

Only snake with heat sensors

The pit viper (subfamily Crotalinae), found in the hilly parts of India, is able to locate warm- looded prey using two heat sensors between its nostrils and eyes.

Snake at the highest altitude

No other species of snake has been found at an altitude higher than the Himalayan pit viper (*Gloydius himalayanus*). Herpetologist Frank Wall (1868– 1950), who lived in Sri Lanka and India, claimed to have seen one at an altitude of 3,658 m (12,000 ft) in Kashmir and one was captured at the foot of the glacier at Dharamshala at an altitude of 4,877 m (16,000 ft).

First time discovery of new species

As per a study published in the Journal of Asia-Pacific Biodiversity, a team of seven researchers, Zeeshan Mirza, Soham Pattekar, Sourabh Verma, Bryan Stuart, Jayaditya Purkayastha, Pratyush Mohapatra, and Harshil Patel, discovered a new snake species, *Ahaetulla longirostris*, the long-snouted vine snake. The two specimens were discovered miles apart – in Bihar and in Meghalaya. It was only after a detailed analysis and DNA testing that the discovery of this new species, which can be bright green or orange brown in colour, could be confirmed.

Russell's viper

Ornate flying snake

Only 'flying' snake

The ornate flying snake (*Chrysopelea ornata*) is capable of gliding by launching itself from a height. An instance of this species gliding for a distance of 50 m (164 ft) has been recorded. This snake inhabits the hilly forests of the southwest and the north-east, besides the Andaman Islands.

Only snake that builds a nest

The female king cobra (*Ophiophagus hannah*) is the only snake that builds a nest and is found in the Western Ghats, parts of north India, eastern India, the north-east and the Andaman Islands. It builds a 30 cm (11.8 in.) nest by scraping leaves, weeds and loose vegetation together.

Loudest hiss

Russell's viper (*Daboia russelii*) hisses the loudest among all Indian snakes – nearly as loud as the hiss of a pressure cooker.

King cobra

TORTOISES AND TURTLES

Largest rookery

The 12 km long sandy beach in the Gahirmatha region of Odisha is one of the largest rookeries for marine sea turtles. During February and March, olive ridley turtles (*Lepidochelys olivacea*) come out here in hundreds of thousands to mate and nest. The olive ridley is one of the seven endangered species of turtles in the world due to the disturbance and destruction of their habitat.

Olive Ridleys galore!

Between 23 February and 2 March, Odisha's Ganjam District saw the arrival of a record 6.37 lakh Olive Ridley turtles for mass nesting. This huge number was attributed to the emergence of new beaches that remained unaffected by extreme weather conditions. These turtles, labelled as vulnerable by the IUCN, dig holes in the sand using their flippers, lay eggs, and cover them before returning to the sea. The eggs hatch after 40–60 days and the hatchlings make their way back into the sea. The Gahirmatha Beach in the Kendrapara District of Odisha also sees the arrival of turtles and is known as the world's largest rookery.

Rarest freshwater turtle

India's rarest freshwater turtle is considered to be the Assam leaf turtle (*Cyclemys dentata*), found in the hill streams of Assam. It grows to a length of around 24 cm (9.4 in.).

Smallest tortoise

The Indian star tortoise (*Geochelone elegans*) grows to a length of around 15 cm (5.9 in.).

Smallest carapace

The Cochin cane forest turtle (*Vijayachelys silvatica*) has a carapace that is 13 cm (5.1 in.) long.

Largest turtle

The leatherback sea turtle (*Dermochelys coriacea*) has a shell length averaging 2.5 m (8 ft) and weighs 700 kg. It feeds mainly on jellyfish.

Largest terrapin

The Batagur terrapin (*Batagur baska*), found in the river estuaries of the Sundarbans, West Bengal, is the largest terrapin and a critically endangered species. The carapace of this terrapin is 59 cm (23 in.) long.

Below: Leatherback sea turtle; *bottom*: Batagur terrapin

FISH AND MOLLUSCS

Oldest freshwater fish

Fossil remains of the Dipnoi subclass of fish or lungfish (*Ceratodus agassiz*) were found in the Maleri beds of the Godavari Valley in the late Triassic period (237–201.3 million years ago). The genus *Ceratodus* evolved in the northern hemisphere in the early Triassic period (251–247 million years ago).

Lightest/smallest fish 

The dwarf pygmy goby (*Pandaka pygmaea*) is 1 cm (0.39 in.) long and weighs 4–5 mg.

Only fish with suction plates

The remora or suckerfish (family Echeneidae) can swim but is usually found attached to sharks, turtles, dolphins and even ships. The first dorsal fin is modified into a suction apparatus, and the erection of the plate where the fish joins its host creates a vacuum, enabling the fish to stay attached.

Only fish without a bony skeleton

Sharks (and their relatives, the guitarfish and swordfish) do not have a bony skeleton. They have cartilage or gristle. They are predominantly marine fish with a few freshwater representatives.

WR Largest recorded subterranean fish

A fish measuring around 45 cm (17.7 in.) was discovered in a cave in Meghalaya in February 2019. It was discovered by Daniel Harries, a biologist from Heriot-Watt University in Edinburgh, UK.

Shortest-living fish

Small fish such as the *Pandaka pygmaea* and those from the families Oreichthys and Gambusia (such as mosquito fish) live hardly for a year.

Longest-living fish

The common carp, a freshwater fish that is found in ponds, lakes and large rivers, is said to live for over 50 years if left alone.

WR Largest recorded cave fish 

Inside a secluded cave in the Jaintia Hills of Meghalaya, the largest species of cave fish in the world – growing to a length of about 40 cm, or around one and a half feet, was discovered. In February 2019, a group of researchers from India and around the world discovered the fish, which is linked to the Golden Mahseer. It has no eyes and is white because it lacks melanin pigmentation. It is the largest troglobitic fish recorded so far.

Only anadromous fish

Hilsa (*Tenualosa ilisha*) is India's only anadromous fish, which migrates from the sea or estuarine waters up rivers for breeding. This fish is found mostly in the Gangetic estuary.

Only male fish producing young

Seahorses (Genus *Hippocampus*) are predominantly marine. The male fish carries a kangaroo-like pouch in its belly. The female passes her eggs into this pouch where the father incubates them. The young are thus born from the father.

Largest clam

The giant clam (*Tridacna gigas*) grows to a length of 1 m (3 ft 3.4 in.) and weighs over 100 kg. This clam has been exploited throughout its Asia-Pacific range, but is fortunately plentiful in the coral reefs of the Andaman and Nicobar Islands.

Heaviest fish

The whale shark *(Rhincodon typus)* is the largest and heaviest shark in India, weighing up to 60 tonnes.

Left: Hilsa; *centre*: Giant clam; *bottom*: Whale shark

PLANTS

Oldest plant fossils

Fossils, which are 1.6 billion years old and appear to contain red algae, were found embedded in mats of cyanobacteria in phosphaterich sedimentary rocks in Chitrakoot in central India, in May 2017. Until this discovery, the oldest known red algae were 1.2 billion years old.

Fastest-maturing trees

The eucalyptus and the subabul (*Leucaena leucocephala*) trees mature very fast and are both ready for cutting in 6–7 years.

Tallest trees

The fir (*Abies pindrow*) and deodar (*Cedrus deodara*) grow to an average height of 76.2 m (250 ft).

Biggest tree trunk

The deodar (*Cedrus deodara*) found in Jammu and Kashmir, Himachal Pradesh, and Uttarakhand have trunks with a circumference of around 12 m (39 ft 4 in.) or more.

Largest hollow tree

A baobab or monkey-bread tree (*Adansonia digitata*), which is a species of African origin, stands amid the ruins of the eastern part of the historic Golconda Fort near Hyderabad, Telangana. Reportedly, its 3.3 sq. m (35.5 sq. ft) hollow trunk can comfortably accommodate 10–12 people.

Largest tree canopy

A banyan tree identified in Anantapur District of Andhra Pradesh in 1988, by freelance photographers 'Regret Iyer' and K.S. Ramakrishna from Bangalore (now Bengaluru), Karnataka, was reported to have a canopy covering 2.1 hectares (5.19 acres) and was believed to be over 600 years old.

Banyan Tree

Longest-living tree species

The banyan tree (*Ficus benghalensis*), found in most parts of India, is known to have lived for more than 250 years.

Plants at the highest altitude

- The *Ermania himalayensis* grows at 6,000 m (19,685 ft) in the Himalayas.
- *Christolea himalayensis*, a herb usually about 10–15 cm (3.9–5.9 in.) tall, is found at 5,000–6,000 m (16,404–19,685 ft).

Longest creeper

The elephant creeper (*Argyreia nervosa*) grows to a length of 1.5 km, making it the longest creeper in the country and one of the longest in the world.

Above: Elephant creeper; *below*: Water lily leaves

Largest family of plants

The Family Poaceae is the largest plant family in the country, and is represented by as many as 263 genera and 1,291 species. Poaceae or Gramineae is a ubiquitous family of monocotyledonous flowering plants known as grass. The Poaceae family includes cereal grass, bamboo and grasses of natural grasslands as well as the grasses of cultivated lawns and pastures.

Rare flowering

Found in southern and eastern India, the talipot palm (*Corypha umbraculifera*) flowers once in 25–80 years and then dies.

Heaviest fruit

The jackfruit tree (*Artocarpus heterophyllus*) is planted (but also grows wild) in the Western Ghats and elsewhere in India. The tree bears fruit of enormous size – weighing up to 40 kg.

Lightest wood

Balsa (*Ochroma lagopus*) has a specific gravity of 0.12 to 0.15.

Heaviest wood

Anjan (*Hardwickia binata*) wood is the heaviest, with a specific gravity of 0.61–0.73.

Dragon bamboo

Tallest bamboo/grass

The tallest bamboo (*Dendrocalamus giganteus*), known as dragon bamboo, is found in Assam and West Bengal. It grows up to 40 m (130 ft) with a diameter of around 20–25 cm (8–10 in.).

Largest leaf

The leaf of the water lily (*Victoria amazonica*) may measure up to 1.5 m (5 ft) in diameter.

MEGHALAYA – Halfway to Heaven

Only double-decker living root bridge

Located in Nongriat village near Cherrapunji, Meghalaya, the only double-decker living root bridge in India is formed by guiding the aerial roots of rubber fig trees (*Ficus elastica*) across streams. With two levels of intertwined roots, it is over 150 years old and continues to serve the Khasi community and visitors during the monsoon.

Cleanest river

The Umngot River in Meghalaya, also known as the Dawki River, with its crystal-clear waters where boats appear to float on air, is the cleanest river in India. Originating in the Shillong-Peak region and forming a natural boundary between the Khasi and Jaintia Hills, it passes through Mawlynnong village – which is considered Asia's cleanest village. Local communities, known as the 'Keepers of Umngot', protect it by banning destructive fishing, enforcing heavy fines, and promoting sustainable practices, ensuring the river's pristine beauty and ecological balance remain intact.

Bio-engineering marvel
Bio-engineering is the application of biological processes and living systems to create sustainable solutions for human needs. The living root bridges of Meghalaya illustrate this principle, as they are grown and strengthened naturally over decades, making them resilient, eco-friendly structures that improve with age and integrate seamlessly with the environment.

River cave with most limestone dams
Krem Chympe, located in the Jaintia Hills of Meghalaya, is a resurgence river cave noted for having the most limestone dams (*gours*) in India. The cave contains over 50 such dams, some rising up to 11–12 m, which create a series of striking underground lakes. These crystal-clear pools, some as deep as 8 m, are interconnected by long river passages, making Krem Chympe both a geological wonder and one of India's most fascinating cave systems.

CONSERVING NATURE AND WILDLIFE

Oldest botanical garden

The Acharya Jagadish Chandra Bose Indian Botanic Garden was established in 1787 in Shibpur, Howrah, near Kolkata in West Bengal. It has about 12,000 living plants and 2.5 million dried plant specimens in the herbarium, from all over the world. The garden covers 276.75 acres (112 hectares) in 25 sections.

Oldest zoos

- Raja Rajendra Mallick Bahadur started the Marble Palace Aviary and Zoo in Calcutta (now Kolkata), West Bengal, in 1854 specifically for the education and entertainment of the public.
- The Thiruvananthapuram Zoological Gardens in Kerala is said to have been set up by Maharaja Swathi Thirunal in 1859. Spread over 30 acres (12 hectares), it is the oldest extant zoo.

First conservation organization

The Indian Board for Wildlife (IBWL), with S. Dharmakumar Sinhji as its vice chairman, was set up in 1952 by the Government of India. It was replaced by the National Board for Wildlife (NBWL) in September 2003.

First marine reserve

The Marine National Park and Sanctuary in Jamnagar District, Gujarat, forms the first marine reserve in India. Including Pirotan Island and other islands, it was given the status of a national park in 1980. It is rich in corals, octopuses, giant snails, sponges, crabs, lobsters and fish.

First virtual herbarium

Since February 2017, a virtual digital herbarium of specimens preserved in the Kerala Forest Research Institute at Peechi in Thrissur District, Kerala, can be accessed at the URL http://kfriherbarium.in.

Tallest flower

- The gigantic Himalayan rhubarb (*Rheum nobile*) grows 0.9–1.2 m (3–4 ft) long and is the tallest native species. It is found even at 4,268 m (14,000 ft) in the Himalayan ranges.
- The corpse flower (*Amorphophallus titanum*) or 'titan arum', though not a native species, is the tallest flower (2.4 m/7 ft 10 in.) in India, and the largest by diameter (more than 1 m/3 ft 3.3 in.).

Right: The gigantic Himalayan rhubarb; *far right*: Corpse flower

Oldest NGO to be engaged in conservation and biodiversity research

On 15 September 1883, eight men established the Bombay Natural History Society at the then Victoria and Albert Museum (now Dr Bhau Daji Lad Museum) in Bombay (now Mumbai), Maharashtra. It was established to exchange information on natural history and exhibit interesting specimens. They were E.H. Aitken, Dr G.A. Maconochie, Dr D. MacDonald, J. C. Anderson, Colonel C. Swinhoe, J. Johnston, Dr Atmaram Pandurang and Dr Sakharam Arjun, along with H.M. Phipson.

First national park

Jim Corbett National Park (earlier Hailey National Park and then Ramganga National Park), established in 1936, stretches over 521 sq. km across the two hill districts of Pauri Garhwal and Nainital, Uttarakhand. It is home to around 110 tree species, 50 species of mammals, 580 bird species, and 25 species of reptiles. It was the first to come under the Project Tiger initiative. The elevation of the park ranges from 400 m to 1,200 m (1,300 ft to 4,000 ft).

First wildlife magazine
Indian Wildlife was published by Jim Corbett in the 1930s.

Highest national park
The Kanchenjunga Biosphere Reserve or the Khangchendzonga National Park in Sikkim is the highest national park at 8,585 m (28,166 ft) above mean sea level.

Largest camera trap tiger census
India's tiger census of 2018 became the largest camera trap wildlife survey in the world. Camera traps (outdoor photographic devices fitted with motion sensors that start recording when an animal passes by) were placed in 26,838 locations across 141 different sites and surveyed an effective area of 121,337 sq. km as part of the survey. Individual tigers (excluding cubs numbering 2,461) were identified using the stripe pattern recognition software from the photographs clicked by camera traps.

Largest zoological park
Arignar Anna Zoological Park at Vandalur, near Chennai, Tamil Nadu, is the largest zoological park in South Asia. Spread over 602 hectares (1,487.57 acres), it has more than 100 species of birds, 50 species of mammals, and 20 species of reptiles.

State and UT with most national parks
Madhya Pradesh leads with 10 national parks, with an area of 365,725 sq. km dedicated to them. Andaman and Nicobar Islands follow with nine national parks across 115,394 sq. km.

State and UT with the most wildlife sanctuaries
Andaman and Nicobar Islands have 96 wildlife sanctuaries (389.39 sq. km) and Maharashtra has 46 (7,592.3 sq. km).

Largest collection of bamboo species
Prashant Atmaram Date, a bamboo farmer and entrepreneur from Lakhalgaon Village, Nashik Taluk and District, Maharashtra, has the largest collection of bamboo species in the country. He has a total of 94 species of 22 genera in one place called 'Date Bambusetum', where they are placed in flowerpots. Different species have been collected from bamboo-growing states for conservation away from their place of origin.

GARDENING

Tallest bougainvillea
Prof. Dr Ramesh Babu has grown a 10.33 m (33 ft 11 in.) tall *Bougainvillea spectabilis* in his garden in Bengaluru, Karnataka. The over 16-year-old bougainvillea with white blossoms had a spread of 6.09 m (20 ft) and a base girth of 0.2 m (7.8 in.) as on 29 January 2020. Normally, bougainvillea grows to an average height of 6.09 m (20 ft).

Tallest prickly amaranth plant
In August 2017, T. Damodar and his wife Shobha T. Damodar from Belagavi, Karnataka, grew the tallest prickly amaranth plant (*Amaranthus spinosus*), which measured 4.03 m (13 ft 3 in.) in height. Normally this plant grows to a height of 0.3 m to 2.43 m (1–8 ft).

Biggest lemon
K. Mohanchandran from Kothanur, Bengaluru, Karnataka, grew a lemon measuring 28 cm x 14 cm (11 in. x 5.5 in.) in his garden. The lemon had a circumference of 49 cm (19.2 in.) and weighed 2.365 kg on 22 February 2020.

Longest mango leaf
A mango tree with a leaf measuring 61 cm (2 ft) was found at the primary school of Budapur in Varanasi, Uttar Pradesh, by Dr Bhola Vishwakarma, one of the school teachers, on 30 October 2018.

Largest taro leaf
A taro (*Colocasia esculenta*) leaf measuring 76.0 cm x 64.5 cm (2 ft 5.9 in. x 2 ft 1.39 in.) was cultivated in Boudhgarh, Boudh District, Odisha, by Jayaram Rana on 7 January 2020.

Tallest rose plant
Arunsinh Solanki grew a rose plant 11.88 m (39 ft) tall at his home in Godhra in Gujarat, as recorded on 13 May 2019.

Tallest jamun tree
Prof. Dr Ramesh Babu from Bengaluru, Karnataka, has the tallest *jamun* tree (*Syzygium cumini*) in his garden. On 20 June 2019, the 15-year-old tree was 11.9 m (39 ft) tall with a spread of 6 m (20 ft) and a base girth of 1.04 m (41 in.). The average height of a jamun tree is 9.1–10.6 m (30–35 ft).

Longest money plant
Sapna Popli from Lucknow, Uttar Pradesh, grew the longest money plant

Longest money plant

COASTAL WATER QUALITY INDEX

Moderate · Good · Very Good

2020-21
Out of 9 Coastal States, Number of States in the category of

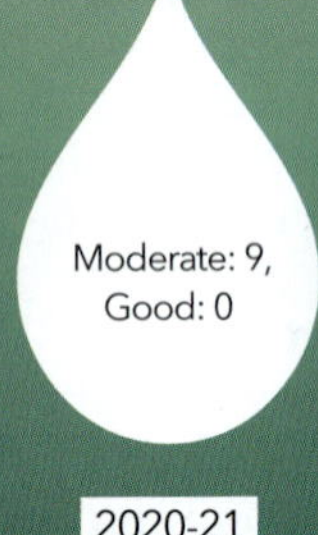

2021-22
Out of 8 Coastal States, Number of States in the category of

Moderate: 8
Good: 1

2022-23
Out of 13 Coastal States/UTs, Number of States/UTs in the category of

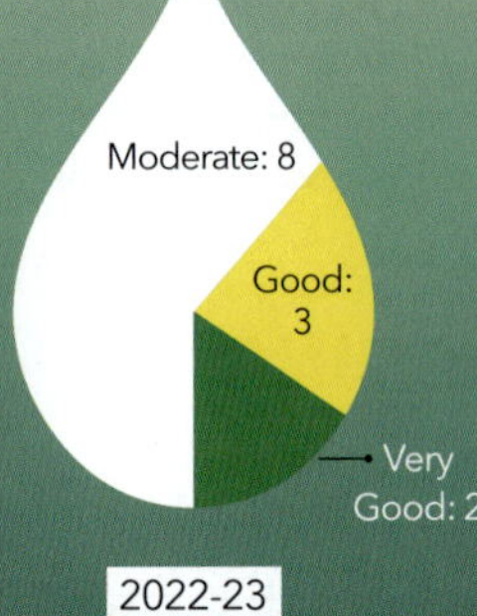

2023-24
Out of 12 Coastal States/UTs, Number of States/UTs in the category of

Moderate: 10
Good: 2

2024-25
Out of 12 Coastal States/UTs, Number of States/UTs in the category of

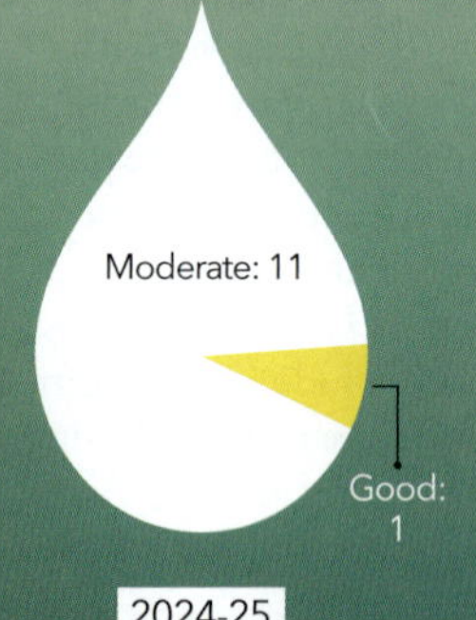

Source: Sustainable Development Goals National Indicator Framework Progress Report 2025, Ministry of Statistics and Programme Implementation, Government of India

PERCENTAGE CHANGE IN CARBON STOCK IN FOREST COVER

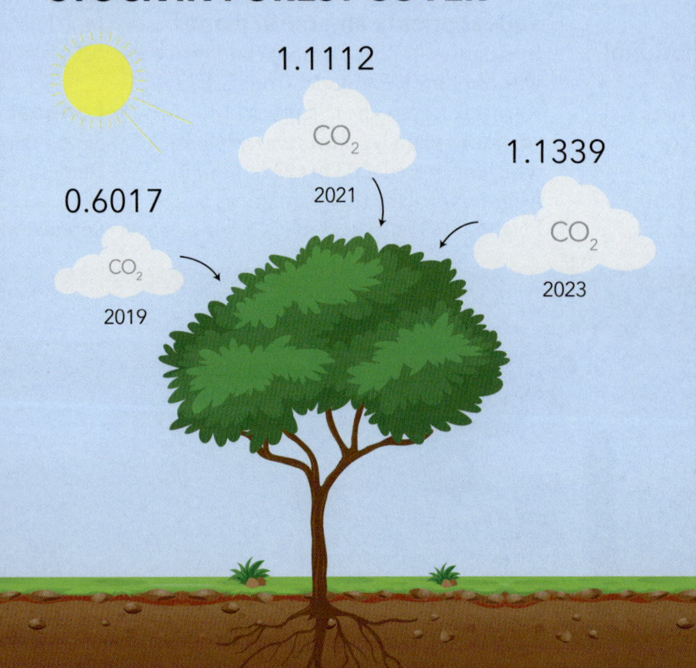

Source: Sustainable Development Goals National Indicator Framework Progress Report 2025, Ministry of Statistics and Programme Implementation, Government of India

in her home. As on 21 April 2023, the length of the stem measured 38.4 ft (460.8 in.).

Tallest coriander plant

Dalbir Maan grew a 2.28 m (7 ft 6 in.) tall coriander plant at his home in Melbourne, Australia, as recorded on 18 November 2020.

Longest drumstick

Longest Drumstick

Rekha K.N. from Kochi, Kerala, grew the longest drumstick (*Moringa oleifera*) on her drumstick tree. As on 17 April 2023, the drumstick measured 116.84 cm (46 in.).

Longest tapioca plant

Satheesha Nayak an anatomy professor at the Manipal Academy of Higher Education, Udupi, Karnataka, has grown the longest tapioca (cassava) plant, measuring 16.76 m (55 ft 10 in.), as on 30 January 2022, in his kitchen garden. The plant is about three years old and was provided support on an adjoining mango tree.

Tallest drumstick tree

Prof. Dr Ramesh Babu from Bengaluru, Karnataka, has the tallest drumstick tree (*Moringa oleifera*) growing in his residential garden. On 20 June 2019, the 11-year-old tree was 8.2 m (26 ft 11 in.) tall with a spread of 3.66 m (12 ft) and a base girth of 47.6 cm (1 ft 6.74 in.). The average height of a drumstick tree is 6.1 m (20 ft).

Tallest musk mallow plant

A.K. Narayanan from Thrissur, Kerala, had, in his garden, a three-year-old musk mallow plant, 2.74 m (9 ft) tall as in June 2016.

Longest green chilli

Krishnalal L.S. of Thiruvananthapuram, Kerala, grew the longest green chilli, measuring 31 cm (12.1 in.) in his terrace garden in February 2020. He used a home-made nutrient mixture or organic and natural material for pest control while maintaining the nutrient grade of the soil.

ENVIRONMENT AND SUSTAINABILITY

First state/UT to place a ban on plastic bags

Sikkim became the first state to ban plastic bags in 1998. Local communities in Yuksom Village were upset by the harmful impact of plastics on the environment and formed the Khangchendzonga Conservation Committee (KCC), which banned plastic bags and bottles in 1996 and collected around 800 kg of plastic waste from trails and trek routes. Encouraged by their success, the state government announced a statewide ban on plastic bags on 4 June 1998.

First forest healing centre

India's first forest healing centre was inaugurated on 7 March 2021 in Ranikhet, Uttarakhand. Spread across an area of around 13 acres (5.26 hectares), it was developed by the research wing of the Uttarakhand Forest Department as a space where visitors can take walks, hug trees and engage in calming activities such as meditation and sky-gazing. The centre draws inspiration from the Japanese therapy of forest bathing (*shinrinyoku*) and ancient Indian traditions.

WR First country to have a cooling action plan

The India Cooling Action Plan (ICAP) is the first cooling action plan in the world. It addresses cooling requirements across all sectors to reduce direct and indirect emissions. ICAP aims to balance socioeconomic and environmental needs while reducing refrigerant transition and cooling demand, enhancing energy efficiency and evolving better technology options.

First green village

Khonoma Village, located in the Sechu-Zubza Subdivision of Kohima District, Nagaland, has become the country's first 'green village'. The first steps were taken by setting up the Khonoma Nature Conservation and Tragopan Sanctuary in 1998, leading to a ban on hunting in a 20 sq. km area. Ecological studies suggest that the village has 250 plant species, 204 species of trees, 45 varieties of orchids, and 19 varieties of bamboo.

Khonoma village, Nagaland

RENEWABLE ENERGY SHARE IN TOTAL INSTALLED ELECTRICITY GENERATION

Source: Sustainable Development Goals National Indicator Framework Progress Report 2025, Ministry of Statistics and Programme Implementation, Government of India

PERCENTAGE OF INDUSTRIES COMPLYING WITH ENVIRONMENTAL STANDARDS

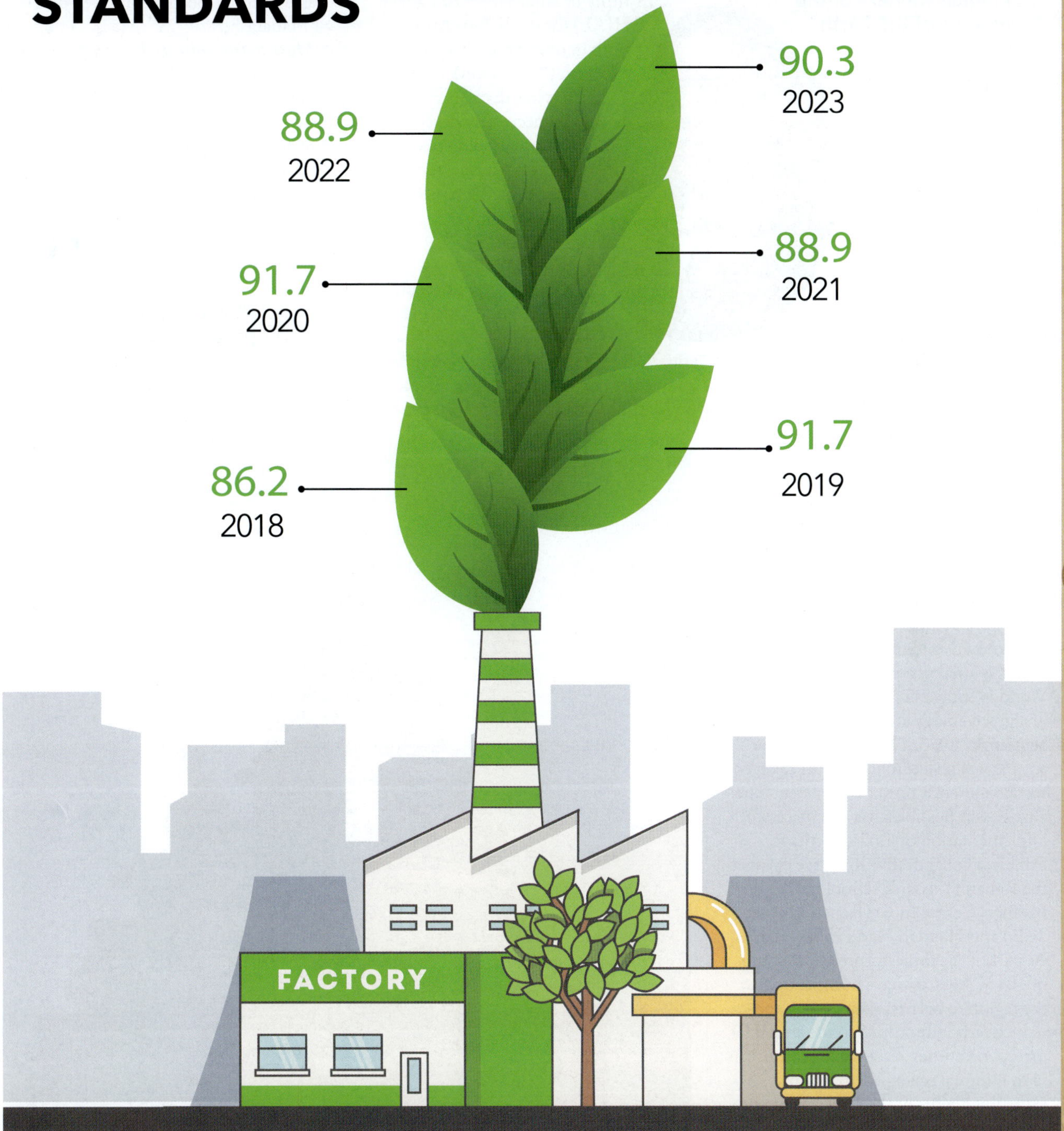

Source: Sustainable Development Goals National Indicator Framework Progress Report 2025, Ministry of Statistics and Programme Implementation, Government of India

The fauna includes 25 varieties of snakes, kinds of lizards, 11 types of amphibians, and 196 bird species, including the Blyth's tragopan, which is categorized as vulnerable on the IUCN Red List.

First Indian winners of the Champions of the Earth Award

Tulsi Tanti, chairman and managing director of the wind turbine manufacturer Suzlon Energy Ltd, was the first Indian recipient of the Champions of the Earth Award in 2009 in the 'entrepreneurial vision' category. Since then, India has won five more awards. The latest recipients of the awards were Prime Minister Narendra Modi for policy leadership and the fully solar-powered Cochin International Airport for 'entrepreneurial vision' in 2018. The award is given by the United Nations Environment Programme.

Tulsi Tanti

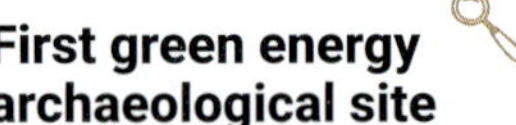

First green energy archaeological site

The Shore Temple in Mahabalipuram (also known as Mamallapuram), Tamil Nadu, is a seventh-century UNESCO World Heritage site that became India's first green energy archaeological site in September 2023. This means that the temple will be illuminated with clean and sustainable solar power completely. The change was possible after the successful implementation of Green Heritage Project, a collaborative initiative between the Renault Nissan Technology & Business Centre India (Renault Nissan Tech) and Hand in Hand India (HiH). As part of the project, three solar plants of 10 kW capacity have been set up in the region to harness solar energy and reduce carbon footprint in the area. The project promotes sustainable ecotourism with minimal ecological footprint. Other highlights of the Green Heritage Project at the temple include women operated electric buggies, solar-operated reverse osmosis plant that provides clean drinking water, dedicated parking shed with three charging units for electric vehicles among others.

WR First solar-heated tent

Considered to be the first in the world, a 10-seater portable tent that can be heated using solar panels was built by engineer and innovator Sonam Wangchuk along with the Himalayan Institute of Alternatives of Ladakh (HIAL) for the Indian Army. Built in four weeks at a cost of ₹5 lakh (0.5 million), the tent weighs less than 30 kg and was specifically developed for Indian soldiers and army personnel serving in areas with very low temperatures.

Most waste collected – beach clean-up – single day

The Maharashtra Navnirman Paryavaran Sena, headquartered in Matunga, Mumbai, Maharashtra, set three records in waste collection on 11 December 2021, based on data available from 16 local governmental bodies:

- ***Most waste collected – multiple venues*:** 13,194 registered volunteers, among others, collected 59.2 tonnes of waste from 37 locations in seven districts of Maharashtra.
- ***Most waste collected – single venue*:** Volunteers collected 27 tonnes of waste from a single location – Uttan Beach, Bhavander, Thane District, Maharashtra.
- ***Most participants in a waste collection campaign – multiple venues*:** The clean-up campaign saw the participation of 13,194 registered volunteers across 37 locations in seven districts of Maharashtra.

WR Plog run with most participants

The biggest plog run (combining jogging with picking up litter – from Swedish *plockaupp*) was organized on Gandhi

Shore Temple in Mahabalipuram

Seeds for a Greener Tomorrow

Most seedballs rolled
2 Tamil Nadu Air Squadron NCC, Coimbatore, Tamil Nadu, prepared 75,000 seedballs in three hours from 8:00 am to 11:00 pm on 16 March 2025 at Dr Mahalingam College of Engineering and Technology, Pollachi, Coimbatore. The seedballs were prepared by 300 NCC cadets with each seedball measuring between 3 cm and 5 cm in diameter.

Jayanti on 2 October 2018 from 55 locations of Bengaluru, Karnataka. Plastic waste weighing 6.5 tonnes (6,500 kg), including bottles and litter, was collected by 6,518 participants in four hours from 7:00 a.m. to 11:00 a.m. The participants, representing five organizations – BBMP (Bruhat Bengaluru Mahanagara Palike), Go Native, Namma Nimma Cycle Foundation, Let's Be the Change, United Way Bengaluru – and an individual, Ramakrishna Ganesh, created awareness on urban cleanliness by proper disposal of waste, especially plastic.

Tallest scrap-metal structure – solo

Sandeep Pisalkar from Vadodara, Gujarat, created a replica of the iconic Eiffel Tower, measuring 21.33 m (70 ft) in height, with 40 tonnes (4,000 kg) of automobile scrap. The three levels of the structure were created separately and then assembled with the help of a crane. The material used included petrol tanks from trucks, C-channels, angles and clutch plates. It was exhibited at the Waste to Wonder Park, New Delhi, in February 2019.

Eiffel Tower replica, Waste to Wonder Park, New Delhi

Most trees planted – 15 mins

Under the supervision of the National Service Scheme (NSS) Programme Officer Shyam Sunder of the Government Dungar College, Bikaner, Rajasthan, a total of 1,05,000 saplings were planted at three locations in Gajsukhdesar Village in 3 min 50 sec by a team of 15,000 participants comprising NSS volunteers, schoolchildren and villagers on 4 August 2008. The total land covered under the plantation was 1,200 bighas (300 hectares).

Most trees planted – 1 hour

As part of the Green India Challenge, an initiative by J. Santhosh Kumar, a member of Parliament (Rajya Sabha) from Telangana, 3,54,900 trees were planted in 1 hr on 4 July 2021 in Durga Nagar, Adilabad, Telangana. The 16,900 people involved in the plantation drive planted 21 trees each.

Most trees planted – single day

The Department of Forests and Wildlife, Uttar Pradesh, planted 258,747,661 saplings in a day on 5 July 2020, with the participation of various departments of the state as well as the general public. Starting at 5:55 a.m., the plantation work at selected plantation sites in all 75 districts concluded at 6:00 p.m. This was part of their larger campaign for tree plantation.

Most trees planted – in a quarter

The Maharashtra Forest Department, with the support of individual volunteers, planted 35,13,76,361 seedlings across the state between 1 July and 30 September 2019. The plantation work was done by 9,51,963.5 million people at 23,986.8 million plantation sites. To integrate the work of the forest department, the government hosted a Plantation Monitoring Information System (PMIS) and captured the plantation data of forest and non-forest agencies.

Most saplings distributed – single day

The Department of Environment, Forest and Climate Change and the Department of Tourism, Government of Uttar Pradesh, along with the Prayagraj District Administration, Uttar Pradesh, distributed 76,824 saplings on 9 August 2019. This was part of their larger campaign for tree plantation.

Largest single rooftop solar plant – by area

On 17 May 2016, a rooftop solar power plant was inaugurated at the Dera Baba Jaimal Singh (Radha Soami sect) premises at Beas, Amritsar District, Punjab. Spread over 42 acres (17 ha),

the plant is the largest single rooftop facility and can generate 11.5 MW of electricity. The solar panels are laid over 82 acres (33.18 hectares) on eight rooftops and the project is planned to cater to 8,000 households.

Largest biogas plant – by capacity

As a step towards clean and green energy, Asia's largest compressed biogas (CBG) plant with a total capacity of 33.23 tonnes CBG per day was commissioned on 12 August 2022 at Bhuttal Kalan village in Sangrur District, Punjab.

First railway station with Green Building Certification

Kevadia railway station in Gujarat, from whose third level platform one can view the Statue of Unity, is India's first railway station with a Green Building Certification by the Indian Green Building Council (IGBC). The railway station features LED lights and star-rated branded electrical appliances to save electricity; water management through rainwater harvesting; a sewage treatment plant; waterless eco-urinals; and drip irrigation. Additionally, the segregated green waste will be reused to produce fertilizers.

Widest scrap-metal structure – group

The Home Designers organization from Jodhpur, Rajasthan, created the widest replica of a blue whale, measuring 104 ft (31.7 m) in width from scrap metal. The team comprised 100 people who began work on the structure on 6 January 2023. It took 10 days to complete the structure.

Tallest scrap-metal structure – group

A group of 120 students, training to be fitters, welders, electricians, plumbers, and painters at the Government ITI in Berhampur, Ganjam District, Odisha, created the tallest scrap-metal structure, a 21.33 m (70 ft) tall guitar, over a period of three months from 17 July 2019. The 'Best out of waste' mission sought to integrate skill development with waste management in an ecofriendly manner. The guitar was exhibited at the open-air Scrap Sculpture Museum of the ITI, along with 10 other smaller sculptures, which were also created from waste.

CLEANEST IN INDIA!

Cleanest city(s)

The Swachh Survekshan Awards 2024–2025 ranked Indore in Madhya Pradesh as the cleanest city of the country for the eighth time in a row. Indore was followed by Surat in Gujarat and Navi Mumbai in Maharashtra for the second and third positions respectively.

Aerial view of Indore, Madhya Pradesh

TRANSPORT

34
57
34 9

AIR

First flight

On 18 February 1911, Henri Pequet flew a Humber-Sommer biplane carrying mail from Allahabad (now Prayagraj), Uttar Pradesh, to Naini Junction. It flew a distance of 10 km. However, proper and official civil aviation began on 15 October 1932, when aviator and industrialist J.R.D. Tata flew 2,092 km on the aircraft D.H. *Puss Moth*. The flight took place under the aegis of Tata Air Services. It delivered mail from the Drigh Road Aerodrome in Karachi (now in Pakistan) to Juhu Aerodrome in Bombay (now Mumbai), Maharashtra, and then continued to Madras (now Chennai).

Humber-Sommer biplane

First airline

Tata Airlines, set up by J.R.D. Tata soon after he piloted India's maiden civil flight in 1932, was later converted into a public company in 1946 under the name Air India Ltd, with him as its chairman. In March 1953, it was raised to be a public corporation and became Air India. The state-run carrier was privatized to the Tata Group in 2021.

First airfield

The grass aerodrome at Juhu in Mumbai opened in 1932. It was the base for Tata Airlines.

First pilot licence

J.R.D. Tata; an aviator, entrepreneur, and chairman of Tata Group; became the first licensed pilot in India when he received his pilot licence No. 1 in 1929.

First flying club

The Aero Club was established in Mumbai by industrial magnate Sir Victor Sassoon in 1928. In September 1929, the club was affiliated to the Royal Aero Club, UK. It was recognized by the Government of India as the coordinating body for flying clubs in India. In 1948, the club was affiliated to the Federation Aeronautique Internationale.

First aircraft designer

S.V. Setty, an assistant engineer with the Public Works Department, Mysore, Karnataka, in 1911–12, designed, piloted and helped manufacture planes at Avro (a British company). With an eight cylinder engine, the Avro biplane had a 9.76 m (32 ft) span and weighed 362.8 kg without a pilot or passenger. The plane touched a speed of around 72–80 km/hr.

First air varsity

The Central Training Establishment in Hyderabad (now in Telangana), an independent training centre of Indian Airlines Ltd, was upgraded to a deemed university in 1997. The centre is equipped with infrastructure and training facilities for courses in civil aviation.

First aeronautical society

On 17 December 1948, the Aeronautical Society of India was inaugurated at Bengaluru to promote advancement in the field of aeronautics and dissemination of knowledge about aeronautical science and aircraft engineering to the public.

Avro Biplane

Juhu Aerodrome

The Malabar Princess

First international flight

The *Malabar Princess*, an Air India passenger flight, with Captain K.R. Guzder in command, flew from Bombay to London, UK, via Cairo (Egypt), and Geneva (Switzerland), on 8 June 1948, carrying 35 passengers.

First helicopter school

Hindustan Aeronautics Ltd (HAL), based in Bangalore (now Bengaluru), Karnataka, established a training school on 1 May 2000 for potential aviators to obtain commercial as well as private helicopter pilot licences.

First air ticket booking office

The first air ticket booking office was opened in 1939 in a building in the Churchgate Reclamation area in Bombay. The space now houses the Asiatic Department Store.

First crash

On 17 July 1950, a DC-3 aircraft was recorded to have crashed near Pathankot, Punjab, tragically killing all 22 passengers.

First radio plane

The twin-engine aeroplane called *de Havilland DH-89 Dragon Rapide*, which was on the Karachi– Bombay–Colombo route, was equipped with wireless transmission facilities on 1 December 1937.

First cargo service

An air cargo service started on 21 May 1927 between Calcutta (now Kolkata), West Bengal, and Bagdogra in Darjeeling District of West Bengal by West Bengal Air Transport, which operated for only a week.

First air freight service

Air Freight Pvt. Ltd was set up in 1945 as handling agents for Tata Airlines and Air India International. It was also the first air cargo clearing agent.

First indigenous helicopter

The advanced light helicopter (ALH) was built at HAL, Bangalore, in 1992. The ALH was used both in defence and civil operations.

First indigenous aircraft

The Hindustan Trainer-2, built by Hindustan Aeronautics Ltd (HAL), Bangalore, made its maiden flight in August 1951. Meant for military use, it was also used by flying schools.

First air traffic control system

A state-of-the-art Air Traffic Control (ATC) system, supported by Raytheon flight data and equipped with radar-processing hardware, was installed at the Indira Gandhi International Airport (IGIA), New Delhi, on 14 January 1999. It provided three-dimensional radial, bearing, and height information regarding the location and situation of any aircraft within a range of 250 nautical miles.

First heliport

India's first heliport was inaugurated at Rohini, Delhi, on 28 February 2017. Built by Pawan Hans Ltd, it is spread over an area of 25 acres (10.12 hectares) and has 4 hangars, 9 parking bays, and a terminal building that has a capacity of 150 passengers. The first such facility

Deadliest air crash

The Charkhi Dadri mid-air collision, which occurred on 12 November 1996 near Charkhi Dadri in Haryana, remains the deadliest air crash in India's aviation history. A Saudi Arabian Airlines Boeing 747 bound for Dhahran collided mid-air with a Kazakhstan Airlines Ilyushin Il-76 cargo plane approaching Delhi, resulting in the deaths of all 349 people on board both aircraft. The tragedy led to major reforms in Indian airspace management, including the mandatory installation of Traffic Collision Avoidance Systems (TCAS) in all commercial aircraft flying in Indian airspace.

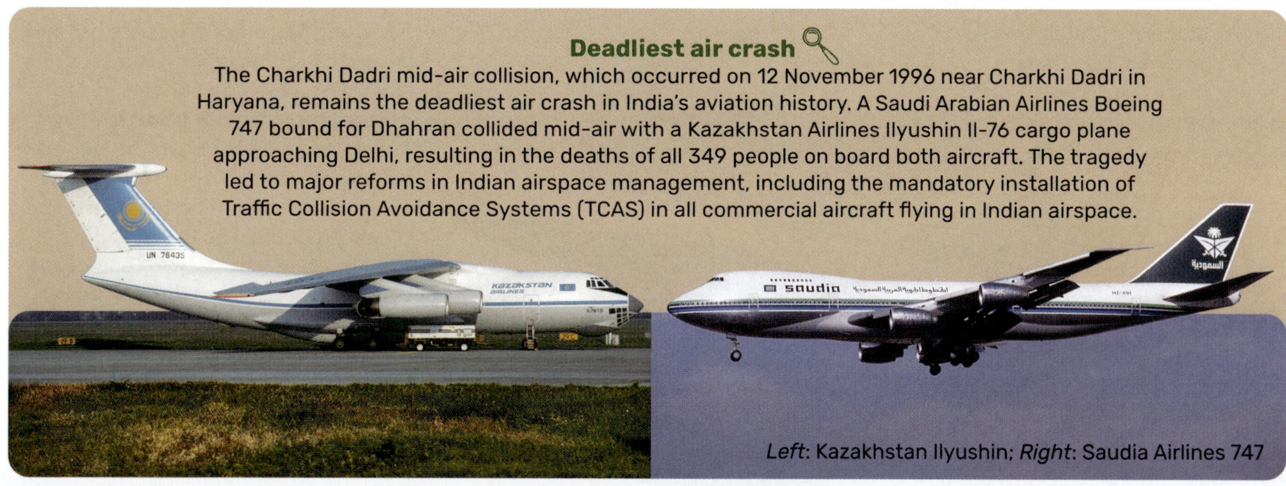

Left: Kazakhstan Ilyushin; *Right*: Saudia Airlines 747

in South Asia, it helps in offshore transport, emergency medical services, promoting heli-tourism, and reducing the congestion on the IGIA, Delhi.

First jet

Air India entered the jet age on 20 April 1960, when its Boeing 707 *Gauri Shankar* flew to London. Soon after, on 14 May 1960, it flew to New York. With this, India became the first Asian country to operate a transatlantic flight. The aircraft was written off after a landing accident at Bombay on 22 June 1982.

Chandigarh Airport

First indigenously assembled plane

The first HS-748 was assembled at the Aircraft Manufacturing Depot, Kanpur, Uttar Pradesh, and delivered to Indian Airlines on 27 June 1967.

Model of the HS-748

First all-jet carrier

WR In 1962, Air India became the world's first all-jet carrier when it replaced Super Constellation planes with a fleet of Boeing 707.

First Boeing 737-900 aircraft

Jet Airways acquired the first Boeing 737-900 aircraft in May 2003. The aircraft can seat up to 190 passengers and is the longest among the Boeing 737 family. It has a maximum flight range of 5,084 km. In 2018, Jet Airways took the delivery of the first 150 Boeing 737 MAX aeroplanes, becoming the first Indian carrier to fly the new variant.

Model of 737-900 aircraft

First airport to install full-body scanner

The first full-body scanner system was installed on a trial basis at Terminal 1D of the Indira Gandhi International Airport, New Delhi, on 10 April 2010. Initially the system was used only on volunteering passengers and the scanning process took less than a minute. The scanning system, called SmartCheck, was built by American Science and Engineering (AS&E). The system works on the X-ray backscatter technology.

Most air freight traffic

Indira Gandhi International Airport, New Delhi, handled over 65,00,000 tonnes of freight traffic by the end of 2023.

First air taxi

India's first air taxi service started at Chandigarh Airport on 14 January 2021 under the UDAN RCS (Regional Connectivity Scheme) of the Central government. With the capacity to seat a pilot and three passengers, the daily flight was of 45-minute duration and it plied on the Chandigarh–Hisar route at a cost of ₹1,755 per seat. This service was discontinued in August 2021, 7 months after its launch.

First airport to install waste recycling machines

The Rajiv Gandhi International Airport (RGIA) in Hyderabad, Telangana, became the first airport in the country to install waste recycling machines. It was launched as a pilot project in October 2017. Operated by the GMR Hyderabad International Airport Ltd (GHIAL), the airport has equipment to crush and recycle plastic PET (polyethylene terephthalate) bottles, steel or aluminium cans, and plastic bags into reusable raw material. These 'Swachh Bharat Recycling Machines' were designed and created by Mumbai-based company Wild West Media, and can be used to manufacture upcycled goods like bags, wallets, and denim. Passengers may make a donation or claim discount coupons in return for submitting their waste and plastic products. The RGIA is also the first airport to have its own composting plant, which processes the food waste generated at the airport.

Oldest to obtain a commercial pilot's licence

Captain Rajagopal Nagarajan (b. 25 April 1962) from Coimbatore, Tamil

Nadu, joined the commercial pilot's course after retiring from the Indian Air Force. He obtained the commercial pilot's licence (CPL) from the Civil Aviation Authority, Philippines, at 48 years on 11 December 2009.

Oldest fleet

Founded in 1932 as Tata Airlines and renamed in 1946 as Air India Ltd, this airline has a fleet size of 125 aircrafts (excluding subsidiaries), making it the oldest fleet in India. The airline has its headquarters in New Delhi.

Highest commercial airport

Kushok Bakula Rimpochee Airport (or Leh airport) in Leh, Ladakh, is the highest commercial airport at 3,256 m (10,682 ft) above mean sea level. The airport is named after Kushok Bakula Rinpoche, whose Spituk Monastery is very close to the airfield. The Indian Air Force handed over the airport to the Airport Authority of India in 2016.

WR First fully solar-powered airport

The Cochin International Airport in Kochi, Kerala, became the first airport in the world to run completely on solar power on 18 August 2015. The solar plant installed at the airport has 46,000 solar panels and can produce 50,000 to 60,000 units of electricity every day. The airport won the Champion of Earth Prize, awarded by the United Nations, in 2018.

Largest passenger airport terminal

On 3 July 2010, Terminal 3 of the Indira Gandhi International Airport, New Delhi, became India's and South Asia's largest aviation hub, with the capacity to handle more than 40 million (four crore) passengers a year. The airport handled over 73.6 million (7.36 crore) passengers in 2023-24.

Inside View of Terminal 3, Delhi

First dual-way elevated taxiway

On 14 July 2023, the country's first dual-way elevated taxiway was inaugurated at the Indira Gandhi International Airport, New Delhi. The elevated taxiway reduces taxi distance for aircraft by 7 km and annual carbon dioxide emissions by 53,000 tonnes. The Eastern Cross Taxiway is 2.1 km long and 44 m wide to allow safe passage for 2 big aircrafts.

First to offer free in-flight Wi-Fi on international flights

Vistara airlines has announced that passengers will now receive 20 minutes of complimentary Wi-Fi on international flights. This service will be available on Vistara's Boeing 787-9 Dreamliner and Airbus A321 neo aircraft.

WR First three-point disembarkation system

IndiGo, a leading Indian airline with its headquarters at Gurugram, Haryana, introduced a three-point disembarkation system in a global first on 4 August 2022. To mark its 16th anniversary, the airline introduced a disembarkation process that was carried out from 2 forward and 1 rear exit ramp.

Longest length of runways

The Indira Gandhi International Airport, New Delhi, has the longest stretch of airport runways in the country, with a length of 4,430 m (14,534 ft).

Largest passenger airline

IndiGo, with its headquarters at Gurugram, is the largest passenger airline in India by passengers carried and fleet size. Since its inception in August 2006, it has grown from 1 plane to a fleet of 269 aircraft. It is also the largest individual Asian low-cost carrier in terms of jet fleet size. It has a destination count of 100 with 74 domestic destinations and 26 international ones.

WR Highest airfield

The Daulat Beg Oldi airstrip in Ladakh is the highest airfield in the world. It is situated at an altitude of 5,065 m (16,617 ft). The Indian Air Force landed a C-130J Super Hercules aircraft at this airfield, reactivating it in 2013.

Plane Taking Off from Daulat Beg Oldi

She Flies, She Conquers

First woman to fly solo

In 1936, Sarla Thakral etched her name in history as India's first woman pilot. Just 21 years old and dressed in a saree, she took to the skies in a Gypsy Moth aircraft for her maiden flight and soon earned her pilot's license. Over the years, she went on to log more than 1,000 hours of flying experience, inspiring generations of women to follow their dreams into the cockpit.

First woman airbus pilot

On 14 May 1987, Durba Banerjee became the first woman to co-pilot a flight – Airbus A300 – on the Calcutta–New Delhi–Calcutta route.

Longest direct-route flight with an all-woman cockpit crew

Air India's flight AI-176 made history on 11 January 2021 when an all-woman cockpit crew flew a distance of 16,000 km from San Francisco, California, to Bengaluru, Karnataka. The flight departed on 9 January 2021 and was flown by four pilots – Captain Zoya Aggarwal, Captain Papagari Thanmai, Captain Shivani Manhas, and Captain Akansha Sonaware. The longest commercial flight to be operated by an Indian airline and longest flight entering India, its flying time was 17 hours and its route remarkably included flying over the North Pole.

Representative image

WR Highest number of women pilots

In a report released by Air Line Pilots Association, International (ALPA), in 2018, India led the charts in the number of female pilots among all countries. Around 13 per cent of the pilots in the country are women whereas the global average is only 5 per cent. This means that out of every 8 flights in India, 1 is flown by a woman. Airlines such as IndiGo, SpiceJet, and Air India have the highest recruitment numbers for women pilots.

WR First woman Airbus commander

Captain Indraani Singh, who joined Indian Airlines in April 1986, was the first Indian and Asian woman to fly the Airbus A320, in 1989, and became the world's first woman commander of the wide-bodied Airbus A300 in August 1996.

First woman chief executive officer of an airline

Harpreet A. De Singh was appointed chief executive officer (CEO) of Alliance Air, a regional subsidiary of Air India, on 30 October 2020. Previously executive director for flight safety in Air India, she became the first woman CEO of an airline. She was also the first woman pilot to be selected by Air India in 1988.

First woman chairperson of the International Civil Aviation Organization (ICAO) Aviation Security Committee

Shefali Juneja was elected chairperson of the ICAO Aviation Security Committee on 17 September 2021. A specialized agency of the UN, ICAO was formed to support and help nations with diplomacy and cooperation in air transport. India held the position 12 years ago. Shefali was also appointed as the representative in the council of ICAO in 2019.

First woman to obtain a pilot's licence

Urmila K. Parekh became the first woman to obtain a pilot's licence, in 1930.

First woman offshore captain

Captain Mayuri V. Deshmukh (b. 11 November 1982) with Commercial Helicopter Pilot Licence 991 became the first woman offshore captain in the country when she flew from Juhu to Mumbai High, Mumbai, Maharashtra, as captain from 11:07 a.m. to 1:25 p.m. on 8 March 2022. She was working for Pawan Hans Ltd (PHL) at the time. She has complied with the syllabus laid down by the Directorate General of Civil Aviation (DGCA) and validated by Oil and Natural Gas Company Ltd.

RAIL AND METRO

First passenger train
India's first passenger train chugged away from Bori Bunder (later renamed Victoria Terminus, and then Chhatrapati Shivaji Maharaj Terminus) station in Mumbai to Thane, Maharashtra, on 16 April 1853. It was pulled by 3 locomotives named *Sindh*, *Sultan*, and *Sahib*, and carried 400 passengers in 14 railway carriages. This historic journey, which was of about 1 hr 15 mins duration, was flagged off with a 21-gun salute.

First rail construction company
R.M. Stephenson, a British railway engineer, formed the East Indian Railway (EIR) Company in 1844 for the construction of railways. In a contract signed on 17 August 1849, the EIR and the Great Indian Peninsula (GIP) Railway Company, England, were authorized to construct and operate railway lines in Kolkata, and Mumbai, Maharashtra.

First indigenous railway carriages
The first railway coaches made in India were built by 2 coach-building firms in Kolkata, Steward and Company, and Seton and Company John Hodgson was the chief engineer of the East Indian Railway Company. then, and the coaches were employed for the first train journey from Howrah to Hooghly in West Bengal on 15 August 1854.

First double-decker coaches
The Bombay, Baroda and Central India (BB&CI) Railway Company in Mumbai, introduced the first double-decker coaches in 1862.

BBCI Logo and BBCI Locomotive at Railway Museum

First tramway company 

The Calcutta Tramway Company was registered in London, in 1880. The Government of West Bengal nationalized it in 1976.

Fastest train
The fastest train in India is the Vande Bharat Express or Train 18, which reached a top speed of 180 km/hr during test runs. Its current operating speed is 130 km/ hr. As of October 2024, 66 Vande Bharat trains are in service which includes 17 sixteen-car services, 4 twenty-car service, and 45 eight-car services.

First public–private partnership railway station
The Habibganj railway station in Bhopal, Madhya Pradesh, is the first railway station to be built under a public–private partnership and at par with international standards. The redevelopment work began in partnership with the Bansal Group on 9 June 2017. It lies on the main Jhansi–Bhopal–Itarsi route. The plan includes airport-like facilities, such as shopping complexes, forex kiosks, and eateries, making it the first of its kind in the country.

First double-decker train
India's first double-decker train was the *Flying Ranee*, a superfast train that runs between Mumbai Central and Surat station. It began operating in 1906, was halted in 1939 due to the Second World War, and resumed in 1950 as a daily service train.

First locomotive factory
The first locomotive factory in India was set up at Chittaranjan in Paschim Bardhaman District, West Bengal, in 1950. The first diesel locomotive, with an imported engine, was manufactured at the Varanasi Diesel Locomotive Works, Varanasi, Uttar Pradesh, on 4 January 1964.

Longest freight train 
Asia's longest freight train, Rudrastra, is a 4.5 km-long train consisting of 354 wagons and 7 engines. It successfully completed a trial run in August 2025. This operational feat by Indian Railways aims to boost freight efficiency, reduce logistics costs, and improve overall goods transport by combining multiple standard freight trains into 1 massive unit.

First green corridor

The Manamadurai–Rameswaram stretch of the Southern Railway was inaugurated as India's first green corridor in July 2016, by installing bio-toilets in 150 coaches of 13 pairs of express and passenger trains on the 114 km-long train route. Developed by Indian Railways and the Defence Research and Development Organization (DRDO), the toilets have no discharge of human waste.

First tramcars

A horse-drawn tramcar ran on a 3.8 km route between Sealdah and Armenian Ghat Street in Calcutta on 24 February 1873.

First air-conditioned train

Before 1936, some coaches on the Bombay, Baroda, and Central India (BB&CI) Railway Company, Mumbai, had double walls lined with lead–zinc sheets filled with ice. The Frontier Mail (now renamed the Golden Temple Mail), which runs between Mumbai and Amritsar, was the first train to get air-conditioned (AC) coaches, in 1934.

Golden Temple Mail Coaches

First electric train

The first electric train operated on the Harbour branch of the Great Indian Peninsula Railway from Victoria Terminus to Kurla in Mumbai over 16 km, on 3 February 1925.

First Vistadome trains

A special seven-coach Vistadome passenger train was introduced on the Visakhapatnam–Araku route in Andhra Pradesh on 16 April 2017 by the Indian Railways. It has features such as see-through glass on all sides, glass roofs, LED lights, a GPS-based information system, and an observation lounge that offers panoramic views throughout the journey.

India's only ticketless train

The Bhakra-Nangal train was launched in 1948. It also played a crucial role in the construction of the Bhakra-Nangal Dam, one of India's tallest and most renowned dams. The Bhakra- Nangal train has been running without charging its passengers for the last 75 years. Over 800 passengers travel by it every day.

Longest rail tunnel

The Pir Panjal railway tunnel, or the Banihal railway tunnel, is 11.215 km long. It is located in the Pir Panjal range of the Himalayas in Jammu and Kashmir, and it opened in 2013.

Busiest railway station

Kanpur Central station, Uttar Pradesh, is the busiest railway station in the country in terms of the number of trains that pass through it every day. As many as 230 trains pass through the station daily. This railway station also has the world's largest interlocking route system.

Most people at a public-service event – multiple venues

Ministry of Railways organized an event on 26 February 2024 which was attended by 40,19,516 people at 2,140 venues. The event was organized for the inauguration of road overW/road under railway bridges and for laying the foundation stones of railway stations by Prime Minister Narendra Modi.

Longest train routes of India

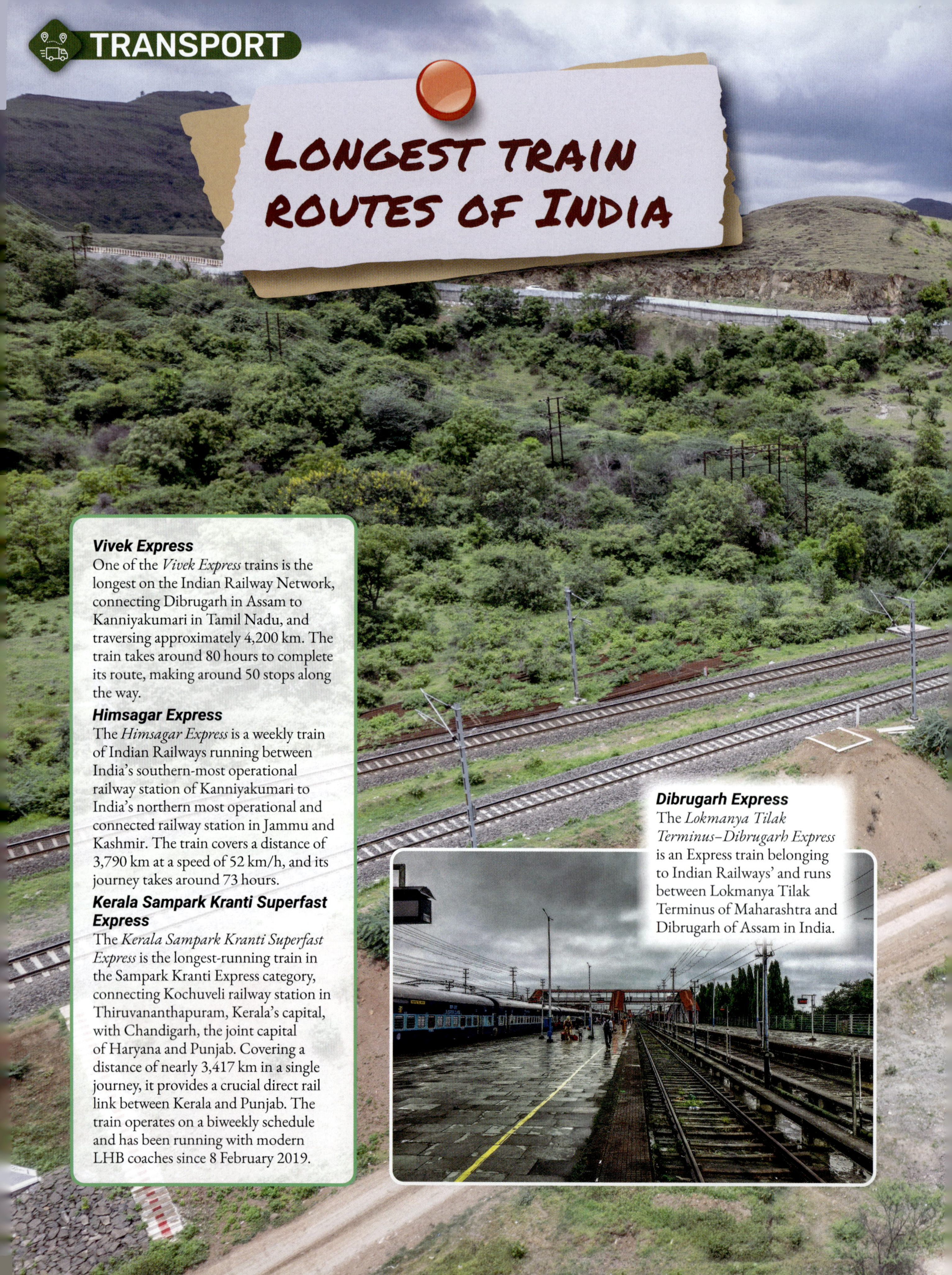

Vivek Express

One of the *Vivek Express* trains is the longest on the Indian Railway Network, connecting Dibrugarh in Assam to Kanniyakumari in Tamil Nadu, and traversing approximately 4,200 km. The train takes around 80 hours to complete its route, making around 50 stops along the way.

Himsagar Express

The *Himsagar Express* is a weekly train of Indian Railways running between India's southern-most operational railway station of Kanniyakumari to India's northern most operational and connected railway station in Jammu and Kashmir. The train covers a distance of 3,790 km at a speed of 52 km/h, and its journey takes around 73 hours.

Kerala Sampark Kranti Superfast Express

The *Kerala Sampark Kranti Superfast Express* is the longest-running train in the Sampark Kranti Express category, connecting Kochuveli railway station in Thiruvananthapuram, Kerala's capital, with Chandigarh, the joint capital of Haryana and Punjab. Covering a distance of nearly 3,417 km in a single journey, it provides a crucial direct rail link between Kerala and Punjab. The train operates on a biweekly schedule and has been running with modern LHB coaches since 8 February 2019.

Dibrugarh Express

The *Lokmanya Tilak Terminus–Dibrugarh Express* is an Express train belonging to Indian Railways' and runs between Lokmanya Tilak Terminus of Maharashtra and Dibrugarh of Assam in India.

Silchar Superfast Express

The *Silchar–Coimbatore Superfast Express* is one of Indian Railways' longest-running trains, operated by the Northeast Frontier Railway. Covering an impressive 3,492 km, it ranks as the eighth longest train route in India. Running once a week, it departs from Silchar in Assam every Tuesday at 20:10 and arrives at Coimbatore Junction in Tamil Nadu on Friday at 12:00.

Celebrating 90th Anniversary of *Deccan Queen*

First deluxe train

The first deluxe train, the *Deccan Queen*, started operating between Victoria Terminus, Bombay and Poona (now Pune), Maharashtra, on 1 June 1930. It had 61 first class, 156 second-class, and 19 attendants' seats.

First stations

Bori Bunder, Byculla, Sion, and Thane stations on the Bori Bunder–Thane line in Maharashtra were the first railway stations built at the time of the inaugural run of the first passenger train from Bori Bunder to Thane in 1853.

Station with most platforms

Howrah Junction, West Bengal, serves around 1 million passengers every day. It has 23 platforms, making it the station with the most platforms in India.

First woman train driver

Surekha Yadav Bhosale was the first woman to drive an Indian Railways train in 1988. She drove the first 'Ladies Special' local train, which started in April 2000 in Mumbai, Maharashtra. She was the first woman to join the Indian Railways as a trainee assistant driver in 1986. In 2011 she became the world's first Asian woman to drive the *Deccan Queen* from Pune to Chhatrapati Shivaji Maharaj Terminus.

WR Most coaches produced in a year

The Integral Coach Factory, which is located at Perambur in Chennai, Tamil Nadu, manufactured 4,166 railway passenger coaches in 2019–20.

WR Most locomotives produced in a year

The Chittaranjan Locomotive Works in Paschim Bardhaman District, West Bengal, produced 700 locomotives in the financial year 2024–25. It surpassed the Railway Board's production target for the period.

WR Longest rails manufactured

The Bhilai Steel Plant, the largest plant of the Steel Authority of India Ltd (SAIL), became the only rail maker in the world capable of producing 260 m (853 ft) long rails, on 23 February 2005. It first manufactures 65 m (213 ft) long rails, which are welded together to form the 260 m tracks for high-speed trains.

WR Oldest steam engine

The *Fairy Queen*, officially called the East Indian Railway Nr. 22, has the world's oldest working steam engine. This train started running in 1855 but was stopped in 1908. It was restored in 1997 by Perambur Loco Works in Perambur in Chennai, Tamil Nadu. In July 1997, this heritage train resumed its route between Delhi and Alwar, Rajasthan, and it still runs occasionally.

WR Longest double decker viaduct

The longest double decker viaduct in India was built by Maharashtra Metro Rail Corporation Limited on Wardha Road, Nagpur. It has a length of 3.14 km. The double decker viaduct carries a highway flyover at the first level and a metro rail at the second level. Along with the already existing highway at ground level this viaduct is a three-tier transportation system.

Longest train route

The *Dibrugarh–Kanniyakumari Vivek Express* has the longest train route on the Indian Railways network, and the ninth longest in the world. It joins Dibrugarh in Assam to Kanniyakumari in Tamil Nadu, covering 4,286 km, while halting at 56 stations along the route. It starts at 11:05 p.m. and reaches at 9:50 a.m. on the fifth day, with a scheduled journey time of 82 hrs 45 mins.

First fully solar-powered railway station

The Guwahati railway station in Assam is India's first fully solar-powered station. Commissioned in 2017, the project has 2,352 solar panels on the roof. This solar project aims to make the railways environmentally responsible and reduce their carbon footprint. The panels have an average power generation capacity of 2,048 kWh per day.

Integral Coach Factory, Chennai

Only railway station listed as a UNESCO World Heritage Site

The first train in the country was flagged off on 16 April 1853 from Bori Bunder in Mumbai. The historic station is one of the busiest railway stations in India and the only one declared as a UNESCO World Heritage Site. The building, featuring a Victorian Gothic style of architecture, was designed and constructed by draughtsman Axel Herman and architect Frederick William Stevens in 1888.

First corporatized train

The Indian Railways launched the *Tejas Express*, India's first corporatized train, on 4 October 2019. The infrastructure is owned and run by the Indian Railway Catering and Tourism Corporation (IRCTC), a subsidiary of the Indian Railways, while the services on board are outsourced to private contractors. They include catering, housekeeping, ticketing and refund, among others. The train shuttles between Lucknow and New Delhi, and has only 2 halts in between – Kanpur and Ghaziabad. Running all week, except Tuesdays, it is contracted under the public– private partnership model.

Interior of the *Tejas Express*

Most railway stations inaugurated simultaneously

On 22nd May 2025, Prime Minister Narendra Modi inaugurated 103 redeveloped Railway Stations through Video Conference, under Amrit Bharat Station Scheme across 18 states and union territories. 103 Plaques were placed and unveiled indicating the inauguration. These railways stations have been redeveloped to include improved toilet access, new seating arrangements, clear signage, new booking offices, better lighting etc.

Deepest metro station

The Hauz Khas station on the Magenta Line and the Yellow Line of the Delhi Metro is the deepest metro station, located at a depth of 32 m (105 ft).

First metro

A 16.3 km underground mass rapid transit system in the country was inaugurated on 24 October 1984 in Kolkata, between Dum Dum and Tollygunge. The carrying capacity of this metro was 1.73 million passengers a day. The trains for the metro system were manufactured at the Integral Coach Factory, Perambur, Madras (now Chennai), Tamil Nadu, during 1981–82.

Most metro stations on a double-decker viaduct

The double-decker viaduct on Wardha Road has 3 metro stations along the length of 3.14 km. Each station has a length of 77.5 m. The 3 stations are Ujjwal Nagar, Jaiprakash Nagar, and Chhatrapati Square.

Deepest metro tunnel

Delhi Metro Rail Corporation (DMRC)

Above: Delhi Metro Blue Line; Below: PM Modi Inaugurating the Underwater Metro Tunnel

completed a metro tunnel at a depth of 45 m (147 ft 7 in.) on 30 April 2009. The 1,556 m (5,105 ft) long tunnel below the underground Rajiv Chowk metro station in New Delhi is part of the 22.7 km long Airport Express Line.

Largest metro network

The Delhi Metro, set up by the Delhi Metro Rail Corporation (DMRC), spread across 391 km, is the largest metro rail network in India in terms of both route length and ridership. It has 12 lines and 286 metro stations.

First underwater metro

The East-West corridor project, India's first underwater metro service under the Kolkata Metro Rail Corporation was completed by June 2023. The metro line connects Salt Lake to Howrah via Kolkata with a 520 m (1,706 ft) stretch below the Hooghly River. It successfully completed a trial journey from Howrah Maidan to Esplanade and vice versa.

WR Station with the longest platform

Shri Siddharoodha Swamiji railway station in Hubballi, Karnataka, has completed the construction of the 1,505 m (4,937 ft 7.97 in.) long Platform No. 1, thus becoming the station with the world's longest railway platform. The platform was inaugurated by Prime Minister Narendra Modi on 12 March 2023.

First driverless metro

The Magenta Line in the Delhi Metro became the first 'driverless' metro line in India. The 12.64 km long line started operating on 25 December 2017, and connected Kalkaji Mandir, New Delhi, to Botanical Garden, Noida, while halting at 9 stations. The line was extended by 24.34 km to Janakpuri West in May 2018. Initially, it was run by an operator, with high levels of automation based on the Communications-based Train Control technology, but began driverless operations in 2020.

ROAD

First state transport system

In June 1932, the Nizam's State Railways Transport Department (NSRTD), Hyderabad (now in Telangana), set up a road transport service on a 24 km route, with 27 buses operating through 3 depots. Each bus could seat as many as 25 passengers.

First regular public transport

The first regular long-distance public road transport was introduced between Aligarh and Kanpur in Uttar Pradesh in November 1841.

First traffic police

The Traffic Department of Calcutta Police in Calcutta came into force in 1874 with 17 sepoys in its ranks.

First trolley bus

Twelve trolley buses were imported to replace tramcars on the Gowalia Tank–Mazagon route in Bombay on 11 June 1962. They were withdrawn in March 1971 in favour of buses.

First zero-emission electric car

REVAi, the environment-friendly electric car, is manufactured by the Reva Electric Car Company, Bengaluru, Karnataka, a joint venture formed by Amerigon Inc. of California, USA, and the Maini Group of Industries based in Bengaluru. This eco-friendly car was first flagged off from New Delhi in March 1998 and sold in 26 countries by 2011. It was acquired by the Indian conglomerate Mahindra & Mahindra in May 2010, and the company launched the electric hatchback e2o in 2013.

Earliest route

In 1926, the Brihanmumbai (then Bombay) Electric Supply & Transport Undertaking (BEST) purchased motor buses, choosing 2 points to try them out. The route covered present-day Afghan Church to Crawford Market through Dadar tram terminus, King's Circle, Opera House, Lal Bagh, and Arthur Road in Mumbai, Maharashtra.

First Indian car manufacturers

Hindustan Motors Ltd, registered in 1942 to manufacture vehicles, was followed by Premier Automobiles (1944) and Standard Motor Products of India Ltd (1948). The first Indian-built car,

First highway 

Lord William Bentinck, the then Governor General of India (1828–35), began metalling work on the 2,400 km long historic Grand Trunk Road from Calcutta to Peshawar (now in Pakistan) and beyond. During his tenure, the initial steps were taken to build a metalled road from Calcutta to Delhi.

Original Grand Trunk Road Between Margalla and Kala Chitta

Hindustan 10, not fully indigenous but identical to the series M10 HP Morris, rolled out of the factory located in Hooghly District, West Bengal, in 1946.

First motor bus

The motor bus was introduced in Mumbai on the Afghan Church–Crawford Market route on 15 July 1926. With a cruising speed of 20 km/hr, it carried 24 passengers, with 2–3 standing ones. Twenty-six buses were bought for ₹12,000 each.

First stainless-steel bus

The first bus with a stainless steel body was built at the Maharashtra State Road Transport Corporation workshop in Aurangabad, Maharashtra. It was inaugurated on the Bombay–Ratnagiri route, Maharashtra, on 12 February 1988.

First car

The first motor car was reportedly imported in 1892 by the then maharaja of Patiala in Punjab. It was a De Dion Bouton car.

First satellite navigation system

Sanjay, a navigation system using a Global Positioning System (GPS) receiver and mapping software, was launched on 15 February 1999 in New Delhi. Once installed in the vehicle, the user could access Delhi's road map and get audio information about routes. It also tracks the vehicle from elsewhere. Developed indigenously at the I.B. Saxena Design Lab in New Delhi, it uses 24 satellites.

First battery-bus fleet

In 1987, for the first time, the Delhi administration introduced 76 battery operated buses on 11 routes in Delhi, through the Delhi Energy Development Agency. Each bus had a laden weight of 3,800 kg, a cruising speed of 40 km/hr, and a maximum speed of 60 km/hr.

A De Dion Bouton Model

First indigenous payment eco-system for transport

The National Common Mobility Card (NCMC) based on the 'One Nation, One Card' model was launched in Ahmedabad, Gujarat, on 4 March 2019, by the Ministry of Housing and Urban Affairs, Government of India. It allows users to make payments across multiple transportation platforms, such as metros, toll taxes, buses, and parking, across India.

First electric buses

- The first electric bus service in India is reported to have commenced in Himachal Pradesh for Rohtang Pass, near Manali, at an altitude of 3,962.4 m (13,000 ft). The bus has been developed by Goldstone Infratech and the Automobile Research Association of India. It had the capacity to carry 30 passengers and can run 200 km on fully charged batteries.
- India's first electric double-decker bus was launched at Y.B. Centre in south Mumbai, Maharashtra, on 19 August 2022. The bus – the 'Switch EiV 22' – is run by the Mumbai civic transport body. Two new electric buses, including the first air-conditioned double-decker bus in the country, joined the fleet of the Brihanmumbai Electric Supply & Transport Undertaking (BEST).

First Advanced Traffic Control system

The Delhi Police installed the first Advanced Traffic Control system at 47 intersections of the capital city in April 2000. The intelligent sensors in this high-tech system are equipped to assess the volume of traffic at each intersection and control the traffic light system accordingly.

First electric cabs

Nagpur in Maharashtra is India's first city to have an electric mass mobility system. It has a fleet of 200 electric vehicles including taxis, buses, e-rickshaws, and autorickshaws, owned by cab aggregator Ola. This multimodal electric vehicle project, the first of its kind in India, was inaugurated on 26 May 2017.

TANGLA

Highest national highway

The 490 km-long Manali–Leh national highway has an average elevation of over 4,000 m (13,123 ft). Its highest elevation is 5,328 m (17,480 ft) at Tanglang La in Ladakh.

First CNG autos

Bajaj Auto Ltd launched the first of its Compressed Natural Gas (CNG) autorickshaws in Delhi on 29 May 2000. With a 3-kg CNG tank and a standby 3-litre petrol tank, it is powered by a 175 cc, four-stroke, overhead camshaft engine, which gives 50 km per kg of CNG and meets the Bharat-II emission norms.

First fully electrical SUV

Hyundai launched India's first fully electric SUV, the Kona Electric, on 9 July 2019. The eco-friendly vehicle can cover approximately 452 km on a single charge and was introduced with 4 drive modes: Eco, Eco+, Comfort, and Sport.

WR Highest filling station

The Indian Oil Corporation Ltd operates a filling station at Kaza, Spiti Valley, Himachal Pradesh, at an elevation of about 3,740 m (12,270 ft) above mean sea level.

WR Shortest national highway

National Highway 327 B, located in West Bengal, is the shortest national highway in India. Only 1.2 km long, it starts from its junction with NH-327 near Panitanki in Darjeeling District, connecting Mechi Bridge and terminating at the Indo-Nepal border.

Above: A CNG Auto; *Below*: Hyundai Kona

Longest highway tunnel

Atal Tunnel, a 9.2 km- long tunnel on the Manali–Leh highway, was inaugurated on 3 October 2020. It cuts down the distance between Manali and Leh by 46 km and reduces travel time by four hours. Equipped with CCTVs and fire hydrants, the tunnel is the only one in India to have an emergency exit tunnel inside.

Delhi–Dehradun Expressway – Asia's Longest Wildlife Corridor

The Delhi–Dehradun Expressway is a flagship infrastructure project spanning approximately 210 km, connecting Delhi to Dehradun via Uttar Pradesh and Uttarakhand. Built as a six-lane, access-controlled highway, it slashes journey time from over 6 hours to just 2.5 hours. Among its standout features is a 12-km elevated wildlife corridor over Rajaji National Park,

Delhi-Dehradun Expressway

along with multiple animal underpasses and elephant crossings, marking it as one of India's greenest expressways in terms of wildlife safety design. The expressway also includes numerous engineering marvels, such as a 340 m three-lane tunnel at Datkali, 113 vehicular underpasses, several ROBs (rail over-bridges), major and minor bridges, making it a milestone in modern highway design in the region

WR Longest highway construction in a single day

National Highway Authority of India (NHAI) has broken a world record by laying a 75 km highway in under 5 days. The highway was laid as a single-layer of bituminous concrete in a single lane between Amaravati and Akola.

Largest automotive company

Tata Motors Ltd (earlier Tata Engineering and Locomotive Company), founded in 1945 and headquartered in Mumbai, Maharashtra, is the largest automotive company with a portfolio of cars, sports vehicles, buses, trucks, and defence vehicles. The company's consolidated net revenue for the fiscal year 2021–22 was ₹2,78,454 crore (₹2,784.54 billion) with 10,86,734 vehicles sold.

Most bituminous concrete poured – single day

Travelling over an approximate linear distance of 18,701 km, Hyderabad-based IJM (India) Infrastructure Ltd (IJMIL) poured 15,656 tonnes (6,068.217 cu.m) of bituminous concrete in 20 hrs 40 mins on 25 February 2021. The laying of the 26.82 km Solapur–Bijapur single lane of the four-lane NH-13 between Maharashtra and Karnataka was implemented under the National Highway Authority of India.

State/UT with the largest fleet of buses

Tamil Nadu State Transport Corporation (TNSTC) has a fleet of 22,000 buses. It is the largest government-owned bus transport corporation in the country (2019).

Logo of Tamil Nadu State Transport Corporation

WATER

Earliest compass

According to the *Bombay Gazetteer*, Vol. XIII, Part II, Appendix A, a crude forerunner of the modern magnetic compass, Matsya Yantra was used around the fifth century CE. It featured an iron fish that floated in a vessel of oil, and pointed north.

Oldest ships

- MV *Safeena* of Ellon Hinengo Ltd, Port Blair, Andaman and Nicobar Islands, built at the government dockyard in Rangoon (now Yangon), Myanmar, in 1942, is the oldest passenger ship.
- HMS *Foudroyant (Trincomalee)*, used for training, was built in Mumbai in 1817 and is now a museum ship in Hartlepool, UK. The *Trincomalee* carried 46 guns and displaced 1,065 tonnes.

HMS *Trincomalee*

First steamboat

The steamboat *Diana* was built in India in 1819 by Jessop & Co. Ltd in Calcutta, and launched on 12 July 1823.

First ship to sail from India

The first ship carrying the flag of an Indian Shipping Company, SS *Loyalty* of the Scindia Steam Navigation Company, sailed with a full complement of passengers from Bombay to the British Isles. A hospital ship, *Loyalty,* was bought on 17 February 1919 and converted to a passenger vessel. National Maritime Day is observed on 5 April, the day on which the ship started this voyage in 1919.

Reshma Nilofer Naha

First woman marine pilot

Reshma Nilofer Naha (b. 4 February 1989) is the first and only Indian woman marine pilot in the country. She joined the Kolkata Port Trust in 2011 and became a trained marine pilot in January 2018. As a river pilot, she guides ships in and out of Sagar, to and from ports at Haldia and Kolkata ports through the Hooghly River.

First solar ferry boat

The first solar-powered boat was launched in the country in December 2017. Named *Aditya*, the boat is 21.18 m (69 ft 7 in) long and 7.0 m (22 ft 11 in) wide. Constructed by the NavAlt Solar and Electric Boats Pvt. Ltd, it accommodates 78 rooftop solar panels and sails at a maximum speed of 7.5 knots. The boat seats 75 passengers and operates on the 2.5 km Vaikom– Thavanakadavu route in Kerala.

First shipping company

Freedom fighter V.O. Chidambaram Pillai set up the Swadeshi Shipping Company at Tuticorin (now Thoothukudi), Tamil Nadu, in 1906.

First diesel engine ship

MV *Dwarka,* a modern D-class passenger and cargo ship of the British India Steam Navigation Company, entered service in 1947. Weighing 4,851 gross tonnes, it was 1,21.6 m (399 ft) long and 16.8 m (55 ft) wide. It had a service speed of 13.5 knots.

First indigenous hovercraft
A twin-engine, air-cushioned hovercraft, made in 1987 by the Scientific Instrument Co. Ltd, Allahabad, had a 55 HP thrust engine for propulsion and an 8 HP engine for lift, with a payload capacity of 500 kg and a speed of 45 km/hr.

First hovercraft ferry
A diesel hovercraft service began between Surat and Ghogha Port in Gujarat on 10 December 1992, linking the 2 ports, 55 nautical miles (101.85 km) apart, in 2 hrs.

Earliest representation of ships
A rectangular seal portraying a vessel with a sharply upturned prow and stem was unearthed in an excavation at Mohenjo-Daro (now in Pakistan). It was dated to 3000 BCE.

First roll-on–roll-off ferry service
A roll-on–roll-off ferry service began on 22 October 2017 between Ghogha Port and Dahej in Gujarat. The 31 km service reduces the travel time between the 2 towns from 7–8 hours to just over an hour. It can carry 1,000 passengers and 150 vehicles.

SS *Jalabala*

First overseas cargo service
On 3 February 1948, a continental line for an overseas cargo service between India and European countries was inaugurated by the Scindia Steam Navigation Company, with the sailing of the cargo steamship SS *Jalabala* from present-day Mumbai, Maharashtra.

Largest covered dock
Hindustan Shipyard houses the largest covered dock at Visakhapatnam

Aerial View of Hindustan Shipyard Dock in Andhra Pradesh. The dock measures 240 m x 53 m x 11.25 m (787 ft x 174 ft x 37 ft) with an intermediate twin gate and undocking draft of 8 m (26 ft). It can accommodate ships of up to 80,000 deadweight tonnage.

First corporatized port
Ennore Port (now Kamarajar Port Ltd) on the Coromandel Coast, Chennai, Tamil Nadu, was the first Indian port that was a public company, and later became a corporatized port in 1999.

WR Longest river cruise

The MV *Ganga Vilas* is a vessel made in India that was flagged off on its journey from Varanasi on 13 January 2023 by Prime Minister Narendra Modi. The cruise covered a distance of 3,200 km in over 46 days. It reached Dibrugarh on 28 February 2023. It covered 27 river systems in India and Bangladesh.

Oldest operating port and largest riverine port

Calcutta Port, Bengal (later called Kolkata Port, and now renamed Syama Prasad Mookerjee Port, West Bengal), built by the East India Company and operating since 1870, is the oldest operating port in India. It is also the only major riverine port and the largest riverine port in the country.

First private sector port

Pipavav Port in Gujarat, which was inaugurated in November 1996, has 3 dry cargo berths built as a single-length jetty of 725 m (2,379 ft), and a liquid cargo berth.

First superfast catamaran service

A superfast catamaran service between Mumbai, Maharashtra, and Goa became operational from 14 November 1994. The 40 m long, 400-seater, twin-hull luxury catamaran was imported by Damania Shipping Ltd from Norway. It moved at 40 knots, covering 225 nautical miles (417 km) in 6 hrs 30 mins.

Transport Tourism

Tourism ferry

The Kochi Water Metro, inaugurated in April 2023, is the first integrated water metro service in India and a pioneering model of sustainable urban transport. Connecting 10 islands around Kochi with the mainland, the service uses a fleet of modern, air-conditioned, battery-powered electric boats designed for both comfort and eco-friendliness. By blending with the existing Kochi Metro rail network, it offers seamless connectivity across land and water, reducing congestion while promoting tourism in Kerala's backwaters. Beyond being a commuter lifeline, the Water Metro doubles as a unique attraction, giving visitors an affordable and scenic way to experience Kochi's famed waterways.

Largest Heli-Tourism Operation in India

The Kedarnath Heli Yatra has emerged as one of India's largest heli-tourism operations, providing pilgrims with swift and convenient access to the sacred Kedarnath shrine in Uttarakhand's Garhwal Himalayas. Operating from helipads such as Phata, Guptkashi, and Sirsi, the service shortens what is otherwise a demanding trek of nearly 16 km into a flight of just 7–10 minutes. During the annual Char Dham Yatra season, thousands of devotees avail of the helicopter service daily, making it a vital link for elderly and differently-abled pilgrims. Beyond religious travel, the Heli Yatra offers stunning aerial views of snow-clad peaks and valleys, turning the journey itself into a memorable tourism experience while easing the pressure on mountain trails.

Maharajas Express

Longest Luxury Train Journey

The *Maharajas' Express*, owned and operated by The Indian Railway Catering and Tourism Corporation (IRCTC), is a luxury tourism train. It operates between the months of October and April and is centered around Rajasthan serving 4 routes across North-West and Central India. It received recognition from the Condé Nast Traveler Readers' Choice Travel Award in 2022. It was voted 'The World's Leading Luxury Train' 7 times in a row at The World Travel Awards from 2012 through 2018 and again in 2024.

Kashi Ropeway

First Ropeway Across a River

The Kashi Ropeway, currently under construction in Varanasi, is set to be India's first public transport ropeway system and one of only a handful worldwide to operate in an urban setting. Designed to ease congestion in the city's narrow lanes, the 3.75 km ropeway will connect Varanasi Cantonment railway station to Godowlia, passing key landmarks along the Ganga. Once operational, it will be able to carry more than 96,000 passengers daily, dramatically cutting travel time from over 30 min by road to just 15 min. Beyond easing commutes, the ropeway is also expected to become a major tourist draw, offering pilgrims and visitors an aerial view of the ancient city and the ghats of the Ganga.

Longest Highway Stretch for Tourism

The Delhi–Mumbai Expressway, India's longest expressway at 1,386 km, is not only a feat of engineering but also a major boost to tourism. Slashing travel time between the national and financial capitals from 24 hrs to just 12, it passes through Rajasthan, Madhya Pradesh, Gujarat, Haryana, and Maharashtra, opening up quicker access to countless heritage sites, wildlife sanctuaries, and cultural hubs. Notably, the expressway has direct connectivity to the upcoming Bharatpur Bird Sanctuary eco-tourism zone, Ranthambore, and Sariska tiger reserves, and several historical cities, transforming it into a tourism corridor as much as a transport link. With dedicated wayside amenities, food plazas, and EV charging stations, it aims to create a seamless and traveler-friendly journey, encouraging both domestic road trips and international tourist itineraries.

Delhi-Mumbai Expressway

BUSINESS AND ECONOMY

PLANNING

First book on political economy

Written in Sanskrit by Chanakya in the fourth century BCE, the *Arthashastra* is an ancient Indian treatise on statecraft, economic policy, and military strategy. It was influential till the 12th century, after which it disappeared. A copy of it was rediscovered in 1905 by R. Shamasastry, a Sanskrit scholar, who published it in 1909. Its first English translation was published in 1915.

The *Arthashastra* places the knowledge of economics at the heart of a king's education. Its discussion on taxation and expenditure gives expression to 3 traditional Indian principles: the taxing power of the state is limited, taxation should not be felt to be heavy or exclusive or discriminatory, and tax increases should be graduated.

First national economic planning

Prasanta Chandra Mahalanobis (1893–1972), an Indian scientist and applied statistician, laid down the framework for modern formal economic planning in India. A member of the first Planning Commission of independent India, Mahalanobis was the first to use statistical tools to forecast, plan, analyse, and evaluate social and economic welfare policies and implementation in India.

First budgets

The first Indian budget was presented by James Wilson on 18 February 1860 in colonial India. Wilson, who founded *The Economist* magazine, was a finance member of the Council of India, which advised the Indian viceroy at the time. The first Union budget of independent India was presented on 26 November 1947 by then finance minister R.K. Shanmukham Chetty. This was an economic review without any new taxes levied, as the Union budget for 1948–49 was only 95 days away. After this, a budget for a short period began to be called an 'interim' budget.

Longest budget speech

• Dr Manmohan Singh holds the record for the longest budget speech in India. His 1991 budget speech consisted of 18,650 words.

Sikkim Legislative Assembly

• Longest budget speech in terms of duration is held by Nirmala Sitharaman. Her 2020 budget speech went on for 162 minutes.

Shortest budget speech

The shortest budget speech record is held by Hirubhai Mulljibhai Patel. His budget speech in 1977 had only 800 words.

Most budgets presented

Morarji Ranchhodji Desai (29 February 1896–10 April 1995), the fourth prime minster of India, also served two terms as finance minister. During the first term, from 22 March 1958 to 31 August 1963, he presented 6 consecutive Union budgets, including an interim budget in 1962. During the second term, from 13 March 1967 to 16 July 1969, he presented one interim budget in 1967 and three full budgets in 1967, 1968, and 1969. The total stands at 10.

Morarji Desai

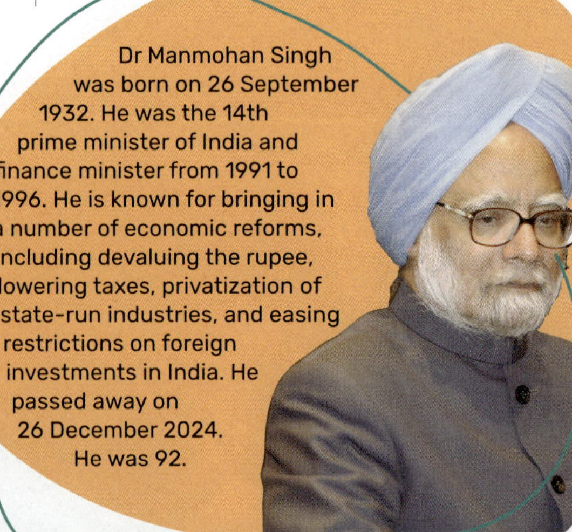

Dr Manmohan Singh was born on 26 September 1932. He was the 14th prime minister of India and finance minister from 1991 to 1996. He is known for bringing in a number of economic reforms, including devaluing the rupee, lowering taxes, privatization of state-run industries, and easing restrictions on foreign investments in India. He passed away on 26 December 2024. He was 92.

Only tax-free state in India

The only state in India where residents don't have to pay income tax is Sikkim. Since 1975, when Sikkim became part of India, the north-eastern state had its own tax laws, according to which Sikkimese people did not have to pay tax to the central government. In 2008, the Government of India repealed the existing tax laws, but the new law also exempted this north-eastern state's residents from tax (under Section 10 (26AAA) of the Income Tax Act). Also the Securities and Exchange Board of India has exempted Sikkimese people from the requirement of having a permanent account number (PAN) for investing in Indian securities market and mutual funds.

First Union budget papers in Hindi

While introducing the budget for 1955–56, then finance minister Sir Chintaman Dwarakanath Deshmukh (14 January 1896–2 October 1982) circulated the Hindi version of the budget speech for the first time. Hindi versions of the Annual

First paperless budget

The Union budget for 2021 was presented on a 'Made-in-India' tablet on 1 February 2021 by Finance Minister Nirmala Sitharaman, doing away with the long-standing tradition of printing the budget papers and also the long-standing convention of carrying them in a briefcase. The budget, presented amid the COVID-19 pandemic, was distributed electronically to members of Parliament (MPs).

Financial Statement and the Explanatory Memorandum were also circulated from then on.

State GST collection from a single state

In FY 24-25, Maharashtra has contributed ₹3.59854 lakh crore from Goods and Services Tax (GST) collection—highest ever for any state since GST was introduced.

First winner of the Nobel Prize in Economics

Dr Amartya Kumar Sen (b. 3 November 1933) received the Nobel Prize in economic sciences in 1998, becoming the first Indian and Asian to do so. Born in Santiniketan, West Bengal, he is considered to be a pioneer of welfare economics.

Amartya Sen

WORKFORCE AND HUMAN RESOURCES

Oldest trade union

The Madras Labour Union, the first organized trade union, was formed in 1918–19 by labour veterans Annie Besant, B.P. Wadia, Thiruvarur Viruttachala Kalyanasundaram, Sakkarai Chettiar, G. Ramanujalu, and G. Selvapathy Chetty.

Earliest public association

The earliest public association in modern India was the Landholders' Society, an association of the landlords, or zamindars, of Bengal (now West Bengal), Bihar, and Orissa (now Odisha), founded in 1837. It was established to look after the interests of landlords.

Workers on board

Delhi Cloth Mills (DCM) was the first company to recognize labour rights by inducting a workers' representative into its board in 1938.

First Labour Day

The International Workers' Day celebrations were first organized by communist leader Singaravelar, or Malayapuram Singaravelu Chettiar, (1860–1946) in Madras (now Chennai), Tamil Nadu on 1 May 1923.

First industrial association

The Industrial Association of Western India was formed in 1890 at the annual conference held at Poona (now Pune), Maharashtra.

First all-India farmers' organization

The All-India Kisan Sabha was formed in 1936 in British India. It was the first pan-India organization of farmers.

First labour legislation

- The Industrial Employment (Standing Orders) Act of 1946 was followed by protective regulations, such as the Factories Act and the Minimum Wages Act in 1948.
- The first effort to protect unorganized labour was the Coal Mines Provident Fund and Bonus Schemes Bill introduced in 1948, which became an Act in the same year.

Largest employers

Government: The record for the largest employer in India belongs to the country's government controlled sector – Indian Railways. On 31 March 2024 the number of regular employees of the Indian Railways stood at 12,52,180.
Private: In the private sector, Tata Consultancy Services continues to be the largest employer with slightly over 6,13,069 employees on 30 June 2025. In June 2023, the number stood at 6,15,316.

Women workers of the Northeast Frontier Railway working at the Guwahati Railway Station

STRIKING RECORDS

First labour strike

The first labour strike in India was that of the palanquin bearers of Calcutta (now Kolkata), West Bengal, in 1827 in pre-Independence India. They refused to wear badges and demanded fare on the basis of the distance they covered instead of time.

First organized strike

In 1877, labourers struck work at the Empress Mills in Nagpur, Maharashtra, following a wage cut. In 1884, as many as 5,000 textile workers of Bombay (now Mumbai), Maharashtra, submitted a petition asking for regular payment of wages, a weekly holiday, and a midday recess.

Largest strike

On 26 November 2020, over 25 crore (250 million) workers struck work for 24 hrs in a nationwide general strike organized by a joint platform of 10 trade unions.

Glimpses of the day of the largest strike in India

Longest-serving chairperson

The longest-serving chairman of an Indian private sector company is Yogesh Chander Deveshwar (4 February 1947–11 May 2019), who served as chairman of ITC Limited for over two decades. He held the position of chairman and CEO from 1996 to 2019. He died in harness.

First LGBTQIA+ job fair

The RISE (Reimagining Inclusion for Social Equity) job fair organized by the Pride Circle on 12 July 2019 in Bengaluru, Karnataka, was the first job fair exclusively for the LGBTQIA+ community. The fair attracted 450 candidates competing for 250 job opportunities in 35 companies. The employers included Goldman Sachs, Uber, Accenture, and Intel.

COINS AND CURRENCY

Earliest coinage

Ingots of silver, with only three dots as a mark, probably represent the earliest form of coinage on the Indian subcontinent (in circulation as early as 600 BCE).

Earliest gold coins

The Kushans (130 BCE–185 CE) issued the earliest gold coins in India. They weighed 121 or 123.1 grains (1 grain = 0.068 g approx.) and appear to be based on the auric standard (122.9 grains) of the Romans with whom the Kushans had regular trade.

Aditya Puri served as the Managing Director and CEO of HDFC Bank for 26 years, from September 1994 to October 2020. He was the longest-serving CEO of a private bank in India.

Highest denomination rupee notes

The highest-denomination note ever printed by the Reserve Bank of India was the ₹10,000 note issued in 1938. This was demonetized in January 1946. The ₹10,000 note was re-introduced in 1954, only to be demonetized again in 1978. The current highest denomination for a rupee-note is ₹500.

Oldest surviving gold coins

The oldest surviving gold coins are from the reign of Kushan emperor Vima Kadphises (c. 45–78 CE) and they were struck in three denominations – the double stater, the stater or dinara, and the quarter stater. On the obverse of these appears either the king's head or bust, or the king seated cross-legged on a couch, or sitting in a chariot drawn by two horses.

First lead coins

The first lead coins were found in the Deccan, dating back to the reign of Sri Satai (c. 150 BCE).

First coins for the visually impaired

On 7 June 2019, in New Delhi, Prime Minister Narendra Modi released a new series of coins, specially conceived to help visually impaired people to identify them. Designed by the National Institute of Design in Ahmedabad, Gujarat, the series has coins in denominations of ₹1, ₹2, ₹5, ₹10, and ₹20. These coins are characterized by increasing size and weight from lower to higher denominations. The newly included coin of ₹20 was designed as a 12-sided coin with no serrations. The other denominations are circular.

First mint

The East India Company started the first mint in India in 1640 at Fort St. George, Madras. In 1671, the first English mint was installed in Bombay through a letter of patent issued by King Charles II of England, but the first coin was minted there only a few years later in 1678.

BANKING

First bank

The Bank of Hindostan was established in 1770 by Alexander and Co. of Calcutta and survived three economic crises before shutting down in the 1830s.

First government banking agency

The Imperial Bank of India, formed in 1921 by merging the Presidency Banks of Bengal, Bombay, and Madras, became the State Bank of India (SBI) on 1 July 1955.

Oldest private bank

The Punjab National Bank Ltd (PNB), the first private bank wholly owned and run by Indians, opened in 1895.

Top: Punjab National Bank, New Delhi
Bottom: Facade of Standard Chartered Bank in Mumbai with classic architecture

First regional rural banks

The first regional rural banks (RRB) in India were opened in Moradabad and Gorakhpur in Uttar Pradesh, Bhiwani in Haryana, Jaipur in Rajasthan, and Malda in West Bengal on 2 October 1975.

First foreign bank

The Chartered Bank, established in 1853 in Madras, was the earliest foreign bank in India. In 1969, it merged with the Standard Bank in London, UK, and was incorporated as the Standard Chartered Bank.

First institution for agri-loans

On 12 July 1982, the National Bank for Agriculture and Rural Development (NABARD) was established, with its headquarters in Bombay, to implement the National Bank for Agricultural and Rural Development Act, 1981. The agricultural credit functions of the Reserve Bank of India (RBI) and refinance functions of the then Agricultural Refinance and Development Cooperation (ARDC) were transferred to NABARD.

First bank for housing development

The National Housing Bank (NHB), a subsidiary of the RBI, was established on 9 July 1988.

First Indian bank with a merchant banking subsidiary

The State Bank of India (SBI) was the first bank to set up a wholly owned merchant banking subsidiary when it set up SBI Capital Markets Ltd in April 1986.

First bank to establish a mutual fund

The SBI launched the SBI Mutual Fund

in July 1987. Managed by its subsidiary, SBI Capital Markets Ltd, it was established under the amended Banking Regulations Act, 1949, to attract funds from small investors in rural and semi-urban areas.

First cooperative bank

The Greater Bombay Cooperative Bank Ltd was registered on 5 November 1952 under the Bombay State Cooperative Act, with 50 members and an initial capital of ₹21,000.

First Indian bank to open a branch overseas

The Bank of India was the first Indian bank to open a branch outside India, in London, UK, in 1946, and also the first to open a branch in Paris, France, in 1974.

First automated teller machine facility

The Hong Kong and Shanghai Banking Corporation (HSBC) started 24-hour banking facilities by installing automated teller machines (ATMs) at its main office in Bombay on 4 September 1987.

Bank with most foreign offices

The SBI has 241 offices in 29 foreign countries to service the bank's foreign customers, in addition to retail operations (as in July 2024). The focus of these offices is India-related business.

Most branches

In August 2025, the SBI had over 22,937 branches – most for any Indian bank.

First Indian bank listed on the New York Stock Exchange

On 22 September 1999, the Industrial Credit and Investment Corporation of India (ICICI) Bank was listed on the New York Stock Exchange (NYSE), with its American Depository Shares priced at $9.80. After the Bank of Tokyo-Mitsubishi, it was the second Asian bank to be listed on the NYSE.

The bank with the largest network

The India Post Payments Bank (IPPB), launched in 2018, currently has 1,58,988 access points (1 controlling branch, 649 banking outlets – 1 in every district – as well as 1,36,078 post offices and 22,251 head and sub post offices both in urban and rural areas, which also work as IPPB's access points). This makes it the largest banking network in the country. It also has more than 2,00,000 postmen or *gramin dak sevak*s who provide doorstep services.

ICICI Bank, Canadian corporate head office

International bank with most branches in India

As reported by the Reserve Bank of India, the Standard Chartered Bank, with the United Kingdom as its country of incorporation, leads the list of international banks in India with the highest number of branches, totalling 100 till July 2024.

First credit card issued by an Indian bank

The Central Bank of India introduced the Central Card in 1980.

First floating ATM

The SBI launched a floating ATM installed on a *jhankar* (ferry) plying between Ernakulam and Vypin (one among a group of islands forming part of Kochi) in Kerala on 9 February 2004. The ship was owned by the Kerala Shipping and Inland Navigation Corporation.

First ATM on Wheels

In December 2002, the ICICI Bank introduced an ATM on wheels using vans equipped with ATM machines and parked at four locations in Mumbai suburbs – Vile Parle (East), Juhu, Andheri (West), and Kandivali – for fixed hours. The mobile ATM was connected to the central database of the bank through GPRS (General Packet Radio Service) technology for a fixed number of hours every day.

State/UT with the most ATMs

Maharashtra ranks first in the country as the state with the highest number of ATMs and WLAs (White Label ATMs) deployed, with 29,392 ATMs as reported in September 2022. Tamil Nadu, with 23,524 ATMs, comes second in the list.

First bank with a satellite network

The SBI installed the first satellite network in September 1988, connecting 134 offices in 64 cities. This network facilitated communication by voice, facsimile, and message switching via digital electronic exchanges.

First indigenous payment card

The National Payments Corporation of India (NPCI) introduced the RuPay debit card in Mumbai, Maharashtra, on 26 March 2012.

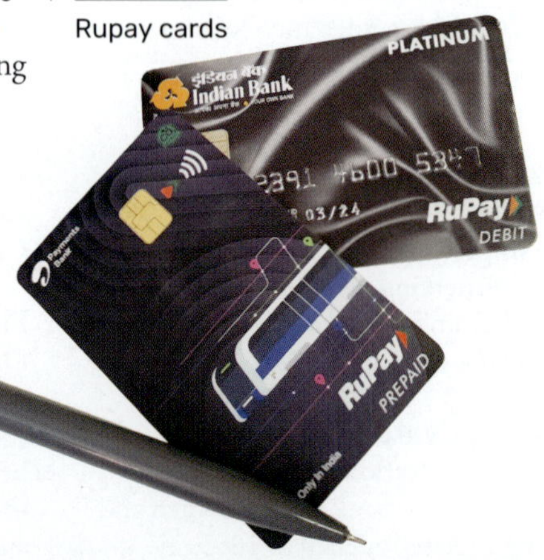

Rupay cards

First woman bank manager
Shanta Kumari became the manager of the Syndicate Bank, Seshadripura, Bangalore (now Bengaluru), Karnataka, in 1962.

First all-woman bank
Bharatiya Mahila Bank (BMB) is India's first bank only for women. This government-owned bank was set up with the vision of economic empowerment of women, and it opened its first branch at Nariman Point in Mumbai, Maharashtra, on 19 November 2013. It was incorporated on 5 August 2013 and received a banking licence from the RBI on 25 September 2013. It was merged with the SBI in April 2017.

First Indian governor of the Reserve Bank of India
Sir Chintaman Dwarkanath Deshmukh, a member of the Indian Civil Service, was the first Indian governor of the SBI – appointed governor in 1943.

Biggest bank fraud
On 14 February 2018, PNB, India's second-largest government-owned lender at the time, declared the largest ever bank fraud in India's financial history. It involved fraudulent letters of undertaking worth around ₹11,400 crore (114 billion) issued by PNB at its Brady House branch in Fort, Mumbai, Maharashtra, to overseas branches of other Indian banks.

First demonetization
In 1946, currency notes of ₹1,000 and ₹10,000 denominations were removed from circulation in the first instance of demonetization. Both notes were then reintroduced in 1954, along with the introduction of ₹5,000 and ₹500 notes.

WR World's most popular payment platform
• According to the global payments hub Paysecure, India's unified payments interface (UPI) processed 3,729.1 transactions per second during the April–July 2024 period.
• UPI processed nearly ₹81 lakh crore transactions in the April–July 2024 period, thus leading all other global digital payment platforms.
• More than 40 per cent of all payments in India are done through UPI, per the Press Information Bureau, 30 October 2023.

INSURANCE

First general insurance company
Triton Insurance Company Ltd, set up by the British in 1850, was the first general insurance company in India.

First life insurance company in India
The Oriental Insurance Company, the first life insurance company in India, started in Calcutta in 1818, but served only the Europeans in India then.

Largest insurance company
The Life Insurance Corporation of India (LIC) was founded on 1 September 1956. It grew into what is now the biggest public sector insurance company in the country and leads in the insurance sector. As of June 2025, its market capitalization is ₹5,92,968.53 crore.

First Indian life insurance company
The Bombay Mutual Life Assurance Society was the first Indian life insurance company. It started in 1870.

FINANCIAL INSTRUMENTS

First secured promissory notes
Tata Iron and Steel Company Ltd (TISCO), now Tata Steel Ltd, issued secured promissory notes in June 1992.

First domestic mutual fund
The Unit Trust of India's (UTI) scheme launched in 1964 was the first domestic mutual fund in the country.

First private sector mutual fund
Shyam Kothari, head of the H.C. Kothari group of companies, floated the Kothari Pioneer Bluechip Fund in November 1993.

India's first depository
The National Securities Depository Limited (NSDL) was jointly promoted by the Industrial Development Bank of India (IDBI), UTI, and the National Stock Exchange (NSE). It started operations in August 1996. C.B. Bhave was the first managing director of the NSDL. In September 2016, when the depository completed 20 years of operations, it had 15 million demat accounts.

LIC building, Bangaluru, Karnataka

Largest mutual fund

SBI Mutual Fund, founded in 1987, is a joint venture between the SBI and the AMUNDI (France). It is the largest mutual fund company in India with its assets under management (AMU) standing at ₹11,90,743 crore as of July 2025.

FINANCIAL INSTITUTIONS

Oldest stock exchange

The Bombay Stock Exchange (BSE) was formed under the shade of a giant banyan tree way back on 9 July 1875 by Premchand Roychand, a cotton merchant. Educated in Elphinstone College, Bombay, he was the first Indian broker able to write, read, and speak in English. Indian brokers doing business in stocks and shares decided to form an association in Bombay to protect the interests of Indian share brokers and stockbrokers. It was also Asia's first stock exchange and tenth oldest in the world.

Stock exchange with most listed companies

As of 20 August 2024, the BSE had 4,939 listed companies with a market capitalization of ₹4,56,17,998.

First stock exchange to cross the 80,000 mark

On 4 July 2024, the 30-stock BSE share index crossed the historic 80,000 mark. First to cross the 100 billion mark in monthly turnover The National Stock Exchange (NSE) is the stock exchange with the highest turnover. In August 2024, GIFT Nifty set an all-time high monthly turnover of $100.13 billion (about ₹8,40,000 crore) for the month of May 2024.

Shares of most companies held by an individual

Rajiv Maheshwari (b. 10 April 1961) held shares of 5,348 companies in dematerialized form in National Securities Depository Ltd (NSDL) and Central Depository Services (India) Ltd (CDSL) depository accounts as on 12 June 2023.

State/UT with the highest contribution to equity trading

Maharashtra continues to lead with unique investors' number at 18.4 million as on 28 March 2025 (16.6 per cent YoY growth). A close second is Uttar Pradesh at 12.8 million. These are the only 2 states that have more than 10 million registered unique investors.

An investor can have multiple demat accounts. Unique investor data track an investor by PAN to avoid double-counting. In terms of investors' accounts, the number stood at 40 million in July 2025.

First automatic exchange and screen-based trading

The automated Over the Counter Exchange of India (OTCEI), set up in 1992 in Bombay, Maharashtra, was the ideal avenue for small and medium-sized companies with an issued capital ranging from ₹30 lakh (3 million) to ₹25 crore (250 million). This exchange failed to live up to its promise and the NSE came into being in November 1994. The NSE started the first screen-based trading system, in which a network of computers is linked to a central computer located in the stock exchange.

Highest single-day transactions

On 5 June 2024, the NSE traded 1,971

First global depository receipts issue

Reliance Industries Ltd issued global depository receipts worth $150 million in March 1992.

Reliance Industries Limited (RIL) chairman, Mukesh Ambani, and his father, Dhirubhai Ambani (right), in Mumbai, in 2000

• As in many other sectors, women-power in the Indian financial sector has had a transformative influence. For a generally considered ultra-conservative sector, finance merits a special mention, as it required extra grit from game changers like **Arundhati Bhattacharya**. She created a record of sorts when, in 2013, she was appointed chairman of the SBI, thereby becoming the first-ever woman chairperson of the largest bank in India.

• In this Hall of Fame **Kalpana Morparia** would be another name to reckon with. She joined the legal department of ICICI in 1975 and rose through the ranks to become a director of the company's board in 2001, and in 2002 she became the executive director in the board. She is credited with steering the merger of ICICI and ICICI Bank. During her time ICICI bank became the second largest bank in the country.

Banking on Women

• In the list of earliest glass ceiling breakers, **Shanti Ekambaram** would be another important name. As part of the Kotak group and currently serving as a member of the executive board, she is credited with setting up various businesses.

• And then, of course, there is **Naina Lal Kidwai**, who happens to be the first Indian woman alumna of the Harvard Business School and the first woman to head a foreign bank in India. Recognized as a distinguished alumna by her alma mater, she took over the charge of HSBC India and was also the group general manager of the HSBC Holdings Plc in 2006.

crore (19.71 billion) orders and 28.55 crore (280.55 million) trades in 6 hrs and 15 mins.

First offshore mutual fund

Unit Trust of India (UTI) and Merrill Lynch promoted the ₹ 750 lakh (75 million) India Fund in 1986.

Highest price for stock exchange membership

A broking card for the Bombay Stock Exchange was auctioned for ₹4.1 crore (41 million) to Jardine Fleming Asia, which later shut down. Before that, Baring Securities India Ltd had paid ₹3 crore (30 million) for one in 1995.

First rating agency

Crisil, formed in 1988, was the first rating agency in India. It was set up jointly by the LIC, ICICI, GIC, and various banks.

First PSU to go public

Indian Petrochemicals Corporation Ltd (IPCL) went public on 16 November 1992, with a ₹320 crore (3.2 billion) equity issue.

First sectoral fund

The first sectoral mutual fund by the name of CanExpo was offered by Canara Bank in February–March 1994 as the first emerging industry fund.

First woman president of a stock exchange

Forty-five-year-old Omana Abraham became the first woman president of a stock exchange in India when she was nominated president of the Cochin Stock Exchange in Kochi, Kerala, in 1991.

First woman managing director and chief financial officer of World Bank Group

Anshula Kant, born in Roorkee (now in Uttarakhand), was appointed managing director (MD) and chief financial officer (CFO) of the World Bank on 12 July 2019. Kant is responsible for managing the International Development Association (which offers concessional loans and grants to the world's poorest developing countries), finance, and risk management of the group. Previously a financial officer of the SBI, Kant became the first woman to become MD and CFO of the international financial institution.

POWER AND ENERGY

First builder of the steam engine

Golak Chandra, who was a blacksmith in Titigur (now Titagarh), near Barrackpore in West Bengal, indigenously built a steam engine to pump groundwater, without any European help, in 1828.

First steam-powered plant

The Calcutta Electric Supply Corporation (CESC) set up a steam-powered plant in 1899 at Emambagh Lane near Prinsep Ghat in Calcutta, marking the start of thermal power generation in India.

First commercial use of electricity

Electricity was first introduced commercially on 10 November 1897 at Sidrapong Hydroelectric Power Station in Darjeeling, West Bengal.

First indigenous atomic power plant

Madras Atomic Power Station (MAPS) at Kalpakkam near Chennai, Tamil Nadu, was India's first fully indigenously built nuclear power station under the Indira Gandhi Centre for Atomic Research (IGCAR). Each of its 2 units generates 220 MW of electricity. The first indigenous 40 MW Fast Breeder Test Reactor (FBTR) was commissioned in August 1985 here.

WR Largest refinery

The Jamnagar Refinery is a private sector crude oil refinery owned by Reliance Industries in Jamnagar, Gujarat. The refinery was commissioned on 14 July 1999 with an installed capacity of 6,68,000 barrels per day. Its current capacity is 1.4 million barrels per day (MMBPD) crude processing capacity and a complexity index of 21.1, which makes it is the largest single-site refinery in the world. In December 2024, it completed 25 years.

Largest private sector thermal power station

The 4,620 MW Mundra Thermal Power Station at Mundra in the Kachchh District of Gujarat is the largest privately operating thermal power plant in India, with nine generating units. It is a coal-based power plant, owned and operated by Adani Power.

First private sector power company

Tata Power Company Ltd (TPCL) was the first private sector power company to start operations, in 1910 in Bombay.

First heavy water plant

The first heavy water plant was set up at Nangal in the Rupnagar District of Punjab in 1962. Heavy water or deuterium oxide was the basic fuel used by first-generation nuclear power plants.

First nuclear power plant

The Tarapur Atomic Power Station (TAPP) in Palghar, Maharashtra, with an installed capacity of 380 MW, was commissioned in 1969. It started with two boiling-water reactor units with an initial generating capacity of 210 MW each (de-rated to 160 MW), fuelled by enriched uranium. It was built by Bechtel Corporation and General Electric

The entrance to the largest refinery in the world, Jamnagar, India

State with the highest installed capacity of renewable power

As on 10 October 2024, Rajasthan's total installed renewable capacity stood at 29.98 GW – the highest in India. A close second is Gujarat with 29.52 GW.

Women constructing solar cookers at the workshop of Barefoot College in Tilonia, Rajasthan

Company, US, under an agreement between the Government of India, the United States, and the International Atomic Energy Agency.

First electrification

Calcutta was the first city in India to go electric when it received current in 1899 with the commissioning of Calcutta Electric Supply Corporation's (CESC's) first generating station at Emambagh Lane the same year.

First state electricity board

On 1 May 1955, the West Bengal State Electricity Board was the first electricity board in the country to become operational.

First solar-powered thermal plant

The country's first 50 MW solar-powered thermal power plant, developed by Chhattisgarh-based Godawari Green Energy Ltd (GGEL) in Nokh Village in Jaisalmer District, Rajasthan, went operational in 2013.

First hydropower station

Sidrapong Hydroelectric Power Station in the foothills of Arya Tea Estate near Darjeeling, West Bengal, is the oldest hydroelectric power plant in India. It was commissioned on 10 November 1897 with a capacity of 2 x 65 kW. This was increased in phases to meet the rising demands and reached 1,000 kW (1 MW) by 1916.

Largest grid-connected rooftop solar plant

The country's largest grid-connected rooftop solar plant, with a capacity of 7.52 MW, started operations in May 2016 at Dera Beas in Amritsar District, Punjab.

Largest thermal power plant

Vindhyachal Super Thermal Power Station in Singrauli District, Madhya Pradesh, with an installed capacity of 4,760 MW, is ranked as the biggest thermal power plant in the country. It is a coal-based power plant, owned and operated by NTPC Ltd.

Largest power supplier

The National Thermal Power Corporation (NTPC) Ltd, set up in 1975, is the country's largest power company. As of April 2024, it has an installed capacity of 76,294 MW (including joint ventures). NTPC's own stations include 27 coal-based, 7 gas-based, 1 hydroelectric, 1 small hydro, and 17 renewable energy–based stations. Under joint ventures, the company has 9 coal-based, 4 gas-based, 8 hydroelectric, 1 small hydro, and 29 renewable energy projects.

First oil well 

• Oil was first located at Borbil (later Digboi) in Assam in 1890, but systematic drilling for oil had begun in Upper Assam in 1866 and oil was struck at Makum near Margherita at a depth of 36 m (118 ft) on 26 March 1867.

• The first offshore well was sunk in the Bombay High oilfield in 1974.

Longest underwater hydrocarbon pipeline

India's longest underwater hydrocarbon pipeline was completed in April 2023. It stretches 1,656 km, from the river island Majuli in Assam to Jorhat in Upper Assam. The pipeline runs under the Brahmaputra River. Its diameter is 24 in., and it cost ₹9,265 crore.

First refinery 

The Assam Railways and Trading Co. built a small refinery at Margherita in present-day Tinsukia District, Assam, in 1893 to refine oil from Makum and Digboi areas.

First pipeline 

The Guwahati–Siliguri petroleum product pipeline (between Assam and West Bengal) was commissioned by the Indian Oil Corporation in 1965.

First public sector oil refinery 

Guwahati Refinery, Assam, built with Romanian collaboration, started operations on 1 Jan 1962. It belongs to Indian Oil Corporation.

WR Oldest running refinery 

The Digboi Refinery, under the Indian Oil Corporation since 1981, was commissioned in 1901 in Assam. It is the world's oldest running refinery. Earlier, it was owned by Assam Oil Company Limited under Burmah Oil Company.

First refinery to produce lead-free products

Mangalore Refineries and Petrochemicals, commissioned on 25 March 1996, has been jointly promoted by the A.V. Birla Group and Hindustan Petrochemicals Ltd. It has an oil processing capacity of 3 million tonnes (MT) per annum and is the first refinery to manufacture lead-free products.

First private branded LPG 

Reliance Gas was launched in 1998 by Reliance Petroleum Ltd in collaboration with the local liquefied petroleum gas (LPG) bottlers for the packaging of the product.

Highest-ever crude throughput and distillate yield

Numaligarh Refinery Limited (NRL) recorded its highest-ever crude throughput of 3.093 MT against its nameplate capacity of 3.0 MT in the FY 2022–23. The company has also announced a distillate yield of 87.6 per cent, which is its highest since inception. NRL has kept its capital expenditure at ₹6,615 crore (66.15 billion) in FY 2022–23, which is the highest ever to date, surpassing its earlier record of ₹3,605 crore (36.05 billion) in the FY 2021–22.

First company to market LPG 

The first company to market LPG in India was Bharat Petroleum Corporation Ltd (BPCL) in 1955. Now BPCL reaches more than 8.5 crore (85 million) households with over 6,500 LPG distributors across the country.

MINING

Largest coal producing company

Coal India Limited (CIL), a government-owned coal-mining company headquartered in Kolkata came into being in November 1975, when the Government of India took over private coal mines. It is now the single largest coal producer in the world. Operating through 84 mining areas, it has seven wholly owned coal-producing subsidiaries as well as a mine planning and consultancy company, across eight states in India. CIL produced an all-time high of 773.65 MT in FY 2023–24 and coal offtake of 753.59 MT.

First coal mining 

The first tonne of coal was struck in Raniganj Coalfield in 1775 by Suetonius

A coal mine in Katni, Madhya Pradhesh

Grant Heatly, the then collector of the East India Company for Palamu and Hazaribagh, in present-day Jharkhand. Records show that John Summer and Grant Heatly jointly obtained a licence from the then British Governor General Warren Hastings in 1774 to exploit what they then called 'Panchet coal'. They were later joined by another Englishman called Redfern.

State/UT with the most mines

There are 1,319 reporting mines (excluding minor, fuel, and atomic minerals) in the country as recorded in 2021–22. Among these, Madhya Pradesh tops the chart with 263 mines, followed by Gujarat (147), Karnataka (132), Odisha (128), Chhattisgarh (114), Andhra Pradesh (108), Telangana (92), Rajasthan (84), and Maharashtra (67). In terms of the value of mineral production, Odisha leads with ₹32,841 crore (328.41 billion), followed by Rajasthan (₹22,776 crore/ 227.76 billion), and Andhra Pradesh (₹17,906 crore/179.06 billion).

Oldest gold mine

India's oldest gold mine was located in Kolar, Karnataka. The production here in the mid-1970s was 3,000 kg a year, but was on a decline ever since, and the mines were closed in 2001.

Only diamond mines

India's only diamond mines are at Panna in Madhya Pradesh and are administered by the government owned National Mineral Development Corporation (NMDC).

India's first international Bullion Exchange

The India International Bullion Exchange (IIBX), India's first international bullion exchange, is located at Gujarat's GIFT (Gujarat International Finance Tec-City) in Gandhinagar. It was inaugurated on 29 July 2022. This exchange is the third such exchange in the world. India's first bullion exchange will sell physical gold and silver. The jewellers registered as trading partners with the exchange, with a minimum net worth of ₹25 crore as a prerequisite, will be able to buy and sell gold and silver in the exchange. Jewellers abroad will also be able to do the same, following certain conditions, after registering with the International Financial Services Centre Association (IFSCA).

Only London Bullion Market Association (LBMA)-accredited refinery

MMTC–PAMP is India's only London Bullion Market Association (LBMA)-accredited gold and silver refinery, producing 24 carat 999.9 purity bullion and digital gold products with international standards of quality and transparency. *MMTC* stands for 'Metals and Minerals Trading Corporation' of India and PAMP stands for '*Produits Artistiques Métaux Précieux*', which is French for 'Artistic Precious Metals Products'. MMTC–PAMP is a joint venture between MMTC Ltd. (a government enterprise) and PAMP SA (a Swiss refiner).

First lithium resource

Geological Survey of India has found lithium for the first time. They discovered 5.9 million tonnes of inferred reserves of lithium in Salal-Haimana area of Reasi District, Jammu and Kashmir, in February 2023.

INDUSTRIES AND COMPANIES

First cigarette company

Imperial Tobacco Company (ITC) was established in Calcutta in 1910.

First cotton textile mill

Though the British had established a cotton textile mill in 1817, the first truly Indian textile mill was set up in July 1854 in Bombay by Cawasji N. Davar. It was called the Bombay Spinning and Weaving Company.

Current trend in India's tourism industry

India's tourism industry has undergone a dramatic, asymmetrical, but ultimately resilient reset from the COVID shock (2020–21) to the present (September 2025). Following the reopening of borders, Indians travelling domestically led the initial phase of recovery (2022–23), with foreign arrivals following in their wake. Ministry data indicates that domestic tourism increased dramatically from 1.73 billion visitors in 2022 to approximately 2.51 billion visitors in 2023. This suggests a robust rebound in road trips, 'workcations', and short-distance travel, all of which are bolstered by more flexible work schedules and easier access to trains and highways.

Pre-pandemic levels of inbound travel have been reached, and in some cases, exceeded. Foreign tourist arrivals (FTAs) rose from 6.44 million in 2022 to 9.52 million in 2023 and 9.95 million in 2024, approaching the 10.93 million in 2019, according to government data. Important long-haul source markets also experienced a notable recovery in 2024. This recovery was aided by restored air capacity, the availability of e-visas, and India's G20-year visibility.

The nature of the demand has evolved. Spiritual and heritage-related travel has done better, particularly since the January 2024 dedication of the Ram Mandir in Ayodhya. This one node has expanded associated services (transport, hospitality, guides, and crafts) and redrawn northern circuits. A staggering 135.5 million domestic tourists visited Ayodhya in 2024, according to Uttar Pradesh government, and the number kept rising into 2025.

The number of eco-stays, homestays, and community-based itineraries has increased as states adopt sustainable tourism playbooks under Swadesh Darshan 2.0 and related programmes, which place an emphasis on waste management, carrying capacity, and decentralized infrastructure.

Two significant structural enablers stand out. First, digital adoption: contactless bookings, dynamic hotel rates, and the pervasive use of QR codes for payments

Most income from tourists in a year

According to the World Travel & Tourism Council (WTTC), India has broken its past record of 2019 in terms of income from tourism. In 2024, international visitor spend reached ₹3.1TN (3,10,000 crore). From domestic tourists, the spending was ₹15.5TN (15,50,000 crore). Overall income from tourism stood at ₹21TN (21,00,000 crores).

have all simplified the traveler experience. The RBI-enabled UPI flows for international travellers, which were first introduced in 2023 and have since expanded through 'UPI One World' wallets, benefit attractions, small businesses, and ride-hailers by reducing foreign spend frictions.

Second, MICE (Meetings, Incentives, Conferences, Events) potential has grown as a result of supply-side investments. These include event-ready spaces, upgraded rail and airports, and new rooms in Tier-2 and Tier-3 cities. The Tourism Ministry's 2024 review emphasizes the growth of conference and destination development initiatives across regions.

However, the recovery is not consistent. Despite global airfare volatility, inbound long-haul segments remain price-sensitive, and seasonal overcrowding puts pressure on top sites. Policymakers are responding by enacting capacity management, sustainability standards, and dispersion to circuits that are less well-known.

All things considered, India's tourism sector has evolved from being predominantly domestic to becoming more diverse, with digital payments, improved infrastructure, and travel for spiritual and historical reasons all contributing to its growth. As FTAs get closer to 2019 levels and domestic travel hits all-time highs, trade prospects seem bright — as long as last-mile connectivity, sustainability, and service quality are preserved.

First five-star hotel

The Taj Mahal Hotel in Mumbai, Maharashtra, said to have been built back to front, was founded by Jamshetji Nusserwanji Tata in 1904. The story goes that in those days, there were very few hotels that permitted entry to Indians and Tata himself had been denied admission to Pyrke's Apollo Hotel, close to the present-day Taj Mahal Hotel. This motivated Tata to build the hotel.

Source: Tourism.gov.in

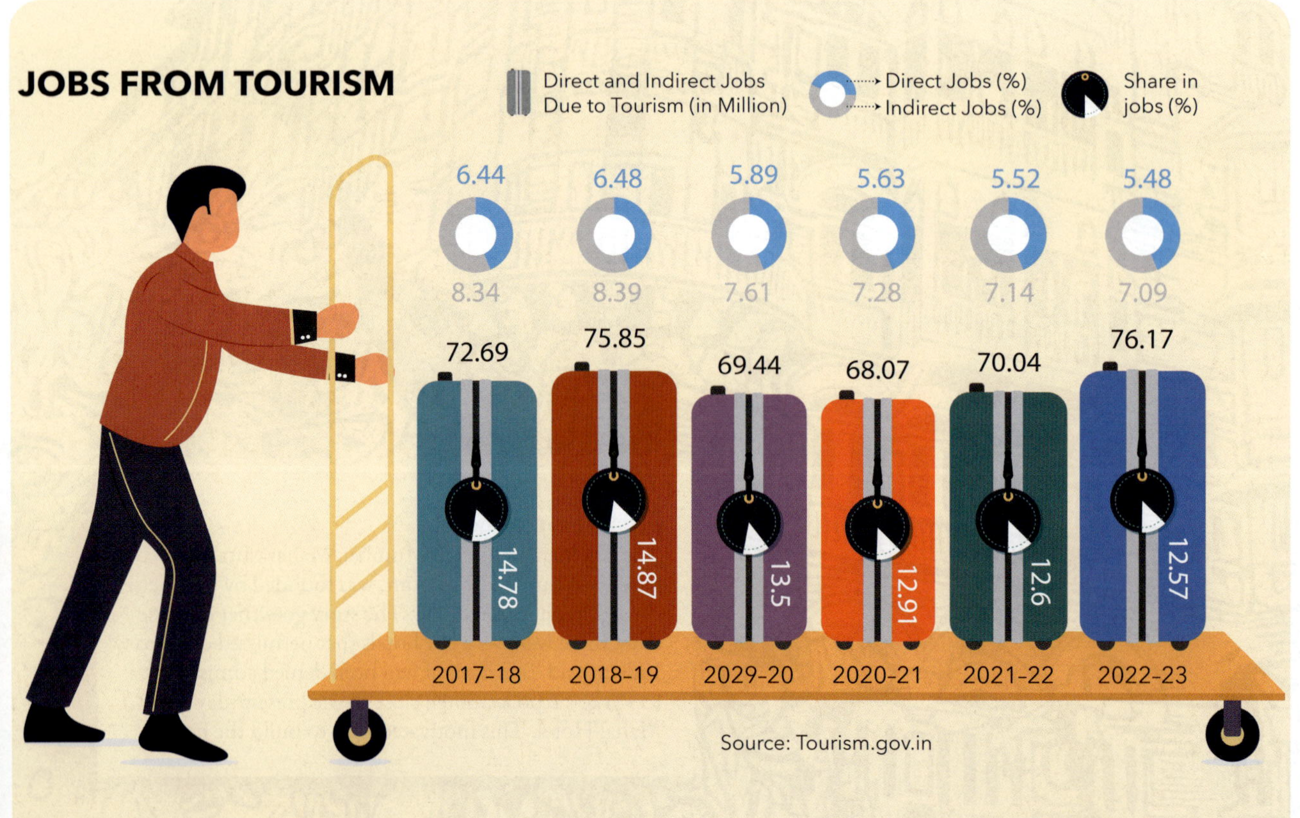

Source: Tourism.gov.in

First commercial production of iron and steel

• In 1830, a unit was set up at Porto Novo (now Parangipettai) in Cuddalore District, Tamil Nadu, to produce iron, but it failed.
• In 1853, the East India Iron Company set up two blast furnaces in South Arcot and Coimbatore Districts, Tamil Nadu. These closed in 1858.
• In 1875, the Barakar Iron Works, Kulti, Bengal, produced pig iron.
• Steel production began in 1892 at the Metal and Steel Factory at Cossipore (now Kashipur, West Bengal), moving to Ichapore (now Ishapur, West Bengal) in 1905.

First factory

The first factory in India, which was a dye-manufacturing unit, was set up by the East India Company with the permission of the then Mughal emperor Jahangir in Surat in 1609, marking the beginning of colonialism.

First ice-cream company

Joy Ice Creams Pvt. Ltd, which was founded by L.C. Java, was the first company to manufacture and market ice cream. In 1948, Java bought a homogenizer and pasteurizer, and set up a small business that became India's first ice-cream company.

Oldest jute mill

Wellington Jute Mill in Rishra, near Serampore (now Srirampur), West Bengal, was established by George Auckland in 1855 as the Rishra Twine and Yarn Mills Ltd, with machinery bought from John Kerr of the Douglas Foundry, the leading manufacturers of flax and manufacturing machines in Dundee, Scotland. The mill had an output of eight tonnes a day. It shut down in 1868 and resumed as Calcutta Jute Mills, which later became Wellington Jute Mills. It is now under AI Champdany Industries Ltd.

First rubber estate and company

The first rubber company, called Malankara Rubber and Produce Company, was started in 1910 by P. John on a 70-acre (28.3-hectare) estate in Thodupuzha, Idukki District, Kerala.

First tea company

Tea seeds were first imported into India from China in 1774. In 1837, the East India Company set up the first tea estate at Chabua, Dibrugarh District, Assam. The Alubari Tea Company, established in 1856 in Darjeeling (now in West Bengal) under the Kurseong and Darjeeling Tea Company, was the first to commercialize tea.

First car factory

In 1928, General Motors had commenced the assembly of cars and trucks in Bombay using imported components. The first indigenous car manufacturing company was the Birlas' Hindustan Motors, which was established at Uttarpara near Calcutta. The first Indian car, 'Hindustan 10', rolled off the assembly line in 1948.

First foreign collaboration

Carr, Tagore and Company was the first Indo-British collaboration under the Charter Act of 1833. There were four partners: W. Carr, Dwarakanath Tagore, D.M. Gordon, and William Prinsep. It closed in 1847.

First retail chain for computers

Computer Point launched the country's first retail chain for computers and computer accessories by establishing the first showroom in Bombay on 31 December 1984. It also had stores in other cities, like New Delhi.

Oldest engineering company

Jessop & Company Ltd, the oldest engineering company in the country, was established in 1788 by two engineers from Britain – Henry and George Jessop.

First champagne manufacturer

In 1987, its very first year, Shyam Chougule's Champagne India, a subsidiary of Indage in Narayangaon, Pune District, Maharashtra, with a 42-acre (17-hectare) vineyard, entered the export market. Champagne Indage Ltd, as it was renamed after being restructured, was the market leader in wines then, with a production of about 1,00,000 cases a year.

First tyre company

The Dunlop Rubber Company (India) Ltd was established on 19 August 1926, with its registered office in Bombay and an authorized share capital of ₹50 lakh (5 million). Dunlop opened its first tyre factory in India at Sahagunj, Hooghly District, West Bengal, in 1936.

First scooter manufacturing company

Lambretta, the first scooter introduced by Automobile Products of India (API), was manufactured in 1956.

First plastic factories

A plastic factory was established in 1926 at Jessore, now in Bangladesh. It manufactured combs, soapboxes, ashtrays, and other articles. It started with machinery that was imported from Germany. The first thermosetting plastic produced in India, starting in 1946, was phenol formaldehyde.

First batch of microchips

The first microchips rolled out of Semiconductor Ltd, located in Chandigarh, in March 1984.

First hosiery company

The Oriental Hosiery Company Ltd, the first hosiery company of India, was started in Calcutta in 1893 by Ananda Mohan Mukherjee.

First power loom

The first power loom for jute cloth was started in 1958 by Henderson and Company, agents of Borneo Jute Company, in present-day Baranagar, Kolkata, in West Bengal. On becoming a limited company, it was named the Baranagore Jute Manufacturing Company and had 512 looms at its peak.

First private sector space launches

On 24 June 2022, the Indian Space Promotion and Authorization Centre (INSPACe) authorized Dhruva Space Pvt. Ltd, Hyderabad, Telangana, and Digantara Research and Technologies Pvt. Ltd, Bengaluru, Karnataka, to launch their payloads. This marked the beginning of private sector space launches in India. Dhruva Space's Dhruva Space Satellite Orbital Deployer (DSOD 1U), a technology payload, along with Digantara's ROBust Integrating Proton Fluence Meter (ROBI), a proton dosimeter payload, were carried onboard the PSLV Orbital Experimental Module (POEM).

First infrastructural index

The Government of India launched a City Liveability Index on 23 June 2017 to measure the quality of life in 116 major cities, based on a set of

79 parameters, such as the availability of roads, education, healthcare, mobility, employment opportunities, emergency response, grievance redressal, pollution, availability of open and green spaces, cultural and entertainment opportunities, and so on.

First commercial payload

India launched its first full commercial payload on 23 April 2007 from Sriharikota in Andhra Pradesh. The payload was an Italian satellite called Agile and was carried by PSLV-C8. The Polar Satellite Launch Vehicle or PSLV has been fully developed by the Indian Space Research Organisation (ISRO). It is an expendable medium lift launch vehicle and has capabilities of launching small size satellites into geostationary orbit. The commercial space service to launch such satellites is called ride-share services as a single such launch can carry multiple payloads. With the launch, India acquired its own independent commercial payload launch capabilities into space and broke into the league of five nations (the United States of America, Russia, France, China, and Japan) in commercial satellite launching market.

India's first small satellite manufacturing company

Set up in 2012, Dhruva Space is India's first small satellite manufacturing company. Based in Hyderabad, they develop scalable and modular satellite platforms that can be used for commercial, defence, and scientific missions in Low Earth Orbit (LEO) and beyond.

First commercial imaging satellite in space

Founded in 2019, Pixxel claims the honour of sending the first commercial Indian imaging satellite into space. It is an Indian space technology start-up focused on building and launching a constellation of hyperspectral Earth imaging satellites. Pixxel has successfully launched its first commercial satellites, named 'Firefly', in January 2025, and secured contracts with NASA and other organizations.

RETAIL

First virtual mall

The Digital Mall of Asia is a virtual e-commerce platform, an amalgamation of digital space and real estate, making it the first virtual mall in the country. The mall is open in Delhi, Noida, Pune, Ahmedabad, Bengaluru, Chennai, Gurugram, Hyderabad, Jaipur, Lucknow, and Mumbai. Each location has a different digital interface and e-shops can be bought or acquired on rent. The mall works 24 hours a day, 7 days a week.

Highest number of stores opened in a single day

On 29 October 2018, the Chinese electronics company Xiaomi opened 500 retail stores, called Mi Stores, in rural regions of India, thereby setting a record for the greatest number of stores opened in a single day. These stores are on the lines of the larger 'Mi Home' stores in metropolitan cities.

Biggest business deal

In August 2018, Walmart Inc., a US multinational retail corporation, announced the deal agreements that made it the largest shareholder in the Flipkart Group, an e-commerce company founded by Sachin Bansal and Binny Bansal in 2007 and based in Bengaluru, Karnataka. Walmart bought roughly 77 per cent stake in the e-retailer for around \$16 billion (approx. ₹1,000 billion then). This was India's largest acquisition and also the world's biggest purchase of an e-commerce company.

ADVERTISING

First known advertisements

Advertising in India began with the first printed newspaper, called *Hicky's Bengal Gazette*, and printed from the 1780s onwards in Calcutta. The advertisements consisted of a series of simple messages 'classified' into different categories for easy reference of readers, or they were lists of the latest merchandise from England.

First ad association

On 21 September 1945, the Advertising Agencies Association of India (AAAI) was registered as a society in Calcutta. In 1961, its headquarters moved to Bombay.

First full-service Indian advertising agency

In 1934, Venkatrao Sista opened Sista Advertising and Publicity Services in Bombay as the first Indian agency offering creative work and space selling in the media. Sista, who came to the financial capital of India as a stenographer of the Great Indian Peninsular Railway, will always be associated with Khatau Voiles, popularized by his agency's campaign.

First patented brand

Horlicks, the first patented brand in the country, was launched in the last decade of the 19th century. In the 1940s, Hindustan Thompson Associates (HTA), an advertising agency, which is now J. Walter Thompson India (JWT), coined the 'Balanced Nourishment' concept for the malt-based beverage to make Horlicks more relevant to India.

First multinational advertising agencies

- Alliance Advertising was set up during the First World War (1914–18), and other foreign (American) agencies, such as L.A. Stronach and D.J. Keymer, followed later.
- The first fully multinational agency in the country was Hindustan Thompson Associates (now JWT) in 1926.

First Indianized foreign brand

Lux toilet soap, sold as the 'favourite beauty soap of film stars', signed on Hindi cinema actor Leela Chitnis as its first Indian model in 1941, in order to Indianize the brand.

Largest LED display screen – on water (aboard a ship/boat/vessel)

On 21 March 2021, Zen Media Ltd LLP, a digital-first Make-in-India start-up, launched Broadcoasters, LED screens

on waters in India, used as an advertising platform on a ship. The vessel *My Blue Papillon*, in the waters near the Bandra–Worli Sea Link, carried a screen measuring 20 m (65.61 ft) x 5 m (16.40 ft) – with a total area of 100 sq m (1076.39 sq ft). The LED screen was powered with a display of 10,000 NITs (Network Interface Taps) and auto-sensors to adjust picture brightness as per daylight.

First ads on TV

The first product to be advertised on TV was Gwalior Suitings in an advertisement that appeared in January 1976.

First ad agency abroad

Interads, a Delhi-based ad agency, was the first Indian advertising agency to open a foreign branch in Moscow, Russia, in 1962.

First commercials on radio

The first commercial came on Vividh Bharati in 1967.

First colour TV ad

An advertisement made for Bombay Dyeing was the first colour TV ad in 1982, the year that colour TV came to India.

Firsts at the Cannes Lions

In 1996, the advertising fraternity bagged three awards at the International Advertising Festival in Cannes, France.

Most awards at the Cannes Lions

In 2022, India won 47 medals including five Grand Prix awards.

Most awards at Cannes by a single agency

In 2025, FCB India won a total of 9 awards including a Grand Prix, the highest by a single Indian agency.

Palais des Festivals in Cannes – the venue of the Lions Festival

EXPORT–IMPORT

Post-COVID global market underwent a significant transformation, leading India to shift its focus on international trade accordingly. During the pandemic, the demand for medicines, active pharmaceutical ingredients (APIs), and medical equipment surged, creating a niche for Indian suppliers. This success propelled the country into the major player league in the global market, particularly in the vaccine segment.

As the market reopened, India began redefining its exportables and market priorities. It expanded its product offerings and explored new market opportunities through treaties and collaborations.

The global situation also favoured India, as the world's understanding of the supply chain and dependency on China as the single major source of inputs underwent a paradigm shift.

In electronics and technology, India stepped out and focused on making the country a major mobile phone manufacturer for the world, alongside IT hardware and components. In the field of green energy, the focus shifted to the export of green technology and solar panels. The focus on exporting refined petroleum products also took on renewed importance.

As for the new markets, Latin America is emerging as a major story for India. The country has started exploring the markets in Latin American countries with renewed gusto. This market, which came into India's trade focus only in 1997 when the foreign ministry drew up a strategy paper to explore the markets there, has seen progress over time. The commerce ministry projects that the trade with this region will exceed $100 billion (about ₹8,80,000 crore), replacing the United Arab Emirates as India's third-largest trading partner.

First export–import bank

The Government of India set up the Export–Import Bank of India (EXIM Bank) in 1982 as a statutory corporation wholly owned by the Union government to provide financial assistance to exporters and importers and to co-ordinate the operations of export–import institutions.

First car to be exported

Hindustan Motors Ltd's Ambassador was the first car to be exported in 1975–76 to Guyana in South America.

India leads in the export of measles vaccines

Ninety per cent of measles vaccines in the world are supplied by India, which also supplies 65 per cent of Diphtheria, Pertussis, and Tetanus (DPT) and Bacillus Calmette-Guerin (BSG) vaccines in the world. The BCG vaccine is used to prevent tuberculosis.

EXPORT-IMPORT

Commodity	Total Exports April 2024-March 2025 ($Mn)	% Share in Total Exports
Engineering Goods	1,16,540.94	26.88
Petroleum Products	60,071.67	13.86
Electronic Goods	38,559.43	8.89
Drugs and Pharmaceuticals	30,379.64	7.01
Gems and Jewellery	29,802.06	6.87
Organic and Inorganic Chemicals	28,631.01	6.60
Readymade Garments of All Textiles	15,974.61	3.68
Rice	12,470.93	2.88
Cotton Yarn/Fabrics/Madeups, Handloom Products, Etc.	12,038.56	2.78
Plastic and Linoleum	8,901.42	2.05
Marine Products	7,393.86	1.71
Meat, Dairy and Poultry Products	5,096.41	1.18
Mica, Coal and Other Ores, Minerals Including Process	4,920.03	1.13
Man-Made Yarn/Fabs./Madeups, Etc.	4,854.06	1.12
Spices	4,447.48	1.03
Leather and Leather Manufactures	4,363.25	1.01
Ceramic Products and Glassware	3,981.54	0.92
Fruits and Vegetables	3,864.71	0.89
Cereal Preparations and Miscellaneous Processed Item	3,091.98	0.71
Iron Ore	2,082.72	0.48
Tobacco	1,976.48	0.46
Coffee	1,802.89	0.42
Handicrafts Excluding Handmade Carpet	1,765.32	0.41
Carpet	1,540.49	0.36
Oil Seeds	1,343.83	0.31
Oil Meals	1,342.58	0.31
Tea	923.86	0.21
Jute Manufacturing (Including Floor Covering)	372.6	0.09
Cashew	337.14	0.08
Other Cereals	270.88	0.06
Others	24,419.85	5.63

Total Exports » **$4,33,562.23 Million**

ADVENTURE

AERO SPORTS

First jump from a microlight

Wing Commander U.K. Palat skydived from a powered hang-glider piloted by Captain K.A. Vasan from 8,000 ft at 7:40 a.m. on 18 October 1999 in Bangalore (now Bengaluru), Karnataka.

First international paramotor medallist

Appasaheb Bhimraj Dhus (b. 26 December 1970) from Maharashtra is the first Indian to win international medals in paramotor games. He won a gold medal in the Pure Economy Task category of the World Paramotor Championship Test Event at Lopburi, Thailand, held from 28 April to 7 May 2017. In the same event, Captain Prafulla Raj Singh won a silver medal in the Pure Navigation Task category.

Microlight flight – representative image

First aerial world circumnavigation in a single-engine plane

Ravinder K. Bansal (b. 26 February 1949) from Clarence, New York, The US, undertook an aerial circumnavigation in a Cessna 400 and flew solo, covering 36 cities over 20,959 nautical miles. He started from Buffalo, New York, US, on 4 July 2017 and returned on 20 August 2017. The expedition was undertaken to raise funds for the Rotary Ambala Cancer and General Hospital.

First paraglide from a high cliff

Anand Munje (b. 7 November 1956) from Kitty Hawk Ground School, Pune, Maharashtra, launched a flight from the 1,646 m (5,400 ft) high Kalsubai Peak, part of the Western Ghats in Maharashtra, on 25 February 1997. The flight covered 4 km in 11 mins.

First at the Mantar Paragliding XC Open Championship

Prakash Chand Thakur won the first prize at the Mantar Paragliding XC Open Championship, organized from 18 to 24 July 2017 by the Asian Continental Paragliding Association in Mantar, Indonesia.

Highest bungee jump – woman

Sudhalakshmi Thanigai Arasu (b. 2 July 1965) performed a 220 m (721 ft 9 in) high bungee jump on 13 August 2010 at Diga Verzasca, Switzerland.

First balloon bungee jump

Major M.K. Yadav jumped from a hot-air balloon, which was at a height of 3,310.73 m (10,862 ft) on 18 August 1995 over Leh, Ladakh.

First Indian woman to skydive over seven continents

Shital Mahajan (b. 19 September 1982) from Pune, Maharashtra, completed 705 skydives across 7 continents during 2017–18, adding to her skydive at Skydiver Empuriabrava in Spain (Europe) in 2014. She skydived at Skydive Go Fly in Boituva, Brazil (South America); Skydive Utti in Sky Dance Skydiving Center, US (North America); Sydney Skydivers in Sydney (Australia); Patriot Hill (Antarctica); Skydive Pretoria, Johannesburg, South Africa (Africa); and Skydive Pattaya, Thailand (Asia), taking the total to 7 continents.

Shital Mahajan also won the Padma Shri in 2011, conferred by Pratibha Patil who was president then. She also won the Tenzing Norgay National Adventure Award in 2006. Shital has jumped from 10 different types of aircraft including hot air balloons, helicopters, paramotors, and powered hang glider. She has also achieved the highest altitude parachute landing at Kala Patthar at 17,444 ft near Mount Everest.

First BASE jump

• *Men*: Lieutenant Colonel Satyendra Verma (b. 24 August 1969), then an officer of the Indian Army from the Corps of Signals, carried out a BASE (Building, Antenna, Span, and Earth) jump from the 137.16 m (450 ft) high deck of the Pitampura TV Tower, New Delhi, on 29 October 2010. This feat was part of the centenary celebrations of the Corps of Signals and the silver jubilee of the Army Adventure Wing.

• *Women*: Archana Sardana (b. 1 April 1972) from Visakhapatnam, Andhra Pradesh, is India's first female BASE jumper. She performed 25 BASE jumps off a 122 m (400 ft) high bridge above a canyon in Utah, US, on 13 July 2010.

The Pitampura TV Tower

First woman skydiver

Rachel Thomas (b. 9 August 1955) from Chittaranjan, West Bengal, was the first Indian woman to skydive from 2,133.6 m (7,000 ft) over the North Pole. She achieved this feat on 20 April 2022 to commemorate 150 years of the Indian Railways. An employee of the Indian Railways, Thomas was also the first woman to represent the country in a skydiving competition in 1987. She was honoured with the Padma Shri in 2005.

Highest BASE jump

Mayank Nagpal (b. 21 September 1983) from New Delhi erformed the highest BASE jump from the 3,080 m (10,105 ft) high point of Eiger Mountain in the Bernese Alps, Switzerland, on 24 July 2019.

Lowest BASE jump

Lieutenant Commander Mahesh V. Birajdar from the Indian Navy performed the lowest BASE jump from a 116 m (380 ft 6 in) high span over a river in the Solang Valley, Himachal Pradesh, on 30 January 2011.

First to complete a BASE jump during day and night

Mayank Nagpal (b. 21 September 1983) from New Delhi became the first Indian to complete a BASE jump from all 4 platforms, during both day and night. For the day BASE number, he jumped from Perrine Bridge, US (5 September 2014), a cliff called Crooked Stick in Idaho, US (11 September 2014), a mobile antenna in Gua Damai Xtreme Park, Malaysia (6 October 2015), and an under-construction building in Delhi, India (31 December 2016). For the Night BASE number he jumped from Perrine Bridge, US (7 September 2014), an antenna in Idaho, US (on 8 September 2014), an under-construction building in Delhi (26 June 2017), and Gua Damai Cliff, Malaysia (28 September 2018).

Highest hot-air balloon take-off

Indradhanush, the hot-air balloon of the Ballooning Club of India, piloted by the then club president Vishwa Bandhu Gupta along with pilot R.K. Wason, took off from the Kushok Bakula Rimpochee Airport (3,310.7 m/ 10,862 ft) in Leh, Ladakh, on 29 September 1988.

Ballooning Club of India

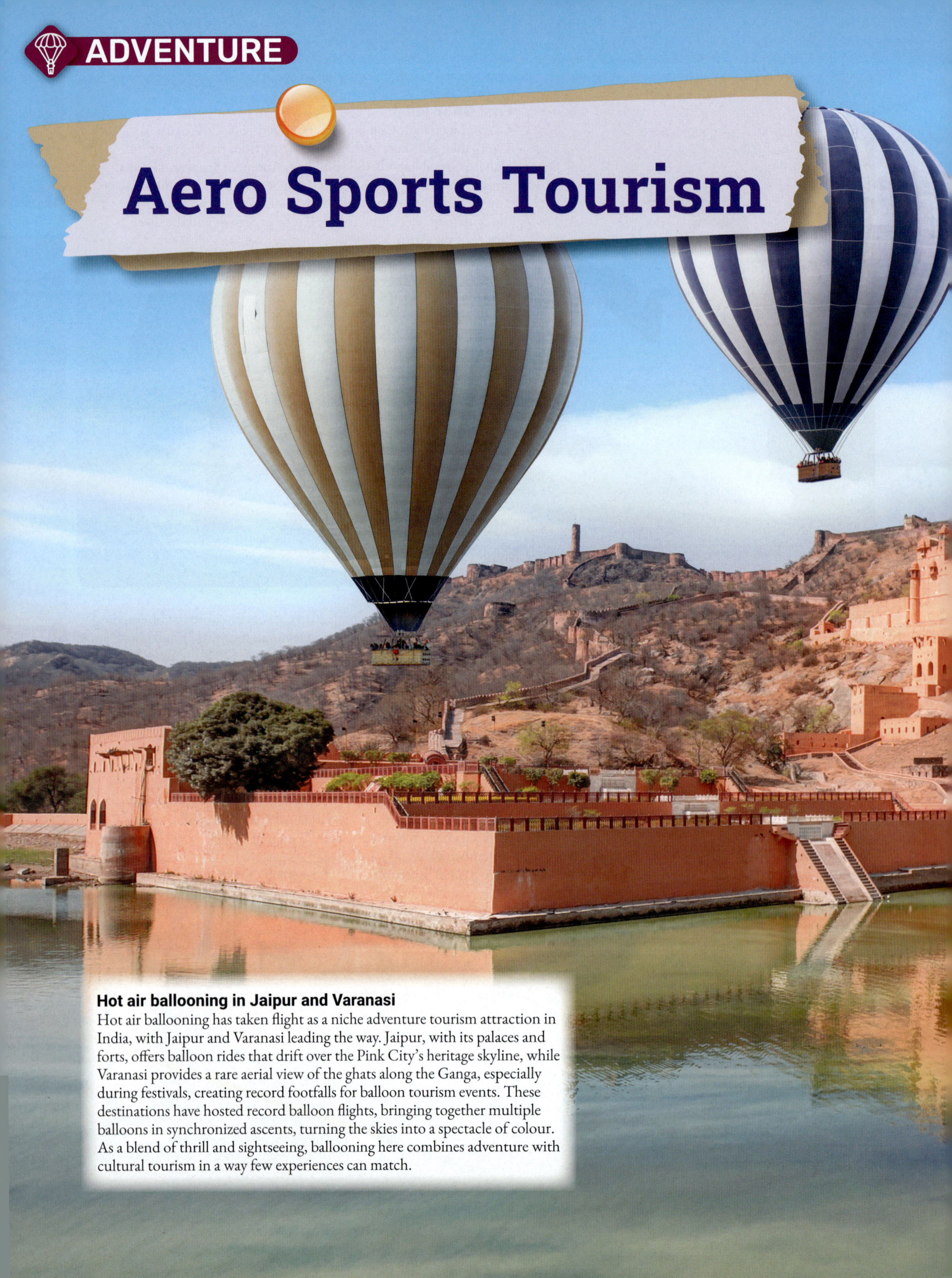

ADVENTURE

Aero Sports Tourism

Hot air ballooning in Jaipur and Varanasi

Hot air ballooning has taken flight as a niche adventure tourism attraction in India, with Jaipur and Varanasi leading the way. Jaipur, with its palaces and forts, offers balloon rides that drift over the Pink City's heritage skyline, while Varanasi provides a rare aerial view of the ghats along the Ganga, especially during festivals, creating record footfalls for balloon tourism events. These destinations have hosted record balloon flights, bringing together multiple balloons in synchronized ascents, turning the skies into a spectacle of colour. As a blend of thrill and sightseeing, ballooning here combines adventure with cultural tourism in a way few experiences can match.

Paragliding at Bir Billing

Nestled in Himachal Pradesh, Bir Billing is acclaimed as the second highest paragliding site in the world, with take-off at 8,000 feet and flights that can soar for over 30 km. Known as India's paragliding capital, it regularly hosts international competitions, including the Paragliding World Cup, and attracts adventure seekers from across the globe. Bir Billing has also seen record-setting events, such as mass paragliding gatherings and endurance flights, making it a premier hub for aerial adventure tourism in India.

Highest skydive landing
Warrant Officer Anshu Kumar Tiwari (b. 3 February 1978) and Wing Commander Gajendra Yadava from the Indian Air Force jumped off an aircraft and landed at Khardung La, 5,481 m (17,982 ft) above mean sea level, on 8 October 2020.

Highest and longest wingsuit flight
Lieutenant Colonel Satyendra Verma (b. 24 August 1969), a retired Indian Army officer, on 31 March 2018, jumped from 5,913.12 m (19,400 ft) using a hot-air balloon platform at Phalodi, Rajasthan. He flew in his wingsuit for 4 mins, covering 10 km across the Jodhpur desert.

Highest flight
Megha Jain (b. 21 September 1988) from New Delhi made the highest flight in an MiG-29 fighter jet, touching 18,400 m (60,367 ft 5 in.) at a top speed of 1,850 km/hr over Sokol Airbase in Nizhny Novgorod, Russia, on 16 February 2017.

Most microlight expeditions
Mountain Eagles, the Indian Army microlight formation flying team, based at Army Adventure Nodal Centre (Microlight and Powered Hang-gliding), Mhow, Madhya Pradesh, conducted 3 expeditions in 13 months from February 2015. The first, with 7 aircrafts, covered 1,800 km in 10 flying days between 13 and 26 February 2015. In the second one, commemorating the golden jubilee of the India–Pakistan war 1965, 3 microlights covered 3,050 km in 10 flying days from 5 to 14 September 2015. The third one, at the 15th reunion of the Corps of Signals, was from 9 to 17 February 2016, with 6 aircrafts covering 1,500 km in 9 flying days. The core team remained the same in all 3 expeditions.

Longest motor glider flight
Captain Surendra Prasad Sinha (b. 26 July 1968), director, Flying Operations, Civil Aviation Department, Government of Jharkhand, flew a Sinus 912 VT-GEE 2-seater aircraft for 1,098.24 km for 8 flying hours, making it the longest motor glider flight in the country. Along with his co-pilot Captain Anil Gill, he took off from Karnal, Haryana, on 13 March 2014 and reached Ranchi, Jharkhand, the next day.

Motor Glider - representative image

Longest cross-country microlight expedition
The Cross India Air Expedition 2011, organized by the Indian Air Force, covered 7,600 km in 80 hrs 15 mins over 20 days. Wing Commander Akhilesh Chauhan piloted the 2-seater microlight, while Squadron Leader Asha Vashisht, Squadron Leader N.D. Gholba, and Sergeant M.P. Singh joined him as co-pilots at different stages of the journey. The flight took off from the air force station at Hindon, Ghaziabad, Uttar Pradesh, on 8 February 2011, proceeded to Udhampur, Jammu and Kashmir, and traversed the length of the country, flying over Delhi, Jodhpur (Rajasthan), Vadodara (Gujarat), Pune (Maharashtra), Bangalore (Karnataka), Sulur (Tamil Nadu), and Thiruvananthapuram (Kerala). It returned to Hindon by the same route on 27 February 2011.

Longest paramotor expedition
The Indian Air Force paramotor team, with Wing Commander M.P.S. Solanki as leader, conducted a circumnavigation-of-India expedition called 'Pradakshina', covering 10,041.7 km in 53 days from 3 February to 26 March 2016. Flagged off from the air force station at Kalaikunda, West Bengal, the team flew along the periphery of the country before returning to Kalaikunda. They followed a clockwise route along the eastern and western coasts and the north-western and eastern regions, covering an average of 218.3 km per day.

Highest zipline by a disabled person
Vijay Kumar Devarkhyani (b. 13 March 1989) from Delhi zipped across Tower 1 and Tower 3 at a height of 473 ft for a distance of 250 ft at 9:58 p.m. on 19 May 2013 at the 40th level of Crown Regency Hotel and Tower, Philippines.

Zipline – Representative image

First Asian triple amputee to complete a bungee jump
Tinkesh Kaushik (b. 21 June 1993) from Jhajjar, Haryana, became the first Asian triple amputee to perform a bungee jump from the world's highest canyon swing. He performed the jump from a height of 160 m (525 ft) on 25 November 2018 at The Last Resort, Kathmandu, Nepal.

First visually impaired person to paraglide
Divyanshu Ganatra, who lost his eyesight due to glaucoma at 19 years, performed a solo paraglider flight over

Kamshet near Pune, Maharashtra, on 30 April 2014. The flight up to 213.36 m (700 ft) lasted 1 min 30 seconds.

First to paraglide with a prosthetic leg

Lieutenant Colonel Dharam Dutt Goel (b. 14 August 1976) from Pune, Maharashtra, successfully performed solo paragliding on 19 October 2013 at Al-Hilal, Himachal Pradesh, thereby becoming the first Indian with a prosthetic leg to paraglide. He performed the paraglider flight from an altitude of 2,400 m (7,874 ft) for 25 mins.

Major D.P. Singh

First disabled skydiver in Asia

Major Devender Pal Singh (b. 13 September 1973) from Gurugram, Haryana, is the first disabled skydiver in Asia. A war-injured amputee veteran, Major Singh skydived from an altitude of 2,743.2 m (9,000 ft) on 28 March 2019 at the military cantonment in Nashik, Maharashtra.

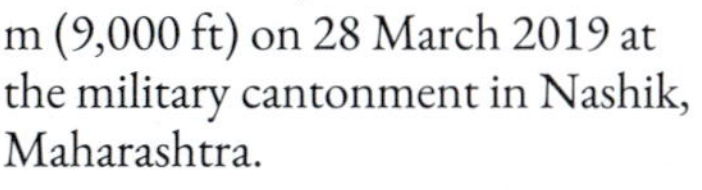

Most podium finishes in FAI F3M Championship

Harshil Virendra Mane (b. 3 March 1999) from Pune, Maharashtra, has 6 international podium finishes in the FAI F3M category championship of aeromodelling, the highest number by an Indian. He is also the first aeromodeller representing India in international championships including the World Cups conducted by the Federation Aeronautique Internationale (FAI).

Harshil Virendra Mane

Daring dives

Wing Commander Gajanand Yadava of the Indian Air Force (IAF) created 4 national records in the field of wingsuit skydive jumping in 2019 in Agra, Uttar Pradesh:

1. First wingsuit skydive jump from a high-speed aircraft (An-32),
2. Highest wingsuit jump from an altitude of 7,437.12 m (24,400 ft),
3. First to do a night-time wingsuit jump from 2,438.40 m (8,000 ft),
4. The only jumper to undertake a high-altitude night-time wingsuit jump from 3,657.60 m (12,000 ft), where he opened the chute at 914.40 m (3,000 ft) after doing wingsuit flying for 2,743.2 m (9,000 ft) Part

of the IAF's skydiving team Akashganga and a parachute jump instructor, Wing Commander Yadava has taken more than 2,900 jumps to date and was awarded the Tenzing Norgay National Adventure Award 2019 in the air adventure category.

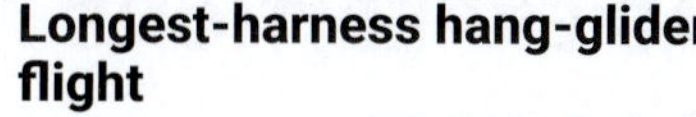

Longest-harness hang-glider flight

Havildar Sanjeev Kumar from the Indian Army Hang-Gliding Team completed the longest-harness hang-glider flight from Suratgarh to Barmer, Rajasthan, on 12 December 2018. He covered 465.33 km on Fox hang-gliders powered by a Mosquito NRG harness. He covered the distance in 8 hrs 43 mins.

Most skydiving jumps

Rajkumar Balakrishnan (b. 1 April 1977) from Theni, Tamil Nadu, started performing skydiving jumps in February 2006 and completed his 10,000th jump on 23 March 2018.

Microlight aircraft flight

• *First:* Flying at a cruising speed of 56 km/hr on a 90 kg tricycle-shaped aircraft, Lieutenant Anil Kumar Yadav covered 3,000 km from Jaisalmer, Rajasthan, to Calcutta (now Kolkata), West Bengal, in 31 days starting 21 September 1994.
• *Fastest:* Squadron Leader B.K. Das flew a microlight aircraft from Jaisalmer, Rajasthan, to Dibrugarh, Assam, covering 3,250 km during 1–23 February 1999.

Most hours logged in free fall

Rajkumar Balakrishnan (b. 1 April 1977) from Theni, Tamil Nadu, has logged a total of 84 hours in free fall while skydiving, up to 6 July 2018.

A Lone Skydiver in Free Fall - Representative Image

Oldest woman skydiver

Neela Ingle from Mumbai successfully performed a freefall from the height of 3,048 m (10,000 ft) at 12 mph on 12 April 2024 at the Old Sarum Airfield in Wiltshire, England at the age of 78 years 7 months.

Skydiving from the highest altitude

Jithin Vijayan skydived from an altitude of 12,933 mt (42,431 ft) at Whiteville, Tennesse, US on 1 July 2023.

ROAD EXPEDITIONS

FOUR-WHEELER

Longest journey within a country – solo

Shashi Kapila (b. 3 November 1942) from New Delhi completed the longest journey in a Honda Mobilio car, covering 8,227 km in 105 hrs 15 mins. He started from Delhi at 6:00 a.m. on 12 November 2016 and reached back at 12:28 p.m. on 22 November 2016. The farthest location he travelled to was Kanniyakumari, Tamil Nadu.

Fastest East–West India expedition – group

Apurba Kumar Deka (b. 27 March 1975), Animesh Deka (b. 15 January 1982), and Md Zillur Rahman (b. 2 December 1975) from Guwahati, Assam, completed the fastest East–West India expedition from Tezu, Arunachal Pradesh, to Koteshwar, Gujarat, covering 3,771.4 km in 70 hrs 52 mins. The team drove a Renault Duster car, starting their journey on 27 October 2015 and ending the expedition on 30 October 2015.

Fastest East–West India expedition by a disabled person – solo

Eric Paul (b. 14 January 1988), a wheelchair-bound paraplegic from Rohini, New Delhi, completed the East–West India solo expedition in a hand-controlled Maruti Swift, covering 3,697 km in 4 days 18 hrs 55 mins. He started from Tezu, Arunachal Pradesh, on 30 November 2017 at 4:13 a.m., reaching Koteshwar, Gujarat, at 11:43 p.m. on 4 December 2017.

Eric Paul

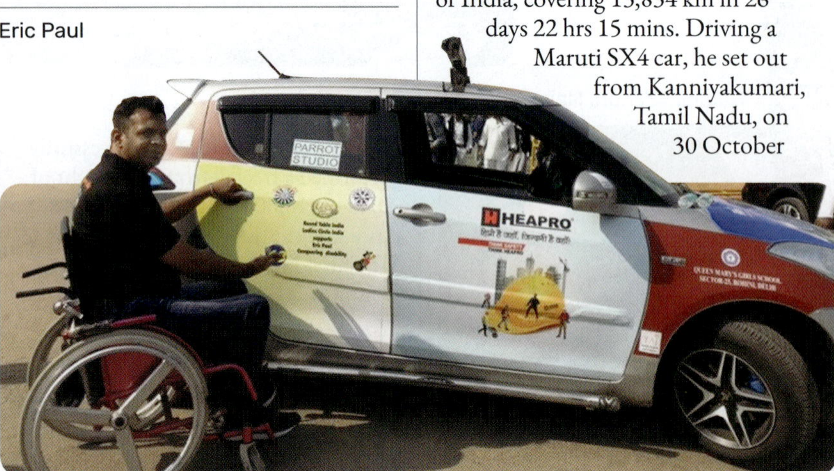

Fastest GQ expedition – group – women

Sukraty Saxena, Rupam Devedi, Swaranjali Saxena, and Apala Rajvanshi completed the Golden Quadrilateral (GQ) expedition, covering a distance of 6,263 km in 6 days 14 hrs 5 mins. They started their expedition at 1:35 a.m. on 10 May 2023 from India Gate, New Delhi, and concluded it at 4:30 p.m. on 16 May 2023 at Subroto Park Air Force Station, New Delhi.

First All-India expedition – group

Arun Kumar Basra and Kamaljit Singh Virdi from Rapid Action India completed an all-India car expedition in their Fiat Padmini, covering 15,179 km in 19 days 19 hrs 5 mins. They were flagged off from Delhi on 5 January 1998 and returned on 25 January 1998.

First Four Corners of India expedition – solo

Dr S.S. Chaudhari (b. 7 March 1962) from Jalgaon, Maharashtra, completed a solo drive connecting the 4 corners of India, covering 13,834 km in 26 days 22 hrs 15 mins. Driving a Maruti SX4 car, he set out from Kanniyakumari, Tamil Nadu, on 30 October 2014. He reached Tezu, Lohit District, Arunachal Pradesh, on 8 November 2014; Leh, Ladakh, on 16 November 2014; Koteshwar, Kachchh District, Gujarat, on 22 November 2014; and concluded the expedition at Kanniyakumari on 26 November 2014.

First North–South India round expedition – solo

Suresh Joseph (b. 14 May 1958) from Tamil Nadu is the first person to complete the trailblazing North–South India round expedition trip in 2012 and, in the process, breaking the record of the fastest North–South solo expedition. He started his expedition from Kanniyakumari, Tamil Nadu, on 2 July 2012 and reached Leh, Ladakh, on 7 July 2012, covering 3,811 km in 129 hrs 30 mins. Four days later, he was back on the trip, taking off from Leh on 11 July 2012. He reached Kanniyakumari on 15 July 2012. He drove a Maruti Swift car for the journey.

First Trans-Himalayan expedition – solo

Suresh Joseph (b. 14 May 1958) from Tamil Nadu set out in a Ford Endeavour to create a new record for a Trans-Himalayan solo trip, which he accomplished in 18 days 13 hrs 15 mins. Starting his journey from Jammu in Jammu and Kashmir on 21 August 2015, he reached Tezu in Arunachal Pradesh on 8 September 2015. Joseph covered 5,845 km across 9 Indian states, Nepal and Bhutan, and crossed altitudes of up to 2,554.2 m (8,380 ft).

Fastest Trans-Himalayan expedition – group

Dr Yagnesh Gohil, Dr Sanjay Karangiya, and Dr Mayur Diwani from Gujarat set a record for the fastest Trans-Himalayan expedition, covering a total distance of 5,464 km in 21 hours and 46 minutes. The trio began their journey from Leh, Ladakh, at 4:45 a.m. on 23 September 2023 and ended their journey in Tezu, Arunachal Pradesh on 1 October 2023 at 4:00 a.m.

Fastest Four Corners of India expedition – solo

Suresh Joseph (b. 14 May 1958) from Tamil Nadu successfully completed the 4 corners of India tour (Kanniyakumari, Tamil Nadu; Koteshwar, Gujarat; Leh, Ladakh; and Tezu, Arunachal Pradesh), covering 13,214 km in 403 hrs. Driving a MahindraXUV500, he started his expedition on 7 May 2015 and ended it on 12 June 2015.

Fastest North–South expedition – group

Sameer A.S. (b. 14 December 1986), Noufal K.N. (b. 30 May 1985), and Bibin Krishnan (b. 20 April 1984) from Kerala set a record for the fastest North–South India group expedition, covering 3,870 km in 49 hrs 34 mins. The trio started from Leh, Ladakh, at 7:05 a.m. on 1 September 2021, reaching Kanniyakumari, Tamil Nadu, at 8:39 a.m. on 3 September 2021.

Sameer A.S., Noufal K.N., and Bibin Krishnan

First disabled person to reach Umling La – solo

Eric Paul (b. 14 January 1988) from Delhi was the first disabled person to reach Umling La, Ladakh on 6 July 2022 at 2:57 p.m. He started on 1 July 2022 from Delhi and covered a distance of 1,260 km in 126 hrs 27 mins. He is paralyzed from below the chest and drove his hand-controlled car to this high altitude.

First West–East India round expedition – solo

Daljit Singh Matharoo (b. 29 September 1986) completed a solo West–East–West India expedition, covering 7,715km in 217 hrs 25 mins. He broke the record for the fastest solo East–West India expedition by covering 3,832km in 94 hrs 44 mins. He started in his Maruti Zen car from Koteshwar, Kachchh District, Gujarat, on 27 April 2018, and reached Tezu, Arunachal Pradesh, on 1 May 2018. He started back on 1 May 2018 and reached Koteshwar on 6 May 2018.

Daljit Singh Matharoo

Dhruveer Singh Gandhi

Fastest North–South expedition – solo

Dhruveer Singh Gandhi (b. 6 March 1985) from Mumbai, Maharashtra, completed the North–South expedition, covering a distance of 3,819.17 km in 56 hrs 20 mins. He started his expedition at 4:45 a.m. on 10 September 2021 from the office of the deputy commissioner GST Division, Srinagar, and concluded it at 1:05 p.m. on 12 September 2021 at the deputy superintendent of police's office at Kanniyakumari.

Fastest Four Corners of India expedition – solo

Suresh Joseph (b. 14 May 1958) from Tamil Nadu successfully completed the four corners of India tour (Kanniyakumari, Tamil Nadu; Koteshwar, Gujarat; Leh, Ladakh; and Tezu, Arunachal Pradesh), covering 13,214 km in 403 hrs. Driving a Mahindra XUV500, he started his expedition on 7 May 2015 and ended it on 12 June 2015.

First North–South India solo drive by a woman

Vinaya Shrikant Ket (b. 17 March 1984) from Pune, Maharashtra, successfully completed her North–South India solo expedition from Leh, Jammu and Kashmir, to Kanniyakumari,

Tamil Nadu, covering 3,911 km in 98 hrs 56 mins. She started the journey from Leh on 25 June 2016 and reached Kanniyakumari on 29 June 2016.

Longest distance travelled across countries – solo

Hitendra Sharma (b. 11 January 1978) from Gwalior, Madhya Pradesh, successfully undertook a solo expedition by road, covering 30,195 km across 11 Asian countries in a Honda Amaze car in 92 days. Starting from Gwalior in Madhya Pradesh, India, on 10 February 2017, he reached Bangladesh, driving through India, Myanmar, Thailand, Laos, Vietnam, Cambodia, Malaysia, Singapore, Bhutan, and Nepal, and returned to India on 21 May 2017.

Longest journey within a country – group

Sagar Thakar (b. 30 June 1982) and Kanak Barsadia (b. 14 February 1984) from Surat, Gujarat, completed the longest journey in a Maruti Swift Dzire car, covering 60,830 km in 82 days. They set off from Bardoli, Gujarat, on 20 March 2017 and reached back on 12 June 2017.

TWO-WHEELER (MOTORCYCLE)

UP TO 150 CC

First Trans-Himalayan expedition – solo

Rajeev Kumar Mondal from Burdwan, West Bengal, successfully completed a solo 2-wheeler expedition along the Trans-Himalayan route covering 7,120 km in 303 hrs 58 mins of travel time. Kick-starting the expedition on a 150 cc Hero Honda Achiever from Guwahati, Assam, on 5 May 2013, he first went to Arunachal Pradesh and then, passing through Bhutan, West Bengal, Nepal, Uttarakhand, and Himachal Pradesh, reached Srinagar in Jammu and Kashmir on 12 July 2013. He crossed 22 passes including Khardung La at 5,602 m (18,380 ft).

151–450 CC

Longest journey within the country – solo

Krishanu Kona (b. 27 September 1991) from Delhi travelled 50,338 km on his motorcycle in 224 days to set the record

Krishanu Kona

for the longest motorcycle journey in India. He started on a Bajaj Pulsar NS200 bike on 30 August 2015 from Delhi and returned on 9 April 2016.

First North–South India round expedition by a disabled person – solo

Vadivel Baluchamy (b. 14 June 1990), a disabled person from Madurai, Tamil Nadu, completed the first North–South solo round expedition by a disabled person, covering 9,136 km in 576 hrs 23 mins. He started on a Royal Enfield Classic 350 bike from Kanniyakumari, Tamil Nadu on 30 August 2018 at 4:25 p.m. and travelled to Leh, Ladakh. He returned to Kanniyakumari on 22 September at 8:18 p.m.

Fastest All-India expedition – solo

Srinath K.A. from Chennai, Tamil Nadu has completed the all-India expedition on 31 March 2024 on his TVS Apache RR310 covering a distance of 16,433 km in 25 days. He began his journey on 7 March 2024 and completed it on 31 March 2024 travelling through 28 states and 8 union territories.

Fastest GQ expedition by a disabled person – solo

Vadivel Baluchamy (b. 14 June 1990), completed the fastest Golden Quadrilateral (GQ) expedition by a disabled person, covering 6,723 km in 14 days 9 hrs 30 mins. He started on a Royal Enfield Classic 350 bike from Chennai, Tamil Nadu, on 25 September

Above: Hitendra Sharma; *below*: Sagar Thakar

388

Fastest East–West India expedition – solo

Dr S.T. Thomas (b. 8 January 1987) from Tamil Nadu covered 3,729 km from Tezu, Arunachal Pradesh, to Koteshwar, Gujarat, in 68 hrs 18 mins to set a new record in the East–West India two-wheeler expedition category. He started his journey on his Honda CBR 250R bike on 20 March 2016 and concluded the expedition on 23 March 2016.

2017 and travelled to Kolkata, Delhi, and Mumbai, returning to Chennai on 9 October 2017.

Longest distance covered within the country by a disabled person – solo

Mahinder Singh Raghuwanshi (b. 2 October 1987), who has 70 per cent disability and a prosthetic limb, covered 5,331.5 km on an Enfield Bullet 350 bike in 17 days. He started from his hometown Mhow, Madhya Pradesh, on 3 June 2016 and went up to Khardung La (5,359 m/17,582 ft) in Leh, Ladakh, returning to Mhow on 19 June 2016.

Fastest Four Corners of India expedition – solo

Vishvesh Dhirendrakumar Mehta (b. 10 June 1980) from Jamnagar, Gujarat, completed the fastest solo expedition connecting the 4 corners of India, covering 11,217 km in 313 hrs 51 mins. Riding a Royal Enfield Classic 350, he set out from Koteshwar, Gujarat, on 21 May 2019 and returned to Koteshwar after covering Kanniyakumari, Tamil Nadu; Leh, Ladakh; and Tezu, Arunachal Pradesh, on 8 June 2019. His break time was 113 hrs.

OVER 450 CC

Fastest All-India expedition – solo

Prashant Kumar (b. 14 July 1987) from Bengaluru, Karnataka, completed the all-India expedition on 7 November 2019 on his Triumph Tiger XCA 800 bike, covering 16,305 km in 23 days 9 hrs 46 mins. He started from Hyderabad, Telangana, on 15 October 2019 and returned on 7 November 2019, travelling through the then 29 states and 5 Union Territories.

Left: Prashant Kumar Vishvesh; *right*: Dhirendrakumar Mehta

Shraiyans Mittal

Fastest GQ expedition – solo
Shraiyans Mittal from Noida, Uttar Pradesh, completed the GQ solo motorcycling expedition, covering a distance of 6116.6 km in 87 hrs 13 mins on a Royal Enfield Interceptor 650 between 18 March 2022 and 21 March 2022.

GENERAL

First to cross Umling La – solo
Pallavi Fauzdar (b. 20 December 1979) from Delhi was the first to cross Umling La pass on 4 August 2017 at 3:16 p.m. It is the highest motorable pass in the world, situated at an altitude of 5,882.64 m (19,300 ft) above sea level. On her expedition, she even named the Bonni La, situated at an altitude of 5,083 m (16,677 ft), which was unnamed before.

Longest ride while standing anywhere on the bike – solo
Vishwajeet Bhatia (b. 22 January 1983) of the Border Security Force (BSF) successfully covered 95.42 km while standing on the side footrest of the Royal Enfield 350. He completed the ride in 2 hrs 36 mins on 28 December 2022 at 25 Battalion, BSF, R.K. Wadhwa parade ground, Chhawla, New Delhi. He performed this stunt without any belts, harnesses, or supporting equipment.

Longest ride while standing on a structure – solo – woman
Satabdi Dhar (b. 23 December 1990) of the Border Security Force performed a continuous ride on a 2.49 m (8 ft 2.4 in) ladder fitted on a Royal Enfield 350 for 2 hr 30 mins on 26 December 2022. She covered a distance of 76 km at 25 Battalion, BSF, R.K. Wadhwa parade ground, Chhawla, New Delhi. She performed this stunt without any belts, harnesses, or supporting equipment.

Satabdi Dhar

Largest rally (less than 100 km) by women riders – multiple venues
The largest 2-wheeler rally by only women riders was organized by the Akhil Bharatiya Terapanth Mahila Mandal on 8 March 2020, International Women's Day. As many as 6,205 women rode distances ranging from 1.5 to 10 km at locations like Udaipur, Ahmedabad, Balotra, Surat, and Delhi. The rally was held as part of their 'I Respect' campaign to emphasize the need for women to respect one another for their choices.

Largest moving human pyramid – women
On 27 December 2022, the female team of 38 women led by Inspector Himanshu Sirohi of the Border Security Force formed a human pyramid on 9 Royal Enfield 350 bikes. They covered more than 1 km in 2 mins 10 secs at Kartavya Path between Vijay Chowk and India Gate, New Delhi. They performed this stunt without any belts, harnesses, or supporting equipment.

Longest ride while standing anywhere on the bike – solo – woman
Inspector Himanshu Sirohi (b. 4 May 1988) of the Border Security Force successfully covered 178 km while standing on the side bracket of a Royal Enfield 350. She completed the ride in 6 hrs 2 mins on 24 December 2022 at 25 Battalion, BSF, R.K. Wadhwa parade ground, Chhawla, New Delhi. She performed this stunt without any belts, harnesses, or supporting equipment.

Longest ride while standing on a structure – group
Inspector Awadhesh Kumar Singh (b. 19 April 1980) and Constable Sudhakar (b. 8 July 1987) of the Border Security Force performed a continuous ride on a 3.35 m (11 ft) ladder fitted on a Royal Enfield 350 for 2.5 hrs. They covered a distance of 75 km at 25 Battalion, BSF, R.K. Wadhwa parade ground, Chhawla, New Delhi. They performed this stunt without any belts, harnesses, or supporting equipment.

Longest ride on a structure facing backwards – solo
Inspector Awadhesh Kumar Singh (b. 19 April 1980) of the Border Security Force performed a continuous ride on a 3.42 m (11 ft 3.6 in) pole fitted on a Royal Enfield 350 for 4 hrs 37 mins while facing backwards. He covered a distance of 169 km at 25 Battalion, BSF, R.K. Wadhwa parade ground, Chhawla, New Delhi. He performed this stunt without any belts, harnesses, or supporting equipment.

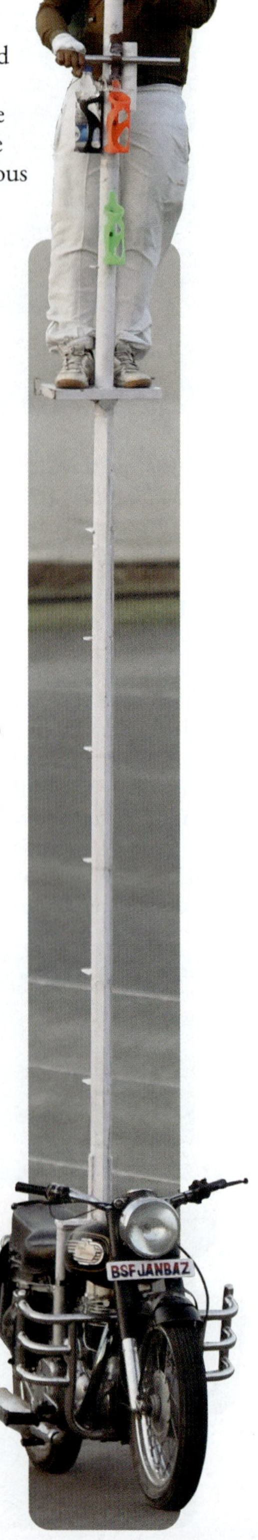

Awadhesh Kumar Singh

Longest ride while sitting on a bike facing backwards – solo – woman

Constable Rajwinder Kaur (b. 1 May 1986) of the Border Security Force performed a continuous ride while sitting facing backwards on a Royal Enfield 350. She covered a distance of 32 km in 1 hr on 28 December 2022 at 25 Battalion, BSF, R.K. Wadhwa parade ground, Chhawla, New Delhi. She performed this stunt without any belts, harnesses, or supporting equipment.

Rajwinder Kaur

TWO-WHEELER (BICYCLE)

GEARED

Fastest East–West expedition – solo

Naresh Kumar Rajendran (b. 3 June 1992) from Vellore, Tamil Nadu, completed the fastest East–West solo expedition on a geared bicycle by covering 3,613 km in 10 days 8 hrs 57 mins. He started from Tezu, Arunachal Pradesh, at 4:00 a.m. on 5 December 2018 and ended at Koteshwar, Gujarat, at 12:57 p.m. on 15 December 2018.

Fastest GQ expedition – solo

Bharat Pannu (b. 8 May 1983) from Bengaluru, Karnataka, completed the Golden Quadrilateral (GQ) solo expedition, covering a distance of 5,938.2 km in 14 days 23 hrs 52 mins on his geared bicycle. He started his expedition at 12:08 a.m. on 16 October 2020 from India Gate, New Delhi, and concluded it at 12:20 a.m. on 31 October 2020.

Fastest North–South expedition – solo

Nimesh Mansukhbhai Jivrajani (b. 11 February 1980) from Bhavnagar, Gujarat, completed a solo North–South India expedition on a geared bicycle, covering 3,400 km in 14 days 16 hrs 20 mins. He started from Jammu, Jammu and Kashmir, at 5:40 a.m. on 24 December 2018 and reached Kanniyakumari, Tamil Nadu, at 10:00 p.m. on 7 January 2019.

Longest distance covered within the country – solo

Karan Singh Jagawat (b. 1 March 1948) covered a distance of 20,948 km on his geared cycle in 178 days. He started his journey on 23 April 2017 from Jaipur, Rajasthan, and returned to Jaipur on 18 October 2017. He travelled through Koteshwar, Gujarat; Tezu, Arunachal Pradesh; Khardung La, Ladakh; and Kanniyakumari, Tamil Nadu.

GEARLESS

Fastest North–South expedition – solo

Saurabh Bharat Zagade (b. 28 October 1996) from Pune, Maharashtra, completed a solo North–South India expedition on a gearless bicycle, covering a distance of 3,440 km in 14 days 7 hrs. He started the expedition from Dharmal, Jammu and Kashmir, at 6:25 a.m. on 15 April 2019 and reached Kanniyakumari, Tamil Nadu, at 1:25 p.m. on 29 April 2019.

Left: Bharat Pannu; *right*: Saurabh Bharat Zagade

Fastest North–South expedition – group

Ashwani Kumar Singh (b. 14 August 1995) from Deoria, Uttar Pradesh, and Akash Yadav (b. 1 February 1990) from Azamgarh, Uttar Pradesh, completed the fastest North–South India expedition by cycle, covering 4,197 km in 14 days 15 hrs 37 mins. The duo started from Leh, Ladakh, on 13 June 2016 and reached Kanniyakumari, Tamil Nadu, on 27 June 2016.

GENERAL

Largest bicycling marathon

Organized by Vodafone India, the second edition of the Vodafone Cycling Marathon held in Bengaluru, Karnataka, on 1 March 2015, attracted 6,123 cyclists. The event was held under four different categories: Champion Race (60 km), Passion Race (40 km), Green Ride (20 km) and Fashion Ride (5 km). It was conducted under the aegis of the Cycle Federation of India, supported by Bengaluru City Traffic Police. Around 5,000 cyclists took part in the first edition of this marathon.

First tandem bicycling

Ashok N. Bhanushali (b. 21 May 1974) from Mumbai, Maharashtra, and Dr Meera Velankar (b. 11 December 1975) from Bengaluru, Karnataka, completed India's first 300 km brevet ride on a tandem bicycle. The feat was part of an event organized by Surat Randonneurs on 10 July 2016. The duo started the ride from M.T.B. College, Surat, Gujarat, and covered a distance of 309 km in 17 hrs 36 mins.

Cycles and Overland Tourism

Trans-India cycling expeditions

Long-distance cycling has become a hallmark of India's adventure tourism, with record-making journeys spanning the length of the country. The iconic Delhi–Kanniyakumari route, covering over 2,500 km, has seen both solo cyclists and large groups attempt endurance rides that test stamina, resilience, and determination. These expeditions, often undertaken for awareness campaigns or record bids, not only showcase the spirit of adventure but also highlight India's diverse landscapes, from the northern plains through the Deccan plateau to the southern tip at Kanniyakumari.

Aerial View of National Highway - 44: One of the Highways on Delhi–Kanniyakumari Route

Camel and horse safaris in the Thar desert

The Thar desert of Rajasthan has long been a hub for camel and horse safaris, with some of the longest desert tourism trails in India. These expeditions, stretching across sand dunes from Jaisalmer to Bikaner and beyond, recreate the traditional caravan routes once used by traders. Safari records often involve large groups travelling together over extended distances, blending adventure with cultural immersion through village stays, folk performances, and desert camping. They stand out as both a test of endurance and a unique way to explore Rajasthan's living heritage.

Mountain biking in Ladakh

With its rugged terrain and high-altitude passes, Ladakh is a premier destination for mountain biking adventures, including some of the highest MTB races in the world. Riders navigate challenging routes across passes like Khardung La (17,582 ft) and Taglang La (17,480 ft), making these events both physically demanding and breathtakingly scenic. The combination of thin mountain air, stark landscapes, and the thrill of racing on the "roof of the world" has given Ladakh a record place in global mountain biking tourism.

Oldest Super Randonneuse

Ela Ghose (b. 8 April 1961) successfully completed 4 brevets organized by Noida Randonneurs and Delhi Randonneurs (a part of Audax India Randonneurs) under the aegis of Audax Club Parisien of France, and earned the title of Super Randonneuse in the 2018–19 season. A randonneuring event is called a randonnée or brevet, and a rider who has completed a 200 km event is called a randonneur. The Super Randonneur/Randonneuse title is awarded on the completion of a series of 4 brevets within a single (cycling) year, say, November 2018–October 2019. The 4 brevets cover 200 km (completed within 13 hrs 30 mins), 300 km (completed within 20 hrs), 400 km (completed within 27 hrs) and 600 km (completed within 40 hrs).

Ela Ghose: Oldest Super Randonneuse

Longest tandem bicycling – women

Sheetal Bambulkar (b. 27 October 1978) from Mumbai, Maharashtra, and Dr Meera Velankar (b. 11 December 1975) from Bengaluru, Karnataka, completed a tandem cycling brevet ride of 206 km in 12 hrs 27 mins in Vadodara, Gujarat, on 20 December 2015.

Fastest Asian to cycle across the world

Vedangi Kulkarni (b. 1998) from Pune, Maharashtra, became the fastest Asian to cycle across the world. She started her expedition from Perth, Australia, in July 2018 and reached Kolkata, West Bengal, on 23 December 2018. She crossed 29,000 km in 159 days, pedalling up to 300 km every day. She covered 14 countries including New Zealand, Canada, Iceland, Portugal, Spain, France, Belgium, Germany, Denmark, Sweden, Finland, and Russia, and endured temperatures ranging between –20°C and 37°C.

Vedangi Kulkarni

Most consecutive cycling expeditions – 100 km

Gurpreet Singh (b. 28 June 1972) from Jalandhar, Punjab, cycled at least 100 km per day consecutively for 300 days from 19 May 2020 to 14 March 2021 with geared Merida Sculptura 400 and Trek FX2 bicycles in Jalandhar, Punjab.

All-India tour on a mono-wheeler

Subrata Chakraborty (b. 5 November 1976) from Kolkata, West Bengal, completed an all-India solo expedition on a monocycle, covering 10,500 km in 256 days. He started his journey from Raj Bhavan, Kolkata, on 8 September 2000 and returned to Kolkata on 21 May 2001. He passed through 17 states of the country, viz., West Bengal, Odisha, Andhra Pradesh, Tamil Nadu, Kerala, Karnataka, Goa, Maharashtra, Gujarat, Rajasthan, Haryana, Delhi, Uttar Pradesh, Madhya Pradesh, Bihar, Assam, and Arunachal Pradesh.

WATER SPORTS

First circumnavigation of the globe – group

On 28 September 1985, 10 sappers, led by Colonel T.P.S. Chowdhury, set off on INS *Trishna*, for a 55,000 km sail in an 11.3 m (37 ft) long, 10.5 tonne fibreglass yacht. They sailed from Mumbai, Maharashtra, to Maldives and Mauritius, and then to St Helena Island. Crossing the Equator for the second time, they sailed into the Port of Belem in Brazil, then through the Panama Canal towards the Galapagos Islands, the Polynesian Islands and Bali, reaching Mumbai on 10 January 1987.

First to sail down the Ganga River

Captain P.P. Sabharwal and Captain S.N. Dubey performed the first sail down the Ganga River in a racing craft from Chandi Ghat at Haridwar, Uttarakhand, to Kolkata, West Bengal, from 26 to 28 July 1960. The total distance they covered was 1,931.23 km.

First circumnavigation of the globe by a disabled sailor

Major Ashok Kumar Singh, a permanent member of the INS *Trishna* crew and winner of the National Adventure Award in 1994, went around the globe in 1985. It was the longest journey undertaken by a disabled person.

First circumnavigation – woman – solo

On 15 October 1988, Ujwala Rai became not only the first Indian woman, but also the first Asian one, to sail around the world after a 17-month voyage in *Jaykus III*, a 9.75 m (32 ft) Vancouver-class sailboat.

First catamaran sailing expedition

A team of sailors from the Artillery Water Sports Association, Hyderabad, Telangana, completed the Sarvatra Sailing Expedition, a 1,364 km long marine voyage along the eastern coast of India. The longest such expedition in the country, it was launched from Marina Beach, Chennai, Tamil Nadu, on 18 December 2011 and culminated at Gopalpur, Odisha, on 3 January 2012. They also set records of sailing 153 km non-stop in a day on 21 December 2011 and of 15 hours of non-stop sailing on 31 December 2011.

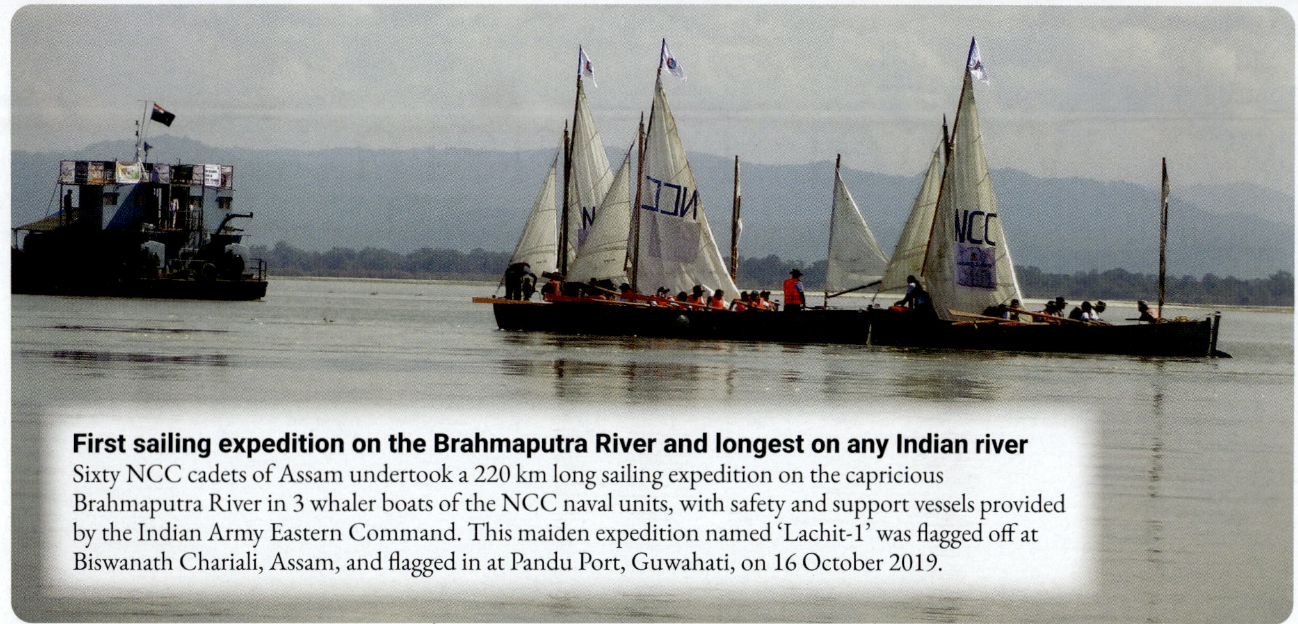

First sailing expedition on the Brahmaputra River and longest on any Indian river

Sixty NCC cadets of Assam undertook a 220 km long sailing expedition on the capricious Brahmaputra River in 3 whaler boats of the NCC naval units, with safety and support vessels provided by the Indian Army Eastern Command. This maiden expedition named 'Lachit-1' was flagged off at Biswanath Chariali, Assam, and flagged in at Pandu Port, Guwahati, on 16 October 2019.

First expedition on the Beas River

A team of 13 people from Atal Bihari Vajpayee Institute of Mountaineering and Allied Sports (ABVIMAS), Manali, Himachal Pradesh, was the first to raft across the length of the Beas River from 23 to 26 October 2019. Led by Colonel Neeraj Rana, the director of ABVIMAS, the 230 km long rafting expedition was undertaken with 2 rafts and 3 kayaks from Manali to Dehra Gopipur Bridge at Pong Dam.

First circumnavigation – man – solo

Commander Dilip Donde of the Indian Navy completed a solo circumnavigation of the globe in 276 days. He covered 21,600 nautical miles sailing on INSV *Mhadei*, a 17-m (56-ft) long sailing boat fitted with high-tech navigation and communication equipment. He embarked on the voyage on 19 August 2009. On return, his boat touched base at Sunk Rock Lighthouse at Mumbai harbour on 22 May 2010. The expedition was part of the Indian Navy's 'Sagar Parikrama' project.

First rafting event in the country

The Indo-US Upper Ganga Rafting Expedition in 1984 was the first rafting expedition in India led by American Ken Warren and Avinash Kohli. The expedition rafted sections of the Bhagirathi and Alaknanda Rivers till Devprayag, and the Ganga River from Devprayag to Rishikesh in Uttarakhand.

Rafting on the Ganga

WR Youngest in the world to complete the Oceans Seven Challenge

Prabhat Koli (b. 27 July 1999) from Navi Mumbai, Maharashtra, became the youngest person in the world, at the age of 23, to complete the Ocean Seven Challenge on 1 March 2023. He completed the challenge in 8 hrs 41 mins, crossing the Cook Strait between New Zealand's North and South Islands amid bad weather. He is also the recipient of Tenzing Norgay National Adventure Award.

First to complete the Ocean Seven Challenge

Rohan Dattatrey More (b. 30 October 1985) from Pune, Maharashtra, became the first Asian swimmer at the age of 32, to complete the Ocean Seven challenge on 9 February 2018 when he swam across the Cook Strait between North and South Islands of New Zealand in 8 hrs 37 mins. He became the ninth swimmer in the world to complete the difficult open-water swimming challenge that includes the English Channel, the North Channel, the Molokai Channel, the Catalina Channel, the Tsugaru Channel, the Strait of Gibraltar, and the Cook Strait.

First canoeing expedition

Sheo Shankar Gope and Ravindra Kumar Bhuyan were team leaders of a canoeing expedition that started from Kolkata on 6 July 1991. They paddled upstream on the Ganga and sailed a distance of 2,000 km, touching Bhagalpur, Mokama, Patna, Allahabad (now Prayagraj), and Etawah, reaching Delhi on 25 September 1991.

First Asian woman to swim across the seven seas

Bula Chowdhury (b. 2 January 1970) from West Bengal was the first Asian woman to swim across the 7 seas: the Arctic Ocean, the North Atlantic Ocean,

Water Tourism

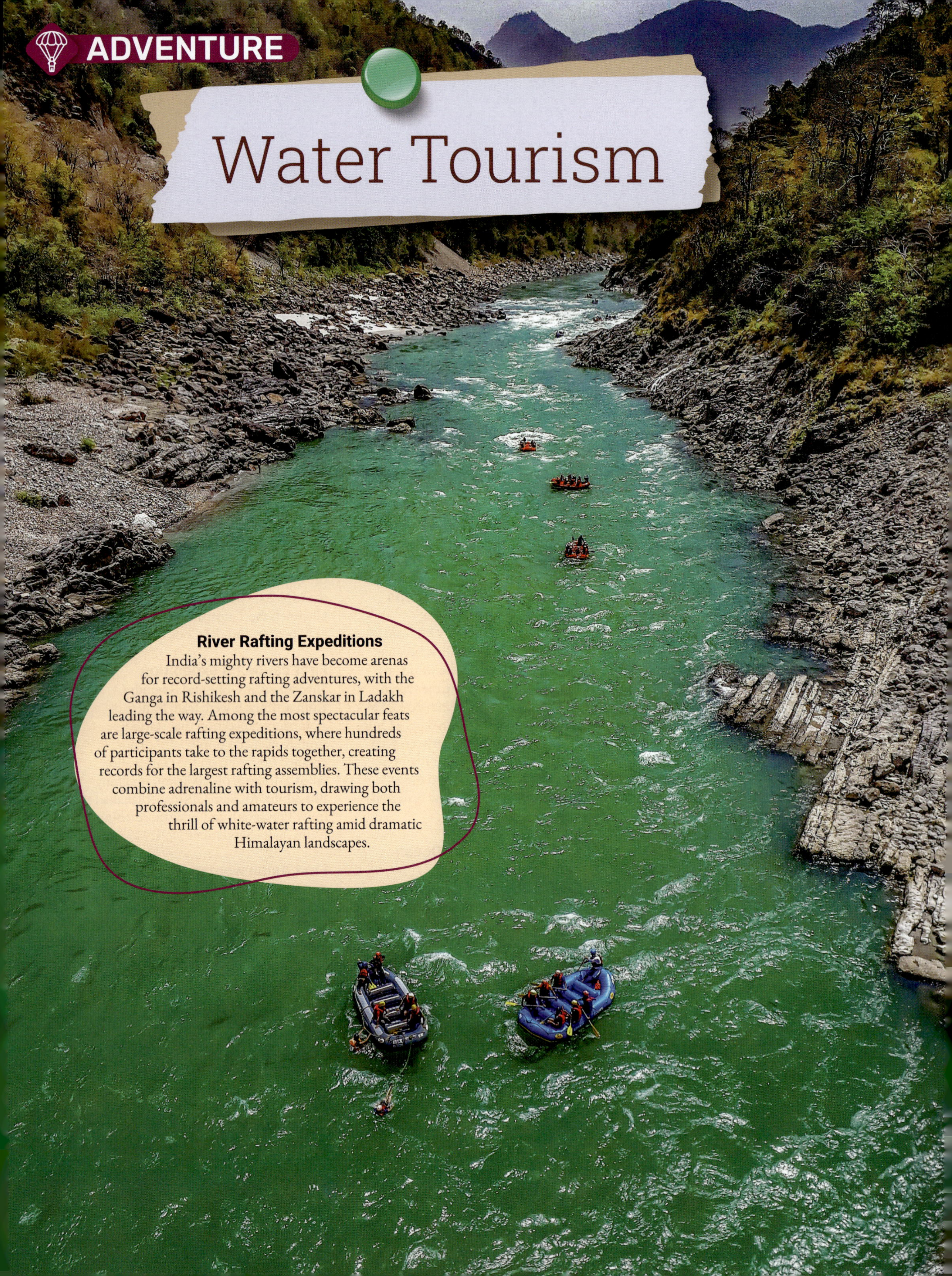

River Rafting Expeditions

India's mighty rivers have become arenas for record-setting rafting adventures, with the Ganga in Rishikesh and the Zanskar in Ladakh leading the way. Among the most spectacular feats are large-scale rafting expeditions, where hundreds of participants take to the rapids together, creating records for the largest rafting assemblies. These events combine adrenaline with tourism, drawing both professionals and amateurs to experience the thrill of white-water rafting amid dramatic Himalayan landscapes.

Scuba Diving Tourism Records

The pristine waters of the Andaman and Nicobar Islands and Lakshadweep have hosted record-setting scuba tourism events, including the largest group dives in India. These coordinated underwater gatherings bring together dozens of divers to explore coral reefs, marine life, and underwater landscapes simultaneously, turning adventure into a collective spectacle. As hubs for eco-tourism, these sites have become magnets for both professional divers and beginners, positioning India as an emerging destination for large-scale scuba diving experiences.

Longest Distance Open-Water Swims

Indian swimmers have made their mark in the world of endurance open-water swimming, conquering some of the toughest channels and straits. Records include successful crossings of the English Channel, often called the 'Mount Everest of swimming,' and the Palk Strait between India and Sri Lanka, an arduous 30 km swim through challenging currents. These feats, achieved by both solo swimmers and relay teams, highlight India's growing adventure tourism in open-water sports while inspiring new generations of long-distance swimmers.

the South Atlantic Ocean, the Indian Ocean, the North Pacific Ocean, the South Pacific Ocean, and the Antarctic Ocean. She crossed the English Channel twice in 1989 and 1999, and in 2005 she became the first woman to swim across sea channels off 5 continents. She received the Arjuna Award in 1990 and the Padma Shri in 2008.

First and youngest Asian woman to swim in Antarctic waters

Bhakti Sharma (b. 30 November 1989) from Udaipur, Rajasthan, is the first Asian woman and the youngest in the world to set a record in open swimming in Antarctic waters. She swam 2.3 km in 41 hrs 14 mins, in temperatures of around 1°C, breaking the record of L. Cox (US) and L. Pugh (Britain). She was awarded the Tenzing Norgay National Adventure Award in 2010.

First saturation dive

Commodore Vimal Kumar of the Indian Navy conducted the first saturation dive in May 1985 in a decompression chamber, using a mix of helium and oxygen, on INHS *Ashvini* in Mumbai. Pratap Singh and T. Vinod Rao were pressurized to a depth of 67 m (219 ft 10 in.) on 16 May 1985 and stayed in saturation for 6 days.

Fastest Asian swimmer to cross the Gibraltar Strait

Shubham Dhananjay Vanmali (b. 20 December 1995) from Mumbai became the fastest Asian swimmer to cross the Strait of Gibraltar, completing 16.7 km from Isla de Tarifa in Spain to Point Cires in Morocco in 3 hrs 16 mins on 14 August 2014. Earlier, Vanmali had also swum the English Channel (England to France), crossing the channel in 12 hrs 42 mins on 4 August 2014, and the 35 km long stretch from Dharamtar in Raigad district, Maharashtra, to the Gateway of India in Mumbai in 8 hrs 1 min 17 secs on 21 January 2014.

First backstroke swimming across the Strait of Gibraltar without neoprene

Tejesh Vishnu Parsekar (b. 30 May 1990) from Mumbai, Maharashtra, became the first Indian and second in the world (since 1928) to successfully complete backstroke swimming across the Strait of Gibraltar from Isla de Tarifa, Spain, to Perejil Island near Morocco on 16 August 2010. He was the first in the world to complete it without neoprene (protective suit). He covered 19. 4 km in 5 hrs 21 mins.

First deep-bounce dive

Commodore Vimal Kumar of the Indian Navy was the first person to dive to a depth of 160 m in a diving bell in the Black Sea in 1970. He explored the bottom of the sea for about 10 mins. After surfacing, he underwent a decompression schedule for 10 hrs.

First to swim from mainland to Anacapa Island

Prabhat Raju Koli (b. 27 July 1999) from Navi Mumbai, successfully swam from Hollywood Beach, Oxnard, to Anacapa Island in 6 hrs 22 mins 17 secs on 10 July 2019. The route was 20 km long in open sea.

WR First woman to cross the English Channel – solo

Arati Saha (b. 24 September 1940) from West Bengal became the first Indian woman to cross the English Channel on 29 September 1959. She swam from Cape Gris Nez, France, to Sandgate, England, in 16 hrs 20 mins.

First to swim the English Channel thrice – solo

• *Men*: Taranath Narayan Shenoy (b. 1958) from Maharashtra became the first person to cross the English Channel 3 times by 1985. Deaf and nearly blind, he had previously swum across the channel in 1983 and 1984.

• *Women*: Rashmi Sharma (b. 1988) from Kolkata became the first woman to cross the English Channel 3 times by 2009. She had previously swum across the channel in 2006 and 2007.

First to complete the Triple Crown

Taranath Narayan Shenoy (b. 1958) from Maharashtra became the world's second swimmer and the first Indian to complete the Triple Crown of Open Water Swimming when he crossed the 32.2 km long Catalina Channel (or San Pedro Channel), separating Santa Catalina Island from the southern Californian mainland, US), on 25 August 1987. Deaf and nearly blind, he had previously swum the 20 Bridges Swim (a 45.9 km circumnavigation of Manhattan Island, New York City, US) on 9 August 1987 and the English Channel on 18 August 1983.

King of Gibraltar

B.R. Ghadge of Mumbai Police, Maharashtra, crossed the shark-infested and freezing Strait of Gibraltar (Spain–Morocco) 4 times. He was conferred the title 'King of Gibraltar' by the Gibraltar Strait Association in August 2002 as he completed the fourth feat in 6 hrs 10 mins on 2 August 2002. He was also the first Indian to cross the 26 km long Toroneos Gulf, Greece, in 10 hrs 43 mins on 20 July 2002.

Most stand-up paddle-boarding

Kumaran M. (b. 2 March 1981) from Chennai had completed standup paddle-boarding on 19 different waterbodies, including 17 in India and 1 each in Sri Lanka and Malaysia, as on 30 June 2016.

Longest kayaking – solo

Kaustubh Kisan Khade (b. 17 January 1987) from Mumbai completed the west coast expedition from Dwarka, Gujarat, to Kanniyakumari, Tamil Nadu, from 17 November 2016 to 7 February 2017. He paddled 1,845 km in 83 days.

First to complete the Round-Trip Angel Island marathon

Shubham Dhananjay Vanmali (b. 20 December 1995) from Mumbai, Maharashtra, was the first Indian to complete the Round-Trip Angel Island marathon swimming. He completed the 16.1 km marathon swim in 10 hrs in San Francisco, California, US, on 24 May 2018. He is also the youngest male swimmer and 12th in the world to complete this challenging bay-water swim marathon.

First woman to swim the Gibraltar Strait

Aarti Pradhan from Maharashtra became the first Indian woman to swim the Strait of Gibraltar in 1988. She covered the distance of 22.2 km in 7 hrs 17 mins from Isla de Tarifa, Spain, to Morocco. She received the Arjuna Award in 1988.

First surfing and stand-up paddle competition

The Surfing Federation of India, with the Kerala Tourism Department, organized Spice Coast Open, India's first official national surfing and stand-up paddle (SUP) competition at Kovalam Beach, Kerala, from 3 to 5 May 2013. The 3-day event had more than a hundred participants in surfing contests under 5 categories and SUP races under 2.

Longest stand-up paddle-boarding – group

Sri Krishnan (b. 31 July 1991) and Siddharth C. (b. 6 July 1992) from Chennai, Tamil Nadu, accomplished the longest stand-up paddle-boarding in the open sea, covering 31 km in the Bay of Bengal on 15 April 2016. They started at Kovalam Beach, Kerala, and paddled to reach Marina Beach, Tamil Nadu, covering the distance in 6 hrs 27 mins.

Most rivers rafted in a month

National Institute of Mountaineering and Allied Sports (NIMAS), Dirang, Arunachal Pradesh, conducted an expedition with 7 members, namely, Colonel Sarfaraz Singh, Naib Subedar Jadhav Laxman Vishnu, Havaldar Loushambam Labango Singh, Havaldar Darshan Singh, Lance Naik Patil Suraj Ravindra, Lance Naik Himmat Singh, and Mr Tosap Rime, and rafted 7 rivers in a month. They rafted on Kameng, Dibang, Noa Dihing, Lohit, Subansiri, Siyom, and Siang in Arunachal Pradesh from 23 November 2020 to 23 December 2020, covering a total distance of 720.21 km.

Longest social campaign through an adventure sport

The National Mission for Clean Ganga, operated under the Department of Water Resources, River Development, and Ganga Rejuvenation, Ministry of Jal Shakti, Government of India, organized the Ganga Aamantran Abhiyaan – a river-rafting and kayaking expedition on the Ganga River, conducted between 10 October and 12 November 2019 with a team of 9 members. The expedition started from Devprayag and culminated at Ganga Sagar after covering 2,500 km. They spread the message of water conservation and river rejuvenation.

Longest kayaking – group

Tarun K. Roy and Brij Mohan Bisht from New Delhi completed the Himalaya-to-Ocean Ganga Expedition from Rishikesh, Uttarakhand, to Ganga Sagar Island in the Bay of Bengal from 5 January to 19 March 2003. They paddled 2,443 km in 74 days.

First sailing expedition around the Indian peninsula

Alok Kumar Yadav (b. 20 June 1984) from EME Sailing Association completed the first sailing expedition around the Indian peninsula. He started from Haldia, West Bengal on 21 October 2018 and reached Porbandar, Gujarat on 1 December 2018. He covered a distance of 4,597 nautical miles in 41 days.

Alok Kumar Yadav *(middle)*

Fastest to swim across the English Channel

Anita Sood from Maharashtra remains the fastest Indian to swim the Great English Channel. She swam in the year 1987 and took 8 hrs 15 mins (England to France).

Longest white-water rafting expedition

Aqua Scullers, the 9-member rafting team of the Indian Air Force, completed the longest white-water rafting expedition on the Ganga River, covering over 3,000 km from Gangotri in Uttarakhand to Ganga Sagar in West Bengal in 16 days from 19 October to 4 November 2013. The first such expedition undertaken by the Indian Air Force, it included the Himalayan portion of the river from Gangotri (3,049 m/ 10,003 ft) to Haridwar (295 m/968 ft), a very challenging white-water stretch with Grade IV–V rapids.

WR Long-distance swimming by a paraplegic woman

Deepa Malik (b. 30 September 1970) is an Indian athlete from New Delhi. She swam against the current in the Yamuna River at Allahabad (now Prayagraj), Uttar Pradesh, covering a distance of 1 km in 35 mins 36 secs on 15 June 2008. She received the Khel Ratna award in 2019.

Non-stop rafting expedition

Eight members of the Bihar Adventure Foundation, led by Sanjay Kumar Dutta, set off on a non-stop rafting expedition on the Ganga River. They began from Haridwar, Uttarakhand, on 29 October 1991 and covered 2,400 km in 621 hrs, ending at Calcutta (now Kolkata), West Bengal, on 24 November 1991.

Swimming at the highest altitude

Petty officer R.L. Sharma and leading seaman Dhani Ram swam a distance of 4,746 m (15,571 ft) across the breadth of Kedartal, a glacial lake at an altitude of 4,750 m (15,584 ft) in Uttarakhand, on 25 September 1995.

Oldest to complete the Triple Crown

Srikaanth Viswanathan (b. 15 July 1972) from Bengaluru, Karnataka, at the age of 47, completed the 20 Bridges Swim in New York City, US, in 8 hrs 7 mins on 31 August 2019, becoming the oldest Indian to complete the Triple Crown of Open Water Swimming. He had previously swum across the English Channel (14 hrs 7 mins) on 21 July 2018 and the Catalina Channel (13 hrs 4 mins) on 16 August 2019.

Longest open-sea swimming by a paraplegic

M.S.A. Shaikh (b. 17 July 1986) from Mumbai, a paraplegic with 100 per cent disability due to a spinal cord injury, participated in open-sea swimming from Sinquerim to Baga and back to Candolim Beach, Goa, on 8 April 2017 at the UMOJA #BeachFest 2017. He completed the 8 km swim in 4 hrs 4 mins.

Mohd Shams Aalam Shaikh

Oldest to cross English Channel

Siddhartha Agarwal from Bengaluru, Karnataka crossed the English Channel on 29 August 2024 at the age of 49 becoming the oldest Indian to do so. He covered the 42 km stretch between England and France in 15 hrs and 6 mins.

Marathon windsurfing

Rahul Rastogi from Hyderabad, Telangana, was the first Asian to windsurf 400 km from Kavaratti, Lakshadweep, to Kozhikode, Kerala. He started on 22 April 1988 and completed the marathon 3 days later. His average windsurfing timing was 14 hrs a day.

Yachting at the highest altitude

Captain Gautama Dutta from Mumbai, carted his laser boat to an altitude of 5,460m (17,913 ft) at Devtal Lake, Uttarakhand, and yachted there on 18 September 1993.

Deepest underwater cycling – ocean – solo

Nishant K. Patel (b. 15 February 1982) from Mumbai, successfully attempted underwater cycling at a depth of 32.7 m (107 ft 3 in) on 25 October 2016. He covered a distance of 100 m in 6 mins 47 secs in the Bay of Bengal off Puducherry coast. He used a Firefox Vortex 20 cycle and tied weights of 5 kg in the front and 2 kg at the back of the cycle to avoid floating. He had a 12-litre (200 bar) air tank attached for breathing support.

Fastest to complete Cape2Rio race

Indian Navy's Captain Atool Sinha (b. 1 August 1968) from Pune, Maharashtra, skippered INSV *Mhadei* in the Transatlantic Intercontinental Cape2Rio Race 2017 and completed the race in a record time of 20 days 19 hrs 27 minutes. The crew began the race on 1 January 2017 at 12:00 noon and finished the race on 22 January 2017 at 7:27 a.m., covering a distance of 3,800 nautical miles (7,038 km). The boat had 6 crew members including the skipper.

MARATHONS

First 4 Deserts Grand Slam winner

Atul Patki (b. 8 November 1965), a US citizen of Indian origin, completed the 4 Deserts Ultramarathons Series on 8 November 2014. He became the first Indian to complete all 4,250 km events in a calendar year.

WR First to complete all six World Marathons

Siddhartha Ghosh (b. 21 February 1975) from Kolkata, was the first person to complete all 6 World Marathons in a calendar year during 2013. He is also the first recipient of the 6 Star World Marathon certificate and has received the same 5 times consecutively from 2012 to 2016. The World Marathon Majors consist of 6 races annually across cities and are accredited by the International Association of Athletics Federations.

Siddhartha Ghosh

First to complete the 7 Emirates Run

M.A. Shaikh (b. 29 September 1974) from Mumbai, became the first Indian to successfully complete the 7 Emirates Run, an ultramarathon across all 7 emirates of the United Arab Emirates (UAE). He covered a distance of 575 km in 12 days from 21 November to 2 December 2014.

First Ultraman triathlete

Arunaabh Shah (b. 11 August 1990) from Delhi completed the Ultraman Triathlon (a 10 km swim, 421.1 km of cycling and an 84.3 km run) in Australia on 16 May 2016. He is the first Indian to do so in Ultraman's 33-year-long history.

First Ironman triathlon

The first Indian Ironman triathlon was held in Goa with over 1,000 participants on 20 October 2019. Considered the most prestigious endurance triathlon event worldwide, the race included 1.9 km of swimming, 90 km of cycling, and 21.1 km of running, which were all done sequentially in a single day. Bishworjit Singh Saikhom from Pune, completed the triathlon in 4 hrs 42 mins 44 seconds, securing the first place.

Ironman Triathlon – representative image

First to complete Grand-to-Grand Ultramarathon

Arpita Maitra (b. 31 October 1978) from Kolkata, became the first Indian to successfully complete the Grand-to-Grand Ultra (G2G) marathon, a gruelling week-long foot race from the Grand Canyon to the Grand Staircase in the US, in which she covered the 273 km route in 76 hrs 21 mins 43 secs in six stages from 22 to 28 September 2013.

First to complete the World Marathon Challenge – full marathon

Aditya Raj (b. 22 June 1983) from Gurugram, Haryana, became the first Indian to complete the World Marathon Challenge, in 2020, in which runners travel across the globe, completing 7 marathons (each 42.2 km) in 7 days on 7 continents. Starting on 6 February 2020 in Novo, Antarctica, Raj travelled to Cape Town in Africa, Perth in Australia, Dubai in Asia, Madrid in Europe, and Brazil in South America, finishing his seventh marathon in Miami, North America, on 12 February 2020. His total running time was 36 hrs 47 mins 36 secs.

Most consecutive half-marathon distance runs

Abhishek Singh Pandher (b. 27 September 1977) from Ahmedabad, Gujarat, completed 685 half-marathon distance (21.1 km) runs in 685 days from 15 July 2020 to 30 May 2022. The runs were conducted in Gujarat and Madhya Pradesh.

Marathons and Ultra Runs Tourism

Beach and Desert Runs

From the shimmering sands of the Rann of Kutch and Jaisalmer's Thar Desert to the rugged Konkan coastline, India's marathon scene has expanded into some of the most dramatic terrains in the world. These events, often organized as ultra runs or trail marathons, have set records for participation in extreme climates, showcasing runners braving searing desert heat or humid coastal winds. Blending endurance sport with landscape tourism, they turn India's deserts and beaches into open-air stadiums for record-breaking runs.

Cross-Country Ultra Runs

India has witnessed extraordinary feats in ultra-distance running, with athletes undertaking solo cross-country runs spanning thousands of kilometres across multiple states. These journeys, such as Delhi to Mumbai or Kanyakumari to Kashmir, test endurance, mental strength, and logistics over weeks of running. Often undertaken to raise awareness for social causes, these ultra runs have created records for the longest solo endurance journeys on foot, blending adventure with advocacy and tourism.

Marathon Tourism in Ladakh

The Ladakh Marathon, held at altitudes of over 11,500 ft, is recognized as the world's highest marathon and a flagship event for adventure tourism in India. Attracting thousands of participants from across the globe, it combines extreme endurance with breathtaking Himalayan landscapes. With steadily increasing participation each year, it has set records for the largest number of runners at a high altitude, turning Ladakh into a bucket-list destination for both athletes and adventure travellers.

First to finish the Ultraman World Championship

Gaurav Makkar (b. 26 November 1979) from Gurugram, became the first Indian to finish the Ultraman World Championship. The championship is a 3-day, 515 km multi-sport race held annually in Hawaii, US. He completed a 10 km swim (in 4 hrs 24 mins), a 421 km bicycle ride (in 16 hrs 20 mins), and an 84 km run (in 8 hrs 56 mins) during 23–25 November 2018. He also completed the Ultraman Florida 2018 during 16–18 February 2018, thereby completing 2 Ultraman races, the most by an individual in a year.

Most half-marathons organized in a single day – multiple venues

The Indian Air Force organized half-marathons simultaneously across 100 air force stations as part of the centenary celebrations of the marshal of the Indian Air Force, Arjan Singh on 14 April 2019. The marathon began at 5:30 a.m. and concluded at 9:30 a.m. and saw the participation of 12,600 air force officers. The marathon distance was 21 km and it was conducted in three age categories: below 35 years; between 35 and 45 years; and above 45 years. Marshal of the Indian Air Force, Arjan Singh, was the first and only officer of the Indian Air Force to hold a 5-star rank.

Most triathlons completed in a year

Adil S. Nargolwala (b. 31 August 1969) from Gurugram, Haryana, completed the most triathlon races in a year in 2019. He completed the Triathlon Sprint at the Delhi International Triathlon 2019, the Triathlon Olympics at the New Delhi Triathlon Championship, the Ironman (113 km/70.3 mi) in Kazakhstan, the Ironman in Sweden, and the Ultraman India Race conducted in Delhi-NCR.

Adil S. Nargolwala

Longest relay race

As part of its golden jubilee celebrations, while also paying tribute to former president A.P.J. Abdul Kalam, the Border Security Force (BSF) Sector Headquarters in West Bengal organized the BSF Golden Jubilee Baton Relay Race 2015. The event saw 1,785 BSF jawans in commando uniform cover a distance of 174.2 km in relay format in 8 hrs 55 mins 36 secs on 24 August 2015.

Longest distance covered while running – single day

Ullas Narayana from Bengaluru, ran 250.3 km in 24 hours on 1 December 2018, becoming the first to cover this distance in a day. He completed the non-stop run at the 2018 International Association of Ultra Running (IAU) 24-Hour Asia and Oceania Championships in Taipei, Taiwan.

Most half-marathons in a year

Vijay Boddupalli (b. 1 September 1988) from Chennai, completed 17 half-marathons, the most by an individual in a year, from 1 June 2017 to 31 May 2018. The 17th half-marathon was completed at the H2O Run on 22 April 2018. The half-marathons were conducted across 7 states in India.

Most half-marathons by an individual

B. Srinivasan from Chennai, Tamil Nadu has completed 301 half-marathons, the most by an individual, beating the previous record of 164. These marathons were conducted at different venues in India including Gurgaon, Haryana, and Madurai, Tamil Nadu. He has run a total distance of 7037.77 km.

Longest cross-country run

Long-distance runner Raj Vadgama (b. 18 June 1967) from Mumbai, successfully undertook 'Bharathon 10,000', a unique run across 70 cities in 17 states of India to spread the message of unity. He covered a distance of 9,902 km from 15 August 2014 to 26 January 2015, making it the first and longest such self-supported cross-country run. He ran about 60 km a day on an average for 165 days.

Most full marathons in a year

Sivabalan Pandian (b. 21 September 1958) from Mumbai, completed 114 full marathons, the most by an individual in a year, from 6 January to 31 December 2019. These full marathons were conducted at venues both within India and abroad. The count also includes 14 ultramarathons.

Most ultramarathons in a year

Sivabalan Pandian (b. 21 September 1958) from Mumbai, has run and completed 18 ultramarathons in a year from 16 June 2018 to 23 December 2018.

Fauja Singh

WR Oldest marathoner

Fauja Singh (b. 1 April 1911) of Indian origin, residing in the UK, is the world's oldest marathon runner. He completed the London Marathon, covering a distance of 42.2 km in 6 hrs 2 mins on 22 April 2012. His marathon record, for age 90-plus, was 5 hrs 40 mins at the Toronto Waterfront Marathon held in Canada in 2013.

Only Asian to complete Ironman triathlons in six continents

Kaustubh Radkar has completed the Ironman triathlon in 6 continents between March 2014 and November 2016, and is the only Asian to do so. He has completed 25 Ironman triathlons since he ran his first triathlon in 2008.

Fastest at Badwater Ultramarathon

Brij Mohan Sharma (b. 1 January 1974) of the Indian Navy, from Mumbai, is the fastest Indian at the Badwater Ultramarathon, one of the world's toughest foot races, held in California, US, from 18 to 20 July 2016. He completed the 217 km run in 40 hrs 47 mins.

First disabled Ironman

Praveen Kumar (b. 17 July 1985) from New Delhi became India's first disabled Ironman on 17 November 2018 in the Ironman event organized in Langkawi, Malaysia. He completed a 3.86-km long swim in 1 hr 36 mins 7 secs, 180 km of cycling in 7 hrs 49 mins 50 secs, and a 42-km long run in 5 hrs 40 mins 55 secs.

Kumar is a battle-casualty soldier who was injured during the terrorist attack in Mumbai, in November 2008.

Most visually impaired athletes completing marathons

Six visually impaired athletes – Nandeesh J., Sunita N.D., Renuka Rajput, Kavya Ramesh, and Ajay and Mala Kolkar – ran a full marathon in 7 hrs 21 mins on 21 October 2018 at Sree Kanteerava Outdoor Stadium, Bengaluru, Karnataka. Helped by guide runners, the students, who were from the Samarthanam Trust for the Disabled, Bengaluru, were led by their coach, Bhumika Patel.

MOUNTAIN ADVENTURES

First club

The Himalayan Club was founded in February 1928 in the room of Field Marshal Sir William Birdwood, then commander-in-chief of the British Indian Army.

First to scale Mt Kun

In 2023, members from the Jawahar Institute of Mountaineering & Winter Sports scaled the 7077 m peak of Mt Kun. They began their expedition on 12 July 2023 and ended it on 4 August 2023. Nun Kun is a mountain massif of the greater Himalayan range, located on the border of Jammu and Kashmir and Ladakh in northern India.

First mountaineering expedition

In 1951, Gurdial Guru Singh from Dehradun, Uttarakhand, led an expedition to the 7,120 m (23,360 ft) high Trishul 1 Peak in the Garhwal Himalayas, Uttarakhand.

Members of The Himalayan Club

Garhwal Himalayas

First to complete the Seven Summit challenge

Mastan Babu Malli (3 September 1974–24 March 2015) was an Indian mountaineer best known for his 2006 world–record–setting feat of climbing each continent's highest peak in the shortest period at the time – a total of 172 days – with the first climb on 19 January 2006 and the seventh on 10 July 2006. This feat made him the fastest Seven Summiteer in the world by 2006, and the first Indian and South Asian to climb the Seven Summits.

First to walk the Siachen Glacier

Siachen Glacier, lying along India's border with China, is about 700 sq km in area and situated at an altitude touching 5,753 m (18,875 ft) above mean sea level. Under Indian Army protection since 1984, it is the highest battlefield in the world. In 1984, Captain (now Colonel) Ashok Pratap Tanwar became the first person to cover the entire glacier on foot. Appointed as the official photographer of a military formation, he walked the length and breadth of the 76 km long and 3–5 km broad glacier.

First to summit the Volcanic Seven and youngest to climb both the Seven Summits and Volcanic Seven summits

At 34 years, Satyarup Siddhanta (b. 29 April 1983) from Bengaluru, completed the Volcanic Seven Summits (Messner list) on 15 December 2017 becoming the first Indian to do so. The Volcanic Seven Summits include Mt Kilimanjaro (5,895 m/19,341 ft – Africa), Mt Ojos del Salado (6,893 m/ 22,615 ft – South America), Mt Elbrus (5,642 m/18,510 ft – Europe), Mt Damavand (5,628 m/18,465 ft – Asia), Mt Giluwe (4,367 m/14,327 ft Australasia), Mt Pico de Orizaba (5,610 m/18,406 ft – North America), and Mt Sidley (4,181–4,285 m/13,717–14,058 ft – Antarctica). He also completed the Seven Summits challenge on 15 January 2019, becoming the youngest Indian to climb both the Volcanic Seven Summits and Seven Summits.

Most Himalayan summits

Sange Sherpa from Darjeeling, West Bengal, has 6 summits to his credit, which include Mt Everest 3 times, Aqtash in 1993, Jaloni in 1994, and Nanda Devi in 2000. He is the only person in the world to climb Mt Everest from 3 faces: from South Col in 1992, North Col in 1996, and Kangshung face in 1999. He received the National Adventure Award in 1998.

First Indian to summit the three highest peaks of South America

Vikas Shukla (b. 6 December 1989) from Bhusawal, Maharashtra, is the first Indian to summit the 3 highest peaks of South America. He scaled Mt Aconcagua (6,961 m/22,838 ft) on 16 February 2019; Mt Pissis (6,793 m/22,287 ft) on 24 February 2019; and Mt Ojos del Salado (6,893 m/22,615 ft) on 1 March 2019.

First to summit four unscaled peaks above 6,000 m

A team of 8 mountaineers from the Nehru Institute of Mountaineering, Uttarkashi in collaboration with Uttarakhand Tourism Development Board, summited 4 unscaled and unnamed peaks in the Gangotri region of the Garhwal Himalayas in 8 days between 9 October and 16 October 2018. The team, led by Colonel Amit Bisht, SM, scaled peaks 6,566 m (21,542 ft), 6,557 m (21,512 ft), 6,126 m (20,098 ft), and 6,086 m (19,967 ft) high.

First mountaineering institute

The Himalayan Mountaineering Institute at Darjeeling, West Bengal, the first in India, was formed in 1954 by the then prime minister Jawaharlal Nehru, along with Major Nandu Jayal of the Corps of Engineers of the Indian Army, who was its first director.

Himalayan Mountaineering Institute

Mt McKinley

Oldest to climb the Seven Summits

Ankur Bahl (b. 25 January 1961) from Haryana, became the oldest, at 57 years, to complete the Messner list of the Seven Summit challenge in 2018, which involves the summiting of the highest mountains in each continent. These include Mt Kilimanjaro (5,895 m/19,341 ft – Africa), Mt Elbrus (5,642 m/18,510 ft – Europe), Mt Denali/McKinley (6,190 m/20,310 ft – North America), Mt Aconcagua (6,961 m/22,838 ft – South America), Mt Everest (8,848.86 m/29,031 ft 8 in – Asia), Mt Kosciuszko (2,228 m/7,310 ft – Australia), and Mt Vinson (4,892 m/16,050 ft– Antarctica).

First woman to scale Mt Everest

Bachendri Pal (b. 24 May 1954) became the first Indian woman to reach the summit of Mt Everest in 1984.

First to summit Mt Everest without supplemental oxygen

Phu Dorjee was the first to summit Mt Everest (then measured at 8,848 m/ 29,028 ft) without supplemental oxygen on 9 May 1984 through the south-east ridge route. He was part of the third Everest expedition led by Captain M.S. Kohli in 1965. Dorjee died in 1987 on the Kangchenjunga Expedition of the Assam Rifles.

Oldest to scale Mt Everest

- *Men*: S.C. Negi (b. 8 March 1950), additional deputy inspector general of the Border Security Force, became the oldest to scale Mt Everest on 24 May 2006 at the age of 56 years.
- *Women*: Sangeeta Sindhi (b. 9 February 1965) from Gurugram, became the oldest Indian woman to summit Mt Everest on 19 May 2018 at the age of 53 years.

Fastest scaling of Mt Everest

Kazi Sherpa climbed Mt Everest in 20 hrs 24 mins in 1998, breaking the earlier record of 22 hrs 29 mins.

TREKKING

Longest desert trek – group

The 22nd battalion of the Mahar Regiment, part of the Golden Katar Division of the Indian Army, successfully completed the 'Golden Katar Desert Trek 2017–18'. A 10-member team of soldiers trekked 700 km through the Thar Desert, Rajasthan, in 21 days from 22 December 2017 to 12 January 2018. The arduous journey on foot

Mahar Regiment Logo

through the Great Indian Desert began from Bakhasar, Barmer District, and concluded in Gajjewala, Bikaner District, Rajasthan.

Oldest trekker

Gopal Vasudev Lele (b. 8 March 1932) from Pune, then 81 years of age, made a week-long trek to Rupin Pass (4,680 m/15,354 ft) in Himachal Pradesh from 21 to 28 September 2013. He completed a 70-degree climb. Lele has completed 20 treks since 1972.

Fastest to scale most 8,000 m peaks

Baljeet Kaur became the first Indian to summit 4 out of the 14 peaks at altitudes of 8,000 metres or more in less than a month. The 27-year-old from Solan, Himachal Pradesh, started her journey by summitting Mt Annapurna I (8,091 m) on 28 April 2022 and Mt Kanchenjunga (8,586 m) on 12 May 2022, and became the first Indian woman to summit these peaks in less than 2 weeks. She continued her journey 2 weeks later and summitted Mt Everest (8,849 m) on 21 May 2022 and Mt Lhotse (8,517 m) on 22 May 2022, the first and fourth highest mountains in the world, respectively.

First women's team to complete Snowman Trek

A team of 11 women led by iconic Indian mountaineer Bachendri Pal successfully completed the Snowman Trek in Bhutan, considered one of the toughest in the world. Starting at Paro Valley on 4 June 2011, the trek was completed at Sephu Village on 27 June 2011. It involved crossing 11 high mountain passes and other difficult terrain. This expedition was sponsored by the Tata Steel Adventure Foundation in Jamshedpur, Jharkhand.

Fastest Everest Base Camp trek by a disabled person

Mahinder Singh Raghuwanshi (b. 2 October 1987) completed the longest trekking in Nepal, with a prosthetic leg, to the Everest Base Camp from an altitude of 2,859.9 m – 5,642.7 m (9,383 ft – 18,513 ft). He started his trek on 28 April 2018 and ended it on 11 May 2018, covering 150 km in 14 days. He started his trek from Lukla, Nepal, and covered Kala Patthar (5,550 m/18,209 ft), Cho La (5,368 m/17,612 ft), Gokyo (4,790 m/15,715 ft), Renjo La (5,360 m/17,585 ft), and Everest Base Camp (5,364 m/17,598 ft). He was accompanied by a friend and a guide.

THE POLES

First at Antarctica

Meher Moos (b. 1944) from Maharashtra was the first woman to set foot on the icy continent of Antarctica way back in 1976, long before any of the scientific expeditions went there.

First to reach North Pole by surface

Dr M.R. Shetty from Bangalore (now Bengaluru), Karnataka, reached the North Pole by surface on 5 August 2001 with a 100-strong team, by *Yamal*, a nuclear-powered ice-breaking ship, starting from Longyearbyen, Svalbard's administrative centre in Norway, on 1 August 2001.

First at the Geographic South Pole

On 17 January 1989, Colonel J.K. Bajaj became the first Indian to reach the Geographic South Pole at 22:15 hrs (GMT). He was the only Indian in this 11-member international expedition that skied over 1,200 km in 50 days to the Geographic South Pole. The 5-nation expedition was organized by Mountain Travel, US, and the International Adventure Network, Canada.

First route recce to the South Pole

Major Anand Swaroop and Captain R.R. Bhat of the Corps of Engineers of the Indian Army were the first to recce the route from the Maitri base, Antarctica, to the Polar/Antarctic Plateau in 2000.

First at the Arctic

Sharat Kumar Roy (1897–1962) was the first to reach the Arctic as a member of the Rawson–Macmillan Arctic Expedition in 1927.

First organization to reach 'three' poles

Indian Navy teams have been to 3 poles: Mt Everest, the vertical pole, in 2004; the Geographic South Pole in 2006; and the Geographic North Pole in 2008. Commander Satyabrata Dam and 2 POMAs (petty officer medical assistants) Vikas Kumar and Rakesh Kumar were the first to reach all 3 poles.

Longest stay in Antarctica

Shaik Mastan (b. 12 February 1968) from Gudavalli Village, Guntur District, Andhra Pradesh, had the longest uninterrupted stay of 490 days in Antarctica at the Indian Antarctic research station, Bharati, from 16 November 2011 to 19 March 2013. He was a member of the 35th Indian expedition to Antarctica.

First to ski to the North Pole

Ajeet Bajaj is the first Indian to ski to the North Pole and complete the polar trilogy, which entails skiing to the North Pole and South Pole and crossing the Greenland Ice Sheet. He started his ski expedition to the North Pole from the Russian Arctic Polar Research Station called Barneo and reached the North Pole on 26 April 2006, along with 3 other skiers.

Indian Station, Maitri

SPORTS

GENERAL

First Indian president of the International Cricket Council
Jagmohan Dalmiya became the first Indian president of the International Cricket Council (ICC) in 1997. He served till 2000.

First Indian chairman of the ICC
N. Srinivasan was the first ICC chairman from India (2014–15).

First Indian independent chairman of the ICC
Shashank Manohar was the first independent chairman of the International Cricket Council in 2016, and he was re-elected for another two years.

First Indian president of the World Squash Federation
Indian squash administrator Narayana Ramachandran was president of the World Squash Federation (WSF) for two terms from 2008 to 2016.

First Indian president of the International Kabaddi Federation
Sports administrator Janardan Singh Gehlot was the founder president of the International Kabaddi Federation from 1985 to 2013. He became the life president from May 2013.

First Indian to become a FIFA World Cup match commissioner
Former All India Football Federation president Priya Ranjan Dasmunsi was the match commissioner in a FIFA World Cup 2006 game. It was a group stage match between Australia and Croatia.

First sportsman to be nominated to the Rajya Sabha
Wrestler Dara Singh was the first sportsman to be nominated to the Rajya Sabha, the Upper House of the Indian Parliament, in 2003.

Dara Singh

First sportsperson to receive the Padma Vibhushan
In 2008 the Padma Vibhushan was first awarded to sports persons and the first to receive the award was the chess wizard Viswanathan Anand. There are only three other recipients of the same from sports, mountaineer Edmund Hillary, cricketer Sachin Tendulkar, and boxer M.C. Mary Kom.

First sportsperson to be awarded the Padma Shri
Triple Olympian gold medallist Balbir Singh Sr. (1924–2020) became the first sports person to be awarded the Padma Shri in 1957. The versatile centre forward played a key role in India's victories in the Olympics in 1948 in London, in 1952 in Helsinki, and in 1956 in Melbourne.

Balbir Singh Sr

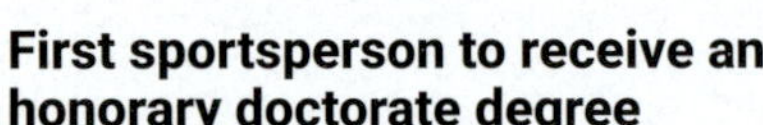

First sportsperson to receive an honorary doctorate degree
Man: Raja Randhir Singh, former shooter, was conferred with a honorary doctorate degree in Literature by the Lakshmibai Institute of Physical Education, Gwalior, Madhya Pradesh on 8 September 2000. He had represented India in six Olympic Games: Tokyo (1964), Mexico City (1968), Munich (1972), Montreal (1976), Moscow (1980) and Los Angeles (1984).
Woman: P.T. Usha was conferred with an honorary doctorate degree by Kannur University, Kerala on 1 November 2000 for her contribution to athletics. She represented India in four Olympic Games, five Asian Games, and five Asian Championships. She also won the most medals ever by an Indian athlete at the Jakarta Asian Championships in 1985, with five gold medals and a bronze medal.

First sweep in the Asian Para Games
At the 2018 Asian Para Games, Indian para-athletes occupied all three positions in high jump when Sharad Kumar (1.90 m), Varun Bhati (1.82 m), and Thangavelu Mariyappa (1.67 m) got the gold, silver, and bronze medals respectively, in the T-42/63 category (lower limb deficiency, leg length difference, impaired muscle power and impaired range of movement).

First sports magazine
Bengal Sporting was first published in 1837. It was edited by British journalist Joachim Hayward Stocqueler.

First Indian woman to participate in the World Transplant Games
Reena Raju (b. 4 December 1982) from Bengaluru, Karnataka, was the flag bearer in the opening ceremony at the World Transplant Games 2017 in Malaga, Spain. She represented India in the 100 m sprint and badminton mixed doubles. She was the first Indian to undergo a repeat heart transplant on 22 October 2017 at Frontier Lifeline Hospital, Chennai, for cardiac allograft vasculopathy.

Olympic Order

First recipient of the Olympic Order (Gold)
The Olympic Order (Gold), the highest award of the Olympic movement, is given for distinguished contribution to the movement. Former Indian prime minister Indira Gandhi was its first recipient in 1983. The Olympic Order is also awarded in silver and bronze categories.

First international rugby 15s win
The Indian women's rugby team scripted history by clinching their first ever international 15s victory against a higher ranked Singapore for a bronze medal in the Asian women's Division 1 Rugby 15s Championship 2019.

First to win a world title in motorsport
Aishwarya Pissay from Bengaluru, Karnataka, became the first Indian to win a world title in motorsport. She won the Federation Internationale de

Motocyclisme (FIM) Bajas World Cup (women's category) with 65 points on 13 August 2019 in Varpalota, Hungary. She won the first round in Dubai, UAE, was placed third in Portugal, fifth in Spain, and fourth in Hungary.

Indian postal stamp commemorating Commonwealth Games 2010

Best performance in the Olympic Games

India capped off its best-ever performance in the 2020 Tokyo Olympics with a haul of seven medals, including a gold, two silver, and four bronze medals.

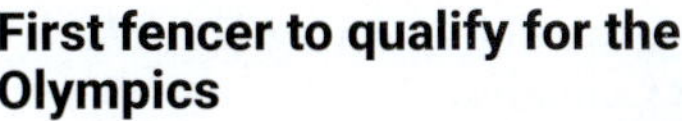

First fencer to qualify for the Olympics

C.A. Bhavani Devi became the first Indian fencer to qualify for the 2020 Tokyo Olympics on 14 March 2021 at the Women's Sabre World Cup in Budapest, Hungary. Chennai based Devi secured her slot through the Asia/Oceania Zone of the Adjusted Official Ranking (AOR).

M.C. Mary Kom

First Indian fencer to win a medal at the Asian Fencing Championships

C.A. Bhavani Devi became the first Indian fencer to win a medal at the Asian Fencing Championships by winning the bronze medal in 2023. She defeated Misaki Emura with a remarkable score of 15-10 in the quarter-finals but in the semi-finals she had to settle for a bronze because she lost 14-15 to Uzbekistan's Zaynab Dayibekova.

Pullela Gopichand

Best performance in the Asian Para Games

Indian para-athletes won 72 medals in the 2018 Asian Para Games in Jakarta, Indonesia, bagging 15 golds, 24 silvers, and 33 bronzes.

Best performance in the Asian Games

India participated in the 2018 Asian Games in Jakarta and Palembang, Indonesia (from 18 August to 2 September) and had the best ever haul with 69 medals, including 15 gold, 24 silver, and 30 bronze medals from 465 events. After 67 years, since the inaugural edition of the Games in Delhi in 1951, India matched its best haul of 15 golds.

Best performance in the South Asian Games

India bagged 174 gold, 93 silver, and 45 bronze medals in the 13th South Asian Games 2019 in Kathmandu, Nepal.

Best performance in the Commonwealth Games

India's best performance was in the 2010 CWG held in New Delhi, when India won 101 medals in all.

Most national awards

Woman: M.C. Mary Kom, six-time world champion, was the recipient of the Arjuna Award in 2003, the Rajiv Gandhi Khel Ratna Award in 2008–09, the Padma Shri in 2006, the Padma Bhushan in 2013, and the Padma Vibhushan in 2020.
Man: Pullela Gopichand, the second Indian to win All England Open Badminton Championships in 2001, was the recipient of the Arjuna Award in 1999, the Rajiv Gandhi Khel Ratna Award in 2000–01, the Dronacharya Award in 2009, the Padma Shri in 2005, and the Padma Bhushan in 2014.

Youngest to receive the Padma Bhushan

Badminton player P.V. Sindhu, at 24 years, became the youngest sportsperson to receive the Padma Bhushan in 2020. Sindhu is the third badminton player to be awarded the honour after Pullela Gopichand received it in 2014 and Saina Nehwal in 2016.

ARCHERY

GENERAL

First to win back-to-back titles

Deepika Kumari became the first Indian archer to win titles back-to-back when she won the cadet individual recurve title in 2009 at Ogden in Utah, USA, and the junior individual recurve gold in 2011 at Legnica, Poland.

Deepika Kumari

First compound para medal

Indian compound mixed pair of Shyam Sundar Swami and Jyoti Bullyan made history with a silver at the World Archery Para Championships 2022 in Dubai.

First Indian to win World Archery Award

Sheetal Devi became the first Indian to win a World Archery Award, clinching the para women's category in 2023. She is also the first female para-athlete without arms to compete internationally. Additionally, Aditi Swami won the breakthrough archer of the year award, making her the first able-bodied Indian recipient.

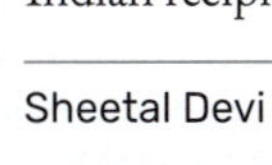

Sheetal Devi

ASIAN CHAMPIONSHIP

First medal in the Asian Championships – men

Limba Ram became the first Indian archer to win an Asian Archery Championships medal in 1988.

Most medals in the Asian Championship

Indian recurve archers won one gold, four silver and two bronze medals at the 2021 Asian Archery Championships in Dhaka (Bangladesh). In the Asian Championships in 2019 too, in Bangkok, Thailand, during 22–28 November 2019, India had won seven medals: one gold, two silver and four bronze medals.

ASIAN PARA GAMES

First gold medal in the Asian Para Games

Harvinder Singh won India's maiden archery gold in the Asian Para Games 2018 in the men's individual recurve. He outplayed China's Zhao Lixue 6–0 in the W2/ST category.

Harvinder Singh

COMMONWEALTH GAMES

Most medals in the Commonwealth Games

The Indian team won three gold, a silver and four bronze medals in archery at the 2010 Commonwealth Games in Delhi.

INTERNATIONAL

First Junior World Championships title – men

Palton Hansda won the World Junior Archery Championships (compound – men's) in 2006 at Merida in Mexico.

First individual international medal

Shyam Lal won a bronze in the 50 m event at the fifth Asia Cup championship in Calcutta (now Kolkata), West Bengal, in January 1988. He represented India in the 1988 Seoul Olympics in South Korea.

First Archery World Cup team gold – women

Rimil Buriuly, Bombayla Devi Laishram, and Deepika Kumari toppled Olympic champions South Korea 219–215 to win the first back-to-back World Cup titles at the Archery World Cup (stage 4) at Wroclaw, Poland, on 25 August 2013, after winning the first medal at the World Cup (stage 3) in Medellin, Colombia, in July.

First international gold

In October 1989, India took the gold in the team event at the Asian Archery Championships in Beijing, China, with 1,850 points, while reigning Olympic champion South Korea stood second with 1,842 points. The Indian team comprised Limba Ram, Shyam Lal and Skalzang Dorje.

First Olympics representation – men

The Indian national archery team, with Shyam Lal, Limba Ram, and Sanjeeva Singh, participated in the individual and team archery events at the Olympics in 1988 at Seoul, South Korea.

First international gold – individual

Jayanta Talukdar won an individual gold medal at the Federation Internationale de Tir a l'Arc (FITA) Meteksan World Cup, in 2006 in Merida, Mexico.

First international gold – women

Dola Banerjee outclassed Tatyana Dorkhova of Ukraine 102-96 in the women's recurve final at the 18th Golden Arrow Grand Prix Championship 2005 at Antalya, Turkey.

First Olympics representation – women

Dola Banerjee, Reena Kumari and Sumangala Sharma were the first women to represent India in archery at the 2004 Olympic Games in Athens, Greece.

First gold medal in a World Cup

Dola Banerjee from West Bengal is the only Indian archer to win gold in a World Cup final, in the women's individual recurve event at the World Cup in Dubai, UAE, in November 2007.

Abhishek Verma

First World Cup compound title – men – individual

Abhishek Verma won an archery World Cup (stage 3) event at Wroclaw, Poland, on 15 August 2015.

First World Cup compound title – men – team

The men's compound archery team of Abhishek Verma, Chinna Raju Srither and Amarjeet Singh bagged the World Cup (stage 1) on 20 May 2017 in Shanghai, China, scoring 226–221 against Colombia.

First World Championship medal

The Indian men's archery team won a silver medal, behind Korea, at the 43rd World Outdoor Target Archery Championship 2005 in Madrid, Spain. The recurve team comprised Tarundeep Rai, Gautam Singh Sardar, Jayanta Talukdar and Robin Hansda.

Jayanta Talukdar

Most medals in the World Championship

India won a silver and two bronzes in the World Archery Championships during 10–15 June 2019 at 's-Hertogenbosch, Netherlands. The men's team of Tarundeep Rai, Atanu Das and Pravin Yadav won silver. The women's compound team of Jyothi Surekha Vennam, Muskan Kaur and Raj Kaur won the bronzes.

Most medals in a World Cup

India won one gold, two silver and two bronze medals in the Archery World Cup (stage 4) at Wroclaw, Poland, in August 2014. The team of Deepika Kumari, Bombayla Devi Laishram and Laxmirani Majhi won the gold in the women's recurve team event. The men's recurve team, with Tarundeep Rai, Jayanta Talukdar and Atanu Das,

Dola Banerjee

won a silver medal. Abhishek Verma and Purvasha Shende clinched the silver in the compound mixed pair event. Deepika Kumari bagged two bronze medals in the women's recurve individual event and in the mixed team event with partner Jayanta Talukdar.

Most gold medals at the World Cup by an individual

India won three gold medals in the Archery World Cup (stage 3) 2021 in Paris, France: the individual gold – Deepika Kumari; the mixed team event – Deepika Kumari with her husband Atanu Das; and the women's team event trio of Deepika Kumari, Komalika Bari and Ankita Bhakat.

First to equal women's compound archery world record of qualification round

Indian archer Jyothi Surekha Vennam equalled the world record in the women's compound qualification at the 2023 Archery World Cup in Antalya, scoring 713 out of 720 points. Her performance matched Sara Lopez's 2015 record and broke the Asian record of 709 set by Korea's So Chaewon in 2017.

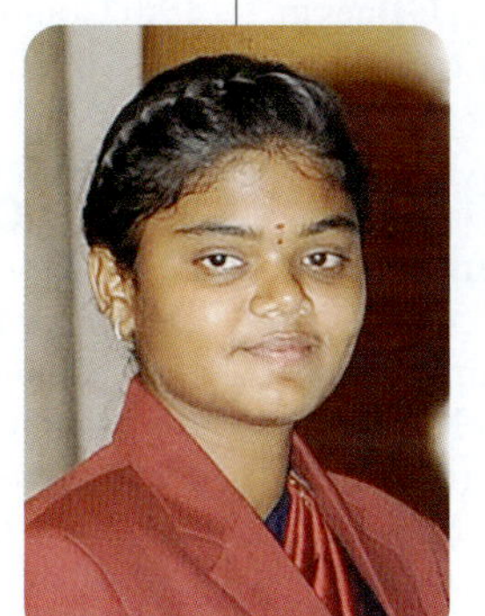

Jyothi Surekha Vennam

First to break U-18 world record

Aditi Gopichand broke the U-18 World record with 711 points out of possible 720 (72 arrows) during the qualification round of the World Cup Stage III in Medellin. The 16-year-old broke the previous age group record of 705 held by Riko Arreola of the USA.

First Indian to win Youth World Champion in recurve – men

Parth Salunkhe became the first Indian male archer to win recurve under-21 men's individual champion during the World Archery Youth Championships 2023 in Limerick. The 19-year-old archer defeated Korea's Song In Jun in the gold medal match.

Best medal show at Archery World Cup

India's archery team achieved a historic milestone of eight medals at the 2024 Archery World Cup Stage 1 in Shanghai, securing their highest-ever medal tally at a single edition. The Indian contingent took home five golds, two silvers, and one bronze. Notably, the men's recurve team of Tarundeep Rai, Pravin Jadhav, and Dhiraj Bommadevara captured gold, while Deepika Kumari claimed silver in the women's individual recurve event. The mixed team, comprising Ankita Bhakat and Dhiraj, added a bronze. This stellar performance, driven by the compound archers (non-Olympic event) who secured four golds.

PARALYMPICS

First archery medal in Paralympics

Harvinder Singh clinched India's first-ever archery at the 2020 Paralympics. He won the bronze medal in the men's singles recurve archery at the 2020 Summer Paralympics in Tokyo, Japan.

World's first armless archer to reach World Championship final

Sheetal Devi became the first female armless archer to make a World Championship final as she won the silver medal in the compound women individual category in Pilsen. She lost the gold medal match to Turkey's Oznur Cure after defeating compatriot Sarita in the semis.

World record in Women's Team

Sarita and Sheetal Devi set a New World Record in the Compound Women Team Open category with a score 1386/1440 in the qualification round. The duo also won the bronze medal, defeating Iran.

First World Archery Para Championship gold

Sarita and Rakesh Kumar set world record in the Compound Mixed Team Open category with a score of 1398 out of possible 1440 in the qualification round. The duo went on to win the gold medal as well by beating Brazil in the final, winning India's first para archers to win gold medal in World Archery Para Championships.

ATHLETICS

ASIAN ATHLETICS CHAMPIONSHIPS

Bahadur Singh Chouhan

Triple excellence in shot put

Former shot putter Bahadur Singh Chouhan is the only Indian to receive the Arjuna Award, the Dronacharya Award as well as the Padma Shri. Between 1973 and 1985 he won three gold, two silver and three bronze medals at the Asian Games and Asian Championships.

Best performance in the Asian Athletics Championships

India clinched five gold, one silver and three bronze medals in the 2017 Asian Athletics Championships in Bhubaneswar, Odisha, to top the medal tally for the first time in the championships.

Biggest point-haul in pentathlon – women

Swapna Barman set the pentathlon record with a point haul of 4119 points (out of 5000) while clinching the Asian Indoor Championships silver medal. She omitted the old record held by Purnima Hembram of 4062 points (in 2017).

First to win gold at Asian Athletics Championship – women

Jyothi Yarraji won the first gold for India in the women's 100m hurdles at the Asian Athletics Championship held in Bangkok in July 2023. She clocked in 13.09 seconds.

ASIAN GAMES

First Asian Games medals – women

In the 1951 Asian Games in Delhi, Roshan Mistry won the silver in the 100 m race, while Mary D'Souza (200 m) won a bronze. The women's 4 x 100 m relay team of Nilima Ghose, Stephie D'Souza, Mary D'Souza and Roshan Mistry also won a silver.

First gold medal – women – team

Christine Brown, Stephie D'Souza, Violet Peters and Mary D'Souza won the gold in the 4 x100 m relay, clocking 49.5 secs at the second Asian Games held in Manila, Philippines, in 1954.

First Asian Games gold – men – individual

Ranjit Singh won a gold in the 800 m marathon on 8 March 1951 at Delhi, clocking 1 hr 59 mins 3 secs. Indian men won 10 golds in this edition of the Asian Games.

First double gold at the Asian Games

Lavy Pinto won the first double gold at Asian Games in the 100m and 200m races in Delhi, 1951. Six other athletes have won atleast two golds each in a single Asian Games event.

First Asian Games gold – women – individual

Kamaljeet Sandhu won the 400 m race in 57.3 secs at the sixth Asian Games held in Bangkok, Thailand, in 1970.

Only Asian Games gold medal in marathon

Chhota Singh won a gold in the men's marathon in 1951 in Delhi with a timing of 2 hrs 42 mins 58 secs 6 microseconds.

First to win three golds successively in the Asian Games

Manjeet Kaur was the first Indian to win three consecutive gold medals in the women's 4 x 400 m relay race in the Asian Games (2002, 2006 and 2010).

Most individual golds in the Asian Games

Two sportspersons have won four gold medals each at the Asian Games:

- Milkha Singh won four golds in two Asian Games in 1958 and 1962.
- P.T. Usha won four golds in the 1986 Asian Games at Seoul, South Korea, in the 200 m, 400 m, 400 m hurdles and the 4 x 400 m relay.

Milkha Singh

P.T. Usha

ASIAN YOUTH ATHLETICS CHAMPIONSHIP

Best performance in the Asian Youth Athletics Championships

India clinched six gold, eleven silver and three bronze medals in the 2022 Asian Youth Athletics Championships, held in Kuwait between 13 and 16 October 2022, topping the medal tally.

COMMONWEALTH GAMES

First gold medal in throws at the Commonwealth Games – men – individual

This feat was achieved by the 6 ft 9 in. tall Vikas Gowda in discus throw. Gowda won this event in 2014 in Glasgow, Scotland, with a throw of 63.64 m.

First medal in the Commonwealth Games – women

Anju Bobby George won the bronze medal in long jump with a best of 6.49 m at the 2002 Commonwealth Games in Manchester, UK, followed by Neelam J. Singh, who won a silver in the women's discus throw.

First Commonwealth Games gold medal – women

The first Commonwealth Games gold medal for women came when Krishna Poonia won the discus throw (61.51 m), while the quartet of Sini Jose, Mandeep Kaur, Manjeet Kaur and Ashwini Chidananda Akkunji won the women's 4 x 400 m relay (3 mins 27.77 secs) at the 2010 New Delhi Games.

First to win a gold medal in triple jump in the Commonwealth Games

Eldhose Paul became the first Indian to win a gold medal in the men's triple jump at the Commonwealth Games 2022, recording a massive 17.03 m.

First high jump medal in the Commonwealth Games

Tejaswin Shankar, the 2015 Commonwealth Youth Games gold medallist in high jump, became the first Indian to win a medal – a bronze – in high jump with a jump of 2.22 m at the 2022 Commonwealth Games.

First medal in race walk – women

Priyanka Goswami is the first Indian woman to win the silver medal in the women's 10,000 m race walk at the 2022 Commonwealth Games. It is India's second medal in the race walk at the Commonwealth Games after Harminder Singh's bronze in the 20 km event in the 2010 Commonwealth Games.

First javelin throw medal in the Commonwealth Games – women

Annu Rani, a javelin thrower, is the first Indian woman to win a medal, a bronze, in the 2022 Commonwealth Games in Birmingham, UK.

Best Commonwealth performance

India won 12 medals – two golds, three silvers and seven bronzes – during the 19th Commonwealth Games in New Delhi in 2010.

First title in the Commonwealth Fencing Championship

Chennai-born fencer C.A. Bhavani Devi made history in November 2018 by becoming the first Indian to win the gold medal at the Commonwealth Championship. The 42nd ranked Indian fencer and the first ever Indian fencer to have qualified for an Olympics (Tokyo 2020) Bhavani Devi defeated second-seeded Australian Veronika Vasleva 15-10 in the senior women's sabre individual category final in London, UK, in the Commonwealth Championship in August 2022.

COMMONWEALTH AND ASIAN GAMES

Gold medal in Commonwealth and Asian Games

Milkha Singh won gold in the 440 yards (the quarter-mile dash) race at the 1958 British Empire and Commonwealth Games in Cardiff, Wales, with a timing of 46.6 secs. He also won the 400 m races back-to-back in the Asian Games in Tokyo, Japan (1958), in 47.0 secs, and Jakarta, Indonesia (1962), in 46.9 secs. He was the first Indian to win individual gold medals in both the Asian Games and the Commonwealth Games. He was also the first Indian athlete to win a gold medal in the Commonwealth Games.

INTERNATIONAL

First international medal in a marathon – women

Asha Agarwal won the Hong Kong Marathon on 27 January 1985. She

later won the Asian track and field gold at Jakarta, Indonesia, in 1985, and the Trinidad Marathon in 1986.

First Indian elected to the International Association of Athletics Federations (IAAF) Council

Adille J. Sumariwalla was elected to the IAAF (now World Athletics) Council at the IAAF Congress in 2015.

First clean sweep in a major international meet

Krishna Poonia, Harwant Kaur and Seema Antil bagged the gold, silver and bronze medals respectively in the women's discus throw in the 2010 Commonwealth Games in New Delhi.

First athlete to win a medal at the IAAF Continental Cup

Arpinder Singh, the 2018 Asian Games gold medallist in triple jump, was the first Indian to win a medal in the IAAF Continental Cup. He won a bronze medal in triple jump with a distance of 16.59 m.

First individual gold medal in track events at the IAAF World U-20 Championships

Hima Das won the gold in the 400 m race in the IAAF (now World Athletics) World U-20 Championships in Tampere, Finland, on 12 July 2018 with a timing of 51.46 secs. She holds the current Indian national record in 400 m with a timing of 50.79 secs set at the 2018 Asian Games in Jakarta, Indonesia.

First Indian to win gold at the IAAF World U-20 Championships

Neeraj Chopra, by clinching the gold on 23 July 2016 at the IAAF (now World Athletics) World U-20 championships in Bydgoszcz, Poland, with a winning javelin throw of 86.48 m, became the first Indian to win a gold medal at any event in the championships and the first Indian to set a junior world record in athletics. In 2018, he became the second Indian after the legendary runner Milkha Singh to win both Commonwealth and Asian Games gold medals in the same year, breaking the national record on both occasions. At 20 years, he was the youngest ever flagbearer of the Indian contingent at the 2018 Jakarta Asian Games.

First to receive IAAF Veteran Pin

Indian track and field legend P.T. Usha was presented the Veteran Pin by the World Athletics governing body – IAAF (now World Athletics) on 24 September 2019.

First World U-20 Athletics Championships twin medals

Quarter-miler Rupal Chaudhary is the first Indian to win twin medals in a single edition of the 2022 World U-20 Athletics Championships. She won silver in 4x400 m relay silver and a bronze medal in the women's 400 m.

First to finish among podium places at Diamond League

Murali Sreeshankar became the first long jumper to finish among the podium places of a Diamond League as he finished third in the Paris Diamond League 2023 with an attempt of 8.09m. He is overall the third Indian to finish in top three of Diamond Leagues after discus thrower Vikash Gowda (2015) and Neeraj Chopra (2022).

Hima Das

MARATHONS

Most appearances in marathons

Sunita Godara has completed 85 half- and 69 full marathons in 24 different countries. Starting with the Rath Marathon in 1984, she finished first in 25 marathons, second in 12 and third in 14 of them. She has won 25 gold medals in half-marathons.

OLYMPICS

First Olympic marathoner

Phadeppa Dareppa Chaugule represented India in the 1920 Antwerp Olympic Games. He finished 19th in 2 hrs 50 mins 45.2 secs.

Phadeppa Dareppa Chaugule

First women participation at the Olympics

Mary D'Souza and Nilima Ghose participated in the 1952 Helsinki Olympics. They were both eliminated in the heats of the 100 m and 200 m races, and 80 m and 100 m hurdles, respectively.

First woman captain

Shiny Wilson captained the Indian athletes' contingent at the 1992 Olympic Games in Barcelona, Spain.

Shiny Wilson

Best performances in the Olympics

Milkha Singh and P.T. Usha finished fourth in the 400 m and the 400 m hurdles in the 1960 Rome and the 1984 Los Angeles Olympic Games respectively.

WORLD ATHLETICS

First gold at World Athletics final

In the World Athletics Championships held in Monte Carlo in September 2005 Anju Bobby George from India came second in long jump. The gold medallist, Tatyana Kotova, from Russia, was later disqualified following a failed retest for doping, and Anju Bobby George was upgraded to gold medallist, India's first, in January 2014.

Anju Bobby George

First Indian to win gold at World Athletics Championships

Neeraj Chopra wrote history when he became the first Indian to win a gold medal at the World Athletics Championship. He had a big throw of 88.17 m in the men's javelin final.

Neeraj Chopra

WORLD CHAMPIONSHIPS

First World Championship medal

Anju Bobby George won a bronze in long jump at the 2003 World Championship in Paris, France, in August, with a leap of 6.70 m. She surpassed this at the 2004 Olympics in Athens, Greece, finishing sixth with 6.83 m.

WORLD UNIVERSIADE

First gold at the World Universiade

Dutee Chand, the current national champion in the women's 100 m race, became the first Indian to win the gold at the World Universiade, Naples, Italy, in the 100 m race with a timing of 11.32 secs on 10 July 2019. She is also the first Indian to win a gold in the 100 m race at a global championship. She also won a silver in the 100 m race at the 2018 Asian Games in Jakarta.

Dutee Chand

PARA ATHLETICS

First participation in the Paralympics

In 1968, India made its Paralympics debut at the Tel Aviv Games. India did not participate in the first two Games, in 1960 and 1964. India competed again in 1972 and then consistently from the 1984 New York Games in the USA to Tokyo 2020 in Japan.

First triple medal in the Paralympics

India's Joginder Singh Bedi had won three medals – a silver each in javelin and shot put, and a bronze in the discus throw – at the 1984 Paralympics in Stoke Mandeville and New York, USA.

First gold in javelin

Sumit Antil won the gold medal in the men's javelin throw F64 category at the 2020 Summer Paralympics in Tokyo, Japan. He holds the current world record, having thrown 68.55 m in the Paralympics final.

First bronze medal at the World Para Athletics Championships

Varun Kumar Bhati won the bronze medal in the men's T-42 category high jump and Karan Jyoti Dalal settled for bronze in the discus throw F-55 at the World Para Athletics Championships in London in 2017.

Best performance in the World Para Athletics Championships

India won two gold, two silver, and five bronze medals (a total of nine) at the World Para Athletics Championships 2019 held in Dubai.

Best javelin throw – men

Sumit Antil's world record javelin throw of 68.55 m in the F64 category came at the 2020 Tokyo Olympics. He threw the spear to a record distance of 68.62 m in the Open National Para Athletics Championships.

Deepthi Jeevanji sets T20 400m world record – women

Deepthi Jeevanji clinched India's first gold at the 2024 World Para Athletics Championships by winning the women's T20 400m event in a world-record time of 55.07 seconds on May 20. She broke Breanna Clark's previous record of 55.12 seconds. Earlier In the qualifying rounds, Deepthi set a new Asian record of 56.18 seconds and secured a Paris 2024 Paralympics quota.

Best throw – discus F-36 (para-athletics) – men

Yogesh Kathuniya smashed the world record in men's discus F-36, when he threw 45.18 m to win the gold medal in the World Para Athletics Grand Prix in Berlin, Germany, on 1 July 2018.

Yogesh Kathuniya

First Paralympics gold – women

Deepa Malik became the first Indian woman to win a medal at the Paralympics by bagging a silver medal in shot put in the 2016 Paralympic Games. She also won gold in the F-53/54 javelin event at the para-athletic Grand Prix held in Dubai in 2018.

Deepa Malik

First para-athlete to get the Rajiv Gandhi Khel Ratna Award – women

Deepa Malik was the first woman para-athlete to receive the Rajiv Gandhi Khel Ratna Award in 2019.

WR

Best javelin throw F64 – men

Sumit Antil won gold in the Hangzhou Asian Para Games javelin throw F64 event with a world record of 73.29m, surpassing his previous record of 70.83m set at the 2024 World Para Athletics Championships. He also set a world record with a 68.55m throw at the Tokyo Paralympics.

Best javelin throw F46 – men

Sundar Singh Gurjar set a new world record with a 68.60m throw in the men's javelin throw F46 event, winning gold at the Asian Para Games in Hangzhou on 25 October 2023. He broke the previous world record of 67.79m held by Sri Lanka's Dinesh Priyantha.

NATIONAL GAMES

Fastest 100 m hurdles – women

In the women's-only 100 m hurdles, Jyothi Yarraji became the first Indian woman to finish the race with a sub-13 timing, as she clocked 12.82 seconds at the 61st National Open Athletics Championships in Bengaluru on October 2022.

Fastest 3000m steeplechase – men

Avinash Sable improved his national record in the 3000m steeplechase at the Paris Diamond League on July 7. Sable clocked 8:09.91 to finish sixth while shaving over a second off his earlier personal best of 8:11.20. Sable has been re-setting the national record several times since 2019 when he clocked 8:28.94 at the Federation Cup in Patiala.

Fastest 4x400m mixed relay – team

The Indian 4x400m mixed relay team, consisting of Muhammad Ajmal, Jyothika Sri, Amoj Jacob, and Subha Venkatesan, set a new national record at the 2024 Asian Relay Championships on May 20. They secured gold with a time of 3:14.12, breaking the previous record of 3:14.34 set at the 2023 Asian Games, in which Ajmal and Subha also participated.

Fastest 400m – U-18 – women

Neeru Pathak clocked 52.85 seconds to break the under-18 national record in the girls' 400m at the 19th National Youth Athletics Championships in Bilaspur on June 16. The 17-year-old quarter-miler from Delhi surpassed Rezoana Mallick Heena's previous record of 52.98 seconds and qualified for the U-20 World Championships.

Fastest 5000m and 10000m – men

Gulveer Singh set two new national records in 2024. On June 10, he broke the men's 5000m record with a time of 13:18.92 at the Portland Track Festival, surpassing Avinash Sable's previous mark. Later, at The Ten in California, Gulveer shattered a 16-year-old men's 10,000m record, clocking 27:41.81 and beating Surendra Singh's 2008 record by over 20 seconds.

Avinash Sable

Fastest 110m hurdles – men

Tejas Shirse set a new national record in the men's 110m hurdles at the World Athletics Continental Tour meeting in Jyvaskyla, Finland on 22 May. Shirse clocked 13.41 seconds to win the final, surpassing the previous record of 13.48 seconds held by Siddhanth Thingalaya since 2017.

Fastest 1500m – women

KM Deeksha set a new national record in the women's 1500m at the Sound Running Track Fest in Los Angeles on May 11, surpassing Harmilan Bains' three-year-old mark. The 25-year-old distance runner from Madhya Pradesh clocked 4:04.78, improving her personal best by over a second. Deeksha had previously won gold at the Inter-State Nationals by defeating Harmilan.

Highest pole vault

Women: At the 36th National Games Rosy Meena Paulraj cleared a height of 4.20 m to break the eight-year-old record of 4.15 m held by V. S. Surekha in the women's pole vault in the National Games 2022. A week later, she rewrote her own record by vaulting 4.21 m on 15 October 2022 at the National Open Athletics Championships 2022 in Bengaluru.
Men: At the 36th National Games, held between 29 September and 12 October 2022, Siva Subramani (5.31 m) eclipsed his own record of 5.30 m in the men's pole vault, set four years back.

Fastest race walk

Ram Baboo clocked 2.36.34 to break the previous national record in the men's 35 km race walk (2.40.16) by nearly four minutes in the 36th National Games in 2022.

Oldest gold medallist 

Rambai, at 105 years, won gold in the 100 m race at the National Open Masters Athletics Championships on 21 June 2022 in Vadodara, Gujarat.

Longest triple jump – women

On 13 June 2022, Aishwarya Babu made a record in the triple jump among Sumit Antil: best javelin throw – para athletics women at the 2022 National Inter-State Athletics Championships in Chennai, Tamil Nadu, leaping 14.14 m and breaking the national record of 14.11 m set by Mayookha Johny set at the Asian Championships in Japan in 2011.

Youngest athletics champion

Henry Rebello won the triple jump at Bangalore (now Bengaluru), Karnataka, in 1946 when he was only 17 years old. He set a record of 50 ft 2 in. at the 1948 National Games, which was surpassed only after a gap of 23 years by Mohinder Singh in 1971.

Longest shot put – women

Abha Khatua set a new women's shot put national record with a throw of 18.41m at the Federation Cup 2024 on 13 May, breaking Manpreet Kaur's previous record of 18.06m. The 28-year-old shot putter from Maharashtra achieved this mark on her fifth attempt, surpassing her previous joint national record of 18.06m set at the 2023 Asian Athletics Championships.

INDOOR ATHLETICS

Fastest 60m indoor hurdles – women
India's Jyothi Yarraji set a new National Record of 8.12 seconds to win gold in the women's 60m hurdles at the Asian Indoor Athletics Championships in Tehran on 17 February 2024.

BADMINTON

INTERNATIONAL

First doubles pair to reach World No. 1
Indian men's doubles pair Satwik Sairaj Rankireddy and Chirag Shetty achieved the world No. 1 ranking in the BWF rankings for the first time in their careers after winning gold in the men's doubles at the 2023 Asian Games in Hangzhou. Satwik-Chirag, popularly known as 'Sat-Chi', have also set new record as the longest-reigning world No. 1 Indian badminton players, holding the top spot in men's doubles for 11 weeks after regaining top spot on 23 January 2024. They surpassed Saina Nehwal, who held the world No. 1 rank for nine weeks in 2015.

OLYMPIC GAMES

First medallist
Saina Nehwal became the first Indian medallist, winning a bronze medal in London, UK, in 2012.

First silver medallist
P.V. Sindhu finished runner-up in Rio de Janeiro, Brazil, in 2016.

First two-time medallist
P.V. Sindhu remains the only two-time medallist with the silver medal in Rio de Janeiro, Brazil (2016), and the bronze medal in Tokyo, Japan (2020).

WORLD CHAMPIONSHIP

First individual medallist – men – singles
Prakash Padukone claimed the men's singles bronze medal in Copenhagen, Denmark, in 1983.

First individual medallist – women – singles
P.V. Sindhu received the women's singles bronze medal in Guangzhou, China, in 2013.

First doubles medallists – women
Jwala Gutta and Ashwini Ponnappa became the first Indian bronze medallists in women's doubles in London, UK, in 2011.

Jwala Gutta and Ashwini Ponnappa

First doubles medallists – men
Satwiksairaj Rankireddy and Chirag Shetty finished with a bronze in the men's doubles in Tokyo, Japan, in 2022.

First world champion
P.V. Sindhu claimed the honour by winning the women's singles in 2019.

Highest number of medals
P.V. Sindhu has five medals – a gold, two silver and two bronze medals – from the premier championship.

ASIAN GAMES

First medal – men – team
The men's team comprising Prakash Padukone, Dinesh Khanna, Davinder Ahuja, Partho Ganguli and Raman Ghosh won a bronze medal in Tehran in 1974.

First medal – women – team
The women's team comprising Ami Ghia, Madhumita Goswami, Amita Kulkarni, Hufrish Nariman, Kanwal Thakur Singh and Vandana Chiplunkar claimed a bronze medal in New Delhi in 1982.

First to win a medal – mixed – doubles
Leroy D'Sa and Kanwal Thakur Singh received a bronze medal in New Delhi in 1982.

First to win a medal – men – singles
Syed Modi claimed a bronze in New Delhi in 1982.

First to win a medal – women – singles
Saina Nehwal received a women's singles bronze in Jakarta-Palembang in 2018.

First to win a medal – men – doubles
Leroy D'Sa and Pradeep Gandhe claimed a bronze medal in New Delhi in 1982.

Chirag Shetty and Satwiksairaj Rankireddy

First gold medal at Asian Games

The Indian men's doubles badminton duo of Satwiksairaj Rankireddy and Chirag Shetty made history on 7 October 2023 by securing India's first-ever gold medal in badminton at the Asian Games. The dynamic pair emerged victorious after defeating the formidable Korean duo with a scoreline of 21-18, 21-16 in final match.

Multiple medal–winner in a single edition

Leroy D'Sa received three bronze medals – for the men's team, the doubles and the mixed doubles – in New Delhi in 1982.

Two medallists in a single event

P.V. Sindhu (silver) and Saina Nehwal (bronze) made it to the podium in the women's singles in Jakarta-Palembang in 2018.

P.V. Sindhu

COMMONWEALTH GAMES

First medallist – men – singles

Dinesh Khanna claimed a bronze medal in 1966 in the British Empire and Commonwealth Games. (In 1978, these Games were rechristened as the Commonwealth Games.)

Dinesh Khanna

First medallist – women – singles

Aparna Popat received a bronze medal in women's singles in Manchester in 2002.

First medallists – men – team

The team comprising P. Gopichand, Abhinn Shyam Gupta, George Thomas, Jaseel P. Ismail, Marcos Bristow, Nikhil Kanetkar and Vincent Lobo claimed a silver medal in Kuala Lumpur in 1998.

First medallists – women – team

The team comprising Manjusha Kanwar, P.V.V. Lakshmi, Madhumita Bisht, Aparna Popat, Archana Deodhar, K. Neelima Chowdhary and C. Deepthi won a bronze medal in Kuala Lumpur in 1998.

First gold medallist – mixed – team

The team comprising K. Srikanth, Saina Nehwal, P.V. Sindhu, H.S. Prannoy, Ashwini Ponnappa, Sikki Reddy, Ruthvika Shivani, Chirag Shetty, Satwiksairaj

Saina Nehwal

Rankireddy and Pranaav Chopra won the title in Gold Coast in 2018.

First medallist – women – doubles
Ami Ghia and Kanwal Thakur Singh claimed a bronze in Edmonton in 1978.

First gold medallist – men – singles
Prakash Padukone won the men's singles title in Edmonton in 1978.

Prakash Padukone

First medal – women – singles
Meena Shah claimed a women's singles bronze in Lucknow in 1965.

First medal – men – doubles
Dipu Ghosh and Raman Ghosh received a bronze at Jakarta in 1971.

First medal – women – doubles
Jwala Gutta and Ashwini Ponnappa received a bronze medal in Gimcheon in 2014.

First gold medallist – women - singles
Saina Nehwal won in New Delhi in 2010.

First gold medallists – women – doubles
Jwala Gutta and Ashwini Ponnappa won gold in Delhi in 2010.

First gold medallists – men – doubles
Chirag Shetty and Satwiksairaj Rankireddy won the title in Birmingham in 2022.

ASIAN CHAMPIONSHIP

First gold medal at Badminton Asia Team Championships
India's women's badminton team won their first-ever gold medal at the Badminton Asia Team Championships 2024 in Shah Alam, Malaysia. This historic victory marks the first time India's women made the podium, with the men's team previously earning two bronze medals in 2016 and 2020. The winning team members were P.V. Sindhu, Anmol Kharb, Ashmita Chaliha, Gayatri Gopichand-Treesa Jolly (doubles), and Tanisha Crasto-Ashwini Ponnappa (doubles). The Indian men's team had previously won two bronze medals in 2016 and 2020 while the women's team reached podium first time.

First gold medal from Asian championship
Dinesh Khanna won the men's singles gold medal in Lucknow in 1965.

First bronze medal – men – singles
Suresh Goel claimed a men's singles bronze in Lucknow in 1965.

First medal – mixed – doubles
Owen Roncon–Sarojini Apte and A.I. Sheikh–Achala Karnik received bronze medals in Lucknow in 1965.

WORLD JUNIOR CHAMPIONSHIP

First medallist – girls – singles
Saina Nehwal received a silver medal in the girls' singles in Incheon, South Korea, in 2006.

First gold medallist – girls – singles
Saina Nehwal won the girls' singles in Pune in 2008.

First medallist – boys – singles
R.M.V. Gurusaidutt claimed a bronze medal in the boys' singles in Pune in 2008.

BWF SUPER SERIES MASTERS FINALS/BWF WORLD TOUR FINALS

First medallist – women – singles
Saina Nehwal received a bronze in Kota Kinabalu, Sabah, Malaysia in 2008.

First medallist – men – singles
K. Srikanth received a bronze medal in Dubai in 2014.

First gold medallist – women – singles
P.V. Sindhu won the title in Guangzhou, China, in 2018 when the event was rechristened as BWF World Tour Finals.

Highest world ranking – women – singles
Saina Nehwal became the world no. 1 in the women's singles in April 2015.

Highest world rankings – mixed – doubles
Jwala Gutta and V. Diju were ranked world no. 6 in August 2010.

Highest world ranking – men – singles
K. Srikanth became the world no. 1 in the men's singles in April 2018.

Highest world ranking – women – doubles
Jwala Gutta and Ashwini Ponnappa were ranked world no. 10 in August 2015.

Highest world ranking – men – doubles
Chirag Shetty and Satwiksairaj Rankireddy were ranked world no. 7 in November 2019.

OTHER INTERNATIONAL COMPETITIONS

Indonesian postal stamp commemorating Thomas Cup

First medal in the Thomas Cup – men – team championship
India defeated 14-time champion Indonesia at the Thomas Cup 3-0 to win the prestigious title in 2022 for the first time ever, with World Championships medallist Lakshya Sen, K. Srikanth and the current world no. 8 doubles duo of Chirag Shetty and Satwiksairaj Rankireddy.

First duo to win Super 1000 title
Satwiksairaj Rankireddy and Chirag Shetty became the first Indian pair to win Super 1000 title as they won the men's doubles final at Indonesian Open 2023. They are also the first Indian pair to win a BWF World Tour Title at all levels.

Two semi-finalists at the All England
Prakash Nath and Davinder Mohan reached the men's singles semi-finals in 1947. Interestingly, the two players chose not to play each other. They tossed a coin, Prakash Nath called it right and advanced to the final.

First winner of the World Cup – men – singles
Prakash Padukone won in Kuala Lumpur, Malaysia, in 1981.

First winner at the All England Championship
Prakash Padukone won in London in 1980.

First finalist at the All England – men – singles
Prakash Nath reached the men's singles final in 1947 in London.

First medal in the Uber Cup – women's – team
India claimed its first bronze medal in New Delhi in 2014.

Most titles – women
Saina Nehwal won 10 titles in the BWF Superseries from 15 appearances in the final.

Most titles – men
K. Srikanth won six titles in the BWF Superseries in seven appearances in the final.

PARALYMPICS

First gold medallist – men – singles
Pramod Bhagat became the first gold medallist after winning the men's singles in the SL3 category in the 2020 Tokyo Paralympics.

DOMESTIC: NATIONALS

First National champions
Vijay Madgavkar (men's singles in 1934); T.P. Boland (women's singles in 1935); D. Minas–V. Minas (men's doubles in 1934); T.P. Boland–Cameron (women's doubles in 1935); and N. Knight-I. Brydges (mixed doubles in 1936).

Most titles – men – doubles
Rupesh Kumar was part of the men's doubles title winning pair for nine successive years between 2002 and 2010. Rupesh partnered Markose Bristow in 2002 and 2003, and thereafter joined hands with Sanave Thomas.

Most titles – men – singles
Prakash Padukone holds a unique record of winning all his nine singles titles in a row from 1971 to 1979.

Aparna Popat

Most titles – women – singles
Aparna Popat matched Prakash's record by winning her nine singles titles on the trot from 1997 to 2005.

Most titles – women – doubles
Jwala Gutta formed part of the title-winning combination 10 times between 2000 and 2013. She won with Shruti Kurien in 2000 and again from 2002 to 2008. She paired with Ashwini Ponnappa in 2009 and 2013.

Most titles – mixed – doubles
Madhumita Goswami-Bisht won the mixed doubles title 12 times with five different partners. She won in 1981, 1986-88 (with Sanat Mishra); In 1989-1990 (with Harjeet Singh); in 1994-97 (with Vinod Kumar); in 2000 (with Vincent Lobo); and 2001 (with Markose Bristow).

First gold medal – Paralympics
Pramod Bhagat of Odisha won India's first ever Paralympics Gold in badminton. (Badminton made its debut at the 2020 Tokyo Olympics). He clinched Gold in men's singles badminton (SLB) event.

BASKETBALL

First appearance in the Asian Games
India took part in the first Asian Games at New Delhi in 1951, under the captaincy of Ranbir Chand. In its best performance at the Games to date, the team came fourth.

Longest sequence of Nationals titles
• Services won the men's national title 26 years in a row from 1957 to 1982.
• Railways won the women's title 17 years in a row from 1986 to 2002.

First Indian-born player in the NBA
Satnam Singh Bhamara set a milestone in the history of Indian basketball when he was drafted into the National Basketball Association (NBA), the premier professional basketball league in the USA, in June 2015. Selected by the Dallas Mavericks, he played his Summer League debut match against the New Orleans Pelicans, scoring four points for his team, on 11 July 2015.

Satnam Singh Bhamara

Most appearances in the Asian Games – women
Prashanti Singh is the only woman basketball player to represent the Indian team in two Asian Games, in 2010 and 2014. She also represented the national team in the 2006 CWG. She has won 22 medals in national championships and federation events.

Prashanti Singh

Best win
Indian basketball's biggest win was at the 2014 FIBA Asia Cup, held in Wuhan, Hubei, China, winning against home favourites and against the most successful Asian team, China, by 7 points.

BOXING

Most golds in an international meet
India won 10 gold and two silver medals at the 1995 South Asian Games (SAG; formerly SAF) in Chennai, Tamil Nadu.

This achievement is second only to South Korea's haul of all 12 gold medals in the 1986 Seoul Asian Games.

Most successive professional wins
Vijender Singh demolished former Commonwealth champion Charles Adamu to claim his 12th straight win in November 2019. The winning streak ended when he was defeated by Russian opponent, Artysh Lopsan, in Goa in March 2021.

Best youth boxer – men
Sachin Siwach was named Asian Boxing Confederation's Best Youth Boxer of 2017.

Sachin Siwach

Oldest existing boxing association
The Maharashtra Amateur Boxing Association was formed in 1924.

AIBA

First boxer in the AIBA athletes' commission
In November 2019, veteran Indian boxer Laishram Sarita Devi was elected unopposed to the AIBA's first ever athletes commission to represent the Asian bloc. She is an eight-time Asian Championship medallist, with five being gold medals.

AIBA LEGEND

First Indian woman boxer to receive AIBA Legends Award
M.C. Mary Kom received the AIBA Legends Award at AIBA's 70th anniversary gala in Montreux, Switzerland, in 2016.

First male boxer to win the APB Best Boxing trophy
Asian Games gold medallist Vikas Krishan was awarded the APB Best Boxing trophy at AIBA's 70th anniversary in Montreux, Switzerland, 2016.

Vikas Krishan

Vijender Singh

World no. 1
- In 2009, AIBA announced Vijender Singh as the top-ranked boxer in the annual middleweight category.
- In January 2019, M.C. Mary Kom (48 kg category) was the top ranked boxer in the AIBA World Ranking (women)

ASIAN CHAMPIONSHIPS

Most medals in the Asian Championship – women
M.C. Mary Kom (46 kg), L. Sarita Devi (54 kg), Jenny R. Lalremliani (63 kg) and Jyotsna (80 kg and 86 kg) won two golds each at the 2003 and the 2005 Asian Women's Boxing Championship, in Hisar, Haryana, and Kaohsiung, Taiwan, respectively.

Best performance at the Asian Championship
Indian boxers won two gold, four silver and seven bronze medals in Bangkok, Thailand, in April 2019 to finish at the third position with 13 medals. Pooja Rani (81 kg) and Amit Panghal (52 kg) won gold medals; Deepak Singh (49 kg), Kavinder Singh Bisht (56 kg), Ashish Kumar (75 kg) and Simranjit Kaur (64 kg) won silvers; Nikhat Zareen (51 kg), Manisha Moun (54 kg), Sonia Chahal (57 kg), L. Sarita Devi (60 kg), Shiva Thapa (60 kg), Ashish (69 kg) and Satish Kumar (91 kg) won bronze medals.

ASIAN GAMES

First Asian Games medal – men
Hari Singh won the silver in the middleweight category at the 1958 Manila Games in the Philippines. Sunder Rao and Ranganathan won the bronze in the lightweight and the welterweight categories respectively.

First Asian Games gold – men
Padam Bahadur Mal won the gold medal in the lightweight category in 1962 in the Asian Games held in Jakarta, Indonesia.

Best performance in the Asian Games
India won two gold, three silver and four bronze medals in the 2010 Asian Games, its best haul at an Asian Games. The gold medallists were Vikas Krishan (60 kg) and Vijender Singh (75 kg). Silver medals were won by V. Santosh Kumar (64 kg), Dinesh Kumar (81 kg) and Manpreet Singh (91 kg). The bronze went to Suranjoy Singh (52 kg), Paramjeet Samota (+91 kg), M.C. Mary Kom (51 kg) and Kavita Goyal (75 kg).

Best performance in Asian Games – gold – women
India won a gold and two bronze medals at the 2014 Incheon Asian Games in South Korea. M.C. Mary Kom won the gold in the women's flyweight (51 kg) event. L. Sarita Devi (lightweight, 60 kg) and Pooja Rani (middleweight, 75 kg) won bronze medals.

Most Asian Games golds
Hawa Singh (heavyweight) won two golds at the 1966 and 1970 Asian Games, both held in Bangkok, Thailand.

Hawa Singh

COMMONWEALTH CHAMPIONSHIPS

Most Commonwealth Championship gold medals
India won six gold medals and the overall title at the Commonwealth Championship in New Delhi in March 2010. Amandeep Singh (49 kg), Suranjoy Singh (52 kg), Jai Bhagwan (60 kg), Vijender Singh (75 kg), Dinesh Kumar (81 kg) and Paramjeet Samota (+91 kg) won a gold medal each.

Amandeep Singh

COMMONWEALTH GAMES

First Commonwealth Games gold
Mohammed Ali Qamar won the gold medal in the lightweight category, defeating Darren Langley 27–25 at the Commonwealth Games in Manchester, UK, in 2002.

Best performance at the Commonwealth Games
At the 2018 CWG in Gold Coast, Australia, India won three gold, three silver and three bronze medals. M.C. Mary Kom in women's lightweight (48 kg), Gaurav Solanki in flyweight (52 kg) and Vikas Krishan in middleweight (75 kg) won gold medals. Amit Panghal in light flyweight (49 kg), Manish Kaushik in lightweight (60 kg) and Satish Kumar in superweight (+91 kg) won silver medals. Mohammed Hussamuddin in bantamweight (56 kg), Manoj Kumar in welterweight (69 kg) and Naman Talwar in heavyweight (91 kg) won bronze medals.

Amit Panghal

INTERNATIONAL

Most international titles
• Heavyweight boxer Kaur Singh won gold at four major international events: the 1980 Asian Boxing Championship (Bombay, now Mumbai, Maharashtra) and 1982 (Seoul, South Korea), the 1982 Delhi Asian Games and the 1982 King's Cup in Bangkok, Thailand.
• Super heavyweight boxer Rajkumar Sangwan also won four golds: at the 1991 Asian Invitational Championship in Bangkok, Thailand; the 1993 China Invitational Championship in Beijing, China; the 1993 South Asian Federation (SAF) Games at Dhaka, Bangladesh; and the 1994 Asian Boxing Championship at Tehran, Iran.

NATIONALS

First National Championship
The very first National Boxing Championship in the country, organized by the Indian Amateur Boxing Federation, was held in Bombay (now Mumbai), Maharashtra, from 18 to 22 March 1950.

OLYMPICS

First Olympic appearance
India entered a boxing team in seven divisions for the first time at the 1948 London Olympics but could not reach the quarterfinals.

First Olympic medal – men
Vijender Singh won a bronze medal (middleweight) in the 2008 Beijing Olympics.

First Olympic medal – women
Six-time women's world champion M.C. Mary Kom won a bronze medal (51 kg) in the 2012 London Olympics. Lovlina Borgohain (69 kg) became the second Indian woman to win a bronze medal at Tokyo 2020 after losing to Turkey's Busenaz Surmeneli 0-5 in the semi-finals.

WORLD BOXING CHAMPIONSHIP

First medal in the World Boxing Championships – men
• Amit Panghal was the first Indian male boxer to win a silver medal in the World Boxing Championship 2019.
• Parveen Kumar won a bronze medal in the lightweight category in the World Junior Championship in Budapest, Hungary, in November 2000.

First World Boxing Championships medal – women
• M.C. Mary Kom from Manipur bagged a silver medal in the 48 kg category in the USA in December 2001.

Most medals in the World Boxing Championships
In October 2019, M.C. Mary Kom became the first boxer in the world (male or female) to win eight World Championship medals (six gold, a silver and a bronze).

Best performance in the World Boxing Championships – women
India won four gold, one silver and three bronze medals in the fourth World Women's Boxing Championship 2006 in New Delhi. M.C. Mary Kom (46 kg), L. Sarita Devi (52 kg), Jenny R. Lalremliani (63 kg) and Lekha K.C. (75 kg) won gold medals. N. Usha (57 kg) won a silver. The bronze winners were Chhotu Loura (50 kg), Aruna Mishra (60 kg) and Renu (82 kg).

WORLD CHAMPIONSHIP

First medal in the World Championship – senior – men
Vijender Singh won a bronze medal in the 2009 Milan World Cup in Italy.

Most World Championship titles – women
M.C. Mary Kom is the first female pugilist to win the World Championship crown six times (2002, 2005, 2006, 2008, 2010 and 2018). She also won the most world titles (five) in a row between 2002 and 2010. Others to have won gold medals in the World Championships are Sarita Devi (2006), Jenny R. Lalremliani, (2006), Lakha K.C. (2006) and Nikhat Zareen (2022).

WORLD CUP

First medal at the World Cup – men
Zoramthanga defeated teammate Dharmender Yadav 17–4 on points to win the light flyweight bronze on 17 November 1990 in Bombay (now Mumbai), Maharashtra.

Most medals in the World Cup – men
The Indian team won a silver and a bronze medal, and the sixth position overall, in the AIBA Boxing World Cup in October 2019 in Yekaterinburg, Russia.

YOUTH BOXING CHAMPIONSHIP

Most medals at the Youth Boxing Championships

The Indian team won five gold, two silver and five bronze medals at the Youth Boxing Championship in November 2019 in Ulaanbaatar, Mongolia.

Best performance in the World Youth Women's Boxing Championship

Seven Indian women boxers clinched gold medals in their respective weight categories in the AIBA Youth World Boxing Championships in Kielce, Poland, in August 2021. They were Gitika (48 kg), Naorem Babyrojisana Chanu (51 kg), Poonam (57 kg), Vinka (60 kg), Arundhati Choudhary (69 kg), T. Sanamacha Chanu (75 kg) and Alfiya Pathan (+81 kg).

Postal stamp from USSR commemorating AIBA Championship

CHESS

GENERAL

Most times world champion

Viswanathan Anand has won the World Chess Championship five times (2000, 2007, 2008, 2010 and 2012).

Oldest to regain the world rapid title

Viswanathan Anand, at 48, became the oldest world champion in the rapid format (25-minute time format) in Riyadh in December 2017. He regained the title won in 2003. Two days later, he also became the oldest medallist in the blitz format (five-minute time format) by claiming the bronze medal.

Viswanathan Anand

Board Prize with a perfect score

Viswanathan Anand scored seven points from seven rounds to win the top Board Prize in the Asian Team Championship in 1989.

Domination in Advanced Chess

Viswanathan Anand won a hat-trick of titles in 1999, 2000 and 2001 in Leon, Spain. In 2000 and 2001 he beat Alexei Shirov of Spain in the final to win the tournament. In Advanced Chess, players have the benefit of using database searches on their computers before making a move.

Longest reign as top-ranked Indian in the world

Viswanathan Anand remained India's top-ranked player in the world for 37 successive years. His supreme reign ended when D. Gukesh overtook him in the World rating list released on 1 September 2023.

Four successive Asian Junior titles

Indians twice won the title for four years in a row. The Indian boys won from 1997 to 2000 and again from 2007 to 2010.

Golden sweep – Asian Youth Championship

India won 18 medals, including all eight gold medals at stake, in the Asian Youth Championship in 2006. Sweety Patel (girls' U-8), Sahajasri (Girls U-10), Padmini Rout (girls' U-12), Bhakti Kulkarni (girls' U-14), Prince Bajaj (boys' U-8), G.V. Sai Krishna (boys' U-10), Vidit Gujarati (boys' U-12) and S. Nitin (boys' U-14) were the gold medal winners.

Grand Slam victories

In chess, the tournaments in Wijk Aan Zee, Linares and Dortmund were considered the equivalent of the Grand Slam in golf. Anand won at Wijk Aan Zee five times, and at Linares and Dortmund, both three times.

Youngest winner of the Candidates Tournament

D. Gukesh, 17, became the youngest winner of the prestigious Candidates Tournament in Toronto in April 2024. The title earned him the right to challenge reigning World champion China's Ding Liren for the world crown, in Singapore, in November-December 2024.

D. Gukesh

Pravin Thipsay

First GM norm

Pravin Thipsay was the first to achieve GM norm in the 1985 Commonwealth championship in London.

First GM norm in National Championship

P. Konguvel was the first Indian to date to gain a nine-game norm from the National 'A' Championship at New Delhi in June 2001.

First Olympiad golden sweep

India became only the third nation – after Russia and China – to make a sweep of team titles in the 2024 edition Budapest, Hungary. Seeded two, India won the Open title with a stupendous tally of 21 match points (out of a maximum of 22) in the 11-round competition for its maiden gold in the games' most prestigious team championship, involving 197 nations/federations. The team members were D. Gukesh, R. Praggnanandhaa, Arjun Erigaisi, Vidit Gujrathi and P. Harikrishna. Coach: N. Srinath. Top seeded Indian women scored 19 points to justify its ranking in a field of 183 nations/federations. The team comprised D. Harika, R. Vaishali, Divya Deshmukh, Vantika Agrawal and Tania Sachdev. Coach: Abhjiit Kunte.

First Grandmaster (GM)
Viswanathan Anand became India's first GM on 28 December 1987 at the Sakthi Finance Grandmaster tournament in Coimbatore.

First International Master (IM) – men
Manuel Aaron of Tamil Nadu became an International Master in 1961.

First International Master (IM) – women
S. Vijayalakshmi got the International Master's title in Sept 2000.

Most individual gold medallists in a single edition of Olympiad
Five Indians won gold medals for their individual performance in Budapest, 2024. D. Gukesh (Open, Board 1), Arjun Erigaisi (Board 3), Divya Deshmukh (Women, Board 3) and Vantika Agrawal (Women, Board 4) played stellar roles in India's historic twin-triumphs.

FIRSTS

First Olympiad gold
Dibyendu Barua won the gold on the second board of the Olympiad in Novi Sad (erstwhile Yugoslavia) in 1990.

First Olympiad gold on top board
D. Gukesh won the gold on top board in Mahabalipuram in 2022. He retained it in 2024 to set a unique record.

First time when India won medals in both sections of Olympiad
India won bronze medals in Open and women sections of the Olympiad in Mahabalipuram in 2022.

First sweep of titles in Grand Swiss
Vidit Gujrathi and R. Vaishali won the Open and women titles in the premier Grand Swiss Chess in 2023 and qualified for their prestigious Candidates Tournaments.

First international recognition

Mir Sultan Khan, born in 1905 in village Mittha, Punjab, received international recognition at a time when there was no system of Elo ratings. In 1928, he won the all-India title scoring 8.5 out of 9 points at the British Championship. He won again in 1932 and 1933. He also defeated world champion Jose Casablanca of Cuba at the Hastings tournament. Considered among the 10 best players in the world then, he returned to India in 1933 but played little chess. He died in Sargodha, Pakistan on 25 May 1966.

Mir Sultan Khan after winning the British Chess Championship

First medal in the Chess Olympiad
India won its maiden medal from the Tromso Chess Olympiad in 2014 in Norway. In the open section, India was represented by Parimarjan Negi, K, Sasikiran, S.P. Sethuraman, B. Adhiban and M.R. Lalith Babu claimed the bronze medal, ahead of traditional powerhouses like Russia, Armenia and Ukraine.

First Olympiad medal
Rafiq Khan won a silver medal in the 1980 Olympiad.

First medal in Asian Games
K Humpy won the gold in the Doha Asian Games in 2006.

First winner of Women World Cup
Divya Deshmukh became the first to win the coveted title by beating compatriot K. Humpy in 2025.

Divya Deshmukh

First team medal in Asian Games
The trio of K. Sasikiran, P. Harikrishna and K. Humpy won the mixed team gold in Doha in 2006.

First World Junior title
Viswanathan Anand was 17 years 225 days when he won the title on 2 August 1987 at Baguio city in the Philippines. P. Harikrishna (2004) and Abhijeet Gupta (2008) are the other junior title winners.

First WGM norm
Bhagyashree Thipsay, 21, was the first to achieve a Woman Grand Master (WGM) norm in 1986 in the Lloyds Bank Master's tournament.

First WIM
Jayshree Khadilkar became a WIM (Woman International Master) in 1978.

First woman to lead a team in the open section
K. Humpy led India 'B' in the open section of the Asian Team Championship at Jodhpur in 2003.

Two World Cups
Viswanathan Anand is the first person in the world to successfully defend the men's World Cup title. He did so at Hyderabad in October 2002.

First country to win both World Junior titles in a single edition
India became the first country to win both the World Junior titles in a single edition in 2008 when Abhijeet Gupta and D. Harika won the open and girls' sections respectively in the World Junior Chess Championship in Gazientep. Parimarjan Negi claimed the silver to give India a rare 1-2 finish in the open section.

MOSTS

Most medals
Indians won 21 medals – seven gold, seven silver and seven bronze – in the Asian Youth Championship held in New Delhi in 2005. This was the biggest haul by India in a continental competition.

Most National titles (in a season)
P. Harikrishna won five National titles in 1997–98 season – the 1997 National Sub-juniors held in January 1998 at Aurangabad, the U-12 in Ahmedabad, the U-18 in Bikaner, the U-14 rapid chess title in Guntur and the 1998 National Sub-junior at Aurangabad.

Most National titles
• *Men*: Manuel Aaron won nine National titles, five of them in a row from 1969-74.
• *Women*: S. Vijayalakshmi has claimed the National title six times, including five times in a row from May 2002.

Manuel Aaron

Most titles in a year
Viswanathan Anand won a string of eight titles in the year 2000. Starting with the World Blitz Cup, he won the Wydra International at Haifa, the Advanced Chess title in Leon, the Giants Classic in Frankfurt, the Dortmund International (joint winner), the World Cup in Shenyang, China, and the Corsica Masters in France, finishing with the World Championship title in December 2000.

City to host most Commonwealth Championships
New Delhi hosted the Commonwealth championship six times between 2007 and 2019.

FASTEST

Fastest to achieve norms
P. Harikrishna achieved three International Master norms – in the Asian Championship in Udaipur, the Goodricke tournament in Kolkata and the Commonwealth Championship in Sangli – in less than two months in 2000.

YOUNGEST

Youngest to achieve an IM norm
R. Praggnanandhaa became the youngest Indian to make an IM norm. At 10 years, six months, he gained the distinction in Cannes (France) in February 2016.

Youngest Grandmaster – male
D. Gukesh became the country's youngest and the world's second youngest Grandmaster in January 2019 at the age of 12 years, 7 months and 17 days.

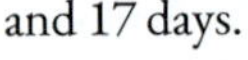

Youngest International Master
R. Praggnanandhaa, at the age of 10 years and nine months, became the youngest International Master in chess history in May 2017 by making his third and final IM norm at Bhubaneswar. His earlier two norms had come in Cannes and Moscow.

S. Vijayalakshmi

R. Praggnanandhaa

Youngest international title winners
Sanskruti Wankhede and Vallabh Kavi were the winners of the Asian Schools' chess (U-5) girls' and boys' titles respectively, in New Delhi in 2011.

Youngest Grandmaster – female
K. Humpy became the youngest female to become a GM at 15 years, 1 month and 27 days in 2002.

K. Humpy

Youngest National champion
Sixteen-year-old G. Akash became the youngest National champion in 2012.

Youngest National Junior – champion
Abhijeet Gupta of Bhilwara became the youngest National Junior champion at Nagpur in 2002. He won the U-19 event at the age of 13 years 10 days.

Youngest to beat a GM
Hetul Shah (9) defeated Kazakh Nurlan Ibrayev in the first round of the Parsvnath International Open chess tournament in New Delhi on 11 January 2009, to become the youngest Indian to beat a Grandmaster. He broke the record of Parimarjan Negi who had achieved the feat at the age of eleven.

Youngest to qualify for the National Championship
• Dibyendu Barua, then 12, remains the youngest to qualify for the National championship in 1978.
• D. Harika holds the unique record of being the youngest girl to qualify for the men's National championship in 2004 as well as for the women's National championship in 2001.

Youngest to win the Commonwealth title
P. Harikrishna, then fifteen, won the gold in London in 2001 after a three-way tie with two British players.

Youngest WIM
K. Humpy became the youngest Woman International Master (WIM) in Asia at 12 years, three months, four days.

Youngest winner of Asian Junior (U-20) title
M. Kasturi, then 14 years old, won the Asian Junior title in Teheran in 2001.

Youngest world champion in any sport
Ivana Furtado claimed the World Girls' U-8 crown at the age of 7 years and 226 days at Batumi, Georgia on 29 October 2006.

Youngest rated player
At 3 years, 8 months and 19 days, Anish Sarkar became the youngest rated

player in the world. Born on January 26, 2021, this prodigy entered the World list with a rating of 1555 in November 2024.

BEST

Best achievement

• *Men*: Viswanathan Anand's rating of 2817 in March 2011 is the highest recorded by an Indian.
• *Women*: Among women, Koneru Humpy's rating of 2623 in July 2009 is the highest.

Best performance (Category 21)

Viswanathan Anand beat a field of seven super Grandmasters at Madrid between Feb 21 and March 10, 1998. The Category 21 tournament attracted seven of the top nine GMs of the world. Anand beat Alexey Shirov, Peter Svidler, Vassily Ivanchuk, Vaselin Topalov 1.5 0.5; lost to Gary Kasparov 0.5-1.5 and drew 1-1 with Vladimir Kramnik.

Best performance in Candidates Tournament (women)

K. Humpy finished runner-up after topping a three-way tie, including compatriot R. Vaishali, for the second spot in the 2024 edition held in Toronto.

Best performance in Asian Team Championship

Indian men won three gold and women claimed five silver medal in the continental championships.

Youngest to win World junior (under-20) title

K. Humpy, 14, won the prestigious title in 2001.

ONLY

First/only winner of Asian Junior and Sub-junior titles

Tejas Bakre won the Asian Junior and Asian Sub-junior titles at the same time, in 1998.

Only Indian to win against computers

Viswanathan Anand simultaneously played six computers and won 4-2, in the Aegon Man versus Computer Chess Event in 1997.

Only Asian to win at Wijk Aan Zee

Viswanathan Anand is the only Asian to win the Hoogovens Chess Tournament (Corus tournament since 2000) at Wijk Aan Zee in 1989, though jointly with three others. He won the title again in 1998, jointly with Vladimir Kramnik, and outright in 2003, 2004 and 2006.

Only Indian to win rapid/ blindfold event

Viswanathan Anand won the first-of-its-kind Melody Amber Blindfold and Rapid chess event in 1994, 1997, 2003 and jointly in 2006.

Only Chess Oscar award winner

Viswanathan Anand is the only Indian to receive the Chess Oscar (founded in 1967) by the Russian chess magazine *64 - Chess Review*. He has claimed the Chess Oscar six times (in 1997, 1998, 2003, 2004, 2007 and 2008).

Only Indian with three World Championship bronze medals

D. Harika claimed three successive bronze medals from the Women's World Championship in 2012, 2015 and 2017.

D. Harika

CRICKET

WOMEN'S CRICKET

GENERAL

Youngest to debut across all formats

Shafali Verma became the youngest Indian cricketer to make her debut across all three formats of the game when she played her first One-Day International (ODI) on 27 June 2021, against England in the UK, when she was 17 years and 150 days old. She made her Test debut on 16 June 2021 in Bristol, UK, against England. Her T20I debut came at the age of 15 against South Africa in September 2019 in Surat, Gujarat. She is also the youngest woman ever to play an ODI, and the first Indian and fourth woman to score a half-century in both innings on a Test debut.

Shafali Verma

Most career runs in women's international cricket

Mithali Raj has scored 10,868 runs in her international career, with 669 runs in Tests, 7,805 in ODIs and 2,364 in T20Is.

Longest career

Mithali Raj's cricketing career spans more than 23 years.

Most capped Indian woman in international cricket

Harmanpreet Kaur became India's most capped woman cricketer during the fifth T20I against England in Birmingham in July 2025. Playing her 334th international match, she went past Mithali Raj's tally of 333 appearances across formats.

Most career wickets across formats

Jhulan Goswami, with 355 wickets in 284 matches, has the most wickets across formats.

TESTS

Highest-ever total in Test - World Record

Indian Women set a new record for the highest-ever team total in Test cricket, scoring 603/6 declared during their match against South Africa Women in Chennai on 29 June 2024. This total surpassed the previous record of 575/9 declared, held by Australia Women, which was set in February 2024 against South Africa in Sydney.

India women also set a new record for the most runs scored by any team in a single day's play in Test history, accumulating a total of 515 runs on the opening day of the same Chennai Test. This achievement surpassed the previous record of 509 for 9 by the Sri Lankan men's team on the second day of the 2002 Colombo Test against Bangladesh.

Fastest Double Hundred in Test Cricket

Shafali Varma set a new record for the fastest double century in Women's Test cricket during the match against South Africa in Chennai on June 28. The 20-year-old batter reached her double hundred in just 194 balls, marking her maiden international century in the longest format. She broke the previous record held by Australia's Annabel Sutherland, who scored 210 runs off 256 balls against South Africa in Sydney in February 2024.

Biggest win in women's Test history (by margin)

India recorded the biggest win in women's Test history by defeating England by a massive 347-run margin in Navi Mumbai on December 16. This victory surpassed Sri Lanka's previous record of a 309-run win over Pakistan set in 1998, setting a new benchmark for the largest win by runs in women's Test cricket.

Most career dismissals by a wicketkeeper

Anju Jain has the most career dismissals by a wicketkeeper with 23 dismissals from 1995 to 2003, including 15 caught and 8 stumped.

Biggest victory margin

India won by an innings and 34 runs while playing against South Africa in Mysuru, Karnataka, on 16 November 2014.

Narrowest victory margin

India won by 5 wickets against West Indies in Patna, Bihar, on 17 November 1976, and then against England at Taunton, UK, on 1 September 2006.

Lowest total

The lowest total ever was 65 runs for 10 wickets in 46 overs against the West Indies at Jammu, Jammu and Kashmir, on 29 November 1976.

Highest total

The highest total by the women's Test cricket team is 467 in 177.1 overs versus England at Taunton, UK, on 17 August 2002.

Mithali Raj

First and only double century

Mithali Raj scored 214 runs in 407 balls, against England at Taunton, UK, on 16 August 2002. She also has the best batting average of 51.00 in 10 matches.

Most runs

Sandhya Agarwal has 1,110 runs in 13 matches. She also holds the record for the most centuries, with four in 13 Tests and 23 innings.

WR Most balls delivered

Former Indian player and left-arm spinner Diana Edulji is the only woman to deliver more than 5,000 balls (5,248) in Test matches.

Most wickets in a Test

Right-arm pacer Jhulan Goswami took 10 wickets in the match against England at Taunton, UK, on 1 September 2006.

Most career wickets in Tests

The record for most wickets in a Test career belongs to Diana Edulji, with 63 wickets taken from 1976 to 1991.

First World Cup win

India won the first ICC Women's World Cup after defeating South Africa by 52 runs at DY Patil Stadium, Navi Mumbai, on 2 November 2025.

Indian Women's World Cup winning cricket team with President Droupadi Murmu (*above*) and Prime Minister Narendra Modi (*right*)

Best bowling average
Jhulan Goswami, with an average of 17.36 with 44 wickets in 12 matches, has an unmatched bowling average in women's Test cricket in India.

Jhulan Goswami

WR Best bowling – innings
Neetu David's 8wickets for 53 runs in the India versus England match at Jamshedpur, Jharkhand, on 27 November 1995, makes her the only bowler in women's Test cricket to have claimed eight wickets in an innings.

Most career catches by a fielder
Sudha Shah has taken 21 catches in as many matches, an Indian record for a fielding position.

ONE-DAY INTERNATIONALS

WR Highest run chase
India chased a target of 339 against Australia in Women's Cricket World Cup 2025 semi-finals at the DY Patil Stadium, Navi Mumbai, on 30 October 2025.

Century on debut
Mithali Raj scored a century on her debut with 114 runs (not out) versus Ireland at Milton Keynes, UK, on 26 June 1999.

Most career catches by a fielder
Jhulan Goswami has notched up 69 catches in 204 matches.

WR Most career stumpings by a wicketkeeper
Anju Jain holds a world record with 51 stumpings across her career.

WR Highest partnership
Deepti Sharma and Poonam Raut made a 320-run stand for the first wicket at the India versus Ireland match at Potchefstroom, South Africa, on 15 May 2017.

Highest individual score
Deepti Sharma was 188 not out at the India versus Ireland match at Potchefstroom, South Africa, on 15 May 2017.

Largest victory margin by runs
India defeated Ireland by 304 runs in the third ODI in Rajkot on January 15, 2025, its biggest victory margin in women's ODIs. The previous record was a 249-run win against the same opponent at Potchefstroom in 2017.

Most career dismissals by a wicketkeeper
Anju Jain has 81 dismissals to her credit, including 30 caught and 51 stumped.

Best bowling average – minimum 50 wickets
Neetu David holds the record with an average of 16.34 (141 wickets in 97 matches).

WR Most runs scored
Mithali Raj has scored 7,805 runs in 232 matches. She is the only woman cricketer to score more than 7,000 runs.

Fastest century
Smriti Mandhana scored the fastest century by any Indian in One-Day Internationals, across men's and women's cricket. She scored a 50-ball hundred against Australia during third ODI in New Delhi on 20 September 20, 2025. It was also the second-fastest century in women's ODI history.

First to score consecutive centuries in ODI
Smriti Mandhana became the first Indian woman to score consecutive centuries in ODIs, achieving this milestone during the first two matches of the India-South Africa series in June 2024. She came close to securing a third consecutive century but fell just 10 runs short in the third ODI.

First Indian woman to score centuries in all formats
Smriti Mandhana became the first Indian woman to score centuries in all three formats of international cricket. She achieved the feat with her maiden T20I hundred, a 51-ball knock against England at Trent Bridge in Nottingham on 28 June 2025.

Most centuries
Smriti Mandhana became the batter with the most centuries in women's ODIs for India when she struck her 8th ton against New Zealand in October 2024, surpassing Mithali Raj's tally of seven. She stretched this record to 13 centuries with a blazing hundred against Australia in the third ODI at New Delhi on 20 September 2025.

Most international runs in a calendar year
Smriti Mandhana surpassed the record for most international runs in a calendar year across formats in women's cricket. During the first ODI against West in Baroda on December 22, 2024, she overtook South Africa's Laura Wolvaardt, who had amassed 1,593 runs in 34 matches. Mandhana ended the year with 1,659 runs.

T20 INTERNATIONALS

Oldest Indian player to debut in T20I

Asha Sobhana Joy made her international debut for India at the age of 33 years and 51 days during the T20I series against Bangladesh in Sylhet on May 6. By doing so, she became the oldest Indian player to debut in the T20I format.

Largest victory margin

- The largest victory margin in terms of runs is 142 runs versus Malaysia on 3 June 2018 at the Kinrara Academy Oval, Kuala Lumpur, Malaysia.
- In terms of wickets, the largest victory margin has been by 10 wickets against the Australian team on 29 January 2016 at Melbourne, Australia.

Highest partnership

Shafali Verma and Smriti Mandhana put on a 143-run stand for the first wicket versus West Indies at the Darren Sammy National Cricket Stadium, Saint Lucia, on 9 November 2019.

Narrowest margin of victory

- By runs, the narrowest margin was 3 runs on two occasions. The first was against the West Indies at North Sound, Antigua, on 19 February 2012, and the second was against New Zealand in Melbourne, Australia, on 27 February 2020.
- By wickets, India's narrowest margin has been against New Zealand, of 3 wickets at Aldershot, England, on 27 June 2011.

Most career runs

Harmanpreet Kaur has scored 2,694 in 137 matches with a batting average of 27.48.

Harmanpreet Kaur

Highest team total

India's highest team total was 198 for 4 wickets in the third match versus England at Brabourne Stadium in Mumbai, Maharashtra, in the Tri-Nation Women's T20I Series in March 2018.

Lowest team total

India scored only 62 runs in 18.2 overs versus Australia at Billericay, Essex, UK, on 23 June 2011.

Most career wickets

Poonam Yadav has notched up 98 wickets in 72 matches.

Best bowling average (minimum qualification of 30 matches)

Poonam Raut has a record bowling average of 9.66.

Best bowling

Jhulan Goswami took 5 wickets for 11 runs in a T20I match against Australia at Visakhapatnam, Andhra Pradesh, on 23 March 2012.

Most career dismissals by a wicketkeeper

Tania Bhatia has 67 dismissals (23 caught and 44 stumped) in 50 matches.

Most career catches by a fielder

Harmanpreet Kaur holds the record of 53 catches in 137 matches, the highest number of career catches.

MEN'S CRICKET

GENERAL

Player with the most IPL titles

Rohit Sharma has earned the most IPL titles, totalling six: one with the Deccan Chargers, Hyderabad (2009) and five with the Mumbai Indians (2013, 2015, 2017, 2019 and 2020).

Only country to win ICC Champions Trophy three times

After winning the 2025 edition, India became the only nation to win the ICC Champions Trophy three times.

Only captain to win all three ICC trophies

M.S. Dhoni is the only captain to lead his team to victory in all the three major ICC tournaments: the World T20 in 2007, the Cricket World Cup in 2011 and the Champions Trophy in 2013.

M.S. Dhoni

TESTS

First victory

India, captained by Vijay Hazare, defeated England by an innings and 8 runs on 10 February 1952 at Madras (now Chennai), Tamil Nadu. The victory came in the fifth match of a five-match series and India managed to draw the series 1–1.

Sunil Gavaskar

First to reach 10,000 runs

Indian cricket legend Sunil Gavaskar first went past the 10,000 mark in 125 matches, reaching 10,122 Test runs in his last series against Pakistan in 1987.

Highest team innings score

The highest innings score was 759 runs for 7 wickets against England at Chennai, Tamil Nadu, in 2016.

Highest score on debut (series)

Legendary batsman Sunil Gavaskar scored 774 runs in his very first Test series against West Indies in 1971, a record that remains unbroken.

Most career wickets

Anil Kumble holds the record with 619 wickets in his Test career spanning from 1990 to 2008.

Most wickets in a debut series

In the India–England Test series from 5 February to 8 March 2021, Axar Patel took 27 wickets in the four-match series. He holds the record jointly with Dilip Doshi, who took the same number of wickets during a six-match home series against Australia in 1979.

Most career runs

Sachin Tendulkar's total of 15,921 runs is an unbroken

world record for the most career runs in men's Test cricket.

Most individual centuries

Sachin Tendulkar scored 100 centuries – three versus West Indies in 19 Tests, 11 versus Australia in 35 Tests, two versus Pakistan in 18 Tests, seven versus England in 28 Tests, four in 22 Tests versus New Zealand, nine in 25 Tests versus Sri Lanka, seven in 25 Tests versus South Africa, five in seven Tests versus Bangladesh and three in nine Tests versus Zimbabwe.

Most runs in an over

Jasprit Bumrah scored 35 runs (not out) in an over off England Stuart Broad at Edgbaston, Birmingham in May 2022. He hit two fours off the first two deliveries, followed by a wide ball, then a six, followed by a no ball, and the next three balls were hit for fours. The penultimate ball went for a six and he scored a single off the last ball.

Highest run chase

India's run chase of 406 runs for 4 wickets against West Indies in Port-of-Spain, Trinidad, in 1976 is its highest successful chase to date.

Highest individual score in a day

Virender Sehwag, in his knock of 293 against Sri Lanka in Mumbai, Maharashtra, during 2009–10, made 284 runs on the second day of the Test match – the highest individual score in a single day to date.

Highest individual innings

Virender Sehwag's 319 against South Africa in Chennai, Tamil Nadu, in 2008 is the highest individual score in a Test match.

Virender Sehwag

Fastest Indian opener to score 1,000 runs

Right-handed batsman Rohit Sharma achieved this landmark in his 17th innings as the Indian opener against England on 5 March 2021.

Lowest team innings score

India recorded an all-time low of 36 runs against Australia in Adelaide in December 2020. It is the fifth lowest in the world.

Highest run aggregate

Sachin Tendulkar's score of 15,921 runs from 1989 to 2013 in 200 Tests is a world record. This score, from 329 innings, amounts to an average of 53.78.

Most 1,000+ runs in a calendar year

Sachin Tendulkar has scored more than 1,000 runs in a calendar year on six occasions. He made 1,000 runs in 12 Tests in 1997; 1,088 runs in 10 Tests in 1999; 1,003 runs in 10 Tests in 2001; 1,392 runs in 16 Tests in 2002; 1,063 runs in 13 Tests in 2008; and 1,562 runs in 11 Tests in 2010.

WR Highest century partnerships

Rahul Dravid has been part of the most three-figure partnerships, on 88 occasions; 3 times for the first wicket, 34 times for the second, 26 times for the third, 8 times for the fourth, 12 times for the fifth, 3 times for the sixth and 2 times for the eighth wicket. He partnered with Sachin Tendulkar in 100-plus stands in a world record 20 times and with V.V.S. Laxman 12 times. Dravid's highest stand was with Virender Sehwag in a 410-run stand against Pakistan at Lahore in 2006. Dravid and Tendulkar have added 6,920 partnership runs, the most by any pair in history.

Rahul Dravid

Highest individual innings

Rohit Sharma scored 118 versus Sri Lanka in Indore, Madhya Pradesh, in 2017.

Best bowling figures on Test debut

Narendra Hirwani took 16 wickets for 136 runs against West Indies at Madras (now Chennai), Tamil Nadu, during 1987–88.

Best bowling in an innings

Anil Kumble took 10 wickets for 74 runs against Pakistan at Delhi in one innings during 1998–99. He became the second bowler after England's Jim Laker to do so, and is now joined by Ajaz Patel of New Zealand.

Best bowling in a match

Narendra Hirwani took 16 wickets for 136 runs versus West Indies at Madras (now Chennai), Tamil Nadu, during 1987–88.

Most catches in an innings

The world record of five catches is held by four individuals (along with eight foreign players): Yajurvindra Singh (versus England at Bengaluru, Karnataka, in 1977); Mohammad Azharuddin (versus Pakistan at Karachi, Pakistan, in 1989); K. Srikkanth (versus Australia at Perth, Australia, in 1992); and Ajinkya Rahane (versus Sri Lanka at Galle, Sri Lanka, in 2015).

Most career dismissals by a wicketkeeper

M.S. Dhoni has dismissed 294 batsmen (caught 256 and stumped 38) in 90 Tests.

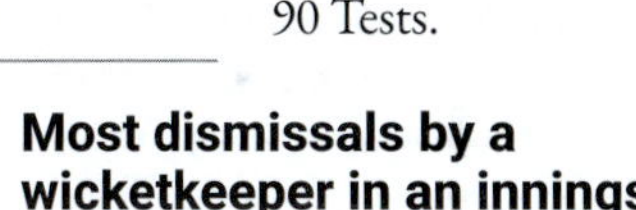

Most dismissals by a wicketkeeper in an innings

The record for dismissals is six, shared by four players: Syed Kirmani, who caught five and stumped one against New Zealand at Christchurch, New Zealand, in 1975–76; M.S. Dhoni, who caught six against New Zealand at Wellington, New Zealand, in 2008–09; Wriddhiman Saha, with five caught and one stumped against West Indies at North Sound, Antigua, in 2016; and Rishabh Pant, with six caught in Adelaide in December 2018 versus Australia.

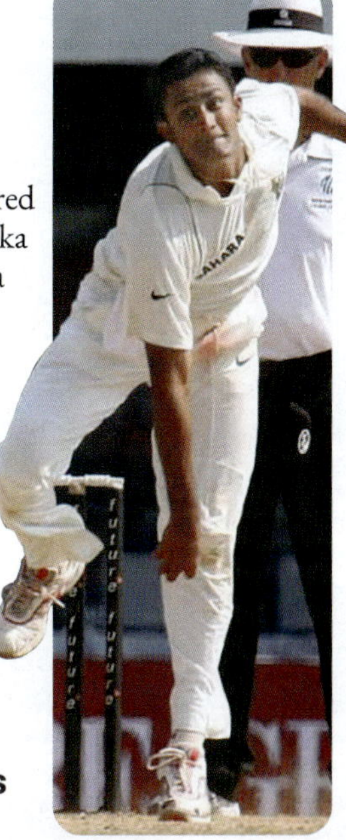
Anil Kumble

Dismissing all 11 batsmen in a match

S. Venkataraghavan dismissed all 11 batsmen in the Delhi Test against New Zealand

RUN MACHINE: VIRAT KOHLI

Fastest to 27,000 international runs

Virat Kohli became the quickest player to reach 27,000 runs in international cricket during the second Test against Bangladesh in Kanpur in September 2024. He achieved the milestone in 594 innings, surpassing Sachin Tendulkar's mark of 623 innings.

Most catches by an Indian fielder in ODIs

Virat Kohli (164) became India's most successful fielder in One-Day Internationals during the 2025 ICC Champions Trophy match against Pakistan in Dubai, surpassing Mohammad Azharuddin's tally of 156. Overall, Kohli now ranks third globally for most catches in ODIs, behind Mahela Jayawardene (218) and Ricky Ponting (160).

Virat Kohli Test Records

- Kohli scored 20 centuries as India's captain, most by an Indian and second overall.
- Kohli's seven double-hundreds are the most by Indian batter in Test. He also scored six of them as captain, the most overall.
- Kohli is the only batter in Tests to score over 1000 runs at an average of 75 or more in two successive calendar years.
- Highest rating points earned by an Indian in men's batting rankings: 937 in 2018
- Most wins as Test captain: 40

Virat Kohli Test statistics

Format	Span	Matches	Innings	Runs	High Score	Average	100s	50s	4s	6s
Test	2011–2025	123	210	9230	254*	46.9	30	31	1027	30

Virat Kohli statistics as Test captain

Matches	Won	Lost	Draw	Tied	W/L Ratio	Away Wins	Home Wins
68	40	17	11	0	2.352	16	24

As he retires from Tests, a look at his Test history...

Virat Kohli Test history

Former India captain Virat Kohli retired from Test cricket on 12 May 2025, bringing the curtain down on a remarkable 14-year journey in the longest format. Kohli played 123 Tests, scoring 9,230 runs with 30 centuries and 31 fifties.

As captain, Kohli created benchmarks never seen before in Indian cricket. He led India in 68 Tests, winning 40: the most by any Indian captain. His aggressive style and fitness standards transformed the team into consistent performers at home and abroad, including 16 overseas wins.

Kohli holds the record for most centuries by an Indian captain in Tests (20), and his seven double-hundreds are the most by an Indian batter. Six of those came as captain, a world record. Between 2016 and 2017, he became the only player in Test history to score over 1,000 runs in consecutive calendar years at an average of 75 or more.

In 2018, Kohli scaled another peak, registering 937 rating points in ICC Test batting rankings – the highest ever achieved by an Indian.

Kohli had earlier retired from T20 internationals in 2024 but will continue to represent India in ODIs, where he remains among the world's leading batters.

WR Most centuries

Virat Kohli has scored 51 centuries in 305 ODI matches.

in 1964–65. His final tally was 12 for 152. He became the second bowler after England's Jim Laker and one among only six bowlers in the world to do this.

Most dismissals by a wicketkeeper in a match

Rishabh Pant shares the world record with England's Jack Russell (versus South Africa, 1995) and South Africa's A.B. de Villiers (versus Pakistan, 2013), with 11 dismissals in Adelaide, versus Australia, in December 2018.

Shubman Gill

Most catches in a match

With eight catches in the match against Sri Lanka at Galle, Sri Lanka, in 2015 (three in the first innings and five in the second), Ajinkya Rahane holds the world record for most catches in a match.

Most dismissals by a wicketkeeper in a series

N.S. Tamhane holds the record with 19 dismissals in five Tests against Pakistan in the 1954–55 series.

Wicketkeeper with the fastest 100 dismissals

Rishabh Pant reached the milestone of 100 dismissals in only 26 matches, with 92 catches and 8 stumpings. He achieved it in the first Test against South Africa at SuperSport Park, Centurion, in December 2021.,

Highest score and fastest 100 on debut

Shikhar Dhawan scored 187 runs in 174 balls (33 fours, two sixes) in his Test debut against Australia at Mohali, Punjab, in 2013. Dhawan reached his 100 in just 85 balls – the fastest by a debutant (where full figures are available).

First Indian wicketkeeper-batter to score two centuries in a Test Match

Rishabh Pant became the first Indian and only the second wicketkeeper-batter overall to score two centuries in a single Test, achieving the feat against England at Headingley, Leeds, in June 2025. The 27-year-old batter also set a new mark for the highest match aggregate by an Indian wicketkeeper-batter, tallying 242 runs and surpassing Budhi Kunderan's 230 against England in Chennai in 1964.

Highest aggregate by an Indian captain in a Test Series

Shubman Gill amassed 754 runs in the 2025 home Test series against England, becoming the highest-scoring Indian captain in a single series. He surpassed Sunil Gavaskar's 732 runs against the West Indies in 1978.

Most Runs by an Indian batter in a Test Match

Shubman Gill scored an aggregate of 369 runs in the 2025 Test against England, setting the record for the highest match tally by an Indian batter during the second Test in Edgbaston on July 5. He went past Sunil Gavaskar's 344 runs against the West Indies in 1971. He also surpassed Virat Kohli's (293) record of most runs by an Indian captain in the same Test.

ONE-DAY INTERNATIONALS

Highest team total

The Indian men's cricket team scored 418 runs for 5 wickets in 50 overs against West Indies at Indore, Madhya Pradesh, on 9 December 2011.

First bowler to take more than three wickets on debut

Prasidh Krishna is the only bowler to take four wickets in an ODI debut. He finished 4/54 in his debut ODI on 23 March 2021, against England, at the Maharashtra Cricket Association Stadium in Pune.

First to score 100 centuries in international cricket

Sachin Tendulkar was the first to score 100 international centuries (51 Test and 49 ODI hundreds). He scored his 100th century at the fourth ODI of the Asia Cup versus Bangladesh on 16 March 2012.

Fastest 50 runs on debut

Krunal Pandya became the fastest-scoring debutant to post a half-century in an ODI match in just 26 balls, finishing at 58 not out in 31 balls on 23 March 2021 at the Maharashtra Cricket Association Stadium in Pune, Maharashtra, against England. He became the 15th Indian to score over 50 runs on an ODI debut.

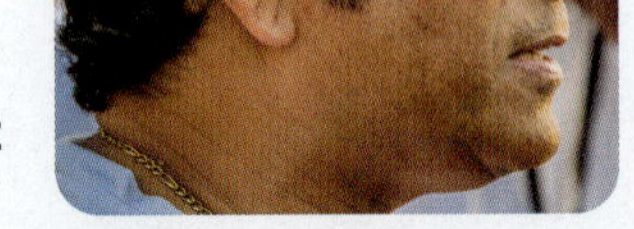

Sachin Tendulkar

Highest score on debut

K.L. Rahul scored an unbeaten 100 against Zimbabwe at Harare, Zimbabwe, on 11 June 2016 – the only Indian to make an ODI century on debut.

Lowest team total

India scored only 54 runs in 26.3 overs against Sri Lanka at Sharjah, UAE, on 29 October 2000.

Most ODI century partnerships

Sourav Ganguly and Sachin Tendulkar have 26 century-plus stands as a pair.

Most career wickets

Anil Kumble holds the record with 337 wickets.

Fastest to 200 ODI wickets

Mohammed Shami became the fastest Indian bowler to claim 200 wickets in One-Day Internationals, achieving the feat in his 103rd innings during the 2025 ICC Champions Trophy match against Bangladesh in Dubai.

Most total career runs

Sachin Tendulkar has made a total of 18,426 runs (including 49 centuries) in his ODI career spanning 463 matches.

Most runs in all World Cups

Sachin Tendulkar scored 2,278 runs in 45 World Cup matches from 1992 to 2011. He also holds the world record for the most centuries in World Cups, with six in 45 World Cup matches; this was equalled by Rohit Sharma in 17 matches.

Most career Man of the Match awards

Sachin Tendulkar has won 62 Man of the Match awards in his

career. He won the first Man of the Match award in the 1992 World Cup against Pakistan.

Most player of the series awards

In the India–England Test series during February–March 2021, R. Ashwin became the first Indian with more than 30 (he took 32) wickets and a century in a four-match Test series, and only the fifth player in the world to do so. He also became the first Indian to take 30 or more wickets in a Test series twice. Ashwin's nine Player of the Series awards in Test cricket are the most won by an Indian, just behind Sri Lankan player Muttiah Muralitharan (11) in this format.

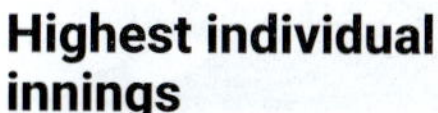

Highest individual innings

Rohit Sharma's 264 runs versus Sri Lanka on 13 November 2014 at Kolkata, West Bengal.

Rohit Sharma

Most sixes in an innings

Rohit Sharma's 16 sixes in his total of 209 runs against Australia in Bengaluru, Karnataka, on 2 November 2013. This record, at the world level, was broken by England's Eoin Morgan who hit 17 sixes against Afghanistan during the 2019 World Cup.

Best strike rate

Hardik Pandya has achieved a record strike rate of 115.59 across 66 matches.

Best bowling

Stuart Binny took 6 wickets for 4 runs against Bangladesh at Mirpur, Bangladesh, on 17 June 2014.

WR Winning four ODI Man of the Match awards in a row

Sourav Ganguly is the only player to have won four consecutive Man of the Match awards in ODIs, a record made against Pakistan at Toronto, Canada, in 1997.

WR Most centuries in a single World Cup

Rohit Sharma notched up five centuries in the 2019 World Cup, breaking Kumara Sangakkara's previous record.

First wins in the World Cup and ICC World Twenty20

India won its first World Cup under the captaincy of Kapil Dev in 1983 and its second World Cup under the leadership of M.S. Dhoni in 2011, thus becoming the third nation after West Indies and Australia to win the World Cup more than once. Dhoni also led India to its first ICC World Twenty20 win in its inaugural 2007 edition.

President Giani Zail Singh receiving the Indian cricket team after the World Cup victory

WR Most career catches

Rahul Dravid holds the record for most career catches, with 210 catches in 164 matches (including one catch for the ICC World XI): 47 versus Australia, 30 versus England, 26 versus West Indies, 21 versus South Africa, 21 versus Zimbabwe; 19 versus Pakistan; 17 versus New Zealand; 16 versus Sri Lanka; and 13 versus Bangladesh.

T20 INTERNATIONALS

Highest team total

The highest team total is 260 for 5, for India versus Sri Lanka in Indore, Madhya Pradesh, on 22 December 2017.

Lowest team total

India scored 74 runs in 17.3 overs against Australia at Melbourne on 1 February 2008.

Most career wickets

Bhuvneshwar Kumar has the most T20I career wickets with 90 in 86 matches.

Virat Kohli

Highest run chase

The Indian team made 211 runs for 4 wickets on 12 December 2009, chasing Sri Lanka's 206 runs for 7 wickets, at Mohali, Punjab.

Best bowling average (minimum 10 wickets)

L. Balaji's bowling average of 12.10 is the best on record for T20I matches.

Best individual bowling

Deepak Chahar took 6 wickets for 7 runs while playing against Bangladesh at Nagpur, Maharashtra, on 10 November 2019.

WR Most career dismissals as a wicketkeeper

M.S. Dhoni holds the record of most career dismissals, with 91 dismissals in 98 matches, including 57 caught and 34 stumped.

WR Best batting average (minimum 50 matches)

Virat Kohli has the best batting average of 52.73 in 115 matches.

Most runs in T20

Virat Kohli has 4,008 runs in 115 matches.

Fastest to 50

Yuvraj Singh's 50 runs in 12 balls against England in Durban, South Africa, on 19 September 2007, is the fastest half-century in T20Is.

Yuvraj Singh

CUE SPORTS

DOMESTIC

First National Championship – billiards

The first National Championship was held in 1931 in Calcutta (now Kolkata), West Bengal, with only eight entries. M.M. Beg won the title.

First National Championship – snooker

The first National Snooker Championship was held in 1939 in Calcutta (now Kolkata, West Bengal). P.K. Deb won the title.

First billiards and snooker hat-trick

Geet Sethi achieved a hat-trick of three consecutive National Championship titles in billiards and snooker from 1985 to 1987. He also won the national titles for both sports in 1988.

WR Highest break – snooker

Geet Sethi had the maximum possible break of 147 against Latif Nazarali at the 54th National Championship in Guntur, Andhra Pradesh, in 1988.

Most national titles – billiards and snooker

Pankaj Advani has won the national titles for both billiards and snooker a record 32 times.

President Giani Zail Singh presenting the World Billiards Championship Cup to Geet Sethi

INTERNATIONAL

First world snooker champion

Om B. Agarwal won the IBSF World Snooker Championship at Dublin, Ireland, in 1984.

WR First world champion on debut

Geet Sethi became world champion on debut when he beat legendary billiards player Bob Marshall, fifty years his senior, to win the 25th World Amateur Billiards Championship in 1985 in Delhi. He was also the first unseeded player to become world champion.

Pankaj Advani

First world billiards team title

India 'B' won a gold while India 'A' bagged a silver in the inaugural World Billiards Team Championship in Glasgow, Scotland, in August 2014. The winning team, with Pankaj Advani, Rupesh Shah, Devender Joshi and Ashok Shandilya, beat India 'A' 5–4.

First World Games snooker title

Aditya Mehta won the Quadrennial World Games snooker gold at Cali, Colombia, in July 2013.

First win at the World Ladies Billiards and Snooker Championship

Chitra Magimairaj and Varsha Sanjeev won the senior goldmedal and the U-21 gold medal respectively at the World Ladies Billiards and Snooker (WLBS) Championship in Leeds, UK, in April 2016.

First snooker team World Cup title

Pankaj Advani and Manan Chandra won the inaugural International Billiards and Snooker Federation (IBSF) Snooker Team World Cup in 2018 in Doha, Qatar.

First World Ladies Billiards and Snooker Association title

R. Umadevi won her maiden, and India's

first, World Ladies Billiards and Snooker Association title, beating the then world no. 13, Eva Palmius, 2–0 in the final at Cambridge, England, in April 2012.

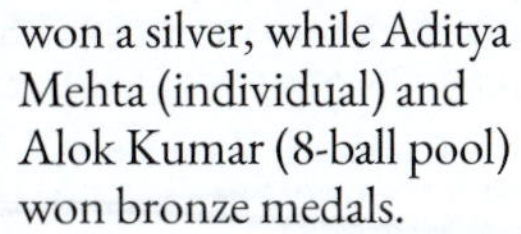

R. Umadevi

First Asian Games title
Billiards was introduced at the 1998 Bangkok Asian Games. India won two golds, a silver and a bronze. Ashok Shandilya won the gold, beating the world champion Geet Sethi 5–4. In the doubles, Ashok Shandilya and Geet Sethi won a gold, beating Devendra Joshi and Balachandra Bhaskar, who won the bronze.

First Asian snooker title
Yasin Merchant beat Udon Khaimuk of Thailand by eight frames in New Delhi on 15 July 1989 to win the Asian Confederation of Billiard Sports (ACBS) Championship.

Most billiards gold medals in the Asian Games
Pankaj Advani won two gold medals in the 2006 Doha Asian Games and in the 2010 Asian Games at Guangzhou, China.

Most world titles – billiards and snooker
Pankaj Advani has the world champion titles for both billiards as well as snooker a record 24 times. Pankaj Advani claimed at least one International Billiard and Snooker Federation world title every calendar year.

Best performance in the Asian Games – snooker
At the 2010 Asian Games held in Guangzhou, China, the Indian team won a silver, while Aditya Mehta (individual) and Alok Kumar (8-ball pool) won bronze medals.

WR Highest break in the World Billiards Championship
Geet Sethi had a break of 1,276 over two sessions in 80 mins against Bob Close of England in the quarter-final of the World Professional Championship in Mumbai, Maharashtra, on 1 October 1992.

Best performance at the Asian Billiards Sports Championship
India won a gold, a silver and three bronze medals in the inaugural Asian Billiards Sports Championship at Al Fujairah, UAE, held from 24 September to 2 October 2016.

WR Highest break under three-pot rule – billiards
Michael Ferreira scored 630 against S.B. Agrawal at the World Championship in Delhi in 1981, a world record for the highest break under the three-pot rule.

Most billiards grand doubles
Pankaj Advani has won four world doubles in billiards (time and points format) in 2005, 2008, 2014 and 2018.

World 6-red title
Laxman Rawat won the 6-red title versus Muhammad Asif of Pakistan in Mandalay, Myanmar, on 20 September 2019.

Most competitive 147 breaks in snooker
Aditya Mehta became the first Indian to make 147 maximum breaks in 2014 at the Paul Hunter Classic snooker tournament.

Aditya Mehta

Most Asian titles
Pankaj Advani – 24-time snooker and billiards world champion – retained the Asian snooker title by defeating former champion Amir Sarkhosh of Iran. Advani had won the title in 2019 before the 2020 edition got scrapped due to COVID-19. Advani's tally of Asian titles across both snooker and billiards stand at 13, including two Asian Games gold medals in 2006 and 2010.

Youngest world champion – snooker
Pankaj Advani was 18 years old when he won the amateur World Snooker Championship title in October 2003.

Youngest to win the World Professional title
Pankaj Advani was 24 years old when he won the World Professional Billiards title at the Northern Snooker Centre, Leeds, England, on 6 September 2009. He outclassed 41-year-old Mike Russell, who has won the World Professional Billiards title a record nine times.

Two titles in 6-red snooker
Pankaj Advani was the world's first player to hold both world and continental titles in 6 red snooker at the same time. He is also the only player to win world titles in both 15-red and 6-red snooker.

Oldest woman champion – billiards
Kamala Devi Chandrababu from Tamil Nadu beat Judy Walia from Karnataka 109–63, 65–112, 53–76, 98–72, 95–74 in the 1995 National Championship at Bangalore (now Bengaluru), Karnataka. At 63 years, it was her fourth championship and the second national title after 1991.

FOOTBALL

GENERAL

Oldest football tournament
The Durand Football Tournament is the third oldest tournament in the world and the oldest in Asia and India. Started by British diplomat and civil servant Sir Henry Mortimer Durand in 1888 for the British troops in India, it was held in Simla (now Shimla, Himachal Pradesh). In 1940, the tournament was moved to New Delhi. The latest edition, the 131st in the history of the tournament, was

held from 16 August to 18 September 2022, with Bengaluru FC winning the tournament.

First Indian team to win the Durand Cup

Mohammedan Sporting won the Durand Cup in 1940 when it was first moved to Delhi and the final played at Irwin Amphitheatre (now Dhyan Chand National Stadium). Mohammedan Sporting beat Royal Warwickshire Regiment 2–1 in the final.

Most wins at the Durand Cup

Mohun Bagan has won the Durand Cup 16 times and finished runner-up 11 times. East Bengal has won 16 times and been runner-up 10 times.

Most clean sheets

The men's national team created a new record of eight consecutive clean sheets between 22 March 2023 and to 24 June 2023. It surpassed the previous record of six clean sheets kept during 1952-53.

Most individual goals at the Durand Cup

Mohammed Habib scored 12 goals for East Bengal in seven matches (both the semi-finals and the final were replayed) in the 1972 Durand tournament.

First football academy

The Tata Football Academy (TFA) was started at Jamshedpur, Jharkhand, in 1986 with Mohammed Habib and Ranjan Chowdhury as coaches, and Subimal 'Chuni' Goswami as technical director. It has produced over 100 junior and senior international players for India. It was followed by the Williamson Magor Football Academy in Assam and the Chandigarh Football Academy that started in the 1990s.

First Indian to be national coach of a foreign country

Syed Nayeemuddin was appointed national coach of Bangladesh in July 2007. He was also the first Indian to coach a club side abroad – the Brothers Union of Bangladesh in 2004. In India, he won 33 trophies with Mohammedan Sporting, East Bengal and Mohun Bagan. As national coach, he led India to victory in the 1987 South Asian Federation (SAF) Games in Calcutta (now Kolkata), West Bengal, the 1997 Kathmandu South Asian Football Federation (SAFF) Championship in Nepal and the 2005 Karachi SAFF Championship in Pakistan.

Syed Nayeemuddin

First Olympic referee

Komaleeswaran Sankar became an Olympic referee when he was selected for the football tournament of the 2000 Sydney Olympics, one among the four matchw officials chosen from Asia. Sankar, who became a referee in 1988 and a national referee in 1994, retired in 2007 at the age of forty-five, as mandated by FIFA rules.

First World Cup referee

Komaleeswaran Sankar was the first World Cup referee from India when he was chosen to officiate at the 2002 World Cup in South Korea and Japan. His first match was a Group G league match between Mexico and Croatia on 3 June 2002. He officiated in three matches.

First international tournament win by a club

- Mohammedan Sporting won the Aga Khan Gold Cup in Dhaka (then Pakistan, now Bangladesh) on 11 October 1960, defeating Makassar XI, Indonesia 4-1 in the final.
- East Bengal, coached by Subhas Bhowmick, won the LG ASEAN Club Cup Championship on 26 July 2003 in Jakarta, Indonesia, beating BEC Tero Sasana of Thailand in the final 3–1.

First Indian club to enter the Asian Football Confederation Cup final

- Bengaluru FC was the first Indian club to enter the final of Asia's prestigious club competition, the Asian Football Confederation (AFC) Cup, in October 2016. They lost the final match against Iraq Air Force 0–1 in Doha, Qatar, on 5 November 2016.
- Dempo SC (Goa) was the first club to enter the semi-finals of the Cup in September 2008.

Bhaichung Bhutia

First hat-trick in Mohun Bagan versus East Bengal match

On 13 July 1997, Bhaichung Bhutia scored a hat-trick for East Bengal versus Mohun Bagan in the KBL Federation Cup semi-final, in which East Bengal won 4-1.

First professional coach

Amal Dutta, India's first professional coach, started his career in 1963, coaching East Bengal. He also coached the other two big Kolkata clubs: Mohun Bagan and Mohammedan Sporting (Dhaka).

First foreign coach

English professional footballer Harry Wright was appointed coach of the Indian football team in 1963. He held the position till 1964, leading India to one of its best performances – a runner-up position at the 1964 Asian Football Confederation (AFC) Cup.

S.A. Rahim

Most appearances as coach in the Olympics

Syed Abdul Rahim (1909–63) from Hyderabad (then in Andhra Pradesh) was the coach of the Indian football team in three consecutive Olympic Games in 1952 (Helsinki), 1956 (Melbourne) and 1960 (Rome).

First Indian club to win a major trophy

The first win in a major domestic tournament was by Mohun Bagan of Calcutta (now Kolkata, West Bengal), who beat East Yorkshire Regiment of Ghaziabad 2–1 in the Indian Football Association (IFA) Shield tournament final at the Calcutta Football Club Ground on 29 July 1911.

First in English professional club

- Mohammed Salim from Calcutta (now Kolkata, West Bengal) was the first from the Indian subcontinent to play for a European club, Celtic FC, in 1936.

- Bhaichung Bhutia was the first Indian footballer to join an English club when he signed a contract to represent second division outfit, Bury FC, from 1999 to 2002.
- Aditi Chauhan was the first Indian woman to play in the English league football on 16 August 2015, as a goalkeeper for West Ham United. She attended Loughborough University, completing an MSc in sports management and represented their football team from 2014 15. Chauhan joined Gokulam Kerala FC for the 2019–20 Indian women's league.

First hat-trick in Indian football

Norman Pritchard scored a hat-trick for St Xavier's College, Calcutta (now Kolkata), West Bengal, against Sovabazar Club in the 1889 Trades Cup.

First woman player to sign a contract with a foreign club

Ngangom Bala Devi made history when she signed a contract with Scottish Giant Rangers FC, a professional football club in Glasgow, UK. She donned a no. 10 jersey for the club and created yet another record on 6 December 2020 when she scored the final goal against Motherwell Women in the Scottish Women's Premier League, becoming the first Indian woman to score in a professional European Club.

Most matches officiated

S.S. Hakim officiated in 33 international matches and was a referee in the final of every major domestic tournament including three Nehru Cups. He represented India in the 1960 Rome Olympics and was the team's assistant coach for the 1982 Delhi Asiad. He is the only individual to have played football, coached the national team and functioned as an international referee.

Most successful coach at the Asian Games

- S.A. Rahim led as coach on five successful occasions – twice at the Asian Games (1951 and 1962), and thrice at the Quadrangular Tournament (1953, 1954 and 1955).
- The foreign coach with the best record is Bob Houghton of the UK with three trophies: the Nehru Cup (2007 and 2009) and the AFC Challenge Cup in 2008.

Most appearances as coach in the Nehru Cup

Syed Nayeemuddin coached the Indian team in the Nehru Cup on four occasions – in 1987 at Kozhikode, Kerala; in 1988 at Siliguri, West Bengal; in 1989 at Margao, Goa; and in 1997 at Kochi, Kerala.

Most successful Indian coaches in domestic tournaments

P.K. Banerjee led domestic teams to 53 trophies, Amal Dutta to 35 and Syed Nayeemuddin to 33 of them.

Most individual goals in an international club match

Bhaichung Bhutia scored six goals, a double hat-trick, for East Bengal against Army FC of the Philippines in the LG ASEAN Cup in Jakarta, Indonesia, on 16 July 2003.

Inder Singh

Longest sequence of wins

Mohun Bagan won 42 consecutive matches in the 1994 season till they lost to Dempo SC (Goa) in the Scissors Cup final in November 1994.

Only Indian coach to gain success with a foreign club

In his eight-year stint in Bangladesh, Syed Nayeemuddin helped his club, Brothers Union of Bangladesh, win three trophies.

Best record against foreign clubs

East Bengal has the best record against foreign clubs: played 239 matches (both exhibition and tournaments), won 97, drawn 40 and lost 102. They scored 343 goals and conceded 348.

Fastest goal

Midfielder Dipankar Roy scored a goal in 9.33 seconds after kick-off for Bengal versus Karnataka in the 2000 Santosh Trophy held in Thrissur, Kerala.

SANTOSH TROPHY RECORDS

Most wins in Santosh Trophy

The National inter-state championships for the Santosh Trophy started in 1941. The football trophy was instituted in the name of maharaja of Santosh, the former president of IFA, the parent body of Bengal football. Bengal won the title 32 times and finished runners-up on 14 occasions. Punjab has won eight times, Kerala seven times, Services six times and Goa five times. Bengal hold the record of winning the trophy six times in a row from 1993-98 and five times in a row from 1975 to 1979.

Most individual goals in the final match

Playing for Bengal, Mohammed Habib scored five goals in the 6-1 win over Services in Nowgong in 1969.

Most individual goals in a single edition

Playing for Punjab, Inder Singh scored 23 goals in the 1974 edition in Jalandhar.

Biggest margin of victory

Bengal beat Tripura 18-0 in Jalandhar in 1974; Punjab beat Gujarat 17-0 in Jalandhar in 1974; Kerala beat Andaman and Nicobar Islands 17-0 in Siliguri in 2014.

All-time top scorers

Inder Singh (Punjab) has 45 goals. Mohmmed Habib and Shyam Thapa (both Bengal) have 34 and 31 goals to their credit.

Success for different teams

Peter Thangaraj won the Santosh Trophy for three different teams – Services (1960), Bengal (1962) and Railways (1966).

INDIAN SUPER LEAGUE (ISL)

Maximum titles

ATK (now ATK Mohun Bagan) has won three titles in 2014, 2016 and 2019-20 season.

Biggest margin of victory

FC Goa defeated Mumbai City FC 7-0 in Margao, Goa, in 2015.

Most individual goals by an Indian footballer

- Sunil Chhetri has played in all editions of the Indian Super League since 2014, scoring 51 goals. He played for Mumbai

City FC and Bengaluru FC.

• Jeje Lalpekhlua, while playing for Chennaiyin FC and SC East Bengal, has 24 goals.

Most goals scored in a match

A total of 11 goals were scored when Odisha FC defeated SC East Bengal 6-5 in the 2020-21 season.

Most goals scored by a team

FC Goa has scored 267 goals, followed by Chennaiyin FC's 199 goals.

Most individual goals by a foreign footballer

Punjab's Nigerian footballer Bartholomew Ogbeche has played four seasons in ISL for NorthEast United, Kerala Blasters, Mumbai City FC and Hyderabad FC, scoring a total of 53 goals. FC Goa's former Spanish striker Ferran Corominas has record 48 goals to his credit for one club.

Left: Bartholomew Ogbeche; *Right*: Ferran Corominas

DOMESTIC EVENTS

First to win three National Football League titles

Mohun Bagan has won three National Football League (NFL) titles: in 1997–98, 1999– 2000 and 2001–02. East Bengal emulated this when they won their third NFL crown in 2003–04. Their earlier wins were in 2000–01 and 2002–03.

Most individual goals in a match in NFL

• Bhaichung Bhutia scored the most goals in an NFL match when he scored five goals playing for JCT against Mahindra in the first NFL in 1997. JCT won the match 6–1.

• In the fourth NFL, Francis Silveira of Churchill Brothers scored four goals in a match against Dempo SC (Goa) for a 5–0 win.

Most goals by a club in the NFL/ Indian League (I-League)

East Bengal has scored 690 goals in 460 matches. Other teams to score are Churchill Brothers with 664 goals in 406 matches and Mohun Bagan with 619 goals in 446 matches.

Most individual goals in a match in the I-League

The most goals by a player in an I-League match are seven by Ranti Martins for Dempo SC (Goa) in their 14–0 win versus Air India in Margao, Goa, on 30 May 2011.

Most individual hat-tricks in the NFL and I-League

Nigerian striker Odafa Onyeka Okolie has scored 14 hat-tricks: nine for Churchill Brothers; four for Mohun Bagan; and one for Sporting Clube de Goa.

Best performance in Olympics

India is the first Asian country to reach the semi-finals of the Olympics. In 1956, in the Melbourne Olympics, captained by Samar Banerjee, India reached the semi-finals and finished fourth.

First International match

With seven barefoot players, India entered the 1948 Olympics under captain Talimeren Ao from Bengal but lost to France 1–2. Sarangapani Raman scored the lone goal. Since then, India has played eight matches in four Olympic Games – 1948, 1952, 1956 and 1960 – won one, drawn one, lost six; scored 10 and conceded 27 goals. After 1960, India has been eliminated in the pre-Olympic stage.

Subimal 'Chuni' Goswami

Biggest margin of victory at the Asian Games

India beat Hong Kong 5–2 at the 1958 Asiad in Tokyo, Japan, in its biggest margin of victory at the Asian Games. Mohammad Rahmatullah scored two goals while Subimal 'Chuni' Goswami, D. Damodaran and T. Balaram scored a goal each. India scored three goals in extra time, the first time India played extra time in an international match.

Only win in Olympics

On 1 December 1956, India beat hosts Australia 4-2 to register their only win in Olympics.

Best performance at the Olympics

India became the first Asian nation to reach the semi finals of an Olympic football event, beating Australia 4-2 at the 1956 Melbourne Games. India took the lead against Yugoslavia but lost 1-4. In the play-off for the bronze, India lost 0 3 to Bulgaria, ending at fourth position. Samar 'Badru' Banerjee was India's captain and S.A. Rahim was the coach.

Biggest margin of victory

In the 1963 pre-Olympics, India won 7–0 against Ceylon (now Sri Lanka) at Bangalore (now Bengaluru), Karnataka, and later 7–0 against Bangladesh in the Aga Khan Tournament at Dhaka, Bangladesh, in 1977.

Biggest defeat at the Asian Games

India lost 1–7 to China in 1974 at Tehran in Iran. Magan Singh scored the lone goal.

Worst defeats

In international tournaments, India's worst defeats have been 1-10 to Yugoslavia at the 1952 Helsinki Olympics and 1–9 to Burma (now Myanmar) in the 1971 Merdeka Tournament in Kuala Lumpur, Malaysia.

India's longest unbeaten run in a year

In 2017, India remained unbeaten in

nine matches, three away games and six at home:

- 1–0 versus Myanmar; 1–0 versus the Kyrgyz Republic; 2–0 versus Macau; 4–1 versus Macau; and 2–2 versus Myanmar (all Asian Cup qualifiers).
- 3–2 versus Cambodia; 2-0 versus Nepal; 2-1 versus Mauritius; and 1-1 versus St Kitts and Nevis (all friendly matches).

Most successful team in Intercontinental Cup (AIFF)

India became the most successful team in the AIFF's Intercontinental Cup with their second title. India defeated Lebanon 2-0 in the final of the 2023's edition in Bhubaneswar. North Korea is the only other winner as the competition has been played thrice since 2018.

INDIVIDUAL RECORDS

Maximum caps earned (top five)

Sunil Chhetri (131 matches), Bhaichung Bhutia (107), I.M. Vijayan (88), Shabbir Ali (81), and Mahesh Gawli (79) have played the maximum number of matches for India.

Maximum goals scored (top five)

Sunil Chhetri (92), Bhaichung Bhutia (42), I.M. Vijayan (39), Shabbir Ali (30), and P.K. Banerjee (26) have scored the maximum goals for India.

Most goals in the Asian Games

P.K. Banerjee scored the highest number of individual goals for India in the Asian Games, He scored six goals – one in 1958, four in 1962 and one in 1966.

P.K. Banerjee

Fastest international goal

I.M. Vijayan scored against Bhutan within 12 seconds after kick off in a Group A league match played on 28 September 1999 at the SAF Games at Kathmandu, Nepal.

Hat-trick in Olympics

Neville D'Souza is the only Indian to score a hat-trick in Olympics. He scored three goals in India's 4-2 win over Australia on 1 December 1956.

Hat-trick on debut

K. Appalaraju scored a hat-trick in his first international appearance against Ceylon (now Sri Lanka) on 22 December 1963 in the pre-Olympics.

Most hat-tricks

Sunil Chhetri is the only Indian to score three hattricks in international matches. Chhetri's three hat-tricks came against Tajikistan (13 August 2008, AFC Challenge Cup, New Delhi), against Vietnam (10 October 2010, Friendly, Pune), and against Chinese Taipei (1 June 2018) in the Hero International Cup, Mumbai.

Jyoti Randhawa

Most successful captain

Bhaichung Bhutia has five tournament wins to his credit as captain: the LG Cup in Vietnam (2002), the SAFF Cup in Karachi, Pakistan (2005), the Nehru Cup in Delhi (2007 and 2009), and the AFC Challenge Cup in Hyderabad and Delhi in 2008. He is also the second highest international scorer, with 42 goals in 107 matches.

Youngest match winner at the Nehru Cup

Bhaichung Bhutia was 19 years old when he scored a goal to beat Uzbekistan 1-0 in 1995 at Calcutta (now Kolkata), West Bengal.

GOLF

GENERAL

Most prize money for an individual event

Golf offers the most prize money in any individual event on the domestic circuit. The prize fund offered in 2024 was Rs. 33 crore spread over 21 tournaments.

Most Indian tournaments on the Asian Tour

In 2002, for the first time, three tournaments – the Royal Challenge Indian Open, the Hero Honda Masters and the Honda-SIEL tournament figured on the Asian Professional Golf Association Tour.

Indian Open record

Jyoti Randhawa won the Indian Open in October 2007 at the Delhi Golf Club course for the third time and equalled the record of Australia's Peter Thomson.

Indians topping the Asian Tour Order of Merit

Jeev Milkha Singh won the Asian Tour Order of Merit in 2006 and 2008. Jyoti Randhawa (2002), Arjun Atwal (2003), Anirban Lahiri (2015) and Shubhankar Sharma (2018) are the other Indians to top the Order of Merit.

Oldest to get hole-in-one

Lt Gen Ajit Singh at the grand old age of 90 achieved his first hole-in-one on 18 October 2005 at the Delhi Golf Club on the 9th hole (par 3; 160 yards).

'Rookie' on a rampage

The Rookie Golfer of the Year award was introduced in 1997–98 on the domestic tour. To date, S. Chikkarangappa remains the most successful 'rookie' on the Tour. He won ₹32,65,313 and finished second to Rashid Khan on the 2013 Order of Merit.

S. Chikkarangappa

Longest hole-in-one
Amit Luthra scored a hole-in-one at the second hole of Delhi Golf Club (par 4 at 258 yards) using a 5-iron on 16 March 1998.

Oldest club
The Royal Kolkata Golf Club founded in 1829 is the oldest club outside Britain. The Kolkata Ladies Golf Club was established in 1891.

Highest golf course
The Yak Golf Club is located at an altitude of 13,025 ft at Kupup, Sikkim.

Series of records – disabled golfer – Ranveer Singh Saini
- Ranveer Singh Saini from Gurugram, Haryana, won three medals in golf, two gold (2015 and 2023) and one silver (in 2019), at the Special Olympics World Summer Games.
- He is the first to win the Macau Golf Masters seven times in 2013, 2014, 2015, 2017, 2019, 2024, and 2025.
- He is also the first autistic golfer to be awarded with 'Shreshth Divyangjan Award' by the president of India Droupadi Murmu on 3 December 2024 at Vigyan Bhavan, New Delhi.

Ranveer Singh Saini

FIRST

First international recognition
India was invited to the 1969 World Cup qualifying event at Singapore. Ruda Valji and Shadi Lal represented India.

First Olympians
Anirban Lahiri, S.S.P. Chawrasia, and Aditi Ashok represented the country in the 2016 Rio Olympics in Brazil.

First to win all three National titles
Arjuna Award–winner Amit Luthra is the first Indian to have won all three National titles: the Junior National (1979), men's National (1993, 1994) and Senior Nationals (2015, 2016).

First victory in Nomura Cup
India's first major victory in an international team event came in the 1973 Nomura Cup at Jakarta where the squad of Raj Kumar Pitamber, P.G. Sethi, Vikramjit Singh and Lakshman Singh was crowned Asia-Pacific Golf champions.

First sweep of gold medals in the Asian Games
Golf was introduced in the Asian Games in 1982. Besides the team gold, India won the individual gold and silver medals through champion Lakshman Singh and runnerup Rajiv Mohta. Two other members of the gold-winning team were Amit Luthra and Rishi Narain.

First to gain qualification for the PGA Tour
Arjun Atwal became the first Indian to gain qualification for the full US Tour after making it through the Q-school for the year 2004.

First to qualify for the British Open
Gaurav Ghei was the first Indian to qualify for the premier event in 1997.

First to play in the US Open
Jeev Milkha Singh was the first to play the US Open in 2002.

Jeev Milkha Singh

First to play the Masters at Augusta
Jeev Milkha Singh was the first to play the Masters at Augusta in 2007.

Arjun Atwal

First to gain a full 'card' on PGA Tour
Arjun Atwal became the first Indian to gain a full card (exemption from playing qualifying rounds) after his stupendous showing in the 2005 season.

First to play the PGA Championship
Arjun Atwal was the first to play the PGA Championship in 2005.

First European–Asian Tour win
Arjun Atwal is the first Asian to win two co-sanctioned titles on the Tour. He won the Caltex Singapore Open in February 2002 and the Carlsberg Malaysian Open in February 2003. Both these events enjoy joint sanction of the European and Asian PGA Tours.

First participation in World Cup
Arjun Atwal and Jyoti Randhawa formed the first Indian team to take part in the World Cup in 2005.

First to play in three WGC events in a year
Jyoti Randhawa became the first Indian to play in three events in the World Golf Championship (WGC) series in 2005.

First to play in a Major
Jeev Milkha Singh became the first Indian to qualify for a Major when he made it to the 2002 US Open in July.

First to qualify for European PGA Tour
Jeev Milkha Singh was the first to qualify for the European Tour for the 1998 season.

First to make the 'cut' in a Major
Jeev Milkha Singh became the first

Indian to make the 'cut' of a Major championship playing all four rounds of the 2002 US Open.

First to win on the Japanese PGA Tour
Jyoti Randhawa won the Suntory Open in 2003.

First win on PGA Tour
Arjun Atwal won the 2010 Wyndham Championship.

First win on the European Tour
Arjun Atwal won the 2002 Singapore Masters.

First win on the European Tour in Europe
Jeev Milkha Singh won the Volvo Masters in Spain in October 2006.

First team to qualify for World championship
The Indian team of Gaurav Ghei and Digvijay Singh qualified for the 2003 World Golf Championship held at Kiawah Island, USA, after finishing joint-second in the Nations Cup.

First to win the Ladies Indian Open
Aditi Ashok became the first to win the Ladies Indian Open in November 2016.

First to secure her card (playing rights) winner on the Ladies European Tour
By winning the Lalla Aicha Tour School, Aditi Ashok secured the Ladies European Tour card for 2016 season. She also became the youngest to win the title.

First woman to qualify for the Olympic Games
Aditi Ashok is the first woman to qualify in golf for the Olympic Games in Rio in 2016. She attained her best finish – fourth – in the 2020 Tokyo Olympics.

First to win LET title outside India
Aditi Ashok won the 2016 Qatar Ladies Open.

First to represent the country in four multi-discipline Games
Aditi Ashok has participated in the 2013 Asian Youth Games, the 2014 Youth Olympic Games, the 2014 Asian Games, and the 2016 and 2020 Olympic Games.

Aditi Ashok

First to win on the Ladies European Tour (LET)
Aditi Ashok is the first to win a title on the Ladies European Tour by claiming the 2016 Ladies Indian Open.

First to qualify for the Ladies PGA Tour
Aditi Ashok gained the playing rights for the 2017 LPGA Tour via the LPGA Final Qualifying School.

First Olympiad golden sweep
India became only the third nation – after Russia and China – to make a sweep of team titles in the 2024 edition Budapest, Hungary.

Seeded two, India won the Open title with a stupendous tally of 21 match points (out of a maximum of 22) in the 11-round competition for its maiden gold in the games' most prestigious team championship, involving 197 nations/federations. The team members were D. Gukesh, R. Praggnanandhaa, Arjun Erigaisi, Vidit Gujrathi and P. Harikrishna. Coach: N. Srinath.

Top seeded Indian women scored 19 points to justify its ranking in a field of 183 nations/federations. The team comprised D. Harika, R. Vaishali, Divya Deshmukh, Vantika Agrawal and Tania Sachdev. Coach: Abhjiit Kunte.

MOSTS

Highest prize money (women)
Aditi Ashok collected US $60,000 in becoming the first to win the Ladies Indian Open title in November 2016.

Tournament with highest prize money
The ₹1.50 crore McLeod Russel Tour Championship in 2014 became the first domestic tournament to offer such high prize money in any individual domestic sport.

Most prize money earned in a season
Veer Ahlawat earned Rs. 1.56 crore in the 2024 season and topped the Order of Merit.

Highest prize money earner in a domestic season
Rashid Khan won two events from 14 tournament appearances in the 2019 season and collected ₹66,27,650 as prize money.

Rashid Khan

Most prize money from a single season of Professional Golf Tour of India (PGTI)
Om Prakash Chouhan earned ₹1,18,26,059 from the domestic PGTI Tour in 2023. He also became the first and the only player to earn over a crore of rupees in a season.

Most birdies
Jyoti Randhawa broke the course record at Shanghai with a seven-under par 65 that included eight birdies at the Volvo China Open Golf tournament in 2000. He finished in a tied fourth place.

Most international titles
Jeev Milkha Singh has won 14 tour titles spread over three tours – four on the European Tour, six on the Asian Tour and four on the Japanese Tour.

Most titles on the Asian Tour
Jyoti Randhawa has won eight titles: the 1998 Hero Honda Masters, the 1999 Hero Honda Masters, the 2000 Indian Open, the 2000 Singapore Open, the 2004 Volvo Masters of Asia, the 2006 Indian Open, the 2007 Indian Open and the 2009 Thailand Open.

Most titles in an Indian Tour season
Mukesh Kumar won six titles during the 2004-05 season.

Most career prize money from the domestic Professional Golf Tour of India (PGTI)
Shamim Khan has earned ₹4,38,03,143 from 265 tournament appearances.

Five titles in a season twice on the Indian Tour
Ashok Kumar won five titles in 2004 and repeated the feat in 2007.

Most appearances for India
Gangesh Khaitan holds the distinction of representing India for 54 years – from 1970 to 2024 – across age-groups. He first represented India as the National junior champion in 1970 and continues to be active on the Seniors Tour. He last captained India in the 2024 APGC Senior Golf championship in Vietnam.

Most individual gold medallists in a single edition of Olympiad
Five Indians won gold medals for their individual performance in Budapest, 2024. .D. Gukesh (Open, Board 1), Arjun Erigaisi (Board 3), Divya Deshmukh (Women, Board 3) and Vantika Agrawal (Women, Board 4) played stellar roles in India's historic twin-triumphs.

BEST

Best finish in a Major
Anirban Lahiri finished tied-fifth in the 2016 PGA Championship.

Anirban Lahiri

Best finish in the European Tour Order of Merit
Jeev Milkha Singh finished 12th on the 2008 European Tour Order of Merit.

Best Indian performance on the PGA Tour
In the 2022 season, Anirban Lahiri has already earned $3,084,598 – the highest by an Indian on the PGA Tour – from 24 events. His best came in the Players Championship where he finished runner-up, earning a $2.18 million pay cheque.

Best world ranking
Jeev Milkha Singh was placed 28th in the World ranking list in 2009.

Best finish on the LET Order of Merit
Aditi Ashok finished second on the 2016 LET Order of Merit and also won the 'Rookie of the Year' award.

Kapil Dev

Best performance based on prize money received
Arjun Atwal became the first Indian to win a title on the PGA Tour by claiming the honours in the Wyndham Championship in August 2010. The first qualifier to win the title in 24 years on the PGA Tour, Atwal collected $918,000 – the highest ever by an Indian golfer.

LOWEST

Lowest winning score on the European Tour
Arjun Atwal's scored title-winning 24-under 260 in the Carlsberg Malaysian Open in February 2003.

S.S.P. Chawrasia

Least putts on the European Tour
Jeev Milkha Singh needed just 94 putts for four rounds of the 2001 Desert Classic. Jeev fell one short of the world record of 93, which stands in the name of Kenny Knox from the USA since 1990.

Lowest winning score on the Asian Tour
Jeev Milkha Singh scored 26 under par in the Philip Morris Championship in Seoul, when he won the four-round tournament on the Asian Tour. This is the lowest score by an Indian in winning an international title.

Lowest winning score on the Indian Tour
Mukesh Kumar fired 30-under 250 to win the DDA Open tournament at the Qutub Golf Course in New Delhi in April 2005.

Lowest round on the Indian Tour
Mukesh Kumar carded 11- under 59 in the third round of the DDA Open tournament at the Qutub Golf Course, New Delhi, in April 2005.

ONLY

Only team title in the USA
Former Test cricketer Kapil Dev led India to the TAG Heuer Invitational Golf title in Boston in Sept 2004. The team comprising Kapil Dev, Rakesh Rao, Nikhil Dewan and Rohit Duggal shot seven 65-under to win ahead of China, Indonesia, South Africa and two teams from North America, among others.

Only Indian to win four European Tour events in India
S.S.P. Chawrasia's all four European Tour titles have come in India: the 2008 Emaar MGF Indian Masters, New Delhi, the 2011 Avantha Masters, Gurugram, the 2016 Indian Open, New Delhi and the 2017 Indian Open, Gurugram.

Only Indian to win four titles on Japanese Tour
Jeev Milkha Singh has won four titles on the Japanese Tour: the 2006 Casio World Open, the 2006 Golf Nippon Series JT Cup, the 2008 Nagashima Shigeo Invitational Sega Sammy Cup and the 2008 Golf Nippon Series JT Cup.

Only Indian to win two European Tour titles in a year
Anirban Lahiri won the Malaysian Open and the Indian Open – both co-

sanctioned events on the European Tour – in 2015.

Quickest to win two European Tour titles

Shubhankar Sharma won two European Tour titles in the space of 55 days. He won the Joburg Open in December 2017 and Maybank Championship in February 2018.

YOUNGEST

Youngest hole-in-one

Viraat Badhwar (b August 28, 1995) was all of 6 years 11 months and 19 days when he scored a hole-in-one at the sixth hole (par 3 at 155 yards) using a 3 wood at the Peacock Course, Delhi Golf Club on 17 August 2002.

Youngest to win two back-to-back international titles

Shubham Juglan won the IMG Academy golf championship in San Deigo and the International Golf Academy titles in Vegas – both for children aged 9–10 – in successive weeks in 2015.

Youngest to win European Tour title

Shubhankar Sharma, at 21 year and four months, won the Joburg Open to become the youngest Indian winner on the European Tour.

Shubhankar Sharma

Youngest to win Asian Tour Order of Merit

Shubhankar Sharma became the youngest to win the Asian Tour Order of Merit in December 2018.

Youngest winner on the domestic PGTI Tour

Playing only his second pro event, amateur Karandeep Kochar became the youngest winner on the PGTI Tour by beating the field in the 2016 Players Championship in Kolkata. Kochar, at 17 years and five months, broke Shubhankar Sharma's record of 17 years and eight months set in 2014.

GYMNASTICS

DOMESTIC

First National Rhythmic Gymnastics event – women

The first National Rhythmic Gymnastics Championships held in 1989 at Kottayam, Kerala, had an event for women, where Neelamjit Kaur won the rhythmic gymnastics title. She won it again in 1990 at Udaipur, Rajasthan, and in 1991 at Delhi.

Most individual titles in the Nationals

- Kalpana Debnath from Madhya Pradesh won the all-round individual title four years in a row from 1976–77 to 1979–80.
- Rajesh Kumar from Chandigarh won the all-round individual title four times in a row between 1990–91 and 1994–95.

First National Championship

The first National Gymnastics Championship was held in 1952 in Madras (now Chennai), Tamil Nadu where Khushi Ram emerged as the all-round individual champion and Punjab won the team championship.

Most successive titles – team

Services won the team National Championship six times in a row between 1954–55 and 1961–62. They won it again six times in a row between 1963–64 and 1971–72. (The tournament was not held for some years in between.)

INTERNATIONAL

First World Cup medal

Aruna Reddy, then 22 years old, from Hyderabad, Telangana, became the first Indian gymnast to win a medal at the Gymnastics World Cup when she won a bronze in vault in Melbourne, Australia, with a score of 13.649 points on 24 February 2018.

Dipa Karmakar

First Olympic appearance

Khushi Ram and Vir Singh were the first gymnasts to represent India at the Olympics, in 1952 at Helsinki.

First appearance in the World Championship

Daljit Inder Singh, Manjit Singh and Vithal Karande participated in the 1970 World Championship held at Ljubljana (in present-day Slovenia).

First appearance in the Commonwealth Games

Manjit Singh, B.S. Nandi and N.B. Bhosle represented India at the 1978 Edmonton Commonwealth Games in Canada.

First medal in the Commonwealth Games – men

Ashish Kumar won the first ever medals (and a rare two at that) in gymnastics: a bronze in the individual floor exercise (score: 14.475) and a silver in the vault (with 15.312 points) at the 2010 Commonwealth Games, New Delhi.

First medal in the Asian Games – men

With a score of 14.925, Ashish Kumar won a bronze in the floor exercise at the 2010 Guangzhou Asian Games in China, which was India's first and only medal in gymnastics at the Asian Games.

First medal in the Asian Championship

Ashish Kumar won a bronze medal in the floor exercise at the third Senior Asian Gymnastics Championship at Pandit Deen Dayal Upadhyay Indoor Stadium, Surat, Gujarat, on 2 August 2006.

First Asian Champion

Dipa Karmakar made history by clinching the gold medal in the women's vault apparatus at the 2024 Asian Gymnastics Championships in Tashkent, Uzbekistan on May 26, 2024. This remarkable achievement marks the first time an Indian gymnast has secured a gold medal at the Asian Championships. Prior to this, Indian gymnasts had earned four bronze medals at the continental event, with Karmakar herself claiming one in the women's vault back in 2015.

Most Olympic representations
Anantram Dogra is the only gymnast who has represented India in two Olympic Games – in Melbourne in 1956 and in Tokyo in 1964. He was also selected for the 1960 Rome Olympic Games, but the Indian Army team was called back due to an emergency.

HOCKEY

GENERAL

First Indian to head the International Hockey Federation
Dr Narinder Dhruv Batra was the first non-European president of the FIH. He was elected twice to the prestigious post, first in 2016 and re-elected in 2022.

First Olympian to head Indian hockey
Dilip Tirkey from Odisha, who had participated in three Olympic Games (in 1996 in Atlanta, USA; in 2000 in Sydney, Australia; and in 2004 in Athens, Greece), was unanimously elected president of Hockey India on 23 September 2022.

Dilip Tirkey

Highest civilian award
Two players – Dhyan Chand and P.R. Sreejesh – were awarded with Padma Bhushan; Dhyan Chand in 1956 and goalkeeper Sreejesh after 69 years in 2025.

Most Arjuna Awards for any sport in a year
Normally, two or three hockey players (both men and women collectively) used to get the Government of India's top sporting award. However, with the success of Indian men's team at the Tokyo Olympics, all the 16 members (except the duo of goalkeeper P.R. Sreejesh and captain Manpreet Singh, who have already received the award earlier) were awarded the honour. P.R. Sreejesh and Manpreet Singh were given the Khel Ratna award.

Most FIH Hockey Star Awards
Indian players and coaches swept all the annual FIH Hockey Star Awards in 2021. The winners include Player of the Year: Harmanpreet Singh (men) and Gurjit Kaur (women); Best Goalkeeper: P.R. Sreejesh (men) and Savita Punia (women); Best Rising Star Vivek Sagar Prasad (men) and Sharmila Devi (women); Best Coach: Graham Reid (national men's team coach) and Sjoerd Marijne (national women's team coach).

Most appearances in the Olympics
Five Indian players played Olympics four times: Leslie Claudius (1948 to 1960, Udham Singh (1952 to 1964), Dhanraj Pillay (1992 to 2004), P.R. Sreejesh (2012 to 2024) and Manpreet Singh (2012 to 2024).

WR First nation to start commercial league for women (where players were auctioned)
India became the first nation to start commercial league for women with Hockey India League 2024-2025 where four teams together bought 96 women hockey players (64 Indian, 32 foreign).

Most Olympics by an Indian goalkeeper

P.R. Sreejesh

P.R. Sreejesh four Olympics (2012 to 2024) surpassing Shankar Laxman's three (1956 to 1964).

Unique Records: Goalkeeper Parattu Raveendran Sreejesh
Only goalkeeper to captain India (2016), only goalkeeper to play in four Olympics, only goalkeeper to play in four World Cups.

WR First nation to start commercial league for men (Where players were auctioned)
India became the first nation to start a commercial league for men with Hockey India League 2023.

Successive Olympic bronze
India won successive bronze only twice, first in the 1972 Olympics when it beat Netherlands 2-1 and then in 2024 with a victory over Spain (2-1) on 8th Oct.

Successive Olympic bronze medallists
1968 & 1972: Three, Ajit Pal Singh, Harbinder Singh, P. Krishnamurthy.
2020 & 2024: Eleven. P.R. Sreejesh, Manpreet Singh, Hardik Singh, Gurjant Singh, Mandeep Singh, Harmanpreet Singh, Lalit Kumar Upadhyay, Sumit, Shamsher Singh, Amit Rohidas and Vivek Sagar Prasad.

DOMESTIC

Oldest tournament – men
The Beighton Cup was started in Calcutta (now Kolkata), West Bengal in 1895 and is considered to be the oldest tournament. Presented by T.D. Beighton, the legal remembrancer of the then Government of Bengal, the Cup was held initially in the form of local matches, evolving into a regular tournament. Its latest edition was held in December 2016, with Indian Oil defeating Bharat Petroleum 5–3.

First National Championship – men
The first National Championship, then known as the Inter-Provincial Championship, was staged in 1928 at Kolkata (then Calcutta). India became

Rare Feat: First to hold two continental hockey championships
New hockey stadium in Rajgir, Bihar, hosted two continental hockey championships on successive years and India won both. Indian women won the Asian Champions Trophy in 2024 winning all 7 matches, followed by men the Asia Cup in 2025. Men won 6 matches while drawing one. The stadium can boast of giving India two Asia titles.

a member of the International Hockey Federation in 1927 and thus became eligible to participate in the 1928 Olympics. The Calcutta edition was held to select the team for participation in the 1928 Olympic Games in Amsterdam.

Oldest tournament – women

First National Championship that was in 1947 in the then Bombay is the oldest domestic tournament for women.

First Domestic League – women

The Khelo India Women Hockey League for U-21 (2021)

First National Championship – women

Various attempts were made to start a National Championship. However, these efforts did not bear any results, after an edition was initially held. Subsequently, when the Bombay Inter-Provincial Hockey Association started in 1947, it got the much elusive consensus of all the states and thus a legacy was born.

Most wins in the National Championship – men

Indian Railways has won 25 times.

Most wins in the National Championship – women

Indian Railways has won 30 times.

INTERNATIONAL

First international appearance – men

In 1926, the Indian Army team went to New Zealand to play 21 matches. They won 18, drew two and lost one match. They scored 192 and conceded 24 goals.

First women professional players

Penalty corner expert Jasjeet Kaur Handa and Subhadra Pradhan played for HC Den Bosch club in the Dutch League in 2007.

First medal and most successful team in the Olympics

The Indian hockey team won its first Olympic medal in 1928, under the captaincy of Jaipal Singh Munda. From 1928 to 1956, the team was unbeaten, winning six gold medals. Since then, India has been adding medals to its Olympic tally, and currently, with a total of eight gold, one silver and two bronze medals, it is the single most successful team at the Olympic Games.

First foreign coach

- *Men*: Gerard Rach from Germany, India's first foreign coach, was with the team at the 2004 Athens Olympics, and till January 2005.
- *Women*: Herman Kruis from the Netherlands was the first foreign coach for the women's hockey team, and was in charge of the Asia Cup in Hong Kong in September 2007.

First Commonwealth Games success – women

At the 2002 Commonwealth Games in Manchester, UK, the Indian women's hockey team won the gold medal, defeating England 3–2. The team was led by Suraj Lata Devi.

First Asia Cup win – men

Led by Dhanraj Pillay, India won the 6th Asia Cup in Kuala Lumpur, beating Pakistan 4-2 in the final in 2003.

First Asia Cup win – women

Coached by M.K. Kaushik, the Indian women's hockey team won the Asia Cup for the first time, beating Japan 1–0 in the final at the National Stadium (now Dhyan Chand National Stadium), New Delhi, in February 2004.

Biggest Victory margin in the Asia Cup – men

India's biggest victory margin in the Asia Cup came in the 7th Asia Cup when India defeated Sri Lanka 20-0, in 2007.

Biggest Victory margin in the Asia Cup – women

India's biggest victory margin in the Asia Cup came in 2007 when it beat Thailand and Singapore on identical 16-0 margin.

First Junior Asia Cup win

India won the fifth Junior Asia Cup in Karachi, Pakistan, in March 2004, beating the hosts 5–2. Tushar Khandekar scored a memorable hat-trick in the final.

First Asian Women's Hockey Champions Trophy win

India, led by Deepika Thakur, won the Asian Women's Champions trophy held in Singapore in 2016, beating China in the final on shoot out.

First Asian Men's Hockey Champions Trophy win

India won the inaugural edition of the tournament held in Ordos City, China, during August–September 2011, by defeating Pakistan 4–2 in the final via penalty strokes.

Inaugural FIH Hockey 5s Championship win

The International Hockey Federation (FIH) introduced a new tournament in 2022. India, led by Gurinder Singh, won, by defeating Poland (4-3) in the final on 7 June 2022 in Geneva, Switzerland.

Dhyan Chand

Most medals by a national team in the men's Asia Cup

India have won most medals with 11 (4 gold, 5 silver, 2 bronze) out of 12 appearances.

Most Olympic goals – individual

Dhyan Chand scored 33 goals in three Olympics – 10 in 1928, 12 in 1932 and 11 in 1936.

Most goals in the Olympics – team

India scored 43 goals in six matches at Moscow in 1980, a record for the most goals in an Olympics. In the 1936 Berlin and 1956 Melbourne Olympics, India notched up 38 goals in five matches. It did not concede a single goal in 1928 and 1956.

Most medals in the Olympics

The world record for the most medals in hockey at the Olympics is held by Leslie Claudius and Udham Singh, who were in four medal-winning teams – with three golds and one silver. Claudius was in the team that won the gold in 1948, 1952 and 1956, and silver in 1960, while Singh played for the gold-winning team in 1952, 1956 and 1964, and the silver-winning team in 1960.

Most Junior Asia Cups — men

India's U-21 hockey team won the Junior Asia Cup in 2024 after defeating Pakistan 5-3 in the final played in Muscat, Oman. This was India's record fifth Asian title at the age group ahead of Pakistan's 3. India previously won in 2004, 2008, 2015 and 2023.

Most capped player
Manpreet Singh (416) followed by Dilip Tirkey (412, retired in 2009). Manpreet Singh is still active in the sport.

Most Asia Cup appearances – men
Four appearances: Dilip Tirkey, Sardar Singh, and S.V. Sunil.

Most Asian Games gold
Colleagues P.R. Sreejesh and Manpreet Singh have won the Asian Games gold twice (2024 & 2018).

Most international caps — women
Striker Vandana Katariya became the first Indian women hockey player to play 300 matches in Indian colours on 31st October 2023 during the Women's Asian Champions Trophy, Ranchi, India. Indian goalkeeper Savita Punia entered the 300th club on 2nd February 2025 during the FIH Pro-league, Bhubaneswar, India.

Most appearance in the Women's World Cup
Deepika Thakur is the only Indian woman hockey player to appear in three World Cups (2006, 2010, 2018). India did not qualify for the 2014 edition.

Most appearances in the World Cup
Three players have the record of figuring in four World Cups. They are Ashok Kumar (1971, 1973, 1975, 1978), Dhanraj Pillay (1994, 1998, 2002, 2006) and P.R. Sreejesh (2010 to 2023) played in four World Cups.

Playing for teams with most Olympic golds
The record for playing for teams winning the most Olympic golds – three each – is held by seven Indians: Richard Allen and Dhyan Chand (1928–36); Balbir Singh, R.S. Gentle, Leslie Claudius and R. Francis (1948–56); and Udham Singh (1952, 1956, 1964).

Most goals in a World Cup
In the fifth World Cup in Bombay (now Mumbai), Maharashtra, during 1981–82, India scored 29 goals in seven matches, winning five and losing two.

Biggest victory margin in the Olympics
India created a world record for the biggest victory margin at the Olympics when they beat the USA 24–1 on 11 August 1932 at Los Angeles, USA.

Best performance in the World Cup – men
India, led by Ajitpal Singh, beat Pakistan 2–1 in the final of the third World Cup at Kuala Lumpur, Malaysia, in 1975, displaying its best performance at the World Cup.

Best performance in the World Cup – women
India, led by Ajinder Kaur, finished fourth in 1974.

Best performance in the Commonwealth Games
Hockey was first introduced in the Commonwealth Games in 1998. India's best performances at the Commonwealth Games include three silver medals (in 2010 in New Delhi 2010, in 2014 in Glasgow and in 2022 in Birmingham).

Best performance on a foreign tour
Dhyan Chand, who led the team to New Zealand in 1935, played 48 matches and won them all. India scored 584 goals and conceded 40 goals. Dhyan Chand alone scored 201 goals, his brother Roop Singh scored 187 and F.C. Wells scored 112 goals.

Best goalkeeping in the Olympics
Richard J. Allen did not concede a single goal in the five matches in the 1928 Olympics. He let in only two goals in 1932 and one in five games in 1936, conceding only three goals in three successive Olympics – a rare feat.

Richard J. Allen (standing extreme left)

Best performances in the Champions Trophy
India reached the final in the 2016 Champions Trophy in London, UK, and the 2018 Champions Trophy in Breda, Netherlands. In both, India lost 1–3 to Australia in the penalty shoot-out. The traditional tournament has not being held after 2018.

Biggest victory margin in the Asian Games – men
India's biggest victory margin at the Asian Games was 26–0 versus Hong Kong in the League phase of the 2018 Jakarta Asian Games in Indonesia.

Biggest win in the Asia Cup finals
India beat South Korea 7–2 in the final of the 2007 Asia Cup in Chennai, Tamil Nadu, on 19 September 2007.

Biggest victory margin in the Asian Games – women
India's biggest victory margin at the Asian Games came in the League phase of the 2018 Bangkok Asian Games when it beat Kazakhstan 21–0 on 21 August 2018.

Best recovery in the Men's Hockey Champions Trophy
- The Indian team rallied from 0–3 at Amstelveen, Netherlands, to beat Pakistan 5–4 in 1982.
- India trailed West Germany 1–5 in 1985 at Perth, but in the last seven minutes levelled at 5–5. Centre half Joaquim Carvalho scored an equalizing penalty stroke.

Highest goal scorer in the Asia Cup
Winger Prabhjot Singh scored 23 goals in the 7th Asia Cup.

Highest goal scorer and double hat-trick in the Youth Asia Cup
Defender Jugraj Singh scored 14 goals, including a double hat-trick, in the Youth Asia Cup in Malaysia in June 2001.

Highest goal scorer at the World Cup
Defender Rajender Singh, who played a solitary World Cup, scored all 12 goals in the 1981–82 tournament in Bombay (now Mumbai), Maharashtra, making him the highest goal scorer at the World Cup.

Fastest goal
Ajit Singh scored within 15 seconds of the start of the League match against Argentina in the 1976 Montreal Olympics – the fastest goal on artificial turf.

Only captain in successive Olympics
Pargat Singh was the captain first at Barcelona in 1992 and then in 1996 at the Atlanta Olympics in the USA, but India did not win a medal at either Games.

Only double hat-trick in the Olympics
Mohammed Shahid scored seven goals, including a double hat-trick, against Thailand (11–0) on 24 September 1986 in the Seoul Olympics in South Korea.

Only hat-trick in the Olympics – women
Vandana Katariya scored a hat-trick against South Africa on 31 July 2021 in the 2020 Tokyo Olympics in Japan.

Vandana Katariya

Only hat-trick in succession
At the 1952 Helsinki Olympics, centre forward Balbir Singh scored three goals in the semi final against Great Britain and netted five, including a hat-trick, against the Netherlands in the final.

Youngest to win a gold in the Olympics
Cinnadorai Desamuthu was the youngest player to be in a gold-winning team, aged 19 years and 272 days, when India won in the 1952 Helsinki Olympics.

Oldest players in the Olympics
Udham Singh (b. 1928) was 36 when he played in the 1964 Tokyo Olympics. Pritipal Singh (b.1932) was also 36 when he was joint captain of 1968 Mexico Olympics. Goalkeeper P.R. Sreejesh (b.1988) was also 36 when he played in the Paris 2024 Olympics.

KABADDI

First Nationals
- The first kabaddi Nationals for men were held in 1951 in Maharashtra. The host state won the title.
- The first Nationals in kabaddi for women were held in 1955 in Calcutta (now Kolkata), West Bengal. Maharashtra won here too.
- The first championships for junior boys and girls were held in 1974 and 1976 respectively at Asansol, West Bengal.

First demonstration in the Olympics
Kabaddi and other indigenous games were the demonstration games in the 1936 Olympic Games held in Berlin, Germany.

First appearance of kabaddi in the Asian Games
Kabaddi was played for the first time in the 11th Asian Games in 1990 in Beijing, China. Pakistan, Japan, China, Nepal, Bangladesh and India participated, with India winning the gold medal.

First demonstration at the Asian Games
Kabaddi was an exhibition sport at the 1982 Asian Games held in New Delhi.

First Asian Championship
The first Asian Championship for men was held at Calcutta (now Kolkata), West Bengal, in 1980, in which teams from Bangladesh, Nepal and India played. India won the gold medal.

First Pro Kabaddi League
The first Pro Kabaddi League was held in 2014, with eight teams participating.

Pro Kabaddi League

Sixty games were played, with the Jaipur Pink Panthers winning the inaugural title, defeating U-Mamba 35–24.

First team to win three consecutive Pro Kabaddi titles
Patna Pirates won three consecutive Pro Kabaddi League titles in 2016–17.

First participation in the Asian Junior Championship
The championship was held for the first time at Faridabad, Haryana, in January 2000, with teams from Bangladesh, Nepal, Sri Lanka and Thailand. India won the gold.

Most World Cup wins – men
The Indian team has won all three Kabaddi World Cups, organized by the International Kabaddi Federation, in 2004, 2007 and 2016, beating Iran in the finals of all three.

Most Asian Games titles – men
Kabaddi was introduced in the Asian Games in 1990 in Beijing, China, and was open only to men at that time. The Indian team has since won the Asian Games gold seven times – in 1990, 1994, 1998, 2002, 2006, 2010 and 2014.

Most Asian Games titles – women
Kabaddi first made an appearance as a competitive sport for women in the 2010 Guangzhou Asian Games in China, 20 years after it was introduced for men. The Indian team won gold in 2010 and 2014, but got a silver in the 2018 Asian Games in Jakarta, Indonesia, losing to Iran in the final.

Most Asian titles — men and women
India won their record eighth Asian Kabaddi Championship title after defeating Iran in the final 42-32 in Busan, South Korea in July. India, under captain Pawan Sehrawat, remained unbeaten in all six games played in the campaign. This was eighth title in nine editions for India with Iran a one-time champion.

Most World and Asian Championship medals – women
Sarala Shetty of Bank Sports Board is the only Indian to win the Asian Kabaddi Championship eight times. Captain of the Indian team on eight occasions, she has also won three World Championship medals.

Most expensive non-cricket player
Raider Monu Goyat from Haryana became India's most expensive non-cricket sportsperson when Haryana Steelers bought him at ₹1.51 crore (15.1 million) for season 6 of the Pro Kabaddi League 2018.

Most expensive player in Pro Kabaddi League (PKL)
Pawan Sehrawat set a new record as the most expensive player in Pro Kabaddi history after being purchased by Telugu Titans for ₹2.605 crores at the 2023 auction. This breaks his own previous record when he was acquired by Tamil Thalaivas for ₹2.26 crores in the 2022 auction.

Pawan Sehrawat receiving the Arjuna Award from President Draupadi Murmu

LUGE

Youngest luge Olympian
India's single representative at luge in the Winter Olympics, Shiva Keshavan from Manali, Himachal Pradesh, was the youngest luge Olympian in history, when he participated in the 1998 Nagano Olympics in Japan at the age of 16 years. Keshavan holds the record of participating in six winter Olympics: 1998 Nagano, Japan; 2002 Salt Lake City, USA; 2006 Turin, Italy; 2010 Vancouver, Canada; 2014 Sochi, Russia; and 2018 Pyeongchang, South Korea. He won the Asian Luge Championships in 2011, 2012, 2016 and 2017. He set a new Asian speed record of 134.3 kmph in 2011.

Shiva Keshavan

MARTIAL ARTS

WUSHU

First world wushu champion – women
In 2017, Pooja Kadian became the first Indian to be crowned World Champion in the women's 75 kg Sanda category.

Pooja Kadian

First world wushu champion – men
Praveen Kumar of the Indian Army became the first Indian to win the gold medal on 23 October 2019 in the Sanda 48 kg category of the 15th World Wushu Championship.

JUDO

First National Championship
The first National Championship was held in Hyderabad in 1965. Till 1981, it was held every two years.

First international medal
India, represented by Sandeep Bayala (below 65 kg), Cawas Billimoria (below 95 kg), Shyam Singh Gurjar (+95 kg) and Bannu Singh (open), won four bronze medals in the 1986 Asian Games in Seoul.

Youngest champion
Sandeep Bayala was 15 years old when he won the Nationals at Srinagar in 1982.

Most wins in the Nationals
Sandeep Bayala of Delhi Police has won 11 titles successively during 1982-93.

First medal in the Asian Games – women
Poonam Chopra won a silver medal in the 56 kg weight category at the 1994 Hiroshima Games in Japan.

First judoka to win a world title
Sixteen-year-old Linthoi Chanambam clinched a historic gold medal at the World Cadet Championship on 22 August 2022. She won the title across age groups.

First medal in the Asian Championship – women
Poonam Chopra won a bronze medal in 56 kg weight category at the Asian Championship in 1993 in Macau, China.

Oldest competitor
Banu Singh was 39 years old when he represented India at the Seoul Games in 1986. He won a bronze in the open category.

Most silver medals in the Commonwealth Games – women
Judoka Shushila Devi Likmabam won two silver medals in the women's 48 kg category, the first in Glasgow in 2014 and the second in Birmingham in 2022.

Sushila Devi

Best performance in the Commonwealth Games
India won two silver and two bronze medals in 2018 at Gold Coast in Australia.

POWERLIFTING

Most medals in one edition of the Asian Championship
V.S.N.L. Renuka won four golds in the 48 kg category in squat, bench, deadlift and overall lift of 310 kg at the Asian Powerlifting Championship in Zarafshan, Uzbekistan, in 2000.

Most Commonwealth Championship golds – individual
Sampa Guha won four gold medals in the first Commonwealth Championship in Newcastle, UK, in September 2005.

Most medals in Asian Championship
In the biggest haul at the Asian Championship to date, Indian powerlifters won 49 medals (22 gold, 19 silver and eight bronze medals), besides

the Women's Team Championship and overall medals (men and women), at the 18th Asian Senior, Junior, Sub-junior and Masters (men and women) Championship 2006 at Taebaek City, Korea.

Best performance in the World Championship

India won all three medals in the World Championship in Akita, Japan, in November 2000. N. Anbu (52 kg) won gold in the deadlift and an overall silver, while Jentry Francis (56 kg) won the bronze medal.

Best performance in the Asian Junior Championship

At the Asian Junior Championship, Indian boys won the team trophy with four gold, four silver and two bronze medals at New Delhi in May 2001. In the same championship, Indian girls also won the team trophy with three gold medals, two silver medals and two bronze medals.

Best performance in the Commonwealth Championship – men

India bagged a total of five gold, three silver and four bronze medals, and were declared runner-up in the team event in the second Commonwealth Championship at Christchurch, New Zealand, held from 6 to 9 December 2007.

Best performance in the Asian Sub-junior Championship

The Indian boys' team won the team trophy with five gold and two silver medals at the inaugural Asian Sub-junior Championship held at New Delhi in May 2001. In the same championship, the Indian girls' team bagged four gold and two silver medals.

First medal in the Commonwealth games in para powerlifting

Sakina Khatun won the bronze medal in the lightweight category at the 2014 Commonwealth Para Games held in Glasgow, UK.

First medal in powerlifting in the Asian Para Games

Farman Basha won India's first medal – a bronze – in the 48 kg category at the inaugural Asian Para Games held in Guangzhou, China, in December 2010.

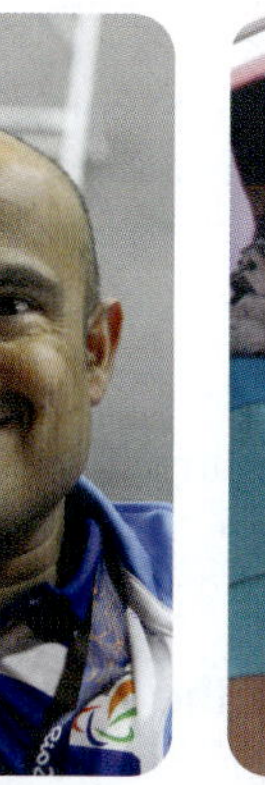

Farman Basha

Mairaj Ahmad Khan

Back-to-back Olympia Pro-Powerlifting wins

Mukesh Singh Gehlot from Delhi is the only Indian to win an individual medal in successive IPL Olympia Pro-Powerlifting. He won the gold on his debut in IPL Olympia Pro-Powerlifting 2017 in the 100 kg open category and a bronze in Las Vegas, USA, in 2018.

First gold in para powerlifting

Sudhir Lath claimed the gold medal in the men's heavyweight para powerlifting event at the 2022 Commonwealth Games in Birmingham. The 27-year-old, who has an impairment due to polio, lifted 212 kg.

SHOOTING

WR World champion with a world record

Rudrankksh Patil became the world champion in men's air rifle in the World Championship in Cairo, Egypt, in October 2022. He had shot a world record 633.9 in the first stage of qualification. 18-year-old Rudrankksh beat Danilo Dennis Solazzo of Italy 17-13 for the gold. He beat two Chinese shooters, including the reigning world and Olympic champion Yang Haoran. He became the second Indian to become world champion in air rifle after Abhinav Bindra in 2006. Rudrankksh also led the Indian team to the gold later, along with Arjun Babuta and Kiran Jadhav, as the trio beat China 16-10.

First skeet gold in the World Cup

Olympian Mairaj Ahmad Khan became the first Indian to win a skeet gold in a World Cup in Changwon, Korea, in July 2022. The 46-year-old Mairaj beat Kin Minsu of Korea 37-36 for the gold. Khan shot 119 in qualification and had to win a shoot-off with four others for the last two slots in the second stage. Mairaj had lost the shoot-off for the gold in the World Cup in Rio de Janeiro in 2016, and won the silver.

First Asian Games medals

• *Men:* India's Asian Games medal haul started with Dr Karni Singh winning silver in the trap event in 1974 at Tehran, Iran.
• *Women:* Soma Dutta won a silver in the individual rifle 3-position event and a bronze medal in air rifle at the 1986 Seoul Games, South Korea.

First World Championship medal

India's first World Championship medal came when Dr Karni Singh from Bikaner, Rajasthan, won a silver medal in the trap event in Cairo, Egypt, in 1962. The gold medal in the event was bagged by Vladimir Zimenko of the USSR.

First ever individual Olympic gold medal

Abhinav Bindra

Abhinav Bindra won India's first individual Olympic gold medal by claiming the honour in the men's air rifle event on 11 August 2008 in Beijing, China.

First World Championship gold

• Ace shooter Abhinav Bindra won India's first gold medal in a World Championship in air rifle at Zagreb, Croatia, on 24 July 2006.
• Manavjit Singh Sandhu won the first shotgun gold medal in a World Championship by beating 124 shooters to the title in the trap event at Zagreb, Croatia, two days after Bindra's effort.

First Asian Games gold

• Randhir Singh won gold in the trap event in the 1978 Games in Bangkok, Thailand, and a bronze in 1982.
• Jaspal Rana won the men's individual 25 m centre-fire pistol event in the 1994 Hiroshima Asian Games with 588 points, a new Asian record then. It was

the only individual gold medal for India that year and the first Asian Games gold in that event.

First woman to win a gold in the Asian Games

Rahi Sarnobat became the first Indian woman to win a gold in the Asian Games (25 m pistol event) in 2018 at Jakarta, Indonesia.

Rahi Sarnobat receiving the Arjuna Award in 2018

First Commonwealth Games gold

- *Men:* Ashok Pandit won the gold in the free pistol event in Auckland, New Zealand, in 1990.
- *Women:* Roopa Unnikrishnan clinched the gold in the rifle prone event in the 1998 Commonwealth Games in Kuala Lumpur, Malaysia. In the 1994 Games in Victoria, Australia, Unnikrishnan won two medals – a silver in the small-bore rifle 3-position and a bronze in the pairs with Kuheli Ganguly.

First World Cup silver and gold medals

Anjali Vedpathak-Bhagwat won the gold in the air rifle event in the World Cup at Milan, Italy, in 2003. She had earlier won the silver in Munich, Germany, in 2002.

First World Cup pistol medal

Sonia Rai from Himachal Pradesh won the bronze in the women's air pistol in the World Cup at Resende, Brazil, on 28 April 2006. She shot a 482.2, after 384/400 in the qualification phase.

Gold in the World Cup

Saurabh Chaudhary won the gold medal in the 10 m air pistol event in the World Cup at Munich, Germany, in May 2019. He shot a 246.3 to break his own world record of 245.5 set in the World Championship. He won gold medals in the 2018 Youth Olympics in Buenos Aires, Argentina, and in the 2018 Asian Games in Jakarta, Indonesia.

First gold in the Asian Championship

Dr Karni Singh won an individual gold in the trap event in 1971 in Seoul, South Korea. This was India's first gold in the Asian Championship.

First medal haul in the Asian Championship

India won two gold, one silver and two bronze medals in Jakarta, Indonesia, in 1983, in its first haul in the Asian Championship. Ashok Pandit and Mohinder Lal won the gold in the centre-fire pistol team event with a world record.

Biggest haul of medals in Asian Championship

The National Rifle Association of India (NRAI) focused on the Asian Championship to field the best and strongest team, with an overall contingent of 182 shooters. There were junior and youth events apart from the main events for men and women. India topped the medals table with 99 medals, including 50 gold. The highlight was the Indian shooters winning 23 gold, 16 silver and 16 bronze in individual events. In the team events, India gathered 21 gold, nine silver and five bronze. India topped in the mixed events as well, with six gold, one silver and two bronze.

Rajyavardhan Singh Rathore

First mixed air pistol gold medal in the World Cup – team

Heena Sidhu and Jitu Rai won the gold in the mixed air pistol team event in the World Cup in Delhi in 2017, when it was officially made a medal event.

First Nationals

The first shooting national tournament was held in Delhi from 9 to 16 November in 1952.

World record in skeet in the Asian Championship

Angad Vir Singh Bajwa shot a perfect 60 out of 60 to win the gold medal in the men's skeet final in the Asian Championship held in Kuwait in November 2018.

First team gold in the Asian Clay Championship

Mansher Singh, Moraad Ali Khan and Manavjit Singh won India's first team gold at the Asian Clay Shooting Championship at Chengdu, China, in July 1995 with a tally of 357/375, equalling Kuwait's Asian record at the 1994 Hiroshima Asian Games in Japan.

First to win two golds in a World Cup

Manu Bhaker, then 16 years old, from Jhajjar, Haryana, won the 10 m air pistol gold medal and partnered with Om Prakash Mitharval for the 10 m air pistol mixed team gold in the 2018 World Cup in Mexico.

First ever Olympic medal in shooting

Rajyavardhan Singh Rathore won the silver medal in double-trap shooting, behind Ahmed Al Maktoum of the UAE, in the 2004 Athens Olympics in Greece. Rathore made his maiden Olympic appearance in the 2004 Olympic Games in Athens, Greece, merely about six years after he had taken up the sport. A year before, he had won the gold medal in the 2003 World Cup in Sydney, Australia.

Most individual medals in the Asian Shooting Championship

Ronak Pandit won seven gold medals and a silver medal in the junior pistol events of the Asian Championship in Kuala Lumpur, Malaysia, in 2004.

World record at the Asian Championship

Suma Shirur shot a perfect 400 out of 400 to win the gold medal in the women's air rifle in the Asian Championship at Kuala Lumpur, Malaysia, in February 2004. She shares the record with eight others.

Most career golds at the South Asian Games

Jaspal Rana won 23 golds and a silver in three editions of the SAF Games (now

South Asian Games). He won eight golds each at Madras (now Chennai), Tamil Nadu, in 1995 and at Kathmandu, Nepal, in 1999; and seven golds and a silver at Islamabad, Pakistan, in 2004.

Jaspal Rana

Best haul in the Asian Clay Shooting Championship

The best performance in the Asian Clay Shooting Championship was five gold medals in Bangkok, Thailand, in September 2005.

Best haul in the World Championship

The Indian team won 34 medals including 12 gold medals in the World Championship for rifle and pistol in Cairo, Egypt, in 2022. It is the best ever performance by India in a World Championship and India finished second in the medals table behind China.

Best haul in the World Cup

The Indian team topped the medals table with a record total of 30 medals in the World Cup in Delhi in March 2021, with 10 gold, eight silver and four bronze medals. The USA came a distant second with four gold, three silver and a bronze medal. Yashaswini Singh Deswal (women's air pistol), Aishwary Pratap Singh Tomar (men's rifle 3-position) and Chinki Yadav (women's sports pistol) won the individual gold medals.

Best Asian Games haul

Indian shooters won three gold, five silver and six bronze medals in the Asian Games at Doha, Qatar, in 2006, for their best haul of 14 medals in an edition of the Asian Games. India had won only 17 medals in all the previous editions put together.

Best haul in the Junior World Championship

The Indian juniors topped the medal standings in the Junior World Championship in Lima, Peru, in October 2021, with a total of 31 medals, including 12 gold and 13 silver medals. Manu Bhaker (women's air pistol), Naamya Kapoor (women's sports pistol), Aishwary Pratap Singh Tomar (men's rifle 3-position), Vijayveer Sidhu (men's standard pistol), Rhythm Sangwan (women's standard pistol) and Arjun Singh Cheema (men's free pistol) won the individual gold medals.

Best performance at the World Cup on debut

Shahzar Rizvi created a world record at the ISSF World Cup when he scored 242.3 points in the final of the 10 m air pistol event on 3 March 2018 at Guadalajara, Mexico. In his debut performance at the World Cup, Rizvi won the gold medal beating the reigning Olympic champion Christian Reitz of Germany.

Best haul in the Commonwealth Games

Indian shooters bagged 27 medals in the 2006 Commonwealth Games in Melbourne, Australia, with 16 gold, seven silver and four bronze medals. Gagan Narang bagged four gold medals (a feat he repeated in the 2010 Commonwealth Games, New Delhi), while Vijay Kumar and Omkar Singh bagged three gold medals each.

Double world record

- Ronjan Sodhi gained the unique distinction of equalling both the qualifying and final world records in double trap while winning the gold in the World Cup in Belgrade, Serbia, in 2008. He shot 147 in the qualifying phase and ended with 194.
- Gagan Narang won the World Cup final gold medal in men's air rifle with two world records in Bangkok, Thailand, in November 2008.

Ronjan Sodhi

Gagan Narang

Best haul in the Olympics

India's win of two medals in the 2012 London Olympics was the best in terms of numbers. Gagan Narang won the bronze medal in the air rifle and Vijay Kumar won the silver in the rapid-fire pistol.

WR Best performance at the Asian Championship

- Ankur Mittal shot 107 to win the double trap gold in the Asian championship in Shymkent, Kazakhstan, in August 2025. It was a world record.
- Naraen Pranav, Himanshu and Abhinav Shaw had a team score of 1890.1, a World Junior record, in men's air rifle, in the Asian championship.

Youngest to win a Junior World Championship gold – men

In 2017, Anish Bhanwala (b. 26 September 2002) became the youngest Indian shooter to win a Junior World Championship gold medal in standard pistol.

Youngest to win a World Cup gold – women

At Guadalajara, Mexico, in March 2018, Manu Bhaker (b. 18 February 2002) was the youngest to win a gold medal in the women's air pistol, and the air pistol mixed gold with Om Prakash Mitharval. She also clinched the gold medals in the unior World Cups in Sydney, Australia, and Suhl, Germany in 2018. She also won the air pistol gold, ahead of compatriot and former world record holder Heena Sidhu, in the 2018 Commonwealth Games in Gold Coast, Australia.

Most medals in a World Cup

India topped the medals table in the 2019 World Cup in Rio de Janeiro, Brazil, with five gold, two silver and two bronze medals.

Most medals in a Junior World Cup

India topped the medals table in the 2018 Suhl World Cup in Germany with 26 medals: 15 gold, two silver and nine bronze medals. This bettered the country's share of 22 out of 66 medals in the 2017 Sydney World Cup in Australia, when it won nine gold, five silver and eight bronze medals, to be placed second behind China (25).

Most medals in four consecutive World Cups

India has topped the medals table in four consecutive World Cups in rifle and pistol events. India topped the table in the 2018 Munich World Cup (with five gold medals and one silver medal), the

2019 New Delhi World Cup (with three golds), the 2019 Beijing World Cup (with three golds and a silver) and the 2019 Rio de Janeiro World Cup (with five golds, two silver and two bronze medals).

First Indian to win two medals at a single edition of Olympics
Manu Bhaker became the first athlete from independent India to win two medals at a single Olympic Games. She achieved this feat with a medal in the individual 10 m air pistol event and another in the 10 m air pistol mixed team event (with Sarabjot Singh). Norman Pritchard was the first Indian athlete to win two Olympic medals, securing silver in both the men's 200 m and 200 m hurdles at the 1900 Paris Olympics.

First shooting team medal
Manu Bhaker and Sarabjot Singh became the first Indian shooting pair to win an Olympic team medal at Paris 2024, marking India's sixth Olympic medal in shooting. The duo secured the bronze by defeating the Republic of Korea's Oh Ye Jin and Wonho Lee 16-10.

Manu Bhaker and Sarabjot Singh

SQUASH

First professionals
In the early 1990s, the first pros were Arjun Singh (men) and Misha Grewal. The latter became a professional in 1993, and played the women's professional circuit in Asia, Europe and the USA. Her best rankings were second in Asia and 27th in the world.

First champion
Rajkumar Narpat Singh won the first squash Nationals in 1953 and made a hattrick, holding the title for two more years.

First junior and senior Nationals title
Anil Nayyar won both the junior and senior titles in the Nationals in 1964, when he was 18 years old.

First junior world no. 1
Saurav Ghosal was the first Indian to be ranked junior world no. 1 when he won the British Junior Open in 2004.

First individual medals in the Asian Championships
- Bhuvaneshwari Kumari won the bronze in the 1990 and 1992 Asian Championships.
- Misha Grewal won a silver in the Asian Championship in 1996 at Amman, Jordan.

First Commonwealth Games gold
India bagged its first gold medal when Dipika Pallikal and Joshna Chinappa defeated Laura Massaro and Jenny Duncalf of England 11–6, 11–8 to win the women's doubles event in the Commonwealth Games in Glasgow, UK, in 2014.

First to win world ranking titles
In August 2003, Ritwik Bhattacharya became the first Indian to win back-to-back international Professional Squash Association (PSA) world ranking tournaments in New Zealand when he won the North Island Championship and the Royal Oak Open titles. In 2005, he annexed two more titles – the Esportiu Rocafort Squash Open in Barcelona, Spain, and the Rochester ProAm Squash Championship in New York, USA. He has won four international squash titles.

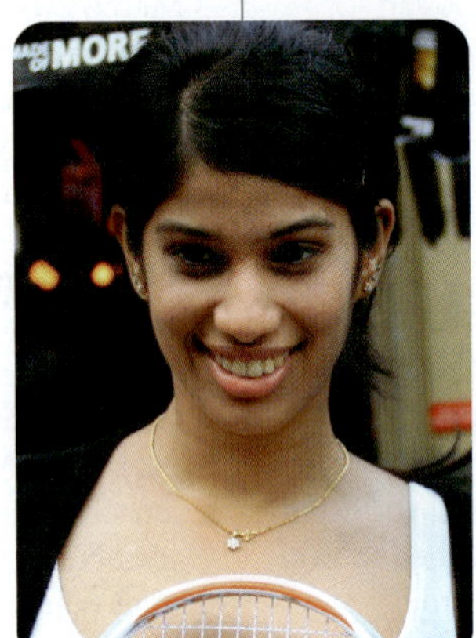
Joshna Chinappa

First international success – women
Joshna Chinappa became the first Indian woman to claim a Women's International Squash Players Association (WISPA) title, defeating Malaysia's Low Wee Wern 11–8, 11–5, 11–3 in the NSC Super Satellite (no. 3) Squash Tournament final at National Squash Centre, Kuala Lumpur, Malaysia, in November 2008.

First to win the Asian junior title – girls
Joshna Chinappa was the first to win the Asian junior title (U-19) in 2003. Later, Dipika Pallikal also won the title in July 2010.

First doubles champions in the Nationals
In the first National Doubles Squash Championship held in Chennai, Tamil Nadu, in 2004. Joshna Chinappa and Dipika Pallikal, representing Tamil Nadu, won the women's title and Saurav Ghosal and Harinder Pal Singh Sandhu, also representing Tamil Nadu, won the men's title.

Best in the Asian Games
For the first time, India won the men's team event gold medal in the 2014 Incheon Asian Games in South Korea, beating Malaysia 2–0. Saurav Ghosal, Harinder Pal Singh Sandhu and Mahesh Mangaonkar represented India in this event. The women's team of Dipika Pallikal, Joshna Chinappa and Anaka Alankamony won the silver medal, losing to Malaysia 0–2 in the 2014 Asian Games team event final.

Dipika Pallikal

First Indians to win World Doubles titles

Dipika Pallikal became the first Indian to win two gold medals at the World Doubles Squash Championships winning the gold in women's and mixed finals. Dipika partnered Joshna Chinappa in the women's final and teamed up with Saurav Ghosal in the mixed doubles in the 2022 edition in Glasgow. The trio are the first Indians to win World Doubles title since the inception of the tournament in 1981.

First Indians to win Asian Mixed Doubles Championship

Dipika Pallikal Karthik and Harinderpal Singh Sandhu won the inaugural Asian Mixed Doubles Squash Championship 2023 in Huangzhou, China. The duo defeated the Malaysian pair of Rachel Arnold and Ivan Yuen 11-10, 11-8 in the final.

Most National titles won

Joshna Chinappa won 18 national titles, the most yet by an Indian.

Best performance in the World Championships

Saurav Ghosal was the first Indian to reach the quarter-finals of the World Championships in Manchester, UK, in October 2013. Though he lost to world no. 1 Ramy Ashour in the match, this is India's best performance to date at the World Championships.

Saurav Ghosal

Most titles in a row in the Nationals – women

Bhuvaneshwari Kumari was the women's national champion 16 times in a row from 1977 to 1992, a record that remains unbeaten.

Bhuvaneshwari Kumari

Best performance in the Asian Juniors

Anaka Alankamony from Chennai, Tamil Nadu, became the youngest winner of the Asian Junior title (U-19) at 16 years when she beat Tsz-Wing Tong of Hong Kong 6–11, 11–8, 10–12, 11–7, 11–7 at Amman, Jordan, in June 2011. India enjoyed triple success in this event: Ramit Tandon (U-19 boys' and Saumya Karki (U-17 girls') won silver medals in India's largest haul at the event.

Youngest national champion – women

Joshna Chinappa became the youngest national women's champion at 14 years in 2001.

Oldest champion

Brigadier R.K. Manchanda was 37 years old when he won the Nationals title in 1983, thus becoming the oldest national champion in squash. He also became the oldest finalist in 1987 when he was 1 years old. He reached the final in the Nationals a record 11 times, as did Anil Nayyar. Manchanda won six of the 11 finals in which he competed.

Youngest champion – men

Adrian Ezra and Ritwik Bhattacharya were both 17 when they won the senior national singles title in 1989 and 1997 respectively, making them the youngest national squash champions to date.

Highest rankings

- Saurav Ghosal is the first Indian to break into the top 10 in the Professional Squash Association (PSA) world rankings. He was ranked 10th with 6,455 points in April 2019.
- Joshna Chinappa is the highest ranked Indian woman in the 27th position with 2,345 points (*at the time of going to press*).
- In 2012, Dipika Pallikal and, in 2016, Chinappa were placed 10th in the world rankings.

SWIMMING

First swimmer in the Olympics

D.D. Mulji of Bengal was the first Indian swimmer in the Olympics, taking part in the 1928 Amsterdam Olympics. Indian women participated in the Olympics for the first time at the 1952 Helsinki Olympics, with Dolly Nazir and Arati Saha representing India.

First woman to participate in the Asian Games

Kumari Rima Dutta participated in the fifth Asian Games in Bangkok, Thailand, in 1966.

First swimmers in the Asian Games

Nine Indian swimmers participated in the inaugural Asian Games in 1951: Sachin Nag, Bimal Chandra, Issar Mansoor, Santosh Bhattacharjee, Kanti Shaw, Protip Mitra, Shambu Shaw,

J.J. Naigamwalla and Bhubaneswar Pandey. The first Indian women to participate in Asian Games were Kumari Rima Dutta in the fifth Asian Games held at Bangkok in 1966.

First water polo team in the Asian Games

- In 1951, the Indian water polo team first participated in Asian Games and won a gold medal. The team members were Ganesh Dass (captain), G. Rattansey, D. Daver, Isaac Mansoor, Jhair Ahir, Rober Dean and Kanti Shaw.
- The Indian water polo team participated in Asian Games in 1970 in Bangkok and won the silver medal. The team included Pijus Mitra (Captain), Samir Kapadia, Tarun Goswami, Abdul Mutlib, Ashok Biswas, Bharat Merchant, Chand Ram, Umed Singh, Avinash Sarang, Pattabhi Raman and Deep Narayan Singh.

First diver in the Asian Games

Three Indian divers participated in the first Asian Games in 1951: K.P. Thakkar, Ashu Dutta and T.T. Dand. Thakkar of Maharashtra won gold medals in the highboard and springboard events, while Dand won a bronze in high-board diving.

First Asian Games gold

India won its first Asian Games gold when Sachin Nag clocked 1 min 4.7 secs to win the 100m freestyle in the 1951 Asian Games in Delhi. In the same Asian Games he won two bronze medals as well. He represented India in two Olympics: in 1948 in London and in 1952 in Helsinki.

First to participate in the Commonwealth Games

- Divers Dum Bahadur and Vasant Gadge were the first to represent India in the aquatics events at the 1978 Commonwealth Games in Edmonton, Canada.
- In 1982, for the first time, Indian swimmers participated in the Commonwealth Games at Brisbane, Australia. The team members were Wilson Cherian, Khazan Singh Tokas, T. Thoiba Singh, Sanjeev Chakraborty, Persis Madaan, Geeta Anand and Giselle Bharucha.

Shikha Tandon

First to qualify for two Olympic events

Shikha Tandon of Bengaluru, Karnataka, qualified for the 50 m and 100 m freestyle events in the 2004 Athens Olympics, but did not win.

First to reach a Commonwealth Games final

During the 2010 Commonwealth Games in New Delhi, two Indian men –Virdhawal Khade and Sandeep Sejwal – reached the finals in their best events. Khade was placed seventh in the 50 m butterfly, while Sejwal came eighth in the 50 m breaststroke.

First relay team in a the Commonwealth Games final

The quartet of Virdhawal Khade, Anshul Kothari, Arjun Jayaprakash and Aaron D'Souza qualified for the 4 x 100 m freestyle relay final at the 2010 Commonwealth Games in New Delhi. They clocked 3 mins 27.14 secs to better their qualifying timing, but only finished sixth.

First National Championship

The first National Championship was held in Mumbai, Maharashtra, in 1945.

First 100 m freestyle – under 1 min.

- The first Indian swimmer to swim under 1 min. in the 100 m freestyle category was Basakha Singh, clocking 59.75 secs in 1971.
- The best performance is by Virdhawal Khade, who clocked 49.47 secs in October 2008. Among women, Shikha Tandon of Karnataka holds the record, with 58.91 secs in 2003.

First para swimmer to win bronze at the Commonwealth Games

Prasanta Karmakar was the first Indian para swimmer to claim a bronze medal in the 50 m freestyle in the S-9 category at the 2010 Commonwealth Games in New Delhi.

First to win a medal in the Asian Indoor Games

Shikha Tandon won a bronze in the 100 m backstroke event at the Asian Indoor Games in Bangkok, Thailand, in November 2005.

Virdhawal Khade

First 200 m freestyle – under 2 mins

Virdhawal Khade of Maharashtra, who clocked 1 min 49.86 secs, holds the record.

First visually impaired swimmer to win a gold

Kanchanmala Pande won gold in the 200 m medley event in the S-11 category on 8 December 2017 at the World Para-swimming Championship in Berlin.

First Indian para swimmer to win gold in the Para Asian games

Jadhav Suyash Narayan won the gold medal in men's 50 m butterfly S7 (6 –7) category at the Para Asian Games held at Jakarta, Indonesia, in 2018. He clocked 32.71 secs.

First Indian para swimmer to qualify for the Paralympic Games

Sharath Gayakwad was the first Indian para swimmer to qualify for the 2012 London Paralympic Games. He secured the ninth position. He also has a bronze at the 2010 Asian Para Games.

First swimmer to make Olympic 'A' cut – 100 m backstroke – men

Srihari Nataraj became the second Indian swimmer to qualify for the 2020 Tokyo

Olympics after FINA approved his 'A' standard qualification time in men's 100 m backstroke time trial at the Sette Colli Trophy in Rome. He clocked 53.77 secs in time trial.

First swimmer to make Olympic 'A' cut 200 m butterfly – men

On 26 June 2021, Sajan Prakash became the first-ever Indian swimmer to breach the 'A' Olympic qualification time by clocking 1:56:38 secs in the men's 200 m butterfly event at the Sette Colli Trophy in Rome. He made the Tokyo Games 'A' standard, set at 1:56:48 secs, by 0.10 seconds at the FINA-accredited Olympic qualifier. Earlier, he was the only Indian male swimmer who represented India in the 2016 Rio Olympics and was the only one to qualify with B timings for Rio.

Sajan Prakash

Participation in two consecutive Olympic Games

Sachin Nag represented India in the 1948 London Olympics and the 1952 Helsinki Olympics. Sajan Prakash represented India at Rio in 2016 and Tokyo Olympics (in 2021).

Participation in two consecutive Paralympics

Suyash Narayan Jadhav represented the country at Rio in 2016 and the 2020 Tokyo Paralympics (in 2021).

Men's 4x200m freestyle relay national record

Swimmers Aryan Nehra, Aneesh Gowda, Sajan Prakash, and Srihari Nataraj set the national record in the 4x200m freestyle relay, securing a gold medal at the Asian Group Aquatics Championships in the Philippines. The Indian quartet clocked an impressive 7:26.64, surpassing the previous best of 7:29.04 achieved by Aryan, Aneesh, Kushagra Rawat, and Tanish George Mathew at the Hangzhou Asian Games last year.

Women's 400m freestyle national record

Hashika Ramachandra set a new National Record in the Women's 400m Freestyle event at the 77th Senior National Aquatic Championships 2024 in Mangaluru, on September 10. The Karnataka swimmer broke the 13-year-old record of 4:25.76, previously held by Jharkhand's Richa Mishra, with an impressive time of 4:24.70.

TABLE TENNIS

GENERAL

Most National singles titles in a row

A. Sharath Kamal among men and Indu Puri among women have won most National singles titles in a row. Kamal won the title five times between 2006 and 2010. Indu was champion six times between 1980 and 1985.

Junior/Senior titles in a year

Four girls have won both titles in one calendar year – Rinku Gupta Acharya (Madhya Pradesh) in 1988; Mantu Ghosh (Bengal) in 1991; Kasturi Chakraborty (Bengal) in 1998 and Poulomi Ghatak (Bengal) in 1998-99.

No games conceded

Farokh Khodaiji was the first to achieve this feat, winning the men's singles title in 1967 in Guwahati, followed by Kaity Chargeman in the women's singles in Kolkata in 1970 and Chetan Baboor in the men's singles in 1999.

FIRST

First to be a medallist in five successive Commonwealth Games

A. Sharath Kamal is the only player to win Commonwealth Games medals in five successive editions – 2006, Melbourne; 2010, New Delhi; 2014, Glasgow; 2018, Gold Coast; and 2022, Birmingham.

First gold medallist in the Asian Championship

Gool Nasikwala won the singles, doubles and mixed doubles gold medals in the 1952 Asian Championship in Singapore.

First woman to play in two Olympics

Mouma Das became the first woman player to qualify for two Olympic Games (2004, Athens and 2016, Rio).

Youngest to qualify for the Olympic Games

Manika Batra became the youngest to play Olympic Games in Rio (2016) at the age of 21 years and two months.

First Commonwealth Games winner – men – singles

A. Sharath Kamal won the men's singles gold at Melbourne in 2006. He regained the medal in Birmingham in 2022.

First Commonwealth Games winner – women – singles

Manika Batra won the women's singles gold at Gold Coast in 2018.

First Commonwealth Games gold – men – team

The Indian men's team won the first Commonwealth Games table tennis gold medal in Melbourne in 2006.

First to regain Commonwealth Games gold – men – team

A. Sharath Kamal was the only member of the Indian team that won the men's team gold in 2006 and again in 2022.

First Commonwealth Games gold – women – team

India's women team won the first Commonwealth Games team gold medal in Gold Coast in 2018.

A. Sharath Kamal

First Commonwealth Games gold medal – mixed doubles

A. Sharath Kamal and Sreeja Akula won the mixed doubles gold in Birmingham in 2022.

First Commonwealth Games gold – men – doubles

A. Sharath Kamal and Subhajit Saha won

the men's doubles gold in New Delhi in October 2010.

First Commonwealth Championship team title – men
India won the Commonwealth men's team title in Kuala Lumpur in 2004.

First Commonwealth Games medal– women – doubles
Poulomi Ghatak and Mouma Das claimed the bronze in the women's doubles in New Delhi in October 2010.

First gold medallist in the Asian Championship
Gool Nasikwala won the singles, doubles and mixed doubles gold medals in the 1952 Asian Championship in Singapore.

First ITTF Pro-Tour title
A. Sharath Kamal won the Egypt Open to become the first Indian to win an ITTF Pro-Tour event in July 2010.

First Indian to be ranked world no. 1 in U-18
Manav Thakkar became the first Indian to be ranked world no. 1 in the boys' U-18 category in February 2018.

First medal in Asian juniors
India won the bronze medal in the 2006 Asian Junior Championship at Kitakyushu, Japan, by reaching the semi-finals of the girls' event.

First National champion
• M. Ayub won the men's singles title in Calcutta (now Kolkata) in 1938.
• P. Lima won the women's singles in Bombay (now Mumbai) in 1939.

First team medal in the World Junior Championship
The Indian boys' team, comprising Soumyajit Ghosh, Harmeet Desai and G. Sathiyan, won India's first ever bronze medal in the 2011 Junior Championship held in in Bahrain.

First title-triumph in the ITTF Junior tour
Harmeet Desai defeated Soumyajit Ghosh in the 2011 Austrian Open junior boys' final to become the first Indian to win a title on the ITTF (International Table Tennis Federation) Junior Tour.

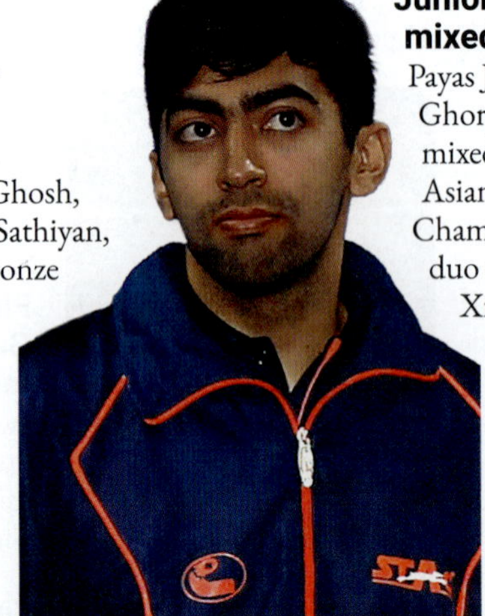
Harmeet Desai

Manika Batra

First professional
Chetan Baboor played as a professional with Enig Club in Kalmar, Sweden, from 1998.

First international league
The first edition of the Ultimate Table Tennis (UTT) was held in July 2017 in Chennai, New Delhi and Mumbai. Six teams took part the event and Falcons Club won the title by beating Shaze Challengers 14-9 in the final.

First Indian in the ITTF's Umpires and Referees Committee
Neelakanta Ganeshan was the first Indian inducted as a member of International Table Tennis Federation's Umpires and Referees Committee (URC) in June 2017.

First pair to win Asian Junior Championship in mixed doubles
Payas Jain and Yashaswini Ghorpade became India's first mixed doubles pair to win Asian Junior Table Tennis Championship in 2022 as the duo defeated China's Han Xinyuan and Qin Yuxuan in the final.

First to win Asian Cup medal — women
Manika Batra became the first Indian woman to win a medal at the Asian Cup in 2022 as she defeated Japan's World No. 6 Hina Hayata in the bronze medal match. She also became the first Indian woman paddler to reach the semis of the continent.

First pair to win WTT Contender title
Manika Batra and G Sathiyan became the first Indian pair to win WTT Contender title after beating Hungary's Nandor Ecseki and Dora Madarasz 3-1 (11-9, 9-11, 12-10, 11-6) in the final in Budapest in 2021.

MOST

Most Commonwealth Games medals won by an individual player in a single edition
• *Men*: A. Sharath Kamal won four medals in the 2022 Commonwealth Games in Birmingham, UK.
• *Women*: Manika Batra won four medals in the 2018 Commonwealth Games in Gold Coast.

Most medals from Commonwealth-level competitions
Mouma Das has claimed 19 medals in both team and individual events of the Commonwealth Games and Commonwealth championships between 2001 and 2018.

Most medals from the Commonwealth Games
Indians won eight medals, including three golds, in the 2018 edition of the Games in Gold Coast. India claimed gold medals in the men's team, women's team and women's singles (Manika Batra); silver medals in the men's doubles (A. Sharath Kamal and G. Sathiyan) and

the women's doubles (Manika Batra and Mouma Das); and bronze medals in the men's singles (A. Sharath Kamal), men's doubles (Harmeet Desai and Sanil Shetty) and mixed doubles (Manika Batra and G. Sathiyan).

Mouma Das

Most World Championship appearances

Mouma Das has played in 16 editions of World Championship since 1997.

Longest mixed doubles reign

Farokh Khodaiji and Kaity Khodaiji of Mumbai won the Susan Barna Cup five years in a row during 1967-71. They had earlier won the title in 1965.

Most state representations at the Nationals

N. Ravichandran represented five different units, including four states in the National Championships: Tamil Nadu, Punjab, Goa and Puducherry apart from the Central Revenue Sports Board at National- level tournaments.

Most appearances in the National Championship

S. Ramaswamy, who first played the Nationals in Allahabad in 1976, appeared in 30 successive National Championships until February 2006.

Most gold medals in the South Asian Federation (SAF) Games

A. Sharath Kamal won four gold medals – men's team event, men's singles, doubles and mixed doubles – in Colombo in August 2006.

Most team titles – men/women

Bombay won the team title for the Barna Bellack Cup 16 times. Maharashtra won the team title for the Corbillion Cup 14 times. The championship was first introduced in 1946 at Madras (now Chennai) where Bombay (now Mumbai) won the title and remained unbeaten till 1952.

Most National titles – singles

• Sharath Kamal has won 10 National singles titles in the men's singles section. Sharath broke Kamlesh Mehta's record of eight singles titles in 2019.

• Indu Puri won the ladies singles title eight times — 1972, 1975 and from 1979-84.

YOUNGEST

Youngest to win the National title

Mantu Ghosh was 16 when she won the title at Jaipur in 1990-91.

BEST

Best team performance in the World Championship

India finished 10th – its best finish till date – in the men's team events of the 1959 World Championship in Dortmund (Germany). In 2018, India produced its second-best performance and took the 13th place.

Best Indian performance (individual): beating three top 20 players in one event

A. Sharath Kamal defeated three players from the world's top 20 list in the Asian Cup held in Jaipur in March 2015. They included world no. 8 Chuang Chih-Yuan (Chinese Taipei), world no. 15 Gao Ning (Singapore) and world no. 16 Joo Sae Hyuk (Korea).

Best performances in the Commonwealth Games – doubles

A. Sharath Kamal holds the distinction of winning the men's doubles medal in four successive Commonwealth Games. He partnered Subhajit Saha to win the gold in the 2010 Commonwealth Games in New Delhi. In 2014, he joined hands with Anthony Amalraj to claim the silver in the men's doubles in Glasgow. In 2018, he and G. Sathiyan settled for a silver medal in Gold Coast and again in 2022 in Birmingham.

Best doubles performance in the Commonwealth Championship

Chetan Baboor and S. Raman won two successive Commonwealth Championship titles in 1997 and 2000.

Second division titles in World championship

Indian men and women won the second division titles in the 2016 World Championship in Kuala Lumpur on 5 March 2016. In the final, Indian men beat Brazil 3-2 and the women defeated Luxemburg 3-1.

TENNIS

GENERAL

Best women's singles result

Karman Kaur Thandi's singles title in the US $60,000 ITF women's tournament in Saguenay, Canada, with a 3-6, 6-4, 6-3 victory over Katherine Sebov (Canada) in the final in October 2022 was a big breakthrough for Indian women's tennis. It was the biggest singles title for an Indian woman since Sania Mirza won the $75,000 tournament in Dubai in 2010. The biggest title ever by an Indian woman was Mirza winning the US $140,000 WTA event in Hyderabad in 2005. The 24-year-old Karman became no. 1 in India with a rank of 217.

Karman Kaur Thandi

Oldest World No. 1 in tennis – men

At 43 years and 331 days, Rohan Bopanna became the oldest world No. 1 in men's tennis. He joined an elite group of Indian tennis players, including Leander Paes, Mahesh Bhupathi, and Sania Mirza, who have reached the top of the tennis rankings during their careers.

BILLIE JEAN KING (FEDERATION) CUP

First world play-offs qualifying team

Earlier known as the Fed Cup, the Billie Jean King Cup is a team event for women's tennis players who represent their country in singles and doubles matches. The Indian Fed Cup team created history by progressing to the play-offs for the first time ever in March 2020, defeating Indonesia in the Asia–Oceania Group I event in Dubai, and finishing second behind China. They lost the world group play-off tie against Latvia. The team comprised Ankita Raina, Rutuja Bhosale, Zeel Desai, Karman Kaur Thandi and Sania Mirza.

ASIAN GAMES

First gold – men – doubles

Leander Paes and Gaurav Natekar won the gold medal in the Hiroshima Asian Games, held in 1994 in Japan – making this the country's first doubles gold medal at the Asian Games. They won by defeating the South Korean duo of Chang Euijong and Kim Chi-wan.

First gold medallist – doubles – mixed

India got its first mixed doubles gold at the Asian Games when the team, with Leander Paes and Sania Mirza, won the gold in the Doha Asian Games in Qatar in 2006. They defeated the Japanese pair of Satoshi Iwabuchi and Akiko Morigami 7–5, 5–7, 6–2.

First singles gold

Somdev Devvarman won the gold medal at the 2010 Guangzhou Asiad in China, defeating Denis Istomin of Uzbekistan 6–1, 6–2.

Somdev Devvarman

DAVIS CUP

Most successful player – doubles

Leander Paes became the most successful doubles player in the history of the Davis Cup with a record 45th victory in March 2020, when he and his partner Rohan Bopanna won India's Davis Cup match against Croatia in the do-or-die round of the World Group Qualifiers.

First appearance

India played in the Davis Cup for the first time in 1921 against France in Paris and won 4–1. The Indian team comprised S.M. Jacob, Mohammed Sleem, A.A. Fyzee and L.S. Dean.

Best Davis Cup record in Asia

Though India has not yet won the Davis Cup, they have managed to reach the finals three times (in 1966, 1974 and 1987). Japan is the only other Asian nation to have figured in the Davis Cup finals (once in 1921).

Most appearances

Leander Paes holds the record of playing the most Davis Cup matches – 128 in 58 ties (as of March 2020). His win/loss records are 48/22 in singles and 45/13 in doubles.

GRAND SLAM TOURNAMENTS

WIMBLEDON

First to play at Wimbledon

Sardar Nihal Singh was the first Indian to play at Wimbledon in 1908. He lost in the first round to Briton Herbert Wilson Fox, who beat him 11–9, 6–2, 6–4.

First junior boys' title

Ramanathan Krishnan won the first junior boy's Wimbledon title in 1954, defeating Ashley Cooper of Australia 6–2, 7–5. Twenty-five years later, Ramanathan's son Ramesh Krishnan won the same title in 1979, creating a unique father-and-son record. Both were recipients of the Padma Shri in 1962 and 1998 respectively. Ramanathan Krishnan was also awarded the Padma Bhushan in 1967.

Leander Paes

First seeded at Wimbledon

Dilip Bose was the first seeded Indian player, at no. 15, in Wimbledon singles in 1950. He was a product of the Calcutta South Club (now in Kolkata, West Bengal), one of Asia's oldest tennis clubs.

First junior girls' title – doubles

Sania Mirza and her Russian partner Alisa Kleybanova won the junior girls' doubles title in 2003.

First men's title – doubles

The dominant Indian tennis pair of

Leander Paes and Mahesh Bhupathi

First title – doubles – mixed
Mahesh Bhupathi and his Japanese partner Rika Hiraki won the French Open title in 1997, defeating the American team of Lisa Raymond and Patrick Galbraith 6–4, 6–1. With this Bhupathi became the first Indian to win a Senior Grand Slam title.

Leander Paes and Mahesh Bhupathi, then popularly known as Lee–Hesh, won India's first men's doubles title at Wimbledon in 1999, defeating Paul Haarhuis (the Netherlands) and Jared Palmer (USA) 6–7, 6–3, 6–4, 7–6.

First title – doubles – mixed

Leander Paes was the first Indian to win a mixed doubles title when he won it with Lisa Raymond (USA) in 1999. They defeated the pair of Anna Kournikova (Russia) and Jonas Björkman (Sweden) 6–4, 3–6, 6–3. Paes was awarded the Padma Shri in 2001.

First Indian woman at Wimbledon

Jenny Sandison was the first woman to represent India in tennis at Wimbledon, way back in 1929. However, she lost in the first round to French player Simone Barbier 6-2, 6-3.

FRENCH OPEN

First all-Indian title – mixed doubles

Mahesh Bhupathi and Sania Mirza won India's first ever all-Indian mixed doubles title in 2012, defeating Klaudia Jans-Ignacik (Poland) and Santiago González (Mexico) 7–6 (7-3), 6–1.

First all-Indian men's title – doubles

Leander Paes and Mahesh Bhupathi won India's first men's doubles title in 1999. The pair defeated Goran Ivanisevic (Croatia) and Jeff Tarango (USA) 6–2, 7–5.

First and only junior champion

Ramesh Krishnan won the juniors title in 1979, the first and only Indian to achieve this feat, and was ranked the world's no. 1 junior player. He became India's Davis Cup captain in 2007.

US OPEN

First title – doubles – women

Sania Mirza was the first Indian to win a women's doubles title in 2015 at the US Open in New York, with Swiss player Martina Hingis. The pair defeated Casey Dellacqua (Australia) and Yaroslava Shvedova (Kazakhstan) 6–3, 6–3.

First title – doubles

Mahesh Bhupathi and his partner Max Mirnyi of Belarus won the US Open doubles title in 2002, defeating the Czech pair of Jiri Novak and Radek Stepanek 6–3, 3–6, 6–4.

First title – doubles – mixed

Mahesh Bhupathi, with his Japanese partner Ai Sugiyama, won the mixed doubles US Open title in 1999, the first Indian to win a mixed doubles title here. The pair defeated Kimberly Po and Donald Johnson of the USA 6–4, 6–4.

First and only junior boys' title

Leander Paes is the first and only Indian to win the junior boy's crown at the US Open in 1991. He beat Karim Alami (Morocco).

AUSTRALIAN OPEN

First men's title – doubles

Leander Paes became the first Indian to win a men's doubles title at the Australian Open, along with Radek Stepanek (Czech Republic) in 2012. They defeated Bob Bryan and Mike Bryan of the USA 7–6 (7–1), 6–2.

First title – doubles – mixed

Leander Paes, with Martina Navratilova of the USA, won the mixed doubles title in 2003, becoming the first Indian to

Sania Mirza

do so. They defeated Eleni Daniilidou (Greece) and Todd Woodbridge (Australia) 6–4, 7–5.

First all-Indian title – doubles – mixed

Mahesh Bhupathi and Sania Mirza won India's first all-Indian mixed doubles Australian Open title in 2009, defeating the pair of Nathalie Dechy (France) and Andy Ram (Israel) 6–3, 6–1.

Yuki Bhambri

First junior boys' champion

Yuki Bhambri defeated Alexandros-Ferdinandos Georgoudas of Greece 6–3, 6– to win the Junior Boys' Championship in 2009.

ATP TOUR

First Indian to win 2 ATP Challengers singles titles in Europe

Sumit Nagal is the first Indian to win two ATP Challengers titles in Europe after he won the Tampere Open title in Finland in July 2023. He surpasses Somdev Devvarman, Rohan Bopanna and Harsh Mankad, who have won a title each. It was also his fourth ATP title overall and second of the season.

World's oldest player to win ATP Masters title — doubles

Rohan Bopanna at 43 became the oldest tennis player to win the ATP Masters 1000 title after he and Mathew Ebden won the Indian Wells in March 2023. Bopanna surpassed the record of Canada's Daniel Nestor, who won the Cincinnati Masters doubles title in 2015 at the age of 42.

Rohan Bopanna

First Indian to win ATP Challenger on European clay

Sumit Nagal became the first Indian to win ATP Challenger on European clay after winning the ATP Rome Challenger in April 2023. He defeated Jasper De Jong in the final 6-3, 6-2.

NATIONALS

First Nationals – grass court

The first tennis Nationals were held in 1946 at the Calcutta South Club lawns in Calcutta (now Kolkata), West Bengal. Sumant Misra beat Manmohan Lal in the final, becoming the first national champion. Khanum Singh (née Haji) was the first women's national champion.

Most Nationals titles

Ramanathan Krishnan won eight grass-court titles in 1953, 1956, 1958 to 1960 and 1962 to 1964.

WEIGHTLIFTING

First medals in the World Championships

Kunjarani Devi from Manipur bagged three silvers at Manchester, UK, in 1989 in India's debut performance at the World Championships. The Indian squad won seven medals in all at the event. Shyamala Shetty and Chhaya Adak won silver medals for individual lifts, while Lalita Polley claimed two bronze medals.

First gold in the Commonwealth Games – men

E. Karunakaran won gold in the flyweight class in the 1978 Edmonton Games in Canada.

First Junior weightlifting gold

Harshada Sharad Garud became the first Indian boy or girl to win a World Junior Weightlifting Championship by lifting a total of 153 kg (clean and jerk 83 kg + snatch 70 kg)

First Olympic-qualifying gold

Saikhom Mirabai Chanu won the gold medal in the women's 49 kg category at the EGAT Cup International Weightlifting Championship, an Olympic qualifying event in Chiang Mai, Thailand, on 7 February 2019. She lifted 82 kg in snatch and 110 kg in clean and jerk to total 192 kg, and took gold on her return to international competition after a nine-month lay-off due to an injury. She had won the gold medal on her last appearance in 2018 at the Gold Coast Commonwealth Games in Australia.

Top: Saikhom Mirabai Chanu; *Left*: Karnam Malleswari

First back-to-back gold medals

Khumukcham Sanjita Chanu made history for the second time when she bagged the gold medal in the women's 53 kg weightlifting event at the 2018 Commonwealth Games at Gold Coast, Australia. Her first gold was at the 2014 Commonwealth Games in the 48 kg category.

First silver medal at the Olympic Games

Saikhom Mirabai Chanu scripted a remarkable performance by winning a silver in the 2020 Olympic Games held in Tokyo, Japan, on day one. With an 87 kg lift in snatch and a 115 kg lift in the clean and jerk section, Chanu finished with a total of 202 kg.

First Asian Games medals – women

Women's weightlifting was introduced in the 1990 Beijing Asian Games in China, where India won two silvers: Bharati Singh (82 kg category) and Jyotsna Dutta (+82 kg); and two bronzes: Kunjarani Devi (44 kg) and Chhaya Adak (52 kg).

First Asian Games medal

Kamineni Eswara Rao won the silver in the 90 kg category in the 1951 Asian Games held in New Delhi. He was also adjudged the 'Strongest Man of India' at the 1954 Senior Nationals.

First gold medal at the Youth Olympic Games

Jeremy Lalrinnunga became the first Indian to win a gold medal at the Youth Olympics Games 2018 held in Buenos Aires, Argentina.

Jeremy Lalrinnunga

Clean and jerk at the Asian Weightlifting Championships

Saikhom Mirabai Chanu set a new world record in the women's 49 kg clean and jerk with a lift of 119 kg on 17 April 2022 at the Asian Weightlifting Championships in Tashkent, Uzbekistan.

Most medals in the Commonwealth Games– women

Yumnam Renu Bala Chanu has won two golds in the Commonwealth Games. Her first came in the women's 58 kg category in Melbourne in 2006. She repeated this in the 2010 Delhi Commonwealth Games in the same category.

Best performance at an Asian meet

India's weightlifters bagged five gold medals and a bronze at Busan, South Korea, in July 1995. Karnam Malleswari won three gold medals, and Kunjarani Devi claimed two gold medals and the overall title. Arun Murugesan won a bronze in snatch in the 54 kg category for men.

Most medals in world and Asian meets

Kunjarani Devi, who holds the record for the highest number of world and Asian meet medals, won 55 medals overall – 21 in six World Championships and the remaining in the Asian Games, and the Asian and Commonwealth Championships.

Yumnam Renu Bala Chanu

Most national titles

Balbir Singh Bhatia won 15 national and all-India titles.

Most medals in the Commonwealth Games

India won five gold, two silver and two bronze medals at the 2018 Gold Coast Commonwealth Games, the most at the Commonwealth Games in weightlifting.

Most gold medals in World Championships

Karnam Malleswari won the gold in the World Championships twice – in 1994 (Istanbul, Turkey) and 1995 (Guangzhou, China).

Oldest national champion

Alok Nath Ghosh won the National Championship title in 1974 at 40 years. He had won the first national title in 1958 in Cuttack, Odisha. His first title was for Services and the last one was for the Railways.

Youngest Commonwealth Games medal winner

Eighteen-year-old Deepak Lather (69 kg) from Haryana became the youngest Indian weightlifter to win a medal at the 2018 Commonwealth Games in Glasgow, UK, by clinching a bronze medal.

WRESTLING

First woman at the Olympics
Geeta Phogat from Bhiwani, Haryana, was the first Indian woman wrestler to compete at the Olympics during the 2012 London Games. However, she did not advance to the quarter-finals.

First at the Olympics
U. Zaw Weik (75 kg), the first to represent India at the Olympics, was placed 15th in the 1936 Olympics in Berlin, Germany.

First Olympics medal – men
Khashaba Dadasaheb Jadhav from Satara, Maharashtra, won a bronze in the bantam weight category (57 kg) in the 1952 Helsinki Olympics.

First winner of both Olympic and World Championship medals
Sushil Kumar is the first Indian to win medals at both the Olympics and the World Championships. He won a bronze at the 2008 Beijing Olympics in the 66 kg freestyle category and a silver medal in the same category at the 2012 London Olympics. He also won a gold in the same category at the Moscow World Championship in Russia in 2010.

First Olympic medal – women
Sakshi Malik created history as the first Indian woman to win an Olympic medal, a bronze, for wrestling, in the women's freestyle 58 kg category in the Rio Olympics in Brazil on 17 August 2016.

First medal at the World Championship – men
India's first medal in the World Championship was a bronze in the freestyle category (67 kg) won by Udey Chand from Hisar, Haryana, in the 1961 World Championships at Yokohama, Japan. He participated in three Olympics: at Rome, Italy, in 1960; at Tokyo, Japan, in 1964; and at Mexico City, Mexico, in 1968.

First Indian woman to win a silver medal at the World Championship
Anshu Malik (57 kg) became the first Indian female wrestler to win a silver medal at the 2021 World Championship in Oslo.

First woman triple winner – World Championships, Asian Games and Commonwealth Games
Vinesh Phogat became the first Indian woman to win medals at the World Championships, Asian Games and Commonwealth Games. While she won bronze at the 2019 World Championships in the 53 kg freestyle and a bronze at the 2014 Incheon Asian Games in the 48 kg category, she was also the first Indian woman to win a gold medal in the 2018 Asian Games in Jakarta and Palembang, Indonesia, in the 50 kg category. She won three consecutive Commonwealth crowns at Glasgow in 2014, Gold Coast in 2018 and Birmingham in 2022.

Vinesh Phogat

First medal at the World Championships – women
Alka Tomar of the Noida College of Physical Education won a bronze in the women's 59 kg class at the Senior World Wrestling Championship in Guangzhou, China, during September–October 2006. She was the first Indian woman wrestler to win a World Championship medal after a gap of 39 years.

First medal in the Asian Games
Vinesh Phogat, competing in the 50 kg freestyle category, bagged India its first gold medal in wrestling in the Asian Games in 2018 in Jakarta, Indonesia. She is the first Indian woman to win a gold medal in wrestling and to win back-to back Asian Games medals, having won a bronze in 48 kg in Incheon, South Korea, in 2014.

First World Championship gold medallist
Sushil Kumar from Delhi was the first Indian to win a World Championship gold medal in the 66 kg freestyle category in Moscow, Russia, in 2010.

First medal in the Commonwealth Games
- Rashid Anwar won a bronze medal at the 1934 Commonwealth Games held in London, UK, in the 74 kg category. This was the country's first medal won in the Commonwealth Games.

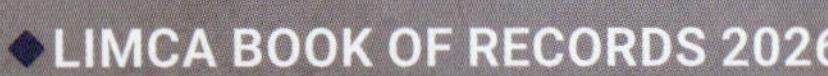

• Lila Ram won the first gold medal in the 1958 Games at Cardiff, Wales, in the heavyweight (100 kg) category.

First and only Indian woman wrestler to win the Laureus World Sports Award

Vinesh Phogat is the first and only Indian wrestler to be awarded the Laureus World Sports Award 2019 in the comeback-of-the-year category. Phogat not only returned from her injury but also won the gold medal in both the 2018 Commonwealth Games at Gold Coast, Australia, and the 2018 Asian Games in Jakarta and Palembang, Indonesia.

First to win gold in U-20 World Championships – women

Antim Panghal became the first to win gold in the U-20 World Championships on 10 September 2022 in Sofia, Bulgaria.

First Asian Games gold – men

Gold medals were won by Maruti Mane in 90 kg freestyle, Malwa Singh in 52 kg Greco Roman and Ganpat Andalkar in 100 kg Greco-Roman section at the 1962 Asian Games in Jakarta, Indonesia.

First Asian Championships gold medal – women

Navjot Kaur from Punjab became the first Indian woman to win the gold at the Senior Asian Wrestling Championships on 2 March 2018 at Bishkek, Kyrgyzstan. She beat Japan's Miya Imai 9–1 to win in the women's 65 kg category.

First Coach of the Year award

Late Yashvir Singh was the first Indian coach to be recognized as the Coach of the Year in 2010 by the Federation Internationale des Luttes Associées (FILA), the then apex body that governed wrestling.

First Junior World Champion

• The first gold medallists at the Junior World Championship were Ramesh Kumar (69 kg) and Palwinder Singh Cheema (130 kg) in 2001.

• Deepak Punia became India's junior world champion after 18 years, winning the gold medal at Tallinn, Estonia, on 14 August 2019. He defeated Russia's Alik Shebzukov in the 86 kg men's freestyle category.

Bajrang Punia

First gold in Greco-Roman wrestling

• Pappu Yadav was the first grappler to win a gold medal in the 48 kg Greco-Roman category at the 1993 Asian Wrestling Championships held in Ulaanbaatar, Mongolia.

• On 19 February 2020, Sunil Kumar (87 kg) won a gold in Greco-Roman wrestling in the Asian Championships, which came 27 years after the first gold in 1993.

First Junior Wrestler of the Year award

Deepak Punia (86 kg freestyle) became the first Indian wrestler to receive the Junior Wrestler of the Year title in 2019 from the UWW.

First gold medal in the Asian Games

The first Indian to win a gold medal in the Asian Games was Kartar Singh in the 1986 Seoul Asiad in South Korea in the 100 kg category.

Ranked as world no. 1

In March 2021, the UWW announced Bajrang Punia (65 kg) and Vinesh Phogat (53 kg) as top-ranked wrestlers.

Best performance in the Asian Championship

India won a record haul of 20 medals (five gold, six silver and nine bronze) across formats and genders in the 2020 Asian Championships.

Best performance at the Commonwealth Games – men

At the Commonwealth Games in 2010 in Delhi, the Indian men's team won seven gold, three silver and three bronze medals in freestyle and the Greco-Roman style.

Best performance in the Greco-Roman event of the Asian Championships

India's best performance in the Greco-Roman category was at the 2020 Asian Championships in New Delhi where Indian grapplers won one gold and four bronze medals.

Most consecutive Commonwealth Games titles – women

Vinesh Phogat became the first to win three consecutive Commonwealth Games crowns at Glasgow, UK, in 2014; Gold Coast Australia in 2018; and Birmingham, UK, in 2022.

Most medals in the Asian Championship

Between 2013 and 2022, Bajrang Punia

won a record eight medals in the 60 kg to 65 kg categories.

Most medals in the Commonwealth Championships

The Indian contingent, with 42 wrestlers, bagged 40 medals – 15 gold, 20 silver and five bronze – in the 2011 Commonwealth Championships in Melbourne, Australia.

Best performance at the World Championship

India has a record haul of five medals at the 2019 World Championship held at Nur-Sultan, Kazakhstan. Deepak Punia won a silver in the 86 kg category. Bronze medals were won by Bajrang Punia (65 kg), Rahul Aware (61 kg), Ravi Dahiya (61 kg) and Vinesh Phogat (women, 53 kg).

Deepak Punia

Best performance in the Commonwealth Games – women

Women's wrestling was introduced in the 2010 Delhi Commonwealth Games, where India bagged three gold medals, two silver medals and one bronze medal in freestyle. Geeta Phogat (55 kg), Alka Tomar (59 kg) and Anita Sheoran (67 kg) won gold medals. The silver medals were won by Nirmala Devi (48 kg) and Babita Phogat (51 kg). Suman Kundu (63 kg) won the bronze medal.

Anita Sheoran

Sushil Kumar

Most medals in the Asian Games – men

Kartar Singh won the gold at Bangkok, Thailand, in 1978, a silver in 1982 at Delhi and another gold at the 1986 Seoul Asian Games in South Korea. He competed in the 90 kg category in 1978 and 1982, and in 100 kg in 1986 (all in freestyle).

Most individual medals in the Commonwealth Championships – men

Sushil Kumar won the title five times between 2003 and 2017. He won the gold medal in 2003 (London, UK), 2005 (Cape Town, South Africa), 2007 (London, UK), 2009 (Jalandhar, India) and 2017 (Johannesburg, South Africa).

Most individual medals in the World Championship

Bajrang Punia won the World Championship medal three times between 2013 and 2019. He won the bronze medal in the 60 kg category in 2013, a silver in the 65 kg category in 2018 and a bronze in 2019.

Most gold medals in the Asian Championship

Sushil Kumar won the title in 2003, 2008 and 2010. Thereafter Ravi Kumar Dahiya won triple gold in Asian Championship titles in 2020, 2021 and 2022.

Most gold medals in the Commonwealth Games – men

Sushil Kumar of the Indian Raiways and an alumnus of the Noida College of Physical Education, Noida, Uttar Pradesh, won India's first ever men's triple gold in the Commonwealth Games (2010, Delhi; 2014, Glasgow, UK; and 2018, Gold Coast, Australia).

Most medals at the Asian Girls Championship (U-15)

Indian girl wrestlers won seven medals in the Asian Girls Championships (U-15) in November 2018 in Fujimi, Japan. The gold medallists were: Pooja Rani (33 kg), Komal (36 Kg) and Sweety (43 kg). Silver medals were won by: Pinki (39 kg), Antim Panghal (46 kg) and Bhagyashreee Fand (58 kg). Pratibha Janghu (54 kg) won the bronze.

Youngest champion in the Asian Games

Malwa Singh won the gold medal in the Greco-Roman style in the light flyweight category at the 1962 Asian Games in Jakarta, Indonesia, at the age of 14 years, thus creating history by becoming the youngest wrestling champion from India.

Youngest gold medallist at the Commonwealth Games

Ved Prakash was 14 years old when he won the gold medal in the light flyweight class at the 1970 Commonwealth Games in Edinburgh, UK.

SYMBOLS

A

B

C

D

E

F

G

H

I

J

K

L

M

N

O

P

Q

R

S

T

U

V

W

Y

Z

NOTE: CCA-SA refers to the Creative Commons Attribution-Share Alike Wikimedia Commons/International Wikimedia Commons licences; PD: Public Domain: (All public domain photographs have been sourced from: Wikimedia Commons/Public Domain); PIB: Press Information Bureau; GODL: Government Open Data Licence – India; GoI: Government of India.

PRELIMS 6–11

Title page: Shaswat Nimesh, CC BY-SA 4.0 <https://creativecommons.org/licenses/by-sa/4.0>, via Wikimedia Commons; **6–11**: **Contents**: images have been credited under the respective chapters below;

HUMAN STORY 12–45

Images are by courtesy of the record holders.
12–13: **Opener pics, from left to right**: Tree planting: Photo by Anna Shvets: https://www.pexels.com/photo/hands-holding-green-plants-5029853/; Coins: Photo by Pratikxox: https://www.pexels.com/photo/heap-of-golden-coins-3222685/; Push-ups: Photo by cottonbro studio: https://www.pexels.com/photo/woman-in-black-and-white-tank-top-and-black-shorts-lying-on-brown-wooden-floor-4753996/; Matchboxes: Photo by Firdevs Birol: https://www.pexels.com/photo/close-up-photo-of-vintage-matchboxes-19442209/; **18–19**: Yuganov Konstantin/Shutterstock.com; **20**: burpees and crunches: Lio putra/Shutterstock.com; **21**: squats: ArtMaris/Shutterstock.com; **22**: **background**: Periodic Table: Shutterstock.com; **35**: **background**: Lata Mangeshkar: Ninety_illustrator/Shutterstock.com; **37**: Hyderabadi meal: PI/Shutterstock.com; Awadhi cuisine: Fanfo/Shutterstock.com;

STRUCTURES 46–75

Opener pic, 46–47: PradeepGaurs/Shutterstock.com; **48–49**: **background**: Iron pillar: Dr Ajay Kumar Singh/Shutterstock.com; **inset**: Kumrahar: Manoj nav (talk)/PD (https://commons.wikimedia.org/wiki/File:Mauryan_Hall_pillar.jpg); **50**: **top**: Sanchi Stupa: Creativecouplestudio/Shutterstock.com; **bottom**: Lothal: DARSHAN KUMAR/Shutterstock.com; **51**: Stepwell: OPIS Zagreb/Shutterstock.com; **52**: Ramanathaswamy Temple CRS PHOTO/Shutterstock.com; **53**: Sultan Garhi Tomb: PRABHAS ROY/Shutterstock.com; **54–55**: Chandeliers: ImagesofIndia/Shutterstock.com; **56**: **top**: Mundeshwari Devi Temple: Lakshya/CCA-SA 3.0 Unreported licence (https://en.wikipedia.org/wiki/File:Maa_Mundeshwari_Devi.jpg); **bottom**: Bairat temple: Raonaresh/CCA-SA 4.0 International licence (https://commons.wikimedia.org/wiki/File:Buddhist_Temple_Viratnagar.jpg); **57**: **top**: Lotus Temple: Media_works/Shutterstock.com; **bottom**: Kapilavastu remains: AnilD/Shutterstock.com; **58**: Largest mosque: Sahil Ghosh/Shutterstock.com; **59**: **top**: shaking minarets: saiko3p/Shutterstock.com; **bottom**: Global Vipassana Pagoda: saiko3p/Shutterstock.com; **60–61**: Se Cathedral at Old Goa: SAHAS2015/Shutterstock.com; **62**: Brihadeeswarar Temple: 2A Stock/Shutterstock.com; **63**: Gommateshwara statue: RAMESH R NAIR/Shutterstock.com; **64**: Tallest Shiva linga: S KUMAR KARAMANA/Shutterstock.com; **65**: **top**: largest bust: Srinivasan.Clicks/Shutterstock.com; **bottom**: Raja Bhoj temple: akimov konstantin/Shutterstock.com; **66–67**: **top left**: Illustration by Surojit Bhattacharya/ © Hachette India; **bottom left**: Col Chewang Rinchen bridge: Press Information Bureau; **top right**: Atal Setu: Bhatakta Manav/Shutterstock.com; **bottom centre**: Chenab Bridge: Lovely Dhiman/Shutterctock.com; **68–69**: **top**: Indira Gandhi Canal: Maninder.dsw/Shutterstock.com; **bottom**: Grand Anicut Dam: Venkatesa Perumal/Shutterstock.com; **70**: **top**: Shivanasamudram Water Falls: Tito George/PD (https://commons.wikimedia.org/wiki/File:Shivanasamudram.JPG); **bottom**: Highest lighthouse: eclicks_by_bunny/ CCA-SA 4.0 (Internaitonal licence (https://commons.wikimedia.org/wiki/File:Vizag_seaport_from_Dolphin_nose_hill_lighthouse.jpg); **73**: Rajgir ropeway: Photo Dharma from Penang, Malaysia/CCA 2.0 Generic licence(https://commons.wikimedia.org/wiki/File:Rajgir_-_034_Chair_Lift_%289244970406%29.jpg); **74–75**: **left**: Reinforced earth structure: by courtesy of record holders; **right**: Underground aquarium: Jim W Kasom/Shutterstock.com;

AGRICULTURE 76–93

Opener pic, 76–77: Parikh Mahendra N/Shutterstock.com; **78**: **top**: Madhu Dandavate: Government of India, GODL-India <https://data.gov.in/sites/default/files/Gazette_Notification_OGDL.pdf>, via Wikimedia Commons; **top right**: Sikkim Organic State: SHEE HENG CHONG/Shutterstock.com; **bottom**: Mango Meadows: AjayThomas/Shutterstock.com; **inset**: N.K. Kurian: Retheeshcochin, CC0, via Wikimedia Commons; **79**: **top**: Archaeological Survey of India (ASI): balajisrinivasan/Shutterstock.com; **middle**: Sir George Campbell: Bourne & Shepherd, Public domain, via Wikimedia Commons; **bottom**: Mohenjo-daro: shozib ali brohi/Shutterstock.com; **inset**: Daya Ram Sahni: The Modern Review. May 1939, Public domain, via Wikimedia Commons; **80**: **top left**: William Carrey: Materialscientist, Public domain, via Wikimedia Commons; **top right**: Central Tuber Crops Research Institute: Rajeev Ramakrishnan, CC BY-SA 4.0 <https://creativecommons.org/licenses/by-sa/4.0>, via Wikimedia Commons; **middle**: Sir Bryce C. Burt: Indian Farming 4(2):66-67., Public domain, via Wikimedia Commons **bottom**: G.B. Pant College of Agriculture: Pranjalyadava, CC BY-SA 4.0 <https://creativecommons.org/licenses/by-sa/4.0>, via Wikimedia Commons; **81**: **top**: Groundwater irrigation system: Shutterstok.com; **bottom left**: Dr BP Pal: India Post, Government of India, GODL-India <https://data.gov.in/sites/default/files/Gazette_Notification_OGDL.pdf>, via Wikimedia Commons; **bottom right**: Dr M.S. Swaminathan: Biswarup Ganguly, CC BY 3.0 <https://creativecommons.org/licenses/by/3.0>, via Wikimedia Commons; **82–83**: **background**: FabrikaSimf/Shutterstock.com; **82**: **inset**: Korakundah Tea Estate: L. Shyamal, CC BY-SA 3.0 <https://creativecommons.org/licenses/by-sa/3.0>, via Wikimedia Commons; **83**: **top right**: Tocklai Tea Research Station: Official anahita, CC BY 3.0 <https://creativecommons.org/licenses/by/3.0>, via Wikimedia Commons; **bottom**: Lord William Bentinck: Based on painting by Sir T. Lawrence (1769 – 1s830), Public domain, via Wikimedia Commons; **84**: **top left**: Dr Rattan Lal: U.S. Department of AgricultureLance Cheung/Multimedia PhotoJournalist, Public domain, via Wikimedia Commons; **top right**: Bt cotton crop: Shutterstock.com; **bottom**: basmati rice: Nataly Studio/Shutterstock.com; **85**: **top**: ash gourd: by courtesy of the record holder; **from middle to bottom**: Mulberry silk: Beniebee6/Shutterstock.com; Oak tussore silk: Sergei Mishchenko/

IMAGE COPYRIGHT INFORMATION

Shutterstock.com; Tropical tussore silk: UP15India/Shutterstock.com; Eri silk: Dr. Nisaphi L. Lyndem/Shutterstock.com; Muga silk: Shutterstock.com; **bottom left**: Bhut jolokia: Shutterstock.com; **88**: **top**: Central Plantation Crops Research Institute (CPCRI): Pmecell, CC BY-SA 4.0 <https://creativecommons.org/licenses/by-sa/4.0>, via Wikimedia Commons; **middle right**: coconut plantation: Shutterstock.com; **middle left**: Indian mangoes: Shutterstock.com; **bottom**: animal husbandry: Shuttertsock.com; **89**: **top**: Indian spices: Dmitr1ch/Shutterstock.com; **bottom**: Dr Alfred Lingard: A description of the Imperial Bacteriological Laboratory, Muktesar and (1940). "Supplement. Imperial Veterinary Research Institute 1890-1940. Golden Jubilee". Indian Farming 1 (11) (COPYRIGHT EXPIRED); **90**: **top left**: Amul: Prolix, Public domain, via Wikimedia Commons; **top right**: Dr Verghese Kurien: Ministry of Railways (GODL-India), GODL-India <https://data.gov.in/sites/default/files/Gazette_Notification_OGDL.pdf>, via Wikimedia Commons; **bottom**: Mathigiri Cattle Farm and District Livestock Centre: Public Information Bureau (PIB); **91**: **middle**: Suguna Foods: Sugunafoods, CC BY-SA 4.0 <https://creativecommons.org/licenses/by-sa/4.0>, via Wikimedia Commons; **bottom**: CMFRI building: Courtesy of Central Marine Fisheries Research Institute (CMFRI), Kochi, Kerala; **92**: **top**: Indian white shrimp: Shutterstock.com; **bottom**: DDT molecule: Shutterstock.com; **93**: **top**: neem leaves and fruit: Anwarul Kabir Photo/Shutterstock.com; **middle**: ladybird beetle: Shutterstock.com; **bottom**: Mahindra tractor: AB-lifepct/Shutterstock.com;

EDUCATION 94–117

Opener pic, 94–95: CatherineLProd/Shutterstock.com; **96**: **clockwise**: Abul Kalam Azad: CCA-SA 3.0 Unported/Jacek Halicki/National Repository of Open Educational Resources/ https://commons.wikimedia.org/wiki/File:Maulana_Abul_Kalam_Azad.jpg; Calcutta Deaf and Dumb School: by courtesy of Sourish Sarkar; St George's School, Chennai: Ramkye, CC BY-SA 4.0 <https://creativecommons.org/licenses/by-sa/4.0>, via Wikimedia Commons; Mizoram Fully Literate State: PIB; **97**: **top**: Children of Andh Vidyalaya: Pranay Chandra Singh/Shutterstock.com; **bottom**: Aurobindo International Centre: Nvvchar, CC BY-SA 3.0 <https://creativecommons.org/licenses/by-sa/3.0>, via Wikimedia Commons; **98–99**: **background**: Old Senate House, University of Madras: PhotopankPL/Shutterstock.com; **98**: **inset**: Sampuranand Sanskrit Vishwavidyalaya: AnilD/Shutterstock.com; **99**: **inset**: Pariksha Pe Charcha: Government of India, GODL-India <https://data.gov.in/sites/default/files/Gazette_Notification_OGDL.pdf>, via Wikimedia Commons; **100**: **top**: Corridor of Presidency University: PD/Taritwan Pal; **bottom**: Sir J.J. School of Art: Satish Parashar/Shutterstock.com; **101**: **clockwise**: University of Mumbai: Bernard Gagnon, CC BY-SA 3.0 <https://creativecommons.org/licenses/by-sa/3.0>, via Wikimedia Commons; Cheena Bhavana: Bodhisattwa, CC BY-SA 4.0 <https://creativecommons.org/licenses/by-sa/4.0>, via Wikimedia Commons; Jawaharlal Nehru University: गंगा सहाय मीणा, CC BY-SA 3.0 <https://creativecommons.org/licenses/by-sa/3.0>, via Wikimedia Commons; Ramakrishna Mission Institute: Biswarup Ganguly, CC BY-SA 3.0 <https://creativecommons.org/licenses/by-sa/3.0>, via Wikimedia Commons; Visva-Bharati University: Biswarup Ganguly, CC BY 3.0 <https://creativecommons.org/licenses/by/3.0>, via Wikimedia Commons; **102–103**: **background**: Mysore University: arun sambhu mishra/Shutterstock.com; **102**: **inset**: Banaras Hindu University: arun sambhu mishra/Shutterstock.com; **103**: **insets**: **top**: Patna University: AnilD/Shutterstock.com; **middle**: Aligarh University: Hhkhan at English Wikipedia, CC BY-SA 3.0 <https://creativecommons.org/licenses/by-sa/3.0>, via Wikimedia Commons; **bottom**: Osmania University: Nbsubbaiah at English Wikipedia, Public domain, via Wikimedia Commons; **104**: Kerala School of Fisheries and Ocean Studies: AjayTvm/Shutterstock.com; **105**: **background**: Shutterstock.com; **clockwise**: students in uniform: WESTOCK PRODUCTIONS/Shutterstock.com; students with laptop: ELAKSHI CREATIVE BUSINESS/Shutterstock.com; Indian languages: stockpexel/shutterstock.com; **106**: IIMC: Hghulam49, CC BY 4.0 <https://creativecommons.org/licenses/by/4.0>, via Wikimedia Commons; **107**: Kadambini Ganguly statue: Salil Kumar Mukherjee, CC BY-SA 4.0 <https://creativecommons.org/licenses/by-sa/4.0>, via Wikimedia Commons; **bottom**: Harpic Toilet College: Outlook India; **108**: Dr Manabi Bandyopadhyay: CCA-SA 4.0 International/ThePortraitLady/https://commons.wikimedia.org/wiki/File:Manabi_Bandyopadhyay.png; **109**: Delhi Public Library: Ramesh Lalwani, CC BY 2.0 <https://creativecommons.org/licenses/by/2.0>, via Wikimedia Commons; **110**: Digital Library: MR.AUKID PHUMSIRICHAT/Shutterstock.com; **111**: **top left**: Anna Centenary Library: Nazeem Fasil, CC BY-SA 4.0 <https://creativecommons.org/licenses/by-sa/4.0>, via Wikimedia Commons; **top right**: National Library, Kolkata: Biswarup Ganguly, CC BY-SA 3.0 <https://creativecommons.org/licenses/by-sa/3.0>, via Wikimedia Commons; **bottom**: National Film Archives: DesiBoy101, CC BY 4.0 <https://creativecommons.org/licenses/by/4.0>, via Wikimedia Commons; **112**: Film Museum: Ritu Manoj Jethani/Shutterstock.com; **113**: Allahabad Terracotta Museum: VibhaSrivastava/Shutterstock.com; **114–115**: **background**: singh_lens/Shutterstock.com; **114**: **left inset**: Rail Transport Museum: Sun_Shine/Shutterstock.com; **right inset**: Dinosaur Fossil: Parthbhatt/Shutterstock.com; **115**: **inset**: Partition Museum: Amritpal Singh Mann, CC BY-SA 4.0 <https://creativecommons.org/licenses/by-sa/4.0>, via Wikimedia Commons; **116**: The Conflictarium: Shubhsadhwani, CC BY-SA 4.0 <https://creativecommons.org/licenses/by-sa/4.0>, via Wikimedia Commons; **117**: Quiz: Andrzej Rostek/Shutterstock.com;

PERFORMING ARTS 118–137

Opener pic, 118–119: Govind Jangir/Shutterstock.com; **120**: **top left**: Apsara: Metropolitan Museum of Art, CC0, via Wikimedia Commons; **top right**: Krishnanattam Mudra: Jean-Pierre Dalbéra, CC BY 2.0 <https://creativecommons.org/licenses/by/2.0>, via Wikimedia Commons; **bottom**: Sculptures of Odissi: by courtesy of Abhishek Roy; **121**: **top**: Raja and Radha Reddy: Ministry of Information & Broadcasting (GODL-India), GODL-India <https://data.gov.in/sites/default/files/Gazette_Notification_OGDL.pdf>, via Wikimedia Commons; **bottom left**: Devadasi: Fedor Jagor, Public domain, via Wikimedia Commons; **bottom right**: Uday Shankar: AnonymousUnknown author, Public domain, via Wikimedia Commons; **122–123**: **background**: ShaikhMeraj/Shutterstock.com; **122**: **top**: Lady in mudra: Kitreel/Shutterstock.com; **bottom**: Natyashastra statue: CCA 2.0 Generic; **124**: **top**: T. Balasaraswati: India Post, Government of India, GODL-India <https://data.gov.in/sites/default/files/Gazette_Notification_OGDL.pdf>, via Wikimedia Commons; **bottom**: Sonal Mansingh: ShaikhMeraj/Shutterstock.com; **125**: **top**: Birju Maharaj: Dmitry Rukhlenko/Shutterstock.com; **bottom**: Theyyam:

Chitranakshatra/Shutterstock.com; **126**: **top**: folk variety dance: PIB; **bottom**: Tansen: AnonymousUnknown author, Public domain, via Wikimedia Commons; **127**: **top**: excerpt from Sama Veda: Ms Sarah Welch, CC BY-SA 4.0 <https://creativecommons.org/licenses/by-sa/4.0>, via Wikimedia Commons; **middle**: Amir Khusrau illuminated manuscript: Public Domain, Wikipedia; **bottom**: Purandara Dasa: savi.art/Shutterstock.com; **128**: **top**: Bangalore Gayana Samaja: Naveenbm (talk) (Uploads), CC BY-SA 3.0 <http://creativecommons.org/licenses/by-sa/3.0/>, via Wikimedia Commons; **bottom**: earliest extant musical instruments: Los Angeles County Museum of Art, Public domain, via Wikimedia Commons; **129**: **from left to right**: Anoushka Shankar: Alicelapen, CC BY-SA 4.0 <https://creativecommons.org/licenses/by-sa/4.0>, via Wikimedia Commons; Hariprasad Chaurasia: Suyash Dwivedi, CC BY-SA 4.0 <https://creativecommons.org/licenses/by-sa/4.0>, via Wikimedia Commons; Shreya Ghoshal: Behindwoods, CC BY-SA 3.0 <https://creativecommons.org/licenses/by-sa/3.0>, via Wikimedia Commons; **middle**: Ustad Ali Akbar Khan: Unknown source, Public domain, via Wikimedia Commons; **bottom left**: Gauhar Jaan: Paper Jewels, CC BY 4.0 <https://creativecommons.org/licenses/by/4.0>, via Wikimedia Commons; **bottom right**: Shehnai: Vaibhavbhatia16/Shutterstock.com; **130**: **top**: Yehudi Menuhin: Yehudi_Menuhin_&_Stephane_Grappelli_Allan_Warren.jpg: Allan warrenderivative work: Parzi, CC BY-SA 3.0 <https://creativecommons.org/licenses/by-sa/3.0>, via Wikimedia Commons; **middle**: Sharan Rani: Public domain, via Wikimedia Commons; **bottom**: Nadaswaram: Serene View/Shutterstock.com; **131**: **top left**: Sandeep Das: Hum Ensemble, GFDL <http://www.gnu.org/copyleft/fdl.html>, via Wikimedia Commons; **top right**: John McLaughlin: Hantsheroes, CC0, via Wikimedia Commons; **bottom**: Talking Machine Hall: https://bajakhana.com.au/tag/h-bose/, Public domain, via Wikimedia Commons; **132**: **top**: Resul Pookutty: Featureflash Photo Agency/Shutterstock.com; **bottom**: Zubin Mehta: Barone Firenze/Shutterstock.com; **133**: **top**: Sunburn Music Festival: © Vyacheslav Argenberg / http://www.vascoplanet.com/, CC BY 4.0 <https://creativecommons.org/licenses/by/4.0>, via Wikimedia Commons; **bottom**: Ravanhatha: Clément Bardot, CC BY-SA 4.0 <https://creativecommons.org/licenses/by-sa/4.0>, via Wikimedia Commons; **134**: **top**: Ilaiyaraaja: Dani Charles Silverscreen Media Inc. (https://silverscreen.in), CC BY-SA 3.0 <https://creativecommons.org/licenses/by-sa/3.0>, via Wikimedia Commons; **134–135**: Nukkad Natak Performance: PradeepGaurs/Shutterstock.com; **135**: **top**: Nil Darpan: Sufe, CC BY-SA 4.0 <https://creativecommons.org/licenses/by-sa/4.0>, via Wikimedia Commons; **136**: **top left**: Raja Ravi Varma's Painting: Raja Ravi Varma, Public domain, via Wikimedia Commons; **top right**: Annasaheb Kirloskar: Abhinavgarule, CC BY-SA 4.0 <https://creativecommons.org/licenses/by-sa/4.0>, via Wikimedia Commons; **bottom**: Jalabala Vaidya: Nisaschette, CC BY-SA 4.0 <https://creativecommons.org/licenses/by-sa/4.0>, via Wikimedia Commons; **137**: **top**: London Opera: https://commons.wikimedia.org/wiki/File:London_Coliseum.jpg; **bottom**: Asvagosha: Daderot, CC0, via Wikimedia Commons;

VISUAL ARTS 138–163

Opener pic, **138–139**: Doctors photography/Shutterstock.com; **140**: **top**: Dadasaheb Phalke: Shutterstock.com; **middle**: Lumière Brothers: Natata/Shutterstock.com; **bottom**: Still from *Alam Ara*: PD–India; **141**: **clockwise**, **from top**: Still from *Sairandhri*: PD–India; Bilwamangal ad: PD–India; Raj Kapoor: Natata/Shutterstock.com; *Sholay* set: Kamni Jethani/Shutterstock.com; *Kisan Kanya* poster: PD–India; **142**: **top**: Canterbury Plains: Shutterstock.com; **top left**: *Love in Tokyo* poster: Fair Use/Kailash29792; **middle**, **from left to right**: *Dil se...* poster: Fair Use/Theo's Little Bot; *Anek* poster: Fair Use/Sush150; *Neelakasham Pachakadal Chuvanna Bhoomi* poster: Fair Use/DatBot; *Rangoon* poster: Fair Use/Ghost No One; **bottom left**: *Gangs of Wasseypur* poster: Fair Use/DatBot; **bottom right**: Pollachi taluk: Shutterstock.com; **inset**: *Malaikkallan* poster: Fair Use/Kailash29792; **143**: **top**: *16 Vayathinile* poster: Fair Use/DatBot; **top left**: *Sholay* poster: Fair Use/Theo's Little Bot; **top right**: Chapora Fort: Santhosh Varghese/Shutterstock.com; **inset**: *Dil Chahta Hai* poster: Fair Use/Theo's Little Bot; **middle left**: Guna Caves: Shutterstock.com; insets, left to right: *Guna* poster: Fair Use/Ajayrangaraj; *Manjummel Boys* poster: Fair Use/DatBot; **middle right**: *Ponniyin Selvan* poster: Fair Use/Kailash29792; **bottom**: Ooty: Shutterstock.com; **inset**: *Anbe Vaa* poster: Fair Use/Kailash29792; **144**: **clockwise**, **from top**: *Shonar Kella* poster: Fair Use/Kailash29792; *Delhi 6* poster: Fair Use/Ghost No One; Hanuman statue: Shutterstock.com; *Dharmatma* poster: Fair Use/Kailash29792; *Khuda Gawah* poster: Fair Use/DatBot; *Haqeeqat* poster: Fair Use/Theo's Little Bot; Pangong lake: Shutterstock.com; Manali: Shutterstock.com; *Yeh Jawaani Hai Deewani* poster: Fair Use/Theo's Little Bot; *Junglee* poster: Fair Use/Kailash29792; *Mission Kashmir* poster: Fair Use/DatBot; Mumbai: Snehal Jeevan Pailkar/Shutterstock.com;

145: **clockwise**, **from top**: *Sangam* poster: Fair Use/Theo's Little Bot; Egypt: Shutterstock.com; Giraffe: Image by Herbert Aust from Pixabay; *Around the World* poster: Fair Use/Kailash29792; *Zindagi Na Milegi Dobara* poster: Fair Use/Theo's Little Bot; *Jeans* poster: Fair Use/Kailash29792; *Chandni* poster: Fair Use/Kailash29792; Yash Raj statue: fatmagulb/Shutterstock.com; Solheimasandur plane wreck: CC0 1.0 Universal Public Domain Dedication/ Thomas Tucker; **146**: **top**: Reel: Designed by Freepik; **bottom**: Satyajit Ray: Natata/Shutterstock.com; **147**: **top**: Still from *Seeta*: PD–India; **bottom**: Priyanka Chopra: Sam Aronov/Shutterstock.com; **148**: **left**, **from top to bottom**: Mohanlal: by courtesy of PIB; *12th Fail* poster: Fair Use/Kailash29792; *The Kerala Story* poster: Fair Use/Tousif.15; *Jawan* poster: Fair Use/Kailash29792; Vikrant Massey and Shah Rukh Khan: by courtesy of PIB; **right**, **from top to bottom**: Rani Mukherji: by courtesy of PIB; *Sam Bahadur* poster: Fair Use/Sush150; *Rocky aur Rani Kii Prem Kahaani* poster: Fair Use/Sush150; *Hanu-Man* poster: Fair Use/Vikckyy; *Naal 2* poster: Fair Use/DatBot; **149**: **background**: Image by Mattia Verga from Pixabay; **150**: **from top to bottom**: *Alaipayuthey* poster: Fair Use/Kailash29792; *Astitva* poster: Fair Use/Kailash29792; *Badri* poster: Fair Use/Theo's Little Bot; *Gaja Gamini* poster: Fair Use/Kailash29792; *Hera Pheri* poster: Fair Use/Kailash29792; *Hey Ram* poster: Fair Use/Kailash29792; **right**: *Bariwali* poster: Fair Use/Aung Phyoe; **151**: **from top to bottom**: *Kaho Naa... Pyaar Hai* poster: Fair Use/DatBot; *Mohabbatein* poster: Fair Use/Begoon; *Mission Kashmir* poster: Fair Use/DatBot; *Nuvve Kavali* poster: Fair Use/Ab207; *Paromitar Ekdin* poster: Fair Use/Aung Phyoe; *Phir Bhi Dil Hai Hindustani* poster: Fair Use/DatBot; *Pukar* poster: Fair Use/Kailash29792; *Kandukondain Kandukondain* poster: Fair Use/Kailash29792; **152**: **left**, **from top to bottom**: *Sasurbari Zindabad* poster: Fair Use/DatBot; *Vaanathaippola* poster: Fair Use/Kailash29792;

IMAGE COPYRIGHT INFORMATION

Uttara poster: Fair Use/Kailash29792; Fiza poster: Fair Use/Kailash29792; Bharathi poster: Fair Use/Theo's Little Bot; *Kochu Kochu Santhoshangal* poster: Fair Use/Sreejithk2000; **right**, **from top to bottom**: *Refugee* poster: Fair Use/DatBot; *Utsab* poster: Fair Use/Aung Phyoe; **153**: **clockwise**, **from top**: *Gandhi* poster: Fair Use/TrebleSeven; *Agantuk* poster: Fair Use/DatBot; *Bhuvan Shome* poster: Fair Use/Aung Phyoe; Jaane Bhi Do *Yaaro* poster: Fair Use/DatBot; Clipboard: Image by OsloMetX from Pixabay; **inset**: NFDC logo: PD; *Charulata* poster: Fair Use/Theo's Little Bot; **155**: Museo camera museum: Sudarshan Jha/Shutterstock.com; **156–157**: Ajanta Caves: Emdadul Hoque Topu/Shutterstock.com; **158–159**: **background**: Image by Dorothe Wouters from Pixabay; **Insets**, **clockwise**, **from top**: Raja Ravi Varma: Shutterstock.com; Scene from the Mahabharat: PD–Art/Raja Ravi Varma/ https://commons.wikimedia.org/wiki/File:Draupadi_humiliated_RRV.jpg; The Maharashtrian Lady: PD–Art/ Raja Ravi Varma/https://en.wikipedia.org/wiki/File:Raja_Ravi_Varma,_The_Maharashtrian_Lady.jpg; The Lady playing the Swarbat: PD–Art/Raja Ravi Varma/https://commons.wikimedia.org/wiki/File:Ravi_Varma-Lady_playing_the_swarbat.jpg; Goddess Lakshmi: PD–Art/ Raja Ravi Varma/https://en.wikipedia.org/wiki/File:Lakshmi_by_Raja_Ravi_Varma.jpg; Scene from the Ramayan: PD–Art/ Raja Ravi Varma/https://commons.wikimedia.org/wiki/File:Ravi_Varma-Ravana_Sita_Jathayu.jpg; **160**: **top**: Lalit Kala Akademi: historicalpitara7/Shutterstock.com; **middle**: Indian Institute of Cartoonists logo: CCA-SA 4.0 International/ IIC-Info/ CSG-Info/ https://commons.wikimedia.org/wiki/File:Logo_pic_IIC.jpg; **bottom**: Frederick Corbyn: PD–US/Colesworthey Grant; **161**: **background**: Umar defeats a Dragon: PD; **162**: **top**: M.F. Husain: CCA-SA 4.0 International/Gower/Abrsinha/ https://commons.wikimedia.org/wiki/File:Husain_with_Rammanohar_(cropped).jpg; **bottom**: by courtesy of the record holder; **163**: Images are by courtesy of the record holders;

LITERATURE 164–177

Opener pic, **164–165**: Shutterstock.com; **166**: **left and middle**: PD–India; **right**: Fakeer of Jungheera and Other Poems: PD; **167**: **left**: Bhagvadgita: CCA-SA 4.0 International/Ms Sarah Welch/https://commons.wikimedia.org/wiki/File:1785_Bhagavad_Gita_translation_English.jpg; **top right**: Shakespeare's folio: PD; **middle right**: Benjamin Schultze: PD; **bottom**: Lavanyavati: PD; **168**: **background**: Shutterstock.com; **169**: **top**: Pustakach gaav: Fair use/DatBot/ https://en.wikipedia.org/wiki/File:Logo_of_Pustakanch_Gaav.jpg; **bottom**: World Book Fair: Photo For Everything/Shutterstock.com; **170**: Bookaroo: Images by courtesy of Swati Roy and Venkatesh M.; **171**: **top**: Jaipur Literature Fest: Radiokafka/Shutterstock.com; **bottom left**: Dan Brown: Markus Wissmann/Shutterstock.com; **bottom right**: Rhonda Byrne: Everett Collection/Shutterstock.com; **172**: **from top to bottom**: Akshat Gupta: CCA 3.0 Unported/Bollywood Hungama/https://commons.wikimedia.org/wiki/File:Akshat_Gupta_at_a_book_launch_event.jpg; Daaji Kamlesh D. Patel: CCA-SA 2.0 Generic/Xiantec/Heartfulness Photos/https://commons.wikimedia.org/wiki/File:Kamlesh_D_Patel_(Daaji).jpg; Sudha Murty: GODL–India/President's Secretariat; Pradeep Chakravarthy and cover of A History of South India for Children: by courtesy of Hachette India; **173**: **top left**: Makhanlal Chaturvedi: GODL–India/India Post, Government of India; **top right**: Rabindranath Tagore: Ninety_illustrator/Shutterstock.com; **middle**: Amrita Pritam: PD–India; **bottom left**: Dr Radhakrishnan: CCA-SA 4.0 International/Barbera-Ivanoff/https://commons.wikimedia.org/wiki/File:Portrait_DR._Sarvepalli_Radhakrishnan.jpg; **bottom right**: Jhumpa Lahiri: Roberto Cano/Shutterstock.com; **174**: **top**: Dhan Gopal Mukerji: PD–US/Bodhisattwa/The Hindusthanee Student; **bottom left**: Harivansh Rai Bachchan: Czajnikolandia/Shutterstock.com; **bottom right**: Arundhati Roy: CCA-SA 2.0 Generic/WikiPedant/jeanbaptisteparis/https://commons.wikimedia.org/wiki/File:Arundhati_Roy_3.jpg; **175**: Amitav Ghosh: CCA-SA 2.0 Generic/Gage Skidmore/Amitav Ghosh/ https://commons.wikimedia.org/wiki/File:Amitav_Ghosh_(33200056540).jpg; **176–177**: **background**: Image by Paolo Berretta from Pixabay;

MEDIA AND COMMUNICATION 178–199

Opener pic, 178–179: Savvapanf Photo/Shutterstock.com; **180**: **top**: Reference Image of a Printing Press: Public Domain via Wikimedia Commons; **middle**: Serampore College: cc-by 3.0, CC BY 3.0 <https://creativecommons.org/licenses/by/3.0>, via Wikimedia Commons; **bottom**: A typewriter: CCA SA 4.0 International; **181**: **top left**: Hicky's Bengal Gazette: Wikimedia Commons/Fair Use/James Augustus Hicky; **top right**: Times of India building: E.O.S. and Company, Public domain, via Wikimedia Commons; **bottom left**: Azdarar newspaper: Harutyun Shmavonyan, Public domain, via Wikimedia Commons; **bottom middle**: Harutyun Shmavonyan: 23artashes, CC BY-SA 4.0 <https://creativecommons.org/licenses/by-sa/4.0>, via Wikimedia Commons; **bottom right**: William Carrey: Public domain, via Wikimedia Commons; **182**: **top**: Chintamani Ghosh: The Modern Review. September 1928, Public domain, via Wikimedia Commons; **middle left**: The Indian Ladies Magazine: Public domain, via Wikimedia Commons; **middle right**: Malayala Manorama stamp: SUDARSHAN BHATLA/Shutterstock.com; **bottom**: Khabar Lahariya: by courtesy of Khabar Lahariya team; **183**: **top left**: Reference image of newspapers: Harshit Srivastava S3/Shutterstock.com; **top right**: Femina Magazine: Amanda Alamsyah/Shutterstock.com; **bottom left**: Chandamama: Anshumanjakhmola, CC BY-SA 4.0 <https://creativecommons.org/licenses/by-sa/4.0>, via Wikimedia Commons; **bottom right**: Tushar Kanti Ghosh: Unknown - found in book published by subject, Public domain, via Wikimedia Commons; **185**: **top**: Bombay Samachar: PP Yoonus, CC BY-SA 3.0 <https://creativecommons.org/licenses/by-sa/3.0>, via Wikimedia Commons; **middle**: Emblem of Akashvani Bhavan: Biswarup Ganguly, CC BY 3.0 <https://creativecommons.org/licenses/by/3.0>, via Wikimedia Commons; **186**: **top**: Pandit Ravi Shankar: John Malmin, Los Angeles Times, CC BY 4.0 <https://creativecommons.org/licenses/by/4.0>, via Wikimedia Commons; **bottom**: Ameen Sayani: Bollywood Hungama, CC BY 3.0 <https://creativecommons.org/licenses/by/3.0>, via Wikimedia Commons; **187**: **top**: Doordarshan Kendra: mrinalpal/Shutterstock.com; **bottom**: DD stamps: India Post, Government of India, GODL-India <https://data.gov.in/sites/default/files/Gazette_Notification_OGDL.pdf>, via Wikimedia Commons; **188**: **top**: Podhigai Tower: Rasnaboy, CC BY-SA 3.0 <https://creativecommons.org/licenses/by-sa/3.0>, via Wikimedia Commons; **bottom left**: Aaj Tak: Piotr Swat/Shutterstock.com; **bottom right**: Representative Image of Satellite Dish: Robert Kneschke/Shutterstock.com; **189**: Madras General Post Office: Williamsatish25, CC BY-SA 3.0 <https://creativecommons.org/licenses/by-sa/3.0>, via Wikimedia Commons; **190**: Dak Chowki:

Sarmad Mahmud, CC BY-SA 3.0 <https://creativecommons.org/licenses/by-sa/3.0>, via Wikimedia Commons; **191**: **top**: Official Letter with stamps: Stiftung historische Museen Hamburg - Museum für Hamburgische Geschichte, Public domain, via Wikimedia Commons; **bottom**: Mumbai GPO: Sailko, CC BY 3.0 <https://creativecommons.org/licenses/by/3.0>, via Wikimedia Commons; **192–193**: **background**: spatuletail/Shutterstock.com; **194**: **clockwise from top left**: 1: SUDARSHAN BHATLA/Shutterstock.com; 2: rook76/Shutterstock.com; 3, 4: SUDARSHAN BHATLA/Shutterstock.com; **middle**: Miniature stamp sheet: Muddy Rhino, CC BY-SA 4.0 <https://creativecommons.org/licenses/by-sa/4.0>, via Wikimedia Commons; **bottom**: Polygonal Stamp and Circular Stamp: Sir Bartle Frere (1815–1884), of the East India Company, the Chief Commissioner of Sindh, Public domain, via Wikimedia Commons; Raja Ram Mohan Roy stamp: brandonht/Shutterstock.com; **195**: **top**: Jai Hind Stamp: Image by India Post, GODL-India <https://data.gov.in/sites/default/files/Gazette_Notification_OGDL.pdf>, via Wikimedia Commons; **middle**: Samuel Hoare: George Grantham Bain Collection (Library of Congress), Public domain, via Wikimedia Commons; **bottom**: A wildlife stamp: Post of India, GODL-India <https://data.gov.in/sites/default/files/Gazette_Notification_OGDL.pdf>, via Wikimedia Commons; **196**: **top**: Stalls to make STD calls: Victorgrigas, CC BY-SA 3.0 <https://creativecommons.org/licenses/by-sa/3.0>, via Wikimedia Commons; **middle**: Stamp depicting Arvi Space Station: rook76/Shutterstock.com; **bottom**: Airtel store: Surya S Nair/Shutterstock.com; **197**: **top**: Jio building in Navi Mumbai: Nairspecht, CC BY-SA 4.0 <https://creativecommons.org/licenses/by-sa/4.0>, via Wikimedia Commons; **bottom**: Telephone lines in Old Delhi: PhotographerIncognito/Shutterstock.com; **198**: **top**: VSNL Manhole Cover: 19Tarrestnom65, CC BY-SA 4.0 <https://creativecommons.org/licenses/by-sa/4.0>, via Wikimedia Commons; **bottom**: BHIM App: Funstock/Shutterstock.com; **199**: **bottom**: Jio: PradeepGaurs/Shutterstock.com;

GOVERNMENT 200–223

Opener pic, 200–201: Snehal Jeevan Pailkar/Shutterstock.com; **202**: Chandragupta: KaeroMan/CCA-SA 4.0 International licence (https://commons.wikimedia.org/wiki/File:Chandragupta_Maurya_and_Bhadrabahu_-_at_the_entrance_to_Chandragupta_Basadi_(cropped).jpg); **203**: **top**: Largest electorate: Hafiz Ahmed/Shutterstock.com; **bottom**: Congress headquarters: PradeepGaurs/Shutterstock.com; **204–205**: **background**: Diu fort: arun uppadhyay/Shutterstock.com; **insets**, **clockwise from top**: Basilica of Bom Jesus: Darkwisper S/Shutterstock.com; relics of St Francis Xavier: Darkwisper S/Shutterstock.com; Portuguese gun: Markeliz/Shutterstock.com; **206**: EVM: John1107/Shutterstock.com; **207**: **top left**: Diya Kumari: Sumit Saraswat/Shutterstock.com; **top right**: Mahua Moitra: Exposure Visuals/Shutterstock.com; **bottom**: Lakshadweep: Nesru Markmedia/Shutterstock.com; **208**: **top**: women voters: Talukdar David/Shutterstock.com; **bottom**: voter ID distribution: Raj Bhaskar/Shutterstock.com; **right**: Pratibha Patil: praszkiewicz/Shutterstock.com; **209**: **top**: S. Radhakrishnan, R. Venkataraman, and A.P.J. Abdul Kalam: Illustrations by Surojit Bhattacharya/© Hachette India; **middle**: Indira Gandhi: Natata/Shutterstock.com; **bottom**: Jawaharlal Nehru: Ninety_illustrator/Shutterstock.com; **210**: **top**: Narendra Modi: Ninety_illustrator/Shutterstock.com; **middle, left**: Jayaprakash Narayan: Natata/Shutterstock.com; **middle, right**: Atal Bihari Vajpayee: Natata/Shutterstock.com; **bottom**: Sardar Vallabhbhai Patel: masterstrokes/Shutterstock.com; **211**: **top**: sreetamo/Shutterstock.com; **bottom**: Tirupati, Andhra Pradesh: Rahul D'silva/Shutterstock.com; **212**: **top**: All Illustrations by Surojit Bhattacharya/© Hachette India; **213**: **top right**: Kiran Bedi: bodom/Shutterstock.com; **bottom left**: T.G. Sanjeevi Pillai: KANISHKAKADPHISES/CCA 4.0 International licence (https://commons.wikimedia.org/wiki/File:PRIME_MINISTER_OF_INDIA_STANDING_INFRONT_OF_THE_INSIGNIA_OF_THE_DIRECTOR_OF_INTELLIGENCE_BUREAU_(DIB)_AT_THE_NATIONAL_POLICE_MEMORIAL,_CHANAKYAPURI,_NEW_DELHI,_DURING_ITS_INAUGURATION_IN_OCTOBER_2018.png); **214–215**: **background**: Greater Chennai Corporation: sivananthan2001/Shutterstock.com; **inset**: Arya Rajendran: Illustration by Surojit Bhattacharya/© Hachette India; **216**: Calcutta High Court: cphotog/Shutterstock.com; **217**: **top**: Allahabad High Court: Harshit Srivastava S3/Shutterctock.com; **bottom**: S. Subramania Iyer: PD (https://commons.wikimedia.org/wiki/File:S_Subramanya_Aiyer_Calcutta_Review_1921_-_2.jpg); **218**: Cornelia Sorabji: Agence Rol, restored by Adam Cuerden/PD (https://commons.wikimedia.org/wiki/File:John_Campbell_Hamilton-Gordon,_1st_Marquess_of_Aberdeen_and_Temair_and_Cornelia_Sorabji,_first_Indian_woman_to_practice_at_the_bar_in_India.jpg); **219**: Sikkim: Panda Koushik/Shutterstock.com; **220**: **top**: Cellular Jail: mrinalpal/Shutterstock.com; bottom: Women from Ladakh: Sandycinecam/Shutterstock.com; 221: top: U.P. Vidhan Sabha: Roshp/Shutterstock.com; **bottom**: Rajasthan State Legislative Assembly: Manmohan chhandwal/Shutterstock.com; **222–223**: Indian Parliament: Mr Subir Halder/Shutterstock.com;

DEFENCE AND MILITARY AFFAIRS 224–253

Opener pic, 224–225: NareshSharma/Shutterstock.com; **226**: **top, left to right**: K.M. Cariappa: CCA-SA 4.0 International/Ank gsx/ https://commons.wikimedia.org/wiki/File:Bust_of_Field_Marshal_K_M_Cariappa,_National_Military_Memorial,_Bengaluru,_Karnataka,_India_(Ank_Kumar,_Infosys_Limited).jpg/; Major Somnath Sharma: Ritu Manoj Jethani/Shutterstock.com; General Bipin Rawat: GODL–India/PIB Press Releases; **middle**: Victoria Cross: Shutterstock.com; **bottom left**: PD–UK; **bottom right**: PD; **227**: **top**: by courtesy of PIB; **bottom, left to right**: Sam Manekshaw: Natata/Shutterstock.com; Dr Punita Arora: GODL–India/ADG (M&C) DPR (Ministry of Defence - India); Lieutenant General Sadhna Saxena: GODL–India/Government of India; **228**: **top**: Artillery company: PD–India/Charles Gold; **middle**: Stringer Lawrence: Flickr's The Commons/Unknown author/British Library Flickr Stream; **bottom**: Maratha light infantry: PD/Alfred Crowdy Lovett; **229**: **top**: Bengal Sappers: PD/National Archives UK; **middle**: RFI logo: GODL–India/Rifle Factory Ishapore; **bottom**: Sarath: CCA 2.0 Generic/Flickr user cell105/SuperTank17; **230–231**: **background**: GODL–India/Defense Research and Development Organisation; **inset**: Cut-away diagram: CCA-SA 4.0 International/Norbert Brügge/Editor8220/https://commons.wikimedia.org/wiki/File:Agni-V_ICBM_Cutaway_diagram.png; **232**: **top**: Vijayanta: :Om_Joshi/Shutterstock.com; **bottom**: CIJWS insignis: Fair use/Kulbhushan Jhadav; **233**: **top left**: Siachen: CCA 2.0 Generic/Pranav21391/Abhishek_Kumar/https://commons.wikimedia.org/wiki/File:

Dogra_Siachen.jpg; **top right**: Fort William: PD–US/Thomas Daniell; **bottom**: Directorate of Military Intelligence Corps insignia: PD–India/Jean-Paul GIBERT; **234**: **top**: National War Memorial: Arnav Pratap Singh/Shutterstock.com; **bottom left**: Bactrian Camel: PD–US; **bottom right**: rail launch: by courtesy of PIB; **235**: **top**: CCA-SA 4.0 International/Dananjaii/ https://commons.wikimedia.org/wiki/File:Mudhol_hound_dog_3.png; **bottom**: Vice Admiral Ram Dass Katari: GODL–India/Indian Navy; **236**: INS Nistar: by courtesy of PIB; **237**: **top**: INS Aditya: GODL–India/Indian Navy; **middle**: INFAC T-80: GODL–India/ Indian Navy; **bottom**: INS Sarvekshak: GODL–India/Ministry of Defence; **238–239**: **background**: SNEHIT PHOTO/Shutterstock.com; **insets, from left to right**: IAC Vikrant: GODL–India/ Indian Navy Western Fleet; INS Vikramaditya and INS Vikrant: CCA-SA 2.0 Generic/CharlieMehta/Sarvajanik Puralekh/ https://commons.wikimedia.org/wiki/File:INS_Vikramaditya_(in_Left)_and_INS_Vikrant_(in_Right).jpg; INS Viraat: PD–US; **240**: **top**: Bombay Harbour: PD; **middle**: GRSE headquarters: CC0 1.0 Universal Public Domain Dedication; **bottom left**: Naval Academy: CCA-SA 4.0 International/ Faraaz16/https://commons.wikimedia.org/wiki/File:Academy_pic.jpg; **bottom right**: Signal School: GODL–India/Indian Navy; **241**: **from top to bottom**: PD/PD-Art; **242–243**: **background**: Image by tadeyco from Pixabay; **244**: **top**: Vice Admiral Arun Prakash: CCA-SA 3.0 Unported/Demiurge1000/Arun Prakash/ https://commons.wikimedia.org/wiki/File:Arun_Prakash.jpg; **middle**: all-women crew: GODL–India/Indian Navy; **bottom left**: dry dock: GODL–India/Indian Navy; **bottom right**: INSV Tarini: CCA-SA 4.0 International/KCVelaga/Krishna Chaitanya Velaga/ https://commons.wikimedia.org/wiki/File:Model_of_INSV_Tarini.jpg; **245**: **middle**: air chiefs: PD–India; **bottom left**: Admiral Sunil Lanba: GODL–India/Ministry of Defence; **bottom right**: Air chief marshal Arjan Singh: PD–UK; **246**: **background**: by courtesy of PIB; **insets, clockwise, from top**: Jeejeeboy P. Bomanjee: PD–US; Indra Lal Roy stamp: GODL–India/India Post, Government of India; Sardar Hardit Singh Malik stamp: GODL–India/India Post, Government of India; Errol Sharat Chandra Sen stamp: GODL–India/India Post, Government of India; Errol Sen: PD; Lieutenant S.G. Welingkar: CC0 1.0 Universal Public Domain Dedication; **247**: **top**: Air Marshal Padma Bandopadhyay: CCA-SA 4.0 International/Mistral&monsoon/ https://commons.wikimedia.org/wiki/File:Padma_Bandopadhyay.jpg; **bottom left**: Group Captain Shaliza Dhami: CCA-SA 4.0 International/ Akshay Daniel/ https://commons.wikimedia.org/wiki/File:Gp_Capt_Shailza_Dhami,_commanding_the_91st_IAF_Day_parade.jpg; **bottom right**: Flying Officer N.J.S. Sekhon: Ritu Manoj Jethani/Shutterstock.com; **249**: **top**: Air Commodore Bouchier: PD–UK; **bottom**: 44 Squadron: CCA-SA 4.0 International/ Vprajkumar/https://commons.wikimedia.org/wiki/File:44-IAF.png; **250**: **top**: Westland Wapiti: PD–UK/Royal Air Force; **middle**: Apache Attack Helicopter: GODL–India/Indian Air Force; **bottom left**: 5 Squadron: Fair Use/Johnxxx9; **bottom right**: 1 Squadron: D–India/Bharat Rakshak; **251**: **from top to bottom**: Havilland Vampire: CCA-SA 3.0 Unported/aeroprints.com/ https://commons.wikimedia.org/wiki/File:ID606_De_Havilland_Vampire_NF.54_Indian_Air_Force_(8447284877).jpg/; HAL Ajeet: CCA-SA 4.0 International/Ank gsx/Ank Kumar/https://commons.wikimedia.org/wiki/File:HAL_Ajeet_based_on_Folland_Gnat_Jet_at_HAL_Museum,_Bengaluru_(Ank_Kumar).jpg; HAL Tejas: GODL–India/Ministry of Defence; Line diagram: CCA 4.0 International/FoxtAl/ https://commons.wikimedia.org/wiki/File:HAL_Tejas_Mark_1A_3-view_line_drawing.png; **bottom right**: Rudram-1: GODL–India/Defence Decode; **252**: Dhruv MK-III: PD/ Indian Coast Guard/Echo1Charlie; **253**: **middle left**: ICGS *Sachet*: GODL–India/Goa Shipyard; **middle right**: Flag of ICG: CCA-SA 4.0 International/ Flag Creator/ https://commons.wikimedia.org/wiki/File:Flag_of_the_Indian_Coast_Guard.svg; **bottom**: INS *Kirpan*: GODL–India/Ministry of Defence;

SCIENCE AND TECHNOLOGY 254–277

Opener pic, 254–255: metamorworks/Shutterstock.com; **256**: Apastamba and Madhava: illustrations by Surojit Bhattacharya/© Hachette India; **257**: Vainu Bappu Observatory: Prateek Karandikar/CCA-SA 4.0 International 3.0 Unported, 2.5 Generic, 2.0 Generic and 1.0 Generic license (https://commons.wikimedia.org/wiki/File:93-inch_telescope_seen_from_the_40-inch_telescope_at_Vainu_Bappu_Observatory.JPG); **258–259**: Hanle Observatory: thaisign/Shutterstock.com; **260**: **top**: Pole star: alionaprof/Shutterstock.com; **bottom left**: Radha Gobinda Chandra: Unknown author/PD (https://commons.wikimedia.org/wiki/File:Scientist_Radha_Gobinda_Chandra.jpg); **bottom right**: Ooty Radio Telescope: Razimantv/CCA 3.0 Unported licence (https://commons.wikimedia.org/wiki/File:Ooty_Radio_Telescope.jpg); **261**: **top**: Bhabha Atomic Centre: Sobarwiki/PD (https://commons.wikimedia.org/wiki/File:BARC_nuclear_reactor.JPG); **261**: **bottom**: Raman Research Institute: Sanal6535/CCA-SA 4.0 International licence (https://commons.wikimedia.org/wiki/File:Raman_Research_Institute_front_view,_Bengaluru,_India_(2014).jpg); **262–263**: **background**: Sergey Nivens/Shutterstock.com; **insets, from top**: Apsara-U Pool and Apsara Reactor complex: Press Information Bureau; Nuclear power plant: Reetesh Chaurasia/CCA_SA 4.0 International licence (https://commons.wikimedia.org/wiki/File:Kudankulam_Nuclear_Power_Plant_Unit_1_and_2.jpg); **264**: **top**: Raman microscope-spectroscope: Artur Wnorowski/Shutterctock.com; **bottom**: National Physical Laboratories: Shishirdasika /CCA-SA 4.0 International licence (https://commons.wikimedia.org/wiki/File:National_physical_laboratories_in_Delhi..jpg); **265**: **top**: Velocity-distribution data: NIST/JILA/CU-Boulder/PD (https://commons.wikimedia.org/wiki/File:Bose_Einstein_condensate.png); bottom: Nuclear fusion: Darkfoxelixir/Shutterstock.com; **266**: **top**: Bengal Chemicals: Biswarup Ganguly/CCA-SA 3.0 Unported licence; **middle**, **left**: Old ad: The Bombay Chronicle/ PD (https://commons.wikimedia.org/wiki/File:Bengal_Chemical_Pharmaceutical_Works_Print_Ad_1943.png); middle, right: Old products of Bengal Chemicals: Biswarup Ganguly/CCA 3.0 Unported licence (https://commons.wikimedia.org/wiki/File:Old_Products_Of_Bengal_Chemical_-_Acharya_Prafulla_Chandra_Ray_Life_And_Science_Of_A_Legend_Exhibition_-_BITM_-_Kolkata_2011-01-17_0183.JPG); **267**: **top**: Quality Stock Arts/ Shutterstock.com; **bottom**: Carbon dioxide laser: Quality Stock Arts/Shutterstock.com; **268**: GSI members in 1870: Herbert Giess, Switzerland/PD (https://upload.wikimedia.org/wikipedia/commons/3/31/GeologicalSurveyIndia1870.jpg); **269**: **top**: Rama Brahma Sanyal: Mukul Patrika/PD (https://commons.wikimedia.org/wiki/File:Ram_Brahma_Sanyal_in_Mukul_Patrika_1908.png); **bottom**: Hepatitis E virus: CDC/ (PHIL #5605) (https://commons.wikimedia.org/wiki/File:Hepatitis_E_virus.jpg); **270–271**: **background**: kudla/Shutterstock.com; **inset**: Dr Kamaljit Bawa: The Royal Society/CCA-SA 3.0 Unported licence (https://commons.wikimedia.org/wiki/File:Kamaljit_Singh_Bawa_FRS.

jpg); **272–273**: Buckyball: Arunlovy/CCA-SA 3.0 Unported licence (https://commons.wikimedia.org/wiki/File:Buckyball,_JNCASR,_Bangalore,_India.JPG); **274**: **top**: Dr Raj Reddy: Debramtobin/CCA-SA 4.0 International licence (https://commons.wikimedia.org/wiki/File:RRCMU1998.jpg); **bottom**: Indigenous microprocessor: FOTOGRIN/Shutterstock.com; **275**: ISRO: Indian Space Research Organisation (GODL-India) (https://commons.wikimedia.org/wiki/File:ISRO_Headquarters_Bengaluru.jpg); **276**: Rakesh Sharma statue: DeepchandDC2/Shutterstock.com; **277**: **left**: LVM3 M5: Indian Space Research Organisation (GODL-India) (https://commons.wikimedia.org/wiki/File:LVM3_M5_during_liftoff.jpg); **right**: XpoSat: Indian Space Research Organisation (GODL-India) (https://commons.wikimedia.org/wiki/File:X-ray_Polarimeter_satellite_(XPoSat).jpg)

MEDICAL SCIENCES 278–297

Opener pic, 278–279: Africa Studio/Shutterstock.com; **280**: **top**: Al-Beruni stamp: The original uploader was Romanm at Slovenian Wikipedia., Public domain, via Wikimedia Commons; **middle**: microscopic view of IVF procedure: Rohane Hamilton/Shutterstock.com; **bottom**: PM-JAY: NEERAZ CHATURVEDI / Shutterstock.com; **281**: **top**: Dr Muthulakshmi Reddy: Abecedare, Public domain, via Wikimedia Commons; **middle**: Mahesh Chandra Bhattacharya: Lakshmikanta Manna, CC0, via Wikimedia Commons; **bottom**: Rajiv Gandhi Hospital: Vkraja, CC BY-SA 4.0 <https://creativecommons.org/licenses/by-sa/4.0>, via Wikimedia Commons; **282**: **clockwise from top left**: Dr Rafiuddin Ahmed: Dr. Joji George, CC BY-SA 4.0 <https://creativecommons.org/licenses/by-sa/4.0>, via Wikimedia Commons; Dr Mukesh Batra: Bollywood Hungama, CC BY 3.0 <https://creativecommons.org/licenses/by/3.0>, via Wikimedia Commons; P.D. Hinduja Hospital: Jkl0101, CC BY-SA 4.0 <https://creativecommons.org/licenses/by-sa/4.0>, via Wikimedia Commons; Apollo Hospitals: Taiyo_no_hono/Shutterstock.com; Postal stamp on Tata Memorial Centre: India Post, Government of India, GODL-India <https://data.gov.in/sites/default/files/Gazette_Notification_OGDL.pdf>, via Wikimedia Commons; Calcutta Medical College: Bratish Kar; **283**: **clockwise from top left**: Serum Institute: MudaCom/Shutterstock.com; **inset**: Serum Institute: T. Schneider; AIIMS New Delhi: Vishnoi M, CC BY-SA 4.0 <https://creativecommons.org/licenses/by-sa/4.0>, via Wikimedia Commons; Lakeshore Hospital: Shady59, CC BY-SA 4.0 <https://creativecommons.org/licenses/by-sa/4.0>, via Wikimedia Commons; Sir Ganga Ram stamp: A. Marino/Shutterstock.com; rotavac: Nays photo/Shutterstock.com; **284–285**: background: Monthira/Shutterstock.com; **286**: **top**: Dr Rupa Bai Furdoonji: Unknown (1891 AD), Public domain, via Wikimedia Commons; **middle**: Kadambini Ganguly: public domain, https://commons.wikimedia.org/wiki/File:Kadambini_Ganguly.jpg#file; **bottom**: Pandit Madhusudan Gupta: S. C. Belnos, Public domain, via Wikimedia Commons (COPYRIGHT EXPIRED); **287**: **top**: PGIMER Chandigarh: PradeepGaurs/Shutterstock.com; **bottom**: Christian Medical College: Lubap at English Wikipedia, CC BY 3.0 <https://creativecommons.org/licenses/by/3.0>, via Wikimedia Commons; **288–289**: background: Bukhta Yurii/Shutterstock.com; **289**: **inset**: Mahadeva Lal Schroff: public domain; **290**: **top**: Sushruta: Anuja Mukhopadhyay/Shutterstock.com; **middle**: Dr Naresh Trehan: World Economic Forum/CCA-SA 2.0 Generic (https://commons.wikimedia.org/wiki/File:Naresh_Trehan_at_the_World_Economic_Forum_on_India_2012.jpg); **bottom**: VAT surgery: Cancer Research UK, CC BY-SA 4.0 <https://creativecommons.org/licenses/by-sa/4.0>, via Wikimedia Commons; **291**: **clockwise from top left**: Coronary artery bypass: Pitchyfoto/Shutterstock.com; Cochlear implant: BruceBlaus, CC BY-SA 4.0 <https://creativecommons.org/licenses/by-sa/4.0>, via Wikimedia Commons; Implantation of pacemaker: Meeter099/Shutterstock.com; Biventricular pacemaker: J-THE PHOTOHOLIC/Shutterstock.com; **292**: Heartbeat vector: Kaya Ra/Shutterstock.com; **294**: Human organ transplant: Dan Race/Shutterstock.com; **296–297**: all images are by courtesy of the record holders;

THE NATURAL WORLD 298-329

Opener pic, 298–299: Elephants in Kaziranga – PRASUN KUMAR CHAKRABORTY/Shutterstock.com; **300**: **top**: Himalayan view from Kullu valley: Dmitry Rukhlenko/Shutterstock.com; **middle**: Aerial view of Ganga in Rishikesh: SauravRawat/Shutterstock.com; **bottom**: Chilika lake: sreymisan/Shutterstock.com; **301**: **top**: Aerial view of Sundarbans: davide bonaldo/Shutterstock.com bottom; Wular lake: Danish23564/Shutterstock.com; **302**: **top**: Amarnath cave: Manoej Paateel/Shutterstock.com; **middle**: Lonar crater: Purva Joshi/Shutterstock.com; **bottom**: Thar desert: Dmitry Rukhlenko/Shutterstock.com; **303**: **top**: Mt Kanchenjunga: jayanta basu/Shutterstock.com; **bottom**: Andaman island: zelvan/Shutterstock.com; **304**: **top**: Ladakh: Suraj Naik 2307/Shutterstock.com; **middle**: One-horned rhino: Som Moulick/Shutterstock.com; **bottom right**: Pygmy shrew: Wirestock Creators/Shutterstock.com; **bottom left**: W.H. Sleeman: public domain via Wikimedia Commons http://www.1902encyclopedia.com/T/THU/william-henry-sleeman.jpg by Pahari Sahib; **305**: **top**: Finless porpoise: Pavaphon Supanantananont/Shutterstock.com; **middle**: Asian elephant: Agent from heaven/Shutterstock.com; **bottom**: langur: Shutterstock.com; **306**: **clockwise from top left**: Western hoolock gibbon: Mihirjoshi/Shutterstock.com; Snow leopard: Shutterstock.com; Tiger: PhotocechCZ/Shutterstock.com; Rusty-spotted cat: Shutterstock.com; **307**: **top**: Kharai camel: Pravin Indrekar/Shutterstock.com; **middle**: Bearded vulture: Dario Pautasso/Shutterstock.com; **bottom right**: sarus crane egg: Eric Isselee/Shutterstock.com; **bottom left**: Nilgiri flowerpecker: Mihirjoshi/Shutterstock.com; **308**: **top left**: Rosy pelican: Matyas Rehak/Shutterstock.com; **top right**: Dalmatian pelican: Palanga Bogdan- Claudiu/Shutterstock.com; **bottom**: Baya bird nest: Sunjoy Monga/Shutterstock.com; **309**: **top**: Malabar gliding frog: ananth-tp/Shutterstock.com; **middle right**: Indian flying lizard: Atul Haldankar/Shutterstock.com; **bottom**: Galaxy frog: Anuradha Marwah/Shutterstock.com; **310**: **background**: Indian atlas moth: Jiri Vlach/Shutterstock.com; **inset**: Grass jewel butterfly: Joey Bom/Shutterstock.com; **311**: **background**: Blue apollo butterfly: KRIACHKO OLEKSII/Shutterstock.com; **inset**: Golden birdwing butterfly: Matee Nuserm/Shutterstock.com; **312**: **top**: Water monitor lizard: Panusak Isariyanet/Shutterstock.com; **middle**: Norvill's flying lizard: Rizky Putra Ramadhan/Shutterstock.com; **bottom**: Chameleon: Shutterstock.com; **313**: **top**: Mugger crocodile: Shutterstock.com; **middle right**: Reticulated python: Shutterstock.com; **middle left**: Romulus Whitaker: Dr. Raju Kasambe, CC BY-SA 3.0 <https://

creativecommons.org/licenses/by-sa/3.0>, via Wikimedia Commons; **bottom**: Madras Crocodile Bank Trust: Kiran-Sharma/Shutterstock.com; **314**: **top**: Russell's viper: jaroslava V/Shutterstock.com; **middle**: Ornate flying snake: Polbkt/Shutterstock.com; **bottom**: King cobra: Padodo/Shutterstock.com; **315**: **top**: Leatherback sea turtle: Agami Photo Agency/Shutterstock.com; **bottom**: Batagur terrapin: Humus/Shutterstock.com; **316**: **top**: Hilsa: Oqbas/Shutterstock.com; **middle**: Giant clam: Christopher D. Morgan/Shutterstock.com; **bottom**: Whale shark: Adam Leaders/Shutterstock.com; **317**: **clockwise from top left**: Banyan tree: Shutterstock.com; Dragon Bamboo: Wagner Campelo/Shutterstock.com; Water lily leaves: Maria Shakhmatova/Shutterstock.com; Elephant creeper: Turrasno/Shutterstock.com; **318–319**: background: Root bridge: WanderDream/Shutterstock.com; **318 inset**: Umngot river aerial: Raj – Contributor/Shutterstock.com; **inset in inset**: Umngot river with boat: mukulb16/Shutterstock.com; **319 inset**: Krem Chympe river cave: I.H.Photography/Shutterstock.com; **320**: **middle left**: Rhubarb: Shutterstock.com; **middle right**: Corpse flower: Evenfh/Shutterstock.com; **bottom**: Jim Corbett National Park: Sourabh Bharti/Shutterstock.com; **321**: by courtesy of the record holder; **323**: **left**: by courtesy of the record holder; **bottom**: Khonoma village: Balajisrinivasan/Shutterstock.com; **326**: **top**: Tulsi Tanti: Shimansh, CC BY-SA 3.0 <https://creativecommons.org/licenses/by-sa/3.0>, via Wikimedia Commons; **bottom**: Shore temple: CCA-SA 4.0 International/Swarna1311 (https://commons.wikimedia.org/wiki/File:Shore_Temple_-Mamallapuram_-Tamil_Nadu_-N-TN-C55.jpg); **327**: by courtesy of the record holder; **328**: **left**: Eiffel tower replica: Shutterstock.com; **328–329**: Indore: PradeepGaurs/Shutterstock.com;

TRANSPORT 330–353

Opener pic, 330–331: Dinesh Hukmani/Shutterstock.com; **332**: **top**: Humber Sommer biplane: NicolaEFurness (WMUK), CC BY-SA 4.0 <https://creativecommons.org/licenses/by-sa/4.0>, via Wikimedia Commons; **middle**: Aero biplane: Kev Gregory/Shutterstock.com; **bottom**: Juhu Aerodrome: Hamehta3 at English Wikipedia, Public domain, via Wikimedia Commons; **333**: **top**: Malabar Princess: Swissair, CC BY-SA 4.0 <https://creativecommons.org/licenses/by-sa/4.0>, via Wikimedia Commons; **bottom left**: Kazakhstan plane Ilyushin: Felix Goetting (GFDL 1.2 <http://www.gnu.org/licenses/old-licenses/fdl-1.2.html> or GFDL 1.2 <http://www.gnu.org/licenses/old-licenses/fdl-1.2.html>), via Wikimedia Commons; **bottom right**: Saudi airlines: Lewis Grant, CC BY 2.0 <https://creativecommons.org/licenses/by/2.0>, via Wikimedia Commons; **334**: **top**: Chandigarh airport: Biswarup Ganguly, CC BY 3.0 <https://creativecommons.org/licenses/by/3.0>, via Wikimedia Commons; **middle**: Model of the HS-748: Ken Fielding/https://www.flickr.com/photos/kenfielding, CC BY-SA 3.0 <https://creativecommons.org/licenses/by-sa/3.0>, via Wikimedia Commons; **bottom**: Model of 737-900 aircraft: Boeing Dreamscape, CC BY 2.0 <https://creativecommons.org/licenses/by/2.0>, via Wikimedia Commons; **335**: **middle**: Terminal 3, Delhi airport: Sumit.Kumar.99/Shutterstock.com; **bottom**: Daulat Beg Oldi: Manas.chafekar, CC BY-SA 4.0 <https://creativecommons.org/licenses/by-sa/4.0>, via Wikimedia Commons; **336–337**: **background**: Craig Dingle/Shutterstock.com; **336**: **top inset**: Sarla Thakral: Public domain, via Wikimedia Commons; **middle inset**: Durba Banerjee: Medhavigandhi, CC BY 4.0 <https://creativecommons.org/licenses/by/4.0>, via Wikimedia Commons; **bottom inset**: Zoya Aggarwal: Zephyrinthesky1, CC BY-SA 4.0 <https://creativecommons.org/licenses/by-sa/4.0>, via Wikimedia Commons; **338**: **top**: Calcutta Tramways Company: © Vyacheslav Argenberg / http://www.vascoplanet.com/, CC BY 4.0 <https://creativecommons.org/licenses/by/4.0>, via Wikimedia Commons; **middle**: BBCI logo: RegentsPark, CC BY-SA 3.0 <https://creativecommons.org/licenses/by-sa/3.0>, via Wikimedia Commons; **bottom**: BBCI locomotive: Shamim Mohamed from Republic of San Francisco, CC BY-SA 2.0 <https://creativecommons.org/licenses/by-sa/2.0>, via Wikimedia Commons; **339**: **top**: Green Corridor: Shaswat Nimesh, CC BY-SA 4.0 <https://creativecommons.org/licenses/by-sa/4.0>, via Wikimedia Commons; **bottom**: Golden Temple Mail: Ian Peter Morton/Shutterstock.com; **340–341**: **background**: Dinesh Hukmani/Shutterstock.com; **340**: **inset** Dibrugarh Station: Sai Rung Wanoak/Shutterstock.com; **341 inset**: Silchar Superfast Express: Smeet Chowdhury, CC BY 2.0 <https://creativecommons.org/licenses/by/2.0>, via Wikimedia Commons; **342**: **top**: Deccan Queen: Dinesh Hukmani/Shutterstock.com; **bottom**: Integral Coach Factory: Saiphani02, CC BY-SA 4.0 <https://creativecommons.org/licenses/by-sa/4.0>, via Wikimedia Commons; **343**: **top**: Chattarpati Shivaji Terminal: ravirsn/Shutterstock.com; **bottom**: Interior of Tejas Express: Ministry of Railways (GODL-India), GODL-India <https://data.gov.in/sites/default/files/Gazette_Notification_OGDL.pdf>, via Wikimedia Commons; **344**: **top**: Delhi Metro Blue Line: WillaMissionary, CC0, via Wikimedia Commons; **middle**: PM Modi inaugurating underwater metro tunnel: Prime Minister's Office (GODL-India), GODL-India <https://data.gov.in/sites/default/files/Gazette_Notification_OGDL.pdf>, via Wikimedia Commons; **345**: **top**: Original Grand Trunk Road between Margalla and Kala Chitta: Khalid Mahmood, CC BY-SA 3.0 <https://creativecommons.org/licenses/by-sa/3.0>, via Wikimedia Commons; **bottom**: De Dion Bouton: Stas Kozlovskiy, CC BY-SA 4.0 <https://creativecommons.org/licenses/by-sa/4.0>, via Wikimedia Commons; **346–347**: **background**: Tanglang La: mrinalpal/Shutterstock.com; **348**: **top**: CNG Auto: Melnikov Dmitriy/Shutterstock.com; **middle**: Hyundai Kona: Alexander Migl, CC BY-SA 4.0 <https://creativecommons.org/licenses/by-sa/4.0>, via Wikimedia Commons; **bottom**: Delhi-Dehradun Expressway: Bhatakta Manav/Shutterstock.com; **349**: **top**: Reshma Nilofer Naha: Ministry of Women and Child Development (GODL-India), GODL-India <https://data.gov.in/sites/default/files/Gazette_Notification_OGDL.pdf>, via Wikimedia Commons; **middle**: HMS Trincomalee: Ian Petticrew, CC BY-SA 2.0 <https://creativecommons.org/licenses/by-sa/2.0>, via Wikimedia Commons; **bottom left**: Logo of Tamil Nadu State Transport Corporation: File:Emblem of Tamil Nadu.svg:User:NikNaksFile:Emblem of India.svg: Various(see file)File:Flag_of_India.svg: various (see file)Derivative work:Perumalism Chat 08:23, 19 July 2013 (UTC), Public domain, via Wikimedia Commons; **350**: SS *Jalabala*: The Scindia Steam Navigation Company Ltd., Public domain, via Wikimedia Commons; **351**: **top**: Aerial View of Hindustan Shipyard Dock: Hslvizag, CC BY-SA 4.0 <https://creativecommons.org/licenses/by-sa/4.0>, via Wikimedia Commons; **350–351**: **bottom**: Ennore Port: nektofadeev/Shutterstock.com; **352–353**: **background**: AnilD/Shutterstock.com; **352**: **top**: Kochi Water Metro: Thilsebatti,

CC BY-SA 4.0 <https://creativecommons.org/licenses/by-sa/4.0>, via Wikimedia Commons; **352**: **bottom**: Kedarnath Heli-Tourism: AjayTvm/Shutterstock.com; **353**: **top**: Maharajas Express: Aswin Krishna Poyil, CC0, via Wikimedia Commons; **353**: **middle**: Kashi Ropeway: Vanilllla/Shutterstock.com; **353**: **bottom**: Delhi-Mumbai Expressway: Memories Over Mocha/Shutterstock.com;;

BUSINESS AND ECONOMY 354–377

Opener pic, 354–355: Travel mania/Shutterstock.com; **356**: **top**: Sikkim Legislative Assembly: Dr Arpan Chatterjee/Shutterstock.com; **middle**: Morarji Desai: Illustration by Ayesha Syed; **bottom**: Dr Manmohan Singh: imagemaker/Shutterstock.com; **357**: **top**: Nirmala Sitharaman: PradeepGaurs/Shutterstock.com; **middle**: Amartya Sen: Sk Hasan Ali/Shutterctock.com; **bottom**: Railway employees: Talukdar David/Shutterstock.com; **358–359**: **background**: Saikat Paul/Shutterstock.com; clockwise, from top: SFI strike: Im_rohitbhakar/Shutterstock.com; Farmer's strike at Delhi border: V. Arun Kumar/Shutterstock.com; Strike in front of JU: Saikat Paul/Shutterstock.com; **360**: **top**: Yogesh Chander Deveshwar: St Gallen Symposium/CCA-SA 4.0 International licence; **bottom left**: Aditya Puri: TERumel/CCA-SA 4.0 International licence (https://commons.wikimedia.org/wiki/File:Aditya_Puri.jpg); **bottom right**: 500-rupee notes: Narottam Rabha/Shutterstock.com; **361**: **top**: PNB: mrinalpal/Shuttertock.com; **bottom**: Standard Chartered: NEKOMURA/Shutterstock.com; **362**: **top**: ICICI: sockagphoto/Shutterctock.com; **bottom**: RuPay: by courtesy of Yukta Vats; **363**: LIC: Albin Raj/Shutterctock.com; **364**: Ambanis: Manoej Paateel/Shutterstock.com; **365**: **background**: Tapati Rinchumrus/Shutterstock.com; insets: all illustrations by Surojit Bhattacharya/© Hachette India; **366**: Jamnagar refinery: Snapshots Profile/Shutterstock.com; **367**: Solar cooker: PradeepGaurs/Shutterstock.com; **369**: Coal mine in Katni: arun sambhu mishra/Shutterstock.com; **370–371**: **background**: SAHAS2015/Shutterctock.com; **inset**: Tourists buying perfume: Dr. Nagaraja Sharma/Shutterstock.com; **374–375**: Cannes: hansleyfr/Shutterstock.com; **376**: Export-import: mapsandphotos/Shutterstock.com;

ADVENTURE 378–407

Opener pic, 378–379: touringdiaries/Shutterstock.com; **380**: **top**: Microlight flight: ovbelov/Shutterstock.com; **bottom left and right**: by courtesy of the record holders; **381**: **top**: **background**: BASE jump: Salienko Evgenii/Shutterstock.com; **top, inset**: Pitampura TV tower: Tarunpant, CC BY-SA 3.0 <https://creativecommons.org/licenses/by-sa/3.0>, via Wikimedia Commons; **bottom**: Ballooning Club of India: आशीष भटनागर, CC BY-SA 3.0 <https://creativecommons.org/licenses/by-sa/3.0>, via Wikimedia Commons; **382–383**: **background**: muratart/Shutterstock.com; **382**: **inset**: Paragliding at Bir Billing: Sudip Jotshi/Shutterstock.com; **384**: **top**: Satyendra Verma: by courtesy of record holder: **middle**: zipline: NeydtStock/Shutterstock.com; **bottom**: Motor Glider: dean bertoncelj/Shutterstock.com; **385**: **top**: Major DP Singh: Amit Vermaz, CC BY-SA 4.0 <https://creativecommons.org/licenses/by-sa/4.0>, via Wikimedia Commons; **bottom left**: Harshil Virendra Mane: by courtesy of record holder; **bottom right**: Skydiver in free fall: Sky Antonio/Shutterstock.com; **386**: **top**: GQ – women: by courtesy of record holder; **bottom**: Eric Paul: by courtesy of record holder; **387**: **top**: by courtesy of record holder; **middle**: by courtesy of record holder; **bottom**: by courtesy of record holder; **388**: **all images**: by courtesy of record holders; **389**: **top**: road image: आर्यावर्त, CC BY-SA 4.0 <https://creativecommons.org/licenses/by-sa/4.0>, via Wikimedia Commons; **bottom left and right**: by courtesy of record holders; **390–391**: images are by courtesy of record holders; **392–393**: background: Paulose NK/Shutterstock.com; **393**: **top**: Camels at Thar dessert: Harshal Sathe/Shutterstock.com; **bottom**: Mountain Biking in Ladakh: Yogifromhills/Shutterstock.com; **394–395**: images are by courtesy of record holders; **396**: **background**: Ashish Lingwal/Shutterstock.com; **397**: **background**: Summer Paradive/Shutterstock.com; **398–399**: images are by courtesy of record holders; **401**: **top**: Siddhartha Ghosh: image by the courtesy of record holder; **bottom**: Ironman Triathlon: Maridav/Shutterstock.com; **402–403**: **background**: Soham Chhajer/Shutterstock.com; **402**: **inset**: Beach Run: SubhadipRudra/Shutterstock.com; **403**: **inset**: Cross-Country Ultra Runs: nkumarm/Shutterstock.com; **404**: **top**: Fauja Singh: HiraV, CC BY-SA 3.0 <https://creativecommons.org/licenses/by-sa/3.0>, via Wikimedia Commons; **bottom**: Adil Nargolwala: by courtesy of record holder; **405**: **top**: Garwal Himayalas: Paul Hamilton, CC BY-SA 2.0 <https://creativecommons.org/licenses/by-sa/2.0>, via Wikimedia Commons; **bottom**: The Himalayan Club: Sumita Roy Dutta, CC BY-SA 4.0 <https://creativecommons.org/licenses/by-sa/4.0>, via Wikimedia Commons; **406**: **top**: Denali National Park and Preserve, Public domain, via Wikimedia Commons; **bottom left**: Himalayan Mountaineering Institute: Nomad Tales, CC BY-SA 2.0 <https://creativecommons.org/licenses/by-sa/2.0>, via Wikimedia Commons; **bottom right**: Mahar regiment logo: Jean-Paul GIBERT, Public domain, via Wikimedia Commons; **407**: Indian Station, Maitri: Ministry of Science & Technology (GODL-India), GODL-India <https://data.gov.in/sites/default/files/Gazette_Notification_OGDL.pdf>, via Wikimedia Commons;

SPORTS 408–466

Opener pic, 408–409: PeopleImages/Shutterstock.com; **410**: **top**: Balbir Singh Sr: Balbir Singh (Senior), Public domain, via Wikimedia Commons; **middle**: Olympic Order: Pistaun, CC BY-SA 4.0 <https://creativecommons.org/licenses/by-sa/4.0>, via Wikimedia Commons; **bottom**: Dara Singh: Camaal Fotografia, CC BY-SA 4.0 <https://creativecommons.org/licenses/by-sa/4.0>, via Wikimedia Commons; **411**: **clockwise from top left**: Commonwealth Games stamp: rook76/Shutterstock.com; Deepika Kumari: CCA-SA 3.0 Unported/Rajivranprasad; Sheetal Devi: Press Information Bureau, CC BY-SA 4.0 <https://creativecommons.org/licenses/by-sa/4.0>, via Wikimedia Commons; Pullela Gopichand: reddees/Shutterstock.com; M.C. Mary Kom: Sudarshan Jha/Shutterstock.com; **412**: **top right**: Abhishek Verma: Government Open Data License–India(GODL)/President's Secretariat; **middle left**: Harvinder Singh: Prime Minister's Office (GODL-India), GODL-India <https://data.gov.in/sites/default/files/Gazette_Notification_OGDL.pdf>, via Wikimedia Commons; **middle right**: Jayanta Talukdar: Government Open Data License–India(GODL)/President's Secretariat; **bottom**: Dola Banerjee: Luis Felipe Paulinyi, Public domain, via Wikimedia Commons; **413**: **top right**: Bahadur Singh Chouhan: [1], Public domain, via Wikimedia Commons; **middle**: : Jyothi Surekha Vennam: President's Secretariat (GODL-India), GODL-India <https://data.gov.in/sites/default/files/Gazette_Notification_OGDL.pdf>, via

IMAGE COPYRIGHT INFORMATION

Wikimedia Commons; **414**: **top**: Milkha Singh: Sanyam Bahga, CC BY-SA 3.0 <https://creativecommons.org/licenses/by-sa/3.0>, via Wikimedia Commons; **bottom**: P.T. Usha: Ministry of Youth Affairs and Sports (GODL-India), GODL-India; **415**: **clockwise from top left**: Phadeppa Darappa Chaugule: Undetermined (Photo uploaded by Dmuc (talk) (Uploads), Public domain, via Wikimedia Commons; Shiny Wilson: Ministry of Information & Broadcasting (GODL-India), GODL-India <https://data.gov.in/sites/default/files/Gazette_Notification_OGDL.pdf>, via Wikimedia Commons; Hima Das: Denis Kuvaev/Shutterstock.com; **416**: **top left**: Anju Bobby George: CCA-SA 4.0 International/Jyothishvijay; Neeraj Chopra: DD News, CC BY 4.0 <https://creativecommons.org/licenses/by/4.0>, via Wikimedia Commons; **bottom clockwise from left**: Dutee Chand: Athletics Federation of India, CC BY-SA 4.0 <https://creativecommons.org/licenses/by-sa/4.0>, via Wikimedia Commons; Yogesh Kathuniya: Prime Minister's Office (GODL-India), GODL-India <https://data.gov.in/sites/default/files/Gazette_Notification_OGDL.pdf>, via Wikimedia Commons; Deepa Malik: Government Open Data License–India(GODL)/Prime Minister's Office, Government of India; **417**: Avinash Sable: U.S. Army, CC BY 2.0 <https://creativecommons.org/licenses/by/2.0>, via Wikimedia Commons; **418**: Jwala Gutta and Ashwini Ponnappa: Government Open Data License–India(GODL)/Ministry of Youth Affairs and Sports; **419**: **clockwise from top**: Chirag Shetty and Satwiksairaj Rankireddy: ryanko/Shutterstock.com; Saina Nehwal: BUGNUT23 / Shutterstock.com; P.V. Sindhu: Abdul Razak Latif/Shutterstock.com; Dinesh Khanna: CCA-SA 4.0 International/Vkg wifi; **420**: **top**: Prakash Padukone: CCA-SA 3.0 Unported/Mussarat Kang; **middle right**: Indonesian stamp commemorating Thomas Cup: aniejasin/Shutterstock.com; **421**: **clockwise from top left**: Aparna Popat: Government Open Data License–India(GODL)/President's Secretariat; Satnam Singh Bhamara: All Elite Wrestling, CC BY-SA 4.0 <https://creativecommons.org/licenses/by-sa/4.0>, via Wikimedia Commons; Prashanti Singh: CCA-SA 3.0 Unported/Risingprincess; **422**: **clockwise from top left**: Sachin Siwach: Akshaysiwach1, CC BY-SA 4.0 <https://creativecommons.org/licenses/by-sa/4.0>, via Wikimedia Commons; Vijendra Singh: Bollywood Hungama, CC BY 3.0 <https://creativecommons.org/licenses/by/3.0>, via Wikimedia Commons; Hawa Singh: Sanjukta663, CC BY-SA 4.0 <https://creativecommons.org/licenses/by-sa/4.0>, via Wikimedia Commons; Vikas Krishan: Shivam.suppal1010, CC BY-SA 4.0 <https://creativecommons.org/licenses/by-sa/4.0>, via Wikimedia Commons; **423**: **top**: Amandeep Singh: Ministry of Youth Affairs and Sports (GODL-India), GODL-India <https://data.gov.in/sites/default/files/Gazette_Notification_OGDL.pdf>, via Wikimedia Commons; **bottom**: Antim Panghal: Prime Minister's Office (GODL-India), GODL-India <https://data.gov.in/sites/default/files/Gazette_Notification_OGDL.pdf>, via Wikimedia Commons;
424: **clockwise from top left**: AIBA stamp: Pavel Kapysh/Shutterstock.com; D. Gukesh: CC BY-SA 2.0 Generic/Frans Peeters; Pravin Thipsay: CCA-SA 4.0 International/Swaralithipsay; Viswanathan Anand: Wolfgang Jekel, CC BY 2.0 <https://creativecommons.org/licenses/by/2.0>, via Wikimedia Commons; **425**: **top**: Mir Sultan Khan: Unknown Cameraman of 1932, CC BY-SA 4.0 <https://creativecommons.org/licenses/by-sa/4.0>, via Wikimedia Commons; **bottom**: Divya Deshmukh: Frans Peeters, CC BY-SA 2.0 <https://creativecommons.org/licenses/by-sa/2.0>, via Wikimedia Commons; **426**: **top**: Manuel Aaron: Jack de Nijs for Anefo, CC0, via Wikimedia Commons; **middle left**: S. Vijayalakshmi: GFHund, CC BY-SA 4.0 <https://creativecommons.org/licenses/by-sa/4.0>, via Wikimedia Commons; **middle right**: R. Praggnanandhaa: CC BY-SA 2.0 Generic/Frans Peeters; **bottom**: K. Humpy: Government Open Data License–India(GODL)/President's Secretariat; **427**: **top**: D. Harika: Artsmith.concepts, CC BY-SA 4.0 <https://creativecommons.org/licenses/by-sa/4.0>, via Wikimedia Commons; **bottom**: Shafali Verma: CCA-SA 4.0 International/Bahnfrend; **428**: **top**: Mithali Raj: CCA-SA 3.0 Unported/Sadhguru (https://www.youtube.com/watch?v=KJF5C00BSRY); **bottom**: Indian Women's Cricket Team with the President and the PM: both the images by courtesy of the Press Information Bureau (PIB); **429**: **top**: Jhulan Goswami: paddynapper, CC BY-SA 2.0 <https://creativecommons.org/licenses/by-sa/2.0>, via Wikimedia Commons; **bottom**: Smriti Mandhana: Ministry of Youth Affairs and Sports (GODL-India), GODL-India <https://data.gov.in/sites/default/files/Gazette_Notification_OGDL.pdf>, via Wikimedia Commons; **430**: **top**: Sunil Gavaskar: Bollywood Hungama, CC BY 3.0 <https://creativecommons.org/licenses/by/3.0>, via Wikimedia Commons; **bottom right**: M.S. Dhoni: Suhail Suri/Shutterstock.com; **bottom right**: Harmanpreet Kaur: CCA-SA 4.0 International/Bahnfrend; **431**: **top**: Rahul Dravid: Chubby Chandru, CC BY 2.0 <https://creativecommons.org/licenses/by/2.0>, via Wikimedia Commons; **bottom right**: Anil Kumble: CCA-SA 3.0 Unported/lensbug.chandru; **bottom left**: Virendra Sehwag: Flying Cloud, CC BY 2.0 <https://creativecommons.org/licenses/by/2.0>, via Wikimedia Commons; **432–433**: Virat Kohli background: Alex Davidson-ICC/Contributor/gettyimages.in; **434**: **top**: Shubman Gill: Bollywood Hungama, CC BY 3.0 <https://creativecommons.org/licenses/by/3.0>, via Wikimedia Commons; **bottom**: Sachin Tendulkar: PIXATHON/Shutterstock.com; **435**: **top**: 1983 World Cup picture: Institution:President's Sectretariat, GODL-India <https://data.gov.in/sites/default/files/Gazette_Notification_OGDL.pdf>, via Wikimedia Commons; **middle**: Rohit Sharma: Prime Minister's Office (GODL-India), GODL-India <https://data.gov.in/sites/default/files/Gazette_Notification_OGDL.pdf>, via Wikimedia Commons; **bottom left**: Virat Kohli: lensbug.chandru, CC BY 2.0 <https://creativecommons.org/licenses/by/2.0>, via Wikimedia Commons; **bottom right**: Yuvraj Singh: Chubby Chandru, CC BY 2.0 <https://creativecommons.org/licenses/by/2.0>, via Wikimedia Commons; **436**: **top**: Geet Sethi: President's Secretariat, GODL-India <https://data.gov.in/sites/default/files/Gazette_Notification_OGDL.pdf>, via Wikimedia Commons; **bottom**: Pankaj Advani: Benutzer:Bill da Flute, CC BY-SA 3.0 <https://creativecommons.org/licenses/by-sa/3.0>, via Wikimedia Commons; **437**: **top**: R. Umadevi: Government Open Data License–India(GODL)/Ministry of Women and Child Development; **bottom**: Aditya Mehta: Martin Rulsch, Wikimedia Commons, CC BY-SA 4.0, CC BY-SA 4.0 <https://creativecommons.org/licenses/by-sa/4.0>, via Wikimedia Commons; **438**: **top**: Baichung Bhutia: CCA-SA 3.0 Unported/Baichung Bhutia; **middle**: S.A. Rahim: Wikimedia Commons/Fair Use/The Hindu; **bottom**: Syed Nayeemuddin: CCA-SA 3.0 Unported/Biswarup Ganguly; **439**: Inder Singh: CCA-SA 4.0 International/Vickrem3; **440**: **top**: Subimal Chuni Goswami: Wikimedia Commons/Fair Use/Vidmarp; **middle left**: Bartholomew Ogbeche: CCA-SA 4.0 International/Rufyrosh; **middle right**: Ferran Corominas: Sahil200034, CC BY-SA 4.0 <https://creativecommons.org/licenses/by-sa/4.0>, via

Unported/Pvt Pauline; **bottom right**: S. Chikkarangappa: SurajInswamy, CC BY-SA 4.0 <https://creativecommons.org/licenses/by-sa/4.0>, via Wikimedia Commons; **bottom left**: P.K. Banerjee: Wikimedia Commons/Fair Use/Unknown Author; **442**: **top**: Arjun Atwal: CC BY-SA 2.0 Generic/Keith Allison; **middle**: Ranveer Singh Saini: by courtesy of the record holder; **bottom**: Jeev Milkha Singh: mooinblack/Shutterstock.com; **443**: **top**: Aditi Ashok: CHEN WS/Shutterstock.com; **bottom**: Rashid Khan: Yu Chun Christopher Wong/Shutterstock.com; **444**: **top**: Kapil Dev: Bollywood Hungama, CC BY 3.0 <https://creativecommons.org/licenses/by/3.0>, via Wikimedia Commons; **middle**: S.S.P. Chawrasia: CCA-SA 3.0 Unported/Pvt Pauline; **bottom**: Anirban Lahiri: CCA-SA 4.0 International/Punishar; **445**: **middle**: Shubhankar Sharma: Yu Chun Christopher Wong/Shutterstock.com; **bottom**: Dipa Karmakar: Ministry for Development of North-East Region (GODL-India), GODL-India <https://data.gov.in/sites/default/files/Gazette_Notification_OGDL.pdf>, via Wikimedia Commons; **446**: **top**: Prime Minister's Office (GODL-India), GODL-India <https://data.gov.in/sites/default/files/Gazette_Notification_OGDL.pdf>, via Wikimedia Commons; **middle**: Dilip Tirkey: Government Open Data License–India(GODL/Ministry of Youth Affairs and Sports; **447**: Dhyan Chand: Wikimedia Commons/Fair Use/Faizhaider; **448**: Richard J. Allen: Wikimedia Commons/Fair Use/Unknown author; **449**: **middle**: Vandana Katariya: Prime Minister's Office (GODL-India), GODL-India <https://data.gov.in/sites/default/files/Gazette_Notification_OGDL.pdf>, via Wikimedia Commons; **bottom**: Pro Kabaddi: ARTDOWN/Shutterstock.com; **450**: **clockwise from top left**: Pooja Kadian: Government Open Data License–India(GODL)/President's Secretariat; Sushila Devi: Prime Minister's Office (GODL-India), GODL-India <https://data.gov.in/sites/default/files/Gazette_Notification_OGDL.pdf>, via Wikimedia Commons; Shiva Keshavan: Sandro Halank, Wikimedia Commons, CC-BY-SA 3.0, CC BY-SA 3.0 <https://creativecommons.org/licenses/by-sa/3.0>, via Wikimedia Commons; Pawan Sehrawat: President's Secretariat (GODL-India), GODL-India <https://data.gov.in/sites/default/files/Gazette_Notification_OGDL.pdf>, via Wikimedia Commons; **451**: **middle**: Abhinav Bindra: Open Government Licence version 1.0/British High Commission, India; **bottom right**: Mairaj Ahmad Khan: CCA SA 2.0 Generic/U.S. Army; **bottom left**: Farman Basha: CCA-SA 3.0 Unported/Laura Hale; **452**: **top left**: Rahi Sarnobat: President's Secretariat (GODL-India), GODL-India <https://data.gov.in/sites/default/files/Gazette_Notification_OGDL.pdf>, via Wikimedia Commons; **middle right**: Rajyavardhan Singh Rathore: Ministry of Youth Affairs and Sports (GODL-India), GODL-India <https://data.gov.in/sites/default/files/Gazette_Notification_OGDL.pdf>, via Wikimedia Commons; **453**: **top**: Jaspal Rana: Government Open Data License–India(GODL/Ministry of Petroleum and Natural Gas; **middle**: Ronjan Sodhi: Government Open Data License–India(GODL)/President's Secretariat; **bottom**: Gagan Narang: Ministry of Youth Affairs and Sports (GODL-India), GODL-India <https://data.gov.in/sites/default/files/Gazette_Notification_OGDL.pdf>, via Wikimedia Commons; **454**: **top**: Joshna Chinappa: CC BY-SA 2.0 Generic/Simitha T.Singam; **middle**: Manu Bhaker and Sarabjot Singh: ProPhoto1234/Shutterstock.com; **455**: **clockwise from top left**: Dipika Pallikal: julesgriff from Burlington, CT, USA, CC BY-SA 2.0 <https://creativecommons.org/licenses/by-sa/2.0>, via Wikimedia Commons; Saurav Ghoshal: Caravanum, CC BY-SA 2.0 <https://creativecommons.org/licenses/by-sa/2.0>, via Wikimedia Commons; Bhuvaneshwari Kumari: CCA-SA 4.0 International/Tpsn98290; **456**: **top**: Shikha Tandon: Government Open Data License–India(GODL)/President's Secretariat; **middle**: Virdhawal Khade: Pratham Books from India, CC BY 2.0 <https://creativecommons.org/licenses/by/2.0>, via Wikimedia Commons; **457**: **top**: Sajan Prakash: Ministry of Youth Affairs and Sports (GODL-India), GODL-India <https://data.gov.in/sites/default/files/Gazette_Notification_OGDL.pdf>, via Wikimedia Commons; **bottom**: A. Sharath Kamal: Government Open Data License–India(GODL/Ministry of Youth Affairs and Sports; **458**: **top**: Manika Batra: Government of Odisha, CC BY 4.0 <https://creativecommons.org/licenses/by/4.0>, via Wikimedia Commons; **bottom**: Harmeet Desai: CC BY-SA 2.0 Generic/XIAOYU TANG; **459**: **top**: Mouma Das: Ministry of Youth Affairs and Sports (GODL-India), GODL-India <https://data.gov.in/sites/default/files/Gazette_Notification_OGDL.pdf>, via Wikimedia Commons; **bottom**: Karman Kaur Thandi: CC BY-SA 2.0 Generic/si.robi; **460**: **top**: Leander Paes: Romain Biard/Shutterstock.com; **bottom**: Somdev Devvarman: CCA-SA 3.0 Unported/Photo by DAVID ILIFF; **461**: **top left**: Leander Paes and Mahesh Bhupati: Public domain, via Wikimedia Commons; **top right**: Mahesh Bhupati: Chris Harvey/Shutterstock.com; **bottom**: Sania Mirza: BUGNUT23/Shutterstock.com; **462**: **clockwise from top**: Rohan Bopanna: Wikimedia CC BY-SA 2.0 Generic/si.robi; Saikhom Mirabai Chanu: Government Open Data License–India(GODL/Ministry of Youth Affairs and Sports); Karnam Malleswari: Government of India, GODL-India <https://data.gov.in/sites/default/files/Gazette_Notification_OGDL.pdf>, via Wikimedia Commons; Yuki Bhambri: CC BY-SA 2.0 Generic/si.robi; **463**: **top**: Yumnam Renu: Government Open Data License–India(GODL)/President's Secretariat; **bottom**: Jeremy Lalrinnunga: cc-by-sa 3.0 © Marcus Cyron, CC BY-SA 3.0 <https://creativecommons.org/licenses/by-sa/3.0>, via Wikimedia Commons; **464**: Vinesh Phogat: Azamat Mukanov/Shutterstock.com; **465**: Bajrang Punia: Azamat Mukanov/Shutterstock.com; **466**: **top**: Sushil Kumar: Ten Sports, CC BY 3.0 <https://creativecommons.org/licenses/by/3.0>, via Wikimedia Commons; **middle**: Deepak Punia: Zandersyn, CC BY-SA 4.0 <https://creativecommons.org/licenses/by-sa/4.0>, via Wikimedia Commons; **bottom**: Anita Sheoran: Prime Minister's Office (GODL-India), GODL-India <https://data.gov.in/sites/default/files/Gazette_Notification_OGDL.pdf>, via Wikimedia Commons;

Special notebox designs throughout the book:
Window frame: Ana Nefedova/Shutterstock.com; Marker highlighter yellow design element: rzarek/Shutterstock.com; Blob-shaped illustration: Maria_Petrishina/Shutterstock.com.

RULES AND GUIDELINES

PREAMBLE

Limca Book of Records ('LBR'), as a record-keeping publication, has been compiling records since 1987 and has seen over 30 editions. It is India's first and longest continuously published book of records.

It is, however, a private book, run and managed by a private organization with no public funding whatsoever. The retail price is also subsidized by the owner Coca-Cola India Private Limited ('CCIPL'). The *LBR* also accepts absolutely no funding or payment or any other charges from record applicants or record holders for entries or for claims processing or for publication acceptance.

Consequently, it is important to understand that all decisions are taken by applying a set of standards that are specific and stringent, but equally are subjective, and based on what the editors and staff of *LBR*, and Consultants ('*LBR* Team') think are most suitable for the book. And that decision is solely *LBR*'s, and *LBR* is not answerable to or the decision is not affected by any other individual, entity, or by what another entity (including other record books), may do or accept.

I. INTRODUCTION

1. *LBR* is a catalogue of achievements made by Indians. It catalogues unique milestones and landmarks including, but not limited to, firsts, bests, mosts, inventions, discoveries, and honours and awards received by Indians at home or abroad in all fields – both human and natural – that can be qualified in superlatives and that conform to the prevailing editorial policy in force during any year.

While this is primarily a catalogue of superlatives and achievements, it is also a book of records, and a work of reference, and therefore in the spirit of empirical record keeping, it will record other milestones that may not always be celebratory or laudatory and may even be negative but are notable and are records, such as 'longest trial in a court of law' or records pertaining to disasters or crime. Any such record is a statement of fact on record, and is not meant to downplay any entity, nor encourage anyone to attempt to beat such records. *LBR* does not solicit or accept claims for negative records.

LBR encompasses an extensive range of information and is thus divided into chapters and record categories. Prospective entries under these chapters and categories may include, but are not limited to, any of the following headings: a record, a quantifiable skill, a superlative or historical landmark/phenomenon/man-made or natural event/process/structure considered as remarkable as a record by the *LBR* Team

2. Anyone with a reasonable claim for a record may write to *LBR* for possible inclusion (subject to acceptance under *LBR* criteria).

3. Entry into *LBR* and attempt of any record are subject to compliance with the general Terms and Conditions (the 'Terms') as well as the specific rules and guidelines applicable to each type of record attempt or claim (the 'Attempt'). Where pre-existing terms are not there to cover a particular record or claim, a relevant policy shall be decided by the *LBR* Team and that shall be binding. Earlier policies and parameters go under continuous review and modifications, and the *LBR* Team is not bound to any previously existing parameters.

4. Individuals or groups interested in attempting to set or break a record must understand and accept *LBR*'s general policy, study the Terms and the specific Rules and Guidelines applicable to the Attempt, and sign the Disclaimer and Indemnity Form (available before the commencement of any Attempt) in order to be considered for inclusion in *LBR*. Records already set and sent for inclusion ex post facto are also bound by all these Rules and Guidelines; acceptance of all Terms and Conditions is a necessary qualifier to any record being accepted.

5. All Terms, Rules, and Guidelines apply to a person/persons making a record Attempt ('Applicant'/'Applicants') who send an Application(s) to *LBR* as well as any and every person/persons ('Participant'/'Participants') part of such an Attempt (for example, in an Attempt by a group or organization).

6. *LBR* is owned by CCIPL, which reserves the right to modify these Terms and any other Rules and Guidelines established in relation to an Attempt or general policy. CCIPL does not implement or involve itself in editorial policy and does not process submissions. *LBR* is collated and published by publishers Hachette Book Publishing India Pvt. Ltd/Hachette India, who will process the entries, make all decisions on acceptance and inclusion, and publish the book autonomously as is required for an independent book of records. Publication dates and content design are decided and implemented in conjunction with CCIPL.

All such modifications of the Terms and Conditions, and policy, will be updated on the webpage: https://www.hachetteindia.com/home/rulesandguidelines (for the latest Rules and Guidelines, and updates), and anyone attempting to enter their record in *LBR* must review the Terms and the corresponding rules for each Attempt regularly to remain informed of any changes or modifications therein.

7. *LBR* and its representatives do NOT charge any fee or accept any money for the application, review, processing, or acceptance of records [please see clauses III.(A)18 and III.(A)19 of 'General Guidelines' pertaining to certificates and discount on sale of copies to Applicants].

NOTE: *LBR* emphasizes safety and compliance very clearly in all its guidelines. No record application is reviewed or even considered without all due process being completed in an approved submission including all safety checks and regulatory compliance (the onus of listing and procuring which lies on the Applicant(s)) being certified by the authorities in question (see also Section VIII Safety Precautions).

II. ELIGIBILITY CRITERIA

1. To be eligible for consideration by the *LBR* Team for a successful Attempt, 'Applicant(s)' must fulfil the following conditions:

a. The Applicant should be a resident Indian or non-resident Indian (NRI)/overseas citizen of India (OCI)/Person of Indian Origin (PIO) (at least one grandparent should be Indian), and must submit ID and residence proofs and other documents as required by law to establish this.

b. The Applicant must have read and consented to the Terms, the specific Rules and Guidelines applicable to the Attempt, and must have signed and submitted the Disclaimer and Indemnity Form before undertaking the Attempt.

2. The Attempt must be corroborated by a valid proof of age, i.e., above 18 years:

a. The Applicant must be above eighteen (18) years of age.

b. The Applicant must have carefully read and consented to the Terms, and the specific Rules and Guidelines set down for the Attempt. Before engaging in the Attempt, the Applicant must have submitted the Disclaimer and Indemnity Form as well as a Certificate of Medical Fitness (with the medical practitioner's registration number mentioned on it) to attempt any physical feat or one involving mental exertion, or one deemed so by the *LBR* Team.

NOTE: The *LBR* Team may still include records related to official sports events (associated with only officially recognized national or international bodies like BCCI, IOA, ICC, FIFA, etc.), and medical science (like heaviest baby, lightest baby, etc., where the minor is not an active participant or being exhorted to perform or create a record that is beyond a minor's normal capability). Further, the *LBR* Team may choose to include certain records from the public domain, which may have the involvement of a minor. All these exceptions are subject to the sole discretion and decision of the *LBR* Team.

3. The onus and responsibility of being compliant in the particular context of a record claim lies with the Applicant, and a submission to *LBR* means that all laws, rules, regulations, permissions, and necessary approvals from the right authority have been taken. For example, a driving record means that the Applicant has the necessary and valid driving licence; or a structure erected means that the Applicants have got the necessary approvals including but not limited to all safety clearances needed (structural, mechanical, electrical, fire, etc.) or an event held means that the necessary law and order permissions, etc., have been taken. *LBR* accepts no responsibility for damage or harm to public property that may result from necessary clearances and approvals not being taken and reserves the right to prosecute Applicants found in breach of such safety standards. Above all, safety of people attending or in the vicinity is paramount.

III. GENERAL GUIDELINES

A. GENERAL

1. Standard norms and rules should be adhered to while setting national and world records. In some cases there may be additional event-specific norms that need to be observed.

2. The onus of proving a record claim rests on the Applicant. The claim, signed by the Applicant, should be backed by adequate and satisfactory documents without which it will not be accepted. Materials submitted as supporting evidence, such as press clippings, audio/video tapes, flash/pen drives, CDs, DVDs, hard drives, and photographs, become the property of the publisher, Hachette Book Publishing India Pvt. Ltd/Hachette India and the Copyright Owner, CCIPL, and only copies should be submitted with the originals kept safe by the claimant for Life after the claim has been accepted (see also Section V [Evidence]). Forms such as the Application Form duly signed by the Applicant and validating/witnessing authorities as indicated by the *LBR* Team and/or the Rules and Guidelines need to be submitted in the original (hard copy) and a copy retained by the Applicant(s) for Life after the claim has been accepted. *LBR* does not take any responsibility for lost material(s) if the record is questioned, disputed, or objected to by any person. In case of a query or objection raised, the responsibility of providing the evidence again for reverification (see also Reverification of Evidence clause V.13) and all expenditures therein lies with the Applicant.

3. It is not necessary or binding for someone from *LBR* to be present at the recordmaking event, but proper authentication of the same must be ensured. Authentication should be by someone who is competent and in a responsible position, such as a gazetted officer, district magistrate, or principal of a government school/college, unless specified otherwise.

4. The Applicant(s) must update themselves with the latest record before making any Attempt to break it. Potential record-breakers should inform *LBR* at least 30 days in advance about the record Attempt details and procedure in order to avoid disqualification on technicalities.

5. Confirmations from Consultants are not to be treated as final. The final confirmations are only issued post ratification by the *LBR* Editorial Team. Applicants are advised to check the existing record with the *LBR* Team just before their Attempts as well, so that they may be intimated of any updates.

6. While breaking an existing record, the Applicant(s) must follow the rules, technical specifications, and set precedents. For example, if the needle-threading record specifies a no. 13 needle, no other needle may be used.

7. Records should be absolute and not technical offshoots. For example, if one is setting a typing record, it is assumed that it is normal typing. One-finger or two-finger typing will not be registered as separate records. Records have to be quantifiable and comparable, and overly specific variables may not be considered.

8. While *LBR* does accept new categories, these will have to be of high interest value and have definable and comparable parameters, and these are entirely subject to the *LBR* Team's decision. For example, even if no record exists, a 'two-hour marathon for guitar playing' will not be accepted because in this case, while doing an activity continuously for two hours maybe impressive, but does not necessarily qualify as a record with definable universal parameters.

9. Not every record set by women is eligible for entry as the sub-category 'First woman to...'.

10. Collections should have a basic 'standard'. Limited numbers of obscure articles may not be accepted unless of exceptional interest value, and that acceptance shall be the sole decision of the *LBR* Team.

11. For distance records, only basic types of vehicles are recognized: four-wheelers and plus, two-wheelers, geared bicycles, gearless bicycles, tandem bicycles, and electric vehicles. Cross-country or intra-country motoring/cycling or other vehicular records must get prior clearance from the *LBR* Team for inclusion. In speed-related records, vehicles may be categorized according to engine capacity: up to150 cc, 151–450 cc, and over 450 cc.

12. Before attempting any driving record, Applicants have to submit a copy of the following document/documents, as applicable, attested by a gazetted officer or notary public: their valid driving licence/earlier experience certificate in case of motor sport or bicycling record; pilot's licence/aero-sports course certificate/earlier experience certificate in case of aero-sports record; mountaineering/mountain sports course certificate/earlier experience certificate in case of a mountain sports record; and water sports course certificate/earlier experience certificate in case of a water sports record to the *LBR* office for prior approval.

13. All claimants must send in supporting photographs for their Claim to the *LBR* Team. These should be clear, and should clearly demonstrate the record. No tampering or enhancement of pictures should be done. In physical evidence with documents or photographs, these should not be stapled to the entry. Detachable clips should be used. In cases where applicable and as indicated by the *LBR* Team, time- and date-stamped video recordings of the Attempt must be provided.

14. Attempts that may result in physical harm, such as 'hitting head against a wall', or mental/emotional duress for the Applicant, such as 'isolating oneself for 100 days', will not be considered, and are entirely left to the decision of the *LBR* Team.

15. Any record in the book may be reconsidered or dropped without prior intimation.

16. Certificates issued are valid only as on or for the date or period specified and will be considered ended if surpassed by a new record, and/or change in criteria, measuring methods, or if disputed and found to be erroneous on reverification (see clause V.13). *LBR* is not bound to report an update to previous record holders.

17. For reasons of space or any other reasons, a confirmed entry may at times need to be dropped at the time of going to press. The *LBR* Team reserves the right to do so and may inform the Applicant of the change in status but is not bound to do so.

18. Record holders within India or with a postal delivery address within India are entitled to ONE complimentary copy of their certificate postage free, if eligible. Other modes of despatch may be chargeable. Further copies of certificates need to be ordered by writing to the *LBR* Team and on payment (including GST) as indicated. Record holders outside India are entitled to ONE complimentary copy of their certificate but will need to pay courier and/or postal charges (including applicable taxes/surcharges). Requests for reissue of older certificates issued in previous years are considered on a case-by-case basis and such certificates are reissued on payment within reasonable time as per printing schedules, provided the record is accessible in *LBR*'s archived editions.

19. Record holders are not entitled to any remuneration or free copies of *Limca Book of Records*. They may, however, avail a 30 per cent discount on the declared MRP/cover price of the book by writing to the *LBR* Team and following the payment process.

20. If new record holders do not receive their certificate within two months after the release of the book, they should contact the *LBR* office.

21. The *LBR* Team reserves the sole right to decide on the suitability of all records for inclusion in the book. The Team's decision on all such matters is final. Any attempt to browbeat or threaten the *LBR* Team or representatives shall result in instant disqualification.

22. OBJECTIONS/DISCREPANCIES

a. Any typographical error or inaccuracy in the statement of a record or certificate should be pointed out by the record holder immediately.

b. Objections raised by any person regarding any published entry shall be entertained only within a period of three (3) years from the date of publication or acceptance/certification of a record/entry. However, discrepancies identified by the *LBR* Team suo moto shall be addressed regardless of passage of time. Applicants must note that, in accordance with the prevailing laws, there is no limitation in respect of criminal liability should it arise. Falsification of evidence is a criminal activity.

B. CHAPTERS AND CATEGORIES

LBR reserves the right to include or exclude any chapter or category, or section or record category as otherwise listed below and is under no obligation to publish all or any of the listed chapters or categories in *LBR* or any of its publications.

The list provided here is only for illustrative and explanatory reasons, and for the clarity of persons seeking to engage in an Attempt. Further, the following list consists only of chapters and categories that have been published in current and previous editions and is non-exhaustive. *LBR* may, at its sole discretion, include additional chapters or categories, delete a chapter or category, or even merge two or more chapters or categories as the *LBR* Team deems appropriate. Any such addition, deletion, or merging of chapters or categories creates no obligation on the part of *LBR* Team and/or CCIPL to inform any person making an Attempt of such addition, deletion, or merger. Records after acceptance may also be changed or deleted if suitable circumstances warrant it, and this also shall be the sole decision of the *LBR* Team. Further, the guidelines mentioned here, pertaining to *LBR* chapters and their respective categories, are generic guidelines and in no way represent an exhaustive list for the record claim to be accepted. Specific guidelines for individual record claims will be shared on email by the *LBR* Team.

1. THE HUMAN STORY

This chapter contains records, talents, and information, and includes, but is not limited to, unique achievements, uncommon talents, collections, community development initiatives, and other human feats. Applicants under this category are required to not break any laws, and must sign and submit the Disclaimer and Indemnity Form, Self-Declaration of Medical Fitness and Certificate of Medical Fitness, as applicable, at least one month prior to the Attempt. *LBR* prohibits and will not accept any Attempt that is likely to cause harm or be of nuisance to the general public, or is likely to cause unnecessary waste of essential goods or resources such as food items, or is likely to harm the environment; and of course possible physical, mental, or emotional harm to oneself.

a. Records involving alcohol consumption as an event or performance measure will not be considered.

d. For the section on Online feats, *LBR* will accept both single and multiple sessions for a single event. The number of platforms will not be a parameter.

c. *LBR* does not have categories related to religious traditions and ceremonies, unless they form general records.

d. Records indicating or involving harm to physical or mental health, such as 'maximum blood donated in a day', or 'starving for the most number of days', or 'isolating oneself for the longest period' will not be considered.

e. For collection claims, minor changes like changes in colour and/or slight tweaks will be considered as duplicated, and will not be counted separately.

f. For claims related to 'smallest/largest/biggest' forms of an object, the form has to closely resemble the original object as a replica, and creative representations will not be accepted from both functionality and outer look and feel perspectives.

g. For claims under 'Physical Feats', the gendered categories are not applicable anymore. All attempts are comparable.

2. STRUCTURES

This chapter contains records related to general, modern, residential, religious, mechanical and historical structures, bridges, dams and flyovers, and various other specialized structures.

a. There are no set parameters of the claim regarding fastest construction as each construction would have multiple aspects of difference and the *LBR* Team does not wish to encourage the fastest construction of public services or private buildings.

b. Any structure should have the necessary permissions, and structural safety certified and the Applicant should confirm such certification.

3. AGRICULTURE

This chapter contains records and information, and it may include, but shall not be limited to, topics such as agricultural crops, farm machinery, milk and milk products, poultry, animal sciences, fisheries, agricultural research, and awards. Specific rules are to be complied with for Attempts under this chapter.

4. EDUCATION

This chapter contains records and information related to literacy, schools, higher education, archives, libraries, museums, and quizzes. *LBR* has discontinued the 'youngest' category as a record claim. Record claims with qualifications beyond postgraduation are considered. Record claims pertaining to online courses, or qualifications based on the University Grants Commission–National Eligibility Test (UGC–NET), or publication of research papers will not be considered.

5. PERFORMING ARTS

This chapter contains records related to talent and information in the fields of dance, music, and theatre (including but not limited to puppetry and other local theatre types depending on parameters), and dance drama and dance–martial arts crossovers. The records are further divided into marathon events or group events. All Attempts under this chapter are required to follow the specific rules for both types of events as provided by the *LBR* Team. Record claims pertaining to fastest performances will not be considered.

6. VISUAL ARTS

This chapter contains records and information related to cinema, photography, painting, and some categories of drawing and cartooning. The records related to national and regional commercial and art cinema is based on information collected from the National Film Archive of India (NFAI), public domain, magazines, and national newspapers. The records about box-office collection are obtained from the website www.boxofficeindia.com, the standard source in India for collecting such details, or similar sources.

a. Individual record claims for cinema may be submitted for consideration under this chapter, subject to compliance with the basic criteria laid down:
   i. The film should have been cleared by the Central Board of Film Certification (CBFC) and given a censor certificate.
   ii. Certification requirements for over-the-top (OTT) content/films/drama series will be decided on a case-by-case basis and as per the laws of the land.
   iii. The film should be screened at film festivals or at public theatres/auditoriums.

b. Information related to painting and photography is collected from newspapers, magazines, the Internet, and any other verified source. Individual record claims may be submitted for consideration under this chapter, subject to compliance with the basic criteria laid down:
   i. No miniature paintings in any medium are considered in this chapter currently. They may be eligible for entry in the Human Story chapter depending on parameters.
   ii. All rangoli, alpana and kolam records have been categorized under one category of 'Traditional floor art'.
   iii. Considering that art is a subjective concept, the *LBR* Team reserves the final decision regarding the artwork so produced. Random repetition of patterns, block colour patches, strokes of paint, or smearing paint randomly on the canvas would lead to the rejection of the claim. Similarly, geometric shapes, haphazard lines, and arbitrary usage of colour would also lead to rejection. The artwork so produced should have a coherent sense of pattern, colour, and tone. It should depict a certain level of skill and creation of aesthetics. For photography claims, repetitive, fragmented, and haphazard images would not be considered. The images should have a coherent sense of posture, alignment, and lighting.
   iv. The largest art competition would be a single-day category following the rules of continuous events and being a maximum of 12 hours.
   v. Portrait categories: A portrait should have only a single person in the painting/mosaic. A portrait is considered to be a drawing/painting of the head and shoulder of a person for the purposes of record claims.
   vi. Origami claims have been sorted into the following categories:
      1. Largest origami mosaic – solo/group
      2. Single-item origami (single sheet, single item): A) Tallest/Longest; B) Widest
      3. Multiple-item origami (multiple sheets, multiple items): A) Tallest – solo/group; B) Widest – solo/group
      4. Marathon origami (single day, single venue) – solo
      5. Most towel origami made – solo/group – in 1 hour
   vii. Claims regarding pencil carvings (graphite) have been sorted into the following categories:
      1. Largest collection of carved pencils
      2. Most pencil carvings done – single day
      3. Most pencil carvings done – 1 hour
      4. Smallest pencil carving

7. LITERATURE

This chapter contains records and information from the field of literature. Applicants willing to undertake an Attempt under this chapter must ensure compliance with the basic criteria laid down:

a. Only published works will be considered unless the work created is an art installation or superlative, or an artefact.
b. No long ghazals/poems, rewriting of religious texts, or anthologies will be considered.
c. A work infringing copyright or violative of any other prevailing laws will not be considered.
d. General category claims: Book(s) self-published or published by a publishing house should be available for purchase at bookshops or on a recognized online platform. Sales records must be certified by publishers who have audited accounts, or by Nielsen BookScan.

8. MEDIA AND COMMUNICATIONS

This chapter contains records and information related to the broad fields of (a) media and (b) communications, and may be divided into six sections: (i) print, (ii) radio, (iii) television, (iv) post and philately, (v) telecom, and (vi) Internet, social media and applications (apps). Applicants wishing to undertake an Attempt under this chapter must ensure compliance with the specific guidelines provided by the *LBR* Team.

9. GOVERNMENT

This chapter contains information and records. This category may include, but shall not be limited to, such subjects as nationhood, parties, elections, the Parliament, states, administration, government officials, civics, judiciary, and law and order.

10. DEFENCE AND MILITARY AFFAIRS

This chapter contains records and information pertaining to all the branches of the armed or paramilitary forces and related military records. This chapter does not accept entries unless routed through the appropriate defence authority/organization with the understanding that no official secrets, or confidential information, are being revealed in the process. An independent entry by current or former defence personnel should be accompanied with a self-declaration that no official secrets or confidential information is being revealed. The chapter is otherwise compiled by the *LBR* Team from news sources originating with government ministries and information sources such as the official websites of the Indian Navy, the Indian Army, the Indian Air Force, and the Coast Guard of India as well as the Press Information Bureau, Government of India.

11. SCIENCE AND TECHNOLOGY

This chapter contains absolute records like oldest planetarium and first nuclear reactor along with discoveries and records in, but not limited to, mathematics, physics, chemistry, biology, engineering, environmental sciences, computers, information technology, and space technology. All Attempts under this chapter are required to follow the specific rules for both types of events as provided by the *LBR* Team. For a new invention to be considered as a record, it must be patented with a recognized national/international body. This chapter also includes records and relevant information compiled by the *LBR* Team.

12. MEDICAL SCIENCES

This chapter contains records and information from the field of medical sciences such as medical breakthroughs, medical camps, 'firsts', and in selective medical procedures, medical devices, and equipment.

Claims are acceptable only from registered medical practitioners and related to government-approved medical practices and institutions, such as those affiliated to the Indian Medical Association, the Ministry of Health and Family Welfare, and any others as deemed eligible by the *LBR* Team.

The *LBR* Team will reject any Attempts that may potentially or otherwise harm or endanger persons/patients, e.g., speed-related records, such as 'most kidneys transplanted in a day' or 'most LASIK surgeries performed in a day', whether at a medical centre or in camps, charitable or otherwise.

LBR may accept camp-related statistics that turn out to be records, but may not process or encourage any camps set up to create records, especially speed-related medical science Attempts because such Attempts may jeopardize patient safety and health.

For all surgery-related claims, only successful surgery applications will be accepted, where the patient has not died on the operation table.

13. THE NATURAL WORLD

This chapter contains information and records, and the entries are compiled from multiple and deemed verified reports in magazines, newspapers, and Internet resources available to *LBR* on topics including, but not limited to, geographical features, flora, fauna, environment, and conservation. Information related to flora and fauna is verified with nature conservation authorities, well-known wildlife institutions, government websites, and relevant international websites.

All claims related to rainwater harvesting and pollution control are counterchecked with government sources and/or authoritative expert bodies. Gardening records relating to non-agricultural production and claims, such as largest pumpkin, will require scale-comparative photographs as well as other indicated documentation.

14. TRANSPORT

This chapter contains records and information, and the sections under this chapter include road, rail and metro, water, and air transport. Applicants who claim records under any of these sections shall provide evidence of the same, including authentication documents as required by the *LBR* Team.

15. BUSINESS AND ECONOMY

This chapter contains records and information, and the sections under this chapter may include, but shall not be limited to, the economy, financial institutions, financial instruments, banking, industries and companies, workforce, housing and real estate, and advertising.

Applicants who claim records under any of these sections shall provide proof of the same, including authentication letters from independent observers including at least one expert in the field. Industry company data must be from authentic authorized bodies such as the Registrar of Companies and the Securities and Exchange Board of India (SEBI), or in the case of own company figures, audited figures must be submitted.

a. Claims for 'highest/lowest' sale of product(s) are not accepted.

16. ADVENTURE

This chapter may be divided into various sections, including but not limited to, aero-sports, mountaineering, road expeditions, water sports, marathons (those not classified internationally as athletics track and field events), and other adventure activities. A person undertaking an Attempt under this category may seek the *LBR* Team's guidance/assistance for specific guidelines. Potential Applicants are advised to note that such guidelines or safety advice provided by the *LBR* Team shall merely be explanatory and non-exhaustive, and will not create any responsibilities or liabilities whatsoever on behalf of the *LBR* Team and/or CCIPL.

a. For all claims related to Ironman triathlon, *LBR* refers to the International Triathlon Union and the Indian Triathlon Federation.
b. For swimming records, only solo as well as up to three-person relay crossings (each covering at least 10 km) will be considered. For marathon swimming – with permitted breaks – breaks of only 1.5 minutes will be allowed for each completed hour. Exceptions may be made for para swimmers or extremely remarkable records, subject to the discretion and decision of the *LBR* Team.
c. A minimum altitude of 6,000 m is required to review any mountaineering claim. Claims regarding Mt Kilimanjaro (5,895 m) will not be considered in accordance with this limit. All mountaineering claims must be verified by the Indian Mountaineering Foundation or a similar credible international body.
d. There are separate categories for women in solo attempts and group attempts where Applicants and, if present, Participants are women.
e. Our categories for expedition records for two-wheelers will now be subdivided as:
   i. Up to 150 cc
   ii. 151 to 450 cc
   iii. Over 450 cc
f. Adventure/Marathon and Endurance Claims:
   i. A detailed logbook must be maintained with entries in chronological order. All entries in this logbook must be witnessed and authenticated by reputed individuals/competent authorities (a gazetted officer, district magistrate, or principal of a government school/college, unless specified otherwise). A sample sheet will be given by the *LBR* Team on request. Emphasis will be on events that highlight special skills.
   ii. In cases where applicable and as indicated by the *LBR* Team, time- and date-stamped videos of the Attempt must be provided.
   iii. All adventure/endurance events come under two categories.
      1. Marathon: A five-minute break for rest after every completed hour is allowed as per prevailing international norms. These breaks may be accumulated during the course of the Attempt, but not at the beginning or end (e.g., a 15-minute break may be taken after 3 hours of non-stop action, but finishing the Attempt 15 minutes before the completion of the Attempt cannot be adjusted as break time and will not be added to the tally). The logbook must clearly indicate the rest breaks.
      2. Normal: Breaks permitted as and when necessary.
      NOTE: For marathon attempts, any claimant(s) not using the permissible breaks will still be compared with the claimant(s) using them. All attempts under the marathon categories are comparable regardless of utilizing the permitted breaks or not.
   iv. Attempts jeopardizing individual or public safety and public property are not encouraged.
   v. All adventure feats/stunts/sports, etc., require prior written approval from authorities concerned.

17. SPORTS

The Sports chapter of the *LBR* primarily contains records and sports-related statistics and information. It is prepared by independent

Consultants, who are well-established journalists and/or authorities in particular sports. The Consultants in conjunction with the *LBR* Team are the final authority on all records under this chapter. In cases where an uncommon sport is involved, the decisions will be made in consultation with an expert in the field.

IV. PROCEDURE FOR RECORD ATTEMPTS

1. *LBR* recognizes two types of Attempts by individuals or groups:

a. an Attempt to break a previously existing record; and
b. an Attempt to set a new record.

2. The following procedure must be followed by any person willing to undertake an Attempt to be considered for entry in *LBR*. An application by the person attempting the record should be either emailed to *lbr.entries@hachetteindia.com* or couriered/mailed by registered post (see clause IV.3: Application Procedure).

a. Such application should contain details regarding the unique achievement, or proposal to set a record, for the consideration of the *LBR* Team, along with the complete address and contact number of the person attempting the same, at least one (1) month before the Attempt in order to avoid disqualification on technicalities. For specific requirements in the procedure for an Attempt, please refer to Section III of these Rules and Guidelines/Terms.
b. The person undertaking the Attempt must approach the *LBR* Team regarding the proper procedure and information or documents required for consideration of a successful Attempt.
c. On completion of an Attempt, the Applicant must provide the *LBR* Team detailed and accurate documentation, as required by the *LBR* Team, and these will then be scrutinized by the *LBR* Team.
d. All entries to an edition are confirmed only after the deadline, i.e., the last date for submission of entries. Any Application made after such a date may be considered for a subsequent edition of *LBR*.
e. On confirmation of an entry, a certificate shall be mailed to the Applicant who carried out the successful Attempt. Such certificates shall be sent after the particular edition for which the Attempt has been considered is printed or released.
f. For all Attempts to be undertaken, the person undertaking such an Attempt must sign and submit the Disclaimer and Indemnity Form and Certificate of Medical Fitness (in hard copy), as and when required, to the *LBR* Team, prior to the Attempt. The acceptance of any application for entry in *LBR* shall be conditional on the signing of and adherence to the Disclaimer and Indemnity Form, the Terms, and any other specific rules and guidelines established by *LBR* in relation to a particular category of Attempt.

The following rules will apply to Disclaimer Forms:

i. Disclaimer Forms should have only one party mentioned, i.e., the record claimant. The second party is not applicable. The Disclaimer Forms should have one primary signatory whether it is a team of two or a group application. That signatory should confirm that he/she is authorized to represent the group and all communications with *LBR* will be with this one primary signatory.
ii. Applicants may choose to get the form notarized instead of adding witnesses. Or witnesses can be used, but verification from the notary holds more value.
iii. Disclaimer Forms have to be on a stamp paper of minimum value of ₹10.

3. APPLICATION PROCEDURE

a. All applications must be sent to the following address: Limca Book of Records (Editorial), Hachette Book Publishing India Pvt. Ltd, 4th/5th Floors, Corporate Centre, Plot No. 94, Sector 44, Gurugram 122003, Haryana, India.
Ph: +91 22 35305621, Fax: +91 124 4148900
Email: *lbr*.entries@hachetteindia.com
Hachette Book Publishing India Pvt. Ltd is a company incorporated under the Indian Companies Act, 1956, with CIN U22222DL2007PTC164081.
b. *LBR*'s primary mode of communication is email (and only via its formal email IDs), which is both retrievable and transparent as well as a formal record. No Attempt should be made based on phone or other verbal conversations, or communication on social media/messaging platforms.
c. There is no need for personal visits to the *LBR* office to hand over recordrelated applications, documentation, or evidence, and in case the Applicant does visit personally, the application and requisite documents may be handed over at the reception. *LBR* staff may not be available for personal meetings. Since all claim formats devised are such that they need written submission, everything should be clear from written communication.
d. Submissions must be in English since *LBR* is currently published in the English language (submissions in other languages shall be accepted, but they should be accompanied with an English translation).
e. The primary application shall consist of the following:
   i. Name of the Applicant
   ii. Date of birth of the Applicant
   iii. Complete postal address of the Applicant
   iv. Contact details (phone number and email ID) of the Applicant
   v. Description of the record the Applicant wishes to apply for; and event plan
   vi. Confirmation of acceptance of *LBR* procedures, Terms, and Rules and Guidelines via a formal statement on email or signed hard copy
f. These applications shall be perused by the *LBR* Team, and further correspondence shall take place between the Applicant and the *LBR* Team member concerned, from the assigned chapter/section.
g. On acceptance of the initial application, the general guidelines and record-specific guidelines shall be emailed or couriered to the Applicant by the *LBR* Team along with the procedure and documentation required.
h. On receipt of the correspondence from a member of the *LBR* Team, the Applicant shall send the following documents (in both soft and hard copies) to the addresses mentioned in clause IV.3(a) above:
   i. A covering letter stating the Attempt details
   ii. A signed copy of the Disclaimer and Indemnity Form sent to the Applicant
   iii. A self-attested copy of the Applicant's government-approved identity proof (such as passport, voter ID card, PAN card, Aadhaar, etc.)
   iv. A self-attested copy of the Applicant's government-approved age proof (such as passport, birth certificate, ration card, etc.) together with the 'Required Documents' as indicated by the *LBR* Team.
i. On authentication and verification of the Required Documents, the Applicant shall obtain a confirmation from the *LBR* Team to proceed with the Attempt.
j. After completing the Attempt in accordance with the provisions of Sections III and IV, and collecting evidence of the Attempt in accordance with the provisions of Section V, the Applicant shall send the following to claim a record (the 'Claim'):

i. Details of the supposed record, duly authenticated by gazetted officers, or relevant public authorities, or relevant authorities in charge, or other competent authorities. Such authentication must be on the basis of personal verification of every detail of the Claim.
ii. Material evidence of the event, consisting of all the evidence collected by the Applicant during the Attempt. All CDs/DVDs, flash/pen drives, and other data storage media/devices sent to the *LBR* Team, as part of the application process, should have the Applicant's name and the record category written legibly on it.
iii. Accompanying clearances, permissions and safety certifications as required.

k. Only a claim that is complete and successfully submitted shall be considered for entry in the *LBR*.
l. The application procedure should be completed within the last date of submission. Entries submitted after the deadline may be considered for the subsequent edition unless extension was granted in writing or on email for extenuating circumstances, or at the discretion of the *LBR* Team.
m. In addition to the aforementioned rules, specific requirements provided under the relevant categories must be fulfilled.

V. EVIDENCE

1. The onus of proving a record is on the Applicant. The Claim, signed by the Applicant, should be backed by adequate and satisfactory documentation without which it will not be accepted by the *LBR* Team.

2. The Applicant must, as part of the verification process, submit all supporting documents including at least two authentication letters (originals), verified, stamped, and signed by gazetted officers, preferably on their letter heads, photographs (or CD/DVD/flash/pen drive containing still photos), personal details of the Applicant, including residential address and contact details, along with a covering letter, without which the Claim will not be considered for entry.

3. Outside of moral and creative ownership rights, which will vest in the creator/artist/author, etc., the assigned copyright/publishing rights and any other intellectual property rights in and to any such material evidence shall, to the extent permitted by law, be waived unconditionally by the Applicant and transferred to *LBR* and CCIPL by the submission.

4. The evidence must only be sent after the Required Documents, as indicated by the Rules and Guidelines, have been verified (with copies/scans as stipulated) and the primary application has been duly confirmed and evidence asked for by the *LBR* Team.

5. Only the Claim may be supplemented by evidence of the record with the following to be submitted on the currently prevailing and commonly available and accessible data storage media from where it is easily retrievable, such as a flash/pen drive or hard drive, with the onus of providing a back-up copy/original being on the Applicant:

a. Press clippings of local, national or international newspapers, or press cuttings, or news reports in an electronic form, furnishing direct evidence of the record; or
b. Audio recordings from radio, or any such fact of record which could be heard, furnishing direct evidence of the record; or
c. Direct evidence/audio-visual recording of the record; or
d. Any other fact of record that may be in audio, visual, or audio-visual format, furnishing direct evidence of the record; or
e. Photographs of any such fact of record documented by photographs furnishing direct evidence of the record. (It is advisable to submit high-resolution photographs only, that are pictures 1,500 pixels wide for horizontal images and 1,500 pixels high for vertical images, of 1 Mb or more.)
f. Safety certifications, age proofs, doctor's certificates, etc. where needed.

6. If any of the evidence mentioned above is in a local language, it must be sent along with a copy of an English translation of the said document attested by a gazetted officer/notary public.

7. The evidence must be clear, distinct, and unambiguous.

8. *LBR* reserves the right to refuse the Claim if evidence sufficient to prove the record act beyond reasonable doubt is not furnished, or if safety-related documentation is unsatisfactory, or for any other reason whatsoever at *LBR*'s discretion.

9. The material evidence provided by the Applicant shall NOT be returned. The Applicant is advised to keep all original evidence along with copies (and kept safe so as to be produced in the event of a dispute or reverification).

10. In case of records where giant structures are put in place or super-sized objects are involved, the measurements shall be taken in the presence of appropriate observers and authenticators, such as gazetted officers, a principal of a government school/college, an engineering expert, or others as approved by the *LBR* Team. Structural safety certification must be provided along with the evidence.

11. Originals must not be sent, unless specifically requested by *LBR* for scrutiny. *LBR* will not keep copies longer than twelve (12) months after acceptance of the Claim, but record holders should keep their evidence to be produced for disputes for life (see below V.13: Reverification of Evidence). Evidence and documents of rejected claims will not be kept with *LBR* and will be destroyed within 7 (seven) days of the rejection mail date informing the Applicant of the decision (unless the Applicant has specified that they will pick up the submission themselves or at their cost). It is reiterated that *LBR* should be sent only copies and *LBR* does not take responsibility for safekeeping of documents.

12. All records and evidence are accepted in good faith and normal deep scrutiny. Any submission of fake evidence shall be met with a charge of cheating and other offences as mentioned in the Indian Penal Code and other applicable laws. Similarly, incomplete evidence or improper certification for any record shall see rejection, and if discovered later, may see cancellation of the record and prosecution where applicable.

13. REVERIFICATION OF EVIDENCE

a. In case a discrepancy in the record comes to light, as pointed out by any person/group or independently detected by the *LBR* Team, the onus of providing the evidence again for reverification of the record entry lies entirely with the record holder. If, in the opinion of the *LBR* Team, the discrepancy, irrespective of the reason for its coming to light, is genuine, it shall be communicated to the record holder and evidence sought for reverification. In the meantime, the record will be frozen/suspended and the certificate considered withdrawn until the evidence is reverified by a panel consisting of an *LBR* Team member and a legal consultant. Announcement of such a frozen/suspended record will appear only on the *LBR* website publicly and nowhere else. Subsequent to reverification, the record may either be restored, amended, or struck off completely.

b. *LBR* will not keep any data or records longer than one year (12 months) from acceptance in writing. In the event of any objection or discrepancy needing reverification (see sub-clause [a] above), the record holder must keep all supporting evidence safe and readily accessible.
c. In all matters pertaining to reverification of records/evidence, the *LBR*'s decision shall be final and binding

VI. ACCEPTANCE CRITERIA

1. Each Attempt must be categorized within one of the chapters or categories listed under Sections II and III.B. However, *LBR* reserves the right, to be exercised at its sole and absolute discretion, to accept applications for Attempts.

2. Records must be absolute and not technical offshoots, and they must be quantifiable, comparable, and measurable. Records should be significant in achievement and not frivolous.

3. No Claim shall be considered valid unless it is sent, along with the required evidence, in the manner prescribed in Sections IV and V.

4. *LBR* reserves the right to publish or delete any chapter, section, category, or record in the present or any future edition of *LBR*, without any notice to the Applicants. *LBR* is under no obligation to inform record holders when a record may be dropped. Such decisions shall be the sole prerogative of the *LBR* Team in the larger continuing interests of the book.

5. Records shall be considered for publishing only on the grounds of their interest value and general public acceptance.

6. Further, no entries in violation of any law, rule, regulation, guideline, or any other statutory instrument shall be accepted. No record or feat attempted shall endanger anyone or any property, and if after acceptance a record is found to have caused damage of any sort to the public or individual persons (for example, a building collapse by structural weakness or illness from some food item made, etc.), then such record may be cancelled. However, *LBR* reserves the right to include public domain records of harmful/criminal nature (for example, the first plane crash or the youngest serial killer). This in no way is to be seen as an encouragement to make such records and will not be accepted in a pre-attempt application.

7. Entries for the new edition of *LBR* will be confirmed only after the annual deadline, which is usually 31 May.

8. In all matters pertaining to the *Limca Book of Records*, the *LBR* Team's and/or CCIPL's decision shall be final and binding.

9. Record claims are accepted in good faith and may be considered records and published in the book as such unless disproved with appropriate evidence.

10. It should be borne in mind, that *LBR* by its rejecting a Claim is not stating that the Claim may not be a record, or that the achievement, if any, is belittled. It is merely stating that for its purposes and within the framework of the book, as run by its editorial policy, it does not consider the Claim suitable to feature.

11. Harassment of staff, including overt or covert threats, including threats of legal process for rejecting a Claim, or for any other reason whatsoever, or defaming *LBR* or the *LBR* Team on public platforms will not be acceptable and will be met with all the measures under law. Any such behaviour will also result in automatic disqualification of the Claim.

12. Similarly, due process and timelines shall be followed as has been communicated by the *LBR* team. Attempts to browbeat staff, or bring pressure to bear, including citing official/government/ministry 'priority', may result in rejection of the record. *LBR* does not have a fast-track system either on payment or from any either reason.

VII. STATUTORY COMPLIANCE

1. It is mandatory for Applicants to abide by all local, state, and national laws, rules, and regulations applicable in relation to the Attempt. *LBR* expressly prohibits any Attempt that involves violation of any local, state, or national laws, rules, or regulations. Applicants are under an obligation to ensure that all activities related to the Attempt are neither unlawful, nor against public decency and morality.

Applicants must note that *LBR* strongly discourages Attempts that are likely to offend the sentiments of any community. *LBR* also discourages Attempts that may cause harm to the public or animals, or cause any damage to the environment, and Applicants are requested to refrain from making such Attempts. Applicants shall bear sole responsibility for any consequences arising out of any non-compliance with any applicable laws, rules, or regulations insofar as they relate to the Attempt. *LBR* shall not be liable for any harm caused to the public or the environment in the course of the Attempt, and *LBR* shall not be responsible for any non-compliance with any applicable local, state, national, or international laws, rules, and regulations insofar as they relate to the Attempt.

2. With the submission of any Claim, a record holder agrees to abide by the Terms and Conditions, and Rules and Guidelines, in full and is thereby covenanting that the submission is true with no falsifying of evidence or no mala fide intent of any sort whatsoever.

VIII. SAFETY PRECAUTIONS

1. The Applicant is requested to take all reasonable safety precautions prior to the Attempt including, but not limited to, the testing of all equipment used for the Attempt, the utilization of prescribed safety equipment in relation to the Attempt, the presence of requisite medical personnel and treatment facilities, and any applicable safety permits required under local, state, or national laws, rules, and regulations.

2. The Applicant understands that the Attempt may be dangerous to them, other Participants, and spectators, and that they must identify such risks, with the help of professional advice, such as the risk of accident, illness, paralysis, injury, loss, or death that may be caused by negligence, forces of nature, or other agencies, known and unknown. The Applicant knowingly and freely assumes all such risks, both known and unknown, and assumes full personal responsibility for the Attempt and its consequences.

3. The Applicant shall bear sole responsibility for taking all such safety precautions and acknowledge that CCIPL, the *LBR* Team, and/or their respective directors, publishers, editors, officers, appointed representatives, Consultants, or agents shall not, in any manner whatsoever, be responsible for making any safety arrangements for the Attempt.

4. Safety certifications as stated above in various sections – are an absolute necessity.

IX. PUBLICITY

1. The Applicants undertake and irrevocably and unconditionally permit CCIPL and *LBR* to cover any Attempt through various media including newspapers, radio, television (news and other channels),

IMAGE COPYRIGHT INFORMATION

Internet, mobile apps, social media, etc., and shall not raise any objection, protest, or demur whatsoever to such coverage or in this regard. Whilst *LBR* shall make all reasonable efforts, there is no obligation on the part of *LBR* to air or otherwise engage in publicizing any Attempt. The Applicants must, at the request of CCIPL/*LBR*, participate in all promotional activity (such as publicity and photography) in relation to a successful Attempt, free of charge, and consent to CCIPL and *LBR* using their name and image in all promotional materials, free of charge, should CCIPL/*LBR* Team wish to do so as mentioned under Section X below.

2. In the case of publicity-related interview and other occasions/ opportunities and/or events where the participation or presence of the Applicant may be required, the *LBR*/CCIPL Team will contact the Applicant(s) in writing/on email for their consent and willingness for such an interview and/or event.

3. No applicant should issue any press release or make any statements pertaining to *LBR* or the record until such statement has been approved in writing by the *LBR* Team.

4. No unauthorized use of logo or brand names for own publicity or publicizing/displaying record should occur.

X. LICENCE TO USE NAME, IMAGE, LIKENESS, RECORD

Applicants hereby grant in perpetuity to CCIPL and *LBR*, their authorized agents, successors, and assigns, the worldwide licence to use the name, image, likeness, pictures, video recordings, audio recordings, etc., of the Applicants in relation to any Attempts undertaken by the Applicants (the 'Licensed Property'). Applicants agree and grant to CCIPL and Hachette Book Publishing India Pvt. Ltd/Hachette India a waiver of their privacy and personality rights, and grant the right to use any element of the Licensed Property for any purpose in connection with *LBR* including, but not limited to, the publication and distribution of *LBR*, the promotion of *LBR*, CCIPL, and any of its divisions or products, and the filing of copyright, trademark, and other similar registrations in relation to *LBR* that involve the Licensed Property. All material(s) submitted in connection with a potential entry in *LBR* (whether in written, audio, electronic, or visual form, or a combination of these) or any photographs, video and/or film footage, and/or audio recording taken of Applicants are assigned to *LBR* and CCIPL upon submission and become the property of *LBR* and CCIPL exclusively. *LBR* and CCIPL may use the material(s) in any medium in any reasonable manner they deem fit. Copyright in any such material(s) remains the sole property of *LBR* and CCIPL.

NOTE: Contributions: All *LBR* records and/or information if featured in our book and/or database are copyright *LBR*. *LBR* is also a fact book and therefore has facts that may be available in public domain or provided by experts/consultants/reader-contributors. Such contributions from consultants and or volunteers (which are also facts and/or public domain information) may be acknowledged once in an edition if so contracted or committed but shall have no subsequent continued acknowledgement after the first use.

XI. INTELLECTUAL PROPERTY RIGHTS

The name 'Limca' and the 'Limca' logo are registered trademarks of The Coca-Cola Company, USA, and should not be used for any publicity in relation to an Attempt, or after a Claim has been accepted, without the express permission of CCIPL. All rights, titles, and interests including, but not limited to, the Intellectual Property Rights, in *LBR* and in any and all entries received, shall vest solely and exclusively in CCIPL at all times. CCIPL or any person or entity permitted by CCIPL in this regard shall be entitled to use any information in connection with the entry in any media for future promotional, marketing, publicity, and any other purpose, without any permission and/or payment to the Applicant.

XII. RESPONSIBILITY FOR ALL ASSOCIATED COSTS AND INSURANCE

The Applicant understands and acknowledges that all expenses incurred in relation to the Attempt shall be borne solely by the Applicant. CCIPL and/or *LBR* Team shall in no manner be responsible for reimbursing any expenses incurred in the course of the Attempt, or even in the event that the Applicant is successful at the Attempt. CCIPL/*LBR* Team shall not be responsible for providing any kind of insurance in relation to any Attempt, and shall not be responsible for any emergency medical expenses or any subsequent medical expenses in the event of any incident/accident, illness, or incapacity arising out of the Attempt.

XIII. WAIVER OF CLAIMS AND INDEMNITY

1. Applicants acknowledge and consent on behalf of themselves, their heirs, successors, assignees, personal representatives, and next of kin, to WAIVE ALL CLAIMS AND RELEASE AND HOLD HARMLESS the *LBR* Team, Hachette Book Publishing India Pvt. Ltd/Hachette India and all its employees, directors, parent or affiliate organizations, Consultants, representatives, partners, CCIPL, its directors, publishers, editors, officers, employees and representatives, and its partners, affiliates, subsidiaries, advertising agencies, agents, and their respective directors, officers, employees, and representatives (the 'Released Parties'), with respect to any and all injury, disability, paralysis, death, or loss or damage to person, property, or reputations, arising out of the Attempt, to the fullest extent permitted by law. The Applicants agree to indemnify and hold the Released Parties harmless from all losses, liabilities, damages, costs, or expenses (including but not limited to reasonable legal fees and other litigation costs and expenses) incurred by any of the Released Parties as a result of any claims or suits that any Applicant(s) (or anyone claiming by, under, or through such Applicant[s]) may bring against any of the Released Parties to recover any losses, liabilities, costs, damages, or expenses that may arise during or result from the Attempt in any way.

2. Further,

a. *LBR* retains an indemnity for human error or typographical error, and the right to revise a record because of that; and the right to withdraw or modify a certificate because of such error lies with the narration of the certificate. Any such correction shall also be duly corrected by the Applicant including to any areas the Applicant may have sent publicity information.

b. The right to suspend records/certification on receipt of disputes or objections lies with the *LBR* Editorial Team. In such cases the record verification will be revisited, and the Claimant of the record must provide reverification (see Clause V.13) and, if necessary, further detailing to answer such objections. If the Claimant is not able to furnish a copy of the evidence as per the original claim, the record and certification may be cancelled.

c. The principle of acceptance is basic verification and acceptance in good faith, so records should be clear and detailed. *LBR* reserves the right to do forensic examination or reopen a record case later if found to be suspect.

d. Faking of records and evidence and misrepresenting safety or other regulatory certifications is a criminal offence and shall be dealt with strictly under the prevailing laws. The Application/Claim/Record shall be cancelled and the Applicant/record holder shall be immediately blacklisted and no further applications/claims from them shall be entertained; and the rights to legal prosecution shall be reserved.
e. For records involving mass participation/huge numbers, for example, 'most people at a concert' or 'most vehicles in a rally', the simple principle of sequentially numbered badges should be there with a logbook of a unique identifier (licence/registration number, individual ID card, or any similar clearly visible device).
f. *LBR* is a private body and its editorial criteria solely belongs to it alone and its decisions shall be the ones solely binding on any record.

XIV. SEVERABILITY

Each of the provisions contained in these Terms/Rules and Guidelines is considered to be reasonable by CCIPL, *LBR*, and the Applicants, and each clause, subclause, paragraph, and sub-paragraph shall be construed as independent of any other provision. If any provision of these Terms/Rules and Guidelines proves to be invalid, void, or illegal, it shall not in any way affect, impair, or invalidate any other provision, and the remaining provisions shall remain in full force and effect.

XV. DISPUTE

The courts of competent jurisdiction at Delhi shall have exclusive jurisdiction to determine any and all disputes arising out of, or in connection with, any Attempt undertaken or entry made for the purpose of *LBR*. Further, all issues and questions concerning the construction, validity, interpretation, and enforceability of these Terms/ Rules and Guidelines, or the rights and obligations of the Applicants and/or CCIPL and/or partners of *LBR*, shall be governed and construed in accordance with the laws of the Republic of India.

Note: For general queries and/or specific guidelines pertaining to specific Claims/Records, all Applicants are requested to contact the *LBR* Team by email at *lbr*.entries@hachetteindia.com.

APPENDIX 1

The clauses below are subject to ongoing review and modifications, and Applicants may check this section from time to time to update themselves on categories that may have been discontinued, modified, or changed.

1. SPECIAL NOTE FOR PROSPECTIVE ATTEMPTS

a. There are categories in the book, marked with a single asterisks, indicating that they are one-time categories. These categories will not be carried forward into our subsequent editions and are not contestable.
b. Additional pointers to remember before sending the documentation or Claims:
   i. Applicants should not send any documents unless requested by the *LBR* Team, post-approval.
   ii. Applicants should not send any documentation if their event has not been approved for consideration by the *LBR* Team.
   iii. Documents received by *LBR* for events that are not pre-approved (in writing or on email) will not be reviewed by the *LBR* Team.

2. A NOTE FOR PAST, PRESENT, AND POTENTIAL RECORD HOLDERS

a. The name Limca and the Limca logo are registered trademarks of The Coca-Cola Company, USA, and should not be used for publicity when a record is being attempted or after the Claim has been accepted, without written permission of the publisher.
b. When records are being attempted, it is not obligatory for the *LBR* Team to provide invigilators. However, where possible they may do so.
c. All Attempts at breaking old records and setting new ones are undertaken entirely at the risk of the Applicant. Neither the *LBR* Team nor CCIPL can be held responsible by the Applicant/person undertaking an Attempt or any third party for any liability that may arise out of such an Attempt.
d. Applicants may use the name '*Limca Book of Records*' while attempting the record as long as:
   i. they do not use the logo of the *Limca Book of Records* or Limca brand or any Licensed Property of CCIPL;
   ii. they do not receive or give money in the execution of such an Attempt using *LBR* as a party or implied party or endorser; and
   iii. they do not offer Participants/partners any kind of inducement using *LBR* as a party. This is strictly prohibited and will result in the Applicant's name being blacklisted and rejected for any future application/ attempts.
e. The *LBR* Team reserves the complete and incontestable right to decide which chapters, sections, photographs, categories, and records to publish or delete in future editions. *LBR* will not consider record Attempts by minors (excluding exceptions, please refer II.2.) or any Attempt that is potentially dangerous or violates a law.
f. *LBR* strives to be completely authentic. However, it sometimes happens that an earlier record may come to light or be applied for after the book is released. In such cases corrections/updates will be carried out in the next edition or as deemed fit by the *LBR* Team.
g. Records that are 'firsts' are not entitled to perpetuity and can be dropped from the book without any prior intimation.
h. For reasons of space or any other reasons whatsoever, a confirmed Claim may also be dropped. *LBR* Team members may inform the Applicant of the change in status but are not bound to do so. Such decisions are the sole prerogative of the *LBR* Team in the larger continuing interests of the book.
i. The record holders are not entitled to any prize money, gift(s) or free copies of *Limca Book of Records*.
j. In case the record is subjected to reverification, the onus to prove the same is on the Applicant. So the Applicant must retain copies of documentary, images, audio, and video evidence with them should such a situation arise. The *Limca Book of Records* holds the right to revoke any record that fails reverification and to cancel the issued certificate.
k. In all matters pertaining to *Limca Book of Records*, the *LBR* Team's decision is final.

3. DISCONTINUED CATEGORIES

a. A few categories have been discontinued and will not be featured in any subsequent editions. The website is updated regularly regarding such categories.
b. Most surgeries/medical procedures within a time duration: The category for most surgeries/medical procedures has been discontinued as the quality of the procedure may be compromised during such claims.
c. Tractor service camps: The category for most tractors serviced has been discontinued, as such claims are difficult to monitor and make it an industry-specific claim.

d. Largest blood/organ donation drives.
e. Wrist cracking/wrist rotation.
f. Most couplets written.
g. Holding most burning candles in the mouth.
h. Fastest yoga asanas.
i. Collection of error coins.
j. Longest interview.
k. Limbo skating.
l. One-hand claps.
m. Most postcards sent in a day – solo/group – single/multiple venues.
n. Largest packers and movers of household goods.
o. Most people screened/diagnosed – single/multiple venues.
p. Largest anthology
q. Collections for '786' notes.
r. Fastest construction of structures.
s. Longest preservation of food items/articles.
t. Claims related to number of research papers written or published.
u. Collections based on alphabetical order (A–Z).
v. Longest lesson.
w. Most varieties (of any dish).
x. Largest doodle art – solo/group.
y. Lowest to highest value collections.
z. Longest distance covered barefoot.
aa. Shortest film.

4. WHY WAS YOUR RECORD REJECTED?

Unfortunately, many applications are rejected. The following are the general reasons that lead to the rejection of applications:

a. Not accepted the Terms and Conditions and/or Rules and Guidelines; and/or submission of incomplete form.
b. Insufficient documentation: The details provided do not suffice for verification purposes.
c. Not met criteria/ ineligible: For record purposes, *LBR* has certain criteria and set categories. For instance, in physical feats it has categories for 1 minute or 1 hour claims. Any claim that does not follow the format (for example, most push-ups in 40 seconds) shall not be accepted. Claims involving minors or jeopardizing safety of minors and/or others in any way will not be accepted (please see clause II.2.).
d. Specific titles: Usually, *LBR* measures record titles by one single parameter so that anybody can attempt and break/surpass that record. If the record claim is too specific or has multiple variables, the *LBR* Team would not consider such claims. For example, 'most push-ups in one minute' would be considered whereas 'most push-ups done in 1 (one) minute by a teacher' shall not be accepted.
e. Inappropriate/Offensive: *LBR* does not accept or encourage inappropriate or offensive claims.
f. Claims involving alcohol/smoking/substance usage: *LBR* does not encourage or accept claims involving alcohol, smoking, or substance use.
g. Animal welfare: Any claim that is not in accordance with animal rights laws or involves any mistreatment of animals is neither encouraged nor accepted in *LBR*.
h. Personality-related claims: Claims related to famous personalities, such as 'most people dressed as' or 'most times performing as' will only be considered for internationally recognized, iconic, and universally acknowledged personalities. The *LBR* Team reserves the right of discretion in any such claim.
i. Record claims involving wastage of food/medical supplies, for example, artworks made with fresh food materials would not be considered.
j. Environmentally harmful claims: *LBR* does not support any claim that may have any sort of adverse effect on the environment.
k. Fastest musicians: *LBR* does not consider claims such as fastest guitarist, fastest piano player, etc., as it is not possible to judge the quality of music produced in such claims.
l. Firsts: The firsts in a field are generally not accepted unless they mark change in trend, beginning of a new era, or change the traditional way for the matter. The *LBR* Team reserves the right to accept or reject any such claim.
m. Poetry: *LBR* does not accept claims pertaining to poetry due to its subjective nature.
n. Originality/Uniqueness-based claims: Uniqueness/originality cannot be a parameter of competence for a record. The *LBR* Team reserves the right of discretion in any such claim.
o. Sports achievements: For records directly involving performance in sports, *LBR* only accepts those which occur at a top-level professional, international, or pre-eminent amateur levels, or as per the decision of the relevant Consultant in specific cases.

Limca Book of Records
NEXT EDITION: 2027

The last date for new entries and applications (complete with relevant documentation) for the *Limca Book of Records* 2027 edition:

31 May 2026

Please address all correspondence to:

Limca Book of Records (Editorial)
Hachette Book Publishing India Pvt. Ltd
4th/5th Floors, Corporate Centre
Plot No. 94, Sector 44
Gurugram 122003, Haryana, India
Phone: +91 7292027373
Fax: +91 124 4148900
Email: *lbr.entries@hachetteindia.com*
Websites:
https://www.coca-colaindia.com/limca-book-of-records
https://www.hachetteindia.com/home/rulesandguidelines

Note: In order to have an accessible, credible, and reproducible record of interactions, email (and where it is unavailable, registered postal mail or courier service) is the preferred form of communication and correspondence.